Legal Terminology with Flashcards

FOURTH EDITION

Legal Terminology with Flashcards

FOURTH EDITION

Cathy J. Okrent, J.D.
Member, New York State Bar

DELMAR
CENGAGE Learning™

Australia • Brazil • Japan • Korea • Mexico • Singapore • Spain • United Kingdom • United States

**Legal Terminology with Flashcards,
Fourth Edition**
Cathy J. Okrent, J.D.

Vice President, Editorial: Dave Garza

Director of Learning Solutions: Sandy Clark

Senior Acquisitions Editor: Shelley Esposito

Managing Editor: Larry Main

Senior Product Manager: Melissa Riveglia

Editorial Assistant: Danielle Klahr

Vice President, Marketing: Jennifer Baker

Marketing Director: Deborah Yarnell

Marketing Manager: Erin Brennan

Marketing Coordinator: Erin DeAngelo

Production Director: Wendy Troeger

Production Manager: Mark Bernard

Senior Content Project Manager: Betty Dickson

Senior Art Director: Joy Kocsis

Senior Technology Project Manager: Joe Pliss

Photo Credit: ©stocker1970/Shutterstock

For product information and technology assistance, contact us at
Cengage Learning Customer & Sales Support, 1-800-354-9706
For permission to use material from this text or product,
submit all requests online at **www.engage.com/permissions.**
Further permissions questions can be e-mailed to
permissionrequest@cengage.com

Library of Congress Control Number: 2011920074

ISBN-13: 978-1-1111-3679-6

ISBN-10: 1-1111-3679-3

Delmar
5 Maxwell Drive
Clifton Park, NY 12065-2919
USA

Cengage Learning is a leading provider of customized learning solutions with office locations around the globe, including Singapore, the United Kingdom, Australia, Mexico, Brazil, and Japan. Locate your local office at: **international.cengage.com/region**

Cengage Learning products are represented in Canada by Nelson Education, Ltd.

To learn more about Delmar, visit **www.cengage.com/delmar**

Purchase any of our products at your local college store or at our preferred online store **www.cengagebrain.com**

Notice to the Reader
Publisher does not warrant or guarantee any of the products described herein or perform any independent analysis in connection with any of the product information contained herein. Publisher does not assume, and expressly disclaims, any obligation to obtain and include information other than that provided to it by the manufacturer. The reader is notified that this text is an educational tool, not a practice book. Since the law is in constant change, no rule or statement of law in this book should be relied upon for any service to the client. The reader should always refer to standard legal sources for the current rule or law. If legal advice or other expert assistance is required, the services of the appropriate professional should be sought. The reader is expressly warned to consider and adopt all safety precautions that might be indicated by the activities described herein and to avoid all potential hazards. By following the instructions contained herein, the reader willingly assumes all risks in connection with such instructions. The publisher makes no representations or warranties of any kind, including but not limited to, the warranties of fitness for particular purpose or merchantability, nor are any such representations implied with respect to the material set forth herein, and the publisher takes no responsibility with respect to such material. The publisher shall not be liable for any special, consequential, or exemplary damages resulting, in whole or part, from the readers' use of, or reliance upon, this material.

Printed in the United States of America
1 2 3 4 5 6 7 14 13 12 11

CONTENTS

FOREWORD

Sixty-five years ago I began my legal career with the understanding that the written word was the foundation of all good law, whether it was legislation passed by Congress and state legislatures, pleadings produced by legal counsel, or the orders of the court. My job focused on reading the pleadings and preparing the orders. During my career, a constant avalanche of pleadings populated my desk, requesting relief for plaintiffs and defendants. Sometimes I gently coaxed attorneys to rewrite or amend pleadings where necessary, and I made friends when they had the wisdom to accept my advice. You see, the purpose of my job was the smooth functioning of one of the busiest courts in America's largest city. My goal was to ensure that proposed orders of the court required no further action by the judge—except his or her review and signature.

When my daughter Cathy embarked on writing *Legal Terminology with Flashcards*, my simple advice was always "focus on the quantity and the quality." In other words, she wanted enough terms in each area of law to effectively impart an understanding of its importance without overwhelming the student. The definitions needed to be succinct and clear. Fortunately, the times had changed to embrace "plain English" in legal writing instead of the arcane Latin phrases that vexed me as a law student. In addition to taking my advice, Cathy wisely added the terms that have transformed legal research to a largely online experience today. Ideally, readers of this book will find the "quantity and quality" necessary to become facile in reading law, researching, writing pleadings, reporting, and all the other legal communications found in your legal career. Good luck!

Charles I. Okrent
Chief Clerk, New York State Supreme Court,
Special Term, Part Two, Jamaica, Queens (retired)

PREFACE

The fourth edition of *Legal Terminology with Flashcards* is the only legal terminology textbook anchored by the most recent cases, providing a fundamental understanding for 19 areas of law. This book is the most definitive legal terminology text ever published, with over 2,000 terms and definitions from a robust dictionary/thesaurus feature based on two decades of research and authority. Just like the game *Jeopardy!,* the answers are all provided up front while the questions follow in the exercises. Whether the student opts for the new electronic flashcard program on the Premium Website or the easily accessible flashcards provided inside the book, mastery of terms, pronunciations, meanings, and spellings is quickly achieved. The philosophy of the book is to isolate each legal subject into separate areas of law. In essence, the students need concentrate on only one area of law at a time without distraction.

Reorganization

In the new edition, units are organized into 10 parts, placing interrelated areas of law together for a more logical focus. For example, Part 1 includes areas of law that represent the court systems: civil and criminal. Because each part is self-contained, using all parts in order or rearranging to suit a particular curriculum, syllabus, semester, trimester, quarter, or independent self-paced course of study is achieved as easily as with prior editions that were organized alphabetically.

What's New?

All 10 parts begin with objectives and every unit kicks off with "Case and Comment," 80 percent of which are new cases decided since the last edition. A pithy comment follows each case, placing the area of law in context. Hot-button issues from the cases include: murder in Texas, "Obamacare," harassment in the U.S. Air Force, *Fox Television v. FCC, Brooks Brothers* bow ties suit, Claudia Cohen's estate, fen-phen litigation, Mexican immigration, "Don't ask, don't tell," child support shared by same-sex couples, luxury rent control, medical malpractice, child welfare, Eminem's iTunes contract, and more. Units conclude with an exciting new feature, "The Last Word." Cutting-edge legal words and phrases illustrate trends influencing the legal lexicon, such as copyright troll, stock market "flash crash," and "internalizers," frivolous lawsuits and tort reform, reverse mortgage, risk management, media law, posthumous birth, birth tourism, and Madoff's Ponzi scheme, to name but a few.

Premium Website

As always, flashcards of every term appear in the book, but an exciting new Premium Website features an Audio Library with an electronic flashcard program including audio pronunciations of each term for quick mastery of legal terminology.

Pedagogy

Now entering its third decade, *Legal Terminology with Flashcards,* Fourth Edition offers the tried-and-true pedagogy that has helped tens of thousand of students master difficult legal terms with ease. Each unit explores the most up-to-date case briefs by immersing the students in interesting issues of each area of law. Following the cases is the dictionary/thesaurus feature where students learn the definitions and usages of each term. Application of the terms is provided by over 2,000 exercises divided over the units in the forms of missing words, multiple choice, matching, true/false, synonyms, self-test, and word scramble. Finally, reinforcement of all terms, definitions, and pronunciations is provided by the flashcards in the book as well as the new electronic flashcard program at the student website as well as the Audio Library on the Premium Website.

New Terminology

Finally, what would a new edition be without lots of new terms? Throughout the book, readers will spot new words and terms like *civilogue, flipping, flopping, nanny state laws, keylogger, racial profiling, COPP, Internet piracy, foreclosure defense, robo signers,* and *underemployed* to name just a few. Existing terms were subjected to the most thorough updating since the book was first published and all unit introductions were expanded. C-o-n-f-i-d-e-n-c-e: is the word that describes what readers will take away from reading this book and mastering its terms. Never again will you be embarrassed by mispronouncing legal terms in a law office interview, using the wrong words in a legal document or e-mail and sounding unprepared on a conference call with clients or at a deposition. Like technology, law is a fast-moving business and keeping up with all the current terminology is part of the career you have chosen. And you will have the confidence to be successful because of mastering a new language called legal terminology.

Supplemental Materials

Premium Website

The Premium Website includes the online Audio Library which features all the terms in the Dictionary/Thesaurus from each unit. Pronunciations are provided for each term. You can also search by "term only" or by "terms and definitions."

The card in the text includes an access code for this book's Premium Website. Go to login.cengagebrain.com to access the Audio Library.

Instructor's Manual

The Instructor's Manual has been revised to incorporate changes in the text and to provide comprehensive teaching support. The Instructor's Manual contains the following:

- Chapter outlines
- Teaching ideas and student assignments
- Testbank and answer key

The Instructor's Manual is also posted on our website in the Online Resources section.

Web Page

Visit our website at www.paralegal.delmar.cengage.com, where you will find valuable information such as hot links and sample materials to download, as well as other Delmar Cengage Learning products.

Please note that the Internet resources are of a time-sensitive nature and URL addresses may often change or be deleted.

Acknowledgments

The author and Delmar Cengage Learning would like to thank the reviewers who made valuable suggestions for improving this text.

Kristen Brown
Guilford Technical Community College, Jamestown, NC

Paula Montlary
Florida Career College, Tampa, FL

Anne Conti
Hilbert College, Hamburg, NY

Roger E. Stone
Hilbert College, Hamburg, NY

Terri Lindfors
Globe University Minnesota School of Business, Richmond, MN

Anita Whitby
Kaplan University, Fayetteville, AR

Dictionary/Thesaurus

Examples Are Provided to Illustrate Term

Usage Provides Term in a Phrase or Sentence

Bold-faced Term ▸ **intestate**
[in.*tess*.tate]

adj. Pertaining to a person, or to the property of a person, who dies without leaving a valid will. EXAMPLE: "John died without a will and left an intestate estate." *See* intestacy. *Compare* testate.

n. 1. A person who dies without leaving a valid will. USAGE: "John is an intestate." 2. The status of a person who dies without leaving a valid will. USAGE: "John died intestate." *See* intestacy. *Compare* testate.

Phonetic Spelling with Stressed Syllable in Italics

Parts of Speech

Terms of Like or Similar Meaning (Synonym)

Terms of Like or Opposite Meaning (Antonyms)

A Number of Definitions Are Provided from Most Accepted to Least Used

n. A reason for being relieved from a duty or obligation.
v. 1. To relieve from liability. 2. To relieve from a duty or obligation.

• *v.* pardon, vindicate, exculpate, forbear; absolve, liberate ("excuse from duty")
• *n.* explanation, vindication, defense, rationalization ("a lame excuse")

Additional Terms Listed in Thesaurus Format

Latin Terms Have Phonetic Spelling

pro se
▸ [pro say]

(*Latin*) means "for one's self." Refers to appearing on one's own behalf in either a civil action or a criminal prosecution, rather than being represented by an attorney.

exclusionary rule
[eks.kloo.zhen.air.ree rule]

Legal Rules

The rule of constitutional law that evidence secured by the police by means of an unreasonable search and seizure, in violation of the Fourth Amendment, cannot be used as evidence in a criminal prosecution.

Acronyms ▸ **IOLTA**
[eye.ol.ta]

Acronym for Interest on Lawyers' Trust Accounts. In states with IOLTA programs, lawyers who hold funds belonging to clients deposit such money into a common fund, the interest on which is used for charitable, law-related purposes such as legal services to the poor. Some states' IOLTA programs are voluntary, some are mandatory.

Major Legislative Acts

Administrative Procedure Act
[ad.min.is.tray.tiv *pro*.see.jer akt]

A statute enacted by Congress that regulates the way in which federal administrative agencies conduct their affairs and establishes the procedure for judicial review of the actions of federal agencies. The Act is referred to as the APA.

Abbreviations ▸ **IRS**

Abbreviation of Internal Revenue Service.

Legal Terminology with Flashcards

FOURTH EDITION

1

Civil and Criminal Court Systems

- Learn about the courts.

- Master the similarities and differences in definitions of key terms.

- Master the pronunciations and spellings of legal terms.

- Recognize the synonyms used in legal terminology.

- Practice the usage of terms, definitions, and synonyms.

- Complete unit exercises in the forms of missing words, matching, multiple choice, true/false, synonyms, self-test, and word scramble.

- Work with a legal dictionary/thesaurus.

1

Civil Litigation (Pretrial)

INTRODUCTION

When parties fail to resolve their differences privately, they can try to settle their disputes through the court system; this process is known as civil litigation. Unlike criminal litigation, which is brought by the government against the accused, civil litigation is brought by one party (the plaintiff) against another party (the defendant). Distinguishing a civil matter from a criminal case is key. Civil procedure is very different from criminal procedure and the damages sought in a civil case are usually monetary in nature, as opposed to a jail or prison sentence.

Prior to trial, a lot of work must be done to prepare a case for trial. An attorney must always assume that her case won't settle and do all necessary work in anticipation of a trial. Typically, a client will come in for an initial interview, talk with the attorney about the case, find out if the case has merit, and learn the kind of attorney's fee and other costs that are involved.

Initially, an attorney might send a letter or make a telephone call to the opposing party, or his attorney (if represented by an attorney), in an effort to see if an amicable settlement can be agreed upon. If the parties can't agree to resolve the matter informally, litigation attorneys and their teams of assistants engage in the time-consuming task of discovery for trial: investigating the facts, interviewing witnesses, researching the law, and drafting legal documents (briefs, interrogatories, memoranda of law, as well as pleadings). Some clients won't understand why there will be years of work involved before their case is set for trial, where a friend's case, which the client thought was similar, is ready for trial in a matter of months. Before the evidence ever reaches a judge or jury in the courtroom, legal teams may spend years in preparation for trial or settlement before trial.

Depending on the court involved, and the particular court's rules, a judge assigned to the case will schedule a conference with the parties to review the progress of the case and determine if it can be settled. It is important that the judge determine if the case has been brought to the proper court and that the correct procedure has been followed. At any point in a lawsuit, or even prior thereto, a party might make a request to the court for the purpose of obtaining an order or rule directing that something be done in favor of the applicant. This is called a motion. There are many different kinds of motions. A motion might be made orally or in writing. A party might bring a motion to dismiss a lawsuit without having to proceed to trial, or for a protective order limiting a party's discovery requests. In the following case, a preliminary injunction is requested as a pretrial motion.

CASE AND COMMENT

United States District Court Eastern District of Michigan, Southern Division
Thomas More Law Center, et al., Plaintiffs

v.

Barack Hussein Obama, in his official capacity as
President of the United States, Defendant
Case # 10-CV-11156

Facts: On March 23, 2010, President Obama signed into law "The Patient Protection and Affordable Care Act." It required that every American purchase health insurance or be fined.

Procedural History: Plaintiffs Thomas More Law Center, et al., sought a preliminary injunction halting the overhaul of health care, challenging the constitutionality of the law.

Issue: Whether the Congress possesses the authority to require that every American purchase health insurance.

Rationale: Plaintiffs sought a declaration that Congress lacked authority under the Commerce Clause to pass health-care reform, and a declaration that the penalty provision for not buying insurance per the law was an unconstitutional tax. The judge found that the interstate health-care market is affected and said, ". . . decisions to forego insurance coverage in preference to attempting to pay for health care out of pocket drive up the cost of insurance. The costs of caring for the uninsured who prove unable to pay are shifted to health-care providers, to the insured population in the form of higher premiums, to government, and to taxpayers . . ." and that the provision requiring everyone to have health coverage was essential to the Act's larger goal of regulating "the interstate business of health insurance."

Ruling: The court denied the plaintiff's motion for a preliminary injunction to stop health-care reform.

Comment: The above case illustrates that pretrial remedies (in this case, a preliminary injunction) are not always the most strategic. This action was most likely brought in order to have a speedy resolution of the issue rather than wait years for a trial to be scheduled.

DICTIONARY THESAURUS

Term
[phonetic pronunciation]

Note: All dictionary/thesaurus terms appear on flashcards at the back of the book and on the student website.

acknowledgment
[ak.*naw*.lej.ment]

1. The signing of a document, under oath, where the signer certifies that he is, in fact, the person who is named in the document as the signer. 2. The certificate of the person who administered the oath, for EXAMPLE, a clerk of court, justice of the peace, or notary.

- *n.* confirmation, admission, ratification, declaration, endorsement ("acknowledgment of paternity")

action
[*ak*.shen]

A judicial or administrative proceeding for the enforcement or protection of a right; a lawsuit. It is important to distinguish a civil action from a criminal action.

- *n.* legal proceeding, lawsuit, dispute, litigation ("an action for divorce")

action at common law
[*ak*.shen at *kom*.en law]

A lawsuit governed by the common law rather than by statutes.

action at law
[*ak*.shun at law]

A lawsuit brought in a court of law as opposed to a court of equity. *Compare* equitable action.

adversary
[*ad*.ver.sa.ree]

1. An opponent; an enemy. 2. The opposite party in a lawsuit.

- *n.* opponent, enemy, competitor, foe, challenger, litigant, opposing party, adverse party

adversary proceeding
[*ad*.ver.sa.ree pro.*see*.ding]

A trial or other proceeding in which all sides have the opportunity to present their contentions; a proceeding involving a contested action.

adversary system
[*ad*.ver.sa.ree *sis*.tem]

The system of justice in the United States. Under the adversary system, the court hears the evidence presented by the adverse parties and decides the case.

affidavit
[a.fi.*day*.vit]

Any voluntary statement reduced to writing and sworn to or affirmed before a person legally authorized to administer an oath or affirmation (EXAMPLE: a notary public). A sworn statement. *See also* verification.

- *n.* affirmation, oath, statement, testimony, avowal, averment, declaration, sworn statement

affidavit of service
[a.fi.*day*.vit ov *ser*.viss]

An affidavit that certifies that process (EXAMPLES: a summons; a writ) has been served upon the parties to the action in a manner prescribed by law.

affirmation
[a.fer.*may*.shen]

A formal statement or declaration, made as a substitute for a sworn statement, by a person whose religious or other beliefs will not permit him to swear.

- *n.* statement, oath, declaration, assertion, avowal, confirmation ("out-of-court affirmation")

affirmative defense
[a.*fer*.ma.tiv de.*fense*]

A defense that amounts to more than simply a denial of the allegations in the plaintiff's complaint. It sets up a new matter that, if proven, could result in a judgment against the plaintiff even if all the allegations of the complaint are true. EXAMPLES of affirmative defenses in civil cases include accord and satisfaction, act of God, estoppel, release, and statute of limitations.

allegation
[al.e.*gay*.shen]

A statement in a pleading of a fact that the party filing the pleading intends to prove.

- *n.* assertion, accusation, avowal, claim, charge

amend
[a.*mend*]

To improve; to make better by change or modification; to correct; to adjust. Thus, a motion to amend is a motion by which a party seeks the court's permission to correct

DICTIONARY   THESAURUS *continued...*

an error or omission in a pleading or to modify allegations and supply new ones. *See also* amendment of pleading.

- *v.* correct, remedy, adjust, change, revise, alter, modify

amendment of pleading
[a.*mend*.ment ov *plee*.ding]

Although every jurisdiction imposes different restrictions, all jurisdictions permit pleadings to be amended for the purpose of correcting errors and omissions and to modify allegations and supply new ones. *See also* amend.

amicus curiae
[a.*mee*.kes *koo*.ree.eye]

(*Latin*) "Friend of the court." A person who is interested in the outcome of the case, but who is not a party, whom the court permits to file a brief for the purpose of providing the court with a position or a point of view that it might not otherwise have; often referred to simply as an amicus.

amount in controversy
[a.*mount* in *kon*.tre.ver.see]

A term relevant to determining a court's jurisdiction, when jurisdiction is based upon either a minimum dollar amount with which the court is permitted to concern itself, or a maximum amount that represents the upper limit of its jurisdiction.

answer
[*an*.ser]

n. A pleading in response to a complaint. An answer may deny the allegations of the complaint, demur to them, admit to them, or introduce affirmative defenses intended to defeat the plaintiff's lawsuit or delay it. One may also assert counterclaims against the plaintiff.
v. 1. To reply. 2. In pleading, to respond to the plaintiff's complaint by denying its allegations or by introducing affirmative defenses containing new matter.

- *n.* defense, reply, denial, rebuttal, refutation, counterclaim ("file an answer to a complaint")
- *v.* reply, respond, defend, controvert ("He answered the plaintiff's complaint by denying the allegations")

appear
[a.*peer*]

To enter an appearance in a case.

- *v.* surface, attend, arrive, come in, materialize ("appear in court")

appearance
[a.*peer*.ense]

1. The action of an attorney in declaring to the court that he represents a litigant in a case before the court (also referred to as "entering an appearance"). 2. The act by which a party comes into court. EXAMPLES: the filing of a complaint by a plaintiff; the filing of an answer by a defendant.

- *n.* actualization, entrance, exhibition, materialization, emergence ("The appearance of his attorney was timely")

appearance docket
[a.*peer*.ense *dok*.et]

A docket kept by the clerk of court in which appearances are entered.

bill of particulars
[bill ov per.*tik*.yoo.lerz]

In civil actions, a more detailed statement of the pleading. An adverse party is entitled to be informed of the precise nature of the opposite party's cause of action or defense, in order to be able to prepare for trial and to protect himself against surprise at the trial.

caption
[*kap*.shen]

A heading. As applied in legal practice, when "caption" is used to mean "heading," it generally refers to the heading of a court paper. EXAMPLE:

Miriam Brown	In the Court of Common
Plaintiff	Pleas of Bucks County,
v.	
Stanley Brown,	
Scott Lang,	Pennsylvania
Defendants	Civil Action No. 1234
	September Term, 2011

- *n.* heading, title, inscription ("the caption of the case")

cause of action
[koz ov *ak*.shen]

Circumstances that give a person the right to bring a lawsuit and to receive relief from a court. *See also* complaint.

change of venue
[chanj ov *ven*.yoo]

Moving the trial of a case from one county or judicial district to another county or judicial district. The most common reasons for a court to permit a change in the venue of a civil trial are "in the interest of justice," or "for the convenience of the parties." A venue change in a criminal trial may be permitted due to the defendant's inability to receive a fair trial because of publicity. The issue is put before the court by means of a motion for change of venue.

civil law
[*siv*.el law]

1. Body of law that determines private rights and liabilities, as distinguished from criminal law. 2. The entire body of law adopted in a country or a state, as distinguished from natural law (sometimes called moral law) and from international law (the law governing relationships between countries). 3. The law of the Roman Empire, or modern law that has been handed down from Roman Law. 4. The name of the body of law by which the State of Louisiana is governed.

civil procedure
[*siv*.el pro.*see*.jer]

The rules by which private rights are enforced by the courts and agencies. There are both Federal Rules of Civil Procedure, followed in the federal courts, and rules of civil procedure for each of the states.

claimant
[*clay*.ment]

One who claims or makes a claim; an applicant for justice; a plaintiff.

- *n.* petitioner, challenger, plaintiff, appellant, litigant, party, pleader

class action
[klas *ak*.shen]

An action brought by one or several plaintiffs on behalf of a class of persons. A class action may be appropriate when there has been injury to so many people that their voluntarily and unanimously joining in a lawsuit is improbable and impracticable. In such a situation, injured parties who wish to do so may, with the court's permission, sue on behalf of all. A class action is sometimes referred to as a representative action.

clear and convincing evidence
[kleer and kon.*vinss*.ing *ev*.i.denss]

A degree of proof required in some civil cases, higher than the usual standard of preponderance of the evidence.

DICTIONARY / THESAURUS *continued...*

complaint
[kom.*playnt*]

The initial pleading in a civil action, in which the plaintiff alleges a cause of action and asks that the wrong done to him be remedied by the court. ("Susan was served with a complaint.")

- *n.* petition, charge, pleading. In criminal cases: indictment or accusation

concurrent jurisdiction
[kon.*ker*.ent joo.ris.*dik*.shen]

Two or more courts having the power to adjudicate the same class of cases or the same matter. *See also* jurisdiction.

counterclaim
[*kown*.ter klame]

A cause of action on which a defendant in a lawsuit might have sued the plaintiff in a separate action. Such a cause of action, stated in a separate division of a defendant's answer, is a counterclaim. *See also* cross-action; cross-claim; cross-complaint.

court of equity
[kort ov *ek*.wi.tee]

A court having jurisdiction of non-money or equitable actions; a court that administers remedies that are equitable in nature, such as an injunction. *Compare* court of law.

court of general jurisdiction
[kort ov *jen*.e.rel joo.ris.*dik*.shen]

Generally, another term for trial court; that is, a court having jurisdiction to try all classes of civil and criminal cases except those that can be heard only by a court of limited jurisdiction.

court of inferior jurisdiction
[*kort* ov in.*feer*.ee.er joo.ris.*dik*.shen]

A court of original or limited jurisdiction, as opposed to an appellate court, or a court that has jurisdiction to hear many kinds of cases. *See* court of limited jurisdiction.

court of law
[kort ov law]

1. A court having jurisdiction of actions at law, as distinguished from equitable actions. 2. Any court that administers the law of a state or of the United States. *Compare* equitable action.

court of limited jurisdiction
[kort ov *lim*.i.ted joo.ris.*dik*.shen]

A court whose jurisdiction is limited to civil cases of a certain type (EXAMPLE: probate court) or that involve a limited amount of money (EXAMPLE: small claims court), or whose jurisdiction in criminal cases is confined to petty offenses and preliminary hearings.

cross-action
[*kross*-ak.shen]

1. An action brought by a defendant in a lawsuit against another named defendant based upon a cause of action arising out of the same transaction on which the plaintiff's suit is based. *See also* counterclaim. 2. An independent action brought by a defendant in a lawsuit against the plaintiff.

cross-claim
[*kross*-klame]

A counterclaim against a coplaintiff or a codefendant.

cross-complaint
[*kross*-kem.*plaint*]

A complaint a defendant in an action may file: (a) against the *plaintiff*, based upon *any* cause of action she has against him; or (b) against *anyone* (including persons not yet involved in the lawsuit) if she alleges a cause of action based upon the same transactions as those upon which the complaint against her is based.

defendant
[de.*fen*.dent]

The person against whom an action is brought.

- *n.* accused, respondent, responding litigant, the party charged
- *ant.* plaintiff

demur
[de.*mer*]

1. To make a demurrer. 2. To object to; take exceptions to; to disagree. When a demurrer is used, it is a method of raising objection to the sufficiency of a pleading and asking that the case be dismissed. In most jurisdictions, demurrers have been replaced by the use of motions or answers, which can perform the same function.

deposition
[dep.e.*zish*.en]

1. The transcript of a witness's testimony given under oath outside of the courtroom, usually in advance of the trial or hearing, upon oral examination or in response to written interrogatories. *See also* discovery. 2. In a more general sense, an affidavit, a statement under oath.

- *n.* testimony, sworn testimony, testimony under oath, affidavit, declaration

digest
[*die*.jest]

A series of volumes containing summaries of cases organized by legal topics, subject areas, and so on. Digests are essential for legal research. Some digests are limited to certain regions. Digests are updated continually to ensure they are current.

discovery
[dis.*kuv*.e.ree]

A means for providing a party, in advance of trial, with access to facts that are within the knowledge of the other side, to enable the party to better try her case. A motion to compel discovery is the procedural means for compelling the adverse party to reveal such facts or to produce documents, books, and other things within his possession or control. *See also* deposition; interrogatories.

- *n.* exposure, uncovering, disclosure, investigation, finding, breakthrough, pretrial device

dismiss
[dis.*miss*]

To order a case, motion, or prosecution to be terminated. A party requests such an order by means of a motion to dismiss.

diversity jurisdiction
[di.*ver*.se.tee joo.ris.*dik*.shen]

The jurisdiction of a federal court arising from diversity of citizenship where parties are residents of different states and the jurisdictional amount has been met.

diversity of citizenship
[di.*ver*.se.tee of *sit*.i.zen.ship]

A ground for invoking the original jurisdiction of a federal district court, the basis of jurisdiction being the existence of a controversy between citizens of different states.

equitable action
[*ek*.wi.tebl *ak*.shen]

Although the distinction between a suit in equity and an action at law has been abolished in most states, all actions now being simply civil actions, the concept of an equitable action still exists with respect to the remedy sought, as historically certain types of relief were available only in a court of equity (EXAMPLES: an injunction; specific performance). Equitable actions are designed to remedy injuries that cannot adequately be redressed by an action at law.

ex parte
[eks *par*.tay]

Means "of a side" (i.e., by one party). The term refers to an application made to the court by one party without notice to the other party.

in personam action [in peer.*soh*.nam *ak*.shen]	A legal action whose purpose is to obtain a judgment against a person, as opposed to a judgment against property. Most lawsuits are in personam actions. *See also* jurisdiction in personam. *Compare* in rem action; quasi in rem action.
in rem action [in rem *ak*.shen]	A legal action brought against property (EXAMPLES: an action to quiet title; a civil forfeiture), as opposed to an action brought against the person.
injunction [in.*junk*.shen]	A court order that commands or prohibits some act or course of conduct. It is preventive in nature and designed to protect a plaintiff from irreparable injury to his property or property rights by prohibiting or commanding the doing of certain acts. An injunction is a form of equitable relief.

- *n.* ban, stay, order, enjoinder, interdiction, restraint, mandate, prohibition

interplead [in.ter.*pleed*]	To file an interpleader in a lawsuit.
interpleader [in.ter.*pleed*.er]	A remedy that requires rival claimants to property held by a disinterested third party (EXAMPLES: a stakeholder; a person who is in debt to the claimants) to litigate their demands without entangling him in their lawsuits.
interrogatories [in.te.*raw*.ge.toh.reez]	Written questions put by one party to another, or, in limited situations, to a witness in advance of trial. Interrogatories are a form of discovery and are governed by the rules of civil procedure. They must be answered in writing. *Compare* deposition.

- *n.* questions, inquiries

judgment [*juj*.ment]	1. In a civil action, the final determination by a court of the rights of the parties, based upon the pleadings and the evidence; a decision or decree. 2. In a criminal prosecution, a determination of guilt; a conviction.
jurisdiction [joo.ris.*dik*.shen]	A term used in several senses: 1. In a general sense, the power and authority of a court to decide lawsuits and bind the parties. EXAMPLES: the right of juvenile courts to hear cases involving juvenile offenders; the power of federal courts to adjudicate federal questions. 2. In a specific sense, the right of a court to determine a particular case; in other words, the power of the court over the subject matter of, or the property involved. 3. The power of a court to hear cases only within a specific territorial area (EXAMPLES: a state; a county; a federal judicial district). *See also* venue. 4. Authority; control; power. 5. District; area; locality. *See also* diversity jurisdiction; subject matter jurisdiction.

- *n.* capacity, authority, authorization, right, charter, judicature, license, sovereignty; territory, region, domain, district, circuit, state, quarter, field, province ("The matter has not been decided in this jurisdiction.")

jurisdiction in personam [joo.ris.*dik*.shen in per.*soh*.nam]	The jurisdiction a court has over the person of a defendant. It is acquired by service of process upon the defendant or by her voluntary submission to jurisdiction. Voluntary submission may be implied from a defendant's conduct within the jurisdiction, for

EXAMPLE, by doing business in a state or by operating a motor vehicle within a state. Jurisdiction in personam is also referred to as personal jurisdiction. *See also and compare* jurisdiction in rem; jurisdiction quasi in rem.

jurisdiction in rem
[joo.ris.*dik*.shen in rem]

The jurisdiction a court has over property situated in the state. *See also and compare* jurisdiction in personam; jurisdiction quasi in rem. *See also* in rem action.

jurisdiction quasi in rem
[joo.ris.*dik*.shen *kway*.sye in rem]

The jurisdiction a court has over the defendant's interest in property located within the jurisdiction. *See also and compare* jurisdiction in personam; jurisdiction in rem.

jurisprudence
[joor.is.*proo*.dense]

The science of law; legal philosophy.

- *n.* philosophy, theory, legal foundation, philosophy of law, system of laws

legal research
[*lee*.gl *ree*.serch]

A study of precedents and other authority for the purpose of developing or supporting a legal theory or position. Most legal writing is based upon research and involves application of the law to the facts.

lis pendens
[liss *pen*.denz]

A pending suit or pending action. The doctrine of lis pendens states that a pending suit is notice to all, so buying real estate subject to suit binds the purchaser.

litigation
[lit.i.*gay*.shen]

A legal action; a lawsuit.

- *n.* judicial contest, prosecution, action, lawsuit, case, cause ("Massive amounts of litigation have backlogged the courts.")

long arm statutes
[long arm *stat*.shoots]

State statutes providing for substituted service of process on a nonresident corporation or individual. Long arm statutes permit a state's courts to take jurisdiction over a nonresident if she has done business in the state (provided the minimum contacts test is met), or has committed a tort or owns property within the state.

memorandum of law
[mem.o.*ran*.dum ov law]

A written statement submitted to a court for the purpose of persuading it of the correctness of one's position. Similar to a brief, although usually not as extensive, it cites case law and other legal authority.

motion
[*moh*.shen]

An application made to a court for the purpose of obtaining an order or rule directing something to be done in favor of the applicant. (EXAMPLE: a defendant's motion to dismiss is a formal request to the court that the plaintiff's lawsuit be terminated without further consideration.) The types of motions available to litigants, as well as their form and the matters they appropriately address, are set forth in detail in the Federal Rules of Civil Procedure and the rules of civil procedure of the various states. Motions may be written or oral, depending on the type of relief sought and on the court in which they are made. Some common motions are motion to produce, motion for summary judgment, motion for entry upon land, and motion to dismiss.

- *n.* request, petition, proposition, plan, demand, offering

motion for summary judgment
[*mo*.shen for *sum*.e.ree *juj*.ment]

A method of disposing of an action without further proceedings. Under the Federal Rules of Civil Procedure, and the rules of civil procedure of many states, a party against whom a claim, counterclaim, or cross-claim is asserted, or against whom a

DICTIONARY | THESAURUS *continued...*

declaratory judgment is sought, may file a motion for summary judgment seeking judgment in her favor if there is no genuine issue as to any material fact. *See also* motion.

motion to compel discovery
[*mo*.shen to kom.*pel* dis.*kuv*.e.ree]

To force a response; to force a response to discovery. A person who fails to answer interrogatories or to respond appropriately to an attempt to take his deposition may be forced to comply by a motion to compel discovery.

motion to dismiss
[*moh*.shen to dis.*miss*]

Motion requesting a case, motion, or prosecution to be terminated.

order
[*or*.der]

1. A determination made by a court; an order of court. 2. A determination made by an administrative agency.

- *v.* dictate, require, rule, demand, ordain, prescribe
- *n.* decree, command, mandate, demand, judgment ("order of the court")

order to show cause
[*or*.der to show koz]

An order of court directing a party to appear before the court and to present facts and legal arguments showing cause why the court should not take a certain action adversely affecting that party's interests. Orders to show cause are often granted ex parte (by one side, without notice to the other party). A party's failure to appear, or having appeared, his failure to show cause, will result in a final judgment unfavorable to him.

permission to enter upon land
[per.*mish*.en to *en*.ter up.*on* land]

During the discovery process, a party might request permission to enter upon the land of another. EXAMPLE: For a "slip and fall" case, the plaintiff's attorney would want to enter on the land of another to see the scene of the accident.

petition
[pe.*tish*.en]

1. A formal request in writing, addressed to a person or body in a position of authority (EXAMPLES: a city council; an administrative agency), signed by a number of persons or by one person. 2. The name given in some jurisdictions to a complaint or other pleading that alleges a cause of action. 3. An application made to a court ex parte.

- *n.* appeal, request, plea, motion, application
- *v.* plead, seek, solicit, ask, urge, entreat, apply for ("We petitioned the court for mercy.")

plaintiff
[*plain*.tif]

A person who brings a lawsuit.

- *n.* complainant, accuser, suitor, petitioner, opponent, litigant

pleadings
[*plee*.dingz]

Formal statements by the parties to an action setting forth their claims or defenses. EXAMPLES of pleadings include: a complaint; a cross-complaint; an answer; a counterclaim. The various kinds of pleadings, and the rules governing them, are set forth in detail in the Federal Rules of Civil Procedure and, with respect to pleading in state courts, by the rules of civil procedure of several states. *See also* amendment of pleading.

**preponderance
of the evidence**
[pre.*pon*.der.ense ov the *ev*.i.dense]

The degree of proof required in most civil actions. It means that the greater weight and value of the credible evidence, taken as a whole, belongs to one side in a lawsuit rather than to the other side. In other words, the party whose evidence is more convincing has a "preponderance of the evidence" on its side and must, as a matter of law, prevail in the lawsuit because she has met her burden of proof. The expression "preponderance of the evidence" has nothing to do with the number of witnesses a party presents, only with the credibility and value of their testimony.

pretrial
[pree.*try*.el]

Prior to trial. "Pretrial" is applied to any aspect of litigation that occurs before the trial begins. USAGE: "pretrial proceedings"; "pretrial motions"; "pretrial conference."

pretrial conference
[pree.*try*.el kon.fer.ense]

A conference held between the judge and counsel for all parties prior to trial, for the purpose of facilitating disposition of the case by, among other actions, simplifying the pleadings, narrowing the issues, obtaining stipulations to avoid unnecessary proof, and limiting the number of witnesses. Often leads to resolution or settlement of case.

pretrial motions
[pree.*try*.el *moh*.shenz]

Motions that may be filed prior to the commencement of a trial. EXAMPLES: a motion to suppress; a motion to dismiss.

primary source
[*pry*.mer.ee sors]

An original or firsthand document or reliable works that are generally created at the time the event occurred. These are considered binding authority, or the law itself, as opposed to secondhand information or interpretation or analysis of information. One of the goals of legal research is to find primary sources.

procedural law
[pro.*seed*.jer.el law]

The means or method by which a court adjudicates cases (EXAMPLES: the Federal Rules of Civil Procedure; the Federal Rules of Criminal Procedure; rules of court), as distinguished from the substantive law by which it determines legal rights.

- *n.* process, system, method, policy, routine, action, operation ("Federal Rules of Civil Procedure")

proceeding
[pro.*seed*.ing]

1. In one sense, every procedural aspect of a lawsuit, from beginning to end, including all means or process by which a party is able to cause a court to act; a suit; an action. 2. In another sense, any procedural aspect of a lawsuit undertaken to enforce rights or achieve redress. EXAMPLE: a hearing on a motion. 3. A specific course of action.

- *n.* undertaking, course, happening ("The divorce proceeding took longer than I thought."); records, minutes, report, account, transactions ("The proceedings from GALA are kept in a file.")

quasi in rem action
[*kway*.zye in rem *ak*.shen]

An action that adjudicates only the rights of the parties with respect to property, not the rights of all persons who might have an interest in the property. *See also and compare* in personam action; in rem action.

remand
[ree.*mand*]

n. The return of a case by an appellate court to the trial court for further hearing or proceedings for a new trial, or for entry of judgment in accordance with the order of the appellate court.
v. To return or send back.

reply [re.*ply*]	1. In pleading, the plaintiff's response to the defendant's setoff or counterclaim. 2. A response; an answer. • *n.* rejoinder, replication, retort, refutation, retaliation, response, answer • *v.* answer, counter, acknowledge, return
request for admission [re.*kwest* for ad.*mish*.shen]	Written statements concerning a case, directed to an adverse party, that must be admitted or denied. All will be treated by the court as having been established and need not be proven at trial.
request for physical or mental examination [re.*kwest* for *fiz*.i.kel or *men*.tel eg.zam.i.*nay*.shen]	Demands that can be made during the discovery process. The physical examination or inspection of a party is only requested when the person is claiming bodily harm or hurt (known as personal injury) and has put her physical condition at issue, typically from a car accident or slip and fall. A request for a mental examination is much less common. Again, only where a party has put her mental condition at issue, with a claim of brain damage, distress, fright, or emotional disturbance, can such a request be made. Because of privacy concerns, there are many restrictions on these forms of discovery depending on the jurisdiction.
request for production [re.*kwest* for pro.*duk*.shen]	During the discovery process either party may request that the other side make available for inspection relevant documents or things related to the case that are in its possession. A party is neither required to create or obtain documents it doesn't have in its possession.
sanctions [*sank*.shenz]	An action taken by a tribunal, for EXAMPLE, a court or administrative board, to enforce its judgment, decision, or order. EXAMPLES of sanctions are fines or a penalty, or even the suspension or revocation of a license.
secondary source [*sek*.en.dare.ee sorse]	As opposed to case law, which is binding authority, a secondary source is merely persuasive authority, it is not law itself, but simply commentary upon or a summary of the law. EXAMPLES of secondary sources are legal treatises, law review articles, legal encyclopedias, and dictionaries.
service [*ser*.viss]	The delivering of process; short for service of process. • *n.* notice, notification ("service by mail" or "service by posting")
service by mail [*ser*.viss by mail]	In circumstances where permitted by statute, service of process occurs by mailing a copy of a summons, writ, complaint, or other process to the party to be served at his last known address or by mailing it to his attorney.
service by publication [ser.*viss* by pub.li.*kay*.shen]	In circumstances where permitted by statute, service of process occurs by publishing a copy of a summons, writ, complaint, or other process in a newspaper of general circulation in a particular region.
service of process [ser.*viss* ov *pross*.ess]	Delivery of a summons, writ, complaint, or other process to the opposite party, or other person entitled to receive it, in such manner as the law prescribes, whether by leaving a copy at her residence, by mailing a copy to her or her attorney, or by publication.

statutes of limitations
[*stat*.shootz ov lim.i.*tay*.shenz]

Federal and state statutes prescribing the maximum period of time during which various types of civil actions and criminal prosecutions can be brought after the occurrence of the injury or the offense.

subject matter jurisdiction
[*sub*.jekt *mat*.er joo.ris.*dik*.shen]

The jurisdiction of a court to hear and determine the type of case before it. EXAMPLE: the jurisdiction of a family court to try cases involving matters of family law.

subpoena
[sub.*peen*.ah]

A command in the form of written process requiring a witness to come to court to testify; short for subpoena ad testificandum [ahd *tes*.te.fe.*kan*.dem]. The Latin term means "testify under penalty."

subpoena duces tecum
[sub.*peen*.ah *doo*.ses *tee*.kum]

The Latin term duces tecum means "bring with you under penalty." A subpoena duces tecum is a written command requiring a witness to come to court to testify, and at that time to produce for use as evidence the papers, documents, books, or records listed in the subpoena. Depending on the jurisdiction and the documents requested, court approval may be needed for a subpoena. Other subpoenas can be served with an attorney's signature rather than a judge's approval.

substantive law
[*sub*.sten.tiv law]

Area of the law that defines rights and responsibilities, law, and facts, as opposed to procedural law, which governs the process by which rights are adjudicated.

summons
[*sum*.enz]

In a civil case, the process by which an action is commenced and the defendant is brought within the jurisdiction of the court.

- *n.* citation, mandate, process, notification, command, direction

third-party complaint
[third-*par*.tee kum.*plaint*]

A complaint filed by the defendant in a lawsuit against a third person whom he seeks to bring into the action because of that person's alleged liability to the defendant.

trial court
[*try*.el kort]

A court that hears and determines a case initially, as opposed to an appellate court; a court of general jurisdiction.

venue
[*ven*.yoo]

The county or judicial district in which a case should be tried. In civil cases, venue may be based on where the events giving rise to the cause of action took place or where the parties live or work. Venue is distinguishable from jurisdiction because it is an issue only if jurisdiction already exists and because, unlike jurisdiction, it can be waived or changed by consent of the parties.

- *n.* county, district, zone, area, neighborhood, place of jurisdiction

verification
[vehr.i.fi.*kay*.shen]

A sworn statement certifying the truth of the facts recited in an instrument or document. Thus, for EXAMPLE, a verified complaint is a pleading accompanied by an affidavit stating that the facts set forth in the complaint are true.

- *n.* confirmation, proof, evidence, corroboration

DICTIONARY THESAURUS *continued...*

verified
[*vehr*.i.fide]

Sworn; sworn to; stated under oath.

- *adj.* sworn, sworn to, authenticated

verify
[*vehr*.i.fy]

1. To certify the accuracy or truth of a statement under oath; to make a verification.
2. To establish the accuracy or truth of anything, whether or not by oath.

- *v.* attest, authenticate, confirm, debunk, document, justify, establish, certify; swear, declare, state, avow

Missing Words

Fill in the blanks.

1. A(n) _____ motion is a method of disposing of an action without further proceedings.

2. A(n) _____ is a sworn statement certifying the truth of the facts recited in an instrument or document.

3. A(n) _____ is an affidavit that certifies that process has been served.

4. A(n) _____ action is designed to remedy injuries that cannot adequately be redressed by an action at law.

5. _____ are statutes prescribing the maximum period of time during which various types of actions can be brought.

6. A(n) _____ is a court that hears and determines a case initially.

7. A(n) _____ is the action of an attorney in declaring to the court that he represents a litigant in a case.

8. In a civil action, the final determination by a court of the rights of the parties is a _____.

9. A remedy that requires rival claimants to property held by a disinterested third party to litigate their demands without involving the third party in their lawsuit is called _____.

10. A(n) _____ is the plaintiff's answer to the defendant's setoff or counterclaim.

11. A(n) _____ is a defense that amounts to more than simply a denial of the allegations of the plaintiff's complaint.

12. _____ is a means for providing a party, in advance of trial, with access to facts that are within knowledge of the other side, to enable the party to better try the case.

13. A(n) _____ is a cause of action on which a defendant in a lawsuit might have sued a plaintiff in a separate action.

14. A(n) _____ is a counterclaim against a coplaintiff or a codefendant.

15. Service of process is the delivery of a(n) _____, writ, complaint, or other process.

16. A(n) _____ is the person against whom an action is brought.

17. Written statements directed to an adverse party that must be either admitted or denied are called
_____.

18. A degree of proof required in some civil cases is _____, which is higher than the proof required in most civil actions.

STUDY AID: Use flashcards for this unit before completing the exercises.

Matching

Match the letter of the definition to the term.

P **19.** preponderance of the evidence   **A.** lawsuit

G **20.** interrogatories   **B.** sworn statement

T **21.** summons   **C.** request to court for relief

C **22.** motion   **D.** jurisdiction the court has over the person of a defendant

A **23.** litigation   **E.** the name given in some jurisdictions for a complaint

B **24.** affidavit   **F.** substitute for sworn statement

L **25.** judgment   **G.** written questions put by one party to another

D **26.** jurisdiction in personam   **H.** the jurisdiction of a court to hear and determine the type of case before it

M **27.** cross-claim   **I.** the process by which a civil action is commenced and the defendant is brought within the jurisdiction of the court

J **28.** interpleader   **J.** a remedy that requires rival claimants to property held by a disinterested third party to litigate their demands without entangling the third party in the lawsuit

N **29.** jurisdiction   **K.** a court order that commands or prohibits some act or course of conduct

F **30.** affirmation   **L.** in a civil action, the final determination by a court of the rights of the parties

O **31.** trial court   **M.** a counterclaim against a coplaintiff or a codefendant

_E_ **32.** petition

N. in a general sense, the right of a court to adjudicate lawsuits and bind the parties

_H_ **33.** subject matter jurisdiction

O. a court that hears and determines a case initially

_K_ **34.** injunction

P. the degree of proof required in most civil actions

_Q_ **35.** court of inferior jurisdiction

Q. a court of original or limited jurisdiction

Multiple Choice

Select the best choice.

_B_ **36.** A means for providing a party with access to facts that are within the knowledge of the other side, to enable the party to better try the case is:
- **a.** diversity.
- **b.** discovery.
- **c.** injunction.
- **d.** equitable action.

_C_ **37.** A person who brings a lawsuit is the:
- **a.** defendant.
- **b.** respondent.
- **c.** plaintiff.
- **d.** stenographer.

_a_ **38.** A caption is:
- **a.** the heading on a pleading or motion.
- **b.** a cause of action.
- **c.** an affirmation.
- **d.** an action.

_D_ **39.** The initial pleading in a civil action in which a plaintiff alleges a cause of action and asks that the wrong done him be remedied by the court is the:
- **a.** counterclaim.
- **b.** answer.
- **c.** cross-claim.
- **d.** complaint.

_B_ **40.** An order of the court directing a party to appear and present facts and legal arguments showing cause why the court should not take a certain action adversely affecting that party's interests is a(n):
- **a.** deposition.
- **b.** summons.
- **c.** petition.
- **d.** order to show cause.

_C_ **41.** A long arm statute provides for:
- **a.** service on a resident.
- **b.** substituted service on a resident.
- **c.** substituted service on a nonresident.
- **d.** service on a nonresident.

_a_ **42.** A written statement submitted to the court for the purpose of persuading it of the correctness of one's position is a(n):
- **a.** memorandum of law.
- **b.** interrogatory.
- **c.** bill of particulars.
- **d.** verification.

_B_ **43.** The means or method by which a court adjudicates cases, as distinguished from the substantive law by which it determines legal rights is:
- **a.** substantive law.
- **b.** procedural law.
- **c.** long arm statute.
- **d.** statute of limitations.

_C_ **44.** The jurisdiction of a federal court arising from a controversy between citizens of different states is:
- **a.** jurisprudence.
- **b.** personal jurisdiction.
- **c.** diversity jurisdiction.
- **d.** in personam jurisdiction.

___D___ **45.** A formal request to the court that the plaintiff's lawsuit be terminated without further consideration is a(n):
  a. interpleader.
  b. jurisdiction.
  c. order.
  d. motion to dismiss.

___A___ **46.** The county or judicial district in which a case should be tried is the:
  a. venue.
  b. deposition.
  c. caption.
  d. class action.

___C___ **47.** A statement in a pleading of a fact that the party filing the pleading intends to prove is a(n):
  a. affidavit.
  b. verification.
  c. allegation.
  d. action.

True/False

Mark the following T or F.

___T___ **48.** An action is a judicial proceeding for the enforcement or protection of a right.

___T___ **49.** An application to the court for the purpose of obtaining an order or ruling is a motion.

___F___ **50.** A more detailed statement of the pleadings is the summons.

___F___ **51.** The person who brings a lawsuit is the defendant.

___T___ **52.** A class action is an action brought by one or several plaintiffs on behalf of a class of persons.

___T___ **53.** A counterclaim is a cause of action on which the defendant might have sued the plaintiff in a separate action.

___T___ **54.** Litigation is a term for a legal action.

___T___ **55.** Civil law is from the law of the Roman Empire.

___T___ **56.** A court order that commands or prohibits some act or course of conduct is an injunction.

___F___ **57.** A court's jurisdiction is the right of a court to adjudicate lawsuits of a certain kind.

___T___ **58.** A deposition is the transcript of a witness's testimony given under oath outside of the courtroom, usually in advance of trial.

___F___ **59.** The process by which an action is commenced and the defendant is brought within the jurisdiction of the court is called an affidavit.

___T___ **60.** Statutes of limitations detail the maximum period of time during which various types of actions can be brought.

___T___ **61.** A verification is a sworn statement certifying the truth of facts recited in an instrument or document.

___T___ **62.** An equitable action is brought to remedy injuries that cannot be resolved by an action at law.

Synonyms

Select the correct synonym in parentheses for each numbered item.

63. ACTION
(proceeding, motion, interpleader)

64. ANSWER
(demand, inquiry, response)

65. ORDER
(determination, complaint, reply)

66. PLEADINGS
(allegations, venue, action)

67. PLAINTIFF
(respondent, claimant, interpleader)

68. MOTION
(summons, request, judgment)

69. AFFIDAVIT
(appearance, discovery, statement)

70. DEFENDANT
(respondent, petitioner, juror)

71. LITIGATION
(jurisdiction, lawsuit, reply)

72. VENUE
(place, caption, pleadings)

73. DISCOVERY
(order, cross-claim, disclosure)

74. PETITION
(answer, complaint, reply)

75. AFFIRMATIVE DEFENSE
(interrogatories, action, excuse)

76. AMENDMENT OF PLEADING
(correction, appearance, equitable relief)

77. ADVERSARY
(complaint, opponent, judge)

78. JURISPRUDENCE
(legal philosophy, legal psychology, trial practice)

79. REPLY
(surrender, response, settle)

80. VERIFY
(certify, lis pendens, dismiss)

81. CROSS-CLAIM
(summons, bill of particulars, counterclaim)

82. APPEARANCE
(allegation, amend, represent)

Self-Test

Place the number of the correct term in the appropriate space.

83. motion

84. plaintiff

85. litigation

86. counterclaim

87. summons

88. complaint

89. affirmative defenses

90. answer

91. civil procedure

92. discovery

93. defendant

94. order

95. allegations

96. proceeding

The rules of procedure by which private rights are enforced are _____. Usually, a dispute or problem arises.

In most instances, the parties work their differences out. If not, an attorney might be consulted. Sometimes a simple

letter or telephone call is all that is needed. Where the parties refuse to budge from their positions, _____

might be needed, and a judge or jury resolves the dispute. The _____, the person who brings the action,

will need to supply the attorney with a set of facts supporting one or more causes of action entitling him to relief.

A(n) _____ and _____ will then be drafted and served upon the defendant to start the action

or _____. The _____ must then respond to the _____ contained in the complaint.

The defendant usually responds with a(n) _____ denying the plaintiff's claims, and sometimes sets forth

new issues. The defendant might allege a new matter that, if proven, could result in a judgment against the plaintiff.

These are called _____. Occasionally, defendants will have a(n) _____ in their answer, a cause

of action on which a defendant in a lawsuit might have sued the plaintiff in a separate action. At any point, the parties

can decide to settle their dispute. If not, the case proceeds toward trial. Both sides usually conduct _____

to obtain facts within the knowledge of the other side. A(n) _____, or request to the court for an order or

ruling, may be needed if the parties do not voluntarily reply to discovery requests. The judge will then issue a(n)

_____ or determination resolving the request.

Word Scramble

*Unscramble the following words and write the correct word(s) that match(es) the definition
for each word or phrase.*

97. sweran – a pleading in response to a complaint

    _____

    _____

98. tiffplain – a person who brings a lawsuit _____

    _____

99. nueve – the county or judicial district in which
    a case should be tried _____

    _____

100. otionm – an application made to the court for a
    rule directing something to be done in favor of the
    applicant _____

    _____

101. dictionjuris – the power and authority of the court
    to decide lawsuits and bind the parties _____

    _____

102. ationlitig – a lawsuit; a legal action _____

_____

103. iaffdavit – a sworn statement _____

_____

104. smmonsu – In a civil case, an action is commenced and the defendant is brought within the jurisdiction of the court with the service of this legal document _____

_____

105. pleaderinter – a remedy that requires rival claimants to litigate their demands without entangling in the procedure the third party who holds the property _____

_____

106. deror – a determination made by a court _____

_____

107. verydisco – a means of providing the parties before trial with access to the facts that are within the knowledge of the other side _____

_____

108. claimcounter – a cause of action on which a defendant in a lawsuit might have sued the plaintiff in a separate action _____

_____

109. ialrt ourtc – a court that hears and determines a case initially _____

_____

110. earappance – the action of an attorney in declaring to the court that he represents a litigant

_____

_____

111. deror ot hosw ausec – an order of the court directing a party to appear before the court and present facts and arguments showing cause why the court should not take a certain action

_____

_____

The Last Word

While statistics in your state might differ, only 1.2 percent of federal civil cases went to trial nationwide in 2009. Fifty years ago that percentage was nearly 10 times higher. What are the top 10 reasons for this change?

1. Alternative Dispute Resolution (ADR) is required by more contracts today, reducing the need for trials.
2. Attorneys' cost benefit analysis of cases allows them to better measure which cases would be worth litigating.
3. Clients are more cost conscious before rushing to sue.
4. Risk management policies at corporations often support settlement before trial.
5. Class actions like sexual harassment have matured, allowing for quicker settlements.
6. Statutes like the Americans with Disability Act have codified law, obviating the need to sue.
7. Increasing costs of electronic discovery discourage litigants.
8. The 24/7 news cycle constantly highlights runaway juries and verdicts, increasing fears of both parties.
9. International disputes are increasingly settled by arbitration.
10. The time from pretrial to final verdict is often so lengthy that it encourages the parties to settle before trial.

Can you think of more reasons why this declining trend in court cases actually going to trial will or will not continue?

 Access an interactive eBook, chapter-specific interactive learning tools, and more in your Paralegal CourseMate, accessed through www.CengageBrain.com

2

Civil Litigation (Trial and Appeal)

INTRODUCTION

The majority of civil cases are settled before trial. Even fewer cases are appealed than go to trial. Appeals are the exception rather than the rule.

There are separate rules of civil procedure for the federal and state court systems. At the federal level, there are Federal Rules of Civil Procedure that govern trial practice. At the state level, some states have enacted their own rules of civil procedure, where other states follow a combination of the two sets of rules.

Generally, a trial by jury is not automatic. It is a privilege that must be requested, and is not granted or permitted in all situations. Some matters are heard by a judge alone and are referred to as bench trials. Even where a jury trial is granted, a judge always remains in the courtroom. The plaintiffs generally have the burden of proof to demonstrate that they have a cause of action against the defendant at the time of trial.

To avoid the long wait for a trial date, some litigants are selecting alternative dispute resolution (ADR) where methods other than a formal court trial are used to resolve disputes. Some of the methods used are arbitration, conciliation, mediation, and mini-trials. These alternatives are usually quicker, cheaper, and easier for all the parties and do not contribute to the congestion of the courts. What makes these proceedings particularly attractive for some parties is that they are private proceedings, and not a matter of public record.

A court that hears and determines cases initially is called a trial court. There are many specialized courts that only hear certain types of cases, such as the family court, probate court, bankruptcy court, drug court, teen court, truancy court, domestic violence court, mental health court, business court, and community courts to name a few. The list of problem-solving courts keeps growing to address social changes and needs.

When a case is called to trial, depending on the issue involved, the parties may spend just a few hours or even months, selecting a jury. Attorneys must be fully versed in the rules of evidence and civil procedure. There are many rules for selecting a jury that must be followed precisely, or the parties risk having to start again with a new group of potential jurors.

Many cases settle during the period when the jury is selected; this process is called voir dire examination. The parties and their attorneys are fully assembled, the court is ready to proceed, and the pressure to settle and have some input into the resolution of the case greatly influences the parties. Other clients want to be heard, and insist on having their "day in court."

Once the trial begins, it proceeds in an orderly manner. The plaintiff proceeds first; the defendant can then cross-examine the plaintiff's witnesses. The attorney can have the best witnesses and evidence, but if he doesn't follow the specific rules, he may not be able to introduce key evidence and witnesses during the trial. When the plaintiff feels he has made a prima facie case, he will rest. Then it is the defendant's turn to proceed in much the same manner. At any time during the trial, a case can settle or either side can make a motion to have the claims against it dismissed. Each side seeks a judgment in its favor. Many clients don't understand that they may not necessarily receive a check when their case is resolved in their favor. Often, great effort must be taken by attorneys to collect on a judgment and go after a defendant's assets.

Sometimes, a party will request that a higher court review the decision of a lower court. This process is called an appeal. Such reconsideration is normally confined to review of the record from the lower court, with no new testimony taken and no new issues raised. Only the judge, or a panel of judges (depending on the court), will hear the appeal. A review by a higher court may result in affirmance, reversal, modification, or remand of the lower court's decision for further hearing. In the following case, an appeal was necessary because of a failure to follow simple civil procedure.

CASE AND COMMENT

State of Wisconsin, Court of Appeals, District II
Robert Johnson, Plaintiff-Respondent
v.
Cintas Corp. No. 2, Defendant-Appellant, and
United Healthcare, Defendant
Appeal No. 2009AP2549
Dated and Filed November 17, 2010

Facts: Robert Johnson, an employee of Cintas No. 2, was injured when his vehicle, which was being driven by his friend, collided with another vehicle. Johnson was required to use his personal vehicle in the course of his employment and had automobile liability insurance through Cintas No. 2. Johnson's crash-related injuries required medical treatment and resulted in permanent disability. After Cintas No. 2 refused to pay any insurance benefits through its health insurance provider, United Healthcare, Johnson filed suit against them both.

Procedural History: Johnson served the registered agent for Cintas No. 2 with a summons and complaint that named the wrong corporate entity, Cintas Corp., as the defendant. While Cintas No. 2 is a subsidiary of Cintas Corp., Cintas Corp. is a foreign corporation not registered to do business within Wisconsin. When neither Cintas Corp. nor Cintas No. 2 responded to the complaint, Johnson moved for summary judgment. Upon notice of a hearing for summary judgment, Cintas Corp. filed an Emergency Motion to Strike and Dismiss for Lack of Subject Matter Jurisdiction. However, Johnson was allowed to orally amend the summons and complaint, naming the "correct" defendant Cintas No. 2 at the default judgment hearing. Summary judgment was granted to Johnson and a hearing was ordered to determine damages.

Cintas No. 2 filed a motion for relief of judgment and the court vacated the default judgment. Johnson filed a motion for reconsideration and the court reinstated the default judgment. Cintas Corporation No. 2 appeals from a default judgment entered in favor of Johnson.

CASE AND COMMENT *continued...*

Issue: Whether the default judgment is void because the original summons and complaint named the wrong corporate entity.

Rationale: "Personal jurisdiction is acquired by personal service of a summons naming the party as a defendant . . . (and) Johnson did not simply mislabel the right defendant, he named the wrong corporate entity, Cintas Corp.," the court said.

Ruling: The default judgment against Cintas No. 2 is void because the court did not have the requisite personal jurisdiction to enter a default judgment. Because neither party challenged the amended pleadings, the case is remanded to the trial court for further proceedings.

Comment: This appellate case shows that failure of a law office to carefully follow civil procedure may be both costly and disastrous for the client.

DICTIONARY / THESAURUS

Term [phonetic pronunciation]	*Note: All dictionary/thesaurus terms appear on flashcards at the back of the book and on the student website.*

adjudication
[a.joo.di.*kay*.shen]

The final decision of a court, usually made after trial of the case; the court's final judgment.

- *n.* decision, ruling, holding, disposition, pronouncement, verdict, judgment

admissible evidence
[ad.*mis*.ibl *ev*.i.dense]

Evidence that a court may admit under the rules of evidence and consider in a case before it.

admission
[ad.*mish*.en]

1. A statement of a party to an action that is inconsistent with his claim or position in the lawsuit and which therefore constitutes proof against him. 2. A voluntary statement that something asserted to be true is true. EXAMPLE: the admission of testimony in a trial.

- *n.* confession, acknowledgment, affirmation, declaration, disclosure ("his admission of guilt"); admittance, access, passage ("admission to the bar")

affirm
[a.*ferm*]

In the case of an appellate court, to uphold the decision or judgment of the lower court after an appeal. *Compare* disaffirm.

- *v.* 1. uphold, validate, confirm, ratify ("The decision was affirmed."); declare, assert, maintain, allege ("He affirmed his innocence.") 2. To state formally instead of making a statement under oath; to make an affirmation, a substitute for a sworn statement. This can be used by a person whose religious or other beliefs will not permit him to swear.

DICTIONARY   THESAURUS *continued...*

alternative dispute resolution
[all.*ter*.ne.tiv dis.*pyoot* res.e.*loo*.shen]

A term for speedier and less-costly methods for resolving disputes than going to court. EXAMPLES: arbitration; conciliation; mediation; mini-trial; rent-a-judge; summary jury trial. Also known as ADR.

alternative pleading
[all.*ter*.ne.tiv *plee*.ding]

A form of pleading in which the pleader alleges facts that may be inconsistent with each other and contradictory. Such pleading is permissible in most jurisdictions as long as the inconsistent statements, standing alone, are sufficient grounds for a lawsuit.

amicus curiae
[a.*mee*.kes *koo*.ree.eye]

(*Latin*) "Friend of the court." A person who is interested in the outcome of the case, but who is not a party, whom the court permits to file a brief for the purpose of providing the court with a position or a point of view that it might not otherwise have. An amicus curiae is often referred to simply as an amicus.

appeal
[a.*peel*]

1. The process by which a higher court is requested by a party to a lawsuit to review the decision of a lower court. Such reconsideration is normally confined to a review of the record from the lower court, with no new testimony taken or new issues raised. Review by a higher court may result in affirmance, reversal, modification, or remand of the lower court's decision. 2. The process by which a court or a higher-level administrative body is asked to review the action of an administrative agency. *See also* cross-appeal.

- *n.* petition, review, reexamination ("his appeal to a higher court")

appeal bond
[a.*peel* bond]

Security furnished by the party appealing a case to guarantee that the appeal is bona fide and made in good faith.

appellant
[a.*pel*.ent]

A party who appeals from the lower court to a higher court.

- *n.* appealer, litigant, petitioner, party

appellate court
[a.*pel*.et kort]

A higher court to which the appeal is taken from a lower court.

appellate jurisdiction
[a.*pel*.et joo.ris.*dik*.shen]

The authority of one court to review the proceedings of another court or of an administrative agency. USAGE: "In our system, the Supreme Court of the United States has ultimate appellate jurisdiction."

appellate review
[a.*pel*.et re.*vyoo*]

Review of facts by an appellate court of a case appealed to it from a lower court.

appellee
[a.pel.*ee*]

A party against whom a case is appealed from a lower court to a higher court.

- *n.* respondent, defendant

arbitration
[ar.bi.*tray*.shen]

A method of settling disputes by submitting a disagreement to a person (an arbitrator) or a group of individuals (an arbitration panel) for decision instead of going to court. If the parties are required to comply with the decision of the arbitrator, the process is called binding arbitration; if there is no such obligation, the arbitration is referred to as nonbinding arbitration. Compulsory arbitration, arbitration required by law, most notably occurs in labor disputes. *See also* alternative dispute resolution. *Compare* conciliation; mediation.

award
[a.*ward*]

1. The decision, decree, or judgment of an arbitrator or administrative law judge. 2. A jury's determination with respect to damages. 3. A court's order for the payment of damages or costs.

- *v.* To confer, grant, or give

bar
[bar]

1. The attorneys permitted to practice before a particular court, taken collectively. 2. The court itself, when one speaks of the "case at bar" or the "bar of justice."

- *v.* To prevent. EXAMPLE: The case was barred by the statute of limitations.

below
[be.*loh*]

1. The court below; a lower court. USAGE: "The appeals court may not uphold the judgment of the court below." 2. In a position of lower rank; inferior.

- *adv.* beneath, down, underneath

bench trial
[bench *try*.el]

A trial before a judge without a jury; a nonjury trial.

bifurcated trial
[*by*.fer.kay.ted *try*.el]

A trial that is divided into two parts to provide separate hearings for different aspects of the same matter, for EXAMPLE, guilt and punishment, guilt and sanity, or liability and damages. Bifurcated trials avoid the time and expense of proving damages at trial where liability is not established.

brief
[breef]

1. A written statement submitted to a court for the purpose of persuading it of the correctness of one's position. A brief argues the facts of the case and the applicable law, supported by citations of authority. 2. A text that an attorney prepares to guide her in the trial of a case. Called a trial brief, it can include lists of questions to be asked of various witnesses, points to be covered, and arguments to be made. 3. An outline of the published opinion in a case, made by an attorney or a paralegal for the purpose of understanding the case.

- *n.* legal argument; summary, abstract, digest, outline, synopsis, review, abridgement, restatement

bringing suit
[*bring*.ing sut]

Beginning a lawsuit by filing papers that will result in the court's issuing process compelling the defendant to appear in court.

burden of proof
[*bir*.den ov pruf]

The duty of establishing the truth of a matter; the duty of proving a fact that is in dispute. In most instances the burden of proof, like the burden of going forward, shifts from one side to the other during the course of a trial as the case progresses and evidence is introduced by each side. *See also* prima facie case.

calendar
[*kal*.en.der]

A list of cases ready for the court to dispose of, whether by trial or otherwise; a court calendar. A court calendar is also referred to as a docket. *See also* trial calendar.

- *n.* diary, journal, register, schedule, lineup, program, chronology

calendar call
[*kal*.en.der kol]

The reading aloud of the calendar in court, to determine whether the cases listed are ready for trial or to set trial dates.

certification of record on appeal
[ser.tif.i.*kay*.shen ov *rek*.erd on a.*peel*]

The trial judge's signed acknowledgment of the questions to be decided on appeal. *See also* appeal.

certiorari
[ser.sho.*rare*.ee]

(*Latin*) "To be informed." A writ (written order) issued by a higher court to a lower court requiring the certification of the record in a particular case so that the higher court can review the record and correct any actions taken in the case that are not in accordance with the law. The Supreme Court of the United States uses the writ of certiorari to select the state court cases it is willing to review. *See also* certification of record on appeal.

challenge for cause
[*chal*.enj for koz]

An objection, for bias, prejudice, or other stated reason, to a juror being allowed to hear a case. *Compare* peremptory challenge.

conciliation
[kon.sil.ee.*ay*.shen]

The voluntary resolution of a dispute in an amicable manner. One of the primary uses of conciliators, also called mediators, is in settling labor disputes. Professional conciliators are available for that purpose through the Federal Mediation and Conciliation Service. Conciliation differs from arbitration in that a conciliator, unlike an arbitrator, does not render a decision. *See also* alternative dispute resolution; mediation.

confession of judgment
[ken.*fesh*.en ov *juj*.ment]

The entry of a judgment upon the admission and at the direction of the debtor, without the formality, time, or effort involved in bringing a lawsuit.

court
[kort]

1. A part of government, consisting of a judge or judges, and, usually, administrative support personnel, whose duty it is to administer justice; the judicial branch of government. 2. A place where justice is judicially administered. 3. All judges of the same jurisdiction. For EXAMPLE, all persons who sit as judges of the United States District Court for the Southern District of Texas, taken collectively, constitute "the court" for that judicial district. *Note* that in many instances the words "court" and "judge" are used interchangeably and, in context, have the same meaning.

- *n.* unit of government, forum, chamber, panel, bench, bar, justice, judge, session

court below
[kort be.*loh*]

A term used by an appellate court, or by attorneys appearing before an appellate court, to refer to the trial court.

court costs
[kort kostz]

1. Court fees. 2. The expenses involved in litigating an action (EXAMPLES: witness fees; filing fees, the cost of a transcript), including court fees but excluding attorney fees.

court fees
[kort feez]

The charges for the services of a public officer, particularly the clerk of court, rendered in connection with litigation. These are fixed by law. EXAMPLES: the fee for a certified copy of a document; filing fees.

court of appeals
[kort ov a.*peelz*]

Often abbreviated as CA, C.A., or Ct. App. 1. A Court of Appeals. 2. The intermediate appellate court in most states, although it is the highest appellate court in some, including New York. 3. A court in which appeals from a lower court are heard.

Court of Appeals of the United States
[kort ov a.*peelz* ov the yoo.*ny*.ted states]

The intermediate appellate court in the federal court system, which is divided into 12 geographical circuits (each designated the United States Court of Appeals for that circuit), plus the United States Court of Appeals for the Federal Circuit, which hears appeals in patent, copyright, and customs cases, as well as some appeals from lower courts.

court of record
[kort ov *rek*.erd]

Generally, another term for trial court.

court order
[kort *or*.der]

1. An adjudication by a court. 2. A ruling by a court with respect to a motion or any other question before it for determination during the course of a proceeding.

court reporter
[kort re.*port*.er]

A person who stenographically (*see also* stenographic notes) or by "voice writing" records court proceedings, from which, when necessary, he prepares a transcript that becomes a part of the record in the case.

court reports
[kort re.*ports*]

Official, published reports of cases decided by courts, filing the opinions rendered in the case, with headnotes prepared by the publisher.

cross-appeal
[kros-a.*peel*]

An appeal filed by the appellee from the same judgment, or some portion of the same judgment, as the appellant has appealed from. A cross-appeal is generally made as part of the review proceedings set in motion by the original appeal.

cross-examination
[kross-eg.zam.in.*ay*.shen]

The interrogation of a witness for the opposing party with questions designed to test the accuracy and truthfulness of the testimony the witness gave on direct examination.

defendant in error
[de.*fen*.dent in *err*.er]

The party against whom an appeal is taken to a higher court; an appellee.

dicta
[*dik*.ta]

Plural of dictum, which is short for the Latin term obiter dictum. Dicta are expressions or comments in a court opinion that are not necessary to support the decision made by the court; they are not binding authority and have no value as precedent. If nothing else can be found on point, an advocate may wish to attempt to persuade by citing cases that contain dicta.

direct examination
[de.*rekt* eg.zam.in.*ay*.shen]

The first or initial questioning of a witness by the party who called her to the stand. *Compare* cross-examination.

DICTIONARY | THESAURUS *continued...*

directed verdict
[de.*rek*.ted *ver*.dikt]

A verdict that a jury returns as directed by the judge. A judge directs a verdict when the party who has the burden of proof has failed to meet that burden. A motion for directed verdict is the procedural means by which a litigant requests the court to direct a verdict.

dismissal
[dis.*miss*.el]

An order for the termination of a civil action without a trial of its issues, or without further trial. Whether a dismissal is a final judgment against the plaintiff depends upon whether it is a dismissal with prejudice or a dismissal without prejudice.

- *n.* termination, discharge

docket
[*dok*.et]

1. A list of cases for trial or other disposition; a court calendar. 2. A list of cases and a summary of what occurred in these cases, although not a record in the sense of a transcript.

- *v.* To make an entry in a docket

execution of judgment
[ek.se.*kyoo*.shen ov *juj*.ment]

A writ or process for the enforcement of a judgment. A judgment is usually enforced by a sheriff seizing and selling property to satisfy the judgment.

exhibit
[eg.*zib*.it]

1. Any paper or thing offered in evidence and marked for identification. 2. A document attached to and made a part of a pleading, transcript, contract, or other legal paper.

expert witness
[*eks*.pert *wit*.nes]

A person who is so qualified, either by actual experience or by careful study, as to enable him to form a definite opinion of his own regarding a subject about which persons having no particular training, experience, or special study are incapable of forming accurate opinions.

fact finder
[fak*t fine*.der]

A judge, jury, person, board, or body appointed by business, government, or by court, that is empowered to make findings of fact and conclusion with respect to disputed facts. The finding of fact is reasoned or inferred from the evidence.

high court
[hy kort]

An informal way of referring to the Supreme Court of the United States or the highest court in a state judicial system. *See also* highest court.

highest court
[*hy*.est kort]

The highest court of a state; the Supreme Court of the United States; a court whose decisions are not subject to review by a higher court.

hung jury
[hung *joo*.ree]

A jury that cannot reach a unanimous verdict.

impanel
[im.*pan*.el]

To enroll; to list. The act of the clerk of the court in listing the names of persons who have been selected for jury duty. *See also* jury panel.

- *v.* list, enroll, enter, schedule, docket

impartial juror
[im.*par*.shel *joo*.rer]

A juror who will render a verdict solely on the basis of the evidence.

judgment
[*juj*.ment]

In a civil action, the final determination by a court of the rights of the parties, based upon the pleadings and the evidence; a decision. *See also* confession of judgment.

judgment notwithstanding the verdict
[*juj*.ment not.with.*stan*.ding the *ver*.dikt]

Also referred to as a judgment NOV, a judgment rendered by the court in favor of a party, notwithstanding the fact that the jury has returned a verdict against that party.

judgment NOV
[*juj*.ment en.oh.vee]

Short for judgment non obstante verdicto (judgment notwithstanding the verdict).

judgment on the merits
[*juj*.ment on the *mehr*.its]

A judgment based on the substantive rights of the parties, as distinguished from a judgment based on procedural points.

judgment on the pleadings
[*juj*.ment on the *plee*.dingz]

A judgment rendered in favor of the defendant when the plaintiff's complaint fails to state a cause of action, or in favor of the plaintiff when the defendant's answer fails to state a legally sufficient defense.

juror
[*joor*.er]

A person on a jury.

- *n.* factfinder, trier of fact, appraiser, arbiter

jury
[*joor*.ee]

A group of women and men selected according to law to determine the truth. Juries are used in various types of legal proceedings, both civil and criminal. *See also* hung jury, petit jury, polling the jury.

- *n.* factfinder, trier of fact, reviewers, panel, venire, array, arbiters

jury challenge
[*joor*.ee *chal*.enj]

See challenge for cause; peremptory challenge.

jury instructions
[*joor*.ee in.*struk*.shenz]

Directions given to the jury by the judge just before she sends the jurors out to deliberate and return a verdict, explaining the law that applies in the case and spelling out what must be proven and by whom.

jury panel
[*joor*.ee *pan*.el]

1. The jury list. 2. The jury impaneled for the trial of a particular case. *See also* impanel.

jury trial
[*joor*.ee *try*.el]

A trial in which the jurors are the judges of the facts and the court is the judge of the law. Trial by jury is guaranteed in all criminal cases by the Sixth Amendment, and in many civil cases by the Seventh Amendment. *Compare* bench trial.

leading question
[*lee*.ding *kwes*.chen]

A question put to a witness that suggests the answer the questioner desires. (EXAMPLE: "You did as you were told, didn't you?") Leading questions are generally not allowed on direct examination, but are permitted on cross-examination.

DICTIONARY THESAURUS *continued...*

mediation
[mee.dee.*ay*.shen]

The voluntary resolution of a dispute in an amicable manner. One of the primary uses of mediators, also called conciliators, is in settling labor disputes. Professional mediators are available for that purpose through the Federal Mediation and Conciliation Service. Mediation differs from arbitration in that a mediator, unlike an arbitrator, does not render a decision. *See also* alternative dispute resolution; conciliation.

mistrial
[*mis*.try.el]

A trial that has been terminated by the judge prior to its conclusion because the jury is unable to reach a verdict (*see also* hung jury), because of prejudicial error that cannot be corrected or eliminated by any action the court might take (EXAMPLE: the plaintiff's use of racial slurs), or because of the occurrence of some event that would make it pointless to continue (EXAMPLE: the death of a juror). A mistrial is the equivalent of no trial having been held.

notice of appeal
[*noh*.tess ov a.*peel*]

The process by which appellate review is initiated; specifically, written notice to the appellee advising her of the appellant's intention to appeal.

oath
[ohth]

1. A calling on God to witness what one avers is true. 2. Any form of attestation incorporating an appeal to a sacred or revered being by which a person signifies that he is bound in conscience to perform an act or speak faithfully and truthfully. In most jurisdictions, the question "Do you swear to tell the truth?" has been replaced by "Do you swear or affirm?" In other jurisdictions, the term "oath" has been construed to include affirmation. *See* affirm.

oral argument
[*ohr*.el *ar*.gyoo.ment]

A party, through her attorney, usually presents her case to an appellate court on appeal by arguing the case verbally to the court, in addition to submitting a brief. Oral argument may also be made in support of a motion.

out-of-court settlement
[out-ov-kort *setl*.ment]

1. The ending of a controversy by agreement, before it gets to court. 2. The settlement of a lawsuit after the complaint has been served, and without obtaining or seeking judicial approval.

peremptory challenge
[per.*emp*.ter.ee *chal*.enj]

A challenge to a juror that a party may exercise without having to give a reason. *Compare* challenge for cause.

perfecting an appeal
[per.*fek*.ting an a.*peel*]

Completing all of the steps required by statute for obtaining appellate court review of a judgment.

petit jury
[*pet*.ee *joo*.ree]

The jury in a trial court.

polling the jury
[*pole*.ing the *joo*.ree]

Individually examining the jurors who participated in a verdict to ascertain whether they unanimously support the verdict.

preliminary injunction
[pre.*lim*.i.ner.ee
in.*junk*.shen]

An injunction granted prior to a full hearing on the merits. Its purpose is to preserve the status quo until the final hearing. A preliminary injunction is also referred to as a provisional injunction or temporary injunction, where a permanent injunction is granted after a final hearing on the merits. *See also* temporary restraining order.

prima facie case [*pry*.muh *fay*.shee case]	A cause of action or defense that is sufficiently established by a party's evidence to justify a verdict in her favor, provided the other party does not rebut that evidence; a case supported by sufficient evidence to justify its submission to the trier of fact and the rendition of a compatible verdict.
rebuttal [re.*but*.el]	The stage in a trial or hearing at which a party introduces rebuttal evidence, presenting evidence that denies, refutes, or contradicts. It occurs after the opposite party has rested her case.
record on appeal [*rek*.erd on a.*peel*]	The papers a trial court transmits to the appellate court, on the basis of which the appellate court decides the appeal. The record on appeal includes the pleadings, all motions made before the trial court, the official transcript, and the judgment or order appealed from.
reversal [re.*ver*.sel]	1. The act of an appellate court in setting aside, annulling, or vacating a judgment or order of a lower court. 2. The act of turning a thing or person around, or being turned around.
reverse [re.*verse*]	Opposite; contrary. ■ *v.* To turn around or in the opposite direction. If a judgment is found for the plaintiff, a reverse decision would find for the defendant.
settlement [*set*.el.ment]	The ending of a lawsuit by agreement. *See also* out-of-court settlement. ■ *n.* resolution, termination ("to reach a settlement")
subpoena [sub.*peen*.ah]	*n.* A command in the form of written process requiring a witness to come to court to testify; short for subpoena ad testificandum. *v.* To issue or serve a subpoena. ■ *v.* order, command, summon, beckon, demand ■ *n.* order, command, mandate, citation, summons, writ, call, directive
subpoena ad testificandum [sub.*peen*.ah ad *tes*.te.fe.*kan*.dem]	(*Latin*) The term ad testificandum means "testify under penalty." A subpoena ad testificandum is a subpoena to testify. Often, the shortened term for this is used: subpoena. *Compare* subpoena duces tecum.
subpoena duces tecum [sub.*peen*.ah *doo*.ses *tee*.kum]	(*Latin*) The term duces tecum means "bring with you under penalty." A subpoena duces tecum is a written command requiring a witness to come to court to testify and, at that time, to produce for use as evidence the papers, documents, books, or records listed in the subpoena.

DICTIONARY   THESAURUS *continued...*

summary jury trial (SJT)
[*sum*.e.ree *joor*.ee *try*.el]

A court-ordered form of alternative dispute resolution sometimes used by the federal courts in complex cases that would otherwise require a lengthy jury trial. An SJT is a kind of nonbinding capsule trial that allows the parties to obtain the thoughts of jurors with respect to the merits of the case. The facts are presented in simplified form to a reduced jury, questions of admissibility of evidence are decided with the judge in advance, and counsel interviews the jurors after the verdict. Although the verdict is nonbinding, the parties may agree to be bound by it, or they may settle the case based upon the reactions of the jurors.

summary proceeding
[*sum*.e.ree pro.*seed*.ing]

A proceeding in which a case is disposed of or a trial is conducted in a prompt and simple manner without a jury and without many of the ordinary requirements (such as complaint, summons, indictment, or information). EXAMPLES: a contempt proceeding; trial before a magistrate or a justice of the peace; trial in a small claims court.

summary remedy
[*sum*.e.ree *rem*.e.dee]

In a civil action, a remedy obtainable in a summary proceeding.

temporary restraining order (TRO)
[*tem*.pe.rer.ee re.*strane*.ing *or*.der]

The court is empowered to grant injunctive relief to one party, without notice to the opposite party, if the result would cause "immediate and irreparable harm or loss."

transcript
[*tran*.skript]

A hard copy of the court reporter's stenographic notes of a trial (i.e., a record of the proceedings).

transcript of the record
[*tran*.skript ov the *rek*.erd]

The complete record of a case as furnished to the appellate court when an appeal is taken.

trial
[*try*.el]

A hearing or determination by a court of the issues existing between the parties to an action; an examination by a court of competent jurisdiction, according to the law of the land, of the facts or law at issue in either a civil case or a criminal prosecution, for the purpose of adjudicating the matters in controversy. *See also* bench trial; bifurcated trial; trial by jury; mistrial.

- *n.* citation, hearing, litigation, prosecution, suit ("trial by jury")

trial by jury
[*try*.el by *joor*.ee]

A trial in which the jurors are the judges of the facts and the court is the judge of the law. Trial by jury is guaranteed in all criminal cases by the Sixth Amendment, and in most civil cases by the Seventh Amendment. *Compare* trial by the court. *Also compare* bench trial; *see also* jury trial.

trial by the court
[*try*.el by the kort]

A trial held before a judge sitting without a jury. A trial by the judge alone is also referred to as a judge trial, a bench trial, or a nonjury trial. *Compare* trial by jury.

trial calendar
[*try*.el *kal*.en.der]

A list of cases awaiting trial.

trial court
[*try*.el kort]

A court that hears and determines a case initially, as opposed to an appellate court; a court of general jurisdiction.

trial de novo
[*try*.el deh *noh*.voh]

A new trial, a retrial, or a trial on appeal from a justice's court or a magistrate's court to a court of general jurisdiction. A trial de novo is a trial in which the matter is tried again as if it had not been heard before and as if no decision had previously been rendered.

trial judge
[*try*.el juj]

The judge who presides at the trial of a case.

trial jury
[*try*.el *joor*.ee]

A jury for the trial of a case, as distinguished from a grand jury.

verdict
[*ver*.dikt]

The final decision of a jury concerning questions of fact submitted to it by the court for determination in the trial of a case. In a civil case, the jury may be required to return either a general verdict or a special verdict: making specific findings of fact in response to written questions. *See also* judgment notwithstanding the verdict.

- *n.* adjudication, arbitration, conclusion, decision, decree

verdict against the evidence
[*ver*.dikt a.*genst* the *ev*.i.dense]

A verdict that is contrary to the evidence, or to the weight of the evidence, or that is not supported by sufficient evidence.

verdict contrary to law
[*ver*.dikt *kon*.trare.ee to law]

The verdict of a jury that has failed to follow the instructions of the judge with respect to matters of law. *See also* jury instructions.

voir dire examination
[vwa deer eg.zam.i.*nay*.shen]

Examination of a potential juror for the purpose of determining whether she is qualified and acceptable to act as a juror in the case. A prospective juror who a party decides is unqualified or unacceptable may be challenged for cause or may be the subject of a peremptory challenge. "Voir dire" is from old French meaning "to say the truth."

witness
[*wit*.nes]

1. A person who testifies or gives evidence before a court or at an administrative hearing with respect to something she has observed or of which she has knowledge. *See also* expert witness. 2. A person who is asked to be present at a transaction (for EXAMPLE, the signing of a contract) in order to attest that it took place.

- *v.* 1. To see or observe. 2. To attest; to act as an observer for the purpose of attesting

Missing Words

Fill in the blanks.

1. _____ is a person who is not a party to a case, whom the court permits to file a brief.

2. The first or initial questioning of a witness by the party who called her to the stand is _____.

3. Any paper or thing offered in evidence and marked for identification is called a(n) _____.

4. A group of women and men selected according to law to determine the truth is a(n) _____.

5. Directions given to the jury by the judge just before sending jurors out to deliberate are _____.

6. A(n) _____ is a challenge to a juror that a party may exercise without having to give a reason.

7. The jury in a trial court is known as the _____, as distinguished from the grand jury.

8. Written notice to the appellee advising of appellant's intention to appeal is called a(n) _____.

9. The _____ is a written list of cases awaiting trial.

10. The judge who presides at the trial of a case is known as the _____.

11. _____ is when jurors who participated in a verdict are examined to see whether they unanimously support the verdict.

12. A person who is qualified, either by actual experience or by careful study, to form a definite opinion of his own respecting a subject is a(n) _____.

13. A(n) _____ is a written command requiring a witness to come to court to testify and at that time to bring documents listed in the subpoena.

14. A(n) _____ occurs where a trial is terminated by the judge because the jury cannot reach a verdict.

15. _____ is the voluntary resolution of a dispute in an amicable manner through the use of mediators who do not render a decision.

16. A(n) _____ is another name for a judgment notwithstanding the verdict.

17. A(n) _____ is a writ issued by a higher court to a lower court requiring the certification of the record, so the higher court can review the record and correct any actions not in accordance with the law.

18. In a civil case, a remedy obtainable in a summary proceeding is called _____.

19. A case on appeal is verbally presented to the appellate court by _____.

20. A(n) _____ is empowered to make findings of fact, a conclusion with respect to disputed facts in a legal action.

STUDY AID: Use flashcards for this unit before completing the exercises.

Matching

Match the letter of the definition to the term.

_N_ **21.** record on appeal

_B_ **22.** leading question

_F_ **23.** settlement

_A_ **24.** burden of proof

_G_ **25.** verdict

_I_ **26.** reversal

_C_ **27.** rebuttal

_O_ **28.** alternative dispute resolution

_M_ **29.** confession of judgment

_J_ **30.** transcript

_D_ **31.** subpoena

_K_ **32.** judgment

_L_ **33.** challenge for cause

_E_ **34.** oral argument

_H_ **35.** voir dire

A. the duty of establishing the truth of a matter; the duty of proving a fact that is in dispute

B. a question put to a witness that suggests the answer the questioner desires

C. the stage in a trial or hearing at which a party introduces rebuttal evidence

D. a command requiring a witness to come to court and testify

E. a case is presented to the appellate court by arguing the case verbally to the court

F. the ending of a lawsuit by agreement

G. the final decision of a jury concerning questions of fact submitted to it by the court in the trial of a case

H. examination of a potential juror for the purpose of determining whether she is qualified to act as a juror

I. the act of an appellate court in setting aside, annulling, or vacating a judgment or order of a lower court

J. a hard copy of the court reporter's stenographic notes of a trial

K. a final determination by a court of the rights of the parties

L. an objection, for a stated reason, to a juror being allowed to hear a case

M. entry of judgment upon admission and at the direction of the debtor, without bringing a lawsuit

N. the papers a trial court transmits to the appellate court, on the basis of which the appellate court decides the appeal

O. a term for speedier and less-costly methods for resolving disputes than going to court

Multiple Choice

Select the best choice.

_B_ **36.** The process by which a higher court is requested by a party to a lawsuit to review the decision of a lower court is:
   a. an amicus curiae.
   b. an appeal.
   c. a peremptory challenge.
   d. a challenge for cause.

_A_ **37.** A jury that cannot reach a unanimous verdict is:
   a. a hung jury.
   b. a petit jury.
   c. a grand jury.
   d. none of the above.

_C_ **38.** Any papers or things offered in evidence and marked for identification are called:
   a. expert witnesses.
   b. oral argument.
   c. exhibits.
   d. amicus curiae.

_D_ **39.** Arbitration, conciliation, mediation, and mini-trials are speedier and less-costly methods for resolving disputes than going to court. These are examples of:
   a. certiorari.
   b. impaneling the jury.
   c. voir dire.
   d. alternative dispute resolution.

_A_ **40.** A written statement submitted to the court for the purpose of persuading it of the correctness of one's position is a:
   a. brief.
   b. judgment.
   c. rebuttal.
   d. challenge for cause.

_B_ **41.** The act of the clerk of the court in listing the names of persons who have been selected for jury duty is called:
   a. affirm.
   b. impanel.

   c. appeal.
   d. reversal.

_A_ **42.** The final decision of a jury concerning questions of fact submitted to it by the court for determination in the trial of a case is the:
   a. verdict.
   b. judgment.
   c. judgment NOV.
   d. mistrial.

_C_ **43.** A subpoena duces tecum is a written command requiring:
   a. a witness to tell the truth.
   b. a witness to come to court to testify.
   c. a witness to come to court to testify and bring records listed in the subpoena.
   d. a witness to plead the Fifth Amendment and refuse to testify.

_B_ **44.** Leading questions that suggest the answer the questioner desires are usually used during:
   a. direct examination.
   b. cross-examination.
   c. rebuttal.
   d. jury instructions.

_B_ **45.** A prospective juror whom a party decides is unqualified or unacceptable may be challenged for cause or may be the subject of a peremptory challenge during:
   a. an out-of-court settlement.
   b. voir dire.
   c. oral argument.
   d. jury instructions.

_C_ **46.** In a civil action, the final determination by a court of the rights of the parties based upon the pleadings and evidence is the:
   a. appeal.
   b. notice of appeal.
   c. judgment.
   d. verdict.

_A_ **47.** A trial that has been terminated by a judge prior to its conclusion because of a hung jury, or prejudicial error, is called:
a. a mistrial.
b. arbitration.
c. alternative dispute resolution.
d. confession of judgment.

_D_ **48.** A person who is interested in the outcome of the case, but who is not a party, whom the court permits to file a brief for the purpose of providing the court with a position that it might not otherwise have is a(n):
a. prima facie case.
b. appellant.
c. appellee.
d. amicus curiae.

_D_ **49.** The process by which appellate review is initiated is:
a. oral argument.
b. rebuttal.
c. voir dire.
d. notice of appeal.

True/False

Mark the following T or F.

_T_ **50.** The process by which a higher court reviews the decision of a lower court is called an appeal.

_F_ **51.** The ending of a controversy through a court trial is called an out-of-court settlement.

_T_ **52.** Arbitration is a method of settling disputes by submitting a disagreement to a person, or group of individuals, for decision instead of going to court.

_T_ **53.** A witness is a person who testifies or gives evidence before a court or at an administrative hearing with respect to something observed or of which he has knowledge.

_F_ **54.** Jury instructions are the papers the trial court transmits to the appellate court, on the basis of which the appellate court decides the appeal.

_F_ **55.** A confession of judgment is the stage in a trial or hearing at which a party introduces rebuttal evidence.

_F_ **56.** The act of an appellate court in setting aside, annulling, or vacating a judgment or order of a lower court is called certiorari.

_T_ **57.** The appellee is a party against whom a case is appealed from a lower court to a higher court.

_T_ **58.** An appeal bond is security furnished by the party appealing a case to guarantee that the appeal is bona fide.

_T_ **59.** Direct examination is the first or initial questioning of a witness by the party who called her to the stand.

_F_ **60.** Mediation is the same as arbitration; a mediator resolves a dispute by issuing a decision.

_F_ **61.** The final determination by a jury of the rights of the parties is called a judgment.

_T_ **62.** When an appellate court sets aside a judgment of the lower court, this is a reversal.

Synonyms

Select the correct synonym in parentheses for each numbered item.

63. AFFIRM
(uphold, compare, reverse)

64. JURY
(factfinders, witness, expert)

65. SUBPOENA
(play, command, certiorari)

66. JUDGMENT
(transcript, mediation, ruling)

67. EXHIBIT
(document, appeal, rebuttal)

68. APPEAL
(reverse, review, settle)

69. TRIAL COURT
(higher court, appellate court, court below)

70. DISMISSAL
(termination, continuation, change)

71. SETTLEMENT
(reversal, resolution, continuation)

72. HUNG JURY
(unanimous, undecided, concerned)

73. BENCH TRIAL
(jury trial, nonjury trial, arbitration)

74. TRIAL
(verdict, mediation, hearing)

75. APPELLANT
(respondent, petitioner, defendant)

76. IMPANEL
(to list, to accuse, to defend)

77. MISTRIAL
(jury instructions, hung jury, polling the jury)

78. REVERSAL OF JUDGMENT
(to sustain, to restrain, to set aside)

79. ADJUDICATION
(disposition, summons, petition)

Self-Test

Place the number of the correct term in the appropriate space.

80. appeal

81. verdict

82. subpoena duces tecum

83. petit jury

84. challenges for cause

85. jury

86. burden of proof

87. direct examination

88. judgment

89. witnesses

90. trial

91. leading questions

92. voir dire examination

93. peremptory challenges

94. expert witness

95. proceedings

A(n) _____ is a hearing by a court of the issues existing between the parties to an action. A case might be

heard solely by a judge, or a dispute might be heard by a(n) _____, which is called a(n) _____

to distinguish it from a grand jury proceeding. In order to select a fair and impartial group of jurors to try a matter,

the attorneys first proceed with a(n) _____ to determine if jurors are qualified and acceptable to act as

jurors in a particular case. Attorneys can exercise _____ to eliminate some jurors without reason, and

_____ to eliminate biased or prejudiced jurors. After a group of jurors is determined to be acceptable by

both sides, the jurors will be sworn in to hear the case. The party with the _____ will generally try its side of

the case first. This is done through the introduction of various _____ who will testify about what they said

and observed. A(n) _____ may be used to command a witness to bring documents to court. Sometimes a(n)

_____ is needed to testify about matters concerning his particular field of expertise or training. Information

is initially brought out through _____ of the witnesses. Thereafter, the attorney for the opposing party

will usually conduct cross-examination by use of _____ to narrow the issues in dispute and pinpoint the

weakness in a witness's testimony or recall. At the end of the trial, the jury will issue a(n) _____. Then a(n)

_____ will be entered by the court. It is then up to the losing party to decide if he wishes to continue with

litigation and take a(n) _____ or accept the result of the _____.

Word Scramble

Unscramble the following words and write the correct word(s) that match(es) the definition for each word or phrase.

96. pealap – the process by which a higher court is requested by a party to a lawsuit to review the decision of a lower court _____

_____

97. lementsett – the ending of a lawsuit by agreement.

_____

_____

98. ernativealt sputedi restionolu – a term for speedier and less-costly methods for resolving disputes than going to court _____

_____

99. yruj – a group of people selected to determine the truth of a matter _____

_____

100. ovir dier – the examination of potential jurors to determine if they are qualified to serve _____

_____

101. nesswit – a person who testifies about what he observed _____

_____

102. pertex – a person with special training or experience who is qualified to give an opinion about a subject

_____

_____

103. posubena – a command in the form of written process requiring a witness to come to court and testify _____

_____

104. pellantap – a party who appeals from the lower court to the higher court _____

_____

105. antrscript – a hard copy of the court reporter's notes of trial _____

_____

106. uttalreb – the stage in a trial at which a party introduces rebuttal evidence_____

_____

107. lengechal ofr ausec – an objection to a juror based upon bias or prejudice _____

_____

108. ismtrial – a trial that has been terminated by the judge when a juror dies _____

_____

109. itarbration – a method of settling disputes by submitting a disagreement to a person for a decision instead of going to court_____

_____

110. actf derfin – a person, jury, judge, or board that is empowered to make findings of fact_____

_____

The Last Word

The court of last resort is the United States Supreme Court. However, each year the Supreme Court turns down hundreds of appeals from lower courts, allowing their rulings to stand without comment. Sometimes the Supreme Court may reconsider rejected appeals and accept them for arguments later in the term. In 2010, the high court surprised some observers by rejecting one such high-profile case. Before the case will be considered again, the U.S Solicitor General will respond with a brief in the matter.

The case involves Iraqis who allege they were physically abused by U.S. interpreters and interrogators while held at the notorious Abu Ghraib prison. A federal appeals court threw out the case against CACI International Inc. and Titan (a unit of L-3 Communications) based upon wartime considerations.

Despite being the court of last resort, what considerations make the Court reject an appeal?

UNIT

3

Criminal Law and Procedure

INTRODUCTION

American society has defined the conduct expected from its members so that all may coexist peacefully. Criminal laws were created to describe prohibited acts. In criminal law, the government brings a case on behalf of its people against the accused. The government is represented by an attorney called a district attorney or prosecutor. In civil law, a citizen brings an action against another citizen and both parties have private attorneys.

There are different classes of crimes. The most serious crimes are called felonies, which are generally punishable by one year or more in prison. Less-serious crimes are misdemeanors, usually punishable by fine and/or imprisonment for less than one year. The least-serious crimes are ordinance violations, which are punishable by a fine or probation.

In order to convict a person of a crime there must be evidence that the person performed a prohibited act with criminal intent. Proof beyond a reasonable doubt is required of a prosecutor for a conviction.

Criminal procedure is the process by which an arrest is made, charges are brought against the accused, as well as the stages up to and including the trial. The majority of cases are resolved prior to trial. In plea bargaining, the prosecutor and the defense attorney reach agreement whereby the accused will generally plead guilty to lesser charges in lieu of trial on the more serious charges.

Criminal law and procedure are closely associated with the rights guaranteed by the United States Constitution and are constantly undergoing change by the state courts and legislature, the Congress, and the United States Supreme Court. In the case that follows, the appellant Winfrey's rights were violated. The evidence was not legally sufficient to support a murder conviction.

CASE AND COMMENT

In the Court of Criminal Appeals of Texas
Richard Lynn Winfrey, appellant
v.
The State of Texas
NO. PD-0987-09 (2010)

Facts: In August 2004, Murray Wayne Burr was found murdered in his home. Evidence at trial indicated that the victim had been stabbed 28 times. There was no evidence of forced entry into the victim's home. The evidence indicated that the victim was dragged to his bedroom where the body was found. The only item missing was a bible, the family reported. Investigators collected a variety of forensic evidence during the crime scene investigation, including a partial bloody fingerprint, a bloody shoe print, and several hair samples. Neither the prints not the hair samples matched Richard Lynn Winfrey, who was not considered a suspect at the time. A DNA profile from evidence at the crime excluded Winfrey and his family members. A jailhouse informer came forward to claim Winfrey had told him information he had "heard" about the murder, most of which was false. Also, nearly three years after the murder, a deputy at the sheriff's office conducted a "scent lineup" using three bloodhounds. This involved obtaining scent samples from the clothing the victim was wearing at the time of death and having the dogs "pre-scented" on the victim's scent sample, as well as samples from six males, including Winfrey. The dogs walked a line of cans containing the scent samples and all three dogs alerted on the can containing Winfrey's scent sample. Based on this lineup, the deputy in charge of the dogs concluded that Winfrey's scent was on the victim's clothing and he was charged with murder.

Procedural History: A jury convicted Winfrey based on the jailhouse "informant" and the scent sample lineup testimony of the deputy. Appellant Winfrey petitioned for discretionary review from the Eleventh Court of Appeals San Jacinto County. At trial, the issues were: When Winfrey was interviewed in 2004 he indicated that he was the number one suspect but did not admit to any guilt; a cellmate said that Winfrey "heard" that a gun and knife collection had been taken from the victim's house but Winfrey had never implicated himself in the murder; and on cross-examination, the deputy who conducted the scent lineup said that convicting a person solely on dog scent (evidence) is illegal. The dog scent lineup proved that Winfrey's scent was on the victim's clothes, not that Winfrey had been in direct contact with the victim, but the latter is how the court of appeals decided.

Issue: Whether the evidence is legally sufficient to support a conviction of murder.

Rationale: "When reviewing a case for legal sufficiency, we view all the evidence in the light most favorable to the verdict and determine whether any rational trier of fact could have found the essential elements of the crime beyond a reasonable doubt."

Ruling: The court concluded that "dog-scent discrimination lineups, when used as primary evidence, are legally insufficient to support a conviction." The court overruled the lower court and expressly held ". . . that when inculpatory evidence is obtained from a dog-scent lineup, its role in the court room is merely supportive."

Comment: With apologies to bloodhounds everywhere, the deputy's brand of "this dog won't hunt" forensics was repudiated in Texas.

DICTIONARY / THESAURUS

Term [phonetic pronunciation]	*Note: All dictionary/thesaurus terms appear on flashcards at the back of the book and on the student website.*

accessory
[ak.*sess*.e.ree]

A person who is involved with the commission of a crime but who is not present at the time it is committed. *See also* aiding and abetting.

- *n.* accomplice, abettor, conspirator, collaborator, consort, assistant ("accessory after the fact"); supplement, attachment, addition, extension

accomplice
[a.*kom*.pliss]

A person who knowingly and voluntarily helps another person commit a crime; one who acts as an accessory. *See also* aiding and abetting.

actus reus
[*ahk*.tus *ree*.us]

(*Latin*) An "answerable act" (i.e., an act for which one is answerable); a guilty act. In combination with mens rea (a guilty or criminal intent), actus reus is an essential element of any crime. Thus, for EXAMPLE, the act of killing is the actus reus of murder.

affirmative defense
[a.*fer*.ma.tiv de.*fense*]

A defense that amounts to more than simply a denial of the allegations in the plaintiff's complaint. It sets up new matter that, if proven, could result in judgment against the plaintiff even if all the allegations of the complaint are true. EXAMPLES include alibi, double jeopardy, insanity, and self-defense.

aiding and abetting
[*ay*.ding and a.*bet*.ing]

Helping or encouraging a person to commit a crime.

alibi
[*al*.i.by]

The defense that the accused was elsewhere at the time the crime was committed.

- *n.* defense, excuse, explanation, proof, avowal

arraignment
[a.*rain*.ment]

The act of bringing an accused before a court to answer a criminal charge made against him and calling upon him to enter a plea of guilty or not guilty. *Compare* preliminary hearing.

- *n.* accusation, incrimination, formal accusal, judicial charge

arrest
[a.*rest*]

1. Detention of a person on a criminal charge. 2. Any detention of a person, with or without the intent to take him into custody.

- *v.* apprehend, catch, capture, block, seize ("The thief was arrested."); stop, block, foil, obstruct, hinder
- *n.* apprehension, captivity, capture, confinement, detention, incarceration; stoppage, suspension, halt, cessation ("His arrest was of indefinite duration.")

arson
[*ar*.sen]

The willful and malicious burning of a building. In some jurisdictions, arson includes the deliberate burning of any structure.

- *n.* pyromania, setting a fire, torching

assault [a.*salt*]	An act of force or threat of force intended to inflict harm upon a person or to put the person in fear that such harm is imminent; an attempt to commit a battery. The perpetrator must have, or appear to have, the present ability to carry out the act. ■ *v.* abuse, advance, assail, jump, set upon, bash, violate, storm ("The pedestrian assaulted the child.") ■ *n.* attack, advance, strike, violation ("The assault was aggressive.")
assault and battery [a.*salt* and *bat*.er.ee]	An achieved assault; an assault carried out by hitting or by other physical contact. *See also* battery.
attempt [a.temt]	An act done with the intent to commit a crime, which would have resulted in the crime being committed except that something happened to prevent it.
bail [bayul]	1. The customary means of securing the release from custody of a person charged with a criminal offense, by assuring his appearance in court and compelling him to remain within the jurisdiction. 2. The security given for a defendant's appearance in court in the form of cash, real property, or a bail bond. 3. The person who is the surety on a bail bond. ■ *v.* To secure the release from custody of a person charged with a crime, pending trial, by posting a bail bond ■ *n.* bond, guarantee, security, warrant, collateral
battery [*bat*.ter.ee]	The unconsented-to touching or striking of one person by another, or by an object put in motion by her, with the intention of doing harm or giving offense. Battery is both a crime and a tort. *Compare* assault. *See also* assault and battery. ■ *n.* beating, mugging, flogging, hitting, assault, thrashing, injury ("commit a battery")
behavioral health court [bi.*hav*.yer.le helth kort]	A newer type of court designed to address the needs of the mentally ill, diverting them to treatment programs in the community, and finding creative and appropriate dispositions in order to avoid recidivism.
beyond a reasonable doubt [be.*yond* a *ree*.zen.ebl dout]	The degree of proof required to convict a person of a crime. A reasonable doubt is a fair doubt based upon reason and common sense, not an arbitrary or possible doubt. To convict a criminal defendant, a jury must be persuaded of his guilt to a level beyond "apparently" or "probably." Proof beyond a reasonable doubt is the highest level of proof the law requires.
bigamy [*big*.e.mee]	The crime of marrying while already married.
bribery [*bry*.be.ree]	The crime of giving something of value with the intention of influencing the action of a public official, witness, juror, etc. ■ *n.* corruption, allurement, cajolery, connivance

burglary
[*ber*.gler.ee]

At common law, the offense of breaking and entering a dwelling at night with the intent to commit a felony (EXAMPLES: theft; murder). The crime of burglary has been broadened by statute to include entering buildings other than dwellings, with or without a breaking, and regardless of the time of day or night.

- *v.* robbery, larceny, breaking and entering, housebreaking, looting, crime, forcible entry, raiding

capital crime
[*ka*.pi.tel krime]

A crime punishable by death.

capital punishment
[*ka*.pi.tel *pun*.ish.ment]

The death penalty as a punishment for crime.

commutation of sentence
[kom.yoo.*tay*.shun ov *sen*.tense]

The substitution of a less-severe punishment for a harsher punishment.

consecutive sentences
[ken.*sek*.yoo.tiv *sen*.ten.sez]

Sentences of imprisonment for crimes in which the time of each is to run one after the other without a break.

conspiracy
[ken.*spi*.re.see]

An agreement between two or more persons to engage in a criminal act or to accomplish a legal objective by criminal or unlawful means. Conspiracy is a criminal offense (a criminal conspiracy); it is also a wrong that is grounds for a civil action if damage is suffered.

- *n.* connivance, counterplot, frame, plot, scheme, trickery

crime
[kryme]

An offense against the authority of the state; a public wrong, as distinguished from a private wrong; an act in violation of the penal code; a felony or a misdemeanor. *See also* criminal statute.

- *n.* felony, misdemeanor, criminal act, misconduct, delinquency, corruption, offense, lawlessness

crime scene investigation
[kryme seen in.ves.ti.*gay*.shen]

An inquiry in a criminal matter by law enforcement investigators for the discovery and collection of facts and evidence.

criminal
[*krim*.i.nel]

adj. 1. Pertaining to crime or punishment. 2. Involving crime; guilty of crime.
n. A person who has been convicted of committing a crime.

- *n.* felon, culprit, violator, offender, delinquent, transgressor
- *adj.* unlawful, felonious, illegal, notorious, blameworthy, noncivil ("criminal intent")

criminal act
[*krim*.i.nel akt]

Any act punishable as a crime.

criminal action
[*krim*.i.nel *ak*.shen]

A criminal prosecution.

DICTIONARY   THESAURUS *continued...*

criminal capacity
[*krim*.i.nel ke.*pass*.i.tee]

A person can be guilty of a crime only if he has the capacity to appreciate the criminal nature of his act. In the eyes of the law, certain persons are conclusively presumed to lack criminal capacity. EXAMPLES: insane persons; persons who have not reached the age of reason, and persons not acting voluntarily.

criminal charge
[*krim*.i.nel charj]

An indictment, information, complaint, or other formal charge of the commission of a crime.

criminal law
[*krim*.i.nel law]

Branch of the law that specifies what conduct constitutes crime and establishes appropriate punishments for such conduct.

criminal offense
[*krim*.i.nel o.*fense*]

A crime.

criminal procedure
[*krim*.i.nel pro.*see*.jer]

The rules of procedure that govern criminal prosecutions.

criminal prosecution
[*krim*.i.nel pross.e.*kyoo*.shen]

The process of arresting, charging, trying, and sentencing a person for the commission of a crime. A criminal sentence generally involves the imposition of a fine, imprisonment, or death. A criminal prosecution is brought by the state, as opposed to a civil action, which is brought by a private party.

criminal statute
[*krim*.i.nel *stat*.shoot]

A statute that declares the conduct that it describes to be a crime, and establishes punishment for engaging in it.

critical stage
[*krit*.i.kel stayj]

The point in a criminal proceeding at which a defendant's constitutional right to counsel is violated unless she has counsel or has been advised of her right to counsel.

cruel and unusual punishment
[*kroo*.el and un.*yoo*.zhoo.el *pun*.ish.ment]

Forms of punishment for crime prohibited by the Eighth Amendment. The Supreme Court has determined that corporal punishment inflicted by the state is cruel within the meaning of the Constitution, but that capital punishment is not.

culpable
[*kulp*.abl]

Blameworthy; blameable; responsible; at fault.

death penalty
[deth *pen*.el.tee]

Another term for capital punishment.

defense
[de.*fense*]

The facts submitted and the legal arguments offered by a defendant in support of his claim that the prosecution's case should be rejected. The term "defense" may apply to a defendant's entire case or to separate grounds, called affirmative defenses, offered by a defendant for rejecting all or part of the case against him.

degrees of crime
[di.*greez* ov kryme]

The grades of crime ranked according to seriousness. EXAMPLES: first degree murder; second degree murder.

double jeopardy
[duh.bull *jep*.er.dee]

A rule originating in the Fifth Amendment that prohibits a second punishment or trial for the same offense.

embezzlement
[em.*bezl*.ment]

The fraudulent conversion of property, including but not limited to money, with which a person (EXAMPLES: an employee; a bailee; a trustee) has been entrusted.

- *n.* abstraction, misappropriation, misuse, theft, larceny, pilferage

entrapment
[en.*trap*.ment]

Inducing a person to commit a crime she is otherwise not inclined to commit, in order to bring a criminal prosecution against her. A defendant might assert this as an affirmative defense.

exclusionary rule
[eks.*kloo*.zhen.air.ree rule]

The rule of constitutional law that evidence secured by the police by means of an unreasonable search and seizure, in violation of the Fourth Amendment, cannot be used as evidence in a criminal prosecution.

exculpate
[*eks*.kul.pate]

1. Absolve; exonerate; acquit. 2. Condone; excuse; forgive; pardon.

exculpatory
[eks.*kul*.pe.toh.ree]

Tending to free from blame or to acquit of a criminal charge. USAGE: "I think the defendant will be acquitted; virtually all of the evidence was exculpatory."

excusable homicide
[eks.*kyoo*.zebl *hom*.i.side]

A homicide committed in the course of performing a lawful act, without any intention to hurt (for EXAMPLE, by accident) or committed in self-defense.

excuse
[eks.*kyooz*]

A reason for being relieved of a duty or obligation.

- *v.* pardon, vindicate, exculpate, forbear; absolve, liberate

execute
[*ek*.se.kyoot]

To put a person to death in accordance with a sentence of death. Usage: "The prisoner was scheduled to be executed at 9 a.m."

- *v.* eliminate, condemn, assassinate, liquidate, finish, kill, terminate, destroy

extortion
[eks.*tor*.shen]

The criminal offense of obtaining money or other things of value by duress, force, threat of force, fear, or under color of office.

- *n.* coercion, intimidation, fraud, stealing, oppression ("the criminal extortion of funds")

felony
[*fel*.a.nee]

A general term for more-serious crimes (EXAMPLES: murder; robbery; larceny), as distinguished from lesser offenses, which are known as misdemeanors. In many jurisdictions, felonies are crimes for which the punishment is death or more than one year of imprisonment. Persons convicted of felonies are generally incarcerated in prisons or penitentiaries, as opposed to local jails.

- *n.* gross offense, serious offense, transgression, wrongdoing, crime

DICTIONARY   THESAURUS *continued...*

felony murder rule
[*fel*.a.nee *mer*.der rule]

The rule that a death that occurs by accident or chance during the course of the commission of a felony is first degree murder. (EXAMPLE: If, during the course of an armed robbery by robbers A and B, robber A accidentally shoots and kills the storeowner, robber B as well as robber A are both guilty of murder.) The felony murder rule, which is a common law doctrine, has been modified by statute in most states. *See also* murder.

forensic
[fo.*ren*.sik]

Pertaining to or belonging to the courts of justice.

forensic pathology
[fo.*ren*.sik path.*aw*.le.jee]

Branch of medicine that pertains to the causes of disease and death.

forgery
[*for*.jer.ee]

The false making, material alteration, or uttering, with intent to defraud or injure, of any writing that, if genuine, might appear to be legally effective or the basis for legal liability. Forgery is a crime.

- *n.* falsification, fraudulence, misrepresentation, manipulation

fruits of the poisonous tree doctrine
[frut ov the *poy*.zen.es tree dok.*trin]*

The constitutional law doctrine that evidence, including derivative evidence, obtained as the result of an illegal search is inadmissible. *See* exclusionary rule.

grand jury
[grand *joo*.ree]

A body whose number varies with the jurisdiction, never less than 6 nor more than 23, whose duty it is to determine whether probable cause exists to return indictments against persons accused of committing crimes. The right to indictment by grand jury is guaranteed by the Fifth Amendment.

homicide
[*hom*.i.side]

The killing of a human being. Homicide may be noncriminal (excusable homicide or justifiable homicide) or criminal (felonious homicide). Excusable or justifiable homicide includes killing by accident or in self-defense. A felonious homicide is either murder or manslaughter. Manslaughter homicide includes negligent homicide and vehicular homicide.

- *n.* murder, manslaughter, slaying, assassination, killing, slaughter, felony, termination of life, extermination

identity theft
[eye.*den*.ti.tee theft]

The taking of another's personal data without his permission, usually by use of fraud or deception for personal gain. Congress enacted a new law in 1998 making identity theft a federal crime. Often, a person's personal information, such as his Social Security number, birthday, credit card numbers, telephone card numbers, and bank account numbers, are stolen and used to take funds out of his accounts, and the person committing such acts might even assume the victim's identity while carrying out other crimes, creating huge debt in his name and damaging his reputation.

incest
[*in*.sest]

Sexual intercourse between persons so closely related that the law prohibits their marriage to each other.

inculaptory
[in.*kul*.pe.tor.ee]

That which tends to incriminate. USAGE: "I think the defendant will be convicted because his own testimony was inculpatory." *Compare* exculpatory.

indictment
[in.*dite*.ment]

1. A charge made in writing by a grand jury, based upon evidence presented to it, accusing a person of having committed a criminal act, generally a felony. It is the function of the prosecution to bring a case before the grand jury. If the grand jury indicts the defendant, a trial follows. 2. The formal, written accusation itself brought before the grand jury by the prosecutor. *Compare* information.

information
[in.fer.*may*.shen]

1. An accusation of the commission of a crime, sworn to by a district attorney or other prosecutor, on the basis of which a criminal defendant is brought to trial for a misdemeanor and, in some states, for a felony. 2. In some jurisdictions that prosecute felonies only on the basis of indictment by a grand jury, an affidavit alleging probable cause to bind the defendant over to await action by the grand jury.

- *n.* charge, accusation, complaint, allegation ("felony information")

insane
[in.*sane*]

Of unsound mind. *See also* insanity.

- *adj.* unsound, deranged, demented, absurd, bizarre, mad

insanity
[in.*san*.i.tee]

A term for a condition of the mind, which has no medical or scientific meaning and whose legal meaning depends upon the context in which it is used. Insanity as a criminal defense: Different states use different tests or standards for determining whether a criminal defendant was insane (that is, whether she had the capacity to form criminal intent) at the time she committed the crime. The most important of these tests are the M'Naghten rule, irresistible impulse, and, most frequently used, the Model Penal Code's standard—lack of capacity "as a result of mental disease or defect" to appreciate the criminality of one's conduct or to conform one's conduct to the requirements of law. The law also requires that a criminal defendant be sane at the time of trial, and permits imposition of the death penalty only if the person convicted is sane at the time of execution.

keylogger
[key.*log*.ger]

A thief who deposits a virus on computers to record all keystrokes (passwords, credit, bank, and Social Security numbers, etc.) and sends them to a remote location for later retrieval for illegal purposes.

larceny
[*lar*.sen.ee]

The crime of taking personal property, without consent, with the intent to convert it to the use of someone other than the owner or to deprive the owner of it permanently. Larceny does not involve the use of force or the threat of force. *Compare* robbery. *Also compare* burglary.

- *n.* theft, embezzlement, burglary, pilferage, misappropriation, stealing

lesser included offense
[*less*.er in.*kloo*.ded o.*fense*]

A criminal offense included within the crime for which a defendant has been indicted, and for which he may be convicted under the indictment so long as he is not convicted of the more serious offense; a crime that cannot be committed without at the same time committing one or more other crimes. EXAMPLE: It is impossible to commit first degree murder without also committing second degree murder, voluntary manslaughter, and battery.

DICTIONARY | THESAURUS *continued...*

mala en se
[*mayl*.ah in *saye*]

(*Latin*) Naturally evil or wicked; immoral; illegal from the very nature of the act on the basis of principles of natural, moral, or public law, independent of the fact that it is punished by the state. EXAMPLES: murder; robbery; incest.

mala prohibita
[*mayl*.ah pro.*hib*.i.tah]

(*Latin*) A wrong that is wrong only because it is prohibited by law. EXAMPLE: driving on the left-hand side of the road. *Compare* mala in se.

malice
[*mal*.iss]

State of mind that causes the intentional doing of a wrongful act without legal excuse or justification; a condition of mind prompting a person to the commission of a dangerous or deadly act in deliberate disregard of the lives or safety of others. The term does not necessarily connote personal ill will. It can and frequently does mean general malice. As an element of murder, all those states of mind that prompt a person to kill another person without legal excuse or justification; an intent to do the person great bodily harm. In the law of defamation, to be actionable, malice must be actual malice or express malice.

manslaughter
[*man*.slaw.ter]

The killing of a human being, without premeditation or malice and without legal excuse or justification. Voluntary manslaughter occurs when a homicide is intentional but the result of sudden passion or great provocation. Involuntary manslaughter is an unintentional killing in the course of doing an unlawful act not amounting to a felony or while doing a lawful act in a reckless manner. There are various degrees of manslaughter, which are not consistent from jurisdiction to jurisdiction. *Compare* murder.

mens rea
[menz *ray*.ah]

An "answerable intent" (i.e., an intent for which one is answerable); an evil intent; a guilty mind; a criminal intent. In combination with actus reus (a guilty or criminal act), mens rea is an essential element of any crime except regulatory crimes or strict liability crimes and some petty offenses and infractions. Mens rea may be inferred or presumed.

Miranda rule
[mi.*ran*.da rule]

The Fifth Amendment and the Fourteenth Amendment to the Constitution require that, before a suspect who is in custody may be questioned, he must be informed that he has the right to remain silent and that anything he says may be used against him in court; that he be given the right to have an attorney present during questioning; and that he be advised that if he cannot afford an attorney one will be provided for him. If an interrogation occurs in the absence of these warnings, or in the absence of the suspect's attorney, any confession obtained is inadmissible unless the defendant has intelligently and knowingly waived his "Miranda rights," established by the case *Miranda v. Arizona*.

misdemeanor
[mis.de.*meen*.er]

A crime not amounting to a felony. In many jurisdictions, misdemeanors are offenses for which the punishment is incarceration for less than a year (generally in a jail, rather than in a prison or the penitentiary) or the payment of a fine. EXAMPLE: traffic violation.

- *n.* offense, transgression, wrong, misdeed, violation, trespass, impropriety

M'Naghten rule
[me.*naw*.ten rule]

An accused is not criminally responsible if, by defect of reason from disease of the mind, she did not know the nature of the act, or, if so, did not know it was wrong. *See also* insanity.

Model Penal Code
[*mod*.l *pee*.nel kode]

A proposed criminal code prepared jointly by the Commission on Uniform State Laws and the American Law Institute.

motive
[*moh*.tiv]

The reason that leads the mind to desire a result; that which leads the mind to engage in a criminal act; that which causes the mind to form criminal intent.

murder
[*mer*.der]

The intentional and premeditated killing of a human being (first degree murder); the intentional killing of a human being, without premeditation, but with malice aforethought, express or implied (second degree murder). Under most state statutes, a homicide that occurs during the commission of a felony is first degree murder, as are homicides perpetrated by lying in wait, torture, poison, and other criminal acts from which premeditation or deliberation can be inferred. Similarly, a homicide that results from deliberately doing a dangerous or deadly act with disregard for the safety of others is second degree murder, malice being inferred from the act itself. *Compare* manslaughter. *See also* felony murder rule.

- *n.* liquidation, slaughter, killing, slaying, homicide, execution, unlawful killing

nolo contendere
[*no*.lo kon.*ten*.de.ray]

(*Latin*) "I do not wish to contest it." A plea in a criminal case, also referred to as no contest, which, although it is essentially the same as a guilty plea, and carries the same consequences with respect to punishment, can be entered only with leave of court, because it is not an admission of responsibility and cannot be used against the defendant in a civil action based upon the same facts.

parole
[pa.*role*]

The release of a person from imprisonment after serving a portion of her sentence, provided she complies with certain conditions. Such conditions vary, depending upon the case, but they generally include stipulations such as not associating with known criminals, not possessing firearms, and not leaving the jurisdiction without the permission of the parole officer. Parole is not an act of clemency; it does not set aside the sentence. The parolee remains in the legal custody of the state and under the control of her parole officer. She may be returned to prison if she breaches the specified conditions. However, due process requires that parole cannot be revoked without a hearing.

- *n.* release, freedom, emancipation, conditional release
- *v.* discharge, release, liberate, let out, disimprison

plea bargain
[plee *barg*.in]

An agreement between the prosecutor and a criminal defendant under which the accused agrees to plead guilty, usually to a lesser offense, in exchange for receiving a lighter sentence than he would likely have received had he been found guilty after trial on the original charge.

preliminary hearing
[pre.*lim*.i.ner.ee *heer*.ing]

A hearing to determine whether there is probable cause to formally accuse a person of a crime; that is, whether there is a reasonable basis for believing that a crime has been committed and for thinking the defendant committed it. If the judge concludes that the evidence is sufficient to hold the defendant for trial, and if the offense is a bailable offense, the court sets bail. If the judge concludes that the evidence is insufficient to bind the defendant over for trial, the defendant is discharged from custody. *See also* probable cause.

principal
[*prin*.si.pl]

A principal of *the first degree* is a person who commits a crime, either in person or through an innocent agent; a principal in *the second degree* is a person who is present at the commission of a crime, giving aid and encouragement to the chief perpetrator.

prison
[*priz*.en]

A place of confinement for persons convicted of felonies, as opposed to jail, which is customarily a place of confinement for persons convicted of misdemeanors; a penitentiary.

- *n.* penitentiary, confinement, jail, house of detention, reformatory, guardhouse, pen, cell, facility

probable cause
[*prob*.ebl cawz]

A reasonable amount of suspicion, supported by circumstances sufficiently strong to justify a prudent and cautious person's belief that certain alleged facts are probably true. A judge may not issue a search warrant unless she is shown probable cause to believe there is evidence of crime on the premises. A police officer may not make an arrest without a warrant unless he has reasonable cause, based upon reliable information, to believe a crime has been or is being committed.

probation
[pro.*bay*.shen]

A sentence that allows a person convicted of a crime to continue to live and work in the community while being supervised by a probation officer instead of being sent to prison. A person may also be sentenced to a term of probation to commence after the expiration of his prison term.

- *n.* conditional release, test period, trial period, parole, furlough, exemption

prosecution
[*pross*.e.kyoo.shen]

A criminal action brought by the government.

prosecutor
[pross.e.*kyoo*.ter]

A public official, elected or appointed, who conducts criminal prosecutions on behalf of her jurisdiction. EXAMPLES: the district attorney of a county; the attorney general of a state; a United States attorney.

racial profiling
[*ra*.shul *pro*.fy.ling]

Law enforcement's practice of stopping, detaining, or arresting people based on their race or ethnicity rather than their illegal behavior.

rape
[rayp]

Sexual intercourse with a woman by force or by putting her in fear or in circumstances in which she is unable to control her conduct or to resist (EXAMPLES: intoxication; unconsciousness). Under the common law definition of the crime, only a female can be raped and only a male can perpetrate the crime. In recent years, however, courts in several states have held that the rape statutes of their jurisdictions are gender-neutral and apply equally to perpetrators of either sex.

- *v.* molest, sexually assault, debauch, defile, ravish ("The woman was raped.")
- *n.* violation, assault, sexual assault, nonconsensual sex, defilement, seduction, abuse

robbery
[*rob*.e.ree]

The felonious taking of money or anything of value from the person of another or from his presence, against his will, by force or by putting him in fear. *Compare* larceny.

- *n.* theft, hold-up, piracy, commandeering, embezzlement, expropriation, abduction

scienter
[see.*en*.ter]

Knowledge, particularly guilty knowledge, that will result in one's own liability or guilt.

search warrant
[serch *war*.ent]

An order in writing issued by a magistrate or other judicial officer, commanding her to search for and seize stolen contraband, or illicit property, or other property evidencing the commission of a crime.

self-defense
[self-de.*fense*]

The use of force to protect oneself from death or imminent bodily harm at the hands of an aggressor. A person may use only that amount of force reasonably necessary to protect himself against the peril with which he is threatened; thus, deadly force may be used in self-defense only against an aggressor who himself uses deadly force.

sentence
[*sen*.tense]

The judgment of the court in a criminal case. A criminal sentence constitutes the court's action with respect to the consequences to the defendant of having committed the crime of which she has been convicted. Generally, criminal sentences impose a punishment of imprisonment, probation, fine, or forfeiture, or some combination of these penalties. In some jurisdictions, capital punishment may be imposed in cases involving the commission of a felony of extreme gravity. In some states, depending upon the crime, the jury, rather than the judge, establishes the sentence.

separate counts
[*sep*.ret kounts]

Two or more counts, charging separate offenses, contained in one indictment or information.

statutes of limitations
[*stat*.shoot of *lim*.i.tay.shenz]

Federal and state statutes prescribing the maximum period of time during which various types of criminal actions and prosecutions can be brought after the occurrence of the injury or offense.

stop
[stop]

An arrest; a police officer's action in halting a person's freedom of action, even briefly.

stop and frisk
[stop and frisk]

The detaining of a person briefly by a police officer and "patting him down" with the purpose of ascertaining if he is carrying a concealed weapon.

violation
[vy.o.*lay*.shen]

1. The act of breaking the law; an infringement of the law; a violation of the law.
2. Sometimes used as a synonym for an infraction.

- *n.* abuse, contravention, illegality, misdemeanor, transgression ("a violation of the law")

year and a day rule
[yere and a day rul]

The rule in prosecution for homicide, in many jurisdictions, that if death does not occur within a year and a day after the occurrence of the wrongful act, it will be presumed that death resulted from some other cause.

Missing Words

Fill in the blanks.

1. _____ is the detention of a person on criminal charges.

2. The grades of crime ranked according to seriousness are the _____ of crime.

3. A(n) _____ is the point in a criminal proceeding at which a defendant's constitutional right to counsel is violated unless she has counsel or has been advised of the right to counsel.

4. When a person is released from imprisonment after serving a portion of the sentence provided certain conditions are complied with, this is called _____.

5. A(n) _____ is an agreement between the prosecutor and a criminal defendant where the accused agrees to plead guilty to a lesser offense in exchange for receiving a lighter sentence.

6. _____ is a plea in a criminal case that means, "I don't wish to contest it."

7. _____ are forms of punishment such as torture and banishment that are prohibited by the Eighth Amendment to the Constitution.

8. The branch of medicine that pertains to the causes of disease and death is _____.

9. When one person helps another person to commit a crime, this is _____.

10. A(n) _____ is an offense against the authority of the state, known as a public wrong.

11. The _____ is a proposed criminal code prepared jointly by the Commission on Uniform State Laws and the American Law Institute.

12. _____ is a sentence that allows a person convicted of a crime to continue to live and work in the community instead of being sent to jail.

13. _____ is claimed when one uses force to protect oneself from death or imminent bodily harm at the hands of an aggressor.

14. _____ is an agreement between two or more persons to engage in a criminal act.

15. _____ is used as a criminal defense to show that the accused lacked the capacity to form criminal intent.

16. The crime of marrying while already married is _____.

17. Sexual intercourse with a woman by force is called _____.

18. The criminal offense of obtaining money or other things of value by duress, force, threat of force, fear, or under color of office is _____.

STUDY AID: Use flashcards for this unit before completing the exercises.

Matching

Match the letter of the definition to the term.

___A___ **19.** conspiracy

___H___ **20.** stop and frisk

___C___ **21.** information

___F___ **22.** Miranda rule

___J___ **23.** violation

___L___ **24.** exclusionary rule

___N___ **25.** parole

___O___ **26.** capital punishment

___E___ **27.** misdemeanor

___K___ **28.** degree of crime

___B___ **29.** crime

___G___ **30.** sentence

___D___ **31.** malice

___I___ **32.** rape

___M___ **33.** preliminary hearing

___Q___ **34.** motive

___P___ **35.** forensic

A. an agreement between two or more persons to engage in a criminal act or accomplish a legal objective by criminal or unlawful means

B. an act in violation of the penal code

C. accusation of the commission of a crime sworn to by a district attorney or other prosecutor

D. state of mind that causes the intentional doing of a wrongful act without legal excuse or justification

E. crime not amounting to a felony

F. before a suspect in custody may be questioned he or she must be informed of the right to remain silent

G. judgment of the court in a criminal case

H. detaining of a person by police to see if a concealed weapon is being carried

I. sexual intercourse with a woman by force

J. synonym for an infraction

K. grade of crime ranked according to seriousness

L. evidence secured by police during an unreasonable search and seizure; cannot be used at trial

M. hearing to determine whether there is probable cause to formally accuse a person of a crime

N. conditional release from prison after serving a portion of a sentence

O. the death penalty as a punishment for a crime

P. pertaining to the courts

Q. criminal intent

Multiple Choice

Select the best choice.

___B___ **36.** The security given for a defendant's appearance in court is known as:
  a. incest.
  b. bail.
  c. malice.
  d. extortion.

___D___ **37.** The crime of giving something of value with the intent of influencing a public official is called:
  a. robbery.
  b. larceny.
  c. embezzlement.
  d. bribery.

___C___ **38.** A general term for more serious crimes such as murder and robbery is:
  a. violation.
  b. misdemeanor.
  c. felony.
  d. lesser included offense.

___a___ **39.** The degree of proof needed to convict a person of a crime is:
  a. proof beyond a reasonable doubt.
  b. preponderance of the evidence.
  c. clear and convincing proof.
  d. a scintilla of evidence.

___C___ **40.** The willful and malicious burning of a building is called:
  a. larceny.
  b. embezzlement.
  c. arson.
  d. forgery.

___D___ **41.** The breaking and entering of a dwelling at night with the intent to commit a felony is called:
  a. robbery.
  b. larceny.
  c. extortion.
  d. burglary.

___A___ **42.** Sexual intercourse between persons so closely related that the law prohibits their marriage to each other is:
  a. incest.
  b. bigamy.
  c. sodomy.
  d. rape.

___B___ **43.** When a bank teller has been entrusted with money and converts the property for his own benefit, this is:
  a. larceny.
  b. embezzlement.
  c. aiding and abetting.
  d. extortion.

___A___ **44.** The intentional and premeditated killing of a human being is:
  a. murder.
  b. manslaughter.
  c. misdemeanor.
  d. mens rea.

___C___ **45.** The rule of constitutional law that evidence secured by the police by means of an unreasonable search and seizure cannot be used as evidence in a criminal prosecution is:
  a. strict liability crimes.
  b. lesser included offense.
  c. exclusionary rule.
  d. beyond a reasonable doubt.

___D___ **46.** The charge made in writing by a grand jury based upon evidence presented to it, accusing a person of having committed a criminal act, is the:
  a. preliminary hearing.
  b. arrest.
  c. stop.
  d. indictment.

A 47. The act of bringing an accused before a court to answer a criminal charge, and to enter a plea of guilty or not guilty is:
  a. arraignment.
  b. plea bargain.
  c. grand jury.
  d. trial.

D 48. A crime that cannot be committed without the individual at the same time committing one or more other crimes is:
  a. double jeopardy.
  b. extortion.
  c. exclusionary rule.
  d. lesser included offense.

True/False

Mark the following T or F.

T 49. An accessory is a person who is involved with the commission of a crime but who is not present at the time it is committed.

F 50. A misdemeanor is an offense punishable by one year or more in prison.

T 51. The defense that the accused was elsewhere at the time the crime was committed is called an alibi.

F 52. Extortion is the willful and malicious burning of a building.

T 53. Malice is a state of mind that causes the intentional doing of a wrongful act without legal excuse or justification.

F 54. The unconsented-to touching or striking of one person by another is an assault.

T 55. When the death penalty is a punishment for a crime, this is called capital punishment.

F 56. A detention of a person on a criminal charge is called an indictment.

T 57. The arraignment is when the accused is brought into court to answer a criminal charge and asked to enter a plea.

F 58. A robbery is the breaking and entering of a dwelling at night with the intent to commit a felony.

F 59. The standard of evidence needed for the prosecutor to convict a defendant of a crime is by a preponderance of the evidence.

F 60. An attempt occurs where the accused has committed a crime but has not yet been arrested for the crime.

T 61. M'Naghten rule states that an accused isn't criminally responsible if found to be insane.

Synonyms

Select the correct synonym in parentheses for each numbered item.

62. ALIBI
(arrest, confession, excuse)

63. BRIBE
(kickback, present, request)

64. ATTEMPT
(ponder, try, finish)

65. BATTERY
(beating, frighten, tease)

66. LARCENY
(forgery, lying, pickpocketing)

67. ACCESSORY
(accomplice, violation, sodomy)

68. MURDER
(torture, kill, torment)

69. ARREST
(detention, questioning, arraignment)

70. MALICE
(willfulness, alibi, arson)

71. ASSAULT
(threaten, attack, extortion)

72. FORGERY
(bribery, alteration, bigamy)

73. HOMICIDE
(burglary, robbery, killing)

74. CRIME
(offense, defense, occasion)

75. CONSPIRACY
(doubt, agreement, dispute)

76. CRIMINAL CHARGE
(complaint, answer, demurrer)

77. MENS REA
(crime, charge, intent)

78. ARSON
(torching, incest, insane)

79. BAIL
(attack, security, criminal)

80. PROSECUTION
(persecution, criminal action, alibi)

Self-Test

Place the number of the correct term in the appropriate space.

81. probation

82. misdemeanors

83. arrest

84. degrees

85. indictment

86. parole

87. plea bargain

88. violations

89. crime

90. criminal procedure

91. felonies

92. preliminary hearing

93. arraigned

94. murder

A(n) _____ is an act in violation of the penal code. There are different _____ of crime, meaning the grades of crime ranked by seriousness. The most serious are the _____ such as _____. Less serious are the _____, which are punishable by incarceration for less than a year, or the payment of a fine. The least serious, usually punishable by fine and/or probation, are _____. The rules of procedure by which criminal actions are governed are _____. Generally, some illegal activity occurs. Then, a(n) _____ is made, usually based on a warrant. In some cases, there might be a(n) _____ to see if there is probable cause to formally accuse a person of a crime. Depending on the state, the grand jury then issues a(n) _____ for the more serious crimes. Thereafter, the accused is _____, and a plea is entered by the accused. Not all cases go on to trial. In some instances, a(n) _____ is made, where the accused agrees to plead guilty to a lesser offense in exchange for a lighter sentence. Not all guilty defendants are imprisoned. Some defendants might be placed on _____ instead of being sent to prison. Even if a defendant is imprisoned, she might be released early on _____, provided she complies with certain conditions.

Word Scramble

Unscramble the following words and write the correct word(s) that match(es) the definition for each word or phrase.

95. demeanormis – offense that is punishable by less than a year in jail _____

_____

96. smen are – evil intent _____

_____

97. soryacces – a person involved with the commission of the crime who is not present _____

_____

98. biali – the accused was elsewhere at the time of the crime _____

_____

99. ssaulta – an attempt to commit a battery _____

_____

100. durmer – premeditated killing of a human being

_____

101. liab – security given for a defendant's appearance in court _____

_____

102. licema – state of mind causing the intentional doing of a wrongful act _____

_____

103. glaryrub – breaking and entering _____

_____

104. lonyfe – term for more serious crimes _____

_____

105. tteryba – unconsented to touching _____

_____

106. arcenly – taking personal property without the owner's consent _____

_____

107. tionviola – an infraction _____

_____

108. sonar – willful burning of a building _____

_____

109. dingai and bettinga – helping or encouraging

_____

_____

110. emirc sceen igationinvest – discovery and collection of facts and evidence _____

_____

The Last Word

Electronic privacy is difficult to achieve when today's technology allows the tracking of any individual's whereabouts. Since 1986, the Electronics Communications Privacy Act has allowed law enforcement the low threshold of establishing only "reasonable grounds" to obtain data, not the higher "probable cause" standard needed for warrants. Almost a quarter century later in 2010, the United States Court of Appeals for the Third Circuit found that judges have the right to require warrants before police acquire cell phone records ascertaining a caller's location. While the decision suggests that judges have the discretion to demand more information from law enforcement, it did not say that warrants are always required to obtain cell phone records.

However, the Electronic Frontier Foundation, an advocacy group in favor of electronic privacy rights, believes that lower courts now must look to the higher standard before allowing unconstitutional location tracking as it does when it requires warrants for electronic communications such as a wiretap and the contents of e-mail or a text message.

Whether the decision is a panacea for electronic privacy and a slippery slope for law enforcement remains to be seen, especially if the matter winds up before the Supreme Court. Do you agree with electronic privacy rights, or should law enforcement be favored?

2

Constitutional and Administrative Law

- Learn about constitutional and administrative law.

- Master the similarities and differences in definitions of key terms.

- Master the pronunciations and spellings of legal terms.

- Recognize the synonyms used for legal terminology.

- Practice usage of terms, definitions, and synonyms.

- Complete unit exercises in the forms of missing words, matching, multiple choice, true/false, synonyms, self-test, and word scramble.

- Work with a legal dictionary/thesaurus.

Constitutional Law

The American system of government is set forth in the United States Constitution. Each individual state has its own state constitution as well. Generally, when reference is made to "the Constitution," the federal Constitution is intended. The U.S. Constitution came into effect in 1787 and is composed of seven articles that cover the organization and running of the government.

In time, various amendments to the Constitution have been adopted. The first 10 amendments to the Constitution, which were made to further protect the rights of individual citizens, are known as the Bill of Rights. There have been a mere 27 amendments to the Constitution, the last in 1992.

Much respect is due the Constitution, a document enacted over 200 years ago, yet flexible enough to withstand the great changes in American society and in the world at large. When the Constitution was drafted there was no technology or advanced communications. Yet the Constitution was written to deal with many of the legal problems encountered daily, to wit: separation of church and state, election of the government, freedom of assembly and religion, and illegal search and seizure. Those stated are but a few that will be examined in this unit on constitutional law, including the First Amendment freedom in the following case.

CASE AND COMMENT

United States District Court, Central District of California
Log Cabin Republicans, a nonprofit corporation, Plaintiff
v.
United States of America and Robert M. Gates, Secretary of Defense,
In his official capacity, Defendants
Case No. CV 04-04-08425-VAP (EX) October 12, 2010

Facts: In 1993 the "don't ask, don't tell" policy was enacted by Congress in an effort to reform the military's practice of ferreting out and discharging homosexual personnel. The policy allowed gay and lesbian service members to serve as long as they kept their sexual orientation private. Estimates are that over 13,000 service members have been discharged pursuant to this 17-year policy. Despite efforts to repeal the policy, they failed in Congress as recently as September, 2010.

	CASE AND COMMENT *continued...*

Procedural History: The case was tried in July, 2010. After conclusion of the evidence and closing arguments on July 23, 2010, both sides timely submitted supplemental post-trial briefing on the admissibility of a pretrial declaration brought by Log Cabin Republicans, and the matter stood submitted. Plaintiff's challenge is two-fold: "it contends the Act violates its members' rights to substantive due process . . . and its members' rights of freedom of speech, association, and to petition the government."

Issue: Whether the military's "don't ask, don't tell" policy violates service members' free speech and due process rights under the United States Constitution.

Rationale: The Court declared that the policy "infringes on the fundamental rights of United States service members and prospective service members." It violated constitutional guarantees because it did not permit targeted members "to petition the government for redress of grievances" and to fight for their rights when exposed as homosexuals.

Ruling: Finding violations of both the First and Fifth Amendments, the Court ordered the military to stop "enforcing or applying" the policy and implementing the regulations "against any person under their jurisdiction or command" (and) "immediately to suspend and discontinue any investigation or discharge, separation or other proceedings" now pending against current service members.

Comment: That Republicans won this temporary action to end the ban and that the Obama administration was forced to appeal it drips with irony. Repealing "don't ask, don't tell" was a major campaign promise of President Obama before his election in 2008. In this case, American politics provided strange bedfellows.

DICTIONARY | THESAURUS

Term
[phonetic pronunciation]

Note: All dictionary/thesaurus terms appear on flashcards at the back of the book and on the student website.

amendment of constitution
[*a.mend*.ment ov kon.sti.*too*.shen]

A process of proposing, passing, and ratifying amendments to the United States Constitution or a state or other constitution.

American Civil Liberties Union
[a.*mare*.i.ken *siv*.il *lib*.er.tees *yoon*.yun]

A nonprofit organization, commonly called the ACLU, that is concerned with constitutional rights, particularly individual liberties, and engages in litigation and lobbying.

articles
[*ar*.tiklz]

Plural of article. Distinct divisions, parts, clauses, or provisions that, taken as a whole, make up a constitution, charter, statute, contract, or other written statement of principles or mutual understandings.

balancing test
[*bal*.en.sing test]

A principle of constitutional law that declares that the constitutional rights of each citizen must, in each instance, be balanced against the danger that their exercise presents to others or to the state. EXAMPLE: freedom of speech does not include the right "to cry fire in a crowded theater" if there is no fire, as others might be hurt.

bicameral
[by.*kam*.er.el]

Two-chambered, referring to the customary division of a legislature into two houses (a Senate and a House of Representatives).

Bill of Rights
[bil ov ritz]

The first 10 amendments to the United States Constitution. The Bill of Rights is the portion of the Constitution that sets forth the rights that are the fundamental principles of the United States and the foundation of American citizenship.

civilogue
[*siv*.el.log]

In exercising free speech, those in disagreement agree to conduct a civil dialogue while refraining from insulting each other.

commerce clause
[*kom*.erss kloz]

The clause in Article I, Section 8, of the Constitution that gives Congress the power to regulate commerce between the states and between the United States and foreign countries. Federal statutes that regulate business and labor (EXAMPLES: the Fair Labor Standards Act; the Occupational Safety and Health Act) are based upon this power. *See also* interstate commerce.

constitution
[kon.sti.*too*.shen]

The system of fundamental principles by which a nation, state, or corporation is governed. A nation's constitution may be written (EXAMPLE: the Constitution of the United States) or unwritten (EXAMPLE: the British Constitution). A nation's law must conform to its constitution. A law that violates a nation's constitution is unconstitutional and therefore unenforceable.

Constitution
[kon.sti.*too*.shen]

The Constitution of the United States.

- *n.* charter, code, formation, written law, supreme law

Constitution of the United States
[kon.sti.*too*.shen of the yoo.*nie*.ted states]

The fundamental document of American government, as adopted by the people of the United States through their representatives in the Constitutional Convention of 1787, as ratified by the states, together with the amendments to the Constitution.

constitutional
[kon.sti.*too*.shen.el]

In accordance with the Constitution of the United States; consistent with the Constitution; not in conflict with the Constitution.

- *adj.* approved, chartered, lawful, democratic, enforceable
- *ant.* unconstitutional

constitutional amendment
[kon.sti.*too*.shen.el a.*mend*.ment]

An amendment to a constitution. *See also* amendment of constitution.

constitutional convention
[kon.sti.*too*.shen.el ken.*ven*.shen]

A representative body that meets to form and adopt a constitution. (EXAMPLE: The convention that met in Philadelphia in 1787 to draft and adopt the Constitution of the United States.) Article V of the United States Constitution provides for the calling of a convention as a means of amending the Constitution.

constitutional courts
[kon.sti.*too*.shen.el kortz]

Courts directly established by the Constitution, which are therefore beyond the power of Congress to abolish or alter. EXAMPLE: the Supreme Court of the United States.

DICTIONARY / THESAURUS *continued...*

constitutional law
[kon.sti.*too*.shen.el law]

The body of principles that apply in the interpretation, construction, and application of the Constitution to statutes and to other governmental action. Constitutional law deals with constitutional questions and determines the constitutionality of state and federal laws and of the manner in which government exercises its authority.

constitutional limitations
[kon.sti.*too*.shen.el
lim.i.*tay*.shenz]

The provisions of a constitution that limit the legislature's power to enact laws.

constitutional questions
[kon.sti.*too*.shen.el *kwes*.chenz]

See constitutional law.

constitutional right
[kon.sti.*too*.shen.el ryt]

A right guaranteed by the Constitution of the United States or by a state constitution; a fundamental right. A constitutional right cannot be abrogated or infringed by Congress or by a state legislature.

due process clause
[dew *pross*.ess kloz]

Actually a reference to two due process clauses, one in the Fifth Amendment and one in the Fourteenth Amendment. The Fifth Amendment requires the federal government to accord "due process of law" to citizens of the United States; the Fourteenth Amendment imposes a similar requirement upon state governments. *See also* due process of law.

due process of law
[dew *pross*.ess ov law]

Law administered through courts of justice, equally applicable to all under established rules that do not violate fundamental principles of fairness. Whether a person has received due process of law can only be determined on a case-by-case basis. In all criminal cases, however, it involves, at the very least, the right to be heard by a fair and impartial tribunal, the defendant's right to be represented by counsel, the right to cross-examine witnesses against him, the right to offer testimony on his own behalf, and the right to have advance notice of trial and of the charge sufficient in detail and in point of time to permit adequate preparation for trial. Due process requirements for criminal prosecutions are considerably more rigorous than those for civil cases. "Due process of law" is guaranteed by both the Fifth Amendment and the Fourteenth Amendment. *See also* due process clause.

enumerated powers
[e.*nyoo*.me.ray.ted *pow*.erz]

Powers specifically granted by the Constitution to one of the three branches of government. Another term for enumerated powers is express powers. *Compare* implied power.

equal protection clause
[*ee*.kwel pro.*tek*.shen kloz]

The clause in the Fourteenth Amendment that dictates that no state may "deny to any person within its jurisdiction the equal protection of the laws." *See also* equal protection of the laws.

equal protection of the laws
[*ee*.kwel pro.*tek*.shen ov the lawz]

Constitutional guarantee that specifies that the rights of all persons must rest upon the same rules under the same circumstances. Put another way, every state must give equal treatment to every person who is similarly situated or to persons who are members of the same class. "Equal protection of the laws" is a requirement for the Fourteenth Amendment. *See also* equal protection clause.

Equal Rights Amendment [*ee*.kwel rytz a.*mend*.ment]	A proposed constitutional amendment, passed by Congress in 1972, that failed for lack of ratification by three-fourths of the states. The proposed amendment, generally referred to as the ERA, provided that "equality of rights under the law shall not be abridged by the United States or any state on account of sex."
establishment clause [es.*tab*.lish.ment kloz]	The provision of the First Amendment that states that "Congress shall make no law respecting an establishment of religion, or prohibiting the free exercise thereof." It means that neither a state nor the federal government can set up a state religion; neither can it pass laws that aid one religion, aid all religions, or prefer one religion over another; neither can it force or influence a person to go to or remain away from a church, synagogue, mosque, or other place of worship, or force him to proclaim a belief or disbelief in any religion.
executive branch [eg.*zek*.yoo.tiv branch]	1. With the legislative branch and the judicial branch, one of the three divisions into which the Constitution separates the government of the United States. These branches of government are also referred to as departments of government. The executive branch is primarily responsible for enforcing the laws, it includes the President of the United States and all the federal agencies and departments. 2. A similar division exists in state government.
executive privilege [eg.*zek*.yoo.tiv *priv*.i.lej]	The privilege of the president of the United States to refuse to make certain confidential communications available to public scrutiny or to review by any branch of government other than the executive branch.
federalism [*fed*.er.el.izm]	1. Pertaining to a system of government that is federal in nature. 2. The system by which the states of the United States relate to each other and to the federal government.
Fifteenth Amendment [*fif*.teenth a.*mend*.ment]	An amendment to the Constitution that provides that "the right of citizens of the United States to vote shall not be denied or abridged by the United States or by any state on account of race, color, or previous condition of servitude."
Fifth Amendment [fifth a.*mend*.ment]	An amendment to the Constitution that guarantees the right to grand jury indictment if one is accused of having committed a serious crime, the right not to be placed in double jeopardy, the right not to be compelled to incriminate oneself, the right to due process of law, and the right not to have one's private property taken by the government without just compensation. The Fifth Amendment applies only to the federal government. Its requirements are made applicable to state and local government through the Fourteenth Amendment.
First Amendment [first a.*mend*.ment]	An amendment to the Constitution that guarantees freedom of religion, freedom of speech, and freedom of the press, as well as freedom of association (the right "peaceably to assemble") and the right to petition the government for redress of grievances.
Fourteenth Amendment [*four*.teenth a.*mend*.ment]	An amendment to the Constitution that requires the states (as opposed to the federal government—*compare* Fifth Amendment) to provide due process of law, and to ensure equal protection of the laws, "to any person within (their) jurisdiction." The Fourteenth Amendment also prohibits states from abridging "the privileges and immunities of citizens." *See also* due process clause; equal protection clause; privileges and immunities clause.

DICTIONARY	THESAURUS *continued...*

Fourth Amendment
[fourth a.*mend*.ment]

An amendment to the Constitution prohibiting searches without search warrants and requiring that search warrants be issued only upon probable cause.

free exercise clause
[free *ek*.ser.size kloz]

The clause in the First Amendment that prevents Congress from prohibiting the "free exercise" of religion. *See also* freedom of religion.

freedom of expression
[*free*.dum ov eks.*presh*.en]

A term that covers religious freedom, freedom of speech, and freedom of the press, all of which are protected by the First Amendment.

freedom of religion
[*free*.dum ov re.*lij*.en]

The First Amendment stipulates that "Congress shall make no law respecting an establishment of religion, or prohibiting the free exercise thereof." This provision guarantees the freedom to believe or not believe and, subject to law, the right to act upon one's religious belief or lack of belief. It also prohibits financial assistance to religion from public funds.

freedom of speech and of the press
[*free*.dum ov speech and ov the press]

The First Amendment provides that "Congress shall make no law . . . abridging the freedom of speech or of the press." It embraces the concept that the expression or publication of thought and belief, free from government interference, is essential to the well-being of a free society, and should be limited only to prevent abuse of that right.

full faith and credit
[fel faith and *kred*.it]

A reference to the requirement of Article IV of the Constitution that each state give "full faith and credit" to the "public acts, records and judicial proceedings" of every other state. This means that a state's judicial acts must be given the same effect by the courts of all other states as they receive at home.

HIPAA
[hi.pa]

This is an acronym for Health Insurance Portability and Accountability Act, which was enacted by Congress in 1996. Title I of the Act protects health insurance coverage of workers and their families when they lose or switch jobs. HIPAA also addresses the security and privacy of health records.

implied power
[im.*plide pow*.er]

The power necessary to carry out a power expressly granted. EXAMPLE: the power of a department of an agency of government to perform such acts as are necessary to achieve the objectives of the statute or constitution under which the agency was established. *Compare* enumerated powers.

interstate commerce
[*in*.ter.state *kawm*.ers]

Commerce between states; that is, from a given point in one state to a given point in another. Most federal statutes dealing with business or labor (EXAMPLES: consumer credit protection acts; the Fair Labor Standards Act), as well as many other federal statutes, are based upon the commerce clause of the Constitution, which gives Congress the power "to regulate commerce . . . among the several states." The term "commerce" is often used as a short reference for "interstate commerce." For EXAMPLE, "affecting commerce" means "affecting interstate commerce" and "engaged in commerce" means "engaged in interstate commerce." *See also* commerce clause. *Compare* intrastate commerce.

intrastate commerce
[*in*.tra.state *kawm*.ers]

Commerce that takes place within the boundaries of one state. *Compare* interstate commerce.

judicial branch
[joo.*dish*.el branch]

1. With the legislative branch and the executive branch, one of the three divisions into which the Constitution separates the government of the United States. These branches of government are also referred to as departments of government. The judicial branch, which consists of the court system, is primarily responsible for interpreting the laws. 2. The similar division exists in state government.

legislation
[lej.is.*lay*.shen]

Laws (EXAMPLES: statutes, ordinances) enacted by a legislative body (EXAMPLES: Congress; a state legislature; a city council).

- *n.* law, regulation, statute, ordinances, ruling, measure, act

legislative branch
[lej.is.*lay*.tiv branch]

1. With the judicial branch and the executive branch, one of the three divisions into which the Constitution separates the government of the United States. These branches of government are also referred to as departments of government. The legislative branch, consisting of the House of Representative and the United States Senate, which together form the United States Congress, is primarily responsible for enacting the laws. 2. A similar division exists in state government.

legislature
[*lej*.is.lay.cher]

The branch of government that enacts statutory law, usually consisting of two houses, a Senate and a House of Representatives, made up of members representing districts and elected by the voters of those districts. Congress is the national legislature.

- *n.* house, chamber, assembly, parliament, senate, council

Magna Carta
[*mag*.na *car*.ta]

(*Latin*) "Great charter," a document that was issued by King John of England in 1215 and is the basis of English and American constitutional protections. Its guarantees relating to life, liberty, and property are embedded in the Constitution of the United States and in every state constitution in the United States.

nanny state laws
[nanny stayt lawz]

n. Intrusive state laws legislating or prohibiting those under the age of majority (usually 18) from snowboarding without a helmet, buying soft drinks at school, piercing body parts, getting tattooed, etc.

police power
[po.*leess* pow.er]

1. The power of the government to make and enforce laws and regulations necessary to maintain and enhance the public welfare and to prevent individuals from violating the rights of others. 2. The sovereignty of each of the states of the United States that is not surrendered to the federal government under the Constitution. *See also* Tenth Amendment.

preemption
[pree.*emp*.shen]

The doctrine that once Congress has enacted legislation in a given field, a state may not enact a law inconsistent with the federal statute. Thus, for EXAMPLE, a state may not enact a wage and hour law, applicable to employers who are in commerce, that is inconsistent with the provisions of the Fair Labor Standards Act. A similar doctrine also governs the relationship between the state government and local government.

- *n.* appropriation, substitution, usurpation, replacement, annexation ("preemption doctrine")

DICTIONARY   THESAURUS *continued...*

prior restraint
[pry.er re.*straynt*]

The imposition by the government, in advance of publication, of limits that prohibit or restrain speech or publication, as opposed to later punishing persons for what they have actually said or written.

privileges and immunities clause
[*priv*.i.lejz and im.*yoon*.i.teez kloz]

1. Section 2 of Article IV of the Constitution, which provides that "[t]he citizens of each state shall be entitled to all privileges and immunities of citizens in the several states." 2. The clause of the Fourteenth Amendment that provides that "[n]o state shall make or enforce any law which shall abridge the privileges or immunities of citizens of the United States. . . ." These provisions represent a constitutional requirement that a state give out-of-state residents the same fundamental rights as it gives its own citizens.

procedural due process
[pro.*seed*.jer.el doo *pross*.ess]

The implication that a person has the right to a proceeding to protect one's rights.

ratify
[*rat*.i.fy]

To give approval; to confirm.

rational basis
[*rash*.en.el *bay*.sis]

A reasonable basis, under the law. The courts will not invalidate a statute or overrule an order of an administrative agency that has a "rational basis" in law.

referendum
[ref.e.*ren*.dum]

Under some state constitutions, the process by which an act of the legislature or a constitutional amendment is referred to the voters at an election for their approval.

- *n.* proposition, proposal, election, questions, mandate, plebiscite

Senate
[*sen*.et]

The upper house of Congress. Its 100 members, two from each state, are elected for six-year terms; one-third of the Senate's members are elected every two years.

separate but equal doctrine
[*sep*.ret but *ee*.kwel *dok*.trin]

A doctrine (overruled by *Brown v. Board of Education*), under which the separation of the races in places of public accommodation, including public schools, had been previously held constitutional.

separation of powers
[sep.e.*ray*.shen ov *pow*.erz]

A fundamental principle of the Constitution that gives exclusive power to the legislative branch to make the law, exclusive power to the executive branch to administer it, and exclusive power to the judicial branch to enforce it. The authors of the Constitution believed that the separation of powers would make abuse of power less likely.

stare decisis
[*stahr*.ay de.*sy*.sis]

(Latin) Means "standing by the decision." Stare decisis is the doctrine that judicial decisions stand as precedents for cases arising in the future. It is a fundamental policy of our law that, except in unusual circumstances, a court's determination on a point of law will be followed by courts of the same or lower rank in later cases presenting the same legal issue, even though different parties are involved and many years might have elapsed.

strict scrutiny test
[strikt *skrew*.ten.ee test]

A term the Supreme Court uses to describe the rigorous level of judicial review to be applied in determining the constitutionality of legislation that restricts a fundamental right or legislation based upon a suspect classification: age, sex, etc.

substantive due process [*sub*.sten.tiv doo *pross*.ess]	A right grounded in the Fifth and Fourteenth Amendments, the concept that government may not act arbitrarily or capriciously in making, interpreting, or enforcing the law.
supremacy clause [soo.*prem*.e.see kloz]	The provision in Article VI of the Constitution that "this Constitution and the laws of the United States . . . shall be the supreme law of the land, and the judges in every state shall be bound thereby."
supreme court [soo.*preem* kort]	1. The United States Supreme Court. The United States Supreme Court is the highest court in the federal court system. It is established by the Constitution and has both original jurisdiction and appellate jurisdiction. 2. In most states, the highest appellate court of the state. 3. In some states, a trial court.
taxing power [*tak*.sing pow.er]	The power of government to levy, assess, and collect taxes.
Tenth Amendment [tenth a.*mend*.ment]	An amendment to the Constitution that provides that the powers not delegated to the federal government by the Constitution are reserved to the states or to the people.

Missing Words

Fill in the blanks.

1. The ___judicial___ branch of government is primarily responsible for interpreting the laws.

2. The process by which a constitutional amendment is referred to the voters at an election for their approval is known as ___referendum___.

3. ___taxing power___ is the power of government to levy, assess, and collect taxes.

4. There is a(n) ___due process___ clause in both the Fifth and Fourteenth Amendments to the Constitution.

5. The ___legislature___ branch is the branch of government that enacts statutory law.

6. The ___ACLU___ is a nonprofit organization that is concerned with constitutional rights.

7. The courts will not invalidate a statute so long as the statute has a(n) ___rational basis___ in law.

8. The ___Supreme Court___ is the highest court in the federal court system.

9. The president of the United States may rely on ___executive privilege___ and refuse to make confidential communications available to public scrutiny.

10. ___federalism___ pertains to a system of government that is federal in nature.

11. _Separation_ of powers makes the abuse of power by one branch of government less likely.

12. The _privledges & immunity_ clause guarantees that citizens of each state shall be entitled to the same equal rights.

13. The _U.S. Constitution_ is the fundamental document of American government.

14. The _executive_ branch of government is primarily responsible for enforcing the law.

15. When an act of the legislature is referred to the voters at an election for their approval, this is called a(n) _referendum_.

16. The _Tenth amendment_ provides that the powers not delegated to the federal government are reserved to the states.

17. _Intrastate commerce_ is commerce that takes place within the borders of one state.

18. The _Magna Carta_ is the document that is the basis of both English and American constitutional protections.

STUDY AID: Use flashcards for this unit before completing the exercises.

Matching

Match the letter of the definition to the term.

_____ 19. freedom of expression   A. right not to be compelled to incriminate oneself

_____ 20. Fifth Amendment   B. commerce between states

_____ 21. supremacy clause   C. freedom of religion

_____ 22. Fourth Amendment   D. courts directly established by the Constitution

_____ 23. police power   E. freedom of speech

_____ 24. articles   F. power of government to make laws maintaining public welfare

_____ 25. Magna Carta   G. amendment that prohibits searches without search warrants

_____ 26. free exercise clause   H. The Constitution is the supreme law of the land.

_____ 27. interstate commerce   I. The Constitution is divided into seven of these distinct parts.

_____ 28. constitutional courts   J. a document that is the basis of English and American constitutional protections

____ **29.** bicameral

K. powers specifically granted by the Constitution

____ **30.** Constitution

L. The right to vote shall not be denied based on race, color, or servitude.

____ **31.** enumerated powers

M. two-chambered

____ **32.** Fifteenth Amendment

N. written law

____ **33.** substantive due process

O. prohibits the government from acting arbitrarily or capriciously

____ **34.** procedural due process

P. A person has the right to a proceeding to protect one's rights, per the Fifth and Fourteenth Amendments.

Multiple Choice

Select the best choice.

_B_ **35.** The first 10 amendments to the Constitution are known as the:
   a. Magna Carta.
   b. Bill of Rights.
   c. preemption doctrine.
   d. supremacy clause.

_A_ **36.** The executive branch of government is primarily responsible for:
   a. enforcing the laws.
   b. interpreting the laws.
   c. making the laws.
   d. changing the laws.

_D_ **37.** The principle that requires rights of individual citizens to be balanced against the dangers that their exercise presents to others is called:
   a. strict scrutiny.
   b. equal protection.
   c. due process.
   d. balancing test.

_B_ **38.** Powers specifically granted by the Constitution to one of the three branches of government are called:
   a. secret powers.
   b. enumerated powers.
   c. springing powers.
   d. police powers.

_D_ **39.** A representative body that meets to form and adopt a constitution is called:
   a. legislature.
   b. judicial branch.
   c. bicameral.
   d. convention.

_A_ **40.** This doctrine provided for the separation of races in places of public accommodation:
   a. separate but equal.
   b. equal but adequate.
   c. separate and apart.
   d. separation of powers.

_A_ **41.** The clause in the Constitution prohibiting federal government from setting up a state religion is called the:
   a. establishment clause.
   b. due process clause.
   c. equal protection clause.
   d. privileges and immunities clause.

_A_ **42.** Freedom of speech and expression is a right granted under which amendment to the Constitution?
   a. First Amendment.
   b. Fourth Amendment.
   c. Fifth Amendment.
   d. Fourteenth Amendment.

43. A guarantee in the Constitution that each state will give equal treatment to all persons similarly situated:
a. due process.
b. equal protection.
c. privileges and immunities.
d. strict scrutiny.

44. The legislature is divided into two houses. It is known as:
a. separate but equal doctrine.
b. articles.
c. commerce clause.
d. bicameral.

45. Once Congress has enacted legislation in a given field, a state may not enact a law inconsistent with federal statute. This is called:
a. preemption.
b. prior.
c. separation of powers.
d. rational basis.

46. The upper house of Congress with 100 members, two from each state, is the:
a. Senate.
b. House of Representatives.
c. general court.
d. legislative assembly.

True/False

Mark the following T or F.

47. The judicial branch of government is primarily responsible for enforcing the laws.

48. A document setting forth the fundamental principles of governance is known as a constitution.

49. Freedom of speech and the press is covered under the Fourth Amendment to the Constitution.

50. Enumerated powers are the government's powers to make laws maintaining the public welfare.

51. The executive branch is the branch of government responsible for interpreting the laws.

52. The legislature consists of four houses.

53. The first 10 amendments to the Constitution are known as the Magna Carta.

54. Strict scrutiny test is a term the Supreme Court uses to describe a rigorous level of judicial review.

55. If a law is found to be in accordance with the Constitution, it is said to be constitutional.

56. The establishment clause prevents the government from setting up a state religion.

57. An amendment is a change to the Constitution.

Synonyms

Select the correct synonym in parentheses for each numbered item.

58. FIFTH AMENDMENT
(equal protection clause, due process clause, privileges and immunities clause)

59. ENUMERATED POWERS
(express, implied, changed)

60. AMENDMENT
(correction, protection, preservation)

61. FIRST AMENDMENT
(freedom of expression, double jeopardy, due process)

62. ARTICLE
(part, total, version)

63. CONSTITUTION
(oral law, written law, proposed law)

64. ARTICLES
(provisions, changes, additions)

65. PRIOR RESTRAINT
(freedom, advertising, censorship)

66. EXECUTIVE BRANCH
(president, courts, legislature)

67. SEPARATION OF POWERS
(division, blending, masking)

68. BICAMERAL
(one-chambered, two-chambered, three-chambered)

69. INTRASTATE COMMERCE
(within a state, between states, between nations)

70. DUE PROCESS
(fairness, supremacy, preemption)

71. CONSTITUTIONAL
(lawful, unfair, unenforceable)

72. TAXING POWER
(levy, donate, pledge)

73. FREE EXERCISE CLAUSE
(nutrition counseling, physical education, religion)

74. FIFTEENTH AMENDMENT
(right to vote, right to attend school, right to discussion)

75. EQUAL RIGHTS AMENDMENT
(equality of rights, division of rights, separate but equal)

Self-Test

Place the number of the correct term in the appropriate space.

76. executive

77. legislative

78. Constitution

79. Articles

80. separation of powers

81. enumerated

82. supremacy clause

83. amendments

84. Bill of Rights

85. judicial

86. Fourth Amendment

87. Tenth Amendment

88. Fifth Amendment

89. First Amendment

The fundamental document of American government is the_____. The Constitution is composed of seven

_____ and 27 _____. According to Article VI of the Constitution, which is also known as the _____,

the Constitution is the supreme law of the land. By setting up a system of _____, each branch of government—the

_____ branch, the _____ branch, and the _____ branch—has its own role in government. This

prevents any one branch of government from becoming too powerful. These powers specifically granted to each branch

of government are called _____ powers. After the Constitution was ratified, the people were still concerned with

protecting their individual liberties. The enactment of the first 10 amendments to the Constitution, also known as the

_____, was drafted to ensure that fundamental rights of citizens were protected. Included in the Bill of Rights is the

_____, which guarantees free speech; the _____, which prohibits warrantless searches; the _____,

which protects against double jeopardy; and the _____, which provides that the powers not delegated to the

federal government are reserved to the states.

Word Scramble

Unscramble the following words and write the correct word(s) that match(es) the definition for each word or phrase.

90. laturelegis – the branch of government that enacts laws

_____

_____

91. endamment ssecorp – propose, pass, and ratify changes to the Constitution _____

_____

92. eralfedism – pertaining to a system of government that is federal in nature _____

_____

93. reemptionp – once Congress enacts a law, states can't enact inconsistent laws _____

_____

94. emernuated srewop – powers specifically granted by the Constitution _____

_____

95. erendferum – when voters must approve an act of the legislature through voting _____

_____

96. parseation fo srewop – the three branches of government have different functions _____

_____

97. ued ocpress esualc – is referenced in the Fifth and Fourteenth Amendments to provide due process of law

_____

_____

98. stitconution fo eht teduni setats – fundamental document of the American government _____

_____

99. camerbial – two-chambered legislature _____

100. privegesil and mmunitiesi lausec – each state must give out-of-state residents the same fundamental rights as it gives its own citizens _____

_____

101. lancbaing tset – rights of citizens must be balanced against the danger their exercise presents to others

_____

_____

102. tricts tinyscru tset – a rigorous level of judicial review is used when laws restrict fundamental rights

_____

_____

103. bstansutive eud ssecorp – a government must not act arbitrarily or capriciously in making, interpreting, or enforcing laws _____

_____

104. cedproural ude cesspor – a person has the right to a proceeding to protect one's rights _____

_____

The Last Word

"Birth tourism" has been coined as an expression referring to babies born on American soil to foreign visitors or immigrants. In 2008, the number of these children born in the United States numbered 340,000. Are these children native-born Americans? The Fourteenth Amendment to the U.S. Constitution states, "All persons born or naturalized in the United States, and subject to the jurisdiction thereof, are citizens of the United States and of the State where they reside." In effect, automatic citizenship is granted to all U.S. newborns.

Because 85 percent of the births are to parents who have lived in the United States for over one year and over half of them for five years, "birth tourism" is a misnomer. In fact, the actual number of children born to "vacationing" or visiting foreign nationals is very low. Do you think the Fourteenth Amendment should be changed to prohibit any form of "birth tourism"?

Access an interactive eBook, chapter-specific interactive learning tools, and more in your Paralegal CourseMate, accessed through www.CengageBrain.com

UNIT

5 Administrative Law

INTRODUCTION

The United States Constitution divides the power of the government into three branches: the executive, the legislative, and the judicial. Each of the branches has a separate and distinct function. The idea behind the system was to prevent any one system from becoming too powerful.

As life in the United States became increasingly complex in the twentieth century, it became clear that the three branches of government could not adequately meet all the needs of the American people. Thus, administrative law developed. Although technically there are three branches of government, administrative law is informally referred to as the fourth branch of government. Administrative law deals with the creation and operation of agencies. Legislation has created hundreds of agencies by statute. Each agency handles a variety of problems and resolves them through administrative hearings rather than proceeding in our court system. Unlike the court system, these agencies are designed to conduct hearings that are simpler in procedure, and proceed in a speedier fashion, often within a matter of months rather than years.

Some of the larger agencies are the Department of Justice, the Equal Employment Opportunity Commission, the Internal Revenue Service, the Social Security Administration, the Securities and Exchange Commission, and the Department of Defense. Each covers a distinct and separate area or field of law.

Administrative law is composed of the statutes creating the agency, rules, and regulations drafted by the agency to carry out its particular purpose, and the decisions and orders of the agency tribunals in resolving disputes against the agency. The following case illustrates several corporations' appeal of an administrative policy.

CASE AND COMMENT

United States Court of Appeals for the Second District
Fox Television Inc., et al, Petitioners,
v.
Federal Communications Commission, United States of America, Respondent
Docket Nos. 06-1760-ag, 06-2750-ag, 06-5358-ag
Decided July 13, 2010

Facts: Petitioners complained that an FCC crackdown on fleeting obscenities was unfair and violated their First Amendment rights. Fox and other networks had challenged the FCC's findings that some of their stations had violated indecency rules when broadcasting uncensored expletives on awards shows and other live programming.

CASE AND COMMENT *continued...*

Procedural History: The petition for review followed the Supreme Court's ruling in favor of the FCC on procedural issues pursuant to the Administrative Procedure Act. The case came before the Court of Appeals on remand from the Supreme Court for consideration of petitioners' constitutional arguments.

Issue: Whether the FCC's assertion of authority to regulate the programming with their indecency policy is correct.

Rationale: The court said, "... the indecency policy is impermissibly vague." The first problem arises in the FCC's determination as to which words or expressions are patently offensive. For instance, while the FCC concluded that "bull—" in an "NYPD Blue" episode was patently offensive, it concluded that "d—k" and "d—khead" were not.... The Commission argues that it's "patently offensive" test gives broadcasters fair notice of what it will find indecent. However, in each of these cases, the Commission's reasoning consisted of repetition of one or more of the factors without any discussion of how it applied them."

Ruling: The court grant(ed) the networks' petition for review, and vacate(d) the FCC's order and the indecency policy underlying it.

Comment: The FCC has since sought a rehearing of the matter before the United States Court of Appeals. With its indecency policy vacated, the FCC was left in a position of not being able to regulate decency.

DICTIONARY THESAURUS

Term [phonetic pronunciation]	*Note: All dictionary/thesaurus terms appear on flashcards at the back of the book and on the CD-ROM.*
abuse of discretion [a.*byooss* ov dis.*kresh*.en]	A judicial or administrative decision so grounded in whim or caprice, or against logic, that it amounts to a denial of justice.
adjudicatory [a.*joo*.di.ka.tore.ee]	Refers to the decision-making or quasi-judicial functions of an administrative agency, as opposed to the judicial functions of a court. Thus, for EXAMPLE, an adjudicatory hearing is a hearing before an administrative agency as opposed to a hearing or trial before a court.
administrative act [ad.*min*.is.tray.tiv act]	A routine act by a public official, required by law, as opposed to an act based upon a decision involving a degree of choice; a ministerial act. EXAMPLE: the maintaining of court records by the clerk of the court.
administrative agency [ad.*min*.is.tray.tiv *ay*.jen.see]	A board, commission, bureau, office, or department of the executive branch of government that implements the law, which originates with the legislative branch. EXAMPLES: the FBI (Federal Bureau of Investigation); a county public assistance office.
administrative discretion [ad.*min*.is.tray.tiv dis.*kresh*.en]	The power to choose between courses of conduct in the administration of a public office or in carrying out a public duty.

administrative hearing
[ad.*min*.is.tray.tiv *heer*.ing]

A hearing before an administrative agency, as distinguished from a hearing before a court.

administrative law
[ad.*min*.is.tray.tiv law]

1. The body of law that controls the way in which administrative agencies operate. 2. Regulations and decisions issued by administrative agencies.

administrative law judge
[ad.*min*.is.tray.tiv law juj]

A person, generally a civil servant, who conducts hearings held by an administrative agency. An administrative law judge is variously referred to as an ALJ, a hearing examiner, or a hearing officer.

administrative notice
[ad.*min*.is.tray.tiv *no*.tiss]

See official notice.

Administrative Procedure Act (APA)
[ad.*min*.is.tray.tiv pro.*see*.jer akt]

A statute enacted by Congress that regulates the way in which federal administrative agencies conduct their affairs and establishes the procedure for judicial review of the actions of federal agencies. The Act is referred to as the APA.

administrative proceeding
[ad.*min*.is.tray.tiv pro.*see*.ding]

A proceeding before an administrative agency, as distinguished from a proceeding before a court.

administrative remedy
[ad.*min*.is.tray.tiv *rem*.e.dee]

A remedy that the law permits an administrative agency to grant.

advisory opinion
[ad.*vize*.e.ree o.*pin*.yen]

A judicial interpretation of a legal question requested by the legislative or executive branch of government, or by a private individual or corporation. These opinions have no binding effect.

affirm
[a.*ferm*]

In the case of an appellate court, to uphold the decision or judgment of the lower court after the appeal.

arbitrary and capricious
[*ar*.bi.trare.ee and ke.*prish*.es]

A reference to the concept in administrative law that permits a court to substitute its judgment for that of an administrative agency if the agency's decision unreasonably ignores the law or the facts of a case.

color
[*kull*.er]

An apparent legal right; a seeming legal right; the mere semblance of a legal right. Although they may also refer to activity by private persons, terms such as color of authority, color of law, and color of right generally refer to actions taken by a representative of government, which is beyond her authority, but appears legal because of her official status.

color of right
[*kull*.er ov rite]

A right based upon color of authority, color of law, or color of office.

COPPA
[*kop*.uh]

The Children's Online Privacy Protection Act (COPPA) has been enforced by the Federal Trade Commission (FTC) since 2000 and prohibits website operators from knowingly collecting personally identifiable information (complete name, Social Security number, e-mail address, or telephone number) from children under the age of 13 without parental consent.

| DICTIONARY | THESAURUS *continued...* |

de novo review
[de *no*.vo re.*vyoo*]

(*Latin*) Standard of review under which the reviewing body may find the facts and review all issues without deference to the lower body's findings and conclusions.

declaratory judgment
[de.*klar*.e.toh.ree *juj*.ment]

A judgment that specifies the rights of the parties but orders nothing. Nonetheless, it is a binding judgment and the appropriate remedy for the determination of an actionable dispute when the plaintiff is in doubt as to his legal rights.

declaratory provision
[de.*klar*.e.toh.ree pro.*vizh*.en]

Part of a statute or ordinance that states the need that the legislation was enacted to fulfill (i.e., the statute's purpose). Declaratory provisions often begin with the word "whereas."

declaratory relief
[de.*klar*.e.toh.ree re.*leef*]

See declaratory judgment.

declaratory statute
[de.*klar*.e.toh.ree *stat*.shoot]

A statute enacted to clarify and resolve the law when the correct interpretation has been in doubt.

delegation of powers
[del.e.*gay*.shen ov *pow*.erz]

1. Provisions of the Constitution by which executive powers are delegated to the executive branch of the government, legislative powers to the legislative branch, and judicial powers to the judicial branch. 2. Delegation of constitutional power by one branch of government to another. Such delegation is permissible only if it is consistent with the principle of separation of powers set forth in the Constitution. 3. The transfer of power from the president to an administrative agency.

department
[de.*part*.ment]

An administrative unit within an organization.

- *n.* branch, section, office, agency, bureau, unit, division

department of government
[de.*part*.ment ov *guv*.ern.ment]

1. One of the three divisions into which the Constitution separates the government of the United States. Used in this sense, the term is synonymous with branch of government. 2. A similar division in state government. 3. An administrative unit within a branch of government. EXAMPLES: the Department of Justice (DOJ); the Department of Commerce (DOC).

due process hearing
[dew *pross*.ess *heer*.ing]

An administrative hearing held to comply with the due process clause. EXAMPLE: a parole revocation hearing.

due process of law
[dew *pross*.ess ov law]

Law administered through courts, equally applicable to all, that does not violate principles of fairness. Whether a person has received due process of law can only be determined on a case-by-case basis. In all criminal cases, however, it involves, at the very least, the right to be heard by a fair and impartial tribunal, the defendant's right to be represented by counsel, the right to cross-examine witnesses against him, the right to offer testimony on his own behalf, and the right to have advance notice of trial and of the charge sufficient in detail and in point of time to permit adequate preparation for trial. Due process requirements for criminal prosecutions are considerably more rigorous than those for civil cases. "Due process of law" is guaranteed by both the Fifth Amendment and the Fourteenth Amendment.

Enabling Act
[en.*ay*.bling akt]

A statute that gives the government the power to enforce other legislation, or that carries out a provision of a constitution.

Equal Employment Opportunity Commission (EEOC)
[*ee*.kwel em.*ploy*.ment op.er.*tew*.ni.tee kuh.*mish*.en]

A federal agency whose purpose is to prevent and remedy discrimination based on race, color, religion, national origin, age, or sex with respect to most aspects of employment, including hiring, firing, promotion, and wages. The commission, which is known as the EEOC, enforces many federal Civil Rights Acts and anti-discrimination statutes.

executive
[eg.*zek*.yoo.tiv]

adj. Pertaining to the administration or enforcement of the law.
n. A person who enforces the law, as distinguished from a person who makes the law or a person who interprets the law.

- *n.* chief, supervisor, boss, director, chairperson, president
- *adj.* managerial, presidential, official, administrative

executive agency
[eg.*zek*.yoo.tiv *ay*.jen.see]

See administrative agency.

executive branch
[eg.*zek*.yoo.tiv branch]

1. With the legislative branch and the judicial branch, one of the three divisions into which the Constitution separates the government of the United States. These branches of government are also referred to as departments of government. The executive branch is primarily responsible for enforcing the laws. 2. A similar division exists in state government.

exhaustion of remedy
[eg.*zaws*.chen of *rem*.e.dee]

1. The doctrine that when the law provides an administrative remedy, a party seeking relief must fully exercise that remedy before the courts will intervene. 2. The doctrine, applicable in many types of cases, that the federal courts will not respond to a party seeking relief until she has exhausted her remedies in state court.

fact-finding body
[*fakt*-fine.ding *bod*.ee]

A board or body, usually of an administrative agency, that is empowered to make findings of fact.

federal agency
[*fed*.er.el *ay*.jen.see]

Any administrative agency, board, bureau, commission, corporation, or institution of the federal government, usually in the executive branch of government.

Federal Register
[*fed*.er.el *rej*.is.ter]

An official publication, printed daily, containing regulations and proposed regulations issued by administrative agencies, as well as other rulemaking and other official business of the executive branch of government. All regulations are ultimately published in the Code of Federal Regulations (CFR).

Freedom of Information Act (FOIA)
[*free*.dum of in.fer.*may*.shen akt]

A federal statute that requires federal agencies to make available to the public, upon request, material contained in their files, as well as information on how the agencies function. The Act contains various significant exemptions from disclosure, including information compiled for law enforcement purposes, and to protect the privacy of individuals. *See* privacy.

hearing
[*heer*.ing]

A proceeding in which evidence is introduced and witnesses are examined so that findings of fact can be made and a determination rendered. Although, in a general sense, all trials can be said to be hearings, not all hearings are trials. The difference is in the degree of formality each requires, with the rules of procedure being more relaxed in hearings. A hearing may be conducted by a court, an administrative agency, an arbitrator, or a committee of the legislature, as well as by many other public bodies.

- *n.* trial, inquiry, litigation, adjudication, review, legal proceedings

hearing examiner
[*heer*.ing eg.*zam*.in.er]

The title of the person who functions as a judge with respect to an administrative hearing. In some states, and in the federal system, the title administrative law judge is used instead. *See also* hearing officer.

hearing officer
[*heer*.ing *off*.i.ser]

Same as hearing examiner, although, in some circumstances, a hearing officer, unlike a hearing examiner, does not have the power to adjudicate, her authority being limited to making recommendations to the appropriate administrative agency. *See also* administrative law judge.

in camera
[in *kam*.e.ra]

(*Latin*) In chambers; in private. A term, referring to a hearing or any other judicial business conducted in the judge's office or in a courtroom that has been cleared of spectators and certain excepted parties.

inspection laws
[in.*spek*.shen lawz]

Federal, state, and local laws designed to promote health and safety by protecting the public from hazards such as the unsanitary processing of food, the improper packaging of articles for sale, or unsafe working conditions. EXAMPLES: food inspection laws administered by the FDA (Food and Drug Administration).

judicial review
[joo.*dish*.el re.*vyoo*]

1. Review by a court of a decision or ruling of an administrative agency. 2. Review by an appellate court of a determination by a lower court.

license
[*ly*.sense]

1. A special privilege, not a right common to everyone. 2. Permission (EXAMPLES: a marriage license; a fishing license) to do something that, if it were not regulated, would be a right. 3. A privilege conferred on a person by the government to do something she otherwise would not have the right to do. EXAMPLES: the privilege of incorporation; the privilege of operating as a public utility or a common carrier. 4. A requirement imposed as a means of regulating a business. EXAMPLE: a liquor license. 5. Permission to practice a profession, engage in an occupation, or conduct a business. EXAMPLES: a license to practice law; a business license; a real estate license. 6. A certificate evidencing an official grant of permission or authorization. EXAMPLES: a driver's license; a hunting license.

- *n.* privilege, authorization, sanction, permission, entitlement
- *v.* authorize, legitimize, sanction, approve, validate

licensing
[*ly*.sen.sing]

The act or process of granting or issuing a license.

licensor
[*ly*.sen.*sore*]

The grantor of a license. EXAMPLES: a state (Department of Motor Vehicles); a city (health department); a federal agency (FAA).

official notice
[o.*fish*.el *no*.tiss]

The equivalent of judicial notice by an administrative agency; also referred to as administrative notice.

official records
[o.*fish*.el *rek*.erdz]

Records made by an official of the government in the course of performing her official duties. (EXAMPLE: correspondence; memoranda; data; minutes.) Official records are admissible in the federal courts and in federal administrative proceedings, as well as in most state courts, as an exception to the hearsay rule, to prove the transactions they memorialize.

privacy
[*pry*.ve.see]

The right of privacy is the right to be left alone. It means that personal information of the kind in the possession of, for EXAMPLE, the government, insurance companies, and credit bureaus may not be made public. The right to privacy, which is implied by the Constitution, is supported, and to some extent enforced, by federal and state privacy acts.

- *n.* confidentiality, noninfringement

promulgate
[*prom*.ul.gate]

1. To publish, announce, or proclaim official notice of a public act. 2. To issue a regulation.

quasi-judicial
[*kwa*.zi-joo.*dish*.el]

A term applied to the adjudicatory functions of an administrative agency (i.e., taking evidence and making findings of fact and findings of law).

quasi-legislative
[*kwa*.zi-*lej*.is.lay.tiv]

A term applied to the legislative functions of an administrative agency, for EXAMPLE, rulemaking.

rate fixing
[rate *fik*.sing]

See rate making.

rate making
[rate *may*.king]

The process engaged in by a public service commission in establishing a rate to be charged to the public for a public service.

regulation
[reg.yoo.*lay*.shun]

1. The act of regulating. 2. A rule having the force of law, promulgated by an administrative agency; the act of rule making. *See* rule making. 3. A rule of conduct established by a person or body in authority for the governance of those over whom they have authority.

regulatory
[*reg*.yoo.le.tore.ee]

Pertaining to that which regulates; pertaining to the act of regulation. *See also* regulation.

regulatory agency
[*reg*.yoo.le.tore.ee *ay*.jen.see]

An administrative agency empowered to promulgate and enforce regulations. *See also* regulation.

reporters
[re.*port*.erz]

1. Court reports, as well as official, published reports of cases decided by administrative agencies. 2. Court reporters.

DICTIONARY / THESAURUS *continued...*

ripeness doctrine [*ripe*.ness *dok*.trin]	The doctrine that an administrative agency or a trial court will not hear or determine a case, and an appellate court will not entertain an appeal, unless an actual case or controversy exists.
rulemaking [*rool*.may.king]	The promulgation by an administrative agency of a rule having the force of law (i.e., a regulation).
separation of powers [sep.ar.*ay*.shun ov *pow*.erz]	A fundamental principle of the Constitution that gives exclusive power to the legislative branch to make the law, to the executive branch to administer it, and to the judicial branch to enforce it. The authors of the Constitution believed that the separation of powers would make abuse of power less likely.
statute [stat.*shoot*]	A law enacted by a legislature; an act.
statutory benefits [stat.*shoo*.tore.ee *ben*.e.fits]	Benefits that are provided because the law requires it. EXAMPLES: workers' compensation coverage, unemployment insurance, veterans' benefits, and Social Security.
subpoena [sub.*pee*.nah]	*n.* A command in the form of written process requiring a witness to come to court to testify; short for subpoena ad testificandum. *v.* To issue or serve a subpoena.
substantial evidence [sub.*stan*.shel *ev*.i.dense]	Evidence that a reasonable person would accept as adequate to support the conclusion or conclusions drawn from it; evidence beyond a scintilla. *See also* substantial evidence rule.
substantial evidence rule [sub.*stan*.shel *ev*.i.dense rool]	The rule that a court will uphold a decision or ruling of an administrative agency if it is supported by substantial evidence. *See also* substantial evidence.
substantive due process [sub.*stan*.tiv doo *pross*.ess]	A right grounded in the Fifth and Fourteenth Amendments. The government may not act arbitrarily or capriciously in making, interpreting, or enforcing the law. A person is entitled to both substantive due process and procedural due process.
summary judgment [*sum*.e.ree *juj*.ment]	A method of disposing of an action without further proceedings. A party against whom a claim is made may move for summary judgment in her favor, if there is no genuine issue of any material fact.
sunshine law [*sun*.shine law]	State and federal statutes requiring that meetings and records of administrative agencies be open to the public.

Missing Words

Fill in the blanks.

1. The promulgation by an administrative agency of a rule having the force of law is _____.

2. State and federal statutes requiring that meetings of administrative agencies be open to the public are called _____.

3. The _____ is a federal statute that requires federal agencies to make available to the public, upon request, material contained in their files.

4. When the law provides an administrative remedy, a party seeking relief must fully exercise these _____ before the courts will intervene.

5. A rule having the force of law, promulgated by an administrative agency, is a(n) _____.

6. An administrative decision that is grounded in whim or caprice is a(n) _____.

7. When a representative of government has an apparent legal right, or semblance of, he acts under _____.

8. A(n) _____ is the same as a hearing examiner, but she has the power limited to making recommendations.

9. _____ is the power to choose between courses of conduct in the administration of a public office or in carrying out a public duty.

10. _____ is the body of law that controls the way in which administrative agencies operate.

11. The _____ is a federal agency whose purpose is to prevent and remedy discrimination in employment.

12. A(n) _____ inspection of documents occurs in a courtroom that has been cleared of all spectators.

13. _____ is the act or process of granting a license.

14. Evidence that is beyond what a reasonable person would accept as adequate to support the conclusion drawn from it is _____.

15. A law enacted by a legislature is a(n) _____.

STUDY AID: Use flashcards for this unit before completing the exercises.

Matching

Match the letter of the definition to the abbreviation below.

____ **16.** APA   **A.** Department of Commerce

____ **17.** EEOC   **B.** Administrative Procedure Act

____ **18.** FOIA   **C.** Equal Employment Opportunity Commission

____ **19.** FDA   **D.** Freedom of Information Act

____ **20.** ALJ   **E.** Food and Drug Administration

____ **21.** FCC   **F.** Administrative Law Judge

____ **22.** NLRB   **G.** Federal Communications Commission

____ **23.** OSHA   **H.** National Labor Relations Board

____ **24.** FBI   **I.** Occupational Safety and Health Administration

____ **25.** CFR   **J.** Federal Bureau of Investigation

____ **26.** DOJ   **K.** Code of Federal Regulations

____ **27.** DOC   **L.** Department of Justice

____ **28.** IRS   **M.** Social Security Administration

____ **29.** SSA   **N.** Internal Revenue Service

____ **30.** SEC   **O.** Securities and Exchange Commission

Multiple Choice

Select the best choice.

____ **31.** An adjudicatory hearing is:
   a. the commencement of legal action.
   b. the settlement of legal action.
   c. a hearing before an administrative agency as opposed to a court.
   d. when a new trial is requested.

____ **32.** The process engaged in by a public service commission in establishing a rate to be charged to the public for a public service is known as:
   a. rate of exchange.
   b. rate of interest.
   c. rate of return.
   d. rate making.

_____ **33.** Federal, state, and local laws designed to promote health and safety by protecting the public from hazards such as unsafe working conditions are called:
   a. sunshine laws.
   b. judicial review.
   c. de novo review.
   d. inspection laws.

_____ **34.** The body of law that controls the way in which administrative agencies operate is:
   a. common law.
   b. administrative law.
   c. the Federal Claims Act.
   d. none of the above.

_____ **35.** A rule made by an administrative agency is also known as a(n):
   a. decision.
   b. order.
   c. opinion.
   d. regulation.

_____ **36.** An official publication printed daily containing regulations and proposed regulations issued by administrative agencies is:
   a. Federal Report.
   b. Federal Register.
   c. Administrative News.
   d. Agency News.

_____ **37.** This branch of government is responsible for enforcing the laws:
   a. judicial
   b. executive
   c. legislative
   d. bipartisan

_____ **38.** In camera hearings are hearings held:
   a. in public with press coverage.
   b. at the employers' place of business.
   c. in a courtroom cleared of spectators.
   d. with photographers.

_____ **39.** A court will uphold a decision or ruling of an administrative agency if it is supported by:
   a. substantial evidence.
   b. proof beyond a reasonable doubt.
   c. a preponderance of evidence.
   d. a scintilla of evidence.

_____ **40.** When de novo review is performed by an agency, it:
   a. may review facts and redecide all issues.
   b. must uphold facts found by the administrative law judge.
   c. is the final step in the administrative process.
   d. none of the above.

_____ **41.** The Exhaustion of Remedies Doctrine provides that:
   a. all parties seeking administrative relief are entitled to seek at least two different kinds of remedies.
   b. a claimant has the option of taking his problem to the agency or the courts.
   c. a party must pursue all avenues of agency action before resorting to the court system.
   d. all of the above.

_____ **42.** A judicial interpretation of a legal question is:
   a. an administrative act.
   b. color of right.
   c. rate making.
   d. advisory opinion.

True/False

Mark the following T or F.

_____ **43.** An administrative hearing is a hearing before an administrative agency.

_____ **44.** The body of law that controls the way in which administrative agencies operate is called admiralty law.

_____ **45.** An administrative remedy is a remedy that the law permits an administrative agency to grant.

_____ **46.** When a court reviews a decision or ruling of an administrative agency, this is called inspection laws.

_____ **47.** Courts will uphold a decision of an administrative agency if it is supported by substantial evidence.

_____ **48.** A person who conducts hearings held by an administrative agency is called a justice.

_____ **49.** A remedy that the law permits an administrative agency to grant is called judicial review.

_____ **50.** A court can never substitute its judgment for that of an administrative agency, even if the agency's decision is arbitrary and capricious.

_____ **51.** An administrative agency is a board, commission, bureau, office, or department of the executive branch of government that implements the law, which originates with the legislative branch.

_____ **52.** Administrative notice or official notice is the equivalent of judicial notice.

_____ **53.** A judgment that specifies the rights of the parties but orders nothing is called a declaratory judgment.

_____ **54.** An enabling act is a statute that gives the government the power to enforce other legislation.

_____ **55.** An administrative judge can issue a regulation.

Synonyms

Select the correct synonym in parentheses for each numbered item.

56. EXECUTIVE AGENCY
(administrative agency, agency by estoppel, implied agency)

57. SUBPOENA
(summons, complaint, answer)

58. FOIA
(Freedom of Interstate Agencies, Freedom of Information Act, Full Office Information Advice)

59. RATE MAKING
(antitrust, rate of exchange, rate fixing)

60. ADMINISTRATIVE LAW JUDGE
(hearing examiner, justice of the peace, arbitrator)

61. APA
(Administrative Precedent Act, Administrative Procedure Act, Administrative Policy Act)

62. ADMINISTRATIVE HEARING
(administrative proceeding, court hearing, deposition)

63. STATUTE
(constitution, act, fine)

64. SUNSHINE LAW
(closed meetings, monitored meetings, open meetings)

65. ARBITRARY AND CAPRICIOUS
(abuse of discretion, rational basis, ripeness doctrine)

66. RIPENESS DOCTRINE
(hypothetical case, statutory case, actual case)

67. COLOR OF RIGHT
(color of authority, color of interest, color of remedy)

68. ENABLING ACT
(carries out a provision of a constitution, enables the right to privacy, acts on a promulgation by a public officer)

69. PROMULGATE
(to give official notice, to summon, to abuse one's office)

Self-Test

Place the number of the correct term in the appropriate space.

70. judicial review

71. due process

72. official notice

73. administrative law hearings

74. de novo

75. exhaustion of administrative remedies

76. agencies

77. separation of powers

78. Administrative Procedure Act

79. administrative

80. substantial evidence

81. administrative law judge

82. substantive due process

83. arbitrary and capricious

84. affirm

As modern life gets more and more complex, the court system, Congress, and the executive branch of government can no longer handle all of the problems that arise. Accordingly, _____ are set up to provide specific types of services to the public. Informally, agencies are known as the fourth branch of government. The type of law that sets up and regulates the manner in which agencies operate is _____ law. Unlike the other branches of government, agencies do not have _____, and each agency performs acts of a legislative, judicial, and executive nature. The _____ sets up procedures for judicial review of federal agencies. Although agencies act much like courts in some instances, it should be remembered that they are not courts. It is important that citizens' rights be protected nonetheless. A person's right to _____ and a fair hearing, commonly referred to as _____, should be protected. It is also important that laws bear some relationship to their objective; this is known as _____. A(n) _____ presides over _____ and issues a decision. If a party is not happy with the decision, she may appeal to the agency. The agency may perform a(n)_____ review and refind the facts or redecide the issues without regard to the administrative law judge's findings. When a party is unhappy with an agency's actions, he can go directly to the court system for _____. Before this can happen, a(n) _____ is required. An agency's decision should not be _____, it should be supported by _____ to be upheld. If so, the appellate court will most likely _____ the decision of the agency.

Word Scramble

Unscramble the following words and write the correct word(s) that match(es) the definition for each word or phrase.

85. minadistrative ycnega – a board, commission, bureau, office, or department of the executive branch of government _____

    _____

86. censliing – the act or process of granting or issuing a license _____

    _____

87. makruleing – when an administrative agency enacts a rule that has the force of law _____

    _____

88. raehing – a proceeding where evidence is introduced and witnesses are examined so that a finding of fact can be made and a determination rendered _____

    _____

89. ficialfo tonice – the equivalent of judicial notice by an administrative agency _____

    _____

90. tioninspec swal – laws designed to promote health and safety and protect the public from harm

    _____

    _____

91. traryarbi and riccapious – a court can substitute its judgment for that of an administrative agency, if the agency unreasonably ignores the laws or the facts of a case _____

    _____

92. ed noov weiver – a standard of review where the reviewing body may find the facts and review all the issues without regard to the lower body's actions _____

    _____

93. nessripe enirtcod – an actual case or controversy must exist before before a case can be be heard before a court or agency _____

    _____

94. judadicatory – the decision-making or quasi-judicial functions of an administrative agency _____

    _____

95. paredtment – an administrative unit _____

    _____

96. roloc of trigh – a right based upon color of authority

    _____

    _____

97. promgateul – to announce official notice or to issue a regulation _____

    _____

98. lingenab act – a statute that gives the power to enforce other legislation _____

    _____

99. domfree of formination tca – federal agencies must make information available to the public under this federal law _____

    _____

100. eabus of credistion – a denial of justice because of whim or caprice _____

    _____

101. nshinesu law – meetings and records of administrative agencies must be open to the public _____

    _____

The Last Word

The newest federal agency is the Consumer Financial Protection Bureau. Created as the centerpiece of sweeping financial reform legislation, it intends to protect consumers from the abusive practices of banks, credit card issuers, and other lending institutions. The bureau's broad powers assigned by the Treasury Department, allows it to write consumer protection rules as well as oversee the financial industry for signs of risk. The bureau's regulation of mortgages and other lending will allow banks and credit card companies to ascertain how much credit they may safely extend to the markets. Will this bureau really make a difference, or be an example of overreaching by the executive branch?

 Access an interactive eBook, chapter-specific interactive learning tools, and more in your Paralegal CourseMate, accessed through www.CengageBrain.com

3

The Law of Torts

- Learn about the law of torts and personal injury.

- Master the similarities and differences in definitions of key terms.

- Master the pronunciations and spellings of legal terms.

- Recognize the synonyms used for legal terminology.

- Practice usage of terms, definitions, and synonyms.

- Complete unit exercises in the forms of missing words, matching, multiple choice, true/false, synonyms, self-test, and word scramble.

- Work with a legal dictionary/thesaurus.

6

Torts and Personal Injury

INTRODUCTION

A tort involves a breach of duty and results in an injury to the person or property of another. A tort is a violation of a duty established by law. Some torts are intentional or deliberate acts, while others are caused by negligence, and intent is not a factor.

Often, torts result from a person's failure to exercise reasonable care and avoid injuring others or their property. This is called negligence. A driver might not intend any harm to anyone, but while drinking soda and driving his friend's car, he may become so distracted that he failed to notice pedestrians crossing the road. If his car strikes and injures them, he hasn't committed a deliberate tort, but he may be found negligent for failing to see that which a reasonably prudent driver would have seen and avoided.

Sometimes liability is based on the relationship people have to one another and the duty they owe based on their relationship. To place responsibility in the previous scenario, the operator's relationship as it relates to the owner of the car must be addressed.

The victim of a tort may suffer personal injury. A tort is defined as injury to the body of a person. A person might have suffered a broken bone, swelling and stiffness, or emotional harm such as a nervous breakdown. If personal injury is found to result from the torts of another, the injured party might be entitled to sue for damages by law.

Another class of torts is caused by dangerous instrumentalities such as explosives and fumigation equipment. These are devices that society needs, but they are extremely dangerous. Even when every possible precaution is taken in their use, injuries to others might occur. If these dangerous instrumentalities cause injury, the law may impose liability even if there was no negligence. A dangerous instrumentality is the basis for absolute or strict liability. In the following case, strict liability is addressed.

CASE AND COMMENT

Pennsylvania Superior Court
Lance, Appellant
v.
Wyeth, Appellee
No. 2905 EDA 2008, *slip op.* (Pa. Super Aug. 2, 2010)

Facts: Appellant, a user of the now outlawed weight loss drug fen-phen made by defendant Wyeth, labeled her claim as "negligent and unreasonable marketing" of a product. Her proposed cause of action duplicates a design defect claim, seeking to impose strict liability on the defendant because its drug was unreasonably dangerous. It is akin to a failure to inspect and/or test claim as a separate cause of action.

CASE AND COMMENT *continued...*

Procedural History: Pennsylvania law has not recognized an independent tort for negligent failure to test. In fact, the claim for "negligent failure to test" is not a viable cause of action recognized by Pennsylvania courts.

Issue: Whether the restrictions on strict liability precluded any claim for strict liability design defect involving prescription drugs where there is a failure to test.

Rationale: The Court said, "We begin our analysis by observing that the plaintiff's argument rests on a misperception of the applicable law." There is no common law duty to recall a drug or any product. "Public policy considerations weigh heavily against imposing a duty to recall on a manufacturer. A design defect claim for strict liability is not cognizable under Pennsylvania law when it is asserted against a manufacturer of prescription drugs. For purposes of strict liability a drug cannot be deemed unreasonably dangerous, even it is defectively designed, so long as the drug is manufactured properly and contains adequate warnings," the court said. But the court recognizes a negligent design claim for a prescription drug based on the Restatement of Torts (1) "contains no exemption or special protection for prescription drugs" and that strict liability (2) "is not exclusive and does not preclude liability based upon the alternative ground of negligence."

Ruling: Affirmed, that the restrictions on strict liability precluded any claim for strict liability design defects involving prescription drugs.

Comment: This appellate decision joins a trend, rejecting "failure to test" as a separate cause of action like some other "non-warning" causes of action.

DICTIONARY   THESAURUS

Term [phonetic pronunciation]	*Note: All dictionary/thesaurus terms appear on flashcards at the back of the book and on the student website.*
absolute liability [ab.so.*loot* ly.e.*bil*.i.tee]	Liability for an injury whether or not there is fault or negligence. EXAMPLE: When fire works or dangerous explosives are used and someone is injured, liability is automatically imposed against the user of the dangerous explosives. *See also* strict liability.
act [akt]	*n.* That which is done voluntarily; putting one's will into action. *v.* To put a conscious choice into effect; to do. <ul><li>*n.* performance</li><li>*v.* perform, do, behave, enact, execute, transact</li></ul>
actionable [*ak*.shen.abl]	Conduct is actionable if it furnishes a ground for legal action. EXAMPLES of actionable conduct include defamation, negligence, and trespass.
actual damages [*ak*.chew.al *dam*.e.jez]	Monetary compensation for a loss or injury that a plaintiff has suffered rather than a sum of money awarded by way of punishing a defendant or to deter others. *Compare* punitive damages. *See also* damage.

ad damnum clause
[ad *dahm*.num clawz]

The clause in a complaint that sets forth the plaintiff's demand for damages and the amount of the claim. This is generally substantially more than the plaintiff expects to actually recover.

assault
[a.*salt*]

An act of force or threat of force intended to inflict harm upon a person or to put the person in fear that such harm is imminent; an attempt to commit a battery. The perpetrator must have, or appear to have, the present ability to carry out the act. Accordingly, a child's threat of injury to an adult is rarely considered an assault.

assault and battery
[a.*salt* and *bat*.er.ee]

An achieved assault; an assault carried out by hitting or by other physical contact. *See also* battery.

assumption of risk
[a.*sump*.shen ov risk]

The legal principle that a person who knows and deliberately exposes herself to a danger assumes responsibility for the risk, rather than the person who actually created the danger. Assumption of risk is often referred to as voluntary assumption of risk, and applies to risky sports such as boxing and race car driving.

attractive nuisance
[a.*trak*.tiv *noo*.sense]

An unusual mechanism, apparatus, or condition that is dangerous to young children but is so interesting and alluring as to attract them to the premises on which it is kept. EXAMPLES: an abandoned mine shaft; an abandoned house; a junked car. *See also* nuisance.

attractive nuisance doctrine
[a.*trak*.tiv *noo*.sense *dok*.trin]

The principle in the law of negligence that a person who maintains an attractive nuisance on his property must exercise reasonable care to protect young children against its dangers, or be held responsible for any injury that occurs, even though the injured child trespassed upon his property or was otherwise at fault.

battery
[*bat*.ter.ee]

The unconsented-to touching or striking of one person by another, or by an object put in motion by him, with the intention of doing harm or giving offense. Battery is both a crime and a tort. *Compare* assault. *See also* assault and battery.

breach of duty
[breech ov *dew*.tee]

The failure to do that which a person is bound by law to do, or the doing of it in an unlawful manner. *See also* duty.

breach of warranty
[breech ov *war*.en.tee]

The violation of an express warranty or implied warranty. EXAMPLE: If a product in its promotional material promises to remove rust and it doesn't, there is a breach of warranty.

business invitee
[*biz*.ness in.vy.*tee*]

A person who comes upon premises at the invitation of the occupant, and who has business to contract. If a business invitee is injured as a result of some hazard on the premises, she is more likely to be able to hold the owner or occupant responsible at law than would a social guest or trespasser.

care
[kayr]

1. Custody; safekeeping. 2. Attention; awareness; caution. Care is a word that must always be interpreted in the context in which it appears. It is extremely important as a standard for determining negligence. The context determines the level of care that the law requires under the circumstances. A person should use care not to harm others or their property.

- *n.* custody, safekeeping, interest, regard, attention, awareness, caution
- *v.* beware, be cautious, guard, watch, support, supervise

DICTIONARY   THESAURUS *continued...*

causation
[kaw.*zay*.shen]

The act of causing; the producing of a result. Causation is one of the elements needed to hold a defendant liable in a torts case. *See also* proximate cause.

- *n.* production, origination, root

comparative negligence
[kem.*par*.i.tiv *neg*.li.jense]

The doctrine adopted by most states that requires a comparison of the negligence of the defendant with the negligence of the plaintiff: the greater the negligence of the defendant, the lesser the level of care required of the plaintiff to permit her to recover. The plaintiff's negligence does not defeat her cause of action, but it reduces the damages she is entitled to recover. *Compare* contributory negligence.

compensatory damages
[kem.*pen*.se.to.ree *dam*.ejez]

Damages recoverable in a lawsuit for actual loss or injury suffered by the plaintiff as a result of the defendant's conduct. Also called actual damages, they may include expenses, loss of time, reduced earning capacity, bodily injury, and mental anguish.

consent
[ken.*sent*]

Agreement; approval; acquiescence, being of one mind. Consent necessarily involves two or more persons because, without at least two persons, there cannot be a unity of opinion or the possibility of thinking alike.

- *v.* agree, accept, allow, approve, concede, yield, comply, sanction, ratify
- *n.* agreement, approval, acquiescence, concession, allowance, permission

contribution
[kon.tri.*byoo*.shen]

1. A payment of his share of a debt or judgment by a person who is jointly liable.
2. The right of a person who has satisfied a shared indebtedness to have those with whom she shared it contribute in defraying its cost.

- *n.* indemnification, restitution, reparation, repayment, satisfaction

contributory negligence
[kon.tri.*byoo*.tor.ee *neg*.li.jense]

A failure by the plaintiff to exercise reasonable care that, in part at least, is the cause of an injury. Contributory negligence defeats a plaintiff's cause of action for negligence in states that have not adopted the doctrine of comparative negligence. *Compare* comparative negligence.

conversion
[ken.*ver*.zhen]

Control over another person's personal property that is wrongfully exercised; control applied in a manner that violates that person's title to or rights in the property. Conversion is both a tort and a crime. EXAMPLE: If a man takes a jacket that belongs to someone else, he has converted it when he takes it, hems it, and wears it.

- *n.* theft, larceny, misappropriation, deprivation, embezzlement

culpable negligence
[kulp.abl *neg*.li.jense]

Both in the law of negligence and as used in criminal negligence and manslaughter statutes, a conscious and wanton disregard of the probability that death or injury will result from the willful creation of an unreasonable risk. EXAMPLE: when a person carries a loaded gun on a crowded bus, where she is likely to be bumped, and the gun goes off, injuring bus-riders.

damage
[*dam*.ej]

The loss, hurt, or harm to person or property that results from injury that, in turn, is the negligent or deliberate invasion of a legal right. Although the words damage, damages, and injury are often treated as synonyms, there are important differences in their meanings. Injury is the illegal invasion of a legal right (i.e., a wrong); damage is the loss, hurt, or harm that results from the injury; and damages are the compensation awarded for that which has been suffered. Additional damages may be awarded if the damage resulted from an injury that was inflicted recklessly or with malice. *See also* punitive and special damages.

- *n.* loss, hurt, harm, destruction, impairment
- *ant.* benefit

dangerous instrumentality
[*dane*.jer.*ess*
in.stroo.men.*tal*.i.tee]

A thing so dangerous (EXAMPLES: explosives; hazardous waste; a gun) that if it causes injury, the law may impose liability even though there was no negligence. A dangerous instrumentality is a basis for absolute or strict liability.

defamation
[def.e.*may*.shen]

Libel or slander; the written or oral publication, falsely and intentionally, of anything that is injurious to the good name or reputation of another person. For EXAMPLE: If a person tells a friend that his accountant is a liar and a thief, and knows this is not a true statement, this is an example of slander.

- *n.* libel, slander, defamatory statement, deprecation, belittlement
- *ant.* praise

degree of care
[de.gree ov kayr]

A relative standard by which conduct is tested to determine whether it constitutes negligence. EXAMPLES: due care; extraordinary care; ordinary care; reasonable care.

duty
[*dew*.tee]

1. A legal obligation, whether imposed by the common law, statute, court order, or contract. (USAGE: "When a right is invaded, a duty is violated.") A tort is committed only when there has been a breach of duty resulting in injury. 2. Any obligation or responsibility.

- *n.* responsibility, requirement, assignment, mandatory act, pledge, obligation

emotional distress
[ee.*moh*.shen.l dis.*tress*]

Mental anguish. Nonphysical harm that may be compensated for by damages in some types of lawsuits. Mental anguish can be as limited as the immediate mental feelings during an injury, or as broad as prolonged grief, shame, humiliation, and despair. The misdeed must be so outrageous that a reasonable person would suffer severe emotional distress. Emotional distress can be either the result of intentional, reckless, or negligent acts.

exculpatory clause
[eks.*kul*.pe.toh.ree clawz]

A clause in a contract or other legal document excusing a party from liability for his wrongful act. EXAMPLE: a provision in a lease relieving a landlord of liability for trespass.

excusable
[eks.*kyoo*.zebl]

That which may be forgiven or overlooked.

- *adj.* pardonable, forgivable, permissible ("excusable negligence")

DICTIONARY   THESAURUS *continued...*

excusable neglect
[eks.*kyoo*.zebl neg.*lekt*]

Dilatory neglect that may be forgiven or overlooked by a court, upon a showing of good reason therefore. For EXAMPLE: A court may authorize the opening of a default judgment after expiration of the time normally allowed. The court may authorize belated action in some circumstances if the failure to act was due to excusable neglect.

excusable negligence
[eks.*kyoo*.zebl neg.li.jenss]

See excusable neglect.

false Imprisonment
[fals im.*priz*.en.ment]

The unlawful restraint by one person of the physical liberty of another. Like false arrest, to which it is closely related, it is both a tort and a crime.

foreseeable
[for.*see*.ebl]

That which may be anticipated or known in advance; that which a person should have known. In the law of negligence, a person is responsible for the consequences of his acts only if they are foreseeable. *See also* proximate cause.

- *adj.* imminent, prospective, forthcoming

Good Samaritan doctrine
[good se.*mehr*.i.ten *dok*.trin]

When a person stops to help an injured person in serious danger, through the negligent acts of another, the rescuer cannot be charged with contributory negligence. In this instance, the rescuer risks her life to save another person. However, the attempt must be reasonable and not reckless. Generally, this protection is provided by state statute. Some jurisdictions refer to this as the rescue doctrine.

gross negligence
[grose *neg*.li.jenss]

Willfully and intentionally acting, or failing to act, with a deliberate indifference to how others may be affected. *See also* negligence.

hedonic damages
[hee.*don*.ik *dam*.e.jez]

Damages awarded by some courts for the loss of enjoyment of life's pleasures. For EXAMPLE: A mother who is injured and can no longer hug her children might seek hedonic damages.

immunity
[im.*yo*.ni.tee]

An exemption granted by law, contrary to the general rule. It is a privilege. Immunity may be granted to an individual or a class of persons. *See* Federal Torts Claim Act.

imputed negligence
[im.*pewt*.ed *neg*.li.jenss]

The negligence of one person that, by reason of her relationship to another person, is chargeable to the other person. EXAMPLE: A parent might be responsible for the acts of his child.

injunction
[in.*junk*.shen]

A court order that commands or prohibits some act or course of conduct. It is preventive in nature and designed to protect a plaintiff from irreparable injury to his property or property rights by prohibiting or commanding the doing of certain acts. EXAMPLE: a court order prohibiting unlawful picketing. An injunction is a form of equitable relief.

injury
[*in*.jer.ee]

The invasion of a legal right; an actionable wrong done to a person, her property, or her reputation. (*Compare* "damage," which is the loss, hurt, or harm resulting from "injury.") An injury is not limited to physical harm done to the body; an injury to the body (that is, a personal injury) may mean death as well as mere physical harm.

- *n.* wrong, damage, loss, detriment, harm, offense
- *ant.* benefit

intent
[in.*tent*]

Purpose; the plan, course, or means a person conceives to achieve a certain result. Intent is an essential element of intentional torts but not for negligence. Intent is not, however, limited to conscious wrongdoing, and may be inferred or presumed. *See also* malice.

- *n.* determination, scheme, plan, resolve, goal, will and premeditation

intentional injury
[in.*tent*.shen.al in.je.ree]

An injury inflicted by positive, willful, and aggressive conduct, or by design, as opposed to an injury caused by negligence or resulting from an accident. *See also* injury.

intentional tort
[in.*tent*.shen.al tort]

A harm or wrong inflicted by positive, willful, and aggressive conduct, or by design, as opposed to damage caused by negligence or resulting from an accident.

intervening cause
[in.ter.*veen*.ing kaws]

A cause that intrudes between the negligence of the defendant and the injury suffered by the plaintiff, breaking the connection between the original wrongful act or omission and the injury, and itself becoming the proximate cause of the injury.

invasion of privacy
[in.*vay*.zhen ov *pry*.ve.see]

A violation of the right of privacy. *See also* privacy; which is the right to be left alone. EXAMPLE: If an individual's personal income tax forms or medical records are published in the newspaper without her consent, this is an example of a violation of the right to privacy.

joint and several liability
[joynt and *sev*.rel ly.e.*bil*.i.tee]

The liability of two or more persons who jointly commit a tort (joint tortfeasors). They are responsible individually as well as together.

joint tortfeasors
[joynt *tort*.fee.zerz]

Two or more persons whose acts, together, contribute to producing a single injury to a third person or to property. Joint tortfeasors are jointly and severally liable. *See also* joint and several liability.

last clear chance doctrine
[last cleer chayns *dok*.trin]

A rule of negligence law by which a negligent defendant is held liable to a plaintiff who has negligently placed himself in peril, if the defendant had a later opportunity than the plaintiff to avoid the occurrence that resulted in injury. In some jurisdictions, the doctrine is referred to as the discovered peril doctrine and in others as the humanitarian doctrine.

liability
[ly.e.*bil*.i.tee]

Although broadly speaking "liability" means legal responsibility, it is a general term whose precise meaning depends upon the context in which it appears. A person's responsibility after she has committed a tort that causes injury. *See also* absolute liability; joint and several liability; product liability; strict liability; vicarious liability.

- *n.* responsibility, debt, obligation, indebtedness

libel
[*lie*.bul]

A false and malicious publication, expressed either in printing, writing, or by signs and pictures, tending to harm a person's reputation and expose him to public hatred, contempt, or ridicule. *Note* that "libel" is not "liable." *Compare* slander. *See also* malice; defamation.

- *n.* defamation, slander

loss of consortium
[loss ov ken.*sore*.shem]

The loss of a spouse's assistance, companionship, and a spouse's ability to have sexual relations. If such loss results from a tort, it gives rise to a cause of action.

DICTIONARY | **THESAURUS** *continued...*

malice [*mal*.iss]	1. State of mind that causes the intentional doing of a wrongful, dangerous, or deadly act without legal excuse or justification in deliberate disregard of the lives or safety of others. The term does not necessarily connote personal ill will. It can mean general malice. *Compare* intent. 2. In the law of defamation, to be actionable malice must be actual malice or express malice, as distinct from implied or constructive malice. 3. In the law of damages, additional damages may be awarded if the damage to the plaintiff resulted from an injury inflicted recklessly or with malice. *See also* punitive damages.
malicious prosecution [mel.*ish*.ess us pross.e.*kyoo*.shen]	Civil suit commenced maliciously and without probable cause. After the termination of such a suit in the defendant's favor, the defendant has the right to bring an action against the original plaintiff for the tort of "malicious prosecution."
malpractice [mal.*prak*.tiss]	The failure of a professional to act with reasonable care; misconduct by a professional in the course of engaging in her profession. For EXAMPLE: Attorneys, physicians, accountants, psychiatrists, and even priests have been charged with malpractice of their duties.
misrepresentation [mis.rep.re.zen.*tay*.shen]	The statement of an untruth; a misstatement of fact designed to lead one to believe that something is other than it is; a false statement of fact designed to deceive. EXAMPLE: A jeweler stating to a customer that an inexpensive silver ring is made of platinum would be a misrepresentation.
necessity [ne.*sess*.i.tee]	1. That which is necessary; that which must be done. 2. That which is compelled by natural forces and cannot be resisted.
negligence [*neg*.li.jense]	The failure to do something that a reasonable person would do in the same circumstances, or the doing of something a reasonable person would not do. Negligence is a wrong generally characterized by carelessness, inattentiveness, and neglectfulness rather than by a positive intent to cause injury. *See also* comparative negligence; contributory negligence; gross negligence. ▪ *n.* thoughtlessness, default, breach of duty, oversight, irresponsibility, carelessness, recklessness, inattentiveness ("the doctor's negligence caused the tumor to go undetected")
negligence in law [*neg*.li.jense in law]	1. A breach of the duty to use care; the failure to observe a duty established by law that proximately causes injury to the plaintiff. *See also* proximate cause. 2. Negligence per se.
negligence per se [*neg*.li.jense per say]	Negligence that is beyond debate because the law, usually a statute or ordinance, has established a duty or standard of care that the defendant has violated, as a result of which he has caused injury to the plaintiff. EXAMPLE: failure to stop at a stop sign, as required by law, which is the proximate cause of injury to another driver or a pedestrian. *See also* absolute liability; negligence in law; strict liability.

negligent
[*neg*.li.jent]

1. Being responsible for an act of negligence. 2. Careless; inattentive; lax. 3. Reckless.

- *adj.* careless, inattentive, reckless, irresponsible

negligent homicide
[*neg*.li.jent *hom*.i.side]

The crime of causing the death of a person by negligent or reckless conduct. EXAMPLE: While driving drunk, the driver strikes and kills a pedestrian.

nominal damages
[*nom*.i.nel *dam*.e.jez]

Damages awarded to a plaintiff for a small or symbolic amount ($1.00) where no actual damages have been incurred, but the law recognizes the need to vindicate the plaintiff.

nuisance
[*noo*.sense]

Anything a person does that annoys or disturbs another person in her use, possession, or enjoyment of her property, or that renders the ordinary use or possession of the property uncomfortable (EXAMPLES: noise; smoke; a display of public indecency; an encroachment). What constitutes a nuisance in a particular case depends upon numerous factors, including the type of neighborhood in which the property is located, the nature of the act or acts complained of, their proximity to the persons alleging injury or damage, their frequency or continuity, and the nature and extent of the resulting injury, damage, or annoyance.

- *n.* annoyance, inconvenience, bother, intrusion, aggravation, hindrance, problem
- *ant.* benefit

omission
[o.*mish*.en]

1. Not doing something required by the law. 2. A failure to act; a failure to do something that ought to be done.

- *n.* breach, neglect, disregard, exclusion, oversight

ordinary negligence
[*or*.di.ner.ee *neg*.li.jense]

The failure to exercise the degree of care that a reasonably prudent person would have exercised in similar circumstances; the failure to exercise ordinary or due care. *Compare* gross negligence. *See* negligence.

pain and suffering
[*payn* and *suf*.e.ring]

Mental anguish or physical pain. Damages may be recoverable if the pain and suffering is caused by a tort.

principal
[*prin*.sipl]

In an agency relationship, the person for whom the agent acts and from whom the agent receives her authority to act.

privacy
[*pry*.ve.see]

A reference to the right of privacy. The right of privacy is the right to be left alone. The right of privacy means, among other things, that a person's writings that are not intended for public consumption (EXAMPLES: a diary; personal letters) cannot be made public, that a person's photographs may not be publicly distributed, and that a person's private conversations may not be listened in on or recorded. It also means that personal information of the kind in the possession of, for EXAMPLE, the government, insurance companies, and credit bureaus may not be made public. The right to privacy, which is grounded in the Constitution, is supported, and to some extent enforced, by federal and state privacy acts.

DICTIONARY | THESAURUS *continued...*

product liability
[*pro*.dukt ly.e.*bil*.i.tee]

The liability of a manufacturer or seller of an article for an injury caused to a person or to property by a defect in the article sold. A product liability suit is a tort action in which strict liability is imposed. The manufacturer or seller of a defective product may be liable to third parties (EXAMPLE: bystanders) as well as to purchasers. A contractual relationship is not a requirement in a product liability case.

proximate cause
[*prok*.si.mit cawz]

As an element of liability in a tort case, that cause which, unbroken by any intervening cause, produced the injury, and without which the result would not have occurred; the primary cause; the efficient cause. *Note* that the proximate cause of an injury is not necessarily the final cause or the act or omission nearest in time to the injury.

prudent person
[*proo*.dent *per*.sun]

A reasonable person, or ordinary prudent person. *See also* reasonable person test.

punitive damages
[*pyoo*.ni.tiv *dam*.e.jez]

Damages that are awarded over and above compensatory damages or actual damages because of the wanton, reckless, or malicious nature of the wrong done by the defendant. Such damages bear no relation to the plaintiff's actual loss and are often called exemplary damages, because their purpose is to make an example of the defendant to discourage others from engaging in the same kind of conduct in the future.

reasonable care
[*ree*.zen.ebl kayr]

Due care or ordinary care. The degree of care exercised by a reasonable person. *See also* reasonable person test.

reasonable person test
[*ree*.zen.ebl *per*.sun test]

A standard for determining negligence, which asks: "What would a reasonable person have done in the same circumstances?" In short, it measures the failure to do that which a person of ordinary intelligence and judgment would have done in the same circumstances, or the doing of that which a person of ordinary intelligence and judgment would not have done.

res ipsa loquitur
[race *ip*.sa *lo*.kwe.ter]

(*Latin*) Means "the thing speaks for itself." When an instrumentality (i.e., a thing) causes injury, an inference or rebuttable presumption arises that the injury was caused by the defendant's negligence, if the thing or instrumentality was under the exclusive control or management of the defendant and the occurrence was such as in the ordinary course of events would not have happened if the defendant had used reasonable care. EXAMPLE: The utility company may properly be held liable under the doctrine of res ipsa loquitur for a gas explosion that destroys a building in which its equipment is functioning imperfectly.

slander
[*slan*.der]

A false and malicious oral statement tending to hurt a person's reputation or to damage her means of livelihood. *Compare* libel. *See also* malice; defamation.

- *n.* defamation, slur, vilification, denigration, ("slander of character")

special damages
[*spesh*.el *dam*.e.jez]

Damages that may be added to the general damages in a case, and arise from particular (special) circumstances of the case. For EXAMPLE: a dry cleaning bill or a round-trip airline ticket.

statutes of limitations
[*stat*.shoots ov lim.i.*tay*.shenz]

Federal and state statutes prescribing the maximum period of time during which the various types of civil actions and criminal prosecutions can be brought after the occurrence of the injury or offense.

strict liability
[strikt ly.e.*bil*.i.tee]

Liability for an injury whether or not there is fault or negligence; absolute liability. The law imposes strict liability in product liability cases. EXAMPLE: a defective gas pedal that sticks and the car accelerates by itself, causing injury.

sudden emergency doctrine
[*sud*.en e.*mer*.jen.see *dok*.trin]

The principle that a person who is placed in a position of sudden emergency, not created by his own negligence, will not be held responsible if he fails to act with the degree of care that the law would have required of him had he had sufficient time for thought and reflection.

supervening cause
[soo.per.*veen*.ing cawz]

In the law of negligence, a new or additional event that occurs subsequent to the original negligence and becomes the proximate cause of injury.

supervening negligence
[soo.per.*veen*.ing *neg*.li.jense]

The negligence of a defendant who is held liable under the last clear chance doctrine; the negligence of a defendant whose conduct is the supervening cause of an injury.

tort
[tort]

A wrong involving a breach of duty and resulting in an injury to the person or property of another. A tort is distinguished from a breach of contract in that a tort is a violation of a duty established by law, where a breach of contract results from a failure to meet an obligation created by the agreement of the parties. Although the same act may be both a crime and a tort, the crime is an offense against the public that is prosecuted by the state in a criminal action; the tort is a private wrong that must be pursued by the injured party in a civil action. *See also* intentional injury; joint tortfeasors.

- *n.* wrong, civil wrong, violation, breach of duty

tortfeasor
[*tort*.fee.zer]

A person who commits a tort. *See also* joint tortfeasors.

tortious
[*tore*.shus]

1. Involving a tort; wrongful. 2. Pertaining to a tort.

trespass
[*tress*.pas]

1. An unauthorized entry or intrusion on the real property of another. 2. In the widest sense of the term, any offense against the laws of society or natural law; any wrong; any violation of law. 3. Any misdeed, act of wrongdoing, or sin.

- *n.* breach, contravention, entry, encroachment, obtrusion, poaching

unavoidable accident
[un.a.*voyd*.abl *ak*.si.dent]

An inevitable accident; an inescapable peril; an occurrence that could not reasonably have been foreseen or prevented.

unavoidable casualty
[un.a.*voyd*.abl *kazh*.you.al.tee]

An occurrence or accident that is beyond human foresight or control.

unavoidable cause
[un.a.*voyd*.abl cawz]

In the law of negligence, a cause that could not have been avoided by the exercise of due diligence and foresight; an accidental cause.

unintentional tort [un.in.*ten*.shen.el tort]	A tort that is not done with an intent or knowingly, An unintentional tort is a harm or injury caused by negligence or resulting from an accident. EXAMPLE: A person not paying attention while driving might veer into another car, injuring the occupants. While there was no intent, harm was caused by the driver's negligence.
vicarious liability [vy.*kehr*.ee.us ly.e.*bil*.i.tee]	Liability imposed upon a person because of the act or omission of another. EXAMPLES: the liability of an employer for the conduct of her employees; the liability of a principal for the conduct of her agent, the liability of the owner of a car for the conduct of the driver.
willful and malicious injury [*will*.ful and ma.*lish*.ess *in*.jer.ee]	An injury to a person or property inflicted intentionally and deliberately, without cause and with no regard for the legal rights of the injured party.
willful and wanton act [*will*.ful and *want*.en akt]	1. An act or conduct that the perpetrator knows or should know is likely to result in injury, but about which he is indifferent. EXAMPLES: reckless driving, or shooting a gun in a crowded movie theater. 2. A deliberate and intentional wrong.
willful neglect [*will*.ful neg.*lekt*]	The deliberate or intentional failure of a person to perform a duty to others as required by law. EXAMPLES of such duties include: the duty of a parent to care for a child in some circumstances; the duty of a spouse to provide care to his or her partner; the obligation of a public official to perform a duty required by virtue of her office.
willful negligence [*will*.ful *neg*.li.jense]	Reckless disregard of a person's safety, evidenced by the failure to exercise ordinary care to prevent injury after discovering an imminent peril. *See also* negligence.
wrongful death [*rong*.ful deth]	A death that results from a wrongful act, such as negligence by a doctor in surgery.
wrongful death action [*rong*.ful deth *ak*.shen]	An action arising under a wrongful death statute. The personal representative of the decedent brings an action on behalf of the decedent's beneficiaries that alleges that the death of the decedent was attributable by the negligent act of another. *See* wrongful death statutes.
wrongful death statutes [*rong*.ful deth *stat*.shoots]	State statutes that allow the personal representative of the decedent to bring an action on behalf of the decedent's statutory beneficiaries (EXAMPLES: spouse; children) if the decedent's death was the result of the defendant's wrongful act. This action is for the wrong to the beneficiaries.

Missing Words

Fill in the blanks.

1. _____ occurs when a person who knows and deliberately exposes herself to a danger assumes responsibility for the risk, rather than the person who actually created the danger.

2. A(n) _____ is a court order that commands or prohibits some act or course of conduct.

3. A(n) _____ is anything a person does that annoys or disturbs another person in the use, possession, or enjoyment of his property.

4. A legal obligation is known as a(n) _____.

5. The standard for determining negligence is the _____.

6. _____ is a rule of negligence law where a negligent defendant is held liable to a plaintiff who has negligently placed himself in peril, if the defendant had a later opportunity than the plaintiff to avoid the occurrence that resulted in injury.

7. A(n) _____ is a wrong involving a breach of duty and resulting in an injury to the person or property of another.

8. A(n) _____ is the statement of an untruth designed to deceive.

9. A failure to act is called a(n) _____.

10. A state of mind that causes the intentional doing of a wrongful act without legal excuse is known as _____.

11. The doctrine followed in most states that requires a comparison of the negligence of the parties, where the plaintiff's negligence does not defeat the cause of action, is called _____.

12. _____ can be either libel or slander.

13. An element of liability in a tort case, whose cause, which unbroken by an intervening cause, produced the injury, is called _____.

14. _____ is where liability is imposed upon a person because of the act or omission of another.

15. A(n) _____ is a person who commits a tort.

16. A new or additional event that occurs subsequent to the original negligence is a(n) _____ of injury, and the proximate cause of injury.

17. An unauthorized entry on the real property of another is a(n) _____.

STUDY AID: Use flashcards for this unit before completing the exercises.

Matching

Match the letter of the definition to the term.

_D_ **18.** trespass

_H_ **19.** tortfeasor

_E_ **20.** battery

_I_ **21.** malicious prosecution

_J_ **22.** conversion

_A_ **23.** damages

_B_ **24.** foreseeable

_F_ **25.** vicarious liability

_G_ **26.** product liability

_C_ **27.** contributory negligence

_M_ **28.** tortious

_K_ **29.** prudent person

_L_ **30.** punitive damages

_O_ **31.** general damages

_N_ **32.** hedonic damages

_P_ **33.** nominal damages

_Q_ **34.** special damages

A. the sum of money that may be recovered in the courts as financial reparation for an injury or wrong

B. that which may be anticipated or known in advance; that which a person should have known

C. a failure by the plaintiff to exercise reasonable care that, in part at least, is the cause of an injury

D. an unauthorized entry or intrusion on the real property of another

E. the unconsented-to touching or striking of one person by another

F. liability imposed upon a person because of the act or omission of another

G. the liability of a manufacturer or seller of an article for an injury caused by a defect in the article sold

H. a person who commits a tort

I. a suit commenced maliciously without probable cause

J. wrongfully exercised control over another person's personal property

K. a reasonable person

L. damages awarded over and above compensatory damages because of wanton or reckless conduct

M. pertaining to a tort

N. damages from loss of enjoyment of life's pleasures

O. damages that are the natural and probable result of a wrongful act

P. small or symbolic damages

Q. added damages that arise from a particular circumstance

Multiple Choice

Select the best choice.

A 35. The local newspaper deliberately wrote a false story about a shopkeeper, stating that he was a drunk. This is known as:
    a. libel.
    b. slander.
    c. conversion.
    d. battery.

D 36. Maria Johnson aimed her gun into a busy restaurant, firing three shots. Two people were killed. This is an example of:
    a. trespass to chattel.
    b. transferred intent.
    c. abuse of process.
    d. foreseeability.

B 37. Scott Hansen wants to get a lot of money for his 2008 car. He tells the purchaser the car only has 30,000 miles, when in reality it has 130,000 miles. This is an example of:
    a. necessity.
    b. misrepresentation.
    c. infliction of emotional distress.
    d. contributory negligence.

C 38. Fred Hunt approaches an elevator, which stops 6 inches higher than the floor. The elevator has not been serviced in over 10 years. Fred Hunt is in a hurry and is not looking where he is going. Fred trips and is severely injured. Should the matter go to trial, the court will weigh the evidence comparing the negligence of the plaintiff with that of the defendant. This is known as:
    a. last clear chance.
    b. assumption of risk.
    c. comparative negligence.
    d. invasion of privacy.

B 39. A bank teller is counting up the money in his drawer at the end of the day. Not having enough money to go to the movies that evening, he slips $30 into his pocket, figuring he needs the money more than the bank does. This is an example of:

    a. a reasonable person.
    b. conversion.
    c. sovereign immunity.
    d. attractive nuisance.

A 40. An ex-employee sets fire to the end of the factory where she was previously working. Unknown to her, another employee sets fire to the other end of the factory at the very same time. The entire building burns down and the night custodian is killed. It is unclear which of the fires caused the death. The two employees are held responsible because of:
    a. joint liability.
    b. reasonable care.
    c. trespass to land.
    d. slander.

C 41. A teenager purchases a new car. He wants to show his friends how powerful the engine is. He floors the gas pedal and drives through town going 90 miles per hour in a 30-mile-per-hour zone. An entire family crossing the street is struck and instantly killed by the vehicle. This is an example of:
    a. assault.
    b. joint liability.
    c. gross negligence.
    d. wrongful life.

C 42. To save production costs, the manufacturer of a baby formula deliberately leaves out the iron that is advertised as a major feature of the formula. A baby is fed the formula for several weeks and suffers severe anemia. The baby's parents hire a lawyer to proceed against the manufacturer after they have the product tested at a lab. The lawyer will most likely recommend a suit based on:
    a. wrongful death.
    b. necessity.
    c. product liability.
    d. contributory negligence.

True/False

Mark the following T or F.

_____ T **43.** The violation of an express or implied warranty is called breach of warranty.

_____ F **44.** The principle that the U.S. government or any state is immune from suit except when it consents to be sued is known as zone of danger.

_____ F **45.** The Federal Tort Claims Act allows the federal government to be sued for most torts committed by its employees and agents.

_____ T **46.** A dangerous instrumentality is a thing so dangerous, that if it causes injury the law may impose absolute liability even though there was no negligence.

_____ F **47.** A false and malicious statement that brings into question a person's right or title to property, causing him damage, is trespass.

_____ T **48.** The failure to do something that a reasonable person would do in the same circumstances is known as negligence.

_____ F **49.** The unconsented-to touching or striking of one person by another is an assault.

_____ F **50.** Deceit, deception, or trickery that is intended and induces another to part with something of value is known as invasion of privacy.

_____ T **51.** A state statute that allows the personal representative of a decedent to bring an action on behalf of the decedent's wife and children, where the death was the result of the defendant's wrongful act, is known as a wrongful death statute.

_____ F **52.** A failure to do something that ought to be done is an act.

_____ T **53.** A business invitee is more likely to recover damages then a social guest or a trespasser.

_____ T **54.** Immunity is a privilege or exemption granted by law.

Synonyms

Select the correct synonym in parentheses for each numbered item.

55. TORT
(a measurement, a wrong, a test)

56. DEFAMATION
(libel, fraud, conversion)

57. MALICE
(lunacy, evasiveness, willfulness)

58. TRESPASS
(entry, exit, negotiate)

59. OMISSION
(act, oversight, conversion)

60. FRAUD
(disclosure, honesty, misrepresentation)

61. NUISANCE
(annoyance, conversion, causation)

62. INJUNCTION
(permission, acceptance, prohibition)

63. CONSENT
(permission, refusal, appreciation)

64. DUTY
(obligation, negligence, causation)

65. LIABILITY
(illness, responsibility, forgetfulness)

66. DAMAGES
(battery, assault, compensation)

67. REASONABLE CARE
(little care, ordinary care, extraordinary care)

68. INTENTIONAL TORT
(deliberate, huge, greedy)

69. MALPRACTICE
(exemplary, misconduct, void)

70. FALSE IMPRISONMENT
(lead, follow, confine)

71. STATUTE OF LIMITATIONS
(time limit, money limit, award)

72. ACTIONABLE
(heroic, safe, grounds)

73. PRINCIPAL
(opposite of agent, priority, trespass)

74. GOOD SAMARITAN DOCTRINE
(evil, malice, first aid)

75. UNINTENTIONAL TORT
(deliberate, huge, without intent)

76. IMPUTED NEGLIGENCE
(transferred, equal, different)

Self-Test

Place the number of the correct term in the appropriate space.

77. compensatory damages

78. omission

79. reasonable person

80. contributory negligence

81. foreseeable

82. intentional tort

83. damages

84. pain and suffering

85. proximate

86. strict liability

87. negligent

88. tortfeasor

89. comparative negligence

90. punitive damages

91. malpractice

When a person fails to do something that the _____ would do in the same circumstances, that is known

as _____. This is different than a(n)_____, where an act is done with intent or knowingly. In both

negligence actions and intentional torts, the _____ is punished for wrongs against individuals.

For negligence actions, the court looks for the presence of certain elements. An act or _____ that is

the _____ cause of injury is usually found. A person is responsible for the consequences of his acts only if

they are _____.

In some jurisdictions, the plaintiff must not be even the slightest bit at fault for an incident or they can't recover.

This is known as _____. In contrast, other jurisdictions prefer a system whereby a plaintiff's fault does not stop

her from bringing an action, but merely reduces the amount of her total recovery in an action. This is known as the

theory of _____.

Sometimes, no matter how much care or skill is used, an accident may occur. This is particularly true when

explosives and other dangerous materials are handled. In these instances, a person might be injured despite all possible

precautions being taken. Because society recognizes the need for explosives in the building industry and for other

needed services, a theory of _____ has developed where liability is imposed regardless of fault or negligence

when using dangerous materials.

In the event an injured plaintiff wins her tort action, she might be awarded _____ for loss or harm to

her person or property. Actual or _____ might be awarded for loss of time from work. If the defendant is

found to be reckless, there might be an award of _____. If a plaintiff has suffered physical pain, damages

might be awarded for _____. If the plaintiff was injured as a result of the misconduct of a professional,

this is called _____.

Word Scramble

Unscramble the following words and write the correct word(s) that match(es) the definition for each word or phrase.

92. tynecessi – a must_____

93. ser aspi rutiuqol – it speaks for itself _____

94. missoino – failure to act _____

_____

95. tudy – obligation _____

_____

96. nitent – deliberate plan _____

_____

97. pumasstion fo kris – at your own risk _____

_____

98. tioninjunc – stop an action _____

_____

99. tabtery – unconsented touching _____

_____

100. gligneence – absence of ordinary care _____

_____

101. drauf – deception trickery, deceit _____

_____

102. tenscon – permission _____

_____

103. tiveattrac isancenu trinedoc – protects young children _____

_____

104. bleaseefor – predictable _____

_____

105. tributconion – to give your share _____

_____

106. tributcontroy glenceigne – may defeat a plaintiff's right to bring an action _____

_____

107. olss fo sortconium – loss of a spouse's services

_____

_____

108. lainoemot tresssid – strong feeling of sadness

_____

_____

109. pracmaltice – professional misconduct _____

_____

110. slafe mentprisonim – detain unlawfully _____

_____

111. ablenoitca – conduct that is grounds for legal action

_____

_____

112. retnivening sauce – breaks the connection between an original wrongful act and the injury _____

_____

113. putedim ligenceneg – when an employer might be responsible for the negligence of his employee because of their relationship to each other

_____

_____

The Last Word

The term *sexting*, short for "sex" and "texting," has entered the American lexicon. In 2010 Massachusetts criminalized "sexting," or the sending of sexually graphic instant messages to minors. Arizona, Oklahoma, Rhode Island, and other states are also considering sexting legislation.

If not a crime, the practice of transmitting explicit photos electronically by cell phone or computer can be tortious activity. Recent studies report that at least 20 percent of all teens have sent or received sexual images via e-mail or text message and 60 percent have been pressured to reciprocate. In 2008, an Ohio teen hanged herself after an ex-boyfriend sent naked photos of her to classmates.

While the American Civil Liberties Union has successfully argued in Pennsylvania that sexting is covered by the First Amendment, cases with malicious intent can still be a tort with civil liability. Cases like the Ohio matter could result in wrongful death actions if the facts are supported with evidence and testimony.

Where photos depict nude minors, child pornography laws may already apply. A federal appeals court decision in 2010 raised the issue that future sexting cases may be tried as felonies. Should sexting be treated as a crime or a tort? Does current tort law offer sufficient remedies to address sexting via new and future technologies?

4 Law of Contracts

- Learn about the law of contracts.

- Master the similarities and differences in definitions of key terms.

- Master the pronunciations and spellings of legal terms.

- Recognize the synonyms used for legal terminology.

- Practice usage of terms, definitions, and synonyms.

- Complete unit exercises in the forms of missing words, matching, multiple choice, true/false, synonyms, self-test, and word scramble.

- Work with a legal dictionary/thesaurus.

UNIT

7 Contracts

INTRODUCTION   The law of contracts provides an orderly method for conducting business. People can negotiate and bargain over terms, trying to get the best deal for themselves. When both parties are content and wish to make a binding agreement, they can draft a contract. Contrary to popular belief, it need not always be in writing. For some matters, oral contracts are permissible, but five elements must exist to have an enforceable contract: offer, acceptance, consideration, mutual assent, and capacity; sometimes these elements are combined. An offer is only good for the time set forth in the offer or a reasonable time. An offer can be withdrawn before acceptance. If a person wants to accept an offer but adds additional terms, this voids the offer, and becomes a counteroffer to the offeror, which the offeror has the option to accept or not. A rule called the mail box rule governs the timing as to acceptances. Once an acceptance is properly placed into the mail, this is considered the date of acceptance of an offer.

Under the statute of frauds, a law that exists in one form or another in every state, some contracts, such as real estate transactions, are so important that they must be in writing and signed by the party making the agreement. This greatly reduces misunderstandings as to the precise terms of the contract, provides a system that others can rely on and is designed to avoid fraud. If an individual fails to sign a contract, under the statute of frauds, she still may be able to enforce the contract against the other party, if he signed the contract. It is presumed that the parties trying to enforce a contract have agreed to the terms, hence, no signature is needed.

There are two main kinds of contracts: (1) two-sided, or bilateral, contracts, in which a promise is made for a promise. For example, John says, "I promise to run your printing order for $3,500." Cindy responds, "I promise to pay you $3,500 for printing my order." Each party has made a promise to the other party. (2) In a unilateral or one-sided contract, only one promise is made. A person needs a particular act performed. Another person can only accept a unilateral contract by performing the act requested, rather than trying to accept with a promise. An example of this is a reward situation. The owner of a lost wallet tells his coworkers, "I'll pay $50 to the person who finds my wallet within the next two weeks and returns it to me." In order to accept, you don't make any promises to the owner of the wallet, the offeror. To accept, you must find the wallet and return it following the precise conditions set forth by the wallet owner.

Another law governing the formation and enforcement of contracts is the Uniform Commercial Code, referred to as the UCC. This law covers sales contracts in the United States. Because sales between merchants of differing states is so commonplace, a law was needed to ensure the free flow of goods throughout the country, without regard to the laws of specific states. Most of the most common issues that arise between merchants are covered under the UCC. These provisions are written to encourage commerce and save any valid portion of a contract where possible. Just because one part of a contract is unenforceable, the other parts will still be enforceable where appropriate. Alternatives are provided to merchants, giving them a chance to salvage a contract where for example, goods are late, damaged, or different in quality, quantity, or color than originally requested. A variety of remedies is provided for different situations. Merchants know exactly what they will face if a contract is not carried out properly, or if events occur that are beyond their control, such as acts of nature: fire, floods, and tornadoes. The dispute in the following case concerns the percentage of royalties due under contracts for the recordings of Marshall B. Mathers, III, professionally known as the rap artist Eminem.

CASE AND COMMENT

United States Court of Appeals for the Ninth Circuit
F.B.T. Productions, LLC, Em2M, LLC, Plaintiffs-Appellants
v.
Aftermath Records, Defendants-Appellees
Nos. 09-55817 & 09-56069,
D.C. Nos. 2:07-ev-03314-PSG-MAN & 2:07-cv-03314-PSG-MAN
(Filed September 3, 2010)

Facts: F.B.T. signed Eminem in 1995, gaining exclusive rights to his recordings. In 1998 F.B.T. signed an agreement transferring Eminem's recording services to Aftermath. The "Records Sold" provision of the agreement provides F.B.T. to receive between 12–20% of the adjusted retail price of all "full price records sold in the United States . . . through normal retail channels." In the "Masters Licensed" provision, F.B.T. is to receive 50% of Aftermath's net receipts on masters licensed to others for their manufacture and sale of records or for any other purposes. The contract does not contain a definition of the term "licensed" or "normal retail channels." In 2002, Aftermath concluded an agreement with Apple Computers, Inc. that enabled Eminem's masters to be sold through Apple's iTunes store as permanent downloads to the end-users' computers. Since 2003, Aftermath has also concluded contracts with major cellular telephone network carriers to sell sound recordings as mastertones or ringtones. In 2003, F.B.T. and Aftermath entered into a new agreement that increased some royalty rates but terminated the 1998 agreement while incorporating the wording of the Records sold and Masters Licensed provision of that agreement. In 2004, the agreement was further amended to provide that "sales of albums" by way of permanent download shall be treated as "normal retail channels" for the purposes of increased royalties.

Procedural History: F.B.T brought suit after a 2006 audit showed that Aftermath had been applying the Records Sold provision to calculate the royalties for sales of Eminem's recordings in the form of permanent downloads and ringtones. Before trial F.B.T moved for summary judgment that the Masters Licensed provision unambiguously applied to permanent downloads and ringtones. The district court denied the motion. At trial, the court concluded that the agreements were susceptible to either party's interpretation and the jury returned a verdict in favor of Aftermath. F.B.T. appealed the court's award of $2.4 million in attorneys' fees to Aftermath.

Issue: Whether F.B.T.'s motion for summary judgment should have been granted because the Masters Licensed contract provision unambiguously applies to permanent downloads and ringtones.

Rationale: "Because the agreements were unambiguous and were not reasonably susceptible to Aftermath's interpretation, the district court erred" in denying summary judgment to F.B.T., the court said and "Notwithstanding the Records Sold provision, Aftermath owed F.B.T. a 50% royalty under the Masters Licensed provision for licensing the Eminem masters to third parties for any use. It was undisputed that Aftermath allowed third parties to use the Eminem masters to produce and sell permanent downloads and ringtones."

Ruling: The District court's judgment for Aftermath is reversed, vacating their order awarding attorneys' fees to Aftermath and the case is remanded for further proceedings.

Comment: In light of this case, how can the law evolve fast enough to anticipate the ever-changing technologies of the future?

DICTIONARY	THESAURUS

Term
[phonetic pronunciation]

Note: All dictionary/thesaurus terms appear on flashcards at the back of the book and on the student website.

acceptance
[ak.*sep*.tens]

1. The assent by the person to whom an offer is made, to the offer as made by the person making it. This is necessary for a binding contract. 2. Unspoken consent to a transaction by a failure to reject it. *See also* offer and acceptance. *Compare* rejection.

accord and satisfaction
[a.*kord* and sat.is.*fak*.shen]

An agreement between two persons, one of whom is suing the other, in which the claimant accepts a compromise (usually a lesser amount) in full satisfaction of his claim.

adhesion contract
[ad.*hee*.zhen *kon*.trakt]

A contract prepared by the dominant party (usually a form contract) and presented on a take-it-or-leave-it basis to the weaker party, who has no real opportunity to bargain about its terms. *See also* contract.

age of majority
[aj ov ma.*jaw*.ri.tee]

The age at which a person may legally engage in conduct in which she could not previously engage because she was a minor. EXAMPLES: entering into a binding contract; enlisting in the military service; voting; making a valid will.

agreement
[a.*gree*.ment]

1. A contract. 2. A concurrence of intention; mutual assent. *See also* meeting of the minds. 3. A coming together of parties with respect to a matter of opinion.

- *n.* contract, bargain, compact, arrangement, pact, concurrence, compliance, alliance

anticipatory breach
[an.*tiss*.i.pe.tore.ee breech]

The announced intention of a party to a contract that she does not intend to perform her obligations under the contract; an announced intention to commit a breach of contract. *Compare* repudiation.

avoid
[a.*voyd*]

To cancel, annul, evade, or escape.

DICTIONARY   THESAURUS *continued...*

bargain
[*bar*.gen]

n. An agreement between two or more persons; a contract.
v. To negotiate; to talk about the terms of a contract.

- *n.* treaty, pact, settlement, deal, agreement, transaction, contract, covenant, stipulation

bilateral
[by.*lat*.er.el]

1. Involving two interests. 2. Having two sides.

bilateral contract
[by.*lat*.er.el *kon*.trakt]

A contract in which each party promises performance to the other, the promise by the one furnishing the consideration for the promise from the other. EXAMPLE: a contract for home heating oil (the dealer promises to deliver oil, the homeowner promises to pay). *Compare* unilateral contract.

boilerplate language
[*boy*.ler.plate *lang*.wej]

Language common to all legal documents of the same type. Attorneys maintain files of such standardized forms for use where appropriate. *Compare* adhesion contract.

breach of contract
[breech ov *kon*.trakt]

Failure, without legal excuse, to perform any promise that forms a whole or a part of a contract, including the doing of something inconsistent with its terms. Clear and absolute refusal to perform a contract.

capacity
[ke.*pass*.i.tee]

Competency in law. USAGE: "Generally, a minor does not have the capacity to enter into contracts." A person's ability to understand the nature and effect of an act he has engaged in.

competent
[*kom*.pe.tent]

1. Having legal capacity. 2. Capable; qualified. 3. Sufficient; acceptable.

- *adj.* eligible, qualified, capable, fit, polished, efficient, responsible, able
- *ant.* uncapable

consideration
[ken.sid.e.*ray*.shen]

1. The reason a person enters into a contract; that which is given in exchange for performance or the promise to perform; the price bargained and paid; the inducement. Consideration is an essential element of a valid and enforceable contract. A promise to refrain from doing something one is entitled to do also constitutes consideration. 2. Motivation, incentive, inducement.

- *n.* value, incentive, recompense, inducement, reward, benefit ("Consideration is an essential element of a valid and enforceable contract.")

contract
[*kon*.trakt]

n. An agreement entered into, for adequate consideration, to do, or refrain from doing, a particular thing. The Uniform Commercial Code defines a contract as the total legal obligation resulting from the parties' agreement. In addition to adequate consideration, the transaction must involve an undertaking that is legal to perform, and there must be mutuality of agreement and obligation between at least two competent parties. *See* also bilateral contract. *Compare* unilateral contract.
v. To enter into a contract.

- *n.* agreement, understanding, bargain, compact, mutual promise, covenant, accord, arrangement, promise, assurance
- *v.* agree, promise, engage, undertake, covenant, bargain, obligate, pledge

counteroffer
[*koun*.ter.off.er]

A position taken in response to an offer, proposing a different deal. This negates the original offer. It is considered a rejection of the offer and the proposal of a new counteroffer. Under the UCC, a counteroffer is considered a proposal of additional terms and the original offer is not considered withdrawn.

cure
[kyur]

1. Under the Uniform Commercial Code, a seller has the right to correct ("cure") his failure to deliver goods that conform to the contract if he does so within the period of the contract. 2. To remedy.

- *n.* recovery, improvement, remedy, restoration, correction

damages
[*dam*.e.jez]

The sum of money that may be recovered in the courts as financial reparation for an injury or wrong suffered as a result of breach of contract or a tortious act.

- *n.* restoration, compensation, restitution, repayment, recovery, reparation, expenses

disaffirm
[dis.e.*ferm*]

To disclaim; to repudiate; to renounce; to disavow; to deny.

- *v.* disavow, recant, negate, veto, rescind, renege, renounce, deny, repudiate
- *ant.* affirm

enforceable
[en.*forss*.ebl]

That which can be put into effect or carried out, referring to legal rights. EXAMPLES: a contract; a judgment. If an enforceable contract is breached, a party might seek relief through the court system.

- *adj.* binding, lawful, effective
- *ant.* unenforceable

entire output contract
[in.*tire out*.put *kon*.trakt]

A contract in which the seller binds herself to the buyer to sell to the buyer the entire amount of a product she manufactures, and the buyer binds himself to buy all of the product. *See also* requirement contract.

equity
[*ek*.wi.tee]

A system for ensuring justice in circumstances where the remedies customarily available under the conventional law are inadequate; a system of jurisprudence less formal and more flexible than the common law, available in particular types of cases to better ensure a fair result. EXAMPLE: Instead of awarding money damages, a court might order the opposing party to stop doing a certain act, such as operating a noisy business near a residential area.

executed contract
[ek.se.*kyoot*.ed *kon*.trakt]

A contract whose terms have been fully performed. *Compare* executory contract.

executory contract
[ek.se.kyoo.*tor*.ee *kon*.trakt]

A contract yet to be performed, each party having bound herself to do or not to do a particular thing. *Compare* executed contract.

express contract
[eks.*press kon*.trakt]

A contract whose terms are stated by the parties. *Compare* implied contract.

formal contract
[*for*.mel *kon*.trakt]

1. A signed, written contract, as opposed to an oral contract. 2. A contract that must be in a certain form to be valid. EXAMPLE: a negotiable instrument. *Compare* informal contract.

DICTIONARY   THESAURUS *continued...*

implied contract
[im.*plide kon*.trakt]

Implied contracts are of two types: contracts implied in fact, which the law infers from the circumstances, conduct, acts, or the relationship of the parties rather than from their spoken words; and contracts implied in law, which are quasi-contracts or constructive contracts imposed by the law, usually to prevent unjust enrichment.

impossibility
[im.poss.i.*bil*.i.tee]

That which cannot be done. *Compare* impracticability. When a contract becomes impossible to perform, a party is relieved of the duty of performance. EXAMPLE: A party cannot sell a house that has just burned to the ground.

- *n.* futility, insurmountability, infeasibility, unattainability, failure, unfeasibility, difficulty, failure

impracticability
[im.prak.ti.ke.*bil*.i.tee]

A legal term unique to the Uniform Commercial Code, from the provision of the UCC that excuses a seller from the obligation to deliver goods when delivery has become unrealistic because of unforeseen circumstances. *Compare* impossibility of performance; legal impossibility. *See also* Uniform Commercial Code.

incompetency
[in.*kawm*.pe.ten.see]

1. The condition, state, or status of an incompetent person. 2. Lack of capability to perform a required duty. *Compare* competent.

infancy
[*in*.fen.see]

1. The status of a person who has not reached the age of majority and who therefore is under a civil disability; nonage; minority, generally under the age of 18. 2. A civil disability resulting from the fact that one has not yet attained one's majority. 3. The period of life during which one is a very young child.

- *n.* childhood; inception, start, conception

informal contract
[in.*for*.mel *kon*.trakt]

A contract not in the customary form, often an oral contract. *Compare* formal contract.

intention
[in.*ten*.shen]

Purpose; plan; object; aim; goal. The intention of the parties is the most important factor in interpreting a contract.

- *n.* course, purpose, route, propensity, plan, object, aim, goal ("the intention of the parties")

invitation
[in.vi.*tay*.shen]

An express or implied request by a person for another person to make an offer. EXAMPLE: An advertisement in a newspaper is really an invitation for the public to make an offer to purchase an item.

lapse
[laps]

n. A termination or extinguishment, particularly of a right or privilege; a forfeiture caused by a person's failure to perform some necessary act or by the nonoccurrence of some contingency.
v. To cease: to expire: to terminate. EXAMPLE: An offer can lapse after a reasonable time.

liquidated damages
[*lik*.wi.dated *dam*.e.jez]

A sum agreed upon by the parties at the time of entering into a contract as being payable by way of compensation for loss suffered in the event of a breach of contract; a sum similarly determined by a court in a lawsuit resulting from breach of contract.

mailed [maled]	Describes an item when it is appropriately enveloped or packaged, addressed, and stamped, and deposited in a proper place for the receipt of mail. In contract law, acceptance of an offer takes place when the acceptance is mailed, unless the parties have made another arrangement or a statute provides otherwise. This is sometimes referred to as the "mailbox rule."
majority [ma.*jaw*.ri.tee]	Legal age; full age; the age at which a person acquires the capacity to contract; the age at which a person is no longer a minor. The age of majority varies from state to state and differs depending upon the purpose. ▪ *n.* legal age, full age, age of responsibility
meeting of the minds [*meet*.ing ov the mindz]	The mutual assent of the parties to a contract with respect to all of the principal terms of the contract. A meeting of the minds is essential to the creation of a legally enforceable contract.
misrepresentation [mis.rep.re.zen.*tay*.shen]	The statement of an untruth; a misstatement of fact designed to lead one to believe that something is other than it is; a false statement of fact designed to deceive. ▪ *n.* fraud, deception, deceit, distortion, fabrication, exaggeration
mistake [mis.*take*]	1. An erroneous mental conception that influences a person to act or to decline to act; an unintentional act, omission, or error arising from ignorance, surprise, imposition, or misplaced confidence. "Mistake" is a legal concept especially significant in contract law because, depending upon the circumstance, it may warrant reformation or rescission of a contract. 2. An error; a misunderstanding; an inaccuracy. ▪ *n.* misconception, inaccuracy, confusion ("a mistake of identity")
mutual assent [*myo*.choo.el a.*sent*]	A meeting of the minds; consent; agreement.
mutual mistake [*myoo*.choo.el mis.*take*]	Both sides of a transaction or contract have different perceptions of fact or law. This may warrant the changing or canceling of a contract.
offer [*off*.er]	*n.* 1. A proposal made with the purpose of obtaining an acceptance, thereby creating a contract. *See also* offer, acceptance, mailed. 2. A tender of performance. 3. A statement of intention or willingness to do something. 4. A proposal; a proposition; a bid. *See also* counteroffer. *v.* To propose for acceptance or rejection. ▪ *v.* present, propose, provide, award, suggest ▪ *n.* proposal, suggestion, endeavor, proposition, submission, bid
offer and acceptance [*off*.er and ak.*sep*.tense]	Essential elements in the creation of a legally enforceable contract, reflecting mutual assent or a meeting of the minds. In the case of a bilateral contract, acceptance is the offeree's communication that she intends to be bound by the offer; in the case of a unilateral contract, the offeree accepts by performing in accordance with the terms of the offer.

DICTIONARY | THESAURUS *continued...*

offeree
[off.er.*ree*]

A person to whom an offer is made. *Compare* offeror.

offeror
[off.er.*ror*]

A person who makes an offer.

option
[*op*.shen]

An offer, combined with an agreement supported by consideration not to revoke the offer for a specified period of time; a future contract in which one of the parties has the right to insist on compliance with the contract, or to cancel it, at his election. In other words, "option" is short for option contract.

- *n.* advantage, offer, choice, preference, prerogative ("option to purchase")

oral contract
[*ohr*.el *kon*.trakt]

A contract that is not in writing. Unless the subject of an oral contract is covered by the statute of frauds, it is just as valid as a written contract; often, however, its enforceability is limited because its terms cannot be proven. *See also* contract, informal contract.

- *n.* parol contract

performance
[per.*form*.ense]

1. The doing of that which is required by a contract at the time, place, and in the manner stipulated in the contract; that is, according to the terms of the contract.
2. Fulfilling a duty in a manner that leaves nothing more to be done.

- *n.* fulfillment, effort, production

promise
[*prom*.iss]

1. An undertaking that binds the promisor to cause a future event to happen; an offer that, if supported by consideration, and if accepted, is a contract. 2. An assurance that a thing will or will not be done. It gives the person to whom it is made the right to demand the performance or nonperformance of the thing if she acted in reliance and to her detriment. 3. Under the Uniform Commercial Code, "a written undertaking to pay money signed by the person undertaking to pay."

- *v.* affirm, swear, vow, pledge, covenant, vouch ("I promise I will do this for you.")
- *n.* oath, declaration, affirmation, vow, pledge, assurance, endorsement, covenant

promisee
[prom.i.*see*]

A person to whom a promise is made.

promisor
[prom.i.*sore*]

A person who makes a promise.

quantum meruit
[*kwan*.tum *mehr*.oo.it]

(*Latin*) Literally, it means "as much as is deserved." This doctrine makes a person liable to pay for goods or services she accepts, while knowing the other party expects to be paid, even if no contract exists.

quasi-contract
[*kway*.zye *kon*.trakt]

An obligation imposed by law to achieve equity, usually to prevent unjust enrichment. A quasi-contract is a legal fiction that a contract exists where there has been no express contract. EXAMPLE: a contract implied on the theory of quantum meruit.

ratify
[*rat*.i.fy]

To give approval, to confirm.

- *v.* sanction, confirm, countersign, agree, affirm, authorize
- *ant.* repudiate

reformation
[ref.er.*may*.shun]

To modify or correct the contract to reflect the intent of the parties. An equitable remedy available to a party to a contract provided she can prove that the contract does not reflect the true agreement.

rejection
[re.*jek*.shun]

1. Any act or word of an offeree, communicated to an offeror, conveying her refusal of an offer. 2. The act of rejecting.

- *n.* abandonment, disallowance, denial, refusal, waiver

repudiation
[re.pyoo.dee.*ay*.shun]

A denial of the validity of something; a denial of authority.

- *n.* denial, rejection, renunciation, repeal, retraction, nullification, disaffirmation

requirement contract
[re.*kwire*.ment *kon*.trakt]

A contract under which one party agrees to furnish the entire supply of specified goods or services required by the other party for a specified period of time, and the other party agrees to purchase his entire requirement from the first party exclusively. *See also* entire output contract.

rescission
[ree.*sizh*.en]

The abrogation, annulment, or cancellation of a contract by the act of a party. Rescission may occur by mutual consent of the parties, pursuant to a condition contained in the contract, or for fraud, failure of consideration, material breach, or default. It is also a remedy available to the parties by a judgment or decree of the court. More than mere termination, rescission restores the parties to the status quo existing before the contract was entered into.

- *n.* unmaking, termination, withdrawal, voidance, extricating

restitution
[res.ti.*tew*.shen]

In both contract and tort, a remedy that restores the status quo. Restitution returns a person who has been wrongfully deprived of something to the position he occupied before the wrong occurred; it requires a defendant who has been unjustly enriched at the expense of the plaintiff to make the plaintiff whole, either, as may be appropriate, by returning property unjustly held, by reimbursing the plaintiff, or by paying compensation. *See also* unjust enrichment.

- *n.* compensation, repayment, amends, dues, recompense, reparation

revocation of offer
[rev.e.*kay*.shen ov *off*.er]

The withdrawal of an offer by an offeror before it has been accepted. An offer can be withdrawn anytime before acceptance.

statute of frauds
[*stat*.shoot ov frawdz]

A statute, existing in one form or another in every state, that requires certain classes of contract to be in writing and signed by the parties. Its purpose is to prevent fraud or reduce the opportunities for fraud. A contract to guarantee the debt of another is an EXAMPLE of an agreement that the statute of frauds requires to be in writing.

third-party beneficiary contract
[third-*par*.tee ben.e.*fish*.er.ee *kon*.trakt]

A contract made for the benefit of a third person, other than the parties making the contract. EXAMPLE: Parents buy life insurance for the benefit of their children.

DICTIONARY / THESAURUS continued...

unconscionable
[un.*kon*.shen.ebl]

Morally offensive, reprehensible, or repugnant. An unconscionable contract is a contract in which a dominant party has taken unfair advantage of a weaker party, who has little or no bargaining power, and has imposed terms and conditions that are unreasonable and one-sided. A court may refuse to enforce an unconscionable contract. *See* adhesion contract.

- *adj.* excessive, preposterous, exorbitant, unscrupulous inexcusable, unequal, grossly unfair

undue influence
[*un*.dew *in*.flew.ense]

Inappropriate pressure exerted on a person for the purpose of causing him to substitute his will with the will or wishes of another.

unenforceable
[un.en.*forss*.ebl]

That which cannot be put into effect or carried out. USAGE: "unenforceable contract." Compare enforceable.

Uniform Commercial Code (UCC)
[*yoon*.i.form ke.*mersh*.el kode]

One of the Uniform Laws, which have been adopted in much the same form in every state. It governs most aspects of commercial transactions, including sales, leases, negotiable instruments, deposits and collections, letters of credit, bulk sales, warehouse receipts, bills of lading and other documents of title, investment securities, and secured transactions.

unilateral contract
[yoon.i.*lat*.er.el *kon*.trakt]

A contract in which there is a promise on one side only, the consideration being an act or something other than another promise. In other words, a unilateral contract is an offer that is accepted not by another promise but by performance. EXAMPLE: The Acme Company promises Winton Electronics that if it buys products from Acme, Winton will be the sole Chicago distributor of Acme products. *Compare* bilateral contract.

unilateral mistake
[yoon.i.*lat*.er.el mis.*take*]

A misconception by one, but not both, parties to a contract with respect to the terms of the contract.

unjust enrichment
[un.*just* en.*rich*.ment]

The equitable doctrine that a person who unjustly receives property, money, or other benefits that belong to another may not retain them and is obligated to return them. The remedy of restitution is based upon the principle that equity will not permit unjust enrichment.

valid
[*val*.id]

Effective; sufficient in law; legal; lawful; not void; in effect. USAGE: "Valid contract"; "valid marriage"; "valid defense."

- *adj.* legal, lawful ("valid contract")

void contract
[voyd *kon*.trakt]

A contract that creates no legal rights; the equivalent of no contract at all. *Compare* voidable contract.

voidable
[*voyd*.ebl]

Something that is defective but valid unless disaffirmed by the person entitled to disaffirm.

- *adj.* avoidable, reversible, revocable, nullifiable ("a voidable contract")

voidable contract
[*voyd*.ebl *kon*.trakt]

A contract that may be avoided or disaffirmed by one of the parties because it is defective; for EXAMPLE, a contract induced by fraud.

Missing Words

Fill in the blanks.

1. A(n) _____ can be either implied in fact based on the conduct of the parties or implied in law to prevent unjust enrichment.

2. A contract that must be in a certain form to be valid is a(n) _____ contract.

3. A system for ensuring fairness in circumstances where the remedies customarily available under conventional law are inadequate is known as _____.

4. _____ is the announced intention of a party to a contract that he doesn't intend to perform his obligation under the contract.

5. A contract where one party agrees to furnish the entire supply of specified goods or services required by another is known as a(n) _____.

6. An agreement between two people, one of whom has a cause of action against the other, in which the claimant accepts a compromise in full satisfaction of a claim, is called _____.

7. A contract that has been _____ has been approved.

8. The _____ is the person to whom a promise is made.

9. When an offer is withdrawn by an offeror before it has been accepted, this is a(n) _____.

10. A(n) _____ is a contract where a dominant party has taken unfair advantage of a weaker party.

11. An offer that _____ is terminated or no longer in force.

12. Any act or word of an offeree communicated to an offeror conveying the refusal of an offer is a _____.

13. A remedy that restores the status quo, that returns a person who has been wrongfully deprived of something to his prior position, is known as _____.

14. Language common to all legal documents of the same type is known as _____.

15. A(n) _____ is a contract made for the benefit of a third person.

16. A sum agreed upon by the parties at the time of entering the contract to be payable in the event of a breach is called _____.

17. A minor must wait until reaching the age of _____ before entering into a binding contract.

STUDY AID: Use flashcards for this unit before completing the exercises.

Matching

Match the letter of the definition to the term.

F____ **18.** cure

H____ **19.** performance

G____ **20.** unjust enrichment

C____ **21.** equity

I____ **22.** incompetency

B____ **23.** breach

A____ **24.** infancy

D____ **25.** meeting of the minds

E____ **26.** contract

J____ **27.** unilateral

K____ **28.** restitution

M____ **29.** rejection

L____ **30.** mutual mistake

N____ **31.** quantum meruit

P____ **32.** avoid

P____ **33.** void

O____ **34.** unconscionable

A. one who has not reached the age of majority

B. failure without legal excuse to perform promises that form a contract

C. system for ensuring justice where conventional laws are inadequate

D. mutual consent of the parties to a contract

E. agreement entered into, for adequate consideration, to do, or refrain from doing, a particular thing

F. right of seller to correct his failure to deliver goods

G. equitable doctrine that a person who unjustly receives property of another is obligated to return it

H. doing of that which is required by a contract

I. legal disability that makes a person incapable of understanding the nature of his acts

J. contract in which there is a promise on one side only

K. a remedy that restores the status quo

L. when both sides of a contract have different perceptions of fact

M. when an offeree refuses an offer

N. "as much as is deserved" is the literal meaning

O. a contract to have someone kill your spouse is

P. to cancel or annul

Q. when a person sells bread to someone who is starving and charges 10 times more than she normally would.

Multiple Choice

Select the best choice.

 35. When a person refuses an offer, this is known as:
   a. rejection.
   b. acceptance.
   c. revocation.
   d. termination.

 36. Consideration occurs when:
   a. a person thinks over the offer.
   b. there is a bargained-for exchange.
   c. there is quantum meruit.
   d. there is a novation.

 37. A valid contract is:
   a. an enforceable contract.
   b. an unenforceable contract.
   c. a void contract.
   d. where there is an illusory promise.

 38. In an express contract, the terms are:
   a. oral only.
   b. written only.
   c. implied.
   d. oral or written.

 39. When a lawyer drafts an agreement for his client selling the client's multimillion-dollar business to his lawyer for $10, the court will most likely find there was:
   a. material breach.
   b. impossibility.
   c. minority.
   d. undue influence.

 40. A realtor shows a house to a prospective buyer. When asked about a giant water ring on a ceiling, the realtor lies and says it's just some artwork the owners drew. This is an example of:
   a. misrepresentation.
   b. unilateral contract.
   c. quasi-contract.
   d. merger clause.

 41. When a contract has a liquidated damages clause:
   a. the amount of damages is left to an arbitrator to compute.
   b. the parties at the time of entering a contract agree upon a sum payable in the event of a breach.
   c. this is an example of an exculpatory clause.
   d. the parties seek accord and satisfaction.

 42. Under the mailbox rule, an offer is accepted when:
   a. 24 hours elapse.
   b. 50 hours elapse.
   c. the acceptance is mailed.
   d. the offer is received.

 43. A breach of contract occurs when:
   a. both parties carry out the terms of the contract.
   b. there is a bargained-for exchange of performances.
   c. there is a merger clause.
   d. a party fails to perform a promise that is part of a contract.

 44. Scott offers to sell his automobile for $18,000. John says, "I'll take it if you'll accept $16,000, not a penny more."
   a. John has accepted the contract.
   b. John has used duress.
   c. John has disaffirmed the contract.
   d. John has made a counteroffer.

 45. A contract not in writing is:
   a. illegal.
   b. unenforceable.
   c. oral.
   d. incomplete.

 46. The statute that requires certain types of contracts to be in writing is called:
   a. statute of frauds.
   b. restitution statute.
   c. adhesion contract.
   d. boilerplate statute.

True/False

Mark the following T or F.

_____ **47.** A void contract is the same as no contract at all.

_____ **48.** A contract implied in law is imposed by the court to prevent unjust enrichment.

_____ **49.** A voidable contract is a defective but valid contract unless disaffirmed.

_____ **50.** A requirement contract occurs when one party agrees to furnish the entire supply of specified goods required by the other party.

_____ **51.** The promisor is the party to whom a promise is made.

_____ **52.** UCC is the abbreviation for Uniform Contract Conditions.

_____ **53.** A third-party beneficiary is one of the original parties to a contract.

_____ **54.** A reward is an example of a bilateral contract.

_____ **55.** An offer is made by the promisor.

_____ **56.** An express contract is implied from the conduct of the parties.

_____ **57.** A contract that has been repudiated has been rejected.

_____ **58.** A newspaper advertisement stating that apples are $4.50 a pound is really an invitation to the public to make an offer.

_____ **59.** Bob turns down John's offer to buy Bob's motorcycle for $10,000. Instead, John tells Bob he will take the motorcycle for $10,000 so long as Bob supplies replacement parts for anything that breaks or malfunctions within the next year. This is a counteroffer.

_____ **60.** Reformation occurs when a person completes performance under a contract before the contract date.

_____ **61.** If a building collapses, a contract to repair the building's roof would be impossible to perform or enforce.

Synonyms

Select the correct synonym in parentheses for each numbered item.

62. PROMISE
(vow, cover, cure)

63. OFFER
(accept, propose, guarantee)

64. EXECUTED
(completed, lapsed, rejected)

65. RATIFICATION
(rescission, insanity, confirmation)

66. PERFORMANCE
(cure, effort, agreement)

67. INFORMAL
(casual, implied in law, equity)

68. REVOCATION
(termination, emancipation, best efforts rule)

69. CURE
(make a correction, implied term, severable)

70. IMPOSSIBILITY
(futility, covenant, mistake)

71. MAJORITY
(infancy, adulthood, incompetent)

72. RESCISSION
(cancellation, illusory promise, accord and satisfaction)

73. CAPACITY
(merger, lapse, competency)

74. OFFEROR
(promisor, promisee, beneficiary)

75. LAPSE
(continue, terminate, divide)

76. CONTRACT
(problem, plan, agreement)

77. INFANCY
(competency, minority, majority)

Self-Test

Place the number of the correct term in the appropriate space.

78. rejection

79. voidable contract

80. agreement

81. unilateral contracts

82. offer

83. executory contract

84. consideration

85. contract

86. enforceable

87. void contract

88. counteroffer

89. implied contract

90. acceptance

91. bilateral contract

92. Uniform Commercial Code

93. boilerplate language

94. impossibility

95. cure

96. entire output contract

A(n) _____ between two or more people with the binding effect of the law is known as a(n) _____.

Several elements are needed to complete a valid and _____ contract.

You need a party to make a(n) _____ and you need a(n) _____ without qualification. Should the acceptance have contingencies added, this is really a(n) _____ and a(n) _____. That which is given in exchange for performance of the contract is called _____. It is important to remember that a contract need not be in writing. A contract might be oral, or in writing, or even a(n) _____, a contract that the law

infers from the parties' conduct. Some contracts are one-sided contracts called _____, while others consist

of a promise for a promise and are called _____. Should a contract not be completed, it is called a(n)

_____. Once completed, a contract is called executed. A contract to do something in violation of a statute

would be illegal and is referred to as a(n) _____. Should a contract be executed by a minor, the contract is

called a(n) _____, a contract that is valid but may be disaffirmed.

Most commercial transactions for the sale of goods are governed by the _____, one of the uniform laws

adopted by every state. Attorneys often draft contracts for the sale of goods using _____. A seller has the right

to correct or _____ his failure to deliver goods if done within reasonable time. When a seller binds himself

to sell to a buyer the seller's entire output of a product, this is called an _____. However, if the factory should

burn down, it would be an _____ for the seller to continue to perform under the contract.

Word Scramble

*Unscramble the following words and write the correct word(s) that match(es) the definition
for each word or phrase.*

97. tractcon – an agreement _____

_____

98. efrof – a proposal _____

_____

99. peccatance – when an offer is agreed to

_____

_____

100. eraconsidtion – the reason a person enters into

a contract _____

_____

101. promsie – an assurance that something will be done

_____

_____

102. cutoryexe – a contract that has not yet been fully

performed _____

_____

103. forceableen – when a legal right can be carried

out _____

_____

104. doiv – something that is null and without legal

effect _____

_____

105. takemis – an error or misunderstanding _____

_____

106. reptionmisresenta – a false statement of fact

designed to deceive _____

_____

107. vocationer – to withdraw or cancel _____

_____

108. lamrofin noctract – a contract not in the ordinary

form, often it is oral _____

_____

109. pressex tractcon – a contract whose terms are stated by the parties _____

_____

110. magesad – the sum of money recoverd for an injury or a wrong _____

_____

111. tumquan mertui – "As much as is desired"

_____

_____

112. jormaity – legal age _____

_____

113. romin – a child not of legal age _____

_____

114. tationinvi – a request for an offer _____

_____

The Last Word

A licensing agreement is a contract that grants one party the use of another's personal, real, intellectual, or virtual property for a fee. A perfect example is an agreement offered by game developer Activision and accepted by CBGB Holdings LLC. Activision is allowed to use CBGB's stage as a virtual venue on its new release of *Guitar Hero* video game. Now game players of *Guitar Hero* may practice on the iconic "stage" that was once home to punk rockers like the Ramones and Blondie.

In addition to receiving a $30,000 fee as consideration from Activision, CBGB views the licensing agreement as a way to expose its brand "to a new generation of fans." Lacking capacity because CBGB filed for Chapter 11 protection from creditors, Judge Stuart M. Bernstein of the U.S. Bankruptcy Court in Manhattan had to sign off on the licensing agreement with Activision. Did you note all the basic elements of a contract are the same in the licensing agreement?

1. Offer
2. Acceptance
3. Consideration
4. Mutual Assent
5. Capacity

 Access an interactive eBook, chapter-specific interactive learning tools, and more in your Paralegal CourseMate, accessed through www.CengageBrain.com

5

The Law of Agency and Intellectual Property

- Learn about the law of agency and intellectual property.

- Master the similarities and differences in definitions of key terms.

- Master the pronunciations and spellings of legal terms.

- Recognize the synonyms used for legal terminology.

- Practice usage of terms, definitions, and synonyms.

- Complete unit exercises in the forms of missing words, matching, multiple choice, true/false, synonyms, self-test, and word scramble.

- Work with a legal dictionary/thesaurus.

8 Agency

Gone are the days when people dealt face to face with each and every person who provided them with a service or sold goods to them. More typically, instead of going into a local store or business and meeting the actual owner, there is a good chance people today will be served by an employee with no relation to the owner. Businesses are becoming larger and more impersonal.

A corporation, partnership, or an individual might own several real estate companies. While the original owner might have built his reputation and business on individual customer service, it is physically impossible for an owner to be in all of his stores or businesses at the same time. Thus, the law of agency comes into play. A business owner needs representatives who can act on his behalf. One person would have great difficulty running three offices, in varying locations, all at once.

In an agency relationship, one person gives another person the authority to act and contract on his behalf. The use of an agent is common in buying and selling real estate and buyers and sellers are oftentimes represented by an agent. A large corporation like AT&T may appoint numerous agents to represent it in transactions all over the country. Likewise an insurance agent may represent several companies as a broker.

There are a variety of different agency relationships. Not all businesses wish to give their agents the exact same amount of authority or duties. When a party delegates duties to another person, this is called an agency relationship. The principal, which might be a business owner or employer, delegates certain duties to the agent to act on his behalf. When it is obvious to others that an agent has the authority to act, this is known as an apparent agency, as presumed by law. Should an agent and principal create an agreement setting forth the terms of their relationship, this is known as an agency in fact. This unit fleshes out the distinguishing features of differing agency relationships.

There are special terms used when an agency relationship is the result of an employer/employee situation and the extent to which an employer may or may not be held liable for an employee's actions. Another special type of agency relationship is when one person entrusts goods to another with the expectation that the other person will sell goods for them. This is called a consignment contract, where a consignor authorizes the consignee to sell goods for her. An example of this is where an individual brings lightly worn clothes or furniture to a store, and the store agrees to try and sell the items for her. Agency also comes into play in the entertainment field and in the sports field, where the actors and athletes have a representative to obtain business and conduct business for them. This unit explores the terminology associated with agency. In the case that follows, a sick woman and her husband sign medical authorizations without reading them. Would you think that doctors working in a hospital don't necessarily work for the hospital?

CASE AND COMMENT

The Supreme Court of Tennessee
Amanda Lynn Dewald et al. Plaintiff/Appellant

v.

HCA Health Services of Tennessee, et al. Defendant/Appellee
No. M2006-02369-SC-R11-CV- Filed May 6, 2008

Facts: Mrs. Dewald was admitted to StoneCrest emergency room complaining of lower abdominal pain and nausea. Mr. Dewald signed, on his wife's behalf, a "Consent for Medical Procedure and Treatment" form, which included notice that those "providing medical services are not agents or employees of the hospital." Mrs. Dewald underwent a pelvic ultrasound, the results of which suggested decreased arterial flow to her left ovary. Upon reviewing the results, the emergency room physician released Mrs. Dewald and instructed her to follow up with her primary care physician. Dr. Lambelle, a radiologist with staff priviledges at StoneCrest, dictated and signed a report incorrectly indicating that Mrs. Dewald had undergone chest x-rays that revealed advanced lung cancer. Mrs. Dewald's primary care physician received Dr. Lambelle's report and told Mrs. Dewald to begin treatment for lung cancer. She was admitted to a hospital where she was treated for two days believing she had lung cancer, before it was found that Dr. Lambelle had read a different patient's x-ray.

Procedural History: The plaintiffs filed suit in Rutherford County Circuit Court on January 25, 2005 against StoneCrest Medical Center and Dr. Lambelle, a radiologist, for negligence. The court granted StoneCrest's motion for summary judgment in part as to Plaintiff's claims for negligence but not as to the claims based on an alleged agency relationship between StoneCrest and Dr. Lambelle. The court found that genuine issues of material fact existed as to whether StoneCrest may be held vicariously liable for the negligence of Dr. Lambelle. StoneCrest appealed. The Court of Appeals vacated the trial court's order and remanded the case to trial court for entry of an order granting of summary judgment to Stonecrest on all claims. The plaintiffs appeal by permission from the Court of Appeals, Middle Section Circuit Court of Rutherford County.

Issue: Whether StoneCrest is liable to the Dewalds based on holding Dr. Lambelle out as its agent.

Rationale: Summary judgment is to be granted by a trial court only where the moving party demonstrates that there are no genuine issues of material fact and that judgment is entitled as a matter of law. To hold a hospital vicariously liable for negligence or wrongful acts of an independent contractor physician, a plaintiff must show that, among other things, "the patient accepted those services in the reasonable belief that the services were provided by the hospital or a hospital employee."

Ruling: The Court reversed the Court of Appeals decision granting summary judgment to StoneCrest and remanded this case to the trial court for further proceedings.

Comment: The case is just one example of the agency relationship. Unseen personnel behind the scenes at a hospital can be an agent or not, but how was the couple in this case to know? Do you fully read all the disclaimers placed in front of you to sign?

DICTIONARY	THESAURUS

Term
[phonetic pronunciation]

Note: All dictionary/thesaurus terms appear on flashcards at the back of the book and on the student website.

agency
[*ay*.jen.see]

A relationship in which one person acts for or on behalf of another person at the other person's request. *See also* implied agency.

agency by estoppel
[*ay*.jen.see by es.*top*.el]

An agency created by appearances that lead people to believe that the agency exists. It occurs when the principal, through negligence, permits her agent to exercise powers she never gave him, even though she has no knowledge of his conduct. *See also* estoppel, apparent authority; implied agency; implied authority.

agency by ratification
[*ay*.jen.see by rat.i.fi.*cay*.shen]

A relationship in which one misrepresents one's self as an agent to a principal, when in fact one is not, while the principal accepts the unauthorized act.

agency coupled with an interest
[*ay*.jen.see *cup*.ld with an *in*.trest]

See power coupled with an interest.

agency in fact
[*ay*.jen.see in fakt]

An agency created by the agreement of the principal and the agent, as distinguished from an agency created by operation of law. EXAMPLE: an agency by estoppel.

agency relationship
[*ay*.jen.see re.*lay*.shun.ship]

The relationship that exists in law between a principal and an agent.

agent
[*ay*.jent]

One of the parties to an agency relationship, specifically, the one who acts for and represents the other party, who is known as the principal. The word implies service as well as authority to do something in the name of or on behalf of the principal (EXAMPLE: a person who represents a business person in contract negotiations). Although one can be both an employee and an agent, the usual distinction between the two is that the manner in which an employee does his work is controlled and directed by his employer; in contrast, an agent is free to use independent skill and judgment, his principal's concern being the results he produces, not how he does his work. *See also* del credere agent; general agent; managing agent; special agent; universal agent.

- *n.* assistant, delegate, emissary, assignee, deputy, functionary, proxy, representative

apparent agent
[a.*par*.ent *ay*.jent]

One who is, in law, an agent because she has obvious authority. EXAMPLE: a nurse in uniform working at a doctor's office, who greets patients in the waiting room.

apparent authority
[a.*par*.ent aw.*thaw*.ri.tee]

Authority that an agent is permitted to exercise, although not actually granted by the principal. *See also* agency by estoppel.

commission agent
[ke.*mish*.en *ay*.jent]

An agent who buys or sells on commission; a fee or payment calculated on a percentage basis. *See* factor.

DICTIONARY | THESAURUS *continued...*

consignee
[ken.sine.*ee*]

The person to whom a carrier is to deliver a shipment of goods; the person named in a bill of lading to whom the bill promises delivery; the person to whom goods are given on consignment, either for sale or safekeeping. *Compare* consignor. *See also* factor.

- *n.* receiver, salesperson, representative, seller
- *ant.* consignor

consignment
[ken.*sine*.ment]

The entrusting of goods either to a carrier for delivery to a consignee or to a consignee who is to sell the goods for the consignor.

- *n.* entrusting, distribution, committal, transmittal

consignment contract
[ken.*sine*.ment *kon*.trakt]

A consignment of goods to another (the consignee) with the understanding either that she will sell them for the consignor and forward the proceeds, or, if she does not, that she will return them to the consignor. A consignment is also known as a bailment for sale.

consignor
[ken.sine.*or*]

A person who sends goods to another on consignment; the person named in a bill of lading as the person from whom goods have been received for shipment. *Compare* consignee.

- *n.* shipper, sender
- *ant.* consignee

del credere agent
[*del kreh.de.reh ay.jent*]

(*Italian*) An agent who guarantees his principal against the default of those with whom he contracts.

deviation doctrine
[dee.vee.*ay*.shen *dok*.trin]

The rule that if an agent has digressed only slightly from the instructions of the principal, the principal is not excused from liability for the agent's negligence.

employee
[em.*ploy*.ee]

A person who works for another for pay in a relationship that allows the other person to control the work and direct the manner in which it is done. The earlier legal term for employee was servant. *Compare* independent contractor. *Also compare* agent. *Note* that statutory definitions of "employee" may differ, depending upon the purpose of the statute. For EXAMPLE, although the distinctions between the definitions of employee in the Social Security Act, the Fair Labor Standards Act, and the National Labor Relations Act may seem insignificant, they may, in any given instance, be critical.

- *n.* servant, worker, agent, laborer, helper, personnel, jobholder

employer
[em.*ploy*.er]

A person who hires another to work for her for pay in a relationship that allows her to control the work and direct the manner in which it is done. The earlier legal term for employer was master.

- *n.* master, contractor, director, boss, chief
- *ant.* employee

estoppel
[es.*top*.el]

A prohibition imposed by law against uttering what may actually be the truth. A person may be estopped by his own *acts or representations* (that is, not be permitted to deny the truth or significance of what he said or did) if another person who was entitled to rely upon those statements or acts did so to her detriment. This type of estoppel is also known as equitable estoppel or estoppel in pais.

- *n.* impediment, prohibition, restraint, ban, bar

factor
[*fak*.ter]

A person employed to receive goods from a principal and to sell them for compensation, usually in the form of a commission referred to as factorage. A factor is a bailee (person to whom property is entrusted) who is sometimes called a consignee or commission merchant (e.g., sale of right to collect accounts in exchange for a commission).

- *n.* ingredient, determinant, consideration, instrumentality, point; bailee, consignee, commission, merchant

fiduciary
[fi.*doo*.she.air.ee]

A person who is entrusted with handling the money or property of another person. EXAMPLES: attorney and client; guardian and ward; trustee and beneficiary.

fiduciary duty
[fid.*doo*.she air.ee *dew*.tee]

Duty to act loyally and honestly with respect to interests of another; the duty the law imposes upon a fiduciary.

frolic and detour
[*froll*.ik and *de*.tur]

The negligent conduct of an employee or agent who has departed from doing the employer's or principal's business to do something unrelated to work, for which the employer/principal is not liable.

general agent
[*jen*.e.rel *ay*.jent]

An agent authorized to perform all acts connected with the business of his principal. *Compare* special agent. *See also* agent; managing agent.

implied agency
[im.*plide ay*.jen.see]

An actual agency, the existence of which is proven by deductions or inferences from the facts and circumstances of the situation, including the words and conduct of the parties. *Compare* estoppel; apparent authority.

implied authority
[im.*plide* aw.*thaw*.ri.tee]

The authority of an agent to do whatever acts are necessary to carry out her express authority. EXAMPLE: An attorney retained to commence a legal action has the implied authority to file such pleadings as she feels are appropriate.

imputed
[im.*pew*.ted]

1. That which is attributed to a person, not because he personally performed the act (or personally had knowledge or notice), but because of his relationship to another person for whose acts, omissions, knowledge, or notice he is legally responsible. USAGE: "The neglect by his paralegal in this matter will be imputed to attorney Jones." *See also* agency. 2. Blamed; implicated; ascribed; charged.

- *adj.* attributed, blamed, implicated, ascribed, charged ("The paralegal's neglect is the attorney's imputed neglect.")

imputed knowledge
[im.*pew*.ted *nawl*.edj]

1. An agent's knowledge that is binding upon his principal because of their agency relationship. 2. Knowledge of facts charged to a person because anyone of ordinary common sense would know them. 3. That which a person has a duty to know and the means of knowing.

DICTIONARY   THESAURUS *continued...*

imputed negligence
[im.*pew*.ted *neg*.li.jenss]

The negligence of one person that, by reason of her relationship to another person, is chargeable to the other person. EXAMPLE: An employer is liable for the negligence of his employee that occurs within the scope of employment.

independent contractor
[in.de.*pen*.dent *kon*.trak.ter]

As distinguished from an employee, a person who contracts to do work for another person in her own way, controlling the means and method by which the work is done but not the end product. An independent contractor is the agent of the person with whom she contracts. *Compare* employee.

managing agent
[*man*.e.jing *ay*.jent]

A person to whom a corporation has given general powers involving the exercise of judgment and discretion in conducting the corporation's business. *See* agent. *See also* general agent.

master
[*mas*.ter]

1. An outdated term for employer. *See also* employer; master; servant. 2. A person who has control or authority over others.

- *n.* officer, official, employer, boss, director, leader, commandant, head ("office master")

power coupled with an interest
[*pow*.er *cup*.ld with an *in*.trest]

1. A power of appointment that includes an interest in the thing itself. 2. A power that gives an agent an interest in the subject of the agency. EXAMPLE: the power and interest of a partner in a business who is given the right to manage the business as security for loans he has made to the partnership.

power of attorney
[*pow*.er ov a.*tern*.ee]

A written instrument by which a person appoints another as his agent or attorney in fact and confers upon her the authority to perform certain acts. A power of attorney may be "full" (a general power of attorney) or "limited" (a special power of attorney). The power to sell property without specifying which property, or to whom, is an EXAMPLE of a general power of attorney; the power to sell a particular piece of property to a particular person is an EXAMPLE of a special power of attorney.

principal
[*prin*.sipl]

In an agency relationship, the person for whom the agent acts and from whom the agent receives her authority to act. *See also* undisclosed principal.

respondeat superior
[res.*pon*.dee.at soo.*peer*.ee.or]

(*Latin*) Means "Let the master respond." The doctrine under which liability is imposed upon an employer for the acts of its employees committed in the course and scope of their employment. Similarly, respondeat superior makes a principal liable for a tort committed by her agent, and a master responsible for the negligence of his servant.

servant
[*ser*.vent]

An outdated term for employee. *See also* master. *See also and compare* agent; employee; independent contractor.

special agent
[*spesh*.el *ay*.jent]

An agent authorized to perform a particular or specific act connected with the business of her principal. *Compare* general agent.

third party
[thurd *par*.tee]

A person who is not a party to an agreement, instrument, or transaction, but who may have an interest in the transaction. *See also* third person.

third-party beneficiary [thurd-*par*.tee ben.e.*fish*.er.ee]	The intended beneficiary of a contract made between two other persons. A third-party beneficiary may sue to enforce such a contract (e.g., the child of a couple who signed a separation agreement guaranteeing college tuition for the child).
third person [thurd *per*.sen]	As the term is used in the law, either a person who has an interest in a transaction or a person who has an interest in an action (i.e., a party or a third party).
undisclosed agency [un.dis.*klozed ay*.jen.see]	A situation in which a person who is in fact an agent for another deals with a third person as if he were the principal, the fact that he is an agent being unknown or hidden. *See also* undisclosed principal.
undisclosed principal [un.dis.*klozed prin*.sipl]	The unrevealed principal in a situation involving an undisclosed agency.
universal agent [yoon.i.*ver*.sel *ay*.jent]	An agent who is authorized to do everything her principal is entitled to delegate.
vicarious liability [vy.*kehr*.ee.us ly.e.*bil*.i.tee]	Liability imposed upon a person because of the act or omission of another. EXAMPLES: the liability of an employer for the conduct of its employees; the liability of a principal for the conduct of her agent. *See also* respondeat superior.

Missing Words

Fill in the blanks.

1. A(n) _____ is a relationship in which one person acts for or on behalf of another.

2. A(n) _____ is a person who sends goods to another on consignment.

3. An agent authorized to perform all acts connected with the business of his principal is a(n) _____.

4. An actual agency, the existence of which is proven by deductions or inferences, is a(n) _____.

5. A(n) _____ is an agent authorized to perform a particular act for a principal.

6. A written instrument by which a person appoints another as his agent and confers upon her the authority to perform certain acts is a(n) _____.

7. A(n) _____ is a situation in which a person who is in fact an agent for another deals with a third person as if he was a principal, the fact that he is an agent being unknown.

8. The person for whom the agent acts is called a(n) _____.

9. Liability imposed upon a person because of the act or omission of another is _____.

10. A(n) _____ is an agency created by appearances that lead people to believe that the agency exists.

11. The relationship that exists in law between a principal and an agent is a(n) _____.

12. A(n) _____ is one of the parties to an agency relationship, specifically the one who acts for and represents the other party.

13. A(n) _____ agent guarantees his principal against the default of those with whom he contracts.

14. A power of appointment that includes an interest in the thing itself is called _____.

15. A person who contracts to do work for another in her own way, controlling the method and means by which the work is done (but not the end product), is a(n) _____.

16. An agent's knowledge that is binding upon his principal because of his agency relationship is _____.

STUDY AID: Use flashcards for this unit before completing the exercises.

Matching

Match the letter of the definition to the term.

_____ 17. implied authority

_____ 18. factor

_____ 19. servant

_____ 20. power of attorney

_____ 21. principal

_____ 22. agency

_____ 23. universal agent

_____ 24. consignment

_____ 25. undisclosed agent

_____ 26. agent

_____ 27. respondeat superior

_____ 28. third party

A. one who acts for and represents a principal

B. written instrument giving another authority to perform a certain act

C. entrusting of goods to a carrier for delivery to a consignee

D. authority of an agent to do whatever acts are necessary to carry out express authority

E. person who is not a party to an agreement, but who might have an interest in the transaction

F. an agent who hides the fact that he is an agent to a third party

G. person for whom an agent acts

H. doctrine that an employer is responsible for acts of an employee

I. an agent who is authorized to do everything the principal is entitled to delegate

J. a bailee who is sometimes called a consignee

K. an employee

L. relationship in which one person acts for or on behalf of another person

_____ 29. special agent

_____ 30. vicarious liability

_____ 31. consignee

_____ 32. frolic and detour

_____ 33. deviation doctrine

M. liability imposed upon a person because of the act or omission of another

N. agent authorized to perform a specific act

O. a negligent agent is responsible when departing from doing the principal's business

P. the principal is not excused from liability for the agent's negligence

Q. the person to whom a carrier is to deliver a shipment of goods

Multiple Choice

Select the best choice.

_____ 34. A person employed to receive goods from a principal and to sell them for compensation, usually in the form of a commission, referred to as factorage is:
a. an employer.
b. a factor.
c. a general agent.
d. a managing agent.

_____ 35. An agent's knowledge that is binding upon his principal because of their agency relationship is:
a. power coupled with an interest.
b. respondeat superior.
c. imputed knowledge.
d. implied authority.

_____ 36. A person who is not a party to an agreement, but who may have an interest in the transaction, is a(n):
a. third party.
b. undisclosed agency.
c. universal principal.
d. power of attorney.

_____ 37. A person who contracts to do work for another person in her own way, controlling the means and method by which work is done but not the end product, is:
a. a master.
b. an independent contractor.
c. an employee.
d. a third party.

_____ 38. The intended beneficiary of a contract made between two other persons is a:
a. third-party beneficiary.
b. second-party beneficiary.
c. first-party beneficiary.
d. fourth-party beneficiary.

_____ 39. A power of appointment that includes an interest in the thing itself, such as the power and interest of a partner in a business who is given the right to manage the business as security for loans he has made to the partnership, is:
a. a power coupled with an interest.
b. an implied authority.
c. an undisclosed agency.
d. respondeat superior.

_____ 40. The entrusting of goods either to a carrier for delivery to a consignee or to a consignee who is to sell the goods for the consignor is:
a. a power of attorney.
b. an undisclosed agency.
c. an undisclosed principal.
d. a consignment.

_____ 41. Authority that the principal permits her agent to exercise, although not actually granted by the principal, is:
a. insurance agency.
b. agency by estoppel.
c. implied agency.
d. agency by law.

_____ 42. The doctrine under which liability is imposed upon an employer for the acts of its employees committed in the course and scope of their employment is:

a. third-party beneficiary.

b. apparent agency.

c. respondeat superior.

d. consignment contract.

_____ 43. The authority of an agent to do whatever acts are necessary to carry out her express authority is called:

a. implied authority.

b. partial authority.

c. apparent authority.

d. undisclosed authority.

_____ 44. An agent who is authorized to do everything the principal is entitled to delegate is a(n):

a. third person.

b. universal agent.

c. agent in fact.

d. implied agent.

True/False

Mark the following T or F.

_____ 45. There is a fully disclosed agency when an agent reveals he is acting for a principal and gives the name of the principal he represents.

_____ 46. An agent commits an unauthorized act when he does exactly as the principal instructs.

_____ 47. A man negotiates a fantastic movie role for a star. The star never hired the man to do this but the star thinks it's a great opportunity and wishes to sign the contract. This is an example of agency by ratification.

_____ 48. An insurance agency hires an outside consulting firm to come in and evaluate how to make the insurance company more efficient. It's up to the consulting firm how it will accomplish this job. This is an example of an independent contractor.

_____ 49. When a hospital administrator orders a nurse to paint the outside of the hospital, this is an example of work that is outside the scope of the nurse's employment.

_____ 50. A general power of attorney might be used to allow another to sign a person's checks or conduct business on his behalf while he is out of town.

_____ 51. When an agent is told to negotiate a contract for the sale of diamonds and follows instructions exactly, this is known as an unauthorized act.

_____ 52. When an agent acts on a principal's behalf but does not reveal that he is acting as an agent, or disclose the name of the principal, this is known as an undisclosed agency.

_____ 53. Employers are liable for acts of their employees committed in the scope of their employment. This is known as respondeat superior.

_____ 54. When an ice cream seller drives around a neighborhood wearing a uniform, operating a company truck, and offers to mow peoples' lawns, this is an example of apparent agency.

Synonyms

Select the correct synonym in parentheses for each numbered item.

55. CONSIGNMENT
(entrusting, donation, implied authority)

56. AGENT
(impostor, spy, representative)

57. CONSIGNEE
(obligation, alter ego, receiver)

58. IMPUTED
(denied, blamed, ratified)

59. SERVANT
(third party, principal, employee)

60. VICARIOUS LIABILITY
(conflict of interest, duty of loyalty, respondeat
superior)

61. IMPLIED AUTHORITY
(incidental authority, express agency,
exclusive agency)

62. POWER OF ATTORNEY
(unauthorized act, express agency, frolic and detour)

63. AGENCY COUPLED WITH AN INTEREST
(power coupled with an interest, agency by
ratification, respondeat superior)

64. APPARENT AGENCY
(obvious authority, vicarious liability, coming
and going rule)

65. MASTER
(original, employer, third party)

66. FACTOR
(bailee, del credere agent, deviation doctrine)

67. AGENCY IN FACT
(by agreement, by law, by appearance)

68. ESTOPPEL
(universal agent, encouragement, prohibition)

Self-Test

Place the number of the correct term in the appropriate space.

69. fully disclosed agency

70. agent

71. third persons

72. agency

73. express

74. undisclosed agency

75. agency by ratification

76. principal

77. general agent

78. special agent

79. deviation doctrine

An owner of a successful fast-food chain wishes to start up a second restaurant at another location. The business owner

visits her attorney and tells her of her plans. The lawyer advises:

"Certain situations repeat themselves over and over. The law responds with various solutions. When a person needs

an alter ego, a(n) _____ can be set up with the _____ acting on behalf of a(n) _____.

Typically the principal wishes to delegate certain duties to the agent. When the principal spells out in detail all acts required by the agent, this is known as a(n) _____ agency. Occasionally the agent acts beyond the scope of his agency. Should the principal approve of the actions notwithstanding, a(n) _____ develops. A lot is expected of an agent. Some of the agent's duties are the duty of obedience and a duty of performance. Slightly digressing from a principal's instructions by an agent does not excuse the principal of liability of the agent's negligence under the _____. Sometimes, outsiders known as _____ aren't aware of the existence of an agency relationship between agent and principal. This is known as a(n) _____. In contrast, an agent may tell third persons about her relationship and reveal the principal's name. This is known as a(n) _____. An agent authorized to perform all acts connected with the business of the principal is a(n) _____, whereas a(n) _____ can only perform a particular or specific act connected with the business of the principal."

Word Scramble

Unscramble the following words and write the correct word(s) that match(es) the definition for each word or phrase.

80. entag – representative _____
    _____

81. rincipalp – person for whom an agent acts _____

82. gencya – relationship in which one party acts on behalf of another _____
    _____

83. signconment – when a consignee agrees to sell goods for a consignor _____
    _____

84. cialspe genta – an agent authorized to perform a specific act _____
    _____

85. pliedim ncyage – an actual agency proven by inferences from the facts of the situation _____
    _____

86. werop fo torneyat – an example of this is the power to sell property for another _____
    _____

87. iversunal ntage – an agent who is authorized to do everything his principal is entitled to delegate ____
    _____

88. spondreeat persuior – a Latin phrase that means "let the master respond" _____
    _____

89. putedim ledgeknow – an agent's knowledge that a principal is held responsible for based upon their relationship _____
    _____

90. werpo ledcoup htiw na intesert – an example: when a partner in a business is given the right to manage the business as security for loans he made

to the partnership _____

_____

91. eralgen ntage – the opposite of special agent _____

_____

92. pelestop – when a person cannot deny the truth of her statements where another person relies on what she has said _____

_____

93. viatdeion trinedoc – the principal is responsible for the agent's actions where the agent has only slightly deviated from the principal's instructions _____

_____

94. licfro and toured – an employer is not responsible for an employee's actions where the employee performs tasks unrelated to the prinicpal's business

_____

_____

95. vasernt – an outdated term for employee _____

_____

96. liedimp hautority – the authority of an agent to do whatever acts are necessary to carry out her express authority _____

_____

97. dirth tarpy ficbeniarye – a person who is not a party to an agreement, instrument, or transaction, but who may have an interest in the transaction _____

_____

98. signconee – the person to whom a carrier is to deliver a shipment of goods _____

_____

99. closedundis ncipalpri – the unrevealed principal in a situation involving an undisclosed agency_____

_____

100. miscomsion genta – an agent who buys or sells on commission; a fee or payment calculated on a percentage basis _____

_____

The Last Word

Media Law, or Entertainment Law, involves a combination of traditional areas of law like agency, as well as employment, labor, immigration, securities, security interests, and intellectual property. Media Law caters to the following industries: film, music, television/radio, theater, multimedia/software/game video, Internet (rich and social media), publishing/advertising, and visual arts/design.

Most work involving these agents is transaction based, especially negotiating and drafting contracts. Litigation arising from this work is usually about royalty payments, defamation, personality, and privacy rights. How do you think paralegal education provides a foundation for future careers at a talent agency, television network, recording or film studio?

 **CourseMate**   Access an interactive eBook, chapter-specific interactive learning tools, and more in your Paralegal CourseMate, accessed through www.CengageBrain.com

Intellectual Property

INTRODUCTION

A field of law has developed to protect certain property produced as the result of original thoughts. The broad categories of protected property are known as patents, copyrights, trademarks, and trade secrets. The success of many businesses depends on their ability to protect and use intellectual property to their profitable advantage. When protected property is used without consent this is known as infringement.

When devices or processes that are both new and useful are invented, a patent application can be made by the inventor to gain the exclusive right to manufacture, sell, and use the invention for a period of time. A copyright is the right of an author to exclusively control the reproduction, distribution, and sale of literary and artistic works. Some of the items that may be protected by copyright are written works, music, films, sound recordings, photographs, painting, sculptures, and even some computer programs and chips. Use of a trademark is a method whereby a mark design, title, logo, or motto can be used to sell or advertise products of a particular company and distinguish them from other brands or products. Trade secrets are confidential information and property of a business that describe an industrial process or the way in which the business is conducted.

The following case shows that careful shopping can produce great sales bargains and a lucrative award.

CASE AND COMMENT

United States Court of Appeals for the Federal Circuit
Raymond Stauffer, Plaintiff-Appellant
v.
Brooks Brothers, Inc. and Retail Brand Appliance Inc., Defendants-Appellees
v.
United States, Movant-Cross Appellant
Nos. 2009-1428,-1430, 1453 (August 31, 2010)

Facts: Raymond Stauffer, a patent attorney, was shopping at Brooks Brothers when he noticed a display of bow ties with "Adjustolox" mechanisms. He also noticed that the patent numbers on the mechanisms had expired in 1954 and 1955! Section 292 of U.S.C. prohibits using the word "patent" or "patent numbers" to deceive the public and is grounds for any person to sue for $500 per offense. Any awards must be split with the United States. Brooks Bros. moved to dismiss and the court granted its motion.

CASE AND COMMENT *continued...*

Procedural History: Appellant Stauffer and the government appealed from a decision of the United States District Court dismissing Stauffer's false marketing action for lack of standing. The government also appealed the court's denial of its motion to intervene.

Issue: Whether the provision of Section 292(b) of U.S.C. operated as a statutory "assignment" of the rights of the United States and must Stauffer prove that the government had the right to sue and suffered injury.

Rationale: In enacting the false marketing statute, Congress determined that such conduct is harmful and should be prohibited. It is sufficient injury in fact to confirm standing on the government and therefore on Stauffer as the government's assignee to recover for injury.

Ruling: Stauffer had the right to bring his claim and because the government had the right to intervene, the appeals court reversed on both grounds.

Comment: The ruling may result in scores of cases moving forward against corporations, exposing manufacturers to liabilities under heretofore unenforced patent laws. As the tune goes, "everything old is new again."

DICTIONARY   THESAURUS

Term
[phonetic pronunciation]

Note: All dictionary/thesaurus terms appear on flashcards at the back of the book and on the student website.

abandonment of trademark
[a.*ban*.den.ment ov *trade*.mark]

Loss of trademark rights resulting from nonuse of the mark; demonstrated by sufficient evidence that the owner intends to discontinue use of the mark. May also occur when a mark has lost its distinctiveness or through the owner's misuse of trademark rights.

abstract
[*ab*.strakt]

Summary of the invention that enables the reader to determine the character of the patentable subject matter.

access
[*ak*.sess]

The reasonable opportunity of the defendant to view or hear the copyrighted work.

amendment to allege use
[a.*mend*.ment to a.*lej* yoose]

Amendment to an intent-to-use application indicating use of a mark in commerce; the amendment can only be filed before approval of the mark for publication (or, if there is a rejection, within six months of the response period).

arbitrary mark
[*ar*.bi.trare.ee mark]

Word or image that has a common meaning that does not describe or suggest the goods or services with which it is associated.

architectural work
[ar.ka.*tek*.cha.ral werk]

The design of a building as embodied in any tangible medium of expression, including a building, architectural plans, or drawings; it includes the overall form as well as the arrangement and composition of spaces and elements in the design, but does not include individual standard features.

audiovisual works
[aw.dee.o.*vizh*.u.al werkz]

Works that consist of a series of related images that are intrinsically intended to be shown by the use of machines or devices, such as projectors, viewers, or electronic equipment, together with accompanying sounds, if any, regardless of the nature of the material objects, such as films or tapes, in which the works are embodied.

author
[*aw*.ther]

1. A person who produces a written work. 2. A person who originates something; a maker. In copyright law, a person can be an author without producing any original material, provided she does something beyond copying, such as compiling or editing.

- *n.* producer, maker, originator, biographer, inventor, creator, planner

authorization of agent
[aw.ther.i.*zay*.shen ov *ay*.jent]

Inventor's or patent owner's authorization of representation by a patent agent.

automated database
[*awt*.toh.may.ted *day*.tah.base]

A body of facts, data, or other information assembled into an organized format suitable for use in a computer and comprising one or more files.

basic registration
[*ba*.sik rej.is.*tray*.shen]

The primary copyright record made for each version of a particular work.

collective mark
[ku.*lek*.tiv mark]

A trademark or service mark used to identify a trade association, fraternal society, or union. *See* trademark and service mark.

copyright
[*kop*.ee.rite]

n. The right of an author, granted by federal statute, to exclusively control the reproduction, distribution, and sale of her literary, artistic, or intellectual productions for the period of the copyright's existence. Copyright protection extends to written work, music, films, sound recordings, photographs, paintings, sculpture, and some computer programs and chips. The symbol © is used to show copyright protection. *See also* intellectual property; literary property.
v. To acquire a copyright.

- *n.* authority, grant, license, permit, privilege authorization

copyright infringement
[*kop*.ee.rite in.*frinj*.ment]

Using any portion of a copyrighted material without the consent of the copyright owner. *Compare* fair use doctrine.

copyright notice
[*kop*.ee.rite *no*.tiss]

A notice specifically required in a special form by law in each copy of a published work. EXAMPLE: © or the word copyright.

derivative work
[*de*.riv.e.tiv werk]

A work based upon one or more preexisting works, such as a translation, musical arrangement, dramatization, fictionalization, motion picture version, sound recording, art reproduction, abridgment, condensation, or any other form in which a work may be recast, transformed, or adapted. A work consisting of editorial revisions, annotations, elaborations, or other modifications that, as a whole, represent an original work of authorship is also a derivative work.

DICTIONARY | THESAURUS *continued...*

design patent
[de.*zine pat*.ent]

A patent of a design that gives an original and pleasing appearance to an article.

device
[de.*vice*]

1. In patent law, an invention. 2. An emblem such as a business logo or a union label. 3. An apparatus; machine, appliance, or contrivance.

- *n.* instrument, mechanism, contraption, invention, construction, apparatus ("an eating device")

dilution
[dil.*loo*.shen]

The adverse effect of use of a similar mark on the reputation of a distinctive mark, even though the use may not confuse consumers as to the source of the goods or services; occurs when the defendant's use weakens or reduces the distinctive quality of the mark. A claim of dilution is available only under state laws, sometimes known as antidilution statutes.

disclaimer
[dis.*klame*.er]

Statement that a trademark owner asserts no exclusive right in a specific portion of a mark, apart from its use within the mark.

disparagement
[dis.*pa*.rej.ment]

Discredit; detraction; dishonor; denunciation; disrespect.

disparagement of goods
[dis.*pa*.rej.ment ov goodz]

Criticism that discredits the quality of merchandise or other property offered for sale.

display publicly
[dis.*play pub*.lik.lee]

To show a copy of a copyrighted work, either directly or by means of a film, slide, television image, or any other device or process where the public is gathered or the work is transmitted or otherwise communicated to the public.

distinctive
[dis.*tink*.tiv]

Characteristic, distinguishing, particular, uncommon, idiosyncratic, salient, not indentical, clearly different.

divisional application
[da.*vizh*.an.el ap.li.*kay*.shen]

Application made for an independent invention that has grown out of an earlier application; a method of dividing an original application that contains two or more inventions. Trademark applications may also be divided.

doctrine of equivalents
[*dok*.trin ov ee.*kwiv*.e.lentz]

Right of patent owner to prevent sale, use, or manufacture of a discovery or invention if it employs substantially the same means to achieve substantially the same results in substantially the same way as that claimed.

dramatic works
[dra.*mat*.ik werkz]

Narrative presentations (and any accompanying music) that generally use dialogue and stage directions as the basis for a theatrical exhibition.

drawing (trademark)
[*draw*.ing *trade*.mark]

A substantially exact representation of the mark as used (or, in the case of intent-to-use applications, as intended to be used). A drawing is required for all federal trademark applications and for many state trademark applications.

evaluation agreement [i.val.yoo.*ay*.shen a.*gree*.ment]	Contract by which one party promises to submit an idea and the other party promises to evaluate the idea. After the evaluation, the evaluator will either enter into an agreement to exploit the idea or promise not to use or disclose the idea.
exclusive jurisdiction [eks.*kloo*.siv joo.ris.*dik*.shen]	A court's sole authority to hear a certain type of case.
exclusive license [eks.*kloo*.siv *ly*.sense]	Agreement by patent holder to restrict the grant of proprietary rights to one person.
exhaustion doctrine [eg.*zaws*.chen *dok*.trin]	When a patented product (or product resulting from a patented process) is sold or licensed, the patent owner loses some or all patent rights as to the resale of that particular article.
fair use doctrine [fayr yoos *dok*.trin]	The principle that entitles a person to use copyrighted material in a reasonable manner, including a work's theme or idea, without the consent of the copyright owner. EXAMPLE: teachers photocopying one page of a magazine for students to read.
generic [jen.*err*.ik]	1. Pertaining to a kind, class, or group. 2. General; inclusive. A generic marker or term would lack the distinctiveness for trademark protection. USAGE: A generic drug.
idea [eye.*dee*.uh]	Concept, thought, belief, proposal in the mind of the inventor to be applied to an invention
infringement [in.*frinj*.ment]	A violation of a right or privilege. EXAMPLE: violation of a copyright. • *n.* violation, misfeasance, invasion, encroachment, interference, breach ("infringement of patent")
infringement of copyright [in.*frinj*.ment ov *kop*.ee.rite]	Using any portion of copyrighted material without the consent of the copyright owner. *Compare* fair use doctrine. *See also* copyright.
infringement of patent [in.*frinj*.ment ov *pat*.ent]	The manufacture, use, or sale of a patent or process patent without the authorization of the owner of the patent.
infringement of trademark [in.*frinj*.ment ov *trade*.mark]	A use or imitation of a trademark in such manner that a purchaser of goods is likely to be deceived into believing that they are the goods of the owner of the trademark.
intangible [in.*tan*.jibl]	*adj.* Without physical substance; nonmaterial. *Compare* tangible property. *n.* A thing that may or may not have value, but has no physical substance; an intangible asset or intangible property. EXAMPLES: a copyright; goodwill. *Compare* tangible property. • *adj.* nonphysical, abstract, imperceptible, impalpable
intangible asset [in.*tan*.jibl *ass*.et]	Intangible property that has value. *Compare* tangible property.

intangible property
[in.*tan*.jibl *prop*.er.tee]

1. A right unrelated to a physical thing. EXAMPLES: a right to sue (i.e., a cause of action); a right to inherit property. 2. Property that has no intrinsic value, but evidences something of value. EXAMPLE: a stock certificate (which evidences a share in the ownership of the corporation that issued it). *Compare* tangible property.

intellectual property
[in.te.*lek*.choo.el *prop*.er.tee]

Property (EXAMPLES: copyrights; patents; trade secrets) that is the physical or tangible result of original thought. Modern technology has brought about widespread infringement of intellectual property rights. EXAMPLE: the unauthorized reproduction and sale of videotapes, audiotapes, and computer software. *See also* infringement of copyright, infringement of patent, literary property, piracy.

internet piracy
[in.ter.net *py*.re.see]

Theft conducted on the Internet by illegally copying, downloading, or distributing unauthorized software.

invention
[in.*ven*.shen]

1. The act of creating something patentable. *See also* patent, device. 2. The thing that has been invented. 3. The act of creating something new.

- *n.* finding, discovery, creation

inventor
[in.*ven*.ter]

A person who creates an invention.

- *n.* author, maker, creator, devisor

license
[*ly*.sense]

1. A special privilege, not a right common to everyone. 2. Authorization by the owner of a patent to make, use, or sell the patented article; permission by the owner of a trademark or copyright to use the trademark or to make use of the copyrighted material.

licensee
[ly.sen.*see*]

A person to whom the owner of a patent, copyright, or trademark grants a right to use.

literary property
[*lit*.e.re.ree *prop*.er.tee]

The interest of an author, or anyone to whom he has transferred his interest, in his own work; the exclusive right of an author to use and profit from his own written or printed intellectual production. *See also* intellectual property; literary work; infringement of copyright.

literary work
[*lit*.e.re.ree werk]

In copyright law, "works, other than audiovisual works, expressed in words, numbers, or other verbal or numerical symbols or induced, regardless of the nature of the material objects, such as books, periodicals, manuscripts, phone records, film, tapes, disks, or cards, in which they are embodied."

logo
[*loh*.go]

Graphic symbols that function as a mark. *See also* trademark.

misappropriation of trade secret
[*mis*.a.pro.pree.*ay*.shen ov trayd *see*.kret]

Improper acquisition of a trade secret by a person who has reason to know that the trade secret was obtained by improper means, or the disclosure or use of a trade secret without consent by a person who either had a duty to maintain secrecy or who used improper means to acquire the secret.

moral rights [*mor*.el rytz]	Rights that protect the professional honor and reputation of an artist by guaranteeing the right to claim or disclaim authorship of a work and the right to prevent, in certain cases, distortion, mutilation, or other modification of the work.
motion picture [*moh*.shen *pik*.chur]	Audiovisual works consisting of a series of related images that, when shown in succession, impart an impression of motion with sound, if any.
patent [*pat*.ent]	*n.* 1. The exclusive right of manufacture, sale, or use granted by the federal government to a person who invents or discovers a device or process that is new and useful. *See also* device, invention. 2. The grant of a right, privilege, or authority by the government. The abbreviation "Pat." is often used. *v.* To obtain a patent upon an invention. ▪ *n.* permit, license, certificate, trademark, right, legal right
Patent and Trademark Office [*pat*.ent and *trade*.mark *off*.iss]	Authorized by the Constitution and established by Congress, this office of the federal government registers all trademarks and grants all patents issued in the United States. Its duties also include examining patents, hearing and deciding appeals from inventors and trademark applicants, and publishing the *Official Gazette*.
patent infringement [*pat*.ent in.*frinj*.ment]	*See* infringement of patent.
patent medicine [*pat*.ent *med*.i.sin]	An over-the-counter medication; a medication concocted by a manufacturer, often according to a secret formula. Note that a patent medicine is generally not patented; however, it is often protected by trademark.
patent pending [*pat*.ent *pen*.ding]	The status of a patent application while it is being determined if the invention is new and useful. The symbol used for this is "Pat. Pend."
patent rights [*pat*.ent rytz]	The rights a patentee receives with respect to her invention as a result of having been granted a patent for it.
patentability [*pat*.ent.a.bil.a.tee]	The quality of being patentable.
patentable [*pat*.ent.ebl]	Entitled to receive a patent. To be patentable, an idea must include every essential characteristic of the complete and practical invention.
patentee [pat.en.*tee*]	A person who receives a patent.
pioneer patent [*py*.e.neer *pat*.ent]	A patent in a new field; a totally new device; a basis patent.
piracy [*py*.re.see]	A term for infringement of copyright or for using literary property without permission, plagiarism. ▪ *n.* plagiarism, infringement, appropriation ("Printing an article without the author's permission is piracy.")

DICTIONARY THESAURUS *continued...*

public use
[*pub*.lik yoos]

In patent law, any use of an invention other than a secret or experimental use. If such a use continues for one year or more, prior to the date of patent application, this will prevent the issuance of a patent.

registration
[rej.is.*tray*.shen]

The act of registering.

- *n.* recording, reservation, enrollment, filing, listing

service mark
[*ser*.viss mark]

A mark design, title, or motto used in the sale or advertising of services to identify the services and distinguish them from the services of others. A service mark is the property of its owner and, when registered under the Trademark Act, is reserved for the exclusive use of its owner. *Compare* trademark.

tangible property
[*tan*.jibl *prop*.er.tee]

Property, real or personal, that has physical substance; property that can be physically possessed. EXAMPLES: real estate; automobiles; jewelry.

trade dress
[trayd dres]

The size, shape, texture, color, graphics, and other distinct features of a product that constitute its total appearance used to promote the sale of the product.

trade libel
[trayd *ly*.bel]

A libel that defames the goods or products a person produces in her business or occupation, as opposed to a libel against the person herself.

trademark
[trayd.mark]

A mark, design, title, logo, or motto used in the sale or advertising of products to identify them and distinguish them from the products of others. A trademark is the property of its owner and, when registered under the Trademark Act, is reserved for the exclusive use of its owner. The symbol ® is used to indicate a registered trademark. *Compare* service mark, trade name. *See also* collective mark.

- *n.* logo, brand, identification, mark, design, initials, logotype, stamp

trademark infringement
[trayd.mark in.*frinj*.ment]

Use of a substantially similar mark by a junior user that creates a likelihood of consumer confusion. *See also* infringement of trademark.

trademark license
[trayd.mark *ly*.sense]

Agreement granting limited trademark rights to another.

trade name
[trayd naym]

The name under which a company does business. The goodwill of a company includes its trade name. *Compare* trademark.

trade secret
[trayd *see*.kret]

Confidential information concerning an industrial process or the way in which a business is conducted. Trade secrets are of special value to a business and are the property of the business. EXAMPLE: a secret ingredient in a fried chicken recipe.

transfer of copyright ownership
[tranz.*fer* ov *kop*.ee.rite *oh*.ner.ship]

An assignment, mortgage, exclusive license, transfer by will or intestate succession, or any other change in the ownership of any or all of the exclusive rights in a copyright, whether or not it is limited in time or place of effect, but not including a nonexclusive license.

transmit
[tranz.*mit*]

To communicate a copyrighted work by any device or process where images or sounds are received beyond the place from which they are sent.

tying
[*tye*.ing]

Business practice in which the purchase of a patented item is tied to a second, non-patented item. An unjustified tying arrangement is patent misuse (also called tie-in). EXAMPLE: when someone uses the electronic product of one company, he must use a special device from another company for the first product to function.

unfair competition
[un.*fare* kom.pe.*tish*.en]

A collection of common law principles that protect against unfair business practices. The use or imitation of another firm's name, mark, logo design, or title for the purpose of creating confusion in the public mind and causing the public to believe that a competitor's business or product is one's own. Such practices are illegal.

useful article
[*yoos*.ful *ar*.tikl]

An article having an intrinsic utilitarian function that is not merely to portray the appearance of the article or to convey information. An article that is normally a part of a useful article is considered a useful article.

usefulness
[*yoos*.ful.ness]

An invention must be new and have a use or purpose and must work (i.e., be capable of performing its intended purpose).

use in commerce
[*yoos* in *kom*.erss]

Use of a trademark by placing it on goods or containers, tags or labels, displays associated with the goods (or, if otherwise impracticable, on documents associated with the goods), and selling or transporting the goods in commerce regulated by the United States.

utility patents
[yoo.*til*.i.tee *pat*.entz]

The most common type of patent, granted on the basis that the invention is of benefit to society.

visually perceptible copy
[*vizh*.yoo.e.lee per.*sep*.ta.ble *kop*.ee]

A copy that can be visually observed when it is embodied in a material object, either directly or with the aid of a machine or device.

work of authorship
[werk ov *aw*.ther.ship]

Creation of intellectual or artistic effort fixed or embodied in a perceptible form and meeting the statutory standards of copyright protection.

work of visual art
[werk ov *vizh*.yoo.ul art]

Under the Copyright Act of 1976, either (1) a painting, drawing, print, or sculpture, existing in a single copy, in a limited edition of 200 copies or fewer that are signed and consecutively numbered by the author, or, in the case of a sculpture, in multiple cast, carved, or fabricated sculptures of 200 or fewer that are consecutively numbered by the author and bear the signature or other identifying mark of the author; or (2) a still photographic image produced for exhibition purposes only, existing in a single copy that is signed by the author.

work made for hire
[werk mayd for hyer]

1. A work prepared by an employee within the scope of his or her employment.
2. A work specially ordered or commissioned for use as a contribution to a collective work, as a part of a motion picture or other audiovisual work, as a translation, as a supplementary work, as a compilation, as an instructional text, as a test, as answer material for a test, or as an atlas, if the parties expressly agree in a written instrument signed by them that the work shall be considered a work made for hire.

| DICTIONARY | THESAURUS *continued...* |

writ of seizure
[rit ov *seez*.zher]

Order of the court directing the federal marshal to seize and hold infringing merchandise; granted only upon payment of a bond.

writing
[*write*.ing]

1. Anything that is written. The Uniform Commercial Code defines "written" or "writing" to include "printing, typewriting, or any other intentional reduction (or words) to tangible form." 2. The expression of ideas by visible letters, numbers, or other symbols.

Missing Words

Fill in the blanks.

1. A(n) _____ is a summary of the invention that enables the reader to determine the character of the patentable subject matter.

2. Confidential information concerning an industrial process or the way in which a business is conducted is known as a(n) _____.

3. The _____ doctrine is the principle that entitles a person to use copyrighted material without consent of the copyright owner.

4. The right of an author to control the reproduction, sale, and distribution of literary, artistic, or intellectual productions is known as _____.

5. When any portion of a copyrighted material is used without the consent of the owner, this is called _____ of copyright.

6. A(n) _____ is the name under which a company does business.

7. _____ are the expression of ideas by visible letters, numbers, or other symbols.

8. A person who makes a written work is a(n) _____.

9. The act of creating something patentable is known as a(n) _____.

10. Authorization by the owner of a patent to make, use, or sell the patented article is known as a(n) _____.

11. A mark, design, title, or motto used in the sale or advertising of services is known as a(n) _____.

12. A graphic symbol that functions as a mark is a(n) _____.

13. A work based upon one or more preexisting works such as a translation or musical arrangement is known as a(n) _____.

14. In patent law, another word for an invention is a(n) _____.

15. A trademark used to identify a trade association is a(n) _____.

16. _____ pertains to a kind, class, or group.

17. In patent law _____ is any use of an invention other than a secret or experimental use.

18. _____ is the distinct features of a product used to promote its sale.

STUDY AID: Use flashcards for this unit before completing the exercises.

Matching

Match the letter of the definition to the term.

_____ **19.** writing

_____ **20.** trademark

_____ **21.** inventor

_____ **22.** collective mark

_____ **23.** disparagement of goods

_____ **24.** intellectual property

_____ **25.** dilution

_____ **26.** author

_____ **27.** distinctive

_____ **28.** tying

_____ **29.** pioneer patent

_____ **30.** access

_____ **31.** abstract

A. a trademark or service mark used to identify a trade association, fraternal society, or union

B. the adverse effect of use of a similar mark on the reputation of a distinctive mark

C. the expression of ideas by visible letters, numbers, or other symbols

D. business practice where the purchase of a patented item is tied to a second, nonpatented item

E. a mark, design, title, logo, or motto used in the sale or advertising of products

F. a person who produces a written work

G. criticism that discredits the quality of merchandise or other property offered for sale

H. uncommon or distinguishing

I. a person who creates an invention

J. property that is the physical or tangible result of original thought

K. reasonable opportunity to view or hear copyrighted work

L. summary of an invention

M. patent in a new field

_____ **32.** trade dress   **N.** size, shape, texture, color, and graphics of a product

_____ **33.** piracy   **O.** an invention

_____ **34.** device   **P.** a term of infringement

_____ **35.** licensee   **Q.** a person who is granted a right to use

Multiple Choice

Select the best choice.

_____ **36.** The exclusive right to manufacture a new and useful device is known as:
a. copyright.
b. service mark.
c. trademark.
d. patent.

_____ **37.** The symbol used to show that a writing is copyrighted is:
a. Ⓣ.
b. ®.
c. ©.
d. @.

_____ **38.** In order to protect an original writing, an author might obtain a:
a. patent.
b. copyright.
c. generic name.
d. collective mark.

_____ **39.** The fair use doctrine:
a. entitles a person to use patented materials.
b. entitles a person to use copyrighted material.
c. prohibits a person from using patented material.
d. prohibits a person from using copyrighted material.

_____ **40.** The following abbreviation is used to show an invention has been patented:
a. Pate.
b. Paten.
c. Pa.
d. Pat.

_____ **41.** A graphic symbol that functions as a mark is called a:
a. logo.
b. license.
c. patent.
d. patentee.

_____ **42.** When a business uses a mark in the sale of advertising products and distinguishes them, that is known as:
a. palming off.
b. misappropriation.
c. trademark.
d. invention.

_____ **43.** Confidential information concerning an industrial process or the way in which a business is conducted is known as a:
a. service mark.
b. trade secret.
c. generic name.
d. secondary meaning.

_____ **44.** Copyright protection covers:
a. written works.
b. music and film.
c. photographs and paintings.
d. all of the above.

_____ **45.** Client lists and secret recipes are examples of:
a. generic name.
b. service mark.
c. copyright.
d. trade secrets.

_____ **46.** The owner of a registered trademark is entitled to use which of the following symbols?
  a. Ⓣ
  b. TM
  c. S
  d. ®

_____ **47.** The primary copyright record made for a work is called:
  a. tying.
  b. dilution.
  c. basic registration.
  d. disclaimer.

True/False

Mark the following T or F.

_____ **48.** The fair use doctrine permits teachers to photocopy portions of copyrighted works for use in the classroom.

_____ **49.** A trademark is used in the sale or advertising of a service.

_____ **50.** A musician should obtain a patent to protect a new song.

_____ **51.** Copyright protection is needed to protect an inventor's interest in a new invention.

_____ **52.** An artist who paints a portrait should obtain a service mark to protect her creation.

_____ **53.** A trade secret is of little value to a business.

_____ **54.** When an author has an idea for a new novel, this is an example of a tangible writing.

_____ **55.** Misappropriation of trade secrets occurs when the seller of goods misrepresents himself as someone else to induce a buyer to purchase something.

_____ **56.** Disparagement of goods occurs when someone criticizes the quality of merchandise or other property for sale.

_____ **57.** The office of the federal government that registers all trademarks and grants all patents is known as the Patent and Trademark Office.

_____ **58.** Intellectual property is that property which is the physical or tangible result of original thought.

_____ **59.** Dilution occurs when company A uses a mark that is similar to the mark of company B, thus hurting the reputation of company B, a distinct business.

_____ **60.** To be patentable, an invention must be new and useful.

_____ **61.** A pioneer patent is any patent issued before 1872.

_____ **62.** Intangible property is a right unrelated to a tangible thing.

Synonyms

Select the correct synonym in parentheses for each numbered item.

63. TANGIBLE
    (touchable, imaginary, fake)

64. DISTINCTIVE
    (usual, common, distinguishing)

65. ORIGINAL
    (unique, copy, irregular)

66. MISAPPROPRIATE
    (take, give, review)

67. DISPARAGEMENT
    (praise, criticize, demonstrate)

68. PIRACY
    (infringement, sale, barter)

69. ABSTRACT
    (revelation, secret, summary)

70. PUBLIC USE
    (secret, experimental, non-private)

71. INVENTION
    (edition, distraction, discovery)

72. WRITING
    (print, oral, action)

73. INFRINGEMENT
    (inflation, breach, admission)

74. REGISTRATION OF TRADEMARK
    (filing, typing, copying)

75. COLLECTIVE MARK
    (trade association, individual, government)

76. TRADE NAME
    (trademark, patent, goodwill)

77. INVENTOR
    (piracy, creator, purchaser)

78. LICENSE
    (privilege, fair use, logo)

79. TRANSMIT
    (sell, reduce, communicate)

80. USEFULNESS
    (worthless, purpose, arrangement)

81. GENERIC
    (pertaining to an individual, a group, valuable)

82. DILUTION
    (strengthens, weakens, beautifies)

83. DEVICE
    (invention, infringement, injustice)

84. DISPARAGEMENT
    (praise, control, criticism)

Self-Test

Place the number of the correct term in the appropriate space.

85. patent infringement

86. trade secrets

87. author

88. fair use doctrine

89. trademark

90. copyright infringement

91. unfair competition

92. misappropriation of trade secrets

93. copyright

94. service mark

95. intellectual property
96. patent

97. trademark infringement
98. piracy

Property that is the physical or tangible result of original thought is called _____. Should a(n) _____ produce a written work such as a song or book, and desire exclusive control of the reproduction and sale of the work, he should obtain _____ protection. A person who creates an invention and seeks the exclusive right to manufacture and sell the invention should apply for a(n) _____ through the Patent and Trademark Office. In the event a mark, design, title, logo, or motto is used in the sale or advertising of a product, a(n) _____ should be registered. Another property of a business that is of special value and needs to be protected is _____, the confidential information concerning an industrial process or the way in which a business is conducted. Should a business use a mark, design, title, or motto in the sale or advertising of services, a(n) _____ should be registered.

Much to the surprise of many authors, copyright protection does not guarantee that the public won't be allowed to use copyrighted material. The _____ entitles a person to use copyrighted material in a reasonable manner, without the consent of the copyright owner.

When intellectual property rights are violated, this is called _____. When trade secrets are improperly acquired, this is called _____. When a patent is used without authorization of the owner, _____ occurs. The infringement of copyright protection is called _____. There is _____ when one business uses a mark similar to another company's mark to create consumer confusion. Many unfair business practices are called_____.

Word Scramble

Unscramble the following words and write the correct word(s) that match(es) the definition for each word or phrase.

99. tapent – protection offered to an inventor _____

_____

100. demarktra – a mark used in the advertising of a product _____

_____

101. pyrightco – an author's right to control intellectual property _____

_____

102. llectualinte ertyprop – property that is the result of original thought _____

_____

103. tincdistive – distinguishing, uncommon _____

_____

104. energic mane – pertaining to a kind, class, or group

_____

_____

105. ublicp sue enirtcod – use of another's invention other than for secret use _____

    _____

106. viceser kmar – a mark used to sell a service _____

    _____

107. detra terces – confidential information that is of great use to a company _____

    _____

108. ticmadra kswor – used for theatrical purposes _____

    _____

109. aryliter pertypro – right of an author to profit from her work _____

    _____

110. neepiro tentpa – a patent in a new field _____

    _____

111. gtyin – include a nonpatentable product with sale of patentable product _____

    _____

112. lutiondi – weakening the effect of a mark _____

    _____

113. radet serds – distinct feature of a product, its total appearance used to sell a product_____

    _____

The Last Word

A "copyright troll" is a company whose business model profits from lawsuits against online infringements of copyrighted material. The company surfs the web, trolling or looking for actionable infringements. The nation's first successful copyright troll is Righthaven, an attorney-owned entity that sues on behalf of a newspaper.

Entire stories published by the *Las Vegas Review-Journal* were posted by Dr. Shezad Malik at the Dallas-Ft.Worth Injury Lawyer Blog.

Without notice, Righthaven sued Dr. Malik, who claimed the Nevada court lacked jurisdiction to hear the case because the defendant did not do business in the state. The court disagreed. When Righthaven finds stolen content on the Internet, it purchases copyrights from the pirated party and sues the defendants immediately. Some defendants report being sued for $75,000 and quickly offered settlement for $7,500. The Electronic Frontier Foundation (EFF), an online freedom of speech organization, criticized Righthaven for "seeking to take advantage of copyright (laws') draconian damages in order to bully Internet users into forking over money."

In fact, Righthaven files suits without warnings or notices to take down the content. Typically, sending "cease and desist" letters prior to suit is the prescribed method authorized by the Digital Millennium Copyright Act's "safe harbor" provision. In his defense, Dr. Malik said he was protected because the "safe harbor" provision shields users who had "insufficient notice" of the copyright infringements. Again, the federal judge found for the copyright troll. Is notice to an infringing user of Internet content less important than the owner's right to charge for his intellectual property?

PART

6

Tax Law, and the Law of Wills, Trusts, and Estates

OBJECTIVES

- Learn about the tax law, and wills, trusts, and estates.

- Master the similarities and differences in definitions of key terms.

- Master the pronunciations and spellings of legal terms.

- Recognize the synonyms used for legal terminology.

- Practice usage of terms, definitions, and synonyms.

- Complete unit exercises in the forms of missing words, matching, multiple choice, true/false, synonyms, self-test, and word scramble.

- Work with a legal dictionary/thesaurus.

10 Tax Law

The government uses taxes as a source of raising revenue and regulating the economy. Individuals and businesses are taxed by federal, state, and local levels of government. Taxpayers pay taxes on wages, capital gains, estates, earned income, gifts, real estate, purchases of goods, even on the receipt of services.

Some taxpayers prepare and file their own income tax returns with the Internal Revenue Service (IRS), while others require the services of an attorney, accountant, or other tax preparer. It is no longer necessary to file hard copies of income tax returns; completed tax forms can now be e-mailed directly to the IRS. A taxpayer who needs more time to review and collect documents to prepare tax returns can request an extension of time for the filing of tax returns.

Accurate and detailed records and receipts must be kept. Taxpayers must be able to determine their total income for each year. Most income is taxable income; certain deductions and credits reduce the taxable amount. Married couples can claim a marital deduction for property passing from one spouse to the other upon death. Families receive exemptions for their dependent children. Depending on an individual's tax bracket and the amount of taxes withheld from bonuses and commissions as well as salary, he may still owe the government additional taxes. Upon hire, taxpayers must fill out W-4 forms for payroll purposes, and may claim an exemption for each dependent person in their households. When an employer deducts federal and state income tax and FICA contributions from the pay of employees and remits them to the federal and state governments this is called a withholding tax. Those who have overpaid withholding taxes receive a refund from the IRS. Wage earners who don't receive a regular salary, such as independent contractors, freelancers, or the self-employed, must submit quarterly estimated tax payments to the IRS.

Taxpayers who realize that there have been errors or omissions in their already filed tax return can submit an amended return. Taxes that are owed from a prior date are called back taxes. Those who have falsely reported income, or underpaid taxes, might be the subject of an IRS tax audit. All of the taxpayer's books and records may be examined to determine the accuracy of the return. Tax evasion, also known as tax fraud, is very serious and could result in a felony charge, penalties, and fines. Taxpayers who fail to settle or disagree with the Internal Revenue Service's ruling can file an appeal and can ultimately resort to the tax courts for relief. In the following tax case, the importance of understanding legal terminology comes into play at the expense of the taxpayer.

CASE AND COMMENT

U.S. Court of Appeals for the First Circuit
United States of America, Plaintiff-Appellee
v.
John J. Lavoie, Defendant-Appellant
433 F.3 95
No. 04-1982
December 22, 2005
Appeal from the U.S. District Court of Massachusetts

Facts: Lavoie was the sole owner of a business engaged in installing and repairing heating and air conditioning systems. As a business owner he had to file a Schedule C form showing the details of his business profits and losses. As of 1993, he had yet to file his 1990, 1991, and 1992 tax forms. After being contacted by the IRS, Lavoie contacted an accountant to fill out his tax forms. Lavoie's business records were unorganized, so he created a one-page summary of his business profits and losses rather than giving the actual records to the accountant. The accountant prepared the forms based on the summary and sent Lavoie the signature pages of the forms. Then the IRS contacted Lavoie for a review. When Lavoie turned over his actual records, it was determined that he had grossly underreported his gross receipts.

Procedural History: A jury convicted defendant Lavoie of evading federal income taxes and he was sentenced to 28 months of probation and 4 months of home detention. On appeal Lavoie contended there was not sufficient evidence to show he acted willfully.

Issue: Whether there was sufficient evidence for a jury to find that defendant Lavoie acted willfully in evading federal income taxes.

Rationale: To show Lavoie acted willfully there must be more than a showing that he simply acted with careless disregard for the truth. A mere underreporting does not require a finding of willfulness; it could be caused by negligence or inadvertence. In his defense, Lavoie claims he confused the terminology of gross receipt and net receipt.

Ruling: The evidence of Lavoie's willfulness in evading taxes is not overwhelming. From the evidence presented at trial, inferences could be drawn in favor of willful tax evasion or in favor of a misunderstanding of the difference between gross receipts and net receipts. Convictions are based on the weight of the evidence and not the number of evidentiary submissions. Taking all inferences in favor of the government, we believe that a reasonable jury could find beyond a reasonable doubt that Lavoie willfully evaded taxes. The decision of the lower court is affirmed.

Comment: The court found it probative that the defendant underreported both his gross receipts and his costs of goods by about a factor of two. Do you agree or disagree with the appellate court's decision that this demonstrates willful tax evasion?

DICTIONARY   THESAURUS

| Term [phonetic pronunciation] | *Note: All dictionary/thesaurus terms appear on flashcards at the back of the book and on the student website.* |

accelerated depreciation
[ak.*sel*.e.ray.ted de.pree.shee.*ay*.shen]
Rapid depreciation of the value of a capital asset in order to produce larger tax deductions during the early years of the life of the asset. *Compare* straight-line depreciation. *See also* depreciation.

accrued income
[a.*krewd in*.kum]
Income that a person has earned but has not yet claimed. *See also* income; earned income.

accrued interest
[a.*krewd in*.trest]
Interest that has been earned but has not yet been paid.

ad valorem tax
[ad va.*lore*.em takz]
A tax established in proportion to the value of the property to be taxed. EXAMPLE: a tax of $3 on an antique worth $100 and $9 on an antique worth $300, the tax being 3 percent of the value, as distinguished from a $5 tax regardless of the value of the antique.

adjusted
[a.*just*.ed]
1. Corrected; balanced. 2. Brought into line.

adjusted basis
[a.*just*.ed *bay*.siss]
For the purpose of calculating the amount of income tax due, the original cost of property offset for such things as casualty losses and depreciation.

adjusted gross income
[a.*just*.ed *grose in*.kum]
An income tax term for gross income less the deductions (generally, business expenses) permitted by law. *Compare* taxable income.

amended return
[a.*mend*.ed re.*tern*]
Within the limitations prescribed by law, amended tax returns may be filed to correct inaccuracies and omissions in the original return. *See also* return.

amortization
[am.er.ti.*zay*.shen]
The act of amortizing. *See also* amortize.

amortize
[*am*.er.tize]
1. To gradually pay off a debt by regular payments in a fixed amount over a fixed period of time. 2. To depreciate an intangible asset (EXAMPLES: stock; bills).

appreciation
[a.pree.she.*ay*.shen]
An increase in the value of something. *Compare* to depreciation.

assessment
[a.*sess*.ment]
1. Imposing of tax on the basis of a listing and valuation of the property to be taxed. 2. Requiring a payment above and beyond that which is normal. EXAMPLE: the imposition of a 15 percent penalty on property taxes paid after a certain date.

assessor
[a.*sess*.er]
A public official who makes an assessment of property, usually for purposes of taxation.

- *n.* charger, estimator, collector

DICTIONARY   THESAURUS *continued...*

audit
[*aw*.dit]

1. A formal or official examination and verification of accounts, vouchers, and other financial records as, for EXAMPLE, a tax audit or an independent audit of a company's books and records. 2. Any verification of figures by an accountant.

- *n.* analysis, review, scrutiny, verification ("The audit is complete.")
- *v.* analyze, balance, investigate, examine, monitor, probe ("The accountant audited the books.")

auditor
[*aw*.dit.er]

1. A person who conducts an audit. 2. A civil servant whose duty it is to examine the accounts of state officials to determine whether they have spent public funds in accordance with the law.

- *n.* accountant, bookkeeper, cashier, inspector

back taxes
[back *tak*.sez]

1. Taxes that are owed from a prior date. 2. Taxes on which the ordinary processes for collection have been exhausted.

basis
[*bay*.siss]

In tax law, the cost of property as of a certain date, upon which depreciation can be computed and gain or loss can be calculated when the property is sold or exchanged.

- *n.* cost ("the tax basis of the property")

capital
[*ka*.pi.tel]

adj. Relating to wealth.
n. 1. Broadly, the total assets of a business. 2. Money or property used for the production of wealth. 3. An owner's equity in a business.

- *n.* cash, stock, wealth, holdings, financial assets, funds, resources

capital assets
[*ka*.pi.tel *ass*.ets]

All assets except those excluded from that category by the Internal Revenue Code.

capital gain
[*ka*.pi.tel gayn]

Financial gain resulting from the sale or exchange of capital assets. *See also* gain.

capital gains tax
[*ka*.pi.tel gaynz takz]

Income tax upon financial gain resulting from the sale or exchange of capital assets. *See also* gain.

death taxes
[deth *tak*.sez]

Another term for inheritance taxes or estate taxes.

declaration of estimated tax
[dek.le.*ray*.shen ov *ess*.ti.may.ted takz]

A formal estimate of income anticipated during the forthcoming tax year, required under federal and state tax codes from corporations, trusts, and estates, and individuals who receive income that is not subject to withholding (generally, income other than wages). Such declarations must be accompanied by payment of the estimated tax.

deductible
[de.*duk*.tibl]

Expenses that a taxpayer is permitted to subtract, in whole or in part, in computing her taxable income. EXAMPLES: interest on the mortgage on one's home; casualty losses; charitable contributions. *See also* deduction.

- *adj.* removable, allowable, discountable

deduction
[de.*duk*.shen]

1. The amount allowed a taxpayer in reduction of gross income for the purpose of determining adjusted gross income. 2. That which may be taken away or subtracted, particularly money.

- *n.* subtraction, withdrawal, removal, exemption, allowance ("the home office deduction")

deferred
[de.*ferd*]

Put off to a future time; postponed.

deferred income
[de.*ferd in*.kum]

A tax law term for payments received before they are earned. (EXAMPLE: payment of $1,000 in 2010 to a tutor who is to provide 20 lessons in 2011)

dependent
[dee.*pen*.dent]

In tax law, a person whose relationship to the taxpayer is such that the taxpayer is entitled to claim her as an exemption when filing his income tax return. EXAMPLE: a child of the taxpayer who is less than 19 years of age.

- *n.* minor, charge, ward

depreciation
[dee.pree.shee.*ay*.shen]

1. The lessening in worth of any property caused by wear, use, time, or obsolescence. *Compare* appreciation. 2. In computing income tax, a deduction allowed for the gradual loss of usefulness of a capital asset used in business or in the production of income.

- *n.* devaluation, reduction, deflation
- *ant.* appreciation

direct tax
[dye.*rekt* takz]

A tax (also called a property tax or an ad valorem tax) levied directly on real or personal property based upon value, or directly upon income (i.e., an income tax). Such a tax should be distinguished from an indirect tax, which is levied upon the importation, consumption, manufacture, or sale of articles and upon the privilege of doing business or engaging in a profession.

earn
[urn]

Receive as a result of labor or services.

- *v.* gain, draw, win, acquire ("earn wages")

earned
[urnd]

1. Received as a result of labor or service. 2. Gained; acquired.

earned income
[urnd *in*.kum]

Income received for work or for the performance of some service. Unearned income includes dividends, interest, etc.

earned income credit
[urnd *in*.kum *kred*.it]

A tax credit on earned income for low income workers with dependent children, as defined by the Internal Revenue Code.

equalization of taxes
[ee.kwe.li.*zay*.shen ov *tak*.sez]

Carried out by boards of equalization; the process of adjusting the total assessments on all real estate in a tax district to equalize them with the total assessments in other tax districts in the state, the goal being equality and uniformity in taxation.

DICTIONARY | THESAURUS *continued...*

estate tax
[es.*tate* takz]

A tax imposed by the federal government and most states upon the transmission of property by a deceased person. The tax is imposed upon the net estate of the decedent without reference to the recipient's relationship to the decedent or to the amount a recipient receives. An estate tax is a transfer tax. *See also* inheritance, or death, taxes.

exemption
[eg.*zemp*.shen]

1. An allowance granted by way of a deduction when computing one's taxable income. EXAMPLES: a tax exemption for a dependent; a personal exemption. 2. The person for whom an exemption may be claimed in an income tax return.

extension of time
[eks.*ten*.shen ov time]

1. Modification of an obligation by giving additional time for performance. 2. An enlargement of time.

Federal Insurance Contributions Act
[*fed*.er.el in.*shoor*.ense kon.tri.*byoo*.shenz akt]

The federal statute that funds Social Security and Medicare by taxing employers, the wages of employees, and the earnings of the self-employed. Most people are aware of this law because of the FICA deduction that appears on their pay stub.

FICA
[fy.ka]

See Federal Insurance Contributions Act.

fiscal year
[*fis*.kel yeer]

An accounting period of 12 consecutive months. Both businesses and individuals may choose any such 12-month period as their tax year. A fiscal year is often referred to by its abbreviation, FY.

gain
[gayn]

1. Earnings; profits; proceeds; return; yield; interest; increase; addition. 2. Excess of revenue over expense. *Compare* loss.

- *n.* acquisition, profit, appreciation, enhancement

gift tax
[gift takz]

A tax on the transfer by gift, by a living person, of money or other property. The federal government and most states impose gift taxes. By comparison, there are distinctly different tax consequences if the transfer of the gift occurs upon the death of the donor (*see also* estate tax). Additionally, special tax considerations apply to gifts made by living persons in contemplation of death. A gift tax is a transfer tax.

gross
[grose]

adj. Without deduction; as a whole; entire; total. EXAMPLES: gross earnings; gross income; gross pay. *Compare* net income.

gross estate
[grose es.*tate*]

1. The value of all property left by a decedent, before payment of taxes and expenses. 2. The value of all taxable property in a decedent's estate.

gross income
[grose *in*.kum]

1. Total income. 2. The whole or entire profit from a business. 3. Under the Internal Revenue Code, "all income from whatever source derived," before allowance for deductions or exemptions. *Compare* net income. *See also* adjusted gross income.

head of household
[hed ov *house*.hold]

A single person, other than a surviving spouse, who provides a home for certain persons, generally dependents. Also, married persons who live apart are each a head of household. A head of household is entitled to pay federal income tax at a lower rate than other single persons.

income
[*in*.kum]

The gain derived from capital or from labor, including profit gained through a sale or conversion of capital assets. *See also* adjusted gross income; earned income; gross income; net income; taxable income.

- *n.* wages, salary, earning, profit, livelihood

income tax
[*in*.kum takz]

A tax based on income, personal or corporate. The Internal Revenue Code, which is the federal tax law, taxes income from "whatever source derived." Many states and municipalities tax income as well.

income tax return
[*in*.kum takz re.*tern*]

See tax return.

individual retirement account
[in.de.*vid*.joo.el re.*tire*.ment a.*kount*]

Under the Internal Revenue Code, individuals who are not included in an employer-maintained retirement plan may deposit money (up to an annual maximum amount set by the Code) in an account for the purchase of retirement annuities. No tax is paid on income deposited to an IRA, and the proceeds are taxable only when they are withdrawn.

inheritance tax
[in.*hehr*.i.tense taks]

A tax on the privilege of taking the property of a decedent by descent or under a will, but not as a tax on the decedent's right to dispose of his property or a tax on the property itself. *Compare* estate tax. *See* death taxes.

Internal Revenue Code
[in.*tern*.el *rev*.e.new kode]

A compilation of all federal statutes that impose taxes (EXAMPLES: income tax, estate tax; gift tax; excise tax) or provide for the administration of such laws.

IRS

Abbreviation for Internal Revenue Service.

Internal Revenue Service
[in.*tern*.el *rev*.e.new *ser*.viss]

Popularly known as the IRS, the organization that administers and enforces the Internal Revenue Code. The Internal Revenue Service is an agency within the Department of the Treasury.

joint return
[joynt re.*tern*]

A single income tax return filed by a husband and wife reporting their combined incomes. Although married persons are entitled to file separately, their total tax liability is usually greater if they do.

loss
[loss]

The term is also applied extensively in tax law, where it is used in contradistinction to gain, and refers to transactions involving an excess of expense over revenue.

marital deduction
[*mehr*.i.tel de.*duk*.shen]

In computing the taxable estate, a deduction allowed under both the federal estate tax and gift tax with respect to property passing from one spouse to the other.

DICTIONARY   THESAURUS *continued...*

net income [net *in*.kum]	Gross income less ordinary and necessary expenses; taxable income. *Compare* gross income.
penalty [*pen*.el.tee]	An additional charge because of a delinquency in making payment. The IRS imposes such a penalty on taxpayers who file late tax returns. *Note* that a penalty is not interest, and is usually assessed in addition to interest. ■ *n.* sanction, sentence, forfeiture, castigation, retribution, punishment
return [re.*tern*]	A formal accounting of a person's income; for EXAMPLE, a tax return.
Roth IRA [Rawth eye.rah]	A type of retirement account permitted under the tax laws that allows a tax reduction on some of the money deposited for retirement. Individuals pay income tax and then make their contributions with post-tax dollars. The principal grows tax-free. There are no further taxes when the money is withdrawn for retirement.
straight-line depreciation [strayt-line de.*pree*.shee.*ay*.shen]	A method of depreciating an asset at an even pace by subtracting its estimated salvage value from its cost and dividing the remainder by the number of years of its estimated useful life. *Compare* accelerated depreciation. *See also* depreciation.
tax [takz]	An involuntary charge imposed by the government (whether national, state, or local, or any of their political subdivisions) upon individuals, corporations, or trusts, or their income or property, to provide revenue for the support of the government. Taxes may be imposed on, among other things, sales, gifts, and estates, and may be called, among other things, imposts, duties, excises, levies, and assessments. EXAMPLES of different types of taxes include: ad valorem tax, capital gains tax, estate tax, excise tax, export tax, franchise tax, gift tax, income tax, inheritance taxes, intangibles tax, luxury tax, occupation tax, payroll tax, privilege tax, property tax, sales tax, school taxes, and transfer tax. ■ *n.* levy, assessment, tribute, impost, exaction, imposition, capitulation, tithe ("a graduated tax") ■ *v.* assess, levy, exact, collect, require
tax audit [takz a*w*.dit]	An examination by the IRS of a taxpayer's books and records to determine the accuracy of his income tax return.
tax bracket [takz *brak*.et]	A taxpayer's tax rate category. "Tax bracket" is synonymous with tax rate, and is based upon the amount of the taxpayer's taxable income.
tax credit [takz *kred*.it]	A credit that reduces the amount of income tax owed by a taxpayer, as opposed to a deduction, which merely reduces a taxpayer's taxable income. *See also* exemption.
tax evasion [takz e.*vay*.zhen]	Willfully avoiding payment of taxes legally due; for EXAMPLE, fraudulently concealing or understating one's income. Tax evasion is also referred to as tax fraud and is a felony.

tax exemption
[takz eg.*zemp*.shen]

1. Freedom from the obligation to pay taxes. 2. A personal exemption under the Internal Revenue Code. *See also* exemption.

tax return
[takz re.*tern*]

1. A formal accounting that every person who has income is required to make to the government every tax year; the form on which a taxpayer reports his taxable income annually and on the basis of which he pays his income tax. 2. Independent of income, any formal accounting required by law to be made to any taxing authority with respect to property, gifts, estates, sales, or the like. *See also* return, amended return, declaration of estimated tax, joint return.

taxable
[*tak*.sebl]

Subject to tax; liable to taxation.

- *adj.* liable to taxation, assessable, chargeable, exactable ("a taxable gift")

taxable income
[*tak*.sebl *in*.kum]

With respect to liability for federal income tax; in the case of an individual, adjusted gross income, less itemized deductions, or the standard deduction plus personal exemptions; in the case of a corporation, gross income less deductions.

taxation
[tak.*say*.shen]

The act or process of levying, assessing, and collecting taxes; the act of taxing.

taxing
[*tak*.sing]

The act or process of levying, assessing, and collecting a tax; taxation.

taxpayer
[*taks*.pay.er]

A person who is under a legal obligation to pay a tax; a person who has paid a tax.

W-2 wage and tax statement
[W-2 wayj and takz *stayt*.ment]

A form issued to a taxpayer annually showing earnings summary as well as withholding taxes.

W-4 form
[W-4 form]

A document in which taxpayers state the number of exemptions claimed for employer's payroll purposes per IRS regulations.

withholding tax
[with.*hole*.ding takz]

Federal and state income tax and FICA contributions deducted by an employer from the pay of employees and remitted by the employer to the IRS.

Missing Words

Fill in the blanks.

1. _____ is when someone willfully avoids payment of taxes legally due.

2. _____ is the rapid depreciation of the value of a capital asset.

3. Gross income less the deductions permitted by law is called _____.

4. _____ is the tax imposed by the federal government and, in most states, upon the transmission of property by a deceased person.

5. _____ are taxes that are in arrears.

6. An excess of revenue over expenses is called _____.

7. An allowance granted by way of a deduction when computing one's taxable income is a(n) _____.

8. The _____ is a compilation of all federal statutes that impose taxes or provide for the administration of such laws.

9. _____ is the income received for work or the performance of some service.

10. All income from whatever source derived is _____.

11. A transaction involving an excess of expense over revenue is called a(n) _____.

12. A(n) _____ is imposed upon taxpayers who file late tax returns.

13. A(n) _____ is a single income tax return filed by a husband and wife reporting their combined incomes.

14. A(n) _____ is an involuntary charge imposed by the government to provide revenue for the support of the government.

15. A(n) _____ is a person under a legal obligation to pay a tax.

16. _____ refers to payments received before they are earned.

17. An accounting period of 12 consecutive months is a(n) _____.

18. The lessening in worth of any property caused by wear, use, time, or obsolescence is _____.

19. An examination of a taxpayer's books and records by the IRS to determine accuracy of an income tax return is _____.

20. A public official who makes an assessment of property is _____.

STUDY AID: Use flashcards for this unit before completing the exercises.

Matching

Match the letter of the definition to the term.

_____ **21.** accrued income

_____ **22.** Internal Revenue Service

_____ **23.** exemption

_____ **24.** loss

_____ **25.** tax

_____ **26.** tax bracket

_____ **27.** Form W-2

_____ **28.** IRA

_____ **29.** appreciation

_____ **30.** itemized deduction

_____ **31.** penalty

_____ **32.** amended return

_____ **33.** extension

_____ **34.** fiscal year

A. an allowance granted by way of a deduction

B. income that a person has earned but has not yet claimed

C. charge imposed by government

D. Individual Retirement Account

E. organization that administers and enforces the Internal Revenue Code upon individuals, corporations, or trusts, or their income or property

F. deduction from adjusted gross income used instead of standard deduction

G. withholding statement by employer of federal and state income taxes and FICA contribution deducted from pay

H. transaction involving an excess of expense over revenue

I. an increase in the value of something

J. a taxpayer's tax rate category

K. used to correct inaccuracies and omissions in a tax return

L. accounting period of 12 consecutive months

M. an additional charge because of a delinquency in an original income tax return

N. an enlargement of time

Multiple Choice

Select the best choice.

_____35. A person who is under a legal obligation to pay a tax is known as a:
   a. tax collector.
   b. taxpayer.
   c. dependent.
   d. tax preparer.

_____36. A tax return is:
   a. a refund.
   b. a rebate.
   c. the form on which a taxpayer reports his income.
   d. a deed evidencing the transfer of title.

_____37. A tax credit:
   a. reduces a taxpayer's taxable income.
   b. increases a taxpayer's taxable income.
   c. reduces the amount of income tax owed.
   d. increases the amount of income tax owed.

_____38. A standard deduction is:
   a. when all taxpayers have the same amount added to their taxes.
   b. when a specified standard sum is deducted from adjusted gross income.
   c. the same as an itemized deduction.
   d. the same as depreciation.

_____39. A capital gain is:
   a. a gain resulting from the sale or exchange of capital assets.
   b. a gift.
   c. a donation.
   d. the lessening in worth of any property.

_____40. Appreciation is:
   a. the basis of property.
   b. a loss.
   c. an exemption.
   d. an increase in the value of something.

_____41. Gross income is:
   a. tax evasion.
   b. a capital gain.
   c. appreciation.
   d. total income.

_____42. Straight-line depreciation is:
   a. a method of depreciating an asset.
   b. the same as accelerated depreciation.
   c. a method to rapidly depreciate the value of a capital asset.
   d. used to determine a taxpayer's earned income credit.

_____43. An exemption is:
   a. a contribution.
   b. a dividend.
   c. interest.
   d. an allowance granted by way of a deduction in computing taxable income.

_____44. An amended return is:
   a. needed when taxpayers file their tax return early.
   b. needed when taxpayers fail to file their tax return.
   c. used to correct inaccuracies and omissions in the original return.
   d. used when taxpayers lose their W-2 form.

_____45. The IRS imposes a penalty on taxpayers:
   a. who file late tax returns.
   b. who take exemptions.
   c. who take credits.
   d. who take deductions.

_____46. A tax established in proportion to the value of property to be taxed is:
   a. back tax.
   b. ad valorem tax.
   c. death tax.
   d. direct tax.

True/False

Mark the following T or F.

_____**47.** Tax-exempt income is all income that is taxable.

_____**48.** A tax return is the formal document used by taxpayers to report income to the government.

_____**49.** A tax credit increases the amount of tax owed by a taxpayer.

_____**50.** A deduction is the amount allowed a taxpayer in reduction of gross income.

_____**51.** Depreciation occurs when the worth of a property goes up in value.

_____**52.** Withholding tax is the federal and state income tax and FICA contributions deducted by an employer from an employee's pay.

_____**53.** A joint return is the type of return that a husband and wife file on two separate tax returns to report their income.

_____**54.** FICA is an acronym for the federal statute that funds workers' compensation.

_____**55.** A dependent is a person whom the taxpayer can claim as an exemption when filing a tax return.

_____**56.** A head of household is a single person, other than a surviving spouse, who provides a home for certain persons.

_____**57.** Taxes that are in arrears are back taxes.

_____**58.** A gift tax is a tax imposed by the federal government and most states upon transmission of property by a deceased person.

Synonyms

Select the correct synonym in parentheses for each numbered item.

59. AMORTIZE
(depreciate, round off, recapture)

60. GIFT
(interest, capital asset, donation)

61. EXEMPTION
(offset, deduction, contribution)

62. GROSS INCOME
(taxable income, adjusted income, total income)

63. BASIS
(cost, gain, loss)

64. APPRECIATION
(decrease, increase, appeal)

65. AUDIT
(contribution, examination, standard deduction)

66. ESTATE TAX
(transfer tax, withholding tax, inheritance tax)

67. FISCAL YEAR
(tax year, calendar year, partial year)

68. GAIN
(profits, distribution, cost)

69. INTERNAL REVENUE CODE
(federal law, state law, local ordinance)

70. TAX EVASION
(felony, misdemeanor, violation)

71. JOINT RETURN
(filed by twins, filed by married couple, duplicate return)

72. DIRECT TAX
(importation tax, consumption tax, ad valorem tax)

Self-Test

Place the number of the correct term in the appropriate space.

73. dependents

74. tax return

75. gross income

76. adjusted gross income

77. Internal Revenue Service

78. exemptions

79. taxpayers

80. Internal Revenue Code

81. tax credit

82. deductions

83. amended return

84. audit

Each year as the deadline of April 15 approaches, _____ are reminded of their obligation to the government by the _____. A formal accounting of a person's income, referred to as a(n) _____, must be filed. Under the _____, "all income from whatever source derived" is called _____ and must be listed. Taxpayers are allowed to reduce their gross income through the use of itemized and standard_____.

Allowance is also granted by way of deductions called _____ when computing one's taxable income. A taxpayer is also allowed to claim _____, including one's self, spouse, and children as exemptions when filing a tax return.

After taking all exemptions and credits, taxpayers will determine their_____. Then, instead of reducing taxable income, a(n) _____ may be used to reduce the amount of income tax owed by the taxpayer.

In the event a taxpayer makes omissions in the original tax return that is filed, a(n) _____ should be filed.

By filing an accurate and complete tax return, a taxpayer reduces the chances of a(n) _____.

Word Scramble

Unscramble the following words and write the correct word(s) that match(es) the definition for each word or phrase.

85. axt – an involuntary charge imposed by government to provide funds for the support of the government _____ _____

86. ternalin revueen ersvice – popularly known as the IRS _____ _____

87. 4W-morf – a document on which the employee states the number of exemptions claimed for the employer's payroll purposes _____ _____

88. tensionex – an enlargement of time _____ _____

89. dedtionuc – that which may be taken away or subtracted _____ _____

90. axt ditcre – a credit that reduces the amount of income tax owed _____ _____

91. pendented – a child of the taxpayer who the taxpayer can claim as an exemption _____ _____

92. comein – gain derived from capital or labor _____ _____

93. ointj turren – a single income tax return filed by a husband and wife _____ _____

94. slos – the opposite of gain _____ _____

95. tiespenal – an additional charge because of the lateness in making a payment _____ _____

96. dhea fo shouedohl – a single person other than a surviving spouse, who provides a home for certain persons _____ _____

97. justedad ssaib – the original cost of property offset for such things as losses and depreciation _____ _____

98. gtraihst nile preciationde – a method of depreciating an asset at an even pace _____ _____

99. mortaization – to gradually pay off a debt by regular payments _____ _____

100. duajtsed gossr nomcie – a tax term for gross income less the deductions permitted by law _____ _____

101. xta rackbet – a taxpayer's tax rate category _____ _____

102. intanceheri atx – a tax on the privilege of taking the property of a decedent by descent or under a will _____ _____

103. roth air – a type of retirement account that allows individuals to make their contributions with post-tax dollars _____ _____

The Last Word

The non-partisan Tax Foundation analyzed 2008 data from the Internal Revenue Service and reported that the top 5 percent of taxpayers earn about 35 percent of all income, yet pay almost 59 percent of income taxes in the United States. While this flies in the face of the widespread belief that the wealthy do not pay their fair share of taxes, in fact their share of America's earnings is dropping and their average tax rate is increasing. The decline is due to the wealthy earning more from wages and salaries and less from capital gains and dividends, which are taxed at a lower rate. Further the share of income held by the top 1 percent of wealthy taxpayers was greater in 2000 than it was eight years later. Interestingly, census data report suggest that during the present recession, the wealthy are receiving a disproportionate amount of the nation's wealth while paying lower taxes. Considering that the census data are more recent, do you believe the rich are getting richer because they pay less taxes?

 Access an interactive eBook, chapter-specific interactive learning tools, and more in your Paralegal CourseMate, accessed through www.CengageBrain.com

Wills, Trusts, and Estates

INTRODUCTION

The area of wills, trusts, and estates is one of the most active "bread and butter" areas of practice for law firms and probate and surrogate courts in the United States. The reason it creates interest is that it slices across nearly every other specialty in law, especially real property, corporations, partnerships, agency, contracts, administrative law, intellectual property, tax, insurance, ethics, and family law.

The terminology that professionals use in working with wills, trusts, and estates may be recognized by professionals from these other areas of law. Terminology is an issue of concern because a variety of terms are used interchangeably in describing or defining how an estate is administered and who is administering the estate.

The legal instruments, trusts, and wills that are developed and used in estates administration are the subject of this unit. Wills are testamentary instruments in which a person who dies, known as the testator, has disposed of personal or real property in a predetermined manner. Trusts are fiduciary relations involving a trustee who holds trust property for the benefit or use of a beneficiary. Both are used for the successful arrangement of a person's property, called estate planning. The entire idea is to design an estate in the manner best calculated to maintain and protect the family, both during the testator's lifetime and after the death of the testator. Generally, families are looking to reduce the taxes on an estate and keep the estate out of probate, where a will is authenticated by the court and the administration of the estate is a matter of public record.

CASE AND COMMENT

Superior Court of New Jersey, Chancery Division, Bergen County
Estate of Claudia L. Cohen, by its Executor- Plaintiff Ronald O. Perelman, and
Plaintiff Samantha Perelman,
v.
Robert Cohen and James Cohen, Defendants
Docket NO. C-134-08 Decided August 20, 2010

Facts: "This lawsuit from the beginning (April, 2008) has been a dispute between individuals over millions of dollars," according to the judge. The "individuals" being sued are the former father-in-law and brother-in-law of the executor/plaintiff Ronald Perelman. Claudia Cohen, Perelman's ex-wife, was the *New York Daily News'* "Page Six" reporter and editor as well as one-time girlfriend to former New York Senator D'Amato before her death. Perelman alleges that Robert Cohen made an enforceable promise before 1978 to leave to his daughter (and her children should she pre-decease her father) as much as he left her brother James. Robert Cohen's defense contended that there existed no pre-1978 enforceable promise to bequeath his daughter Claudia a certain share of his estate.

Procedural History: This is the fourth suit Ronald Perelman filed as Executor of Claudia Cohen's Estate against James and Robert Cohen. The suits resulted in 10 judicial decisions. Counsel for the estate engaged in hard-fought litigation that often crossed the boundaries of acceptable litigation tactics, especially the harsh examination of Robert Cohen, who was 84 and terminally ill. The testimony of Perelman did not support the promise claim. On June 20, 2008, the court put plaintiffs on notice that they would be required to prove by clear and convincing evidence that a pre-1978 promise was made. On March 6, 2009, the court reminded plaintiff's counsel of this evidentiary requirement and counsel represented that it would be met.

Issue: Whether plaintiff could prove by clear and convincing evidence that, prior to September 1, 1978, Robert Cohen promised to Claudia that she and her heirs would receive half of Robert and Harriet Cohen's estate.

Rationale: More than required notice was provided by the court to plaintiffs of their burden of proof. "No competent attorney could have missed the frivolous nature of this promise claim, once the unhelpful testamentary documents were received in February of 2009. By that time plaintiffs' counsel . . . lacked any applicable legal authority to proceed with their claim that an enforceable promise was made, but also any evidentiary support for their claim. Cohen's testamentary documents produced no evidence of a promise and evidenced Cohen's continuing desire to keep up with the changes in his estate by eliminating heirs when they died. Yet plaintiff's counsel frivolously included the promissory estoppel claim in their amended complaint."

Ruling: Judge Koblitz found for the Cohens and ordered the plaintiffs to pay $1.96 million in legal fees to the defendants.

Comment: Without any real proof of the purported promise, was Perelman's real end game the hope of a settlement that would obviate his need to produce evidence of the promise in court?

DICTIONARY / THESAURUS

Term [phonetic pronunciation]	*Note: All dictionary/thesaurus terms appear on flashcards at the back of the book and on the student website.*

administrator
[ad.*min*.is.tray.ter]

A person who is appointed by the court to manage the estate of a person either who died without a will or whose will failed to name an executor or named an executor who declined or was ineligible to serve. The administrator of an estate is also referred to as a personal representative.

- *n.* representative, executor, trustee ("the estate's administrator")

administrator cum testamento annexo
[ad.*min*.is.tray.ter kum tes.ta.*men*.to an.*eks*.o]

The court-appointed administrator of the estate of a decedent whose will failed to name an executor or whose named executor cannot or refuses to serve. Cum testamento annexo, a Latin phrase meaning "with will attached," is often abbreviated CTA. *Compare* administrator DBN.

administrator de bonis non
[ad.*min*.is.tray.ter day *boh*.nis non]

The court-appointed administrator of the estate of a decedent whose executor has died or resigned. De bonis non, a Latin phrase meaning "goods not administered," is often abbreviated DBN. *Compare* administrator CTA.

advance directive
[ad.*vanse* de.*rekt*.iv]

A term for the various instruments a person can use to ensure that her wishes with respect to health care are carried out if she is no longer able to speak for herself. EXAMPLES: a health-care proxy; a living will. *See* durable power of attorney.

attest
[a.*test*]

To swear to; to bear witness to; to affirm to be true or genuine. *See also* attestation.

- *v.* adjure, announce, assert, aver, certify, swear, support, sustain

attestation
[a.tes.*tay*.shen]

The act of witnessing the signing of a document, including signing one's name as a witness to that fact.

- *n.* endorsement, affirmation, certification, testimony, evidence ("an attestation clause")

attestation clause
[a.tes.*tay*.shen clawz]

A clause, usually at the end of a document such as a deed or a will, that provides evidence of attestation. EXAMPLES: "signed, sealed, and delivered in the presence of"; "witness my hand and seal."

attesting witness
[a.*test*.ing *wit*.nes]

A person who witnesses the signing of a document. *See also* attestation.

beneficiary
[ben.e.*fish*.ee.air.ee]

1. A person who receives a benefit. 2. A person who has inherited or is entitled to inherit under a will. 3. A person for whom property is held in trust. 4. A person who is entitled to the proceeds of a life insurance policy when the insured dies. 5. A person designated by statute as entitled to the proceeds of a legal action such as a wrongful death action.

- *n.* heir, recipient, successor, legatee, assignee

DICTIONARY   THESAURUS *continued...*

bequeath
[be.*kweeth*]

To leave personal property or money by will; such a gift is called a bequest or a legacy. A gift of real property by will is properly called a devise, although the courts generally construe "bequeath" as synonymous with "devise" when it is used in connection with a testamentary gift of real estate.

- *v.* grant, give, assign, remit, leave, provide

bequest
[be.*kwest*]

Technically, a gift of personal property by will, (i.e., a legacy), although the term is often loosely used in connection with a testamentary gift of real estate as well. *Compare* devise. *See also* bequeath.

- *n.* gift, devise, endowment, heritage, legacy

bypass trust
[*bi*.paz trust]

Also called a credit shelter trust or credit trust. This is used for estate planning purposes so that a deceased spouse's estate passes or goes to a trust instead of to the surviving spouse. This is generally used by married couples to pass money on to their children and bypass as much government estate taxes as is possible.

codicil
[*kod*.i.sil]

An addition or supplement to a will, which adds to or modifies the will without replacing or revoking it. A codicil does not have to be physically attached to the will.

- *n.* addition, supplement, appendix, accessory, addendum, attachment, extension ("codicil to a will")

competency
[*kom*.pe.ten.see]

1. Legal capacity. The ability to execute binding contracts, wills, etc. 2. A testator is considered competent if she understands the general nature and extent of her property, potential beneficiaries of the estate, and the purpose of a will. 3. The right to sue and be sued.

curtesy
[*ker*.te.see]

The rights a man had under common law with respect to his wife's property. These rights have now been modified in every state, and the rights are extended to a wife in her husband's property.

decedent
[de.*see*.dent]

A legal term for a person who has died. *See also* decedent's estate.

- *n.* deceased, testator, intestate, dead individual, departed

decedent's estate
[de.*see*.dents es.*tate*]

The total property, real and personal, that a decedent owns at the time of her death.

devise
[de.*vize*]

n. A gift of real property by will, although it is often loosely used to mean a testamentary gift of either real property or personal property. *Compare* bequest; legacy.
v. 1. To dispose of real property by will. By comparison, "bequeath" is a word used in wills to transfer personal property. However, the term "devise and bequeath" applies to both real property and personal property. *Compare* bequest; legacy.

- *v.* confer, bequeath, convey, endow ("She devised her business operation to her daughter.")
- *n.* inheritance, legacy, transfer, conveyance ("the devise of the family jewels")

devisee
[de.vie.*zee*]

The beneficiary of a devise.

devisor
[de.*vie*.zor]

A testator who makes a devise.

discretionary trust
[dis.*kresh*.en.air.ee trust]

A trust in which broad discretion is vested in the trustee and is to be exercised by her in carrying out the purposes of the trust.

distribution
[dis.tre.*byoo*.shen]

1. The act of the administrator of an estate in allocating the decedent's property among his heirs, or by an executor of the estate where the decedent left a will. 2. Allocation.

dower
[*dow*.er]

The legal right or interest that a wife acquires by marriage in the property of her husband. Dower no longer exists, or has been modified in most states, but every state retains aspects of the concept for the protection of both spouses. *See* elective share.

durable power of attorney
[*dew*.rebl *pow*.er of a.*tern*.ee]

A power of attorney that remains effective even though the grantor becomes mentally incapacitated. Some durable powers of attorney become effective only where a person is no longer able to make decisions for herself. EXAMPLES: A health-care proxy; a living will. *See* advance directive.

elective share
[e.*lek*.tiv share]

In some states, the share a surviving spouse may elect to take in the estate of the deceased spouse. In such jurisdictions, it replaces dower. *See* dower.

estate
[es.*tate*]

1. The property left by a decedent; (i.e., a decedent's estate). 2. The right, title, and interest a person has in real or personal property, either tangible or intangible. Estates in real property (estates in land or landed estates) include both freehold estates (EXAMPLES: a fee simple; a fee tail; a life estate) and estates less than freehold (EXAMPLES: estates for years; estates at will). 3. The property itself.

- *n.* assets, wealth, property, fortune, personality, effects

estate of inheritance
[es.*tate* ov in.*herr*.i.tense]

Also known as a fee, a freehold interest in land that is inheritable; (i.e., an interest that the tenant is not only entitled to enjoy for his own lifetime, but which, after his death, if he leaves no will, his heirs will inherit under the intestate laws).

estate per autre vie
[es.*tate* per *oh*.tre vee]

An estate that is to last for the life of a person other than the tenant. EXAMPLE: "I give Blackacre to my son-in-law, Samuel Jones, for as long as my daughter, Mary Brown Jones, shall live."

estate planning
[es.*tate plan*.ing]

Pre-death arrangement of a person's property and estate best calculated to maximize the estate for the beneficiaries during and after the person's life.

estate tax
[es.*tate* takz]

A tax imposed by the federal government and most states upon the transmission of property by a deceased person. The tax is imposed upon the net estate of the decedent without reference to the recipient's relationship to the decedent or to the amount a recipient receives. An estate tax is a transfer tax.

DICTIONARY | THESAURUS *continued...*

estate upon condition
[es.*tate* up.*on* ken.*dish*.en]

An estate whose existence, enlargement, or termination is conditioned upon the happening of a particular event. Such conditions are either expressed in the deed, will, or other instrument that creates the estate, or they are implied by law.

execute
[*ek*.se.kyoot]

To sign a document. USAGE: "I will not rest until I execute my will."

- *v.* accomplish, perform, achieve, administer, complete ("She was quick to execute her obligations under the contract.")

executed
[*ek*.se.kyoot.ed]

1. Completed, performed, or carried out. 2. Signed

- *adj.* cut, signed

executor
[eg.*zek*.yoo.tor]

A person designated by a testator to carry out the directions and requests in the testator's will and to dispose of his property according to the provisions of his will. *Compare* administrator.

- *n.* administrator, fiduciary, custodian, personal representative

fiduciary
[fi.*do*.she.air.ee]

adj. That which is based upon trust or confidence; the relationship between a fiduciary and his principal.
n. A person who is entrusted with handling money or property for another person. EXAMPLES: attorney and client; guardian and ward; trustee and beneficiary.

fiduciary duty
[fi.*do*.she.air.ee *dew*.tee]

The duty to act loyally and honestly with respect to the interests of another; the duty the law imposes upon a fiduciary.

forced heirs
[forst airs]

Those persons whom the testator or donor cannot deprive of the portion of his estate reserved for them by the law, except in cases where he has reason to disinherit them (i.e., person's spouse).

guardian ad litem
[*gar*.dee.en ad *ly*.tem]

A person appointed by the court to represent and protect the interests of a minor or an incompetent person during litigation.

heir hunters
[air *hunt*.erz]

Persons, often lawyers, who troll probate court filings from public administrators. When documents show missing heirs to a rich estate, hunters locate heirs and offer inheritance information—for a fee.

holographic will
[hol.o.*graf*.ik will]

A will that is entirely written and signed by the testator in his own handwriting. In many states, the requirement that the signing of a will be witnessed is not imposed in the case of a holographic will, because a successful counterfeit of another person's handwriting is very difficult; the requirement that the will be entirely in handwriting is therefore thought to be sufficient protection against forgery.

inter vivos trust
[*in*.ter *vy*.vos trust]

Living trust.

intestacy
[in.*tess*.te.see]

The status of the estate or property of a person who dies without leaving a valid will. *See also* intestate. *Compare* testacy.

intestate [in.*tess*.tate]	*adj.* Pertaining to a person, or to the property of a person, who dies without leaving a valid will. EXAMPLE: "John died without a will and left an intestate estate." *See also* intestacy. *Compare* testate. *n.* 1. A person who dies without leaving a valid will. USAGE: "John is an intestate." 2. The status of a person who dies without leaving a valid will. USAGE: "John died intestate." *See also* intestacy. *Compare* testate.
intestate estate [in.*tess*.tate es.*tate*]	The estate of a person who dies without leaving a valid will.
intestate laws [in.*tess*.tate lawz]	State statutes that set forth the rules by which property passes when a person dies intestate. *See also* intestate succession.
intestate succession [in.*tess*.tate suk.*sesh*.en]	Inheritance from a person who dies intestate. *Compare* testate succession.
issue [*ish*.oo]	All persons who are descendants of one ancestor, including all future descendants. However, when used in a will, "issue" will be taken to mean children or grandchildren, or all living descendants of one ancestor, including all future descendants, if that is the testator's intention.
lapsed devise [lapsd de.*vize*]	A devise that was good when the will was made but has failed since then because of the death of the legatee before the death of the testator.
legacy [*leg*.e.see]	Accurately, a gift of personal property by will, although the term is often used loosely to mean any testamentary gift; a bequest. *Compare* devise. ▪ *n.* grant, bequest, endowment, present; tradition, history, meaning ("the legacy of River Phoenix")
legatee [*leg*.e.*tee*]	A person who receives personal property as a beneficiary under a will, although the word is often used loosely to mean a person who receives a testamentary gift of either personal property or real property. *Compare* devisee, legator. ▪ *n.* recipient, devisee, beneficiary, donee, legal heir
legator [*leg*.a.tor]	A person who makes a gift of property in a will to the legatee.
letters of administration [*let*.erz ov ad.*min*.is.tray.shen]	The formal document issued by the probate court appointing an administrator for an estate.
living trust [*liv*.ing trust]	1. An inter vivos trust. A trust created during the lifetime of its creator and becomes effective in his lifetime, as opposed to a testamentary trust which takes effect at death. 2. An active trust.
nuncupative will [*nung*.kyoo.pay.tiv will]	A will declared orally by a testator during his last illness, before witnesses, and later reduced to writing by a person who was present during the declaration. ▪ *n.* oral will; deathbed will

DICTIONARY THESAURUS *continued...*

per capita
[per *kap*.i.ta]

(*Latin*) Means "by the head"; by the individual. 1. For each person. 2. A method of dividing an estate in which all persons who are equally related to the decedent share equally in the estate. EXAMPLE: Bill has two living children, Mary and Sam, and two grandchildren by Adam, a deceased child. If Bill's $900,000 estate is divided per capita among his heirs, Mary and Sam each receive $450,000 and Adam's children receive nothing. *Compare per stirpes.*

per stirpes
[per *ster*.peez]

(*Latin*) Means "by the root"; according to class; by representation. This is a method of dividing or distributing an estate in which the heirs of a deceased heir share the portion of the estate that the deceased heir would have received had he lived. EXAMPLE: Bill has two living children, Mary and Sam, and two grandchildren by Adam, a deceased child. If Bill's $900,000 estate is divided per stirpes among his heirs, Mary and Sam each receive $300,000, and Adam's children each receive $150,000, sharing the $300,000 portion that Adam would have received had he lived.

pour-over trust
[por-*oh*.ver trust]

Provision in a will that directs that the property be distributed into a trust.

predecease
[preed.i.*ses*]

To die before another person.

pretermitted heir
[pree.ter.*mit*.ed air]

A child of a testator who is omitted from the testator's will. Generally the right of such a child to share in the decedent's estate depends on whether the omission was intentional or unintentional. If there is an unintentional omission, a statute might provide that such child shall share in the estate as though the testator died without a will.

probate
[*proh*.bate]

n. 1. The judicial act whereby a will is adjudicated to be valid. 2. A term that describes the functions of the probate court, including the probate of wills and the supervision of the accounts and actions of administrators and executors of decedents' estates.
v. 1. To prove a will to be valid in probate court. 2. To submit to the jurisdiction of the probate court for any purpose.

- *v.* validate, authenticate, certify, establish, substantiate ("The court must probate this will")
- *n.* validation, adjudication, verification, confirmation

publication clause
[pub.li.*kay*.shen klawz]

Portion of a will that states that the instrument reflects the wishes of the testator.

right to die
[ryt to dy]

This refers to the right of a person to determine what limits, if any, she wishes to impose with respect to efforts to prolong her life if she becomes gravely ill. *See* living will.

surety
[*shoor*.e.tee]

A person who promises to pay the debt or to satisfy the obligation of another person.

surrogate
[*ser*.e.get]

In some states, the title of a judge who presides in probate court.

testacy
[*tes*.te.see]

The status of the estate or property of a person who dies without leaving a valid will. *Compare* intestacy. *See also* testate.

testament
[*tes*.te.ment]

1. A will. The terms "testament," "will," "last will," and "last will and testament" are synonymous. 2. A declaration of faith, belief, or principle.

- *n.* attestation, colloquy, covenant, demonstration, statement, exemplification, testimonial, will, last will

testamentary
[tes.te.*men*.ter.ee]

Pertaining to a will; pertaining to a testament.

testamentary capacity
[tes.te.*men*.ter.ee ke.*pass*.i.tee]

The mental capacity of a testator, at the time of making her will, to be able to understand the nature of her act and, generally if not precisely, the nature and location of her property and the identity of those persons who are the natural objects of her bounty.

testamentary gift
[tes.te.*men*.ter.ee gift]

1. A gift that is the subject of a testamentary disposition. 2. A generic term for a legacy, bequest, or devise.

testamentary instrument
[tes.te.*men*.ter.ee in.stroo.ment]

An instrument whose language clearly indicates that its author intended to make a disposition of his property, or some of his property, to be effective upon his death. A will is an EXAMPLE of a testamentary instrument.

testamentary intent
[tes.te.*men*.ter.ee in.*tent*]

For a court to admit a will to probate, it must determine that the testator intended the instrument to be her last will.

testamentary trust
[tes.te.*men*.ter.ee trust]

A trust created by will.

testate
[*tes*.tate]

adj. Pertaining to a person, or to the property of a person, who dies leaving a valid will. *See* testacy.
n. 1. A person who dies leaving a valid will. 2. The status of a person who dies leaving a valid will. *Compare* intestate.

testate estate
[*tes*.tate es.*tate*]

The estate of a person who dies leaving a valid will.

testate succession
[*tes*.tate suk.*sesh*.en]

Taking property under a will rather than by inheritance. *Compare* intestate succession.

testator
[*tes*.tay.ter]

A person who dies leaving a valid will.

DICTIONARY   THESAURUS *continued...*

trust
[trust]

A fiduciary relationship involving a trustee who holds trust property for the benefit or use of a beneficiary. Property of any description or type may properly be the subject of a trust. The trustee holds legal title to the trust property (also called the res or corpus of the trust); the beneficiary holds equitable title. A trust is generally established through a trust instrument, such as a deed of trust or a will, by a person (known as the settlor) who wishes the beneficiary to receive the benefit of the property but not outright ownership. A trust may, however, also be created by operation of law: implied trust.

trust estate
[trust es.*tate*]

Phrase sometimes used to mean the property held by the trustee for the benefit of the beneficiary, and sometimes used to mean the interest that the beneficiary has in the property.

trust fund
[trust fund]

1. A fund held in trust by a trust company or other trustee. *See also* trust funds.
2. A fund that, although not held in trust in the technical sense, is held under a relationship "of trust" that gives one the legal right to impose certain obligations upon the holder of the funds.

trust funds
[trust fundz]

Money held in a trust account. *See also* trust fund.

trust indenture
[trust in.*dent*.sher]

An instrument stating the terms and conditions of a trust.

trust instrument
[trust *in*.stroo.ment]

A document in which a trust is created. EXAMPLES: a deed of trust; a will.

trust inter vivos
[trust *in*.ter *vy*.vose]

A trust that is effective during the lifetime of the creator of the trust.

- *n.* living trust

trust officer
[trust *off*.i.ser]

An officer of a financial institution who manages trust funds.

trust property
[trust *prop*.er.tee]

Property that is the subject of a trust. It is also referred to as the trust res, the res of the trust, or the corpus of the trust.

trustee
[trust.*ee*]

The person who holds the legal title to trust property for the benefit of the beneficiary of the trust, with such powers and subject to such duties as are imposed by the terms of the trust and the law.

- *n.* guardian, fiduciary, custodian

trustee ad litem
[trust.ee ad *ly*.tem]

A trustee appointed by the court, as opposed to a trustee appointed in a trust instrument.

Uniform Probate Code
[*yoon*.i.form *pro*.bate kod]

An act promulgated in 1969 to streamline and make the probate process more uniform throughout the country. The law was intended to be adopted by all the states; however, less than half have adopted it or some portion of it.

vested
[*vest*.ed]

1. That which cannot be taken away; indefeasible. 2. Absolute; definite; established; fixed. USAGE: "He had a vested devise."

will
[will]

An instrument by which a person (the testator) makes a disposition of her property, to take effect after her death.

- *n.* bequest, bestowal, declaration, disposition, estate, legacy ("last will and testament")
- *v.* bequest, confer, devise, legate, probate ("to will an estate to someone")

will contest
[will *kon*.test]

n. An attempt to defeat the probate of a will, commonly referred to as an attempt to "set aside the will."

Missing Words

Fill in the blanks.

1. A(n) _____ is an addition or supplement to a will.

2. _____ wills are entirely written and signed by the testators in their own handwriting.

3. _____ are gifts of personal property by will.

4. One who _____ to a will swears and bears witness that the instrument is true and genuine.

5. Failure to _____ a will means the testator did not sign the document.

6. _____ are gifts of real property by a will.

7. _____ is a person who makes a gift of property in a will to the legatee.

8. A(n) _____ is an instrument by which a person makes a disposition of property to take effect at death.

9. A(n) _____ is a will or last will in testament, a declaration of faith, belief, or principle.

10. A(n) _____ is a trust that is in effect during the lifetime of the trust's creator.

11. A(n) _____ is a person who is appointed by the court to manage the estate of a person who died without a will.

12. The total property that a decedent owns at death is called _____.

13. A _____ is an attempt to defeat the probate of a will.

14. A(n) _____ is a term for the various instruments a person can use to ensure that her health-care wishes are carried out if she can no longer speak.

15. A power of attorney that remains effective even though the grantor is incapacitated is a _____.

STUDY AID: Use flashcards for this unit before completing the exercises.

Matching

Match the letter of the definition to the term.

A   **16.** attesting witness   **A.** person who observes the signing of a will

D   **17.** attestation clause   **B.** a gift of personal property by will

I   **18.** decedent   **C.** pre-death arrangement of a person's property and estate

F   **19.** devise   **D.** usually at the end of a will, it provides evidence that execution of a will was observed by witnesses

E   **20.** estate   **E.** property left by a decedent

C   **21.** estate planning   **F.** a gift of real property by will

H   **22.** execute   **G.** the status of an estate of a person who dies without a valid will

B   **23.** legacy   **H.** to sign a document, (i.e., a will)

G   **24.** intestacy   **I.** person who has died

N   **25.** testator   **J.** one who makes a devise

L   **26.** devisee   **K.** a will written by hand and signed by testator

O   **27.** codicil   **L.** beneficiary of a devise

J   **28.** devisor   **M.** the judicial act where a will is adjudicated to be valid

K   **29.** holographic will   **N.** one who dies leaving a valid will

M   **30.** probate   **O.** supplement to a will

R   **31.** competency   **P.** the title of the judge who presides in probate court

Q   **32.** surety   **Q.** a person who promises to pay the debt of another

P   **33.** surrogate   **R.** a person's legal capacity

Multiple Choice

Select the best choice.

___ **34.** All persons who receive bequests in a will are:
   a. beneficiaries.
   b. testators.
   c. trustees.
   d. next of kin.

___ **35.** A living trust is also called a(n):
   a. A-B trust.
   b. inter vivos trust.
   c. Totten trust.
   d. pay-on-death trust.

___ **36.** All that a person owns at death is considered:
   a. personal property.
   b. real property.
   c. decedent's estate.
   d. community property.

___ **37.** The personal representative of a decedent's estate could be the:
   a. fiduciary.
   b. executor/executrix.
   c. public administrator.
   d. all of the above

___ **38.** The person who holds the legal title to trust property is a:
   a. trustee.
   b. guardian.
   c. fiduciary.
   d. all of the above

___ **39.** A trustee appointed by the court is a:
   a. trust officer.
   b. trustee ad litem.
   c. testator.
   d. legator.

True/False

Mark the following T or F.

___ **40.** Testamentary capacity is a term referring to the mind of a person who is sane and competent to understand her acts.

___ **41.** A nuncupative will could be a will declared orally by a Roman Catholic nun during her last rites of the church in the presence of priests as long as her wishes are later reduced to writing by those present.

___ **42.** An attestation clause always begins a will.

___ **43.** An attestation clause is a provision in a life insurance policy that after a specified period of time the insurer shall be unable to challenge the policy's validity on the basis of untruths in the application.

___ **44.** The publication clause of a will always announces the obituary information (funeral, place of burial, etc.) that the testator wishes printed in the newspaper.

___ **45.** A trust is a fiduciary relationship involving a trustee who holds trust property for the benefit of a beneficiary.

Synonyms

Select the correct synonym in parentheses for each numbered item.

46. PERSONAL REPRESENTATIVE
(executor, beneficiary, testator)

47. TESTAMENTARY GIFT
(will clause, bequest, trust instrument)

48. FIDUCIARY
(trustee, legacy, bequest)

49. LEGATEE
(beneficiary, optional, void)

50. ESTATE OF INHERITANCE
(fee, codicil, beneficiary)

51. DEVISE
(gift, receiver, thief)

52. BENEFICIARY
(equitable, tangible, heir)

53. ATTEST
(lie, beg, swear)

54. ESTATE TAX
(use tax, transfer tax, receipt tax)

55. PRETERMITTED HEIR
(omitted, included, attested)

56. PROBATE
(will adjudication, indemnification, ratification)

57. INTER VIVOS TRUST
(direct, living, implied)

58. TRUSTEE
(creator, custodian, decedent)

59. TRUST RES
(property, principle, interest)

60. PROBATE
(silent, written, validate)

61. INTESTATE
(mandatory, spendthrift, no will at death)

62. DEVISOR
(improvident, testator, miserly)

63. DECEDENT
(trustee, beneficiary, testator)

Self-Test

Place the number of the correct term in the appropriate space.

64. trust officer

65. devises

66. devisees

67. estate planning

68. bequests

69. wills

70. attest

71. trust instrument

72. trustee

73. holographic

74. estates

75. intestate

76. codicil

77. intestacy

78. administrator

Without the benefit of _____ or witnesses to _____ to their wishes, Heather and her spouse Harold

each executed testamentary instruments called _____ that made _____ or _____ to specific

friends, called _____. Since both Heather and Harold wrote their wills in their own handwriting, the wills are both

_____ (which is not allowed in their state). If they continue to rely on the testamentary instruments they wrote

until they die, both _____ will fall into _____. Could they each execute an addition, or _____,

to their wills with the assistance of an attorney and make the originals valid? No, both will die _____, or without a

valid will, unless they start again and prepare proper wills in the manner prescribed by their state. If the couple dies without

a proper will, the court might need to appoint a(n) _____ to manage their estates.

   If only Heather and Harold had consulted an attorney to review their estate plans. The attorney could have

discussed the benefits of drafting a(n) _____ in addition to a will, so that their children won't inherit all their

money in one lump sum. Then, the couple could have selected a close family friend as the _____, or a(n) _____

_____ of their bank, to administer the trust.

Word Scramble

Unscramble the following words and write the correct word(s) that match(es) the definition for each word or phrase.

79. miniadstrator atc – the court-appointed administrator of the estate of a decedent whose will failed to name an executor _____

_____

80. adstratormini bnd – the court-appointed administrator of the estate of a decedent whose executor has died or resigned _____

_____

81. tatees fo anceinherit – also known as a fee, a freehold interest in land that is inheritable _____

_____

82. statee rep reaut ive – an estate for the life of another person _____

_____

83. tastee – the property left by a decedent _____

_____

84. testatein ccessionsu – inheritance from a person who dies intestate _____

_____

85. mentarytesta pacityca – the mental capacity of a testator _____

_____

86. mittedterpre hire – one who is unintentionally left out of a will _____

_____

87. rusttee ad emlit – a trustee appointed by the court _____

_____

88. rustt statee – a phrase sometimes used to mean the property held by the trustee for the benefit of the beneficiary _____

_____

89. galetee – a person who received personal property under a will _____

_____

90. iwll – an instrument by which a person makes a disposition of her property, to take effect at her death _____

_____

91. cuptivenuna illw – a will declared orally by a testator during his last illness _____

_____

92. eihr terhun – a person who searches probate records to locate missing beneficiaries, for a fee _____

_____

93. dvancea tivedirec – the various instruments a person can use to ensure that her wishes with respect to health care are carried out _____

_____

94. passby rustt – an estate-planning device also called a credit shelter trust or credit trust _____

_____

95. tribudistion – the act of the administrator of an estate in allocating the decedent's property among his heirs, or by an executor of the estate where the decedent left a will _____

_____

96. daburle woper fo rnattoey – a power of attorney that remains effective even though the grantor becomes mentally incapacitated _____

_____

97. petencomcy – legal capacity; the ability to execute binding contracts, wills, etc. _____

_____

98. ciarfiduy – a person who is entrusted with handling money or property for another person _____

_____

99. liwl teconst – an attempt to "set aside the will" _____

_____

The Last Word

Posthumous birth, the birth of a child after the death of a parent, is recognized by only 11 states and establishes the child-parent relationship. New technology, like the use of frozen embryos and the sperm of deceased parents, is starting to impact family law, inheritance laws, and the Social Security Trust Fund.

The Social Security Act requires the federal government to observe a state's law in ascertaining the parent-child relationship. However, most states require a parent to be alive at the time of conception. Courts in jurisdictions as varied as Massachusetts, Arizona, Iowa, and New Jersey have ruled that posthumous birth children are entitled to federal Social Security benefits, while Florida, New Hampshire, and Arkansas have ruled against such benefits for children of posthumous birth.

The Social Security Act was intended to assist the living children of deceased and disabled parents, rather than children who were conceived by choice after the death of their parents. In the laws of every state, if a spouse is pregnant at the time of her spouse's death, their offspring would receive benefits. If a woman conceives one month after her spouse dies, usually benefits are denied. Minnesota refused to change its state law recognizing posthumous conception because it would have required amending state inheritance laws. Today's technology is highlighting the overlapping areas of federal law with family law, as well as wills, trusts, and estates. Does the solvency of Social Security require Congress to amend the Social Security Act, defining the parent/child relationship instead of applying the law of 50 separate states?

Real Property and Landlord/Tenant Law

- Learn about real property and landlord/tenant law.

- Master the similarities and differences in definitions of key terms.

- Master the pronunciations and spellings of legal terms.

- Recognize the synonyms used for legal terminology.

- Practice usage of terms, definitions, and synonyms for terms.

- Complete unit exercises in the forms of missing words, matching, multiple choice, true/false, synonyms, self-test, and word scramble.

- Work with a dictionary/thesaurus.

UNIT

12

Real Property and Landlord/Tenant

INTRODUCTION

The law treats property as either personal or real. Real property is land or whatever is permanently attached to it. These permanently attached items are called fixtures. Examples of fixtures include houses as well as the items permanently attached to the houses such as fireplaces, chimneys, built-in ovens, and window shades; barns built on the property; a cement patio; and water wells. Personal property is defined as anything not attached to the land, such as an automobile, chair, bicycle, picnic table, or even a tree that has been chopped down, but not a tree rooted in the ground.

Rules governing the ownership of property compose the law of real property. There are numerous ways to own property. Some own it alone, while others own property jointly with other people such as family members or friends. The law recognizes different sorts of interests in land, called estates, in real property. Estates might be different by varying property rights, such as the duration of the interest, and whether the property is transferable. The most complete ownership in real property is the fee simple. This is an estate of indefinite duration that can be transferred at will. This is the most popular form of home ownership. Some property might have restrictions listed in the deed or bill of sale. A person might have purchased some property with the condition that the estate will only last for the life of the grantee.

Another kind of right to use land might be very limited. An easement is the right to use the land of another person for a specific purpose. A property owner might grant an easement, such as a right of way to a power or water company, to place its equipment on the owner's property. Or, an owner might sell an easement to another person giving him the right to use water or oil located on the land. Instead of granting a right of specific use, a land owner can also limit the use of property by putting a restrictive covenant in a deed, specifying the kind or size of buildings that can be built on the land.

A person might not enjoy the right of ownership at all, just the right to possess property that belongs to others. This arrangement is descriptive of a landlord/tenant relationship where one rents a house, apartment, or condominium from another for a period of time at a set amount of money, the terms of which are usually written in a lease. There is an entire field of law called "Landlord/Tenant" law that addresses the situation. Generally the terms of the landlord–tenant relationship are set out in a lease (contract) signed by the owner of the property and the persons desiring to use the property. A tenancy might last for several months, a year, or indefinitely depending on the contract agreement made by the parties. In some situations, a tenant might request a lease that is terminable at any time by either party (at will).

Other issues in property law include the searching of title to property, checking that the description of property is verifiable and legal, financing, mortgages, and transfers. All are discussed in this unit. While the following case was brought as a landlord–tenant dispute, the real issue is jurisdictional. The overlapping fields of law provide a maze of challenges to the legal researcher. A search engine could pull this case up under landlord, tenant, administrative law, exhaustion of remedies, rent control, and subject matter jurisdiction, to name a few.

CASE AND COMMENT

Supreme Court of the State of New York, County of New York: IAS Part 61
Paula Gerard, et al., individually and on behalf of others similarly situated, Plaintiffs

v.

Clermont York Associates, LLC, Defendant
Index No. 101150/2010

Facts: The Clermont, located at 444 East 82nd Street in New York City, is a 34-story residential apartment building with 415 rental units. Following the enactment of the Rent Stabilization Law of 1969 and the Tenant Protection Act of 1974, nearly all the units were made subject to rent control. Clermont York has acted as landlord of the Clermont since 2004. In 1994, the Clermont's prior owners took advantage of an amendment (a.k.a. Luxury Decontrol) to the Rent Stabilization Law that allowed for the decontrol of units upon vacancy if rent exceeded $2,000 per month. Further provisions allowed for deregulation when a unit's regulated rent exceeded $2,000 and the tenant's household income exceeded $175,000. During the tax year 1997–1998 the Clermont's former owners accepted a city tax break, known as the J-51 Law, as an incentive for landlords to upgrade properties.

Procedural History: By 2010, market rents at the Clermont ranged between $3,600–$5,600 per month and defendants were sued by plaintiffs in jeopardy of being evicted upon the expiration of their market-rent leases. Plaintiffs' complaint contended that defendant's acceptance of the J-51 tax break made deregulation of their units under "Luxury Decontrol" unwarranted.

Issue: Whether tenants could sue their landlord seeking rental rate reductions on any units deregulated between 1993 and 1997 under the Rent Stabilization Law.

Rationale: While courts have the power to annul Division of Housing and Community Renewal (DHCR) determinations which are irrational or unsupported by substantial evidence, the question of whether a particular unit is subject to rent stabilization falls within DHCR's administrative expertise. DHCR has primary jurisdiction and the Plaintiffs are bypassing the agency with this action.

Ruling: Plaintiffs' complaint is dismissed, with costs and disbursements to the Defendant Clermont.

Comment: Should supply and demand govern the real estate rental market or is government-mandated rent control necessary for even "luxury" tenants? Why?

DICTIONARY THESAURUS

Term [phonetic pronunciation]	*Note: All dictionary/thesaurus terms appear on flashcards at the back of the book and on the student website.*
abstract of title [*ab*.strakt ov *ty*.tel]	A short account of the state of the title to real estate, reflecting all past ownership and any interests or rights, such as a mortgage or other liens, which any person might currently have with respect to the property. An abstract of title is necessary to verify title before purchasing real property. *See also* chain of title; search.
adverse possession [*ad*.verse po.*zesh*.en]	The act of occupying real property in an open, continuous, and notorious manner, under a claim of right, hostile to the interests of the true owner for a period of years. In this manner, the occupier might claim ownership of the property. *See also* tacking.
broker [*broh*.ker]	A person whose business is to bring buyer and seller together; an agent who, for a commission, negotiates on behalf of his principal in connection with entering into contracts or buying and selling any kind of property. A broker does not generally take possession of the property with respect to which he deals. There are both buyer and seller brokers. ▪ *n.* agent, middleman, proxy, representative, emissary, mediator, intermediary
chain of title [chayn ov *ty*.tel]	The succession of transactions through which title to a given piece of land was passed from person to person from its origins to the present day. *See also* abstract of title; search.
color of title [*kull*.er ov *ty*.tel]	That which gives the appearance of title, but is not title in fact; that which, on its face, appears to pass title but fails to do so. EXAMPLE: a deed to land executed by a person who does not own the land.
condition subsequent [ken.*dish*.en *sub*.se.kwent]	In a contract, a condition that divests contractual liability that has already attached (or causes the loss of property rights granted by deed or will) upon the failure of the other party to the contract, deed, or will, to comply with its terms. EXAMPLE: An insurer's obligation to cover losses to a person's home can be void, if she leaves her doors unlocked and she is robbed, provided her insurance contract specified that unoccupied homes must be kept locked.
condominium [kon.de.*min*.ee.um]	A multi-unit dwelling, each of whose residents owns her individual apartment absolutely while holding a tenancy in common in the areas of the building and grounds used by all the residents. *Compare* cooperative apartment house. ▪ *n.* home, multi-unit dwelling, separate ownership
contract for sale of land [*con*.trakt for sale ov land]	A contract in which one party agrees to sell and the other to purchase real estate. *Note* that a contract for the sale of land is not a deed, but merely an agreement to transfer title.
convey [kon.*vay*]	1. To transfer title to property from one person to another by deed, bill of sale, or other conveyance. 2. To transfer, to transmit.

conveyance
[kon.*vay*.ense]

1. The transferring of title to real property from one person to another. 2. Any document that creates a lien on real property or a debt or duty arising out of real estate. EXAMPLES: a lease; a mortgage; an assignment. 3. Any transfer of title to either real property or personal property.

conveyancing
[kon.*vay*.ense.ing]

The act of transferring title to or creating a lien on real estate by deed, mortgage, or other instrument.

cooperative apartment house
[koh.*op*.er.a.tive a.*part*.ment hows]

A multi-unit dwelling in which each tenant has an interest in the corporation or other entity that owns the building as well as a lease entitling her to occupy a particular apartment within the building. *Compare* condominium.

co-ownership
[koh-*ohn*.er.ship]

Ownership of property by more than one person. *See also* joint tenancy; tenancy in common.

covenant
[*kov*.e.nent]

n. In a deed, a promise to do or not to do a particular thing, or an assurance that a particular fact or circumstance exists or does not exist. *See also,* for EXAMPLE, covenant for quiet enjoyment; covenant appurtenant.
v. To contract; to pledge; to make a binding promise.

- *n.* agreement, promise, pledge, vow, bond, compact, commitment ("covenant not to sue")

covenant appurtenant
[*kov*.e.nent a.*per*.te.nent]

See covenant running with the land.

covenant for quiet enjoyment
[*kov*.e.nent for *kwy*.et en.*joy*.ment]

A covenant that title is good and that therefore the grantee will be undisturbed in her possession and use of the property.

covenant running with the land
[*kov*.e.nent *run*.ing with the land]

A covenant that passes with the land when the land is conveyed. Such a covenant imposes upon the next purchaser, and all subsequent purchasers, both the liability for performance and the right to demand performance.

deed
[deed]

n. 1. Document by which real property, or an interest in real property, is conveyed from one person to another. 2. An act or action; something done or completed.
v. To transfer or convey by deed.

- *v.* transfer, convey, grant
- *n.* instrument, release, assignment, conveyance, contact ("warranty deed")

deed of covenant
[deed ov *kov*.e.nent]

See deed of warranty.

deed of gift
[deed ov gift]

A deed conveying property without consideration.

deed of quitclaim
[deed ov *kwit*.klame]

See quitclaim deed.

deed of release
[deed ov re.*leess*]

See quitclaim deed.

deed of trust
[deed ov trust]

A deed that creates a trust in real estate and is given as security for a debt. A deed of trust is in the nature of a mortgage, but differs from a mortgage in that it is executed in favor of a disinterested third person as trustee, where a mortgage is executed directly to the creditor to be secured.

deed of warranty
[deed ov *war*.en.tee]

1. A deed that contains title covenants. 2. A deed that contains covenants concerning the property conveyed and is a separate document from the deed that actually conveys the property.

demise
[de.*mize*]

n. 1. A deed. 2. The transfer of property by will.
v. To convey; to pass on by will or inheritance.

- *v.* bequeath, transmit, confer, endow
- *n.* conveyance, transfer

domicile
[*dom*.i.sile]

The relationship the law creates, between a person and a particular locality or country. Domicile is a person's permanent home or permanent abode. While a person may have only one domicile, she may have many residences.

dominant tenement
[*dom*.i.nent *ten*.e.ment]

Real property that benefits from an easement that burdens another piece of property, known as the servient tenement. *Compare* servient tenement.

dower
[*dow*.er]

The legal right or interest that a wife acquires by marriage in the property of her husband. Dower, which was very important under the common law, ensured that a widow was able to live upon and make use of a portion of her husband's land, usually one-third, as long as she lived. Dower, as such, no longer exists or has been substantially modified in most states, but every state retains aspects of the concept for the protection of both spouses (EXAMPLES: elective share; election by spouse; election under the will). *Note* that "dower" is not "dowry."

easement
[*eez*.ment]

1. A right to use the land of another for a specific purpose. EXAMPLE: a right of way given by a landowner to a utility company to erect and maintain power lines.
2. A right to use water, light, or air. *See also* easement of light and air.

- *n.* privilege, liberty, servitude, advantage, right of way

easement in gross
[*eez*.ment in grose]

An easement in gross does not exist so that the owner of adjoining property may better enjoy his property; rather, it is a personal interest in the use of another's land, unrelated to his own (EXAMPLE: a right to take water from the property of another). An easement in gross may be a right in either real property or personal property, depending upon its intended duration. *See also and compare* dominant tenement; servient tenement.

easement of access
[*eez*.ment ov *ak*.sess]

The right of an owner of real property bordering a public road to come from and go to the highway without being obstructed.

DICTIONARY | THESAURUS *continued...*

easement of light and air
[*eez*.ment ov lite and air]

An easement for the enjoyment of light and air unobstructed by structures on the adjoining premises. This is particularly important to land owners in large cities where there are many multi-story buildings that are next to each other.

eminent domain
[*em*.i.nent doh.*main*]

The power of the government to take private property for a public use or public purpose without the owner's consent, if it pays just compensation. The process by which this is done is called condemnation.

- *n.* condemnation, expropriation, compulsory acquisition

estate
[es.*tate*]

1. The property left by a decedent (i.e., a decedent's estate). 2. The right, title, and interest a person has in real or personal property, either tangible or intangible. Estates in real property (estates in land or landed estates) include both freehold estates (EXAMPLES: a fee simple; a fee tail; a life estate) and estates less than freehold (EXAMPLES: estates for years; estates at will). 3. The property itself.

- *n.* assets, wealth, property, fortune, personality, effects

eviction
[ee.*vik*.shen]

The act of putting a tenant out of possession of premises that she has leased.

- *n.* expulsion, ouster, ejection, dislodgement, removal, dispossession

Fair Housing Act
[fayr *how*.zing akt]

Another name for the Civil Rights Act of 1968, which prohibits practices that deny housing to anyone because of race, color, religion, or national origin.

fair market value
[*fayr mar*.ket *val*.yoo]

Actual value; value in money. The amount a buyer will pay and a seller will accept when neither is under pressure to buy or sell and both have a reasonable degree of knowledge of the relevant facts. Fair market value is virtually synonymous with actual cash value, fair cash value, and fair value. When there is no market, it is sometimes necessary for a court to construct a fair market value, relying upon expert testimony with respect to a hypothetical buyer and seller in the same circumstances.

Fannie Mae
[*fan*.ee may]

From the initials FNMA, Federal National Mortgage Association, it is the agency that supplies a market for mortgages insured by the Federal Housing Administration.

Federal Housing Administration
[*fed*.er.el *how*.zing ad.min.is.*tray*.shen]

Commonly referred to as the FHA; an agency of the United States that supports the availability of housing and of a sound mortgage market by insuring bank mortgages granted to borrowers who meet its standards.

fee
[fee]

An estate in real property that may be inherited. When "fee" is used without words of limitation (for EXAMPLE, base fee, conditional fee, determinable fee, or qualified fee), it always means fee simple.

- *n.* estate, property, inheritance, holding ("absolute fee")

fee estate
[fee es.*tate*]

A fee in land; an estate in fee.

fee simple
[fee *sim*.pl]

Also known as a fee simple absolute; the most complete estate in land known to the law. It signifies total ownership and control. It may be sold or inherited free of any condition, limitation, or restriction by particular heirs. *Compare* fee tail.

fee simple absolute
[fee *sim*.pl *ab*.so.loot]

See fee simple.

fee simple estate
[fee *sim*.pl es.*tate*]

See fee simple.

fee tail
[fee tayl]

An estate in land that is given to a person and her lineal descendants only, the heirs in general being deprived of any interest in the estate. In the absence of lineal descendants, the estate reverts to the donor. A fee tail estate given only to the donor's female lineal descendants is called a fee tail female; a fee tail estate limited to the donor's male lineal descendants is called a fee tail male. *See also* reversion. *Compare* fee simple.

fee tail female
[fee tayl *fee*.male]

See fee tail.

fee tail male
[fee tayl male]

See fee tail.

fixture
[*fiks*.cher]

An article, previously personal property, that, by being physically affixed to real estate, has become part of the real property; something so connected to a structure for use in connection with it that it cannot be removed without doing injury to the structure. EXAMPLES: a chandelier; an outdoor television antenna; a furnace.

- *n.* attachment, permanent addition, immovable object

flipping
[*flip*.ping]

In an illegal "flip" the value of the property is inflated (through high comparable sales and exaggerated appraisals, etc.) to induce the mortgage lender to fund more than the property's true value. Usually a deal is worked with the seller to recoup the difference between the real (lower) selling price and the amount of the buyer's mortgage money. Another way is for the buyer to obtain a "cash out" loan that can be worth up to 125 percent of the property's worth. This scenario only works in a hot, or seller's, market, where home prices are rapidly rising. *See* flopping.

flopping
[*flop*.ping]

v. The near opposite of flipping, it occurs in a softening or down real estate market. The "flop" works by deflating the value of a property to a price where the lender accepts less than is owed in a short sale. Then the buyer (perhaps in cahoots with a broker who may already have another buyer) quickly sells the property to the new party at a higher market price. *See* flipping.

DICTIONARY | THESAURUS *continued...*

foreclosure
[for.*kloh*.zher]

1. A legal action by which a mortgagee terminates a mortgagor's interest in mortgaged premises. *See also* mortgage. 2. The enforcement of a lien, deed of trust, or mortgage on real estate, or a security interest in personal property, by any method provided by law.

- *n.* blockage, obstruction, confiscation, prohibition, removal, dispossession, removal, eviction

foreclosure decree
[for.*kloh*.zher de.*kree*]

A decree that orders the sale of mortgaged real estate, the proceeds to be applied in satisfaction of the debt.

foreclosure defense
[for.*kloh*.zher de.*fenz*]

n. To avoid foreclosure on technical grounds, attorneys representing foreclosed clients take probing depositions from lenders' employees to find lapses in judgment, flaws in the process, or wrongdoing.

foreclosure sale
[for.*kloh*.zher sayl]

A sale of mortgaged premises in accordance with a foreclosure decree.

future interest
[fyu.cher *in*.trest]

An estate or interest in land or personal property, including money, whether vested or contingent, that is to come into existence at a future time. EXAMPLES: a remainder; a reversion; payments or income to be received in the future.

grant
[grant]

n. 1. A word used in conveying real property; a term of conveyance. 2. The conveyance or transfer itself. 3. That which is conveyed, conferred, or given. EXAMPLE: land.
v. 1. To convey; to bequeath; to devise. USAGE (in a deed): "grant, bargain and sell."

- *v.* relinquish; award, donate, assign, allot
- *n.* allocation, gift, contribution, privilege, endowment, donation

grantee
[gran.*tee*]

The person to whom a grant is made; the party in a deed to whom the conveyance is made. *Compare* grantor.

grantee-grantor indexes
[gran.*tee*-gran.*tor in*.dek.sez]

See grantor-grantee indexes.

grantor
[gran.*tor*]

The person who makes a grant; the party in a deed who makes the conveyance. *Compare* grantee.

grantor-grantee indexes
[gran.*tor*-gran.*tee in*.dek.sez]

Volumes maintained in most county courthouses that list every deed, mortgage, secured transaction, and lien of every type ever recorded in the county. All transactions are alphabetically indexed, both by grantor (the grantor-grantee index) and by grantee (the grantee-grantor index).

home
[home]

A word whose legal significance may be either "house," "residence," or "domicile," depending upon the context in which it appears.

- *n.* residence, domicile, house, abode, domain; native land, birthplace, motherland, fatherland

homestead [*home*.sted]	The right to own real property free and clear of the claims of creditors, provided the owner occupies the property as her home.
joint tenancy [joynt *ten*.en.see]	An estate in land (EXAMPLES: a fee simple estate; a life estate; an estate for years) or in personal property (EXAMPLE: a savings account) held by two or more persons jointly, with equal rights to share in its enjoyment. The most important feature of a joint tenancy is the right of survivorship, which means that upon the death of a joint tenant the entire estate goes to the survivor (or, in the case of more than two joint tenants, to the survivors, and so on to the last survivor). *See also* tenancy by the entirety. *Compare* tenancy in common.
land [land]	The soil and everything attached to it, whether naturally (EXAMPLES: trees; water; rocks) or by man (EXAMPLES: buildings; fixtures; fences), extending from the surface downward to the center of the earth and upward endlessly to the skies. "Land" is property used interchangeably with "real estate," "real property," and "realty." "Property" is often used by itself to mean "land." *See also* covenant running with the land. 2. An interest in land or an estate in land. EXAMPLES: a fee simple; a life estate.
	■ *n.* real estate, property, earth, terrain, soil, ground, nation, realty, territory, acreage
land contract [land *kon*.trakt]	A contract for sale of land; installment land contract.
land sale contract [land sale *kon*.trakt]	A contract for sale of land; installment land contract.
land use regulation [land yoos reg.yoo.*lay*.shen]	Government regulation of the way in which land is used. Zoning statutes and ordinances are EXAMPLES of land use regulation. *See also* zoning.
landlord [*land*.lord]	An owner of real property who leases all or a portion of the premises to a tenant. A landlord is also called a lessor; a tenant is called a lessee.
	■ *n.* lessor, landowner, possessor, proprietor ■ *ant.* lessee
landlord's lien [*land*.lordz leen]	A lien for rent that is in arrears, that a landlord has on a tenant's personal property located on the leased premises.
landowner [*land*.oh.ner]	A person who owns real property.
	■ *n.* landlord, owner, proprietor, possessor, title holder
lands, tenements, and hereditaments [landz, *ten*.e.mentz, and he.red.i.ta.mentz]	A term found in deeds and other documents relating to land, which expresses the most inclusive interest a person can own in real property (i.e., an inheritable interest in the land and everything on it or under it) (EXAMPLES: structures, minerals), and all rights arising out of it (EXAMPLES: the right to collect rent; the right to harvest timber).

lease
[lees]

1. A contract for the possession of real estate in consideration of payment of rent, ordinarily for a term of years or months, but sometimes at will. The person making the conveyance is the landlord or lessor; the person receiving the right of possession is the tenant or lessee. 2. Under the Uniform Commercial Code, a contract transferring the right to possession and use of personal property ("goods") for a term in return for consideration.

lease with option to purchase
[lees with *op*.shen to *per*.chess]

A lease that provides the lessee with the option, at the end of the term (or, under some leases, at any time during the term), to purchase the property for a specified sum.

legal description
[*lee*.gl des.*krip*.shen]

In deeds and mortgages, a description of the real estate that is the subject of the conveyance, by boundaries, distances, and size, or by reference to maps, surveys, or plats. *See also* metes and bounds.

levy
[*lev*.ee]

The seizure of property by the sheriff under writ to ensure payment of a judgment debt or to pay it. Such a levy is called levy of execution.

life estate
[life es.*tate*]

An estate that exists as long as the person who owns or holds it is alive. Its duration may also be the lifetime of another person (EXAMPLE: "to Sarah so long as Sam shall live").

listing agreement
[*list*.ing a.*gree*.ment]

A contract between an owner of real property and a real estate agent under which the agent is retained to secure a purchaser for the property at a specified price, for a commission.

lot
[lot]

A tract or parcel into which land has been divided.

lot book
[lot book]

See plat book.

mechanic's lien
[me.*kan*.iks *lee*.en]

A lien created by law for the purpose of securing payment for work performed or materials furnished in constructing or repairing a building or other structure.

metes and bounds
[meets and bowndz]

A property description, commonly in a deed or mortgage, that is based upon the property's boundaries and the natural objects and other markers on the land. *See also* legal description.

mortgage
[*more*.gej]

A written pledge of real property to secure a debt, usually to a bank.

mortgage insurance
[*more*.gej in.*shoor*.ense]

1. Insurance purchased by a mortgagor that pays the mortgage if the mortgagor is unable to because of death or disability. 2. Insurance purchased by a mortgagee insuring him against loss resulting from the mortgagor's inability to make payment. Mortgage insurance is a form of credit insurance.

mortgage loan
[*more*.gej lown]

A loan secured by a mortgage.

mortgage note [*more*.gej note]	A note that evidences a loan for which real estate has been mortgaged.
partition deed [par.*tish*.en deed]	A deed that achieves a partition or splitting of real estate.
perpetuity [per.pe.*tyoo*.i.tee]	A limitation of a contingent future interest in violation of the rule against perpetuities. ▪ *n.* eternity, continuation, indefiniteness, forever
plat [plat]	A map of a tract of land, showing the boundaries of the streets, blocks, and numbered lots. A plat is also referred to as a "plat map" or a "plot." ▪ *n.* map, plan, chart, sketch, diagram ("we needed to see the plat of the city")
plat book [plat book]	An official book of plat maps. *See also* plat.
plot [plot]	Same as plat. ▪ *n.* plat, field, land, area
possibility of reverter [pos.i.*bil*.i.tee ov re.*ver*.ter]	A type of future interest that remains in a grantor when, by grant or devise, he has created an estate in fee simple determinable or fee simple conditional, the fee automatically reverting to him or his successors upon occurrence of the event by which the estate is limited. EXAMPLE: Sam conveys Blackacre to the school district with the condition that it should revert back to Sam or his assigns when the school district ceases to use the land for school purposes. In these circumstances, Sam owns a possibility of reverter. *See also* reversion.
property [*prop*.er.tee]	1. The right of a person to possess, use, enjoy, and dispose of a thing without restriction (i.e., not the material object itself, but a person's rights with respect to the object). 2. Ownership or title, either legal or equitable. 3. In the more common sense, real property and personal property; tangible property and intangible property; corporeal property and incorporeal property. 4. Anything that can be owned. ▪ *n.* possessions, investments, holdings, capital ("his property at death"); realty, territory, acreage ("a beautiful piece of property")
quitclaim deed [*kwit*.klame deed]	A deed that conveys whatever interest the grantor has in a piece of real property, as distinguished from the more usual deed, which conveys a fee and contains various convenants including title covenants.
real property [real *prop*.er.tee]	Land, including things located on it or attached to it directly (EXAMPLE: buildings) or indirectly (EXAMPLE: fixtures). *See also* property. ▪ *n.* real estate
recording [ree.*kore*.ding]	A copy or a record of a transaction for the sale of land. *See also* recording acts.

DICTIONARY   THESAURUS *continued...*

recording acts
[ree.*kore*.ding aktz]

State statutes that provide for the recording of instruments, particularly those affecting title to real estate (EXAMPLES: a deed; a mortgage; a tax lien) and security interests in personal property (EXAMPLES: a conditional sale contract; a security agreement). There are several types of recording acts. In notice act states, an instrument that is not recorded is invalid with respect to a person who subsequently purchases the property who has no actual knowledge of the unrecorded transaction. In race act states, actual notice is immaterial because, in the event of conflicting claims of ownership, absolute priority is given to the first person who "wins the race to the courthouse" to record her instrument. Race-notice acts, which are in effect in some jurisdictions, combine various features of notice acts and race acts.

- *n.* recording laws, recording statutes

remainder
[ree.*mane*.der]

1. An estate in land to take effect immediately after the expiration of a prior estate (known as the particular estate), created at the same time and by the same instrument. EXAMPLE (in a will): "I will leave my land to Joe Jones for life, and after his death to Sarah Green and her heirs." The interest or estate of Sarah Green and her heirs is a remainder; Joe Jones's interest is a life estate. *Compare* reversion. 2. That which is left over; the residue.

- *n.* balance, residue, surplus, excess, remains; estate, interest, property

remainderman
[ree.*mane*.der.man]

A person entitled to receive a remainder.

residence
[*rez*.i.dence]

One's home; the place where a person lives with no present intention of moving. Although in a given context "residence" may have the same meaning as "domicile," the terms are not synonymous, because, while a person may have many residences, she can only have one domicile.

restrictive covenant
[ree.*strik*.tiv *kov*.e.nent]

1. A covenant in a deed prohibiting or restricting the use of the property (EXAMPLE: the type, location, or size of buildings that can be constructed on it). A covenant prohibiting the sale of real property to persons of a particular race is unenforceable because it is an unconstitutional restraint on alienation. 2. A covenant not to sue.

reversion
[re.*ver*.zhen]

1. A future interest in land to take effect in favor of the grantor of the land or his heirs after the termination of a prior estate he has granted; in other words, the returning of the property to the grantor or his heirs when the grant is over. (EXAMPLE: "I leave Blackacre to Joe Jones for life, and after his death to my heirs." The grantor's heirs have a reversionary interest in Blackacre, which will vest when Joe Jones dies; Joe Jones's interest is a life estate.) A reversion arises by operation of law. *Compare* remainder. 2. The interest or estate of an owner of land during the period of time for which he has granted his possessory rights to someone else. Thus, in the above EXAMPLE, the grantor and his heirs may also be said to have a reversionary interest in Blackacre during Joe Jones's life. A landlord's interest in premises that she has leased to a tenant is another EXAMPLE of a reversionary interest.

- *n.* remainder, future interest, residue, estate, interest; return, throwback

reversionary interest
[re.*ver*.zhen.a.ree *in*.trest]

A future interest (i.e., the right to the future enjoyment of a reversion).

revert
[re.*vert*]

1. With respect to an interest in land, to come back to a former owner or her heirs at a future time. USAGE: "After Bill dies, the life estate in Blackacre that Sam granted to Bill will revert to Sam, and if Sam is also dead, it will revert to Sam's heirs." *See also* reversion. 2. Turn backward.

riparian land
[ry.*pare*.ee.en land]

Land along the bank of a river or stream. Only land within the watershed of the river or stream is considered to be riparian.

robo signers
[*row*.bow *syne*.erz]

n. Document processors for mortgage lenders who rapidly sign papers in robotic fashion, without being familiar with the details of the loan or even reading the mortgage documents.

search
[serch]

A title search or examination of all mortgages, liens, debts, etc., that affect ownership of land in order to verify title.

servient tenement
[*serv*.ee.ent *ten*.e.ment]

Real property that is subject to an easement that benefits another piece of property, known as the dominant tenement.

short sale
[short sayl]

In real estate transactions, a sale in which the lender accepts less than what is owed on the mortgage, usually to avoid the time, trouble, and costs of foreclosing.

survey
[*ser*.vey]

n. 1. The method by which the boundaries of land are determined. 2. A map, plat, or other document reflecting a surveyor's determination of the boundary or boundaries of land.
v. 1. To determine the boundaries of land.

- *v.* appraise, outline, assay, canvass, measure ("to survey the land")
- *n.* analysis, study, audit

tacking
[*tack*.ing]

With respect to acquiring title to land by adverse possession, a doctrine allowing an adverse possessor to add her period of possession to that of a previous possessor to establish continuous possession. *See also* adverse possession.

tenancy
[*ten*.en.see]

1. The right to hold and occupy realty or personalty by virtue of owning an interest in it. 2. Possession of a realty under a lease; the relationship existing between a landlord or lessor and a tenant or lessee. 3. A term for the interest a tenant has under the lease.

- *n.* holding, leasing, occupancy, residence, rental

tenancy by the entirety
[*ten*.en.see by the en.*ty*.re.tee]

A form of joint tenancy in an estate in land or in personal property that exists between husband and wife by virtue of the fact that they are husband and wife. As with a conventional joint tenancy, a tenancy by the entirety is a tenancy with right of survivorship. "Tenancy," in this context, means ownership of the jointly held estate or interest, whether, for EXAMPLE, it is a fee simple estate, a life estate, a savings account, or the like. *Compare* tenancy in common.

DICTIONARY | THESAURUS *continued...*

tenancy for life [*ten*.en.see for life]	A life estate.
tenancy for years [*ten*.en.see for yeerz]	A tenancy under a lease or other contract for the period of a year or for a stated number of years.
tenancy from month to month [*ten*.en.see from month to month]	1. A tenancy in which no definite term is agreed upon and the rate is so much per month (i.e., a tenancy under a month-to-month lease). 2. A tenancy at will. 3. The tenancy of a holdover tenant (i.e., a tenancy at sufferance). *Compare* tenancy from year to year.
tenancy from year to year [*ten*.en.see from yeer to yeer]	A tenancy in which no definite term is agreed upon and the rate is so much per year. A tenancy from year to year may also be a tenancy at sufferance or a tenancy at will. *Compare* tenancy from month to month.
tenancy in common [*ten*.en.see in *kahm*.en]	A tenancy in which two or more persons own an undivided interest in an estate in land, for EXAMPLE, in a fee simple estate or a life estate, or in personal property, for EXAMPLE, in a savings account. As opposed to joint tenants, tenants in common have no right of survivorship; when a tenant in common dies, her interest passes to her heirs rather than to her cotenant or cotenants. *Compare* tenancy by the entirety.
tenant [*ten*.ent]	1. A person who holds or possesses realty or personalty by virtue of owning an interest in it. 2. A person who occupies realty under a lease with a landlord; a lessee. *See also* tenancy. ▪ *n.* lessee, occupier, renter, boarder, leaseholder, inhabitant, roomer
tenantable [*ten*.nen.tebl]	Premises that are habitable or ready to live in because plumbing, electricity, heat, and water are all in working condition.
tenants in common [*ten*.entz in *kahm*.en]	Two or more owners of property under a tenancy in common.
timeshare [*tym*.shair]	Interval ownership of a single condominium unit by multiple owners in weekly shares. In practice, each owner buys use of the unit for the week(s) he wants. Pro rata annual fees are assessed to each owner for maintenance/taxes. Ownership is transferable.
trespass [*tress*.pas]	An unauthorized entry or intrusion by one (trespasser) onto the real property of another.
variable rate mortgage [*vair*.ee.ebl rate *more*.gej]	Another term for an adjustable rate mortgage, one in which the percentage rate changes annually, or in some stipulated period.
variance [*var*.ee.ense]	In zoning law, an exception from the strict application of a zoning ordinance, granted to relieve a property owner of unnecessary hardship. A variance allows the land owner to use the land in a matter that the law would not otherwise permit.

warranty deed [war.en.*tee* deed]	A deed that contains title covenants.
warranty of habitability [war.en.*tee* ov hab.it.e.*bil*.i.tee]	A warranty implied by law that leased premises are fit to occupy.
waste [wayst]	1. The destruction, misuse, alteration, or neglect of premises by the person in possession, to the detriment of another's interest in the property. EXAMPLE: a tenant's polluting of a pond on leased land. 2. That which is left over, useless or even dangerous. EXAMPLES: hazardous waste; solid waste; toxic waste. ▪ *n.* decay, desolation, disuse, improvidence, misapplication, squandering; badlands, barrens, brush
zone [zone]	*n.* 1. An area or district created by a zoning board in accordance with zoning regulations. 2. A distinct area that is unlike the surrounding areas. *v.* To engage in zoning. ▪ *n.* area, belt, circuit, district, realm, territory, tract sector
zoning [*zone*.ing]	The creation and application of structural, size, and use restrictions imposed upon the owners of real estate within districts or zones in accordance with zoning regulations or ordinances. Although authorized by state statutes, zoning is generally legislated and regulated by local government. Zoning is a form of land use regulation and is generally of two types: regulations having to do with structural and architectural design; and regulations specifying the use(s) to which designated districts may be put; for EXAMPLE, commercial, industrial, residential, or agricultural.
zoning board [*zone*.ing bord]	An administrative agency of a municipality that administers zoning regulations or ordinances.

Missing Words

Fill in the blanks.

1. _____ is the destruction of premises by the person in possession.

2. A _____ is a multi-unit dwelling where residents own individual apartments.

3. An exception to the strict application of a zoning ordinance is called a(n) _____.

4. A(n) _____ is the transferring of title to real property from one person to another.

5. A person whose business is to bring a buyer and seller together is a(n) _____.

6. _____ is the power of the government to take private property for a public use.

7. A _____ is the most complete estate in land a person can own.

8. A _____ is an estate that exists as long as the person who owns or holds it is alive.

9. A(n) _____ is the transfer of property by a will.

10. When a tenant is put out of possession, it is called an _____.

STUDY AID: Use flashcards for this unit before completing the exercises.

Matching

Match the letter of the definition to the term.

_G_ **11.** deed — **A.** land including things located on it or attached to it

_B_ **12.** abstract of title — **B.** a short account of the state of the title to real estate

_C_ **13.** estate — **C.** right, title, and interest a person has in real or personal property

_A_ **14.** real property — **D.** personal property that becomes part of real estate

_F_ **15.** easement — **E.** the method by which the boundaries of land are determined

_K_ **16.** foreclosure — **F.** right to use land owned by another person for a specific purpose

_M_ **17.** zoning — **G.** document by which real property is conveyed from one person to another

_H_ **18.** mortgage — **H.** a pledge of real property to secure a debt

_J_ **19.** recording — **I.** a contract for the possession of real estate in consideration of payment of rent

_I_ **20.** lease — **J.** the act of making a record

_E_ **21.** survey — **K.** a legal action by which a mortgagee terminates a mortgagor's interest in mortgaged premises

_L_ **22.** co-ownership — **L.** the ownership of property by at least two persons

_D_ **23.** fixture — **M.** restrictions imposed upon owners of real estate within districts or zones

Multiple Choice

Select the best choice.

B **24.** A document by which real property or an interest in real property is conveyed from one person to another is a(n):
  a. mortgage.
  b. deed.
  c. fixture.
  d. easement.

C **25.** The creation and application of structural, size, and use restrictions imposed upon owners of real estate within districts or zones is called:
  a. recording.
  b. partition.
  c. zoning.
  d. trespass.

D **26.** The method by which the boundaries of land are determined is called:
  a. mortgage.
  b. clear title.
  c. foreclosure.
  d. survey.

D **27.** An estate or interest in land or personal property that is to come into existence at a future time is a:
  a. fee.
  b. fee simple estate.
  c. fee tail.
  d. future interest.

A **28.** Ownership of property by more than one person is:
  a. co-ownership.
  b. fee.
  c. covenant.
  d. satisfaction.

A **29.** A short account of the state of the title to real estate, reflecting all past ownership and any interests or rights that a person might currently have with respect to the property, is:
  a. an abstract of title.
  b. satisfaction.
  c. license.
  d. clean title.

C **30.** An agreement to transfer title to land is a:
  a. deed.
  b. mortgage.
  c. contract for sale of land.
  d. lease.

D **31.** Legal action by which a mortgagee terminates a mortgagor's interest in mortgaged premises is a:
  a. mortgage.
  b. license.
  c. recording.
  d. foreclosure.

A **32.** The right to hold and occupy realty or personalty by virtue of owning an interest in it is called a:
  a. tenancy.
  b. partition.
  c. covenant.
  d. fee.

D **33.** In a deed, a promise to do or not do a particular thing, or an assurance that a particular fact or circumstance exists or does not exist, is a:
  a. convey.
  b. survey.
  c. fixture.
  d. covenant.

A **34.** An article, previously personal property, that becomes real property is called:
  a. fixture.
  b. personal property.
  c. real property.
  d. abstract of title.

A **35.** The most complete estate in land known to law that signifies total ownership and control is called a:
  a. fee simple estate.
  b. fee tail.
  c. condominium.
  d. cooperative.

B **36.** An unauthorized entry or intrusion onto real property is called a:
  a. burglary.
  b. trespass.
  c. transgression.
  d. fault.

True/False

Mark the following T or F.

_____T_ **37.** A fee is an estate in real property that may be inherited.

_____F_ **38.** A tenant is the purchaser of real estate.

_____T_ **39.** A fee tail is an estate in land that is given to a person and her lineal descendants only.

_____F_ **40.** An abstract of title is a pledge of real property to secure a debt.

_____T_ **41.** A joint tenancy is an estate in land or in personal property held by two or more persons jointly, with equal rights to share in its enjoyment, with rights of survivorship.

_____T_ **42.** A cooperative is a multi-unit dwelling in which each tenant has an interest in the corporation or other entity that owns the building.

_____T_ **43.** An estate is the right, title, and interest a person has in real or personal property.

_____F_ **44.** The power of the government to take private property for a public use or purpose is called trespass.

_____T_ **45.** An article that was previously personal property that, by being physically affixed to real estate, has become part of the real property is called a fixture.

_____T_ **46.** A tenancy in common is a tenancy in which two or more persons own an undivided interest in an estate in land without rights of survivorship.

_____T_ **47.** An oven built into a wall becomes a fixture that cannot be removed at the time of sale.

_____F_ **48.** If someone occupies real property in an open continuous and notorious manner, under claim of right for a period of weeks, this is adverse possession.

Synonyms

Select the correct synonym in parentheses for each numbered item.

49. CONVEY
(transfer, edit, produce)

50. REAL PROPERTY
(land, goods, money)

51. DEED
(easement, conveyance, mortgage)

52. WASTE
(neglect, preservation, maintenance)

53. TRESPASS
(stroll, convey, intrusion)

54. SURVEY
(recording, easement, outline)

55. MORTGAGE
(sell, pledge, variance)

56. CO-OWNERSHIP
(joint, several, individual)

57. VARIANCE
(exception, conformity, estate)

58. COVENANT
(failure, assurance, satisfaction)

59. ABSTRACT OF TITLE
(chain of title, loss of title, adverse possession)

60. BROKER
(owner, agent, seller)

61. REVERSIONARY INTEREST
(past, future, partial)

62. REVERT
(go forward, turn back, circle around)

63. LAND
(royalty, realty, dower)

64. ZONE
(remainder, revert, district)

65. PLAT
(grant, lease, map)

66. RESTRICTIVE COVENANT
(grants, details, limits)

67. LEVY
(give, seize, divide)

Self-Test

Place the number of the correct term in the appropriate space.

68. condominium

69. eminent domain

70. tenants

71. landlord

72. lease with option to purchase

73. tenancy for years

74. deed

75. abstract of title

76. eviction

77. Fair Housing Act

78. broker

79. tenancy from month to month

80. warranty of habitability

81. contract for sale of land

After the county government took their house by _69 eminent domain_ for the new freeway construction, Sajjad and Kishori

Rajan wanted to buy a new house. While their savings were not quite sufficient to build a new house, they began

searching for a rental property with a(n) _72 lease w/ option to purchase_. Although they wished to be owners instead of _70 tenants_,

they couldn't find a suitable place through an agent or real estate _78 broker_.

So, the Rajans decided to rent for the shortest period of time and began checking the classified advertisements.

They wanted a(n) _79 tenancy from month to month_ that would not obligate them to a long-term lease.

The next day's newspaper had an advertisement for a short-term house rental that attracted the Rajans'

attention and they telephoned the _71 landlord_ of the house. She said it was not ready to be seen because the previous occupants left it a mess after they were ejected in a(n) ___76 eviction___ proceeding. The Rajans insisted on seeing the

house that day and the owner reluctantly agreed. When the Rajans arrived at the house, the owner said, "I'll show it but

it isn't fit to occupy and there is no ___80 Warranty of Habitability___. And if you take it I'll insist on at least a 12-month lease, making it

a(n) ___73 tenancy for years___." The Rajans were upset and wondered if, because of their accents, they were being denied housing

in violation of the ___77 Fair Housing Act___.

Finally, the Rajans found a beautiful apartment that was part of a multi-unit dwelling called a ___68 Condominium___. They

took all the papers pertaining to the sale for their attorney to review. The attorney requested to see the ___74 Deed___, the

___75 abstract of title___, and the ___81 Contract for sale of land___.

Word Scramble

Unscramble the following words and write the correct word(s) that match(es) the definition for each word or phrase.

82. tatees – the property left by a decedent _____

_____

83. lear pertypro – land and everything attached to it

_____

84. eedd – document by which real property is conveyed

_____

85. gagemort – written pledge of real property to secure

a debt _____

_____

86. vicetion – the act of putting a tenant out _____

_____

87. easel – the person making this conveyance is the

landlord or lessor _____

_____

88. mentease – the right to use the land of another for

a specific purpose _____

_____

89. veycon – to transfer title to property _____

_____

90. eef plesim teates – the most complete estate in land

_____

91. tractabs fo tietl – a short account of the state of title

to real estate _____

_____

92. etsaw – the neglect of premises by the person in

possession_____

_____

93. turefix – personal property that becomes attached

to the land _____

_____

94. veysur – to determine the boundaries of land _____

_____

95. nantecy yb het tirenety – a form of joint tenancy

that exists between husband and wife _____

_____

96. verrearysion terestin – a future interest

_____

97. manmainderre – an estate in land to take effect immediately after the expiration of a prior estate

_____

_____

98. anFnie aMe – the agency that supplies a market for mortgages insured by the Federal Housing Administration _____

_____

99. pingflip – an illegal inflation of the value of a property to induce the mortgage lender to fund more than the property's true value _____

_____

100. mitehares – interval ownership of a single condominium unit by multiple owners in weekly shares _____

_____

The Last Word

Reverse Mortgage, also known as a Home Equity Conversion Mortgage, is used by a homeowner age 62 and over to borrow against one's home equity—the appraised value of the home less any amounts owed on loans, taxes, or liens. Borrowers make no payments. In fact, the lender pays the borrower—hence, a reverse mortgage. Options for the borrower include receiving the entire amount of the mortgage in cash, borrowing money as needed, or receiving a monthly check. When the house is sold, the lender collects the original amount of the mortgage plus accrued interest. If the home sells for less than the amount of the mortgage, mortgage insurance (obtained at origination of the mortgage) pays the difference to the lender.

Senior citizen borrowers must occupy the residence and the mortgage is satisfied when the homeowners sell or die. The total amount of the mortgage depends on the age of the borrower (the lowest amount at age 62) and the net value of the property, as well as the lender's limit, which is currently $625,000. What are the pluses of a reverse mortgage for senior citizens versus having their equity locked up in their home?

8 Family Law

- Learn about family law.

- Master the similarities and differences in definitions of key terms.

- Master the pronunciations and spellings of legal terms.

- Recognize the synonyms used for legal terminology.

- Practice usage of terms, definitions, and synonyms.

- Complete unit exercises in the forms of missing words, matching, multiple choice, true/false, synonyms, self-test, and word scramble.

- Work with a legal dictionary/thesaurus.

13 Family Law

Statistics show that approximately 50 percent of all marriages will end in divorce. Couples enter marriage today with less certainty than ever. In order to protect themselves, some couples are drafting prenuptial agreements setting forth the consequences of a possible divorce.

Most states follow principles of community property or equitable distribution in dividing property during a divorce. Issues of custody and support of the children may be addressed before, during, and after divorce proceedings.

Whether or not a man is the true father of a child is an issue that is raised in a paternity proceeding where blood or genetic tests are key evidence.

Sometimes problems arise in the care and raising of children. In some states, parents might find themselves in family court responding to civil charges of failure to properly supervise or support their children. However, charges of abuse, battering, or neglect in a family are usually criminal matters. In the following case of first impression, a precedent may be set in the area of child support.

CASE AND COMMENT

Supreme Court of the State of New York, Appellate Division: Second Judicial
Department
In the Matter of H.M. (Anonymous), respondent,
v.
E.T. (Anonymous), appellant
Docket No. U-110-07 (Submitted June 20, 2008, By Opinion May 4, 2010)

Facts: A lesbian couple agreed to conceive a child through artificial insemination. After the birth, the nonbiological parent, E.T., ended the relationship. H.M. argued that she relied on her former partner's promise of support before she became pregnant. The attorney for E.T. said the appellant "is a stranger to the child and had no formal relationship with the biological mother."

Procedural History: The petitioner H.M., a Canadian citizen, and the biological mother of the subject child, filed a petition pursuant to the Uniform Interstate Support Act, seeking to obtain child support from E.T., her former same-sex partner with whom she allegedly agreed to conceive a child through artificial insemination by a donor, and upon whose promise of support she allegedly relied, in conceiving the child. This court, in a prior decision, concluded that Family Court lacked subject matter jurisdiction and reversed the orders of the Family Court imposing a support order payable by E.T. The Court of Appeals reversed the determination that the Family Court lacked subject matter Jurisdiction, and remitted the matter to this court of whether H.M.'s petition sufficiently states a cause of action for child support.

Issue: Whether a same-sex parent is liable to pay child support pursuant to Family Court Articles 4 and 5-B.

Rationale: In prior rulings, New York State fathers who have denied paternity have still been required to pay child support if they had developed a relationship with the child and had promised to support the child.

Ruling: The court said, "By parity of reasoning, we hold that where the same-sex partner of a child's biological mother consciously chooses, together with the biological mother, to bring that child into the world through [artificial insemination], and where a child is conceived in reliance on the partner's implied promise to support the child, a cause of action for child support…has been sufficiently alleged." The Court ordered "a hearing in the Family Court on the issue of whether E.T. should be equitably estopped from denying her responsibility to support the subject child."

Comment: This first case of an appellate court in New York recognizing child support obligations between same-sex parents exemplified that marriage is a commitment, and a very expensive commitment if broken. This case initiates all gay married couples to the problems of marriage, divorce, children and parenting as well as the need for a domestic relations attorney.

DICTIONARY THESAURUS

Term [phonetic pronunciation]	*Note: All dictionary/thesaurus terms appear on flashcards at the back of the book and on the student website.*

adoption
[a.*dop*.shen]

The act of creating the relationship of parent and child between persons who do not naturally share that relationship.

- *n.* acceptance, embracement, approval, assumption ("their adoption of a hostile stance"); fostering, fosterage, raising ("adoption of the homeless child")

adult
[a.*dult*]

A grown person; one who is no longer a child. "Adult" is not a technical legal word.

adultery
[a.*dul*.ter.ee]

Sexual intercourse by a married person with a person who is not his or her spouse.

- *n.* infidelity, affair, unfaithfulness, cuckoldry

affiliation proceeding
[a.*fil*.ee.ay.shun pro.*see*.ding]

A judicial proceeding to establish the paternity of an illegitimate child and to compel the father to contribute to its support. *See also* paternity suit.

alimony
[*al*.i.moh.nee]

Ongoing support payments by a divorced spouse, usually payments made for maintenance of the former spouse. Alimony is not child support. *See also* palimony.

- *n.* support, maintenance, sustenance, allowance

annulment of marriage
[a.*nul*.ment ov *mar*.ej]

The act of a court in voiding a marriage for causes existing at the time the marriage was entered into (EXAMPLE: the existing marriage of one of the parties). Annulment differs from divorce in that it is not a dissolution of the marriage but a declaration that no marriage ever existed.

antenuptial
[*an*.te.*nup*.shel]

Before marriage.

- *adj.* prenuptial, premarital

antenuptial agreement
[*an*.te.*nup*.shel a.*gree*.ment]

See prenuptial agreement.

arrears
[a.*reerz*]

Payments past due. EXAMPLE: A person may be in arrears in alimony payments or in arrears on a mortgage.

- *n.* unpaid debts, obligations, delinquency, overdue payments ("arrears in alimony")

bigamy
[*big*.e.mee]

The crime of marrying while already married to another.

ceremonial marriage
[sehr.e.*mone*.ee.el *mehr*.ej]

A marriage performed by an appropriate religious or civil official, after the parties have met all legal requirements (EXAMPLE: securing a marriage license). *See also* solemnization of marriage. *Compare* common law marriage.

DICTIONARY   THESAURUS *continued...*

child
[child]

1. A very young person. *Compare* minor. 2. Offspring; progeny; descendent. *Compare* heir. "Child" is not a technical legal term with a definite meaning. Its meaning is always subject to construction in the context in which it is used.

- *n.* kid, adolescent, minor, youth, juvenile

child abuse
[child a.*byooss*]

The physical, sexual, verbal, or emotional abuse of a young person. Child abuse includes the neglect of a child. It is a crime in every state. *See also* child abuse reporting acts.

child abuse reporting acts
[child a.*byooss* re.*port*.ing aktz]

State statutes that make specified persons (EXAMPLES: physicians, teachers) responsible for reporting suspected child abuse.

child stealing
[child *steel*.ing]

The taking or removal of a child from a parent or from a person awarded custody. This is also the crime committed when a child is abducted from the custody of one parent by the other, although it is commonly called parental kidnapping.

child support
[child se.*port*]

1. Money paid, pending divorce and after divorce, by one parent to the other for the support of their children. *See also* support. 2. The obligation of parents to provide their children with the necessities of life.

civil union
[*sih*.vil *yoon*.yen]

An alternative to full marriage for gay couples, also known as "civil partnership." The state confers the rights of inheritance, joint ownership of property, health benefits, and other civil rights to same-sex couples.

cohabitation
[ko.ha.bi.*tay*.shen]

1. Living together as man and wife, although not married to each other. 2. Living together. 3. Having sexual intercourse.

- *n.* living together, common law marriage, alliance, union, residing together
- *ant.* separation

common law marriage
[*kom*.en law *mar*.ej]

A marriage entered into without ceremony, the parties agreeing between themselves to be husband and wife, followed by a period of cohabitation where the parties hold themselves out as actually married. Common law marriages are valid in some states but invalid in most. *Compare* ceremonial marriage.

community property
[ke.*myu*.ni.tee *prop*.er.tee]

A system of law under which the earnings of either spouse are the property of both the husband and the wife, and property acquired by either spouse during the marriage (other than by gift, under a will, or through inheritance) is the property of both. States that have adopted this system are called community property states. *Compare* equitable distribution.

condonation
[kon.do.*nay*.shen]

The forgiveness by one spouse of the other's conduct that constitutes grounds for divorce. Condonation is a defense to a divorce action based upon the conduct that has been condoned.

- *n.* forgiveness, pardon, overlooking, clemency, discharge, acquittal

connivance [ke.*nie*.vense]	As a defense in an action for divorce, fraudulent consent by one spouse to the other spouse's engaging in conduct that constitutes grounds for divorce. *Compare* no-fault divorce. ▪ *n.* conspiracy, collusion, consent, overlooking, condoning
consortium [kon.*sore*.shum]	The rights and duties of both husband and wife, resulting from marriage. They include companionship, love, affection, assistance, comfort, cooperation, and sexual relations. *See also* loss of consortium.
cruelty [*kroo*.el.tee]	The infliction of physical or mental pain or distress. As a ground for divorce, "cruelty" means physical violence or threats of physical violence, or mental distress willfully caused. ▪ *n.* brutality, harshness, spitefulness, viciousness, torture, violence ▪ *ant.* sympathy, kindness
curtesy [*ker*.te.see]	The rights a husband had under the common law with respect to his wife's property. Today these rights have been modified in every state in various ways, but all states that retain curtesy in some form extend the same rights to both spouses. *Note* that "curtesy" is not "courtesy."
custody [*kuss*.te.dee]	As applied to persons, physical contact. (EXAMPLES: Parents customarily "have physical custody" of their children; although, in the event of divorce, one parent may have sole custody, or both parents have joint custody or divided custody.) Custody carries with it the obligation on the part of the custodian to maintain and care for the person in his charge for the duration of their relationship. ▪ *n.* care, control, protection, possession, management, restraint
decree [de.*kree*]	*n.* The final order of a court. For all practical purposes, the distinction between decrees and judgments no longer exists, and all relief in all civil actions, whether legal or equitable, is obtained by means of judgment. *v.* To order, to dictate, to ordain, to enact, to command. ▪ *n.* mandate, commandment, directive, ordinance, statute, decision, ruling
desertion [de.*zer*.shen]	1. As a ground for divorce, a voluntary separation of one of the parties to a marriage from the other without the consent of or without having been wronged by the second party, with the intention to live apart and without any intention to return to the cohabitation. 2. The criminal abandonment of a child in neglect of the parental duty of support.
dissolution of marriage [dis.e.*loo*.shen ov *ma*.rej]	1. The termination of a marriage, whether by annulment, divorce a vinculo matrimonii, or no-fault divorce. 2. A term for divorce in some no-fault states.
divided custody [di.*vy*.ded *kuss*.te.dee]	An arrangement under which the child of divorced parents lives a portion of the time with one parent and a portion of the time with the other. Legal custody, however, remains at all times with one of the parents. *Compare* joint custody. *See also* custody.

DICTIONARY / THESAURUS *continued...*

divorce
[di.*vorss*]

A dissolution of the marital relationship between husband and wife. *Compare* alimony. *See also* no-fault divorce.

- *n.* separation, division, break, break-up, parting, disunion
- *v.* rescind, dismiss, annul, cease, dissolve

divorce a vinculo matrimonii
[di.*vorss* ah *vin*.kyoo.loh mat.ri.*moh*.ni.eye]

A decree that dissolves the marriage because of matrimonial misconduct. Also called absolute divorce. *Compare* no-fault divorce.

divorce from bed and board
[di.*vorss* from bed and bord]

A decree that terminates the right of cohabitation, and adjudicates matters such as custody and support, but does not dissolve the marriage itself. *Compare* divorce a vinculo matrimonii; no-fault divorce.

domestic relations
[de.*mes*.tick re.*lay*.shenz]

The field of law relating to domestic matters, such as marriage, divorce, support, custody, and adoption; family law.

elder law
[*el*.der law]

A field of law with statutes and regulations designed to protect the elderly. Elder law encompasses a variety of legal issues such as wills, trusts and estates, long-term care, guardianships, elder abuse, health care, Social Security, Medicaid, and Medicare.

equitable adoption
[*ek*.wi.tebl e.*dop*.shen]

The principle that a child may enforce in equity a promise to adopt him, at least to the extent that he will be given rights of inheritance with respect to the property of the person who made the promise.

equitable distribution
[*ek*.wi.tebl dis.tri.*byoo*.shen]

Some jurisdictions permit their courts, in a divorce case, to distribute all property obtained during the marriage on an "equitable" basis. In deciding what is equitable, the court takes into consideration factors such as the length of the marriage and the contributions of each party, including homemaking. *Compare* community property.

family
[*fam*.i.lee]

1. A word of great flexibility, the meaning of which varies according to the context in which it appears. In its most common usage, it means the persons who live under one roof and under one head or management. A family is not necessarily limited to a father and mother (or a father or mother) and children. 2. In another of its common uses, "family" refers to persons who are of the same bloodline or are descended from a common ancestor.

- *n.* classification, progeny, descendants, household, family unit, issue

family court
[*fam*.i.lee kort]

A court whose jurisdiction varies from state to state. It may hear domestic relations cases; it may hear juvenile court matters; it may also try child abuse cases and oversee paternity suits.

family law
[*fam*.i.lee law]

Area of the law concerned with domestic relations.

foreign divorce [*forr*.en di.*vorss*]	A divorce granted in a state or country other than the couple's state of residence.
foster child [*foss*.ter child]	A child brought up by a person who is not her biological parent. *Compare* adoption.
foster parent [*foss*.ter *pair*.ent]	A person who rears a foster child.
gay marriage [gay *mehr*.ej]	The relationship of two men or two women legally united as spouses, first legalized by Massachusetts and other foreign jurisdictions. *See also* civil union.
guardian ad litem [*gar*.dee.en ad *ly*.tem]	A person appointed by the court to represent and protect the interests of a minor or an incompetent person during litigation.
HLA testing [HLA *test*.ing]	Abbreviation of human leukocyte antigen testing. An HLA blood test is a paternity test.
imputed income [im.*pew*.ted *in*.kum]	1. The benefit a person obtains through performance of her own services or through the use of her own property. Generally, this is not subject to taxes. EXAMPLE: if you are a carpenter and make repairs to your home, these services would not be subject to tax. 2. Benefits that accrue when no money is received. EXAMPLE: when an employer offers free health insurance to employees and their families, this would be imputed income.
incompatibility [in.kum.pat.e.*bil*.e.tee]	Conflict in personality and temperament. As a requirement for no-fault divorce, a conflict so deep it cannot be altered or adjusted, rendering it impossible for the parties to continue to live together in a normal marital relationship.
infant [in.*fent*]	A person who has not reached the age of majority and who therefore is under a civil disability; non-age, minority. The period of life when one is a young child.
irreconcilable differences [ir.rek.en.*sy*.lebl *dif*.ren.sez]	A requirement for divorce or dissolution of marriage in some states with no-fault divorce laws. The term itself means that because of dissension and personality conflicts, the marriage relationship has been destroyed and there is no reasonable expectation of reconciliation. *See also* irremedial breakdown of marriage.
irremedial breakdown of marriage [ir.re.*mee*.dee.el *brake*.down of *mehr*.ej]	A requirement for no-fault divorce in some states. *See also* irreconcilable differences. ▪ *n.* irretrievable breakdown of marriage
joint custody [joynt *kuss*.te.dee]	An arrangement whereby both parties to a divorce retain legal custody of their child and jointly participate in reaching major decisions concerning the child's welfare.
juvenile [*joo*.ve.nile]	*adj.* Young, youthful, immature. ▪ *n.* infant, youth, youngster, minor, teenager, ward, teen ▪ *adj.* childish, inexperienced, sophomore, irresponsible, infantile, adolescent ▪ *ant.* adult

juvenile court
[*joo*.ve.nile kort]

A court having special jurisdiction over juvenile offenders, as well as abused and neglected children.

juvenile offender
[*joo*.ve.nile o.*fen*.der]

A minor who breaks the law. A juvenile offender is sometimes referred to as a delinquent child or a youthful offender.

legitimacy
[le.*jit*.i.mes.ee]

The state of having been born to parents who are married to each other.

loss of consortium
[los ov kun.*sore*.shem]

The loss of a spouse's assistance or companionship, or the loss of a spouse's ability or willingness to have sexual relations. If such loss results from a tort, it gives rise to a cause of action in favor of the partner of the spouse injured by the tort. *See also* consortium.

maintenance
[*main*.ten.ense]

The support of a person. *See also* support.

- *n.* upkeep, conservation, preservation, care, protection, help, aid, finances, alimony, subsistence, livelihood ("maintenance for her health")

majority
[ma.*jaw*.ri.tee]

Legal age; full age, the age at which a person acquires the capacity to contract; the age at which a person is no longer a minor. The age of majority varies from state to state and differs depending on the purpose. EXAMPLES: eligibility for a driver's license; eligibility to vote; the right to buy alcoholic beverages. *Compare* minor.

marital agreement
[*mehr*.i.tel a.*gree*.ment]

An agreement between two people who are married to each other (a postnuptial agreement), or two people who are about to marry (a prenuptial agreement), with respect to the disposition of the marital property or property owned by either spouse before the marriage, with respect to the rights of either in the property of the other, or with respect to support.

marriage
[*mehr*.ej]

1. The relationship of a man and a woman legally united as husband and wife. Marriage is a contract binding the parties until one dies or until a divorce or annulment occurs. 2. The act of becoming married; the marriage ceremony. *See also* common law marriage, gay marriage, and civil union.

- *n.* matrimony, wedlock, nuptial state, nuptials, sacrament, espousal ("to be joined in marriage")
- *ant.* divorce

marriage certificate
[*mehr*.ej ser.*tif*.i.ket]

A certificate that evidences a marriage, prepared by the person officiating at the ceremony and usually required by state law. *Compare* marriage license.

marriage license
[*mehr*.ej *ly*.sense]

Authorization to marry issued by the state in which the ceremony is to occur. It is a condition precedent to a ceremonial marriage. *Compare* marriage certificate.

merger in judgment
[*mer*.jer in *juj*.ment]

The extinguishment of a cause of action by entry of a judgment. EXAMPLE: the obligation to pay money under a separation agreement is superseded by a judgment for alimony.

minor [*my*.ner]	A person who has not yet attained her majority; a person who has not reached legal age; a person who has not acquired capacity to contract. *See* infant. *Compare* majority.
no-fault divorce [no-fawlt di.*vorss*]	A term for the requirements for divorce in jurisdictions in which the party seeking the divorce need not demonstrate that the other party is at fault. The requirements differ from state to state. EXAMPLES include irreconcilable differences, irremedial breakdown of marriage, and irretrievable breakdown of marriage.
non-marital children [non-*mehr*.i.tel *chil*.drin]	Children not related to or connected with the marriage.
palimony [*pal*.i.moh.nee]	Alimony paid upon the break-up of a live-in relationship between two people who were not married to each other. In some states, such payment may be ordered by a court if the parties entered into an express contract or if the court finds the existence of an implied contract. In others, court-ordered palimony is based upon quantum meruit. In still others, palimony is considered to be contrary to public policy and is not recognized by the law.
partition [par.*tish*.en]	A division made between two or more persons of land or other property belonging to them as co-owners, usually pursuant to a divorce action.
paternity [pa.*ter*.ni.tee]	The status of being a father. ■ *n.* fatherhood, derivation, ancestry, lineage, descent
paternity suit [pa.*ter*.ni.tee sute]	A proceeding to establish the paternity of a child born out of wedlock, usually for the purpose of compelling the father to support the child. *See also* affiliation proceeding.
prenuptial agreement [pree.*nup*.shel a.*gree*.ment]	An agreement between a man and a woman who are about to be married, governing the financial and property arrangements between them in the event of divorce, death, or even during the marriage. Prenuptial agreements are also called antenuptial agreements, antenuptial settlements, or premarital agreements. *See also* marital agreement.
reconciliation [rek.en.sil.ee.*ay*.shen]	The act of resolving differences. In domestic relations law, a resumption of cohabitation by spouses who have been living apart. ■ *n.* restoration, conciliation, rapprochement, concordance, rapport
recrimination [re.krim.i.*nay*.shen]	A defense in an action for divorce based upon the misconduct by the plaintiff that would itself be grounds for divorce if the defendant had brought an action against the plaintiff. ■ *n.* countercharge, retort, rejoinder, counterattack, reprisal, blame, retribution
same-sex marriage [same-sex *mehr*.ej]	*See* gay marriage and civil union.
separation [sep.e.*ray*.shen]	The status of a husband and wife who live separately. The state of being apart or coming apart. ■ *n.* detachment, disrelation, disassociation, partition, parting, rupture, disunion, alienation

DICTIONARY	THESAURUS *continued...*

separation agreement
[sep.e.*ray*.shen a.*gree*.ment]

An agreement between husband and wife who are about to divorce or to enter into a legal separation, settling property rights and other matters (EXAMPLES: custody, child support, visitation, alimony) between them. Separation agreements are subject to court approval. *See also* marital agreement.

solemnization of marriage
[saw.lem.neh.*zay*.shen ov *mehr*.ej]

The performance of the marriage ceremony.

solemnize
[*saw*.lem.nize]

The performance of a formal ceremony; to act with formality. *See also* solemnization of marriage.

spouse
[spouse]

A husband or wife, a marriage partner.
- *n.* wife, husband, mate, companion, partner

step-parent
[step-*pare*.ent]

A wife, in her relationship to her spouse's child by a former marriage; a husband, in his relationship to his spouse's child by a former marriage.

support
[sup.*ort*]

To provide funds or other means of maintenance of a person.

surrogate
[*ser*.e.get]

A person who acts for another.
- *n.* alternate, substitute, agent, vicarious, actor, delegate, proxy, stand-in ("surrogate mother")

surrogate motherhood
[*ser*.e.get *muth*.er.hood]

The status of a woman who "hosts" the fertilized egg of another woman in her womb or who is artificially inseminated with the sperm of a man who is married to someone else and to whom (with his wife) she has agreed to assign her parental rights if the child is delivered.

tenancy by the entirety
[*ten*.en.see by the en.*ty*.re.tee]

A form of joint tenancy in an estate in land or in personal property that exists between husband and wife by virtue of the fact that they are husband and wife. As with a conventional joint tenancy, a tenancy by the entirety is a tenancy with right of survivorship. "Tenancy," in this context, means ownership of the jointly held estate or interest, whether, for EXAMPLE, it is a fee simple estate, a life estate, a savings account, or the like.

tender years
[*ten*.der yerz]

A term used to describe minors, particularly when they are very young. USAGE: "a child of tender years."

visitation
[viz.i.*tay*.shen]

Short for visitation rights (i.e., the right of a divorced parent who does not have custody of his child to visit the child at such times and places as the court may order).

void marriage
[voyd *mehr*.ej]

A marriage absolutely prohibited by law. EXAMPLE: marriage with a person who is not of age.

wedlock
[*wed*.lok]

The state of being married; marriage.
- *n.* marriage, matrimony, connubiality, union

Missing Words

Fill in the blanks.

1. The relationship of a man and woman legally united as husband and wife is called _____.

2. When a spouse loses assistance, companionship, or sexual relations of the other spouse, this is called _____.

3. The status of a husband and wife who live separately is called _____.

4. A minor who breaks the law is known as a(n)_____.

5. The performance of the marriage ceremony is the _____ of marriage.

6. _____ is when people live together as man and wife although not married to each other.

7. The crime of marrying while already married to another is _____.

8. The support of a person is called _____.

9. The infliction of physical or mental pain or distress is _____.

10. _____ is the ongoing court-ordered support payments by a divorced spouse.

11. _____ is an arrangement in which both parties to a divorce action retain legal custody of their child and jointly participate in major decisions concerning the child's welfare.

12. _____ is an agreement between husband and wife who are about to divorce or enter into a legal separation, settling property rights and other matters.

13. _____ are any past due payments such as alimony or child support.

14. The _____ test is a blood test used to test for paternity.

15. A conflict in personality so deep that it cannot be altered, making it impossible for the parties to continue to live together, is _____.

16. _____ is the dissolution of the marital relationship between husband and wife.

17. A husband or wife is called a(n) _____.

STUDY AID: Use flashcards for this unit before completing the exercises.

Matching

Match the letter of the definition to the term.

B 18. alimony

A. principle in equity that a child can enforce a promise to adopt him, at least to the extent that he will be given rights of inheritance

J 19. condonation

B. court-ordered support payments by a divorced spouse to his or her former spouse

G 20. support

C. the crime of marrying while married

K 21. separation agreement

D. the rights a husband has under common law with respect to his wife's property

C 22. bigamy

E. rights and duties of both husband and wife resulting from marriage

E 23. consortium

F. a defense in an action for divorce based upon misconduct by the plaintiff that itself would be grounds for divorce if the defendant had brought an action against the plaintiff

I 24. step-parent

G. to provide funds or other means of maintenance of a person

A 25. equitable adoption

H. status of a woman who "hosts" the fertilized egg of another woman in her womb, or who is artificially inseminated

F 26. recrimination

I. a wife, in her relationship to her spouse's child by a former marriage; or a husband in his relationship to his spouse's child by a former marriage

H 27. surrogate motherhood

J. forgiveness by one spouse of the other's conduct that constitutes grounds for divorce

D 28. curtesy

K. an agreement between husband and wife who are about to divorce or to enter into a legal separation, settling property rights and other matters

M 29. husband

L. infliction of physical or mental pain or distress

L 30. cruelty

M. spouse

N 31. civil union

N. alternative "marriage" for same-sex couples

O 32. legitimacy

O. the state of one born to a married couple

Multiple Choice

Select the best choice.

_D_ 33. A court whose jurisdiction varies from state to state. It may hear domestic relations cases, juvenile court matters, child abuse cases, or even paternity suits:
   a. U.S. Supreme Court
   b. Small Claims Court
   c. U.S. District Court
   d. Family Court

_A_ 34. Ongoing court-ordered support payments by a divorced spouse, usually made by an ex-husband to his former wife are called:
   a. alimony.
   b. child support.
   c. palimony.
   d. curtesy.

_C_ 35. A judicial proceeding to establish the paternity of an illegitimate child to compel the father to contribute to its support is called:
   a. equitable distribution.
   b. cohabitation agreement.
   c. affiliation proceeding.
   d. partition.

_A_ 36. Physical, sexual, verbal, or emotional abuse of a young person is called:
   a. child abuse.
   b. condonation.
   c. connivance.
   d. collusion.

_B_ 37. The act of a court in voiding a marriage for causes existing at the time the marriage was entered into is a(n):
   a. divorce.
   b. annulment.
   c. separation.
   d. modification.

_D_ 38. A person who acts for another is a:
   a. consortium.
   b. connivance.
   c. wedlock.
   d. surrogate.

_D_ 39. Sexual intercourse by a married person with a person who is not his or her spouse is:
   a. marriage by estoppel.
   b. bigamy.
   c. incest.
   d. adultery.

_D_ 40. The right of a divorced parent who does not have custody of his child to visit the child at such times and places as the court may order is called:
   a. merger.
   b. equitable distribution.
   c. emancipation.
   d. visitation rights.

_A_ 41. A person appointed by the court to represent and protect the interests of a minor or an incompetent person during litigation is called a:
   a. guardian ad litem.
   b. guardian.
   c. foster parent.
   d. step-parent.

_C_ 42. The act of creating the relationship of parent and child between persons who do not naturally share that relationship is called:
   a. custody.
   b. paternity.
   c. adoption.
   d. maintenance.

B 43. A conflict so deep that it cannot be altered or adjusted, rendering it impossible for the parties to continue to live together in a normal mutual relationship, is called:
   a. collusion.
   b. incompatibility.
   c. recrimination.
   d. cohabitation.

A 44. First legalized in the United States by Massachusetts, same-sex couples wed by:
   a. gay marriage.
   b. civil union.
   c. legitimacy.
   d. partnership act.

True/False

Mark the following T or F.

T 45. The field of law relating to domestic matters, such as marriage, divorce, support, custody, and adoption, is known as domestic relations.

T 46. When property acquired during the marriage is distributed without regard to whose name the property is in, this is known as community property.

F 47. Money paid by one parent to the other for the support of children is known as alimony.

T 48. When a party seeking a divorce need not demonstrate that the other party is at fault, this is known as a no-fault divorce.

T 49. A marriage entered into without a ceremony where the parties agree between themselves to be husband and wife, which is followed by cohabitation, is called common law marriage.

F 50. The right of a divorced parent who does not have custody of his child to visit the child is known as arrears.

T 51. Generally a husband and wife take property as tenants by the entirety.

T 52. Palimony is alimony that is paid upon the break-up of a live-in relationship between two people who were not married.

F 53. Adopting a child is the same thing as being a foster parent.

F 54. Annulment of a marriage occurs when a court declares that a marriage is void, and that it never existed.

T 55. Solemnization of marriage is the performance of the marriage ceremony.

Synonyms

Select the correct synonym in parentheses for each numbered item.

56. MERGER
(modification, consolidation, dower)

57. DECREE
(order, paternity, necessaries)

58. ARREARS
(separate property, laches, unpaid debts)

59. CUSTODY
(visitation, public policy, control)

60. AFFILIATION PROCEEDING
(paternity suit, alienation of affections,
solemnization of marriage)

61. CONDONATION
(heart balm, recrimination, forgiveness)

62. ADULTERY
(bigamy, infidelity, marital rape)

63. JOINT CUSTODY
(consortium, shared custody, curtesy)

64. COMMUNITY PROPERTY
(shared, divided, sold)

65. DISSOLUTION OF MARRIAGE
(divorce, consensual union, interspousal immunity)

66. DOMESTIC RELATIONS
(corporations, agency, family law)

67. ANTENUPTIAL AGREEMENT
(prenuptial agreement, separation agreement,
legal separation)

68. PATERNITY
(mother, sister, father)

69. MAINTENANCE
(addition, support, subtraction)

70. WEDLOCK
(marriage, divorce, separation)

71. SEPARATION
(divorced, together, apart)

72. JUVENILE OFFENDER
(juvenile delinquent, juvenile player,
juvenile tackler)

73. DESERTION
(forced separation, voluntary separation, support)

74. LEGITIMACY
(child of married couple, dower, bigamy)

75. PALIMONY
(live in, live out, marriage)

76. FAMILY
(descendants, curtesy, void marriage)

77. PARTITION
(divide, combine, forfeit)

78. MAJORITY
(senior citizen, adult, minor)

79. RECONCILIATION
(civil union, fighting, resolution)

Self-Test

Place the number of the correct term in the appropriate space.

80. divorce

81. cohabitation

82. family

83. solemnization

84. common law marriage

85. marriage

86. no-fault

87. separation

88. prenuptial agreement

89. irreconcilable differences

90. recrimination

91. separation agreement

92. connivance

93. annulment

94. custody

95. family law

A(n) _____ is the term commonly used to mean the persons who live under one roof and under one head

or management. A family is not necessarily limited to a father and mother and their children. Generally, a family

starts with the _____ of a marriage. In some states, a marriage can be entered into without ceremony, with the

parties agreeing between themselves to be husband and wife, followed by a period of _____. This is known as

a(n) _____. With dissolution of the marriage arrangement, commonly referred to as divorce, becoming more

prevalent in society, some couples will choose to execute a(n) _____ before marriage, regarding financial and

property arrangements.

In the event a couple finds an irremedial breakdown of the marriage to exist, _____ becomes a requirement

for _____ in some states, with _____ divorce laws. The parties might choose to try a(n) _____,

and live apart for a while before making a final decision.

Should the parties decide that a divorce is necessary, they will have to make many decisions. A(n) _____

can be used to settle property rights and other matters, such as _____ of the children. There are certain defenses

that can be raised in opposing a divorce action, such as _____, a spouse's consent to the other spouse's activities

that constituted grounds for a divorce, or _____, the misconduct by the plaintiff.

Occasionally, the court will agree to void a marriage for causes that existed at the time the marriage was entered

into. This is called a(n) _____. This is different from divorce, in that it is not a dissolution of the _____,

but a declaration that none ever existed. The area of law concerned with these domestic relations issues is _____.

Word Scramble

Unscramble the following words and write the correct word(s) that match(es) the definition for each word or phrase.

96. yamilf – persons who live under one roof under one head or management _____

97. anmentnul – when a court voids a marriage _____

98. diov riagemar – a marriage prohibited by law _____

99. tionparti – a division of property _____

100. nuppretial greeament – an agreement before marriage _____

101. esparation mentagree – an agreement between a husband and wife who are about to divorce _____

102. limonay – support payments _____

103. parseation – when a husband and wife live separately _____

104. pouses – a husband or a wife _____

105. dlich portsup – money paid by a parent to support children _____

106. vodirce – a dissolution of the marital relationship _____

107. lapmonyi – alimony paid on break-up of a live-in relationship _____

108. dopation – creating a relationship of parent and child between people who don't naturally share it _____

109. yag ramriage – relationship of two men or two women legally united as spouses _____

110. fantin – a person who has not reached the age of majority _____

111. jormaity – legal age _____

The Last Word

Hair combs hold the evidence of male pattern baldness. A bathroom wastebasket contains the remnants of dental floss and the tissues used to combat seasonal allergies. So what? Nosy relatives may care. There is an American industry that caters to people ordering covert genetic tests—and it is perfectly legal in most U.S. states. Over 1,500 tests are available on the Internet from scores of businesses to determine parentage and even establish a claim to a family inheritance. The tests can also expose genetic risks to hereditary diseases like diabetes, cancer, and dementia. And that is what attracted the attention of Congress.

The Genetic Information Nondiscrimination Act (GINA) of 2008 was passed to prohibit the improper use of genetic information in health insurance and employment. Now group health plans and insurers may not deny coverage to otherwise healthy people or charge higher premiums solely based on a genetic predisposition to developing a disease in the future. After all, what if you don't live long enough to develop Alzheimer's at 88?

Likewise, employers are barred from making decisions of hiring, firing, job placement, or promotions based on an individual's genetic information. Because all human beings have genetic abnormalities of some kind, Congress was convinced by the National Institute of Health that biomedical research will continue to advance if Americans do not fear their discovery.

What about the thriving private industry in genetic testing? Technological advances in the lab, reduced costs, and almost no regulation are fueling greater testing of items like stray hairs, used Kleenex, and dental floss—all called "abandoned DNA." Even pharmacies are now selling paternity tests alongside home pregnancy tests, both without prescription. While the government is protecting what the late Senator Edward Kennedy called the first civil rights of the twenty-first century with the GINA in 2008, genetic "thieves" are free to test abandoned DNA. Although some states prohibit nonconsensual genetic testing for health purposes, most do not and the federal protection extends only to employment and health purposes.

In most states you can order DNA testing on any sample you have, no matter how it was obtained. Testing firms will store your sample and use it for research or sell it! Even the information derived from your sample may be sold. What is your state law?

Access an interactive eBook, chapter-specific interactive learning tools, and more in your Paralegal CourseMate, accessed through www.CengageBrain.com

9

Legal Ethics, Insurance, and Commercial Law

- Learn about legal ethics, insurance, and commercial law.

- Master the similarities and differences in definitions of key terms.

- Master the pronunciations and spellings of legal terms.

- Recognize the synonyms used for legal terminology.

- Practice the usage of terms, definitions, and synonyms.

- Complete unit exercises in the forms of missing words, matching, multiple choice, true/false, synonyms, self-test, and word scramble.

- Work with a legal dictionary/thesaurus.

UNIT

14 Legal Ethics

INTRODUCTION

The attorney-client relationship is a very special relationship that involves a high degree of trust. Clients might be placing all the property, savings, or even their very lives in their lawyer's hands. It is important that the client completely trust the attorney and feel free to share confidences so that the attorney can adequately represent the client's interests. It is the attorney's job to render professional services and exercise the degree of skill and learning that other members of the profession would exercise under like circumstances.

The American Bar Association (ABA), an organization representing attorneys, has formulated model rules to guide attorneys in their professional conduct. The ABA is interested in protecting the image portrayed by attorneys so that the practice of law continues to be a respected and trusted profession. Each state has adopted portions of the ABA's model rules. Some states follow the ABA's Model Code of Professional Responsibility, whereas other states have adopted the more recent Model Rules of Professional Conduct, or a combination of the two.

Each state's bar association or highest court has a means of enforcing these rules of conduct for attorneys. Depending on the nature of the complaint against an attorney, there might be an investigation followed by a hearing. More serious ethical violations will result in disciplinary proceedings.

Depending on the seriousness of an attorney's actions, there are varying levels of sanctions or discipline. If an attorney fails to pay bar dues, misappropriates client funds, commingles client funds with her own funds, divulges client confidences, misrepresents a case to the court, splits fees with a nonlawyer, fails to represent her client diligently and properly, fails to research the applicable law, or misses an important deadline affecting her client's case, the attorney will be disciplined. Additionally, certain crimes involving moral turpitude, such as stealing, battery, and driving while intoxicated, can affect an attorney's license to practice law.

The ultimate sanction for lawyers is disbarment—the loss of license to practice law. Less-severe discipline might include public or private reprimand or censure, and mandatory remedial education. More serious offenses result in the suspension of license for a specified time period.

Other organizations, including the National Federation of Paralegal Associations (NFPA) and the National Association of Legal Assistants (NALA), also promote ethics for legal professionals. It is the attorney's job to ensure that all employees working for her conduct themselves in an ethical manner. An attorney is responsible for supervising all work done for her, and for signing all documents other than routine correspondence that does not include a legal opinion. The attorney is held ultimately responsible for inappropriate or unethical action by an employee and can be sued for the employee's action. Attorneys are required to carry malpractice insurance to cover damages resulting from legal malpractice. In the following case, the issue of attorney fees is addressed. This is a matter of concern for all clients.

CASE AND COMMENT

Supreme Court of the United States
Purdue, Governor of Georgia, et al.

v.

Kenny A., et al. (2010) No. 08-970

Facts: Lawyers and their clients sought to have the State of Georgia reform its foster-care Program—a system that operated below minimum constitutional acceptability. The state's failure to administer basic health care led to permanent medical disabilities of children. Children were placed in the care of individuals with dangerous criminal records. Children were physically assaulted by staff and punished. Due to improper supervision, 20 percent of the children abused drugs, some became victims of child prostitution, and others were beaten and sexually abused. When Georgia failed to grant the State's Child Advocate office the litigating authority to reform, plaintiffs' attorneys initiated this lawsuit. While the State opposed plaintiffs' attorneys at every turn, it finally entered into a 47-page consent decree agreeing to comprehensive reforms of its foster care system.

Procedural History: Lawyers, on behalf of plaintiff children in Georgia's foster care program, were awarded "reasonable" attorney fees by a trial court under a federal statute permitting winning plaintiffs to recover from losers. Half of the $14 million fee was based on the number of hours worked multiplied by a fixed billing rate called the lodestar method. The other half of the fee was enhanced for "superior work and results," per the attorneys' calculations and request. However, the District Court reduced the awarded "fair and reasonable" fees to $10.5 million because of excessive hours and vague billing entries. The Eleventh Circuit affirmed in reliance on its precedent.

Issue: Whether the calculation of an attorney's fee can ever be enhanced based solely on the quality of the lawyer's performance and the results obtained?

Rationale: The lodestar calculation (# work hours x billing rate) will in virtually every case already reflect attorney performance relevant to a fee award. "Departures from hourly billing may become more common...(and) if hourly billing becomes unusual, an alternative to lodestar method may have to be found," the court said, but not in this case. Fees awarded by the trial court were reduced by several million dollars because the calculation of an attorney's fee based on lodestar may be increased due to superior performance, but only in extraordinary circumstances.

Ruling: The judgment of the Court of Appeals is reversed and the case is remanded for proceedings consistent with this opinion.

Comment: A "reasonable" fee is one that is sufficient to induce a capable attorney to undertake the representation of a meritorious case. The courts believe an hourly billing rate is both equitable and ethical. Experimenting with other methods of calculating fees runs the risk of not gaining court approval and the attorneys not being paid. Is it ethical or unethical to allow attorneys to earn a bonus when they go above and beyond the call of duty?

DICTIONARY | THESAURUS

Term [phonetic pronunciation]	*Note: All dictionary/thesaurus terms appear on flashcards at the back of the book and on the student website.*
abuse of process [a.*byoos* ov *pross*.ess]	The use of legal process in a manner not contemplated by the law to achieve a purpose not intended by the law. EXAMPLE: causing an ex-husband to be arrested for nonsupport of his child in order to secure his agreement with respect to custody. *Compare* malicious use of process.
American Association for Paralegal Education (AAfPE) [a.*mare*.i.ken a.so.see.*ay*.shen for pa.re.*lee*.gal ed.yoo.*kay*.shen]	A national organization of paralegal teachers and educational institutions that provides technical assistance and supports research in the paralegal field, promotes standards for paralegal instruction, and cooperates with the American Bar Association and others in developing an approval process for paralegal education.
American Bar Association [a.*mare*.i.ken bar a.so.see.*ay*.shen]	The country's largest voluntary professional association of attorneys commonly referred to as the ABA. Its purposes include enhancing professionalism and advancing the administration of justice.
attorney [a.*tern*.ee]	An attorney at law or an attorney in fact. Unless otherwise indicated, generally means attorney at law. ▪ *n.* lawyer, counselor, advocate, legal advisor, barrister, counsel, legal eagle
attorney at law [a.*tern*.ee at law]	A person who is licensed to practice law; a lawyer.
attorney fees [a.*tern*.ee feez]	Compensation to which an attorney is entitled for her services. This is usually a matter of contract between the attorney and the client. *See also* retainer. However, where authorized by statute, a court may enter an order in a lawsuit directing the payment of a party's attorney fees by the opposite party. In some types of cases, attorney fees are set by a statute that also requires that the fees be paid by the defendant if the plaintiff or claimant prevails in the action. EXAMPLE: Under many Workers' Compensation acts, the claimant's attorney is entitled to a specified percentage of the claimant's award. *See also* contingent fee.
attorney in fact [a.*tern*.ee in fakt]	An agent or representative authorized by his principal, by virtue of a power of attorney, to act for her in certain matters.
attorney of record [a.*tern*.ee of *rek*.erd]	The attorney who has made an appearance on behalf of a party to a lawsuit and is in charge of that party's interests in the action.
attorney-client privilege [a.*tern*.ee-*klie*.ent *priv*.i.lej]	Nothing a client tells his attorney in connection with his case can be disclosed by the attorney, or anyone employed by him or his firm, without the client's permission. *See also* privileged; privileged communication.
attorney's lien [a.*tern*.eez leen]	A lien that an attorney has upon money or property of her client (including papers and documents) for compensation due her from the client for professional services rendered. It is a possessory lien.

DICTIONARY | THESAURUS *continued...*

attorney's work product
[a.*tern*.eez werk *prod*.ukt]

See work product; work product rule.

canon
[*kan*.on]

A law or rule. Canons of ethical conduct state the standards of behavior expected of attorneys. *See* Rules of Professional Conduct.

- *n.* law, rule, statute, act, code, order, standard, criterion, measure, ethic, norm

censure
[*sen*.shoor]

Severe criticism; condemnation.

- *n.* disapproval, rebuke, reproach, reprimand, criticism, condemnation, denunciation, disapproval, castigation
- *v.* condemn, criticize, scold, reprimand, admonish, reprove, chastise, denigrate

certified legal assistant (CLA)
[*ser*.ti.fide *lee*.gul uh.*sis*.tent]

A legal assistant who has been certified by the National Association of Legal Assistants after passing NALA's examination.

Chinese Wall
[chy.*nez* wol]

The code of ethics prohibits the practice of law where there is a conflict of interest. In order to retain such a case, the attorney or employee with the conflict of interest must conduct herself as if there were a "Chinese Wall" around the case file and the staff working on the case. The person with the conflict of interest cannot handle the case or talk about the case with the persons assigned to the file. In a small town, the chances of a conflict of interest can occur with great frequency. Also with large law firms, an employee might switch her employment, and it is quite possible that the new employer has a case representing a defendant where she worked on the plaintiff's side of the same case.

client
[*klie*.ent]

1. A person who employs an attorney. 2. A person who discusses with an attorney the possibility of hiring the attorney.

- *n.* customer, consumer, patron
- *ant.* seller

Code of Judicial Conduct
[kohd ov joo.*dish*.el *kon*.dukt]

A set of principles and ethical standards promulgated by the American Bar Association, and subsequently adopted by a majority of states, which establish ethical standards, both personal and professional, for judges. *See also* ethics.

commingling of funds
[ko.*ming*.ling ov fundz]

The act of an agent, broker, attorney, or trustee in mingling his own funds with those of his client, customer, or beneficiary. Such conduct is unethical and often illegal as well.

competent
[*kom*.pe.tent]

1. Having legal capacity. 2. Capable; qualified. 3. Sufficient; acceptable.

confidential communication
[kon.fi.*den*.shel kum.yoo.ni.*kay*.shen]

See privileged communication.

confidential relationship
[kon.fi.*den*.shel re.*lay*.shen.ship]

A fiduciary relationship, and any informal relationship between parties in which one of them is duty-bound to act with the utmost good faith for the benefit of the other. Although the terms "confidential relationship" and "fiduciary relationship" are often used interchangeably, there is a distinction between them. "Fiduciary relationship" is a term correctly applicable to legal relationships (EXAMPLES: guardian and ward; trustee and beneficiary; attorney and client), whereas "confidential relationship" includes these as well as every other relationship in which one's ability to place confidence is important, such as, for EXAMPLE, business transactions in which one party relies upon the superior knowledge of the other.

confidentiality
[kon.fi.den.shee.*al*.i.tee]

See privileged; privileged communication.

conflict of interest
[*kon*.flikt of *in*.trest]

1. The existence of a variance between the interests of the parties in a fiduciary relationship. EXAMPLE: the conduct of an attorney who acts both for her client and for another person whose interests conflict with those of her client. 2. The condition of a public official or public employee whose personal or financial interests are at variance or appear to be at variance with his public responsibility. EXAMPLE: ownership, by the Secretary of Defense, of stock in a company that contracts with the Department of Defense for the manufacture of military equipment.

contingent fee
[kon.*tin*.jint fee]

A fee for legal services, calculated on the basis of an agreed-upon percentage of the amount of money recovered for the client by his attorney. *See also* attorney fees; fee.

disbarment
[dis.*bahr*.ment]

The revocation of an attorney's right to practice law. *See also* Rules of Professional Conduct.

- *n.* banishment, discharge, dismissal, ejection, eviction, removal

disciplinary rules
[*dis*.i.plin.eh.ree rulz]

Rules and procedures for sanctioning attorneys guilty of professional misconduct. All jurisdictions have adopted such rules. Sanctions may include disbarment, suspension, probation, or reprimand. *See also* Rules of Professional Conduct.

disqualified judge
[dis.*kwal*.i.fide juj]

A judge who is disqualified to act in a particular case because of personal interest in the subject matter of the suit or because of his preconceived mental attitude. *See also* recusation.

double billing
[*dub*.el *bil*.ing]

To bill twice for the same product or service.

duty of candor
[*dew*.tee ov *kan*.der]

The obligation to be honest. EXAMPLE: Attorneys are charged with the duty of candor.

escrow
[*es*.kroh]

A written instrument (EXAMPLES: stock, bonds, a deed), money, or other property deposited by the grantor with a third party (the escrow holder) until the performance of a condition or the happening of a certain event, upon the occurrence of which the property is to be delivered to the grantee.

- *adj.* separate, designated, specified ("keep the money in an escrow account")

DICTIONARY | THESAURUS *continued...*

escrow account
[*es*.kroh e.*kount*]

A bank account in the name of the depositor and a second person, the deposited funds being returnable to the depositor or paid to a third person upon the happening of a specified event (EXAMPLE: money for the payment of property taxes that a mortgagor pays into the escrow account of the mortgage company or bank).

escrow contract
[*es*.kroh *kon*.trakt]

A contract that describes the rights of the parties to an escrow.

escrow holder
[*es*.kroh *hole*.der]

The third party to an escrow.

ethics
[*eth*.iks]

1. A code of moral principles and standards of behavior for people in professions such as law or medicine (EXAMPLES: the Code of Judicial Conduct (for judges); the Rules of Professional Conduct (for attorneys). 2. A body of moral principles generally.

- *n.* principles, values, morals, mores, criteria, canon, rules

fee
[fee]

1. A charge made for the services of a professional person, such as a lawyer or physician. *See also* attorney fees; contingent fee. 2. A statutory charge for the services of a public officer. EXAMPLE: court fees.

fiduciary duty
[fi.*doo*.shee.air.ee *dew*.tee]

The duty to act loyally and honestly with respect to the interests of another; the duty the law imposes upon a fiduciary.

frivolous pleading
[*friv*.e.les *plee*.ding]

A pleading that is good in form but false in fact and not pleaded in good faith.

frivolous suit
[*friv*.e.les soot]

A lawsuit brought with no intention of determining an actual controversy. EXAMPLE: an action initiated for purposes of harassment.

grievance
[*gree*.venss]

1. Any complaint about a wrong or an injustice. 2. Formal complaint filed by a client who is unhappy with an attorney's work.

- *n.* complaint, protest, allegation, accusation, objection

IOLTA
[eye.*ol*.ta]

Acronym for Interest on Lawyers' Trust Accounts. In states with IOLTA programs, lawyers who hold funds belonging to clients deposit such money into a common fund, the interest on which is used for charitable, law-related purposes such as legal services to the poor. Some states' IOLTA programs are voluntary, some are mandatory.

Juris Doctor
[*joor*.is *dok*.ter]

The primary degree given by most law schools. It is commonly expressed in its abbreviated form, JD or J.D. Although a person might have a JD degree, it doesn't necessarily mean that the person has taken and passed the bar examination or received a license to practice law.

legal assistant
[*lee*.gl e.*sis*.tent]

A legal assistant is the same as a paralegal. *See* paralegal.

- *n.* paralegal, lawyer's assistant

loyalty
[*loy*.el.tee]

Adherence to law or to the government; faithfulness to a person or to a principle.

- *n.* allegiance, fealty, devotion, bond, faith, support ("He has shown great loyalty to his country.")

malicious prosecution
[ma.*lish*.ess pross.e.*kyoo*.shen]

A criminal prosecution or civil suit commenced maliciously and without probable cause. After the termination of such a prosecution or suit in the defendant's favor, the defendant has the right to bring an action against the original plaintiff for the tort of "malicious prosecution."

malicious use of process
[ma.*lish*.ess use ov *pross*.ess]

The use of process for a purpose for which it was intended, but out of personal malice or some other unjustifiable motive (EXAMPLE: to extort money) and without probable cause. It is, in effect, a form of malicious prosecution.

meritorious defense
[mehr.i.*toh*.ree.us de.*fense*]

A defense that goes to the merits of the case; a defense warranting a hearing, although it may not be a perfect defense or a defense assured of succeeding.

National Association of Legal Assistants (NALA)
[*nash*.en.el a.so.see.*ay*.shen of *leeg*.el a.*sis*.tents]

A national organization of legal assistants and paralegals whose purpose is to enhance professionalism and the interests of those in the profession, as well as to advance the administration of justice generally. Among its other undertakings, NALA has established a "Code of Professional Responsibility" for paralegals and legal assistants and provides professional certifications, continuing education, and assistance in job placement. A person who receives certification through NALA is entitled to so indicate by the use of "CLA" (Certified Legal Assistant) after his name.

National Association of Legal Secretaries (NALS)
[*nash*.en.el a.so.see.*ay*.shen of *leeg*.el *sek*.re.tare.eez]

A national organization of legal secretaries whose purpose is continuing legal education and professionalism. Membership in NALS provides publications, seminars and workshops, and other educational tools. NALS also grants professional legal secretary certification to qualified applicants.

National Federation of Paralegal Associations (NFPA)
[*nash*.en.el fed.e.*ray*.shen of pehr.e.*leeg*.el a.so.see.*ay*.shenz]

An association of paralegal and legal assistant organizations nationwide whose purpose is to enhance professionalism and the interests of those in the profession, as well as to advance the administration of justice. Among its other undertakings, NFPA has established the "Affirmation of Responsibility," a code of professional conduct for paralegals and legal assistants, and provides continuing education and assistance in job placement.

paralegal
[*pehr*.e.leeg.el]

The terms *paralegal* and *legal assistant* are used interchangeably. In 1997 the ABA adopted the following definition, "A legal assistant or paralegal is a person, qualified by education, training or work experience who is employed or retained by a lawyer, law office, corporation, governmental agency or other entity and who performs specifically delegated substantive legal work for which a lawyer is responsible." A paralegal is a person who, although not an attorney, performs many of the functions of an attorney under an attorney's supervision and control.

- *n.* legal assistant, paraprofessional, aide, lay advocate, legal technician, lawyer's assistant

privileged
[*priv*.i.lejd]

Entitled to a privilege; possessing a privilege.

- *adj.* protected, excused, immune, exempt, elite ("a privileged class"); confidential, secret, exceptional, top-secret ("privileged records")

privileged communication
[*priv*.i.lejd kem.yoon.i.*kay*.shen]

A communication between persons in a confidential relationship or other privileged relationship (EXAMPLES: husband and wife; physician and patient; attorney and client). The contents of such communications may not be testified to in court unless the person possessing the privilege waives it.

privileged relationship
[*priv*.i.lejd re.*lay*.shen.ship]

A relationship of a type such that communications between the parties to the relationship are protected by law against disclosure (i.e., are "privileged") unless the party whom the law protects waives the right to protection. *See also* privileged communication.

probation
[pro.*bay*.shen]

A sentence that allows a person convicted of a crime to continue to live and work in the community while being supervised by a probation officer, instead of being sent to prison.

pro bono publico
[pro *bone*.oh *poob*.li.koh]

(*Latin*) Means "for the public good." An attorney who represents an indigent client free of charge is said to be representing her client pro bono. Many bar associations require their members to perform a specified amount of pro bono work for the public.

pro hac vice
[pro hak *vy*.see]

(*Latin*) Meaning "for this occasion," an attorney who is not a member of the bar of a particular state may be admitted for one particular case.

pro se
[pro say]

(*Latin*) Means "for one's self." Refers to appearing on one's own behalf in either a civil action or a criminal prosecution, rather than being represented by an attorney.

professional corporation
[pro.*fesh*.en.el kore.per.*ay*.shen]

A corporation formed for the purpose of practicing a profession (EXAMPLES: law; medicine; psychotherapy; dentistry) and to secure certain tax advantages. The members of a professional corporation remain personally liable for professional misconduct. Professional corporations often identify themselves by the abbreviation PC. Thus, for EXAMPLE, a professional corporation composed of attorneys Jessica Smith and Sam Smith might be named "Smith and Smith, Esqs., PC."

professional ethics
[pro.*fesh*.en.el *eth*.iks]

See ethics. *See also* Code of Judicial Conduct; Rules of Professional Conduct.

professional legal secretary
[pro.*fesh*.en.el *leeg*.el *sek*.re.teh.ree]

A person who has met the requirements for certification by the National Association of Legal Secretaries.

professional misconduct
[pro.*fesh*.en.el mis.*kon*.dukt]

1. Malpractice. 2. In the case of an attorney, violating the disciplinary rules of a jurisdiction in which he practices. *See also* Rules of Professional Conduct.

recusation
[rek.yoo.*zay*.shun]

The act of challenging a judge or a juror for prejudice or bias. *See also* disqualified judge.

reprimand
[*rep*.ri.mand]

A severe and solemn rebuke or censure for disobedience or wrongdoing.

- *n.* admonishment, castigation, censure, reprehension, chiding, lecture, warning, reproval
- *v.* chastise, rebuke, reprove, admonish, castigate, deprecate

retainer [re.*tane*.er]	1. The act of hiring an attorney. 2. A preliminary fee paid to an attorney at the time she is retained, in order to secure her services. 3. In certain circumstances, the right of a person (EXAMPLE: an executor) who is rightfully in possession of funds belonging to a person who owes him money (EXAMPLE: money belonging to the decedent's estate that he is administering) to retain an amount sufficient to satisfy the obligation. ▪ *n.* fee, contract, engagement fee, compensation, remuneration
retaining lien [re.*tane*.ing leen]	An attorney's possessory lien, which attaches to a clients' money, paper, or property that the attorney held during the course of his retainer. An attorney has a right to keep such property until a client pays the attorney's fee.
Rules of Professional Conduct [rulz ov pro.*fesh*.en.el *kon*.dukt]	Rules promulgated by the American Bar Association that detail an attorney's ethical obligations to her client, the courts, and opposing counsel. With variations, these rules have been adopted by most states and incorporated into their statutory codes of ethics. *See also* ethics.
sanction [*sank*.shen]	*n.* Action taken by a state bar association or a state's highest court when an attorney has been found to have committed an ethical violation. EXAMPLES of sanctions against attorneys include the imposition of a private or public reprimand, revocation or suspension of license to practice law. *v.* To punish; to penalize. ▪ *v.* punish, ban, boycott ("The bar sanctioned the erring attorney.") ▪ *n.* ban, boycott, decree, injunction, penalty, sentence, punishment ("unimposed sanctions")
solicitation [so.liss.i.*tay*.shen]	1. The act of an attorney in seeking clients. An attorney is permitted to solicit clients but must adhere to the code of ethics. It could be an ethical violation in which an attorney sends dozens of pizzas to an ambulance company's staff at lunch time each week, putting pressure on them to refer all patients to the attorney. 2. Inviting a business transaction. ▪ *n.* petition, requisition
special counsel [*spesh*.el *koun*.sel]	An attorney, employed by the attorney general of the United States or a state, to assist in a particular case as a prosecutor.
suspend [sus.*pend*]	1. To temporarily remove an attorney's right to practice law. USAGE: "The bar association suspended the attorney's law license for six months." 2. To temporarily withdraw a privilege. *See also* suspended. ▪ *v.* withdraw, revoke ("suspend his license")
suspended [sus.*pen*.ded]	Temporarily inactive or temporarily not effective.
unauthorized practice of law [un.*aw*.ther.ized *prak*.tiss ov law]	Engaging in the practice of law without the license required by law. EXAMPLES: giving a legal opinion to a client, setting legal fees, or signing legal documents.

DICTIONARY THESAURUS *continued...*

work product
[werk *prod*.ukt]
Material prepared by counsel in preparing for the trial of a case. EXAMPLES: notes; memoranda, and legal pleadings.

work product rule
[werk *prod*.ukt rool]
The rule that an attorney's work product is not subject to discovery. This includes the materials produced by persons working for the attorney.

Missing Words

Fill in the blanks.

1. A person who employs an attorney is known as a(n) _Client_.

2. Until a real estate closing is completed, all documents and funds are held in _escrow_ by the attorneys for the parties.

3. _Cert. Legal Assistants_ can use the abbreviation CLA after their names.

4. An association of paralegal and legal assistant organizations nationwide, known by the abbreviation NFPA, is called the _Nat'l Federation of Paralegal Associations_.

5. A sanction against an unethical attorney can be the revocation or _suspension_ of the attorney's license to practice.

6. When an attorney represents both the plaintiff and the defendant in an action, this is considered a(n) _conflict of interest_ and is generally prohibited.

7. A(n) _retainer_ is a preliminary fee paid to an attorney to secure his services.

8. When an attorney invites a business transaction this is called _solicitation_.

9. The country's largest voluntary professional association is the _Am. Bar Assoc._.

10. Anything clients tell their attorney in confidence regarding their case is considered a(n) _attorney client privilege_ that cannot be introduced at the time of trial.

11. When defendants choose to represent themselves in a legal matter, rather than being represented by an attorney, this is called _pro se_.

12. Material such as a pleading prepared by an attorney in preparation for the trial is called _work product_ and is not subject to discovery by the opposing party.

13. When an attorney mixes a client's settlement funds with the general bank account of the law office, this is known as the _commingling of funds_.

14. _Ethics_ is a code of moral principles.

15. When an attorney represents a client free of charge, this is called _pro bono_.

16. A(n) _____ is a law or rule.

17. When an attorney's license is revoked, this is known as a(n) ____Disbarment____ by the court.

18. The duty to act loyally and honestly with respect to another's interest is ____duty of. Candor____

> **STUDY AID:** Use flashcards for this unit before completing the exercises.

Matching

Match the letter of the definition to the term.

___A___ **19.** retainer   **A.** preliminary fee paid to an attorney

___G___ **20.** disbarment   **B.** severe criticism

___J___ **21.** professional misconduct   **C.** act or process of granting a license

___H___ **22.** Rules of Professional Conduct   **D.** relationship of a type such that communications between the parties are protected

___F___ **23.** IOLTA   **E.** complaint by client regarding attorney's work

___I___ **24.** certified legal assistant   **F.** fund for depositing client monies

___E___ **25.** grievance   **G.** revocation of an attorney's right to practice law

___D___ **26.** privileged relationship   **H.** rules made by the ABA that detail an attorney's ethical obligation to his client, court, and opposing counsel

___B___ **27.** censure   **I.** legal assistant certified by NALA

___C___ **28.** licensing   **J.** malpractice

___K___ **29.** contingent fee   **K.** fee based upon amount of money collected for client

___N___ **30.** attorney at law   **L.** privileged communication

___L___ **31.** confidentiality   **M.** a suit commenced maliciously and without probable cause

___M___ **32.** malicious prosecution   **N.** person who is licensed to practice law

___Q___ **33.** probation   **O.** a process that allows an attorney to be admitted to the bar for one particular case

___P___ **34.** special counsel   **P.** person who assists in the prosecution of a particular case at the request of the attorney general

___O___ **35.** pro hac vice   **Q.** a sentence that allows a person convicted of a crime not to go to prison

Multiple Choice

Select the best choice.

_C_ **36.** Attorney professional misconduct occurs when:
   a. the attorney is rude to clients.
   b. the attorney practices medicine without a license.
   c. the attorney fails to exercise the degree of care and skill usually used by members of the legal profession.
   d. none of the above

_b_ **37.** When an attorney represents a client free of charge, this is called:
   a. pro se.
   b. pro bono publico.
   c. pro choice.
   d. pro temporare.

_A_ **38.** An attorney must deposit client funds in:
   a. a trust account.
   b. a safe deposit box.
   c. the case file.
   d. a Chinese Wall.

_D_ **39.** When an attorney represents both the husband and wife with differing interests in a divorce proceeding, this is known as a:
   a. privileged document.
   b. confidential relationship.
   c. malicious use of process.
   d. conflict of interest.

_D_ **40.** The country's largest professional association of attorneys is known as the:
   a. Federal Bar Association.
   b. National Bar Association.
   c. United States Bar Association.
   d. American Bar Association.

_A_ **41.** The preliminary fee paid to an attorney is known as a:
   a. retainer.
   b. censure.
   c. work product.
   d. escrow.

_b_ **42.** A contingent fee is collected when:
   a. an attorney works without compensation.
   b. an attorney collects a fee only if successful in the matter.
   c. an attorney is paid a set amount for all services rendered.
   d. an attorney bills the client a specific amount for each hour of work completed.

_D_ **43.** A grievance is:
   a. a client's psychological problems.
   b. the loss of a family member.
   c. a constitutional question of law.
   d. a complaint made by a client against his attorneys.

_A_ **44.** The primary degree given by most law schools:
   a. is a Juris Doctor.
   b. is an IOLTA.
   c. is the same as certification.
   d. can never be revoked.

_D_ **45.** The attorney-client privilege:
   a. prohibits a client from being truthful with his attorney.
   b. requires that anything said to any attorney must be revealed in a court of law.
   c. provides that only judges may hear such privileged communications.
   d. prevents disclosure to others of a client's private conversations with his attorney.

_C_ **46.** The set of principles and ethical standards set by the American Bar Association and adopted by the majority of states to establish ethical standards for judges is known as:
   a. the Constitution.
   b. privileged communication.
   c. Code of Judicial Conduct.
   d. the work product rule.

True/False

Mark the following T or F.

___T___ **47.** A confidential communication is the same as a privileged communication.

___T___ **48.** The National Association of Legal Assistants provides certification for paralegals and legal assistants.

___F___ **49.** A reprimand is the act of challenging a judge or juror for prejudice or bias.

___T___ **50.** Engaging in the practice of law without a license is the unauthorized practice of law.

___T___ **51.** When a person appears on his own behalf in a legal matter, this is known as pro se.

___T___ **52.** A censure is severe criticism.

___T___ **53.** A paralegal is a person who, although not an attorney, performs many of the functions of an attorney, under an attorney's supervision.

___T___ **54.** A privileged communication is a communication between persons in a confidential relationship, such as attorney and client.

___T___ **55.** The Code of Judicial Conduct is a set of principles and ethical standards for judges.

___T___ **56.** The country's largest voluntary professional association of attorneys is the American Bar Association.

___T___ **57.** An attorney's notes are part of her work product and are protected from disclosure.

Synonyms

Select the correct synonym in parentheses for each numbered item.

58. COMMINGLING OF FUNDS
(mixing, separating, controlling)

59. CONTINGENT FEE
(flat fee, hourly fee, percentage fee)

60. PRIVILEGED DOCUMENT
(public, protected, useless)

61. MERITORIOUS DEFENSE
(worthy, worthless, false)

62. CONFIDENTIAL RELATIONSHIP
(fiduciary relationship, estranged relationship, proud relationship)

63. SANCTION
(award, penalty, copy)

64. GRIEVANCE
(complaint, praise, theory)

65. CENSURE
(commend, review, criticize)

66. FRIVOLOUS PLEADING
(truthful, clear, false)

67. COMPETENT
(qualified, loyal, malicious)

68. CLIENT
(canon, customer, expert)

69. SOLICITATION
(buy, seek, lose)

70. LOYALTY
(allegiance, criticize, prejudge)

71. ETHICS
(baseless, malicious, standards)

72. SUSPENDED
(closed, inactive, changed)

Self-Test

Place the number of the correct term in the appropriate space.

73. conflict of interest

74. attorneys

75. disciplinary rules

76. disbarment

77. grievance

78. American Bar Association

79. disqualified

80. Code of Judicial Conduct

81. suspension

82. frivolous

83. solicitation

84. commingling of funds

85. Rules of Professional Conduct

86. recusation

The _____, the code of conduct for lawyers that governs their moral and professional duties, is an issue of great public concern. The media has been calling attention to a variety of cases in which _____ have failed to follow specific _____, resulting in reprimands, sanctions, _____ of license, or even permanent _____ from the practice of law.

When an attorney actively seeks business, this is known as _____ and may be prohibited where direct client contact is made. Another practice that is frowned upon is when a client wishes to leave money or other property to an attorney; that attorney should not prepare the will under which the attorney would benefit. This situation is known as a(n) _____. The attorney cannot zealously represent the client's interests when the attorney may stand to benefit from the matter. It is prohibited as well for attorneys to bring lawsuits for the purpose of harassment, when there is no true actual controversy between parties. These _____ suits are unethical and should be avoided.

A client could have a(n) _____ where his attorney fails to put client funds into a trust account, resulting in a(n) _____ with those of the attorney. The largest professional association of attorneys, known as the _____, has enacted a(n) _____ establishing standards for judges. A judge might be _____

to act in a case because of personal interest. When a judge is challenged for bias, this is called _____.

Word Scramble

Unscramble the following words and write the correct word(s) that match(es) the definition for each word or phrase.

87. lientc – a person who employs an attorney

_____

_____

88. tentcompe – having legal capacity

_____

_____

89. yalolty – faithfulness _____

90. hicset – a code of moral principles and standards of behavior _____

_____

91. fidconential tionrelaship – a relationship between parties where one of them is duty-bound to act with the utmost of good faith for the benefit of the other, where the person's ability to place confidences is important. _____

_____

92. tionsanc – to impose a fine or penalty

_____

_____

93. rievanceg – a complaint

_____

94. crowes – money held by a third party to be delivered to a grantee _____

_____

95. barmentdis – revocation of an attorney's license

_____

_____

96. pendsus – to temporarily remove from employment

_____

_____

97. doce of icialjud duconct – ethical standards for judges. _____

_____

98. orkw ducorpt – materials prepared by counsel for trial of a case _____

_____

99. ticerfied galle sissatnat – a legal assistant certified by NALA _____

_____

100. tionnaal sotaasionci of galle tissasants – a person who receives certification through this group has the title of Certified Legal Assistant (CLA).

_____

_____

101. rkwo ducport lure – this lure protects an attorney's work from discovery proceedings

_____

_____

102. baprotion – instead of being sent to prison, a person might receive this sentence

_____

_____

103. pecsial unsecol – an attorney employed by the Attorney General to assist her in one case

_____

_____

104. orp hac cive – means "for this occasion"

_____

_____

The Last Word

Frivolous lawsuits are unethical if not illegal, according to the beliefs of the U.S. Chamber of Commerce Institute for Legal Reform (ILR). The ILR aims to eliminate frivolous lawsuits by voter education efforts, public education campaigns, grassroots activities, and federal or state legislation.

One state, California, has attempted to reduce certain inappropriate claims filed pursuant to the Americans with Disabilities Act. The most flagrant example of these unethical claims showed one plaintiff alone filing 27 separate lawsuits in a three-month period in 2010 while hundreds more were filed by a tiny number of California attorneys. A lawyer for one small business that was sued complained, "What these guys are doing smells like predatory ambulance chasing that is unethical." What would you do if you discovered that the case you were working on was frivolous, but the attorney said it will settle before trial?

Access an interactive eBook, chapter-specific interactive learning tools, and more in your Paralegal CourseMate, accessed through www.CengageBrain.com

UNIT

15 Insurance Law

INTRODUCTION

A couple buys a home with their savings. Should the house catch on fire, it would take years to save enough money to buy another home. Insurance is a method of providing against known possible losses. A sum of money is paid to another who agrees to cover your loss in the event of a catastrophe or certain conditions occurring.

There are many different kinds of insurance: fire, automobile, collision, theft, home, umbrella policy, title, life, term life, whole life, self, renter's, rental car, leased car, no-fault, malpractice, marine, uninsured motorist, professional liability, business interruption, identity theft, indemnity, flood, mortgage, earthquake, disability, dental, vision, and health insurance. The list is almost endless.

There are some professional models whose work depends on their beautiful hands or legs. The agencies for whom they work have obtained insurance covering their specific body parts in the event of injury or damage. A person with a fear of flying might obtain flight insurance prior to boarding a plane. An elderly couple might purchase travel insurance in the event they can't make their planned cruise due to health reasons. An art museum might insure its multi-million dollar collection of paintings and sculptures against theft or damage.

After weighing the risks of an event occurring, versus the amount of money needed to obtain insurance, a person might decide what types of insurance he wishes to purchase, and how much he is willing to spend for insurance. Insurance can be purchased from an agent or a broker. An insurance agent is the representative of an insurance company, who sells insurance for that one company. An insurance broker does not work for any particular insurance company and might place an order for insurance with the specific company the customer selects. A temporary binder (interim document) might be prepared evidencing that insurance coverage is in effect or has been declined.

The insured—the person buying insurance—needs to decide whether to pay more for insurance and have it cover more eventualities or take affect sooner, versus paying a lower premium (payment) and having less coverage, or having coverage that won't begin until after she has paid for the initial damages up to a certain amount. The amount an insured person pays out of his own pocket for damages before his insurance covers the balance is called the deductible. The beneficiary is the person named in the insurance policy who is to receive the benefit of the insurance. If a purchaser fails to live up to the terms of the policy (contract), such as not paying premiums, or if misstatements are found on the application for insurance, insurance can be cancelled by the company.

This unit explores the kinds of insurance available and the ways that insurance safeguards persons and property. The following case shows how different legal fields intersect.

CASE AND COMMENT

Court of Appeals of the State of California (2nd Appellate District, Div.5)
B 170364
James E. Mitchell, Plaintiff and Appellant,

v.

United National Insurance Company, Defendant and Respondent
Los Angeles County Super. Ct. No. BC279342
March 8, 2005

Facts: Mitchell was issued an insurance policy and was named the insured under an insurance policy issued by United National Insurance Company (United) to provide coverage for a commercial building. During the policy period the building was destroyed by arson. The arsonist, a friend of Mitchell's, died in the fire. As a result of an investigation, United discovered several misrepresentations in Mitchell's application for insurance. United rescinded the policy and offered to give Mitchell the premium back.

Mitchell refused to accept the premium and filed this action. In his application for insurance, Mitchell had claimed he was going to use the building for video production, a studio, and offices, and that it was for a successful and ongoing business. In reality, the building was only used for two days to film a music video, then was leased to a garment business, and then remained vacant thereafter when the garment business could not get a certificate of occupancy from the city. The building had multiple code violations. Mitchell claimed that his friend who died in the fire was supposed to be showing the building to interested parties. Thereafter the friend set the building on fire.

Procedural History: The defendant insurance company was granted summary judgment on the issue of breach of contract. The court concluded that there was no breach of contract on United's part, or breach of the covenant of fair dealing and good faith.

Issue: Whether Mitchell had made material misrepresentations on his application to entitle United to rescind the policy of insurance.

Rationale: Any misrepresentation, whether intentional or unintentional, may be grounds for rescinding a policy of insurance. A party to an insurance contract must disclose in good faith all facts within his knowledge that are, or that he knows to be material to the contract. An entire policy is void if a party has willfully concealed or misrepresented any material fact of circumstance concerning the insurance with the intent to deceive.

Under the Insurance Code, an insurance company may rescind a fire insurance policy based on an insured's negligent or unintentional misrepresentation of a material fact in an insurance application. The fact that the building was vacant, rather than occupied with an ongoing business as was claimed on the insurance application, was a significant misrepresentation of a material fact.

Ruling: Summary judgment affirmed for United National Insurance Company.

Comment: Despite the fact that this is a case regarding insurance, the law of contracts plays a defining role. Even if an attorney specializes in one field of law, he must stay current in a variety of legal subjects.

| DICTIONARY | THESAURUS |

| Term
[phonetic pronunciation] | *Note: All dictionary/thesaurus terms appear on flashcards at the back of the book and on the CD-ROM.* |

adjuster
[a.*just*.er]

A person who makes a determination of the value of a claim against an insurance company for the purpose of arriving at an amount for which the claim will be settled. An adjuster may be an agent for the insurance company or an independent adjuster.

- *n.* reconciler, arbitrator, intermediary, intervenor, mediator

annuity
[a.*nyoo*.i.tee]

1. A yearly payment of a fixed sum of money for life or for a stated number of years.
2. A right to receive fixed periodic payments (yearly or otherwise), either for life or for a stated period of time.

Most annuities are in the form of insurance policies. When payments are made until the death of the beneficiary, the annuity is a life annuity. When payments will be terminated if the beneficiary acts in a specified way (EXAMPLE: accepting full-time employment), the annuity is a term annuity. A contingent annuity is payable upon the occurrence of some stated event beyond the control of the beneficiary (EXAMPLE: the death of the beneficiary's father). A joint and survivorship annuity is paid to two beneficiaries and, after one of them dies, to the survivor (EXAMPLE: continued payment to a widow of an annuity that, prior to her husband's death, was paid to her and her husband jointly). A retirement annuity is generally payable upon retirement from employment.

- *n.* payment, income, pension, subsidy, stipend, allotment

annuity policy
[a.*nyoo*.i.tee *pol*.i.see]

An insurance policy that provides for or pays an annuity.

bad faith
[bad fayth]

A devious or deceitful intent, motivated by self-interest, ill will, or a concealed purpose. The opposite of good faith. Bad faith is stronger than negligence, but may or may not involve fraud. EXAMPLE: An insurance company engages in bad faith when it refuses, with no basis for its action, to pay a claim.

beneficiary
[ben.e.*fish*.ee.air.ee]

A person who receives a benefit.

benefit
[*ben*.e.fit]

A payment made under an insurance policy, pension, annuity, or the like.

- *n.* aid, asset, advantage, profit, gain, utility

binder
[*bine*.der]

1. An interim memorandum, used when an insurance policy cannot be issued immediately, evidencing either that insurance coverage is effective at a specified time and continues until the policy is issued, or that the risk is declined and giving notice of that fact. 2. An earnest money deposit that preserves a buyer's right to purchase real estate.

- *n.* deposit, pledge, stake, collateral, escrow, security ("a binder on the deal")

DICTIONARY | THESAURUS *continued...*

business interruption insurance
[*biz*.ness in.ter.*up*.shen in.*shoor*.ense]

Insurance protecting against loss from the interruption of business, as distinguished from coverage upon merchandise or other property used in the business. *See also* insurance.

cancellation
[kan.sel.*ay*.shen]

The act of a party to a contract ending the contract after the other party has been guilty of breach of contract. Cancellation should be contrasted with termination, which provides the party ending the contract with fewer remedies.

- *n.* abandonment, reversal, recall, nullification, revocation, termination, withdrawal, rescission ("cancellation of the insurance policy")

cancellation clause
[kan.sel.*ay*.shen kloz]

A provision in a contract that allows the parties to cancel the contract without obligation. Also known as an escape clause.

- *n.* escape clause

coinsurance
[*ko*.in.*shoor*.ense]

A division of the risk between the insurer and the insured. EXAMPLE: a health insurance policy under which the insurance company is obligated to pay 80 percent of every claim and the insured pays 20 percent.

collision insurance
[ke.*lizh*.en in.*shoor*.ense]

Automobile insurance that protects the owner or operator of a motor vehicle from loss due to damage done to his property by another.

comprehensive coverage
[kom.pre.*hen*.siv *kuv*.e.rej]

A package of coverage provided by a policy of comprehensive insurance that protects against a myriad of perils (collision, theft, etc.).

comprehensive insurance
[kom.pre.*hen*.siv in.*shoor*.ense]

Insurance that provides coverage for various risks (EXAMPLES: fire; theft; flood; wind; hail), each of which could also be covered under separate policies.

contribution between insurers
[kon.tra.*byoo*.shen be.*tween* in.*shoor*.erz]

The obligation of an insurance company that has issued a policy covering the same loss as that insured by another insurance company to contribute proportionally to the other insurer who has paid the entire loss.

deductible
[de.*duk*.tibl]

In insurance, portion of a loss that the insured must pay from his own pocket before the insurance company will begin to make payment. USAGE: "Because my policy has a $500 deductible, my insurance company will pay only $2,000 of the $2,500 damage to my car."

disability clause
[dis.e.*bil*.i.tee kloz]

A clause in an insurance policy providing for a waiver of premiums in the event of the insured's disability.

disability insurance
[dis.e.*bil*.i.tee in.*shoor*.ense]

Insurance that provides income in the event of disability.

double indemnity
[*du*.bel in.*dem*.ni.tee]

A benefit payable under an insurance policy at twice face value if loss occurs under certain conditions. EXAMPLE: under a life insurance policy, the death of the insured by accidental, as opposed to natural, causes.

double insurance [*du*.bel in.*shoor*.ense]	Coverage of the same risk and the same interest by different insurance companies. *See also* contribution between insurers.
exclusion [eks.*kloo*.zhen]	1. A provision in an insurance policy that removes a specified risk, person, or circumstance from coverage. *See also* exception. 2. The act of keeping out or apart. ■ *n.* rejection, omission, dismissal, elimination, disallowance, nonacceptance, repudiation
fire insurance [*fy*.er in.*shoor*.ense]	Insurance that indemnifies the insured against loss to property (EXAMPLES: a house, the contents of a house; a commercial building) due to fire.
fraud [frawd]	Deceit, deception, or trickery that is intended to induce, and does induce, another person to part with anything of value or surrender some legal right.
group insurance [groop in.*shoor*.ense]	1. A contract providing life, accident, or health insurance for a group of employees. The terms of the contract are contained in a master policy; the individual employee's participation is demonstrated by a certificate of insurance that she holds. 2. A contract providing life, accident, or health insurance for any defined group of people. The contract is a master policy and is entered into between the group policyholder (for EXAMPLE, the American Automobile Association) and the insurance company for the benefit of the policyholder's members.
health insurance [helth in.*shoor*.ense]	Insurance that indemnifies the insured for medical expenses incurred as a result of sickness or accident.
homeowners policy [*home*.ohn.erz *pol*.i.see]	An insurance policy that insures homeowners against most common risks, including fire, burglary, and civil liability.
indemnification [in.dem.ni.fi.*kay*.shen]	1. The act of indemnifying or being indemnified. 2. Payment made by way of compensation for a loss. *See also* indemnity insurance. ■ *n.* restitution, amends, compensation, insurance, payment, reparation
indemnify [in.*dem*.ni.fy]	1. To compensate or reimburse a person for loss or damage. 2. To promise to compensate or reimburse in the event of future loss or damage. *See also* indemnity insurance. ■ *v.* compensate, reimburse, secure, make amends, guarantee, restore, repay, redeem
indemnity insurance [in.*dem*.ni.tee in.*shoor*.ense]	Insurance providing indemnification for actual loss or damage, as distinguished from liability insurance, which provides for payment of a specified sum upon the occurrence of a specific event regardless of what the actual loss or damage may be.
indemnity policy [in.*dem*.ni.tee *paw*.li.see]	*See* indemnity insurance.
insurability [in.shoor.e.*bil*.i.tee]	Having the qualities needed to be insurable: no preexisting health conditions, nonsmoker, under certain ages, etc.

DICTIONARY | THESAURUS *continued...*

insurable
[in.*shoor*.ebl]

Capable of being insured. EXAMPLE: as a condition of purchasing life insurance, being in sound health at the time the policy is issued.

insurable interest
[in.*shoor*.ebl *in*.trest]

An interest from whose existence the owner derives a benefit and whose nonexistence will cause her to suffer a loss. The presence of an insurable interest is essential to the validity and enforceability of an insurance policy because it removes it from the category of a gambling contract. An insurable interest in life insurance, for EXAMPLE, is: (a) one's interest in his own life; (b) one's natural interest in the continued life of a blood relative; (c) any reasonable expectation of financial benefit from the continued life of another (one's debtor, business partner, etc.).

insurance
[in.*shoor*.ense]

A contract (the policy) by which one party (the insurer), in return for a specified consideration (the premium), agrees to compensate or indemnify another (the insured) on account of loss, damage, or liability arising from an unknown or contingent event (the risk). There are almost as many kinds of coverage as there are risks. EXAMPLES of some of the most common types of insurance are accident insurance, automobile insurance, credit life insurance, disability insurance, fire insurance, flood insurance, health insurance, homeowners' insurance, liability insurance, life insurance, major medical insurance, malpractice insurance, mortgage insurance, and title insurance.

The law does not permit a person to insure against the consequences of acts or transactions that violate public policy, for EXAMPLE, gambling losses. Most importantly, the law requires a person to have an insurable interest in whatever she wishes to insure.

- *n.* indemnification, assurance, coverage, policy, warranty, covenant, security, guarantee, indemnity against contingencies, safeguard

insurance adjuster
[in.*shoor*.ense a.*just*.er]

See adjuster.

insurance agent
[in.*shoor*.ense *ay*.jent]

A person authorized by an insurance company to represent it when dealing with third persons in matters relating to insurance. *Compare* insurance broker.

insurance binder
[in.*shoor*.ense *bine*.der]

See binder.

insurance broker
[in.*shoor*.ense *broh*.ker]

A person who acts as an intermediary between the insured and the insurer, who is not employed by any insurance company. The broker solicits insurance business from the public, and having obtained an order, either places the insurance with a company selected by the insured, or, if the insured does not select a carrier, then with a company of the broker's choice. Depending upon the circumstances, an insurance broker may represent either the insured, or the insurer, or both. *Compare* insurance agent.

insurance carrier
[in.*shoor*.ense *kehr*.ee.er]

A company engaged in the business of issuing insurance policies; an insurance company.

insurance company [in.*shoor*.ense *kum*.pe.nee]	A company engaged in the business of issuing insurance policies.
insurance contract [in.*shoor*.ense *kon*.trakt]	The formal name for an insurance policy.
insurance policy [in.*shoor*.ense *pol*.i.see]	A contract to compensate or indemnify a person for loss arising from a contingent occurrence.
insurance premium [in.*shoor*.ense *pree*.mee.um]	Money paid to an insurer for an insurance policy.
insure [in.*shoor*]	1. To enter into a contract of insurance as an insurer; to issue an insurance policy. 2. To guarantee. ▪ *v.* obtain insurance, secure against loss, underwrite, guard, safeguard, shield, back
insured [in.*shoord*]	A person protected by an insurance policy; a person whose property is protected by an insurance policy. One need not be the named insured (i.e., named in the policy) to be covered. A standard automobile insurance policy, for EXAMPLE, usually covers any person operating the insured vehicle with the permission of the named insured.
insurer [in.*shoor*.er]	Generally, an insurance company; that is, the party who assumes the risk under an insurance policy and agrees to compensate or indemnify the insured. ▪ *n.* indemnitor, indemnifier, guarantor, assurer, surety, underwriter
life insurance [life in.*shoor*.ense]	A contract (the policy) in which the insurer, in exchange for the payment of a premium, agrees to pay a specified sum to a named beneficiary upon the death of the insured. *See also* straight life insurance; term life insurance; whole life insurance.
malpractice insurance [mal.*prak*.tiss in.*shoor*.ense]	A type of liability insurance that protects professional persons (EXAMPLES: attorneys; physicians; psychotherapists) from liability for negligence and other forms of malpractice. It is also called professional liability insurance.
marine insurance [ma.*reen* in.*shoor*.ense]	An insurance policy covering the risk of loss to a ship or its cargo from the perils of the sea.
material misrepresentation [mah.*teer*.e.al mis.rep.re.zen.*tay*.shen]	A fraudulent or deliberately inaccurate statement that is intended to cause, or causes, a person to act in reliance. Also called a fraudulent misrepresentation.
no-fault insurance [no-fawlt in.*shoor*.ense]	A type of automobile insurance required by law in many states, under which the insured is entitled to indemnification regardless of who was responsible for the injury or damage. Proof of negligence is not a condition of liability under such a policy. *See also* insurance.
personal liability [*per*.sen.el ly.a.*bil*.i.tee]	Liability to satisfy a judgment, debt, or other obligation from one's personal assets.

preexisting condition clause
[pree.eg.*zis*.ting ken.*dish*.en kloz]

A provision in a health insurance policy that excludes from coverage, for a specified period of time, medical conditions that existed when the insured purchased the policy.

premium
[*pree*.mee.yum]

Money paid to an insurance company for coverage by an insurance policy.

proof of loss
[proof ov loss]

A written statement of the dollar amount of a loss sustained, submitted by an insured. Proof of loss is a standard requirement of casualty insurance policies.

reinsurance
[ree.in.*shoor*.ense]

A contract between two insurance companies under which the second company (the reinsurer) insures the first company (the insurer) against loss due to policyholders' claims.

reinsurer
[ree.in.*shoor*.er]

An insurance company's insurance company. *See also* reinsurance.

replacement value
[ree.*plaiss*.ment *val*.yoo]

In the context of an insurance loss, the cost of replacing insured property at its current value, as opposed to its original cost; that is, at what it costs now, not what it cost when it was purchased.

rider
[*ry*.der]

A sheet or sheets of paper, written or printed, attached to a document, that refer to the document in a manner that leaves no doubt of the parties' intention to incorporate it into the document. Riders are most frequently used with insurance policies to make additions or changes to the original policy.

- *n.* attachment, extension, insertion, supplement, addendum

risk
[rizk]

1. The chance of loss or injury; the hazard or peril of loss that is protected by an insurance policy. EXAMPLES: fire, flood; sickness. 2. A gamble; a peril.

self-insurance
[self-in.*shoor*.ense]

Protecting one's property or business by establishing a fund out of which to pay for losses instead of purchasing insurance. Self-insurance is a means through which employers may provide workers' compensation and health coverage to their employees as an alternative to securing workers' compensation insurance and health insurance.

straight life insurance
[strate life in.*shoor*.ense]

Life insurance in which the cash surrender value of the policy increases as the insured makes premium payments throughout her lifetime. Straight life insurance is also referred to as whole life insurance or ordinary life insurance. *Compare* term life insurance.

subrogation
[sub.ro.*gay*.shen]

The substitution of one person for another with respect to a claim or right against a third person; the principle that when a person has been required to pay a debt that should have been paid by another person, she becomes entitled to all of the remedies that the creditor originally possessed with respect to the debtor. (EXAMPLE: After the insurance company that insures Lloyd's car indemnifies him for the damage done to his car by Mary's negligence, the insurance company has the same cause of action against Mary as Lloyd originally had.) Subrogation is sometimes referred to as substitution.

- *n.* displacement, substitution, transfer, transference, exchange, switch, supplanting

term life insurance [term life in.*shoor*.ense]	Life insurance that provides protection only for a stated number of years and has no cash surrender value. *Compare* life insurance; straight life insurance; whole life insurance.
title insurance [*ty*.tel in.*shoor*.ense]	An insurance policy in which the insurer agrees to indemnify the purchaser of realty, or the mortgagee, against loss due to defective title.
umbrella policy [um.*brel*.a *pah*.li.see]	An insurance policy that provides coverage over and above the liability limitations of the insured's basic liability insurance policies.
waiver [*way*.ver]	The intentional relinquishment or renunciation of a right, claim, or privilege a person knows he has. ▪ *n.* abandonment, abdication, forgoing, refusal, relinquishment, renunciation
whole life insurance [hole life in.*shoor*.ense]	Straight life insurance or ordinary life insurance, as opposed to term life insurance or group insurance.
workers' compensation insurance [*wer*.kerz kom.pen.*say*.shen in.*shoor*.ense]	State statutes provide for the payment by the employer of compensation to employees injured in their employment or, in case of death, to their dependents, without the need to prove any negligence on the part of the employer.

Missing Words

Fill in the blanks.

1. A yearly payment of a fixed sum of money for life or a stated number of years is a(n) _____.

2. A payment made under an insurance policy, pension, or annuity is known as a(n) _____.

3. Money paid an insurance company for an insurance policy is known as a(n) _____.

4. Insurance that indemnifies the insured for medical expenses incurred as a result of sickness or accident is _____.

5. An interim memorandum, used when an insurance policy cannot be issued immediately, is known as a(n) _____.

6. A division of the risk between the insurer and the insured is known as _____.

7. A(n) _____ is an insurance company's insurance company.

8. A person who makes a determination of the value of a claim against an insurance company for which the claim will be settled is a(n) _____.

9. _____ is the written statement of the dollar amount of a loss sustained that is submitted by the insured.

10. A contract by which one party, in return for a specified consideration, agrees to compensate or indemnify another on account of loss, damage, or liability arising from an unknown event is called _____.

11. A type of liability insurance that protects professional persons such as attorneys and physicians is known as _____.

12. The _____ is a person protected by an insurance policy.

13. _____ insurance provides benefits to an employee by an employer for injuries as a result of employment, regardless of whether or not the employer was negligent.

14. A person who receives a benefit is known as a(n) _____.

15. The portion of the loss the insured must pay out of pocket is the _____.

16. A provision in an insurance policy that removes a specified risk, person, or circumstance from coverage is _____.

17. The escape clause in an insurance contract is called the _____.

18. _____ is a benefit payable under an insurance policy at twice the face value.

STUDY AID: Use flashcards for this unit before completing the exercises.

Matching

Match the letter of the definition to the term.

_____ 19. business interruption insurance

    A. payment of compensation to employees who are injured on the job

_____ 20. annuity

    B. insurance that provides coverage for various risks that could be covered under separate policies

_____ 21. whole life insurance

    C. protection against loss from interruption of a business

_____ 22. homeowners' insurance

    D. policy that insures homeowners against most common risks

_____ 23. collision insurance

    E. insurance that protects the owner or operator of a motor vehicle from loss due to damage done to his property by another

_____ 24. workers' compensation

    F. insured is entitled to indemnification regardless of who is responsible for injury or damage

_____ 25. comprehensive insurance

    G. yearly payment of a fixed sum of money

_____ 26. malpractice insurance

    H. straight life insurance

_____ 27. no-fault insurance

    I. protection against loss due to defective title of real property

_____ 28. title insurance

    J. protects professional people from liability for negligence and other forms of malpractice

_____ 29. personal liability insurance

    K. whole life insurance

_____ 30. straight life insurance

    L. provides income in event of disability

_____ 31. term life insurance

    M. liability to satisfy a judgment from one's personal assets

_____ 32. disability insurance

    N. life insurance that provides protection for a stated number of years and has no cash surrender value

_____ 33. bad faith

    O. a person who receives a payment from a policy

_____ 34. beneficiary

    P. a division of risk between the insurer and the insured

_____ 35. coinsurance

    Q. a devious or deceitful intent, motivated by self-interest

Multiple Choice

Select the best choice.

_____ 36. An insurer's right to end an insurance contract when the insured breaches the terms of the contract is known as:
   a. exclusion.
   b. endorsement.
   c. cancellation.
   d. waiver.

_____ 37. Insurance that indemnifies the insured against loss to property due to fire is known as:
   a. health insurance.
   b. term life.
   c. whole life.
   d. fire insurance.

_____ 38. The portion of a loss that the insured must pay is known as a:
   a. deductible.
   b. waiver.
   c. benefit.
   d. rider.

_____ 39. Self-insurance is where:
   a. a person purchases insurance from another.
   b. a person establishes a fund out of which to pay his losses.
   c. an employer purchases insurance for a group of employees.
   d. none of the above

_____ **40.** A written statement of the dollar amount of a loss sustained, submitted by an insured, is known as a(n):
  a. proof of loss.
  b. certificate.
  c. policy.
  d. insurable interest.

_____ **41.** The person who is entitled to the proceeds of a life insurance policy when the insured dies is a(n):
  a. insurance agent.
  b. insurance carrier.
  c. beneficiary.
  d. insurance broker.

_____ **42.** An insurance agent is:
  a. the same as an insurance binder.
  b. the same as an insurance carrier.
  c. a person employed by an insurance company.
  d. none of the above

_____ **43.** After the insurance company that insures Mary Smith's car indemnifies her for damage done to her car by John Wheat's negligence, the insurance company has the same cause of action against John as Mary originally had. This is known as:
  a. subrogation.
  b. self-insurance.
  c. contribution between insurers.
  d. comprehensive insurance.

_____ **44.** A type of automobile insurance in which the insured is entitled to indemnification regardless of who was responsible for the injury or damage is known as:
  a. collision insurance.
  b. title insurance.
  c. no-fault insurance.
  d. comprehensive insurance.

_____ **45.** A person who makes a determination of the value of a claim against an insurance company for the purpose of arriving at an amount for which the claim can be settled is an insurance:
  a. agent.
  b. broker.
  c. carrier.
  d. adjuster.

_____ **46.** When an insurance company refuses without any basis to pay a claim, it is considered:
  a. bad faith.
  b. exclusion.
  c. subrogation.
  d. rider.

True/False

Mark the following T or F.

_____ **47.** An umbrella policy provides coverage over and above the liability limitations of the insured's basic liability policies.

_____ **48.** Subrogation occurs when one person is substituted for another person with respect to a claim or right against a third party.

_____ **49.** A fraudulent or deliberately inaccurate statement intended to cause a person to act in reliance is a material misrepresentation.

_____ **50.** Contribution between insurers occurs when insurers with policies covering the same loss must contribute proportionately to the insurer who has paid for the entire loss.

_____ **51.** Reinsurance occurs when there is a contract between two insurance companies in which the second company agrees to insure the first company against loss due to policyholders' claims.

_____ **52.** The insured is the insurance company who assures the risk under an insurance policy.

_____ **53.** Marine insurance is a policy covering the risk of loss to a ship or its cargo from the perils of the sea.

_____ **54.** Coinsurance is when the risk is divided between the insurer and the insured.

_____ **55.** A rider is used to make additions or changes to the original insurance policy.

_____ **56.** The cost of replacing insured property at its current value, as opposed to its original cost, is known as a double indemnity clause.

_____ **57.** Fire insurance indemnifies the insured against loss to property due to fire.

Synonyms

Select the correct synonym in parentheses for each numbered item.

58. WHOLE LIFE
(straight life, term life, group insurance)

59. DISABILITY
(incapacity, death, competency)

60. EXCLUSION
(inclusion, privilege, exception)

61. BENEFICIARY
(donor, recipient, insurer)

62. INSURANCE POLICY
(contract, release, waiver)

63. INSURED
(agent, buyer, covered person)

64. SUBROGATION
(exclusion, substitution, endorsement)

65. UMBRELLA POLICY
(basic coverage, excess coverage, duplicate coverage)

66. COLLISION INSURANCE
(personal injury insurance, theft insurance, property damage insurance)

67. INDEMNIFICATION
(loss, compensation, revocation)

68. INSURANCE CARRIER
(insurance company, insurance broker, insurance agent)

69. MALPRACTICE INSURANCE
(self-insurance, collision insurance, professional liability insurance)

70. BENEFIT
(return, loss, contribution)

71. INSURE
(cancel, waive, guarantee)

Self-Test

Place the number of the correct term in the appropriate space.

72. insurance agent

73. self-insurance

74. broker

75. policy

76. insurable interest

77. life

78. beneficiary

79. flood

80. homeowners'

81. carriers

82. insurer

83. premium

84. insured

85. title insurance

86. exclusion

87. fraud

There are many risks a person faces throughout the day. People with sufficient resources and foresight might put aside money to cover all possible eventualities. When people or organizations set aside money to cover their own risks, this is known as _____. Other people seek the services of a(n) _____ to obtain insurance for them through a variety of companies. Insurance is a contract (or _____) by which one party (the _____), in return for a specified _____, agrees to compensate another (the _____) for a loss.

There are many different kinds of coverage. The list is almost endless. You need a(n) _____ in whatever you wish to insure. If you are worried about providing for your family after you die, you might obtain _____ insurance. If you live in an area prone to flooding, you might obtain _____ insurance. If you wish to get a mortgage to buy a home, the bank will most likely require you to get _____ insurance and _____, to protect against defective title. Insurance is provided by various companies known as insurance _____. The insurance company might authorize a person known as a(n) _____ to represent it when dealing with third persons. Once a person becomes a(n) _____ to an insurance policy, he will truly appreciate the necessity of insurance. However, if there is any _____ or deceit involved by the insured, a(n) _____ provision in the policy will be relied on by the insurer to see that no one collects under the policy.

Word Scramble

Unscramble the following words and write the correct word(s) that match(es) the definition for each word or phrase.

88. licypo – another name for an insurance contract

_____

89. umpremi – money paid to an insurance company for insurance coverage _____

_____

90. derusni – a person protected by an insurance policy

_____

_____

91. reusnir – an insurance company _____

_____

92. nefbeiciary – a person who receives a benefit ____

_____

93. clusionex – a provision in an insurance policy that removes a specified risk from coverage _____

_____

94. blededucti – portion of a loss that the insured must pay from his own pocket _____

_____

95. iderr – addition or change to a policy _____

_____

96. prehensivecom ercovage – a package of insurance coverage that insures against a variety of perils ___

_____

97. rewaiv – relinquishment of a right, claim, or privilege _____

_____

98. roupg surancein – insurance provided for a group of people _____

_____

99. cosurancein – a division of the risk between the insurer and the insured _____

_____

100. existingpre ditconion – a medical condition that existed at the time the insured purchased a policy _____

_____

101. whoel file – the same as straight life or ordinary life insurance _____

_____

102. brellaum icypol – an insurance policy that provides coverage over and above the liability limitations of the insured's basic policy _____

_____

The Last Word

Ascertaining and planning for risk is the province of law enforcement, attorneys, engineers, financiers, actuaries, public health administrators, private security specialists, and safety experts among others. Their job includes identifying, assessing, and prioritizing uncertainties followed by actions to control or minimize the impact of unfortunate incidents. Risks from legal liabilities, credit exposure, interest and currency rate fluctuations, accidents, disasters, or competing forces all require strategies to manage risk. Methods of managing risk include transferring risk to other parties, avoidance measures, and reducing risk with insurance or other means. Which kinds of insurance do you think are most important?

 Access an interactive eBook, chapter-specific interactive learning tools, and more in your Paralegal CourseMate, accessed through www.CengageBrain.com

16 Commercial Law

A person who regularly trades in a particular type of goods is called a merchant. Years ago, most merchants depended on their family, friends, and relatives who lived nearby to purchase their goods. Most transactions were informal, conducted face to face and settled with a handshake. A merchant usually knew the financial standing of the purchasers and might even accept a barter or trade arrangement to help out friends who were short on cash.

Now business transactions are much more impersonal. Usually a merchant will not be familiar with the person or corporation that wishes to purchase goods. There is a good chance that the purchaser buys online and resides in a different state than where the seller of goods conducts business. A field of law—commercial law—has developed that relates to shipping, insurance, the exchange of money, brokerage, drafts, promissory notes, and other matters of concern to merchants. To protect merchants who are involved in interstate commerce, the Uniform Commercial Code (UCC) was developed, which deals with most areas of commercial transactions and has been adopted in much the same form in most states.

Article 3 of the Uniform Commercial Code regulates commercial paper, also known as negotiable instruments, including checks, drafts, certificates of deposit, and promissory notes. The Uniform Commercial Code defines a negotiable instrument as a signed writing that orders or promises payment of money if: it is unconditional, it is in a fixed amount, it is payable on demand to bearer or to order or at a definite time, and it "does not state any undertaking or instruction by the person promising or ordering payment to do any act in addition to the payment of money."

Commercial paper helps facilitate commercial transactions. It is both a substitute for cash and it can be used as a device to extend credit. The following case demonstrates the importance of knowing the exact definitions in legal terminology. Can a person be charged with forgery when signing his own name to a document?

CASE AND COMMENT

New York Court of Appeals
The People
v.
Gregory P. Cunningham
New York Reports No. 86
June 10, 2004

Facts: Peter Morat opened a small sawmill operation under the name Herkimer Precut, Inc. He engaged the services of Cunningham as a consultant to arrange for finances and related activities. Cunningham was to receive a 20 percent interest in the new business venture. Morat eventually turned over control of the corporate checkbook to Cunningham. Morat would sometimes give Cunningham blank signed checks so he could pay bills, but Cunningham had no authority to sign checks. When Morat discovered that some of the bills were not being paid, he reviewed the company's bank records and found unauthorized payments, some on checks he signed in blank, and others with a signature he did not recognize, that Cunningham used to pay his own personal expenses. Morat claimed that by Cunningham improperly signing or issuing checks, he had stolen thousands of dollars from the company.

Procedural History: This case is before the Court of Appeals to decide whether the decision of the Appellate Division was correct.

Issue: Whether Cunningham's conviction for forgery was correct.

Rationale: Only in rare instances can one commit a forgery by signing one's own name, which is precisely what Cunningham has done. However, if you sign your name to deceive others so that they think you are a third party, an issue of forgery might come up. In most jurisdictions, a forger must act without authority and sign someone else's name. Usually the forger signs the check in someone else's name with the intent of having another person believe he is someone else. This is to mislead the payee to believe that the forger is really someone else, that the maker is a real person, and that the document is authentic. But where the alleged maker and the actual maker of the draft are one and the same, there can be no forgery. Forgery is a crime because of the need to protect commercial instruments and make them freely negotiable.

Ruling: The order of the Appellate Division should be reversed, and the criminal indictment against Cunningham must be dismissed.

Comment: Many legal cases are won or lost by the definition of a single word. Also, the importance of a missed adjective or adverb in law cannot be overemphasized.

DICTIONARY / THESAURUS

Term [phonetic pronunciation]	*Note: All dictionary/thesaurus terms appear on flashcards at the back of the book and on the student website.*

acceptance
[ak.*sep*.tense]

1. With respect to negotiable instruments, the agreement of the bank or other drawer to honor a draft, check, or other negotiable instrument. Acceptance, which must be indicated on the instrument, in writing, is an acknowledgment by the drawee that the drawer has sufficient funds on deposit to cover the draft. *See also* certified check.
2. In the law of sales, the acceptance of the goods that are the subject of the sale has an important bearing upon the passage of title from the buyer to the seller per the contract.

- *n.* acquisition, reception, adoption, compliance, consent, acknowledgment
- *ant.* rejection, opposition

acceptor
[ak.*sep*.tor]

A drawee who has accepted a draft. *See also* acceptance.

accommodation loan
[a.kom.o.*day*.shen loan]

A loan made as a favor, without benefit or without adequate benefit to the person making the loan.

accommodation paper
[a.kom.o.*day*.shen *pay*.per]

A bill or note signed as a favor to another person, known as the accommodated party, to enable that person to receive a loan. The person who grants the favor is the accommodation party or accommodation maker. If the accommodated party and the accommodation party sign jointly, they are known as co-makers. If the accommodated party defaults on the note, the accommodation party is fully liable.

alteration
[al.ter.*ay*.shen]

An erasure, writing, or typing that modifies the content of an instrument or document. EXAMPLE: changing the date on a check (as opposed to securing or writing a new check). Because an instrument can be altered by a person entitled to do so, an alteration is not necessarily a forgery.

- *n.* change, modification, conversion, switch, correction

asset
[*ass*.et]

Anything of value owned by a person or an organization. Assets include not only all real property and personal property, but intangible property such as bills, notes, stock, and accounts receivable.

assignment
[a.*sine*.ment]

A transfer of property, or a right in property, from one person to another.

assignment for the benefit of creditors
[a.*sine*.ment for the *ben*.e.fit of *kred*.it.terz]

An assignment and transfer by a debtor of all her property to a trustee to collect any amounts owned, to sell the property, and to distribute the proceeds among her creditors.

attachment
[a.*tach*.ment]

The process by which a person's property is figuratively brought into court to ensure satisfaction of a judgment that may be rendered against him. In the event judgment is rendered, the property may be sold to satisfy the judgment.

- *n.* seizure, confiscation, garnishment, dispossession

attachment lien
[a.*tach*.ment *leen*]

A lien that arises when property is attached; it is perfected when judgment is entered.

bearer
[*bare*.er]

The holder of a negotiable instrument payable to "bearer" or to "cash" (i.e., a negotiable instrument not payable to a named person). The Uniform Commercial Code defines a bearer as the person in possession of an instrument, document of title, or certificated security payable to bearer or indorsed in blank.

- *n.* carrier, recipient, courier, possessor, holder, payee

bearer instrument
[*bare*.er *in*.stroo.ment]

A negotiable instrument payable to bearer or to cash, or that is in any form that does not specify a payee.

bearer paper
[*bare*.er *pay*.per]

Commercial paper payable to bearer or to cash, or in any other form that does not designate a specific payee.

cash
[kash]

Coin, money; money in hand, either in coin, currency, or other legal tender. A cashier's check or a certified check is the equivalent of cash, because payment is essentially guaranteed.

- *n.* coin, money, funds, currency, notes, legal tender
- *v.* make change, pay, draw, liquidate, redeem ("to cash a check")

cashier's check
[kash.*eerz* chek]

A bill of exchange, drawn by a bank upon bank funds, and accepted by virtue of the act of issuance. The bank's insurance of the check is a guaranty that it will be honored. A cashier's check is the equivalent of cash. *Compare* certified check.

certificate of deposit
[ser.*tif*.i.ket ov de.*poz*.it]

A voucher issued by a bank acknowledging the receipt of money on deposit that the bank promises to repay to the depositor. There are two kinds of certificates of deposit: demand certificates and time certificates. Demand certificates are ordinary savings accounts; the deposit can be withdrawn at any time, without penalty. Time certificates, which pay a higher rate of interest, are designed not to be cashed for a specified number of months or years. A certificate of deposit is often referred to simply as a CD. A treasury certificate is a form of certificate of deposit issued by the United States Treasury.

certified check
[ser.ti.fide chek]

A check upon which the bank has stamped the words "certified" or "accepted," certifying that the check is drawn upon sufficient funds and will be honored when it is presented for payment. A certified check is the equivalent of cash. *See also* acceptance. *Compare* cashier's check.

chattel paper
[*chat*.el *pay*.per]

As defined by the Uniform Commercial Code, a document that reflects both a debt and a security interest in specific goods. *See also* secured transaction.

check
[chek]

A written order ("pay to the order of") directed to a bank to pay money to the person named. *See also* cashier's check; certified check; traveler's check; draft; negotiable instrument.

- *n.* draft, note, negotiable instrument, bank note, inspection, examination

collateral
[ko.*lat*.er.el]

Stocks, bonds, or other property that serve as security for a loan or other obligation; property pledged to pay a debt.

- *n.* deposit, security, endorsement, pledge, promise

commercial paper
[ke.*mer*.shel *pay*.per]

Negotiable instruments, including checks, drafts, certificates of deposit, and promissory notes. Commercial paper is regulated by Article 3 of the Uniform Commercial Code.

consignment
[ken.*sine*.ment]

The entrusting of goods either to a carrier for delivery to a consignee or to a consignee who is to sell the goods for the consignor.

- *n.* entrusting, distribution, committal, transmittal

consumer
[kon.*soo*.mer]

A person who buys and uses products or services and who is affected by their cost, availability, and quality, as well as by laws regulating their manufacture, sale, and financing.

- *n.* buyer, client, patron, purchaser, vendee, customer

consumer credit protection acts
[kon.*soo*.mer *kred*.it pro.*tek*.shen aktz]

Also known as truth in lending acts; federal and state statutes that require, among other things, that contracts for the sale of consumer goods involving credit be written in plain language, that the finance charges be stated as a uniform annual percentage rate, and that goods purchased on credit or with credit cards be returnable within specified periods of time. *See also* credit.

consumer goods
[kon.*soo*.mer gudz]

As defined by the Uniform Commercial Code, articles used primarily for personal, family, or household purposes.

credit
[*kred*.it]

Trust placed in a person's willingness and ability to pay when the obligation to pay is extended over a period of time without security.

- *n.* rating, trust, standing, authority, loan, mortgage ("He has good credit.")

credit bureau
[*kred*.it *byoo*.roh]

A company that collects information concerning the financial standing, credit, and general reputation of others, which it furnishes to subscribers for a fee.

credit card
[*kred*.it kard]

A card issued for the purpose of enabling the owner to obtain goods, services, or money on credit.

The Credit Card Accountability, Responsibility and Disclosure Act of 2009
[the *kre*.dit kard a.kount.a.*bil*.i.tee and dis.*klo*.shur akt ov 2009]

n. The Act's key changes to credit card law included:

Banning retroactive rate increases on existing balances, requiring 45 days notice of rate increases, mandating that statements be mailed 21 days before the due date, and over-limit fees can be charged only after a cardholder authorizes such transactions.

creditor
[*kred*.it.or]

A person to whom a debt is owed by a debtor.

debt
[det]

An unconditional and legally enforceable obligation for the payment of money (EXAMPLES: a mortgage; an installment sale contract) and obligations imposed by law without contract (EXAMPLES: a judgment, unliquidated damages). A debt not presently due is nonetheless a debt.

- *n.* obligation, liability, debit, dues, commitment, encumbrance

defense
[de.*fense*]

With respect to commercial paper, a legal basis for denying one's liability on an instrument.

deficiency
[de.*fish*.en.see]

1. The amount still due the creditor after foreclosure of a mortgage or other security. 2. Shortage, undersupply, lack.

- *n.* insufficiency, lack, shortage, inadequacy, absence, scantiness, want
- *ant.* adequacy

demand loan
[de.*mand* lone]

A loan that is callable (total payment is demanded) at any time.

demand note
[de.*mand* note]

A promissory note payable when payment is demanded.

demand paper
[de.*mand pay*.per]

Commercial paper payable when payment is demanded.

dishonor
[dis.*on*.er]

To refuse to accept or pay a negotiable instrument when it is duly presented for acceptance or payment, or when presentment is excused and the instrument is not accepted or paid.

- *ant.* accept

draft
[draft]

n. An order in writing by one person on another (commonly a bank) to pay a specified sum of money to a third person on demand or at a stated future time. EXAMPLE: a check.

- *n.* money order, check, banknote, negotiable paper ("a bank draft")

draw
[draw]

1. To create, make, or sign a negotiable instrument. 2. To take or accept an advance. 3. To withdraw money from a bank account.

- *v.* extract, deplete, exhaust, withdraw ("Do you wish to draw on your savings account?")
- *ant.* deposit
- *n.* extraction, withdrawal, depletion, advance ("I made a draw on my checking account.")

drawee
[draw.*ee*]

The person upon whom a draft is drawn; the person to whom a draft is presented for acceptance and payment. The drawee of a check is always a bank. *Compare* drawer.

drawer [draw.*er*]	The maker of a draft. *Compare* drawee.
execution [ek.se.*kyoo*.shen]	1. A writ of process for the enforcement of a judgment. 2. The act of an officer in serving a writ or process. 3. The signing of a document or instrument. ▪ *n.* fulfillment, achievement, performance, conclusion ("the execution of a contract")
filing [*file*.ing]	The act of depositing a document with a public officer to preserve it as one of the records of his office.
filing laws [*file*.ing lawz]	Statutes that require the filing of an instrument as a condition of its complete effectiveness.
financing statement [*fine*.an.sing *state*.ment]	A notice of the existence of a security interest in goods, which a creditor is entitled to file with the appropriate public officer, usually the secretary of state. The designated public office varies from state to state. Note that "financing statement" is not "financial statement."
forge [forj]	To commit a forgery; to make falsely with intent to defraud or injure any writing that, if genuine, might appear to be legally effective or the basis for legal liability. Forgery is a crime. ▪ *v.* counterfeit, duplicate, imitate, reproduce, construct. *See* utter.
garnishment [*gar*.nish.ment]	A proceeding by a creditor to obtain satisfaction of a debt from money or property of the debtor that is in the possession of a third person or is owed by such a person to the debtor. EXAMPLE: Because Ron owes back taxes, the IRS (the creditor, also called the garnishor or plaintiff) initiates a garnishment against Ron (the debtor, also called the defendant) by serving a notice of garnishment of Ron's wages upon his employer, the ABC Company (the garnishee). Note that a garnishment is distinguished from an attachment by the fact that the money or property reached by the garnishment remains in the hands of the third party until there is a judgment in the action involving the basic debt. ▪ *n.* attachment, levy, appropriation, collection
holder [*hole*.der]	A person who has the legal right to enforce a negotiable instrument or who is entitled to receive, hold, and dispose of a document of title and the goods to which it pertains. With respect to an instrument payable to or in the name of "bearer," the person in possession is the holder; with respect to an instrument payable to or in the name of an identified person, that person is the "holder" if she is in possession of the instrument. ▪ *n.* owner, possessor, bearer, keeper, recipient
holder for value [*hole*.der for *val*.yoo]	A person who has given consideration for a negotiable instrument that he holds.

DICTIONARY   THESAURUS *continued...*

holder in due course
[*hole*.der in dew kors]

A holder of a negotiable instrument who gave value for it and took it in good faith and without notice of any claim or defense against it.

holder in good faith
[*hole*.der in good faith]

A person who takes or holds property, including a negotiable instrument, without knowledge of any defect in title.

honor
[*on*.er]

To pay or accept a negotiable instrument when it is duly presented.*Compare* dishonor. *See also* acceptance.

- *v.* credit, redeem, make good ("The store honors personal checks.")

indorse
[in.*dorse*]

To sign one's name on the back of a document, especially a check. *See also* indorsement.

indorsee
[in.dor.*see*]

The person to whom a negotiable instrument is indorsed by name. *Compare* bearer. *See also* indorse.

indorsee in due course
[in.dor.*see* in dew korss]

A person who in good faith, in the ordinary course of business, for value, acquires a negotiable instrument duly indorsed to her, indorsed generally, or payable to bearer.

indorsement
[in.*dorse*.ment]

The writing of one's name on the back of a negotiable instrument, by which a person transfers title to the paper to another person.

indorser
[in.*dor*.ser]

The person who indorses a negotiable instrument. *Compare* indorsee.

installment payments
[in.*stall*.ment *pay*.ments]

Payments at fixed intervals until the entire principal and interest on an obligation are satisfied. Installment payments are made under installment contracts, installment notes, or installment sale contracts, as well as other types of agreements. Commercial installment sales and installment loans are regulated by consumer credit protection acts.

judgment
[*juj*.ment]

In a civil action, the final determination entered by a court after it renders its decision on the rights of the parties, based upon the pleadings and the evidence.

- *n.* decree, holding, ruling, conclusion, opinion, award, sentence, finding, adjudication, verdict, arbitration ("the judgment of the court"), decision

lien
[*leen*]

A claim or charge on, or right against, personal property, or an encumbrance on real property, for the payment of a debt. A lien may be created by statute (EXAMPLES: a tax lien, an attachment lien) or by agreement between the parties (EXAMPLES: a mortgage on real estate; a security agreement covering personal property). In some instances, a lien permits the creditor to retain the debtor's property in his possession until the debt is satisfied. Such a lien is called a possessory lien.

- *n.* debt, obligation, mortgage, interest ("The mortgage is a lien on the house.")

lien creditor
[*leen kred*.i.tor]

A creditor whose debt is secured by a lien. EXAMPLES: an execution creditor; a judgment creditor.

liquidated debt [*lik*.wi.day.ted det]	A debt that has been paid or for which it is certain as to how much is due. *See also* debt.
maker [*may*.ker]	A person who obligates himself by executing a check, promissory note, draft, or other negotiable instrument. *See also* drawer.
merchant [*mer*.chent]	1. A person who regularly trades in a particular type of goods. 2. Under the Uniform Commercial Code, "a person who deals in goods of the kind or otherwise by his occupation holds himself out as having knowledge or skill peculiar to the goods involved in the transaction." The law holds a merchant to a higher standard than it imposes upon a casual seller.
mortgage [*more*.gej]	*n.* 1. A pledge of real property to secure a debt. Which one of at least three possible legal principles defines the rights of the parties to a given mortgage depends upon the state in which the mortgaged property is located. In states that have adopted the lien theory, the mortgagee (creditor) has a lien on the property; the mortgagor (debtor) retains legal title and is entitled to possession unless his interest is terminated by a foreclosure decree. In title theory states, a mortgage transfers title and a theoretical right of possession to the mortgagee; title reverts to the mortgagor upon full payment of the mortgage debt. A third group of states employs hybrid versions of the lien and title theories, with characteristics of both. 2. A written agreement pledging real property as security. *v.* 1. To place real property under a mortgage. 2. To obligate; to pledge.
negotiable [ne.*go*.shebl]	Transferable by indorsement or delivery. EXAMPLE: a negotiable instrument. • *adj.* transferable; assignable; alienable; open; undetermined; malleable • *ant.* nonnegotiable, fixed
negotiable instrument [ne.*go*.shebl *in*.stroo.ment]	Under the Uniform Commercial Code, a signed writing that orders or provides payment of money if: it is unconditional, it is in a fixed amount, it is payable on demand to bearer or to order or at a definite time, and it "does not state any undertaking or instruction by the person promising or ordering payment to do any act in addition to the payment of money." (EXAMPLES: a check; a money order; a certificate of deposit; a bond; a note, a bill of lading; a warehouse receipt.) Negotiable instruments are also referred to as commercial paper or negotiable paper. • *n.* draft, check, bond, note, money order, instrument
negotiate [ne.*go*.shee.ate]	To transfer a negotiable instrument to a third person by indorsement or delivery.
negotiation [ne.go.shee.*ay*.shen]	The act of transferring a negotiable instrument to a third person by indorsement or delivery. • *n.* agreement, compromise, mediation, discussion
nonnegotiable [non.ne.*go*.shebl]	1. A document or instrument not transferable by indorsement or delivery. EXAMPLES: a lease, a deed; a mortgage. 2. Not subject to negotiation. • *adj.* nontransferable, non-assignable

DICTIONARY   THESAURUS *continued...*

nonnegotiable instrument
[non.ne.*go*.shebl *in*.stroo.ment]

An instrument that is not negotiable.

note
[note]

A written promise by one person to pay another person a specified sum of money on a specified date; a term used interchangeably with promissory note. A note may or may not be negotiable, depending upon its form. *See also* negotiable instrument.

order paper
[*or*.der *pay*.per]

A negotiable instrument (i.e., an instrument that recites an unconditional promise to pay a fixed amount of money, and that is payable to order and meets all the other requirements of negotiability).

payor
[pay.*or*]

1. A person who makes a payment or is obligated to make a payment. 2. The person who makes a check, bill, or note.

perfecting a security interest
[per.*fek*.ting a se.*kyoo*.ri.tee *in*.trest]

Under the Uniform Commercial Code, a method of protecting a security interest in goods against the claims of other creditors by filing a financing statement with the appropriate public officer (usually the secretary of state). However, a security interest in consumer goods is perfected without such filing.

possession
[poh.*zesh*.en]

Occupancy and dominion over property; a holding of land legally, by one's self (actual possession) or through another person such as a tenant (constructive possession). The holding may be by virtue of having title or an estate or interest of any kind. One need not have a resident on the land to be in actual possession of it.

- *n.* dominion, proprietorship, ownership, holding, guardianship, keeping ("I have possession of my family's land.")

presentment
[pre.*zent*.ment]

A demand to accept (presentment for acceptance) or to pay (presentment for payment) a negotiable instrument, made to the drawee by a person, usually the payee or holder, entitled to enforce the instrument.

primary liability
[*pry*.mer.ee ly.e.*bil*.i.tee]

The liability of a person who, by the terms of the instrument he has executed, or because of some other legal obligation he has incurred, or by virtue of his legal relationship to an injured party, is absolutely required to make payment, satisfy the obligation, or assume full responsibility for the injury; the liability of a maker or principal, as distinguished from that of a guarantor or indorser. *Compare* secondary liability.

promissory note
[*prom*.i.sore.ee note]

A written promise to pay a specific sum of money by a specified date or on demand. A promissory note is negotiable if, in addition, it is payable to the order of a named person or to bearer. *See also* negotiable instrument.

purchase money security interest
[*per*.ches *mun*.ee se.*kyoo*.ri.tee *in*.trest]

A security interest created when a security agreement is executed by a purchaser of personal property.

repossession
[ree.po.*zesh*.en]

1. A remedy of the seller upon default by the buyer under a conditional sale contract or other security agreement. 2. A taking of possession by the owner of real estate after the occupant relinquishes possession or forfeits the right to possession.

- *n.* recapture, restoration, retrieval, seizure, reacquisition, recovery

secondary liability
[*sek*.en.dare.ee ly.e.*bil*.i.tee]

Liability that does not come about until the primary obligor fails to meet her obligation; the liability of a guarantor or indorser as distinguished from that of a maker or principal. *Compare* primary liability.

secured
[se.*kyoord*]

Made certain of payment; given security. *Compare* unsecured.

- *adj.* guaranteed, protected, insured, sheltered ("a secured debt")

secured creditor
[se.*kyoord kred*.it.er]

A creditor who has a perfected security lien for a debt in the form of an encumbrance on property of the debtor. EXAMPLES: a mortgagee; a lienee.

secured transaction
[se.*kyoord* tranz.*ak*.shen]

A transaction that creates or provides for a security interest in personal property. EXAMPLE: a secured loan.

security
[se.*kyoor*.i.tee]

1. Singular of securities. 2. Collateral; a pledge given to a creditor by a debtor for the payment of a debt or for the performance of an obligation. EXAMPLES: a mortgage; a lien; a deposit.

- *n.* warranty, bail, surety, escrow, collateral, debenture, assurance ("security for the mortgage")

security interest
[se.*kyoor*.i.tee *in*.trest]

1. Under the Uniform Commercial Code, "an interest in personal property or fixtures which secures payment or performance of an obligation." *See also* purchase money security interest. 2. With respect to real property, a mortgage or other lien.

sight draft
[site draft]

A bill of exchange or draft payable upon presentment to the drawee. It is the equivalent of a check that is payable on demand.

special indorsement
[*spesh*.el in.*dors*.ment]

An indorsement that specifies the person to whom or to whose order the instrument is to be payable (e.g., "pay to the order of Lisa Whitney").

time draft
[time draft]

A draft payable at a fixed or determinable future time.

traveler's check
[*trav*.lerz chek]

An instrument, usually one of a set, purchased from a bank or other financial institution and similar in many respects to a cashier's check. Traveler's checks must be signed by the purchaser at the time of purchase and countersigned when cashed.

Uniform Commercial Code (UCC)
[*yoon*.i.form ke.*mersh*.el kode]

One of the Uniform Laws, which have been adopted in much the same form in every state. The UCC governs most aspects of commercial transactions, including sales, leases, negotiable instruments, deposits and collections, letters of credit, bulk sales, warehouse receipts, bills of lading and other documents of title, investment securities, and secured transactions.

unsecured
[un.se.*kyoord*]

A term describing debts or obligations for which no security has been given or no perfected security lien exists.

utter
[*ut*.er]

To put counterfeit money or forged checks into circulation. *See* forge.

Missing Words

Fill in the blanks.

1. A card issued for the purpose of enabling the owner to obtain goods, services, or money on credit is a(n) _____.

2. A(n) _____ debt is a debt for which it is certain how much is due.

3. A promissory note payable when payment is demanded is a(n) _____.

4. The act of depositing a document with a public officer is known as _____.

5. A person who regularly trades in a particular type of goods is known as a(n) _____.

6. Money one owes another person is a(n) _____.

7. A security interest created when a security agreement is executed by a purchaser of personal property is a(n) _____.

8. When the contents of a document are modified by erasure, this is called _____.

9. A voucher issued by a bank acknowledging the receipt of money on deposit that the bank promises to repay is a(n) _____.

10. A(n) _____ is the amount still due a creditor after foreclosure of a mortgage.

11. A(n) _____ is the transfer of property, or a right in property, from one person to another.

12. A(n) _____ is an encumbrance on real property or a claim on personal property for payment of a debt.

13. A pledge of real property to secure a debt is called a(n) _____.

14. _____ is a method under the UCC of protecting a security interest in goods against the claims of their creditors by filing a financing statement.

15. A(n) _____ is the holder of a negotiable instrument who gave value for it and took it in good faith and without notice of any claim or defense against it.

16. The _____ is the maker of a draft.

17. Checks, certificates of deposit, drafts, and notes are all examples of _____ or commercial paper.

18. Statutes that require the filing of an instrument as a condition of its complete effectiveness are _____.

19. Payments made at fixed intervals until the entire principal and interest on an obligation are satisfied are _____.

STUDY AID: Use flashcards for this unit before completing the exercises.

Matching

Match the letter of the definition to the term.

D **20.** assignment

    A. deposit a document with a public officer

G **21.** repossession

    B. a person's property is used to satisfy a judgment

J **22.** consumer

    C. promissory note payable when payment is demanded

A **23.** filing

    D. transfer of property or a right in property

L **24.** judgment

    E. written promise to pay a sum of money

C **25.** demand note

    F. method of protecting a security interest in goods

E **26.** promissory note

    G. remedy of a seller upon default by a buyer

I **27.** possession

    H. a notice of the existence of a security interest in goods that a creditor files

F **28.** perfection of a
security interest

    I. occupancy and dominion over property

K **29.** Uniform
Commercial Code

    J. person who buys or uses services

H **30.** financing statement

    K. a uniform law that governs most aspects of commercial transactions

B **31.** attachment

    L. final determination by a court of the rights of the parties

O **32.** check

    M. voucher issued by a bank acknowledging the receipt of money on deposit that the bank promises to repay to the depositor

M **33.** certificate of deposit

    N. material alteration of a writing

N **34.** forgery

    O. written order directed to a bank to pay money to the person named

Q **35.** sight draft

    P. draft payable at a fixed time

P **36.** time draft

    Q. the equivalent of a check that is payable on demand

Multiple Choice

Select the best choice.

 37. Commercial law is the branch of law that is related to matters of concern to:
   a. merchants.
   b. farmers.
   c. food service workers.
   d. wallpaper hangers.

 38. An unconditional and legally enforceable obligation for the payment of money is known as a(n):
   a. filing.
   b. asset.
   c. perfection of a security interest.
   d. debt.

 39. The process by which a person's property is figuratively brought into court to ensure satisfaction of a judgment is known as:
   a. promissory note.
   b. attachment.
   c. assignment.
   d. UCC.

 40. The amount still due a creditor after foreclosure of a mortgage is known as:
   a. deficiency.
   b. lis pendens.
   c. default.
   d. possession.

 41. A financing statement is a notice of the existence of a security interest in goods, which a creditor is entitled to file with the appropriate public officer, usually the:
   a. court.
   b. bank.
   c. secretary of state.
   d. creditor.

 42. Unsecured debt is a debt for which:
   a. there has been no security given.
   b. there has been no lien given.
   c. there has been no contract given.
   d. there has been no writ of execution given.

 43. A consumer loan is a loan made to a consumer for the purpose of purchasing consumer goods, usually under a conditional sales contract involving:
   a. assignment.
   b. attachment.
   c. installment payments.
   d. filing.

 44. In a civil action, the final determination by a court of the rights of the parties is known as:
   a. repossession.
   b. perfection of a security interest.
   c. writ of execution.
   d. judgment.

 45. A claim on or right against personal property or an encumbrance on real property for the payment of a debt is known as a:
   a. lien.
   b. garnishment.
   c. consumer loan.
   d. demand note.

 46. A secured transaction creates or provides a security interest in:
   a. real property.
   b. personal property.
   c. luxury goods.
   d. farm land.

 47. A company that collects information concerning the credit and general reputation of others is known as a:
   a. court.
   b. debtor.
   c. creditor.
   d. credit bureau.

 48. When a demand is made to accept or pay a negotiable instrument, this is called:
   a. overdraft.
   b. presentment.
   c. cancellation.
   d. alteration.

_____ C **49.** Negotiable instruments, including checks, drafts, certificates of deposit, and promissory notes. are called:
  a. business paper.
  b. demand paper.
  c. commercial paper.
  d. working paper.

_____ C **50.** An order in writing by one person on another to pay a specified sum of money to a third person on demand or at a stated future time is called a(n):
  a. draft.
  b. presentment.
  c. certificate of deposit.
  d. indorsement.

True/False

Mark the following T or F.

_____ T **51.** An unsecured debt is a debt for which no security has been given.

_____ F **52.** A time draft is when a buyer has paid off a debt in full.

_____ T **53.** An interest in personal property or fixtures that secures the payment or performance of an obligation is known as a security interest.

_____ F **54.** A person who owes another person money is known as a secured creditor.

_____ F **55.** An agreement to do or refrain from doing a particular thing is known as perfection of a security interest.

_____ T **56.** An obligation for the payment of money is called debt.

_____ F **57.** A security agreement is filed with the court in foreclosure proceedings to give notice that the property listed in the notice is the subject of litigation.

_____ T **58.** An asset is anything of value owned by a person or organization.

_____ T **59.** A deficiency is the amount still due a debtor after foreclosure.

_____ F **60.** An installment payment is a lump sum payment.

_____ T **61.** Primary liability is the liability of a person who is absolutely required to make payment to satisfy an obligation.

_____ T **62.** A certified check is a check upon which the bank has stamped the words "certified" or "accepted," certifying that the check is drawn on sufficient funds and will be honored when presented for payment.

_____ T **63.** The writing of one's name on the back of a negotiable instrument is called an indorsement.

_____ F **64.** The payor is the person to whom a payment is made.

_____ T **65.** A mortgage is an example of a security interest.

_____ F **66.** A maker or principal has secondary liability.

_____ T **67.** The holder of a negotiable instrument not payable to a named person is the bearer.

Synonyms

Select the correct synonym in parentheses for each numbered item.

68. DRAWER
(buyer, maker, consumer)

69. DEBT
(obligation, perfection, possession)

70. HOLDER
(owner, possessor, seller)

71. INDORSE
(sign, attach, breach)

72. NEGOTIATE
(transfer, bargain, collect)

73. POSSESSION
(ownership, execution, judgment)

74. BEARER
(holder, payer, seller)

75. FORGE
(counterfeit, expose, default)

76. DRAFT
(check, note, certificate of deposit)

77. CONSUMER
(buyer, seller, creditor)

78. HONOR
(refuse, copy, pay)

79. NOTE
(order to pay, promise to pay, intention to pay)

80. MERCHANT
(purchaser, consumer, seller)

81. CHECK
(order to pay, promise to pay, intention to pay)

82. MAKER
(payer, possessor, drawer)

83. ALTERATION
(attachment, repossession, modification)

84. ASSIGNMENT
(to transfer, to perfect, to present)

85. EXECUTION
(termination, signing, filing)

86. LIQUIDATED
(paid, owed, refunded)

87. UTTER
(create, keep, circulate)

Self-Test

Place the number of the correct term in the appropriate space.

88. checks

89. installment payments

90. defaults

91. Uniform Commercial Code (UCC)

92. judgment

93. unsecured debt

94. negotiable instruments

95. creditor

96. secured debt

97. repossess

98. Commercial law

99. debt

100. drafts

101. certificates of deposit

_____ is the area of law that relates to concerns of merchants. A uniform law that has been adopted in much the

same form in most states and governs most aspects of commercial transactions is known as the _____. Generally,

some form of an agreement is reached. The purchaser might make payments over time called a(n) _____.

A debtor/_____ relationship may be established with one person owing a(n) _____ to another.

Depending on the particulars of the transaction, different legal documents will be needed to protect the interests of each

party. To protect the creditor, the debtor gives him a(n) _____. Should there be no security interest, the creditor

will find himself with _____, leaving the creditor little protection. Filing a security interest is just one of the

many ways a creditor might protect his interests. In the event a debtor _____ on a loan or other agreement,

a creditor needs to know the remedies available to him. A court action might be needed to foreclose on real estate, or

_____ personal property such as cars or boats. Eventually a(n) _____ may be entered against the

debtor after a court action. Even this does not ensure that a creditor will be paid, and further legal action might still be

required by the creditor to collect against a debtor. Commercial paper is a term used to refer to _____, which

are relied on in business to conduct commercial transactions. These are signed writings that order or promise payment of

money. Examples of commercial paper are _____, _____, promissory notes, and _____.

Word Scramble

Unscramble the following words and write the correct word(s) that match(es) the definition for each word or phrase.

102. bedt – an obligation for the payment of money ___

_____

103. editcr – trust placed in a person's willingness and

ability to pay _____

_____

104. trafd – an order in writing (commonly by a bank)

to pay a specified sum of money to a third person

on demand or at a stated future date _____

_____

105. hoonr – to pay or accept a negotiable instrument

when it is presented _____

_____

106. gorfe – commit a forgery _____

_____

107. warder – the maker of a draft _____

_____

108. ssessionpo – occupancy and dominion over property _____

109. tiatenego – to transfer a negotiable instrument to a third person _____

110. tionfecper – under the UCC, a method of protecting a security interest in goods against the claims of other creditors _____

111. kmaer – a person who obligates himself by executing a check, promissory note, draft, or other negotiable instrument _____

112. dohler in ued crusoe – a holder of a negotiable instrument who gave value for it, and took it in good faith and without notice of any claim or defense against it _____

113. kcech – a written order to pay money to a named person _____

114. sach – coin, money, money in hand, either in coin, currency, or other legal tender _____

115. omissprory noet – written promise to pay a specific sum of money by a specified date, or on demand _____

116. curedse sactrantion – a transaction that creates or provides for a security interest in personal property _____

The Last Word

The Credit Card Accountability and Disclosure Act of 2009 provides a "Bill of Rights" for credit cardholders, aiming to limit how credit card companies can charge consumers. While not addressing price controls, rate caps, or fee setting, the new law **banned**

1. Retroactive rate increases on existing balances in most cases
2. 15-day notice of rate increase (replaced by 45-day notice)
3. Bank over-limit transaction fees without the direct approval of a cardholder to honor such transactions
4. Fees to pay the credit card balance by phone or online
5. 14-day grace period (replaced with 21 days before the due date)
6. Charging interest on debt paid on time
7. Due date gimmicks (pay on same day each month, mail by a certain date, etc.)
8. Misleading terms such as "prime rate" and "fixed rate" deceptively used in advertising and contracts.

Do you think this type of protective law is necessary? Is the phrase "let the buyer beware" still relevant in commercial business transactions?

Access an interactive eBook, chapter-specific interactive learning tools, and more in your Paralegal CourseMate, accessed through www.CengageBrain.com

10

Bankruptcy Law, the Law of Corporations, Partnerships and Sole Proprietorships, and Labor and Employment Law

OBJECTIVES

- Learn about the laws of bankruptcy, corporations, partnerships, sole proprietorships, and labor and employment.

- Master the similarities and differences in definitions of key terms.

- Master the pronunciations and spellings of legal terms.

- Recognize the synonyms used for legal terminology.

- Practice usage of terms, definitions, and synonyms.

- Complete unit exercises in the forms of missing words, matching, multiple choice, true/false, synonyms, self-test, and word scramble.

- Work with a legal dictionary/thesaurus.

UNIT
17 Bankruptcy

INTRODUCTION

Article I, section 8, of the United States Constitution authorizes Congress to create uniform laws on the subject of bankruptcy. From time to time Congress has amended the Bankruptcy code, to help people who could no longer pay their creditors. Under the Bankruptcy Abuse Prevention and Consumer Protection Act, which went into effect in 2005, there has been a significant overhaul in the bankruptcy laws, making them less favorable toward debtors. Each state has one or more judicial districts, with a bankruptcy court for each district. The United States District Courts handle bankruptcy cases. Bankruptcy cases are handled solely in the federal courts to give uniform treatment to this problem. Up until 1833, debtors were sent to debtor's prison until they or their family could pay off their debts.

An individual who petitions for straight bankruptcy files under Chapter 7 of the Bankruptcy Code. Under Chapter 7, a trustee appointed by the court takes over the assets of the debtor, reduces them to cash, and pays off the creditors. Creditors must file a proof of claim to alert the court that they are seeking payment. Debtors have the right to keep certain basic exempt property so that they are not left penniless. Secured creditors have greater protection and are paid off before unsecured creditors. Generally there are few assets in Chapter 7 cases, and the majority of creditors are not paid off. When the bankruptcy case is completed, the debtor will receive a discharge in bankruptcy, exempting the debtor from any personal liability for dischargeable debts. This process generally takes just a few months. Some debtors are reluctant to file for bankruptcy because of the affect it might have on their future credit.

Chapter 11 (reorganization) allows a business to repay creditors and continue in business pursuant to a plan filed with the bankruptcy court. Interested creditors have input and can vote on the proposed plan. Some unprofitable or burdensome contracts and leases may be avoided or restructured. As with other forms of bankruptcy cases, an automatic stay is present during the case, requiring all creditors to cease all debt collection attempts. If the court does not approve of the reorganization plan, or the plan fails, the case may be converted to a Chapter 7 case, where the debtor will have to sell off assets to repay the debtors.

Under Chapter 13, also known as consumer debt adjustment, wage earners with a steady income may pay all or part of their debt to creditors under protection of the court. This must be completed over an approved period of time, usually three to five years. This plan allows a debtor to keep a valuable asset, such as a home, and avoid foreclosure. The debtor submits a repayment plan to the court that must be approved. The debtor might not receive a discharge in bankruptcy for several years until the payment plan is completed.

There is also a bankruptcy provision for family farmers, known as Chapter 12. From time to time, federal legislation updates the Bankruptcy Code to keep pace with inflation, current business conditions (the endangered American family farm), and standards of living.

Under the new law, the bankruptcy court can convert a Chapter 7 (straight bankruptcy) case to either a Chapter 11 or Chapter 13 case with a debtor's consent. Previously, a debtor needed to request such a conversion. Now, the court on its own motion, or that of any party in interest, can move for the dismissal of a case. Previously, this was not permitted. The standard of substantial abuse is no longer needed for dismissal or conversion of a case; only simple abuse need be shown. The previous presumption in favor of granting relief to a debtor has now been changed, with a new presumption that abuse exists if the debtor's monthly income exceeds a certain monthly figure. In order to file a bankruptcy petition, parties must now first receive a briefing from a budget and credit counseling service. All Chapter 7 and Chapter 13 discharges are conditioned upon the debtor's completion of an approved instructional course concerning personal finance management. Clearly it is the intent to prevent some of the abuse that has occurred under the prior laws, which were aimed at granting everyone a "fresh start." The following case is a Chapter 11 bankruptcy case, and shows how matters in bankruptcy court work.

CASE AND COMMENT

United States Court of Appeals for the Third Circuit
Jeld-Wen, Inc. (f/k/a Grossman's Inc.), Plaintiff/Appellant
v.
Van Brunt (In re Grossman's Inc.), Defendant/Appellee
Chapter 11 Case No. 09-1563 (3rd Cir. June 2, 2010)

Facts: Mrs. Van Brunt purchased certain asbestos-containing home improvement products from a Grossman's lumber retailer sometime in 1977, the date that Mrs. Van Brunt said she was exposed to asbestos from Grossman's products. In 2006, Mrs. Van Brunt developed mesothelioma, a disease caused by exposure to asbestos. Ten years before Mrs. Van Brunt discovered her mesothelioma, Grossman's filed bankruptcy, a plan of organization was filed and confirmed, and all the debtor's stock was sold to Jeld-Wen, Inc.

Procedural History: Mrs. Van Brunt commenced suit against Grossman's successor Jeld-Wen, Inc. Moving to re-open the bankruptcy case, Jeld-Wen, Inc. filed an adversary proceeding to determine that Mrs. Van Brunt's liability claim had been discharged in the Grossman's bankruptcy case, and that she was otherwise barred from bringing suit. The bankruptcy court rejected successor company Jeld-Wen's argument. The district court affirmed the substance of the lower court's decision. Jeld-Wen, Inc. appealed that decision.

Issue: Whether under the Bankruptcy Code a "claim" arises when an individual is exposed pre-petition (bankruptcy) to a product or other conduct giving rise to an injury which underlies a "right to payment."

Rationale: The time when a claim arises under the Bankruptcy Code is significant because only "claims" are administered by the bankruptcy court and only "claims" are discharged upon confirmation of a plan or reorganization. The Third Circuit finally joined other circuits by overturning its 1985 decision in *Aveillinot & Beines v. Frenville Co. (In re M. Frenville)*, which looked instead to the time when a payment accrues under state law to determine when a "claim" arose.

Ruling: The court, reversing itself, held that "a 'claim' under section 101(5) of the Bankruptcy Code arises when an individual is exposed pre-petition to a product or other conduct giving rise to an injury which underlies a 'right to payment' under the Bankruptcy Code. The case is remanded back to bankruptcy court for further hearing, to determine if due process would be violated in dismissing the claim.

Comment: Note that 25 years had passed since the Third Circuit's decision in *Frenville* before it realized "that something of a consensus across the country" showed it to be firmly in the minority.

DICTIONARY | THESAURUS

Term [phonetic pronunciation]	*Note: All dictionary/thesaurus terms appear on flashcards at the back of the book and on the student website.*
arrangement with creditors [a.*raynj*.ment with *kred*.i.terz]	1. A proceeding, also called a composition, by which a debtor who is not insolvent may have her failing finances rehabilitated by a bankruptcy court under an agreement with her creditors. *See also* composition with creditors. 2. The plan worked out by the bankruptcy court; also referred to as an arrangement for the benefit of creditors. *See also* bankruptcy.
assets [*ass*.ets]	Property of any value.
automatic stay [awto.*mat*.ik sta]	When a bankruptcy petition is filed with the court clerk, a hold arises that bars creditors from all debt collection efforts against debtors. *See* stay.
bankrupt [*bank*.rupt]	1. A person who is unable to pay her debts as they come due; an insolvent person. 2. A person who is entitled to the protection of the Bankruptcy Code. - *adj.* insolvent, indigent, wiped out, penniless, destitute, broke, out of business
bankruptcy [*bank*.rupt.see]	1. The circumstances of a person who is unable to pay his debts as they come due. 2. The system under which a debtor may come into court (voluntary bankruptcy) or be brought into court by his creditors (involuntary bankruptcy), either seeking to have his assets administered and sold for the benefit of his creditors and to be discharged from his debts (a straight bankruptcy), or to have his debts reorganized (a business reorganization or a wage earner's plan). - *n.* insolvency, failure, disaster, defaulting - *ant.* solvency

DICTIONARY | THESAURUS *continued...*

Bankruptcy Abuse Prevention and Consumer Protection Act
[*bank*.rupt.see a.*byooss* pre.*vent*.shen and kon.*soo*.mer *pro*.tek.shen act]

Enacted in 2005, it is a significant overhaul in bankruptcy that is less favorable than previous bankruptcy legislation for debtors.

Bankruptcy Code
[*bank*.rupt.see code]

Federal bankruptcy legislation. There have been six major statutes, enacted respectively in 1800, 1841, 1867, 1898, 1978, and 2005. The last of these is the Bankruptcy Abuse Prevention and Consumer Protection Act.

bankruptcy courts
[*bank*.rupt.see kortz]

Federal courts that hear and determine only bankruptcy cases.

bankruptcy estate
[*bank*.rupt.see es.*tate*]

All of the property of the debtor at the time the petition in bankruptcy is filed.

bankruptcy judge
[*bank*.rupt.see juj]

A judge of a bankruptcy court.

bankruptcy petition
[*bank*.rupt.see pe.*tish*.en]

See petition in bankruptcy.

bankruptcy proceedings
[*bank*.rupt.see pro.*see*.dings]

Any proceedings under the Bankruptcy Code; any proceedings relating to bankruptcy.

bankruptcy trustee
[*bank*.rupt.see trus.*tee*]

See trustee in bankruptcy.

bond
[bond]

The written instrument that evidences a debt. Trustees and receivers appointed by the court are required to file for a bond in order to take control of the property of the debtor, or to reorganize the debtor's business.

Chapter 11
[*chap*.ter ee.*lev*.en]

Under Chapter 11 of the Bankruptcy Code, the debtor is permitted to continue business operations until a reorganization plan is approved by his creditors. The debtor is not discharged from bankruptcy until the debts are paid off, which could take several years. *See* bankruptcy.

Chapter 7
[*chap*.ter *sev*.en]

A straight bankruptcy is called a Chapter 7 proceeding because it is conducted under Chapter 7 of the Bankruptcy Code. A debtor has his assets collected and sold for the benefit of his creditors, and then is discharged from his debts (a straight bankruptcy). *See* bankruptcy.

Chapter 13
[*chap*.ter ther.*teen*]

Under a Chapter 13 proceeding of the Bankruptcy Code, an individual debtor who is a wage earner and who files a repayment plan acceptable to his creditors will be given additional time in which to meet his obligations, generally three to five years.

Chapter 12
[*chap*.ter twelv]

Chapter 12 of the Bankruptcy Code addresses the debts of "family farmers" or "family fishermen," with regular annual income. Under this chapter, debtors propose a plan to repay all or part of their debts to creditors over a period of three to five years. Chapter 12 is more streamlined, less complicated, and less expensive than Chapter 11 (also a reorganization plan) and better meets the needs of the family farmer or fishermen. *See* bankruptcy.

composition with creditors
[kom.po.*zish*.en with *kred*.i.terz]

1. An agreement between a debtor and her creditors under which, in exchange for prompt payment, the creditors agree to accept amounts less than those actually owed in satisfaction of their claims. *See also* arrangement with creditors. 2. Proceedings under Chapter 13 of the Bankruptcy Code for debt readjustment.

creditor
[*kred*.it.er]

A person to whom a debt (secured by collateral or unsecured) is owed by a debtor. *See also* general creditor, secured creditor, and unsecured creditor.

- *n.* lender, assignee

creditor beneficiary
[*kred*.it.er ben.e.*fish*.ee.ar.ee]

A creditor who is the beneficiary of a contract made between the debtor and a third person.

creditors' meeting
[*kred*.it.erz *meet*.ing]

The first meeting of creditors of a debtor, required for the purpose of allowing the claims of creditors, questioning the debtor under oath, and electing a trustee in bankruptcy.

debtee
[*det*.ee]

A person who lends to a debtor.

- *n.* creditor, lender

debtor
[*det*.er]

1. A person who owes money to another person. 2. A person who owes anything to another person. *See also* debtee.

- *n.* borrower, buyer

debtor in possession
[*det*.er in po.*zesh*.en]

A debtor who continues to operate his business while undergoing a business reorganization under the jurisdiction of the bankruptcy court. *See also* bankruptcy.

discharge in bankruptcy
[dis.*charj* in *bank*.rupt.see]

The release of a debtor from an obligation to pay, pursuant to a bankruptcy proceeding.

- *v.* To perform an obligation or duty; to satisfy a debt. USAGE: "All his debts were discharged by bankruptcy."

dismissal
[dis.*miss*.el]

The release of the debtor's case in totality from protection and jurisdiction of the bankruptcy court.

exemptions
[eg.*zemp*.shenz]

Earnings and property allowed to be retained by a debtor free from claims of creditors in bankruptcy. EXAMPLES: a wedding band, a family bible.

forfeit
[*for*.fit]

To lose, particularly as result of default or neglect, or commission of a crime. One may forfeit money, property, or rights.

DICTIONARY | THESAURUS *continued...*

fraudulent conveyance
[*fraw*.je.lent ken.*vay*.ense]

1. The act of a debtor in making payment to one of her creditors by paying him with the intention of defrauding other creditors. 2. Under the Bankruptcy Code, a transfer of property to a creditor that gives him an advantage over other creditors. Although such a transfer may be disallowed by the trustee in bankruptcy, it is not necessarily a criminal act. *See also* preference.

garnishment
[*gar*.nish.ment]

Attachment of debtor's wages by a creditor.

general creditor
[*jen*.e.rel *kred*.it.er]

One who is not entitled to priority because the creditor's claim is not secured by a mortgage or other lien.

homestead exemption
[*home*.sted eg.*zemp*.shen]

Under homestead exemption statutes, the immunity of real property from execution for debt, provided the property is occupied by the debtor as the head of the family. This can vary by state law, with some states allowing for 100 percent immunity, even for mansions.

involuntary bankruptcy
[in.*vol*.en.te.ree *bank*.rupt.see]

A bankruptcy initiated by one's creditors. *See also* bankruptcy; bankruptcy proceedings. *Compare* voluntary bankruptcy.

judgment creditor
[*juj*.ment *kred*.i.ter]

A creditor who has secured a judgment against his debtor that has not been satisfied.

lien
[leen]

A claim on personal or real property for the payment of a debt or mortgage.

liquidation
[lik.wi.*day*.shen]

1. The extinguishment of a debt by payment or straight bankruptcy. 2. The ascertainment of the amount of a debt or demand by agreement or by legal proceedings. *See also* bankruptcy; receivership.

- *n.* elimination, abolition, rescission

moratorium
[more.e.*toh*.ree.um]

A period during which a person, usually a debtor, has a legal right to postpone meeting an obligation. An individual creditor may declare a moratorium with respect to her debtor, or a moratorium may be imposed by legislation and apply to debtors as a class.

- *n.* grace period

nondischargeable debt
[non.dis.*charj*.ebl det]

Any voidable or fraudulent preferences, taxes, child support, or other debts that cannot be legally discharged in bankruptcy. *See also* voidable preference.

petition in bankruptcy
[pe.*tish*.en in *bank*.rupt.see]

A document filed in a bankruptcy court initiating bankruptcy proceedings. *See also* bankruptcy, petitioning creditor, bankruptcy petition.

petitioner
[pe.*tish*.en.er]

A person seeking relief by a petition.

- *n.* pleader, litigant, applicant, asker, supplicant ("The petitioner asked for relief.")
- *ant.* respondent

petitioning creditor
[pe.*tish*.en.ing *kred*.it.er]

A creditor who initiates proceedings against his debtor in a bankruptcy court. *See also* bankruptcy proceedings; petition in bankruptcy.

preference
[*pref*.e.rense]

1. The act of a debtor in paying one or more of his creditors without paying the others. "Preference" is often confused with priority. However, a priority exists by operation of law; a preference is a transaction that, depending upon the circumstances, the law may consider voidable. *See also* priority. 2. Under the Bankruptcy Code, a transfer of property by an insolvent debtor to one or more creditors to the exclusion of others, enabling such creditors to obtain a greater percentage of their debt than other creditors of the same class. Such a transaction may constitute a voidable preference and be disallowed by the trustee in bankruptcy. *See also* fraudulent conveyance. 3. The right of one person over other persons. *See also* voidable preference.

- *n.* partiality, election, advantage; priority

preferential assignment
[pref.e.*ren*.shel a.*sine*.ment]

An assignment for the benefit of creditors by which the assignor gives a preference to certain of her creditors; any assignment that prefers one creditor over another.

preferential debts
[pref.e.*ren*.shel detz]

Debts that, under the Bankruptcy Code, are payable before all other debts. EXAMPLE: wages owed employees.

preferential transfer
[pref.e.*ren*.shel *tranz*.fer]

See preference and preferential assignment.

priority
[pry.*aw*.ri.tee]

1. In bankruptcy law, the right of a secured creditor to receive satisfaction before an unsecured creditor. 2. The status of that which is earlier or previous in point of time, degree, or rank; precedence. *See also* preference.

- *n.* lead, order, superiority, primacy, preference, precedence, right, seniority, rank

proof of claim
[proof ov klam]

In bankruptcy, a statement in writing, signed by a creditor, setting forth the amount owed and the basis of the claim.

receiver
[re.*seev*.er]

A person appointed by the court to take custody of property in a receivership. In the case of the assets or other property of an insolvent debtor, whether an individual or corporation, the duty of a receiver is to preserve the assets for sale and distribution to the creditors. In the case of assets or other property that is the subject of litigation, the duty of a receiver is to preserve the property or fund in litigation, receive its rent or profits, and apply or dispose of them as the court directs. Such a receiver is called a pendente lite receiver. If the property in dispute is a business, the receiver may have the additional responsibility of operating the business as a going concern. *See* bond.

- *n.* trustee, supervisor, administrator, depository, overseer, manager, collector

receivership
[re.*seev*.er.ship]

A proceeding by which the property of an insolvent debtor, or property that is the subject of litigation, may be preserved and appropriately disposed of by a person known as a receiver, who is appointed and supervised by the court. A corporation as well as an individual may be "in receivership." *See also* receiver.

DICTIONARY   THESAURUS *continued...*

reorganization [ree.or.ge.ni.*zay*.shun]	*See* Chapter 11.
schedule in bankruptcy [*sked*.jool in *bank*.rupt.see]	A schedule filed by a debtor listing, among other things, all of his property, its value, his creditors, and the nature of their claims.
secured creditor [se.*kyoord kred*.it.er]	One who has security for a debt owed in the form of an encumbrance on the property of the person in bankruptcy.

stay
[stay]
	The Bankruptcy Code provides for automatic stops to further proceedings, usually temporarily; to restrain; to hold back; to suspend foreclosures or executions on certain types of debts upon filing of bankruptcy petition. *See also* moratorium and automatic stay.
	
	  ▪ *v.* hinder, postpone, intermit, obstruct, suspend ("stay the creditor's foreclosure")
	  ▪ *n.* deferment, halt, remission, reprieve, standstill, suspension

straight bankruptcy [strait *bank*.rupt.see]	*See* Chapter 7.
trustee in bankruptcy [trust.*ee* in *bank*.rupt.see]	A person appointed by a bankruptcy court to collect any amounts owed the debtor, sell the debtor's property, and distribute the proceeds among the creditors.
unsecured creditor [un.se.*kyoord kred*.it.er]	One who has received no security for the debt owed by the person in bankruptcy.
voidable preference [*void*.ebl *pref*.rense]	Under the Bankruptcy Code, a preference is voidable if it takes place within a specified number of days before the filing of the petition in bankruptcy and if it allows the creditor to obtain more than she would have received from the bankruptcy court.
voluntary bankruptcy [*vol*.en.ter.ee *bank*.rupt.see]	A bankruptcy that the debtor himself initiates, as opposed to an involuntary bankruptcy initiated by a creditor.
wage earner's plan [wayj *ern*.erz plan]	Under Chapter 13 of the Bankruptcy Code, a debtor who is a wage earner and who files a repayment plan acceptable to his creditors and the court will be given additional time in which to meet his obligations.

Missing Words

Fill in the blanks.

1. A(n) _____ is the act of a debtor in making payment to one of her creditors by paying him with the intention of defrauding other creditors.

2. Under _____ statutes, real property is immune from execution for debt.

3. The _____ is federal bankruptcy legislation.

4. A(n) _____ is any voidable or fraudulent preference, taxes, child support, or other debts that cannot be legally discharged in bankruptcy.

5. A(n) _____ is a statement in writing signed by a creditor, setting forth the amount owed and the basis of the claim.

6. The right of a secured creditor to receive satisfaction before an unsecured creditor is _____.

7. The attachment of a debtor's wages by a creditor is _____.

8. A(n) _____ is the release of a debtor's case in totality from protection and jurisdiction of a bankruptcy court.

9. _____ of the Bankruptcy Code is also called the wage earner's plan.

10. A(n) _____ is a creditor who initiates proceedings against his debtor in a bankruptcy court.

11. A(n) _____ is a person who is unable to pay her debts as they come due.

12. A debt under the Bankruptcy Code that is payable before all other debts is called _____.

13. Any proceedings under the Bankruptcy Code are known as _____.

14. An assignment that gives advantage to one creditor over another is a(n) _____.

15. _____ is the extinguishment of a debt by payment or straight bankruptcy.

16. Property of any value is called a(n) _____.

17. One who is not entitled to priority because her claim is not secured by a lien is a(n) _____.

STUDY AID: Use flashcards for this unit before completing the exercises.

Matching

Match the letter of the definition to the term.

_A_ 18. composition with creditors

_F_ 19. preferences

_C_ 20. nondischargeable debt

_I_ 21. Chapter 7

_E_ 22. Chapter 11 reorganization plan

A. an agreement between a debtor and her creditors under which, in exchange for prompt payment, the creditors accept less than actually owed

B. they can file an involuntary petition in bankruptcy

C. child support is an example; a debt that must be paid and can't be discharged in a bankruptcy proceeding

D. when creditors are successful in attaching unpaid judgments by garnishing a debtor's wages prior to bankruptcy

E. when all the debtor's assets are not sold to pay off debts; debts are paid over time

_B_ 23. creditors

F. when payments are made by the debtor to particular creditors

_G_ 24. petition
in bankruptcy

G. when a bankruptcy proceeding is commenced with the filing of forms

_H_ 25. receiver

H. a person who might be appointed by the court to collect rents and profits and preserve the property involved, if a landlord of an apartment building filed for bankruptcy

_D_ 26. garnishment

I. straight bankruptcy

_L_ 27. stay

J. a person appointed by a bankruptcy court to sell the debtor's property

_K_ 28. lien

K. a claim on personal or real property for the payment of a debt

_G_ 29. trustee

L. an automatic stop to further proceedings

_M_ 30. 2005 law

M. Bankruptcy Abuse Prevention and Consumer Protection Act

_Q_ 31. fraudulent
conveyance

N. a creditor not entitled to priority in bankruptcy

_N_ 32. general creditor

O. a creditor who has security for a debt

_O_ 33. secured creditor

P. a creditor who has received no security for debt

_P_ 34. unsecured creditor

Q. a transfer of property to a creditor that gives her an advantage over other creditors

Multiple Choice

Select the best choice.

_C_ 35. A person seeking relief by a petition is a:
   a. bankruptcy trustee.
   b. trustee in bankruptcy.
   c. petitioner.
   d. bankruptcy judge.

_b_ 36. Under Chapter 13 of the Bankruptcy Code, a debtor who is a wage earner and who files a repayment plan acceptable to his creditors and the court will be given additional time to meet his obligations. This is called:
   a. friends and family plan.
   b. wage earner's plan.
   c. head of household plan.
   d. receivership.

_A_ 37. All of the property of the debtor at the time the petition in bankruptcy is filed is called the:
   a. bankruptcy estate.
   b. bankruptcy collection.
   c. bankruptcy holdings.
   d. homestead exemption.

_C_ 38. The release of a debtor from an obligation to pay pursuant to a bankruptcy proceeding is a:
   a. probation in bankruptcy.
   b. parole in bankruptcy.
   c. discharge in bankruptcy.
   d. merger in bankruptcy.

_D_ **39.** A person appointed by a bankruptcy court to collect any amounts owed the debtor, sell the debtor's property, and distribute the proceeds among the creditors is the:
a. adjuster.
b. insurer.
c. administrative law judge.
d. trustee in bankruptcy.

_C_ **40.** When a debtor comes into court seeking to have his assets administered and sold for the benefit of his creditors and to be discharged from his debts, this is called straight bankruptcy or:
a. Chapter 5.
b. Chapter 6.
c. Chapter 7.
d. Chapter 8.

_C_ **41.** A document filed in a bankruptcy court initiating bankruptcy proceedings is the:
a. summons.
b. subpoena.
c. petition in bankruptcy.
d. bankruptcy complaint.

_D_ **42.** A schedule filed by a bankrupt that lists all of his property, its value, his creditors, and the nature of their claims is a:
a. W-2 form.
b. proof of claim.
c. moratorium.
d. schedule in bankruptcy.

_B_ **43.** The business reorganization plan, where the debtor is permitted to continue business operations until a reorganization plan is approved by two-thirds of his creditors, is:
a. Chapter 10.
b. Chapter 11.
c. Chapter 12.
d. Chapter 13.

_B_ **44.** Under the Bankruptcy Code, a preference that takes place within a specified number of days before the filing of the petition in bankruptcy that allows a creditor to receive more than she would have received from the bankruptcy court is a(n):
a. voluntary bankruptcy.
b. voidable preference
c. priority.
d. arrangement with creditors.

_D_ **45.** A written statement by the creditor that includes the amount owed by the debtor is called a:
a. preference.
b. priority.
c. wage earner's plan.
d. proof of claim.

_C_ **46.** The preferred term for a person unable to pay his debts is:
a. broke.
b. penniless.
c. debtor.
d. wiped out.

True/False

Mark the following T or F.

_F_ **47.** Chapter 7 is frequently referred to as the Business Reorganization Plan.

_F_ **48.** Chapter 13 is also called a Liquidation Plan.

_T_ **49.** The automatic stay prevents creditors from contacting the debtor after commencing a bankruptcy proceeding.

_F_ **50.** Exemptions are portions of the debtor's property that are included in the debtor's estate when calculating those assets available to pay the creditor's claims.

_____ **51.** When a debtor receives a discharge in bankruptcy he is relieved from the obligation of paying certain debts.

_____ **52.** The purpose of the Bankruptcy Code is to give individuals and businesses a fresh start after becoming deeply indebted.

_____ **53.** A creditor is a person who owes money to another person.

_____ **54.** Under the homestead exemption statutes, real property is immune from execution for debt.

_____ **55.** A debtor may file a repayment plan under Chapter 13 of the Bankruptcy Code.

_____ **56.** A stay is used to continue with further proceedings in a bankruptcy case.

_____ **57.** A bankruptcy proceeding that a debtor initiates himself is called a voluntary bankruptcy.

_____ **58.** Taxes and child support are considered nondischargeable debts in bankruptcy.

_____ **59.** The bankruptcy petition is the document that ends a bankruptcy case.

Synonyms

Select the correct synonym in parentheses for each numbered item.

60. CHAPTER 7
(straight bankruptcy, reorganization, receivership)

61. PREFERENCE
(priority, garnish, dismissal)

62. DISCHARGE
(foreclosure, lien, release)

63. MORATORIUM
(luxury, security, grace period)

64. LIEN
(claim, retain, surrender)

65. DEBT
(prize, obligation, homestead)

66. CREDITOR
(lender, buyer, borrower)

67. ARRANGEMENT WITH CREDITORS
(maintain, increase, composition)

68. GARNISHMENT
(interest, allowance, attachment)

69. PRIORITY
(strategic, proportional, precedence)

70. BANKRUPT
(frugal, insolvent, conversion)

71. DEBTEE
(lendor, lendee, trustee)

72. PETITIONER
(litigant, respondent, defendant)

73. RECEIVER
(debtor, bankruptcy judge, trustee)

74. CHAPTER 13
(reorganization, straight bankruptcy, wage earner's plan)

75. BANKRUPTCY COURTS
(state courts, small claims, federal courts)

Self-Test

Place the number of the correct term in the appropriate space.

76. creditors

77. assets

78. bankruptcy

79. debt

80. Bankruptcy Code

81. debtors

82. wage earner's plan

83. liquidation

84. reorganization

85. trustee

86. discharge in bankruptcy

87. voluntary bankruptcies

88. involuntary bankruptcies

89. Bankruptcy Abuse Prevention and Consumer Protection Act

All day long, people hear on the radio and the television, *buy now, pay later.* Credit card companies call and write to people telling them they can make the purchases they have been dreaming about if they apply for a certain credit card. Stores invite people to make major appliance purchases with no payments for the first six months after the purchase. The end result is that there are lots of people who are heavily in _____. Since the writing of the U.S. Constitution, Congress has realized that there comes a time when _____ need a fresh start, erasing payments so they may go on with their lives. A common sign that a person has economic problems is when stores and other _____ report to credit bureaus about a person's delinquent payments. A creditor might threaten to repossess a car that is the subject of a loan, or even foreclose on a home. At this point, a debtor will most likely consult an attorney. The attorney will look at the client's complete financial picture, adding up all _____ , deducting all liabilities, distinguishing between luxuries and necessities, such as tools of the trade needed by the debtor to continue to earn a living. The attorney will counsel the client about the different options available from Chapter 7, known as _____ or straight bankruptcy, to Chapter 11, a business _____ plan, or Chapter 13, a _____ . Whatever is decided, the matter will be handled by a(n) _____ court. A(n) _____ will be appointed to monitor the case and the bankruptcy proceeding will be handled under the Federal _____ until a(n) _____ is granted. Most bankruptcy filings are _____. However, under the new _____ of 2005 and prior acts, bankruptcies initiated by creditors are called _____.

Word Scramble

Unscramble the following words and write the correct word(s) that match(es) the definition for each word or phrase.

90. bteede – lendor or creditor _____

_____

91. reditorc – person to who a debt is owed _____

_____

92. tordeb –person who owes money to another person

_____

_____

93. krupbantcy crout – federal court that hears

bankruptcy cases _____

_____

94. ptcybankru – the circumstances of a person who is

unable to pay his debts when they become due ____

_____

95. cybankrupt odec – federal bankruptcy legislation

_____

_____

96. ptcybankru ceedingpro – any proceeding under the

Bankruptcy Code _____

_____

97. ischarged – the release of a debtor of the obligation

to pay _____

_____

98. meptionex – earnings and property allowed to be

kept by the debtor free from claims of creditors

_____

_____

99. reencperfe – when a debtor pays one or more

creditors without paying the others _____

_____

100. dischargenonable ebdt – any voidable or fraudulent

preferences, taxes, child support, or other debts

that cannot be legally discharged in bankruptcy

_____

_____

101. ferpretialen ebtsd – debts that under the

Bankruptcy Code are payable before all other debts

_____

_____

102. positiocomn htiw editcrors – an agreement

between a debtor and her creditors under which, in

exchange for prompt payment, the creditors agreed

to accept a lesser amount than is due in satisfaction

of their claims _____

_____

103. duelsche in ruptcybank – a schedule filed by

a debtor listing, among other things, all of his

property, its value, his creditors, and the nature of

their claims _____

_____

104. lentufraud veyconance – the act of a debtor

in making payment to one of her creditors by

paying him with the intention of defrauding other

creditors _____

_____

105. ergenal itorcred – one who is not entitled to

priority because the creditor's claim is not secured

by a mortgage or other lien _____

_____

The Last Word

The bankruptcy of Bernard L. Madoff Investment Securities LLC is, by far, the most notorious of the twenty-first century and centers around the term "clawback." Bernie Madoff, former NASDAQ chairman, ran his investment firm like a massive scheme, where half of his 2,000 investors lost amounts totaling $65 billion. The "net winners" half are being sued by bankruptcy trustee Irving Picard in "clawback" lawsuits aimed at wresting funds away from investors who were also hoodwinked by Madoff's "Ponzi scheme." (Charles Ponzi was a swindler whose name is synonymous with schemes where early investors are repaid by money from later investors.)

"The people who made money, who got more, have made money at the expense of people who didn't," said Picard, or the ones who withdrew money before the collapse in 2008, are the targets. The bankruptcy trustee has the power under federal bankruptcy law to pursue money withdrawn from Madoff's firm and Picard is pursuing that money with his so-called clawback suits. Some of the targeted investors have appealed a federal bankruptcy judge's decision upholding Picard's efforts against them. If they win, Picard cannot obtain clawbacks and the "net winner" investors could seek more money from the trustee. Is there any merit to their appeal or should clawbacks prevail?

Access an interactive eBook, chapter-specific interactive learning tools, and more in your Paralegal CourseMate, accessed through www.CengageBrain.com

UNIT
18 Corporations, Partnerships, and Sole Proprietorships

INTRODUCTION

Many different forms of organizations conduct business in the United States. Sometimes a person starts his own business and operates as a sole proprietorship. The owner's name doesn't necessarily have to be the name of the business. A business can operate under an assumed trade name. For example, rather than using her own name, an owner might open a financial advice office and do business as (DBA) "Speedy Financial Assistance Services," using a name that explains the type of service she offers to the public. Oftentimes people want to enter a business venture with others.

When two or more individuals carry on a business as co-owners for a profit, this is known as a partnership. The partners must share in the profits as well as losses of the business. Each partner serves as an agent for the partnership, and can perform acts that are binding on the other partners. Any contracts made by one partner become the responsibility of the partnership even though the other partners were not involved in making the agreement. Sometimes a partner might contribute financially to a business, but wish to remain anonymous as a silent or secret partner. If the membership in a partnership changes, this brings about the dissolution of the partnership and the possible formation of a new partnership with another person.

A corporation is a fictitious legal entity created to carry on a business. A corporation is formed pursuant to the particular laws of the state of incorporation. Shareholders invest their money and become owners of the corporation. A shareholder has the opportunity to earn a profit without incurring personal liability for debts of the corporation. Corporations are taxed differently than individuals and can have perpetual existence. These are the primary reasons corporations are formed. A person does not have to risk the loss of a family home and assets if his business is not successful. Corporations can also be formed for charitable reasons and are called charitable corporations, which exist as not-for-profit corporations. Professionals might wish to incorporate and form a professional corporation to practice, for example, law or medicine, and to secure certain tax advantages. Limited liability corporations or limited liability companies are a hybrid, in which a business has the tax advantages of a partnership but the liability protection of a corporation. When a small group of people or family members own all the stock in a corporation, this is known as a close corporation, or a closely held corporation.

Each corporation is bound by strict rules and must elect a board of directors to operate the business, and draft articles of incorporation stating the purpose of the corporation and the rules by which the corporation will conduct itself. It must also conduct an annual meeting of stockholders and issue an annual report detailing the fiscal operations of the business. A corporation must register with the secretary of state in the state where it is formed. Such a corporation is called a domestic corporation. These regulations enable the public to have a means of checking whether a corporation actually exists and whether it has filed all necessary papers with the government. When a corporation is incorporated or formed under the laws of one state, but does business in another state, it is called a foreign corporation.

Corporations issue stock, bonds, notes, and other documentation of indebtedness in order for the corporation to obtain funds. Stock certificates are issued by a corporation to evidence the amount of shares a stockholder owns. The Securities and Exchange Commission (SEC) is the agency that administers and enforces federal statutes relating to corporate securities to protect the public from harm.

Corporations are not required to operate as a single entity. When a company expands, one corporation (called a "parent company") can control another corporation (known as the "subsidiary corporation"). Eventually, a corporation might wish to terminate its existence and liquidate the business, leading to the winding up of the corporation.

CASE AND COMMENT

United States Court of Appeals for the Second Circuit
Esther Kiobel, Plaintiff, et al.

v.

Royal Dutch Petroleum Co., Shell Transport and Trading Company PLC, Defendants
Docket Nos. 06-4800-cv, 06-4876-cv. (2010)

Facts: Plaintiffs were residents of Nigeria who claimed corporations (Dutch, British, and Nigerian) that engaged in oil exploration and production also aided and abetted the Nigerian government in committing human-rights abuses. They sought damages under Alien Torts Statute (ATS), and their suit sought jurisdiction pursuant to tort liability under ATS.

Procedural History: Since 1789, when Congress passed the Alien Tort Statute (ATS), the statute lay dormant until 1980 when the U.S. Court of Appeals recognized that ATS provided jurisdiction over "tort actions brought by aliens for violations of customary international law, including war crimes and crimes against humanity." In the instant case, plaintiffs Kiobel et al. allege that defendant corporations aided the Nigerian government in torturing and murdering Nigerian dissidents in the 1990s.

Issue: Does the jurisdiction granted by ATS extend to civil actions brought against corporations under the law of nations?

Rationale: "The principle of individual liability for violations of international law has been limited to natural persons . . . not corporations—because the moral responsibility for a crime so heinous and unbounded as to rise to the level of an 'international crime' has rested solely with the individual men and women who have perpetrated it," the court said. The U.S. courts have jurisdiction only over alien tort suits against individuals, not companies "because customary international law consists of only those norms that are specific, universal, and obligatory . . ., and because no corporation has ever been subject to *any* form of liability (whether civil or criminal) under the customary international law of human rights . . ." the court said.

Ruling: Plaintiffs' ATS claims must be dismissed for lack of subject matter jurisdiction. The order of the United States District Court for the Southern District of New York is affirmed insofar as it dismissed plaintiffs' claims against the corporate defendants.

Comment: United States law favors corporations with widespread protections and this case is illustrative of it.

DICTIONARY THESAURUS

Note: All dictionary/thesaurus terms appear on flashcards at the back of the book and on the CD-ROM.

Term [phonetic pronunciation]	
accounting [a.*kount*.ing]	An equitable action brought to obtain an adjudication (decision) of the respective rights and obligations of the members of a partnership. *See* partnership.
agency [*ay*.jen.see]	A relationship in which one person acts for or on behalf of another person at the other person's request.
annual meeting [*an*.yoo.el *meet*.ing]	A regular meeting of the stockholders of a corporation, held once a year.
annual report [*an*.yoo.el re.*port*]	A report issued yearly by a corporation, informing its stockholders, the government, and the public, in some detail, of its operations, particularly its fiscal operations, during the year. The contents of an annual report (also called an annual statement), as well as the report itself, are required by law.
articles of incorporation [*ar*.tiklz ov in.kore.per.*ay*.shen]	The charter or basic rules that create a corporation and by which it functions. Among other things, it states the purposes for which the corporation is being organized, the amount of authorized capital stock, and the names and addresses of the directors and incorporators. *See also* certificate of incorporation; incorporation.
articles of partnership [*ar*.tiklz ov *part*.ner.ship]	The same as a partnership agreement. *See* partnership agreement.
association [a.so.see.*ay*.shen]	Also called an unincorporated association, a collection of persons who have joined together for the pursuit of a common purpose or design. Unlike a corporation, an association has no legal existence independent of its members. On the other hand, an association that sometimes functions like a corporation may be treated as a corporation for some purposes by the law. An association may be organized for profit or as a nonprofit.
board of directors [bord ov di.*rek*.terz]	The directors of a corporation or association who act as a group in representing the organization and conducting its business, and may be liable for their actions as such.
bond [bond]	1. A debt owed by a corporation or by the government to an investor. 2. The written instrument that evidences a debt. 3. An obligation to pay a sum of money upon the happening of a stated event. Bonds that represent debt and pay interest are called investment bonds. EXAMPLES of investment bonds issued by corporations include convertible bonds, coupon bonds, guaranteed bonds, registered bonds, serial bonds, and term bonds. Unsecured, long-term corporate bonds are called debentures.

DICTIONARY   THESAURUS *continued...*

business
[*biz*.ness]

The work in which a person is regularly or usually engaged and from which she makes a living.

- *n.* trade, occupation, calling, activity, profession, field ("the cosmetology business"); commerce, manufacture, industry, intercourse, dealings ("doing business")

business corporation
[*biz*.ness kore.per.*ay*.shen]

An ordinary corporation; a commercial corporation; a for-profit corporation. *Compare* nonprofit corporation. *See also* corporation.

business judgment rule
[*biz*.ness *juj*.ment rule]

The principle that courts should be reluctant to second-guess the decisions of corporate directors, even if those decisions are not in the best interests of the stockholders, as long as the decisions are within the power of the directors to make.

business name
[*biz*.ness name]

The name under which a business is operated. In the case of an individual, it may be his real name or a fictitious name. *See also* DBA.

business records
[*biz*.ness *rek*.erdz]

A book of original entry; a book of account; all records kept in the ordinary course of business.

by-laws
[*by*-lawz]

Rules and regulations created by corporations, associations, clubs, and societies for their governance.

C corporation
[see kore.per.*ay*.shen]

Under the Internal Revenue Code, a corporation that has not elected S corporation status. Its income is taxed at the corporate level, its dividends at the shareholder level. *Compare* S corporation.

CEO
[CEO]

Abbreviation of chief executive officer. *See* chief executive officer.

certificate of incorporation
[ser.*tif*.i.ket ov in.kore.per.*ay*.shen]

1. In some states, the same as articles of incorporation. 2. In some states, a certificate issued by the secretary of state attesting that articles of incorporation have been filed and that the filing corporation is therefore a legal entity and capable of being sued. *See also* incorporation.

charitable corporation
[*char*.i.tebl kore.per.*ay*.shen]

A corporation organized and existing solely to engage in charitable activities. It issues no stock and earns no profit. *See also* nonprofit corporation.

chief executive officer (CEO)
[cheef *eg*.sek.yoo.tiv *off*.i.ser]

The officer of a corporation or other organization who has the most responsibility for managing its affairs; commonly referred to as the CEO.

close corporation
[kloz kore.per.*ay*.shen]

1. A corporation in which all the stock is owned by a few persons or by another corporation; sometimes also referred to as a closely held corporation. 2. Another term for a family corporation.

common stock
[*kom*.en stok]

Ordinary capital stock in a corporation, the market value of which is based upon the worth of the corporation. Owners of common stock vote in proportion to their holdings, as opposed to owners of other classes of stock that are without voting rights. By contrast, however, common stock earns dividends only after other preferred classes of stock. *Compare* preferred stock. *See also* stock.

corporate agents
[*kore*.per.et *ay*.jents]

The officers and employees of a corporation who have the authority to act for the corporation.

corporate directors
[*kore*.per.et de.*rek*.terz]

Directors of a corporation; members of the board of directors of a corporation who conduct the company's business.

corporate domicile
[*kore*.per.et *dom*.i.sile]

A corporation is domiciled (legally has its main place of residence) in the state of its incorporation.

corporate officers
[*kore*.per.et *off*.i.serz]

The officers of a corporation. EXAMPLES: the president, the treasurer, the comptroller.

corporate records
[*kore*.per.et *rek*.erdz]

The charter and by-laws of a corporation, the minutes of the meetings of its board of directors and of stockholders' meetings, and the written evidence of its contracts and business transactions.

corporate securities
[*kore*.per.et se.*kyoor*.it.eez]

Stock, bonds, notes, and other documentation of indebtedness issued by a corporation to obtain funds to use in the corporation's business. *See also* securities.

corporation
[kore.per.*ay*.shen]

An artificial person, existing only in the eyes of the law, to whom a state or the federal government has granted a charter to become a legal entity, separate from its shareholders, with a name of its own, under which its shareholders can act and contract and sue and be sued. A corporation's shareholders, officers, and directors are not normally liable for the acts of the corporation. *See also* charitable corporation; close corporation; de facto corporation; de jure corporation; domestic corporation; foreign corporation; nonprofit corporation.

- *n.* business, company, enterprise, organization, association, establishment, firm

DBA
[DBA]

An abbreviation of, and commonly a short way of saying, "doing business as." A person's DBA is his or her trade name. EXAMPLES: a lawsuit involving a business owned by an individual named Gerri Jones, who does business under the trade name Gerri's Jams, might be captioned *Sam Smith v. Gerri Jones DBA Gerri's Jams*; a lawsuit involving a business owned by the ABC Corporation, which does business under the trade name Merry Motels, might be captioned *ABC Corporation DBA Merry Motels v. Sam Smith*.

de facto corporation
[dee *fak*.toh kore.per.*ay*.shen]

A corporation in fact, but one that has failed to comply with the formal requirements for incorporation; an apparent corporation, asserted to be a corporation by its members and acting as a corporation under color of law. Such an organization is deemed a corporation with respect to everyone except the state. *Compare* de jure corporation.

DICTIONARY   THESAURUS *continued...*

de jure corporation
[dee *zhoo*.reh kore.per.*ay*.shen]

A corporation created in compliance with all legal requirements, so that its right to exist and to exercise the powers described in its charter are protected against challenge by the state. *Compare* de facto corporation.

derivative action
[de.*riv*.e.tiv *ak*.shen]

An action brought by one or more stockholders of a corporation to enforce a corporate right or to remedy a wrong to the corporation, when the corporation itself fails to take action.

directors
[di.*rek*.terz]

See corporate directors.

dissolution of corporation
[dis.e.*loo*.shen ov kore.per.*ay*.shen]

The termination of a corporation's existence and its abolishment as an entity. See also liquidate.

dissolution of partnership
[dis.e.*loo*.shen ov *part*.ner.ship]

The change in the relation of partners caused by any partner's ceasing to be associated in the carrying on of the business. Any such change brings about the dissolution of the partnership. *See also* partnership; liquidate.

dividend
[*div*.e.dend]

A payment made by a corporation to its stockholders, either in cash (a cash dividend), in stock (a stock dividend), or out of surplus earnings.

- *n.* profit, benefit, reward, share, allowance, bonus

domestic corporation
[de.*mes*.tick kore.per.*ay*.shen]

A corporation organized under the laws of the state. *Compare* foreign corporation.

dormant partner
[door.*ment part*.ner]

See silent partner.

eleemosynary corporation
[eel.ee.e.*moss*.en.er.ee kore.per.*ay*.shen]

See charitable corporation.

fiduciary duty
[fi.*doo*.she.air.ee *dew*.tee]

The duty to act loyally and honestly with respect to the interests of another.

foreign corporation
[*forr*.en kore.per.*ay*.shen]

A corporation incorporated under the laws of one state and doing business in another. *Compare* domestic corporation.

franchise
[*fran*.chize]

A license granted by the owner of a trademark or tradename to sell the licensor's products or services and retain the profits. Most "chain" fast-food restaurants, for EXAMPLE, are franchises. The franchisor is the person or company that owns and grants a franchise. The franchisee is the person or company that is granted the right to operate a franchise.

general partner
[*jen*.e.rel *part*.ner]

A partner in an ordinary partnership, as distinguished from a limited partnership. "General partner" is synonymous with "partner."

general partnership
[*jen*.e.rel *part*.ner.ship]

An ordinary partnership, as distinguished from a limited partnership. "General partnership" is synonymous with "partnership."

incorporation
[in.*kore*.per.ay.shen]

The act of forming a corporation.

incorporator
[in.*kore*.per.ay.ter]

A person who, alone or with others, forms a corporation.

insider
[in.*sy*.der]

An officer or director of a corporation or any other person who is in a position to acquire knowledge of the business and condition of the corporation through his official position.

- *n.* officer, director, member, intimate, associate
- *adj.* private, protected, nonpublic, undisclosed ("insider information")

issue
[*ish*.oo]

Securities offered for sale at a particular time, either for the public or privately, by a corporation or by government; an offering. EXAMPLES: corporate stock (a stock issue); municipal bonds (a bond issue).

limited
[*lim*.i.ted]

1. A word that follows a company's name and indicates that the business is a corporation, especially in England and Canada, although some American corporations also use the term (or its abbreviation, Ltd.) in place of "Inc." EXAMPLE: "Jack and Jill Limited." 2. A word used to signify a partnership other than a general partnership.

limited liability corporation (LLC)
[*lim*.i.ted ly.e.*bil*.i.tee kore.per.*ay*.shen]

The preferred terminology is "limited liability company." A business form that has both partnership and corporate qualities. A limited liability corporation offers the tax advantages of a partnership while providing liability protection of a corporation.

limited liability partnership
[*lim*.i.ted ly.e.*bilt*.i.tee *part*.ner.ship]

A partnership in which the liability of one or more of the partners is limited to the amount each partner has invested in the partnership. Where the partner takes no part in running the business, the partner incurs no liability beyond that contribution or investment with regard to partnership obligations.

limited partner
[*lim*.i.ted *part*.ner]

A partner in a limited liability partnership whose liability is limited to the sum she contributed to the partnership as capital. A limited partner is not involved in managing the business of the partnership. *Compare* general partner.

liquidate
[*lik*.wi.date]

To break up, do away with, wind up, or dissolve. USAGE: "After Jim died, his partner liquidated the business." *See also* dissolution of corporation and dissolution of partnership; winding up.

- *v.* discharge, clear, cancel, honor, pay off, quit ("liquidate my debts"); cash, convert, exchange, realize ("liquidate the bonds"); remove, wipe out ("liquidate the company")
- *ant.* incur; create

DICTIONARY | THESAURUS *continued...*

merger of corporations
[*mer*.jer ov kore.per.*ay*.shenz]

A joining of two (or more) corporations in which one goes out of existence, leaving a single survivor that possesses the powers and owns the stock and other property of both (or all). Although the terms "merger" and "consolidation" are often used interchangeably, they are actually quite different. In a merger, one of the combining corporations continues in existence and absorbs the others; in a consolidation, the combining corporations are dissolved and lose their identity in a new corporate entity that takes over the property and powers, as well as the rights and liabilities, of the constituent corporations.

nonprofit corporation
[non.prof.it kore.per.*ay*.shen]

A nonstock corporation organized for purposes other than making a profit, generally for charitable or educational purposes. EXAMPLE: a private college or a private university. *Compare* profit corporation. *See* also charitable corporation.

operating agreement
[*op*.e.rate.ing a.*gree*.ment]

An agreement between limited liability company (LLC) members, stating the business, and members' financial and managerial rights and duties.

outstanding stock
[out.*stan*.ding stok]

Shares of stock issued by a corporation. Outstanding stock is an obligation of the corporation.

over-the-counter market
[*oh*.ver-the-*count*.er *mar*.ket]

A market in securities other than the stock exchange; securities transactions directly between brokers. The over-the-counter securities market (the OTC) trades through the NASDAQ system.

par value
[par *val*.yu]

The value of a share of stock or of a bond, according to its face; the named or nominal value of an instrument. The par value and the market value of a stock are not synonymous; there is often a wide difference between them. The issuer of a bond is obligated to redeem it at par value upon maturity.

parent company
[*pair*.ent *kum*.pe.nee]

A corporation that owns all or the majority of the stock of another corporation. The corporation owned by the parent company is called a subsidiary or a wholly owned subsidiary.

partner
[*part*.ner]

A member of a partnership. *See also* general partnership.

- *n.* participant, associate, collaborator, member, teammate

partnership
[*part*.ner.ship]

An undertaking of two or more persons to carry on, as co-owners, a business or other enterprise for profit; an agreement between or among two or more persons to put their money, labor, and skill into commerce or business, and to divide the profit in agreed-upon proportions. Partnerships may be formed by entities as well as individuals; a corporation, for EXAMPLE, may be a partner. For federal income tax purposes, a partnership is a for-profit enterprise that is not a corporation. *See also* articles of partnership; dissolution of partnership; general partnership.

- *n.* federation, alliance, league, association, collaboration, business, enterprise, undertaking

partnership agreement
[*part*.ner.ship a.*gree*.ment]

The agreement signed by the members of a partnership that governs their relationship as partners. It is sometimes referred to as articles of partnership.

partnership assets
[*part*.ner.ship *ass*.ets]

All assets belonging to the partnership, as opposed to the personal assets of the partners.

partnership debts
[*part*.ner.ship detz]

Debts owed by the partnership, as opposed to the personal debts of the partners.

piercing the corporate veil
[*peer*.sing the *kore*.pe.ret vale]

Ignoring the corporate entity to reach or to proceed legally against the corporation's directors, officers, or managers directly and personally. Although a corporation's officers and directors are not normally liable for the acts of the corporation, the courts will hold them responsible for corporate acts if the purpose of organizing the corporation was to perpetrate fraud or if the corporation was a mere shell without substantial assets or capital.

preferred stock
[pre.*ferd* stok]

Corporate stock that is entitled to a priority over other classes of stock, usually common stock, in distribution of the profits of the corporation (i.e., dividends) and in distribution of the assets of the corporation in the event of dissolution or liquidation.

professional corporation
[pro.*fesh*.en.el kore.per.*ay*.shen]

A corporation formed for the purpose of practicing a profession (EXAMPLES: law; medicine; psychotherapy; dentistry) and to secure certain tax advantages. The members of a professional corporation remain personally liable for professional misconduct. Professional corporations often identify themselves by the abbreviation PC. Thus, for EXAMPLE, a professional corporation composed of attorneys Jessica Smith and Sam Smith might be named, "Smith & Smith, Esqs., PC." *See also* corporation.

profit
[*prof*.it]

n. 1. The excess of gross receipts or gross proceeds over the cost or expenses of a transaction; the excess of receipts over expenditures. 2. Gain realized from the investment of capital. 3. For some purposes, the equivalent of income. 4. Gain; benefit. *v.* To gain or benefit; to realize an advantage.

profit corporation
[*prof*.it kore.per.*ay*.shen]

A corporation organized for the purpose of realizing gain (i.e., earning profit) to be distributed among its shareholders; a business corporation. A corporation organized for profit-making purposes is often referred to as a for-profit corporation, as opposed to a nonprofit corporation.

promoter
[pro.*mote*.er]

A person who organizes a business venture or is a major participant in organizing the venture.

- *n.* organizer, incorporator, planner, backer, patron, sponsor

prospectus
[pro.*spek*.tus]

A statement published by a corporation that provides information concerning stock or other securities it is offering for sale to the public. The contents of a prospectus are regulated by the Securities and Exchange Commission.

- *n.* details, list, program, synopsis, statement ("CSX's prospectus is impressive.")

DICTIONARY   THESAURUS *continued...*

proxy
[*prox*.ee]

Authority given in writing by one shareholder in a corporation to another shareholder to exercise her voting rights for her.

- *n.* authorization, power ("I gave her my proxy.")

quorum
[*kwohr*.em]

The number of members of a body (EXAMPLE: a board of directors) who must be present for the body to be able to conduct business.

S corporation
[ess kore.per.*ay*.shen]

A corporation electing to be taxed under Subchapter S of the Internal Revenue Code. Its income is taxed to the shareholders rather than at the corporate level. *Compare* C corporation. *See also* corporation.

secret partner
[*see*.kret *part*.ner]

A partner whose membership in the partnership is not disclosed to the public.

securities
[se.*kyoor*.i.teez]

Certificates that represent a right to share in the profits of a company or in the distribution of its assets, or in a debt owned by a company or by the government. EXAMPLES: stocks; bonds; notes with interest coupons; any registered security.

- *n.* stocks, convertible debentures, negotiables, coupons, bills, warranties

Securities and Exchange Commission (SEC)
[se.*kyoor*.i.teez and eks.*chaynj* kum.*ish*.en]

The agency that administers and enforces federal statutes relating to securities, including the Securities Act of 1933 and the Securities Exchange Act.

shareholder
[*share*.hole.der]

See stockholder.

- *n.* stockholder, owner, investor

silent partner
[*sy*.lent *part*.ner]

A partner whose connection with the partnership is unknown to the public and who takes no part in the conduct of the partnership business. A silent partner who invests in the partnership and shares in the profits is, by definition, a limited partner as well. *See* dormant partner.

sole proprietorship
[sole pro.*pry*.e.ter.ship]

Ownership by one person, as opposed to ownership by more than one person; ownership by a corporation, ownership by a partnership, etc.

stock
[stok]

1. The shares of stock or stock certificates issued by a corporation or a joint-stock company. 2. Shares in a corporation or a joint-stock company owned by shareholders; put another way, the sum of all the rights and duties of the shareholders. 3. The capital of a corporation. *See also* common stock; preferred stock.

- *n.* assets, blue chips, bonds, capital, convertible paper, share ("stock in the company")

stock certificate
[stok ser.*tif*.i.ket]

An instrument issued by a corporation stating that the person named is the owner of a designated number of shares of its stock.

stock market [stok *mar*.ket]	A market where securities are bought and sold. EXAMPLES: a stock exchange; the over-the-counter market.
stockbroker [*stok*.broh.ker]	A person employed in buying and selling stock for others. • *n.* broker, securities broker, agent
stockholder [*stok*.hole.der]	The owner of one or more shares of stock in a corporation or a joint-stock company; a person who appears on the books of a corporation as the owner of one or more shares of its stock. The terms "stockholder" and "shareholder" are used interchangeably.
stockholders' meeting [*stok*.hole.derz *meet*.ing]	A meeting of the stockholders of a corporation called for the purpose of electing directors or transacting other business requiring the consent of the stockholders. *See also* annual meeting.
subsidiary corporation [sub.*sid*.ee.er.ee kore.per.*ay*.shen]	A corporation controlled by another corporation, known as the parent company, which owns all or a majority of its stock.
ultra vires [*ul*.tra *vee*.rayz]	(*Latin*) "Beyond the power." A term that the law applies to a contract, transaction, or other act of a corporation that is beyond those powers enumerated or implied in its articles of incorporation, charter, or by-laws.
winding up [*wine*.ding up]	The dissolution or liquidation of a corporation or a partnership.

Missing Words

Fill in the blanks.

1. A change in relationship of partners caused by a partner's ceasing to be associated with the partnership is known as _____ of the partnership.

2. An equitable action brought by members of a partnership to resolve their respective rights and obligations is called a(n) _____.

3. A(n) _____ is a person employed in buying and selling stock for others.

4. A corporation is domiciled in the state of its _____.

5. A(n) _____ is an action brought by shareholders to enforce a corporate right or to remedy a wrong of the corporation.

6. _____ occurs when the corporate entity is ignored to reach or proceed directly against the corporation's directors, officers, or managers.

7. _____ is corporate stock that is entitled to a priority over other classes of stock.

8. A(n) _____ is a statement issued by a corporation providing information about stock that is for sale to the public.

9. When a corporation transacts business that is beyond its powers, this is a(n) _____ act.

10. The _____ is an agency that administers and enforces federal statutes relating to securities.

11. _____ stock is the shares of stock issued by a corporation.

12. A(n) _____ is an instrument issued by a corporation stating that the person named is the owner of a designated number of shares of stock.

13. The _____ is a meeting of the stockholders of the corporation called for the purpose of electing directors or transacting other business requiring stockholder consent.

14. The _____ of a corporation acts as a group in representing the organization and conducting its business.

15. The _____ are the officers of the corporation such as the president, treasurer, and comptroller.

16. A(n) _____ is the person who organizes a business venture.

17. A corporation organized under the laws of a state is a(n) _____ corporation.

18. _____ Ltd. is a word following a company's name to indicate that a business is a corporation, this term is especially used in England and Canada.

> **STUDY AID:** Use flashcards for this unit before completing the exercises.

Matching

Match the letter of the definition to the term.

___ 19. sole proprietorship

___ 20. S corporation

___ 21. partnership

___ 22. corporation

___ 23. proxy

A. ownership of a business by one person

B. payment made by a corporation to its stockholders

C. value of a share of stock or bond according to its face

D. an artificial person, existing only in the eyes of the law, that can act and contract, and sue and be sued

E. in some states, a certificate issued by the secretary of state attesting that articles of incorporation have been filed

_G_ **24.** shareholder

_E_ **25.** certificate of incorporation

_C_ **26.** par value

_I_ **27.** by-laws

_B_ **28.** dividend

_F_ **29.** professional corporation

_L_ **30.** profit corporation

_M_ **31.** annual meeting

F. corporation formed to practice a profession such as law

G. owner of one or more shares of stock in a corporation

H. when two or more people carry on as co-owners of a business for profit

I. rules and regulations created by corporations

J. authority given by one shareholder in a corporation to another shareholder to exercise voting rights for her

K. corporation whose income is taxed to the shareholders rather than at the corporate level

L. a corporation organized to realize a gain

M. regular meeting of stockholders held once a year

Multiple Choice

Select the best choice.

_B_ **32.** Corporate stock that is entitled to a priority over other classes of stock is known as a:
   a. common stock.
   b. preferred stock.
   c. treasury share.
   d. stock split.

_A_ **33.** A market in securities other than the stock exchange is called an:
   a. over-the-counter market.
   b. under-the-counter market.
   c. both of the above
   d. none of the above

_C_ **34.** Certificates that represent a right to share in the profits of a company or in the distribution of assets, or in a debt owed by a company or by the government, are known as:
   a. proxies.
   b. ultra vires.
   c. securities.
   d. by-laws.

_A_ **35.** A corporation organized and existing solely to engage in charitable activities is known as a:
   a. charitable corporation.
   b. private corporation.
   c. close corporation.
   d. publicly held corporation.

_D_ **36.** Authorization given in writing by one shareholder in a corporation to another shareholder to exercise her voting rights is known as a(n):
   a. stock issue.
   b. stock dividend.
   c. insider trading.
   d. proxy.

_A_ **37.** The directors of a corporation or association who act as a group in representing the organization are known as:
   a. the board of directors.
   b. stockholders.
   c. incorporators.
   d. stockbrokers.

D   **38.** The annual meeting of a corporation is a meeting of:
- a. incorporators.
- b. promoters.
- c. insider traders.
- d. shareholders.

A   **39.** A corporation controlled by another corporation, known as the parent corporation, which owns all or a majority of its stock, is known as a:
- a. subsidiary corporation.
- b. charitable corporation.
- c. private corporation.
- d. close corporation.

B   **40.** When the corporate entity is ignored to reach or to proceed directly against the corporation's directors, officers, or managers, this is known as:
- a. the business judgment rule.
- b. piercing the corporate veil.
- c. stock redemption.
- d. stock manipulation.

A   **41.** The president, treasurer, and comptroller of a corporation are examples of:
- a. officers of a corporation.
- b. directors of a corporation.
- c. shareholders of a corporation.
- d. none of the above

B   **42.** A statement published by a corporation that provides information concerning stock or other securities it is offering for sale to the public is called a:
- a. proxy.
- b. prospectus.
- c. stock certificate.
- d. stock split.

A   **43.** The principle that courts should be reluctant to second-guess the decisions of corporate directors is called:
- a. the business judgment rule.
- b. insider trading.
- c. blue sky laws.
- d. piercing the corporate veil.

True/False

Mark the following T or F.

T   **44.** A partner is a member of a partnership.

T   **45.** All assets belonging to a partnership are known as partnership assets.

F   **46.** The agreement signed by members of a partnership that governs their relationship as partners is known as the Uniform Partnership Act. *Partnership agreement*

F   **47.** A partner's duty to act loyally and honestly with respect to the interests of the other partners is known as indemnification. *Fiduciary Duty*

F   **48.** A partnership in which the liability of one or more partners is limited to the amount of money they have invested is known as a general partnership.

T   **49.** An artificial person existing only in the eyes of the law, to whom a state or federal government has granted a charter to become a legal entity separate from its shareholders, is a corporation.

F   **50.** A corporation electing to be taxed under Subchapter S of the Internal Revenue Code with income taxed to the shareholders is called a private corporation. *S corp.*

T   **51.** A dividend is a payment made by a corporation to its stockholders.

_____ F **52.** An equitable action brought to resolve the respective rights and obligations of the members of a partnership is called the annual shareholders meeting.

_____ T **53.** Insider trading occurs when stock is bought and sold based on information obtained through one's position in a company.

_____ T **54.** The process that takes place when a corporation is broken up or merges with or acquires another corporation is called dissolution.

_____ T **55.** A market in securities other than the stock exchange is the over-the-counter market.

_____ T **56.** A company that owns all or the majority of the stock of another corporation is a subsidiary corporation.

Synonyms

Select the correct synonym in parentheses for each numbered item.

57. SHAREHOLDER
(stockholder, stockmaker, stockseller)

58. DIVIDEND
(debt, payment, liquidation)

59. STOCK
(share, action, prospectus)

60. FIDUCIARY DUTY
(loyalty, public, dissolution)

61. BY-LAWS
(corporate records, corporate laws, corporate officers)

62. ANNUAL MEETING
(first meeting, regular meeting, last meeting)

63. WINDING UP
(dissolution, ultra vires, merger)

64. PROXY
(prohibition, insider, authorization)

65. PROMOTER
(CEO, incorporator, officer)

66. CHARITABLE CORPORATION
(public corporation, nonprofit corporation, C corporation)

67. STOCKBROKER
(securities broker, registered agent, officer)

68. BOND
(assets, debt, collateral)

69. SECURITIES
(stocks, promoters, insiders)

70. SILENT PARTNERS
(dormant, shy, outgoing)

71. ARTICLES OF PARTNERSHIP
(partnership agreement, incorporation, trust agreement)

72. PROFESSIONAL CORPORATION
(Pr.C., PC, P.Corp.)

73. PROFIT
(loss, gain, prospectus)

74. QUORUM
(kind of members, variety of members, number of members)

75. ULTRA VIRES
(below power, super power, beyond its power)

76. PAR VALUE
(face value, facebook value, ebay value)

Self-Test

Place the number of the correct term in the appropriate space.

77. corporation

78. partnership

79. partnership assets

80. professional corporation

81. Securities and Exchange Commission

82. nonprofit corporation

83. S corporation

84. sole proprietorship

85. partnership agreement

86. DBA

87. dissolution of corporation

88. merger of corporations

There are three main forms in which to organize a business. There are pluses and minuses to each of the different types of business organizations. Where a person dreams of having his own business and being his own boss, this is called a(n) _____. However, after working 10-hour days and 7-day weeks, some people decide that this is not the way they want to run a business. They may decide to try a(n) _____, where two or more people agree to carry on a business as co-owners, for a profit. The agreement signed by members of a partnership that governs their relationship as partners is called the _____. All the assets that belong to the partnership, as opposed to the partners' personal assets, are called _____.

Individuals do not need to use their own name to form a business. Some businesses file a(n) _____ certificate when they wish to conduct business under an assumed name.

If business partners wish to protect themselves from unlimited liability as a result of their business affairs, they may wish to form a(n) _____. There are many different types of corporations. Attorneys or doctors might wish to form a(n) _____. A charitable organization that does not seek to earn a profit might form a(n) _____. If shareholders desire that the income of the corporation be taxed to the shareholders rather than at the corporate level, they might consider forming a(n) _____.

Sometimes two or more corporations have a(n) _____ and one of the corporations becomes the single survivor. The corporation that goes out of existence will need to undergo a(n) _____.

The _____ is the agency that administers and enforces the federal statutes relating to securities.

Word Scramble

Unscramble the following words and write the correct word(s) that match(es) the definition for each word or phrase

89. partshipner – two or more persons carry on a business for a profit _____

_____

90. sinessbu – a trade, occupation, or calling _____

_____

91. fitpro – gain _____

_____

92. ertificatec fo orporationinc – written proof that articles of incorporation have been filed _____

_____

93. ed ruje porationcor – corporation created in compliance with all legal requirements _____

_____

94. tocks – shares in a corporation owned by shareholders _____

_____

95. tedlimi bilitylia nershippart – a partnership in which the liability of one partner is limited to the amount he has invested in the partnership

_____

_____

96. denddivi – a payment made by a corporation to its stockholders _____

_____

97. fiiaryduc tudy – to act honestly with the interests of another _____

_____

98. gaency – master and servant is an example of this type of relationship _____

_____

99. rporationco – an artificial person existing only in the eyes of the law _____

_____

100. sloe rshipproprieto – a business owned by one person _____

_____

101. doarb fo rectordis – directors who conduct the business of a corporation _____

_____

102. olhderharse – a stock holder _____

_____

103. oxypr – authorization for another to vote for you

_____

_____

104. etdlimi abilliity porationcor – a business form that has qualities of both a corporation and a partnership _____

_____

The Last Word

On May 6, 2010, the sudden 11 percent decline in American stock markets earned itself the nickname "Flash Crash" and initially stumped the experts as to its cause. Now they believe the culprits are "internalizers," large traders such as investment banks and hedge funds, which have their own vast holdings of off-exchange shares. In fact, only two internalizers accounted for more than half of the share volumes that day.

How did this happen? As the market tanked lower, internalizers kept resubmitting limit (fixed price) orders that could not be filled and "eventually reaching unrealistically low market prices" on the stock exchanges, according to the Flash Crash Report. Should internalizers be legally prohibited from selling their own warehoused shares outside of established markets?

UNIT

19 Labor and Employment

INTRODUCTION

The very core of the American economy is its work force. Historically, employers and employees were free to bargain at will, setting up any type of employment relationship that was desired. With the increase in factories at the start of the Industrial Revolution, the U.S. government could no longer maintain a laissez-faire attitude toward business.

The policy of leaving big businesses completely unregulated and workers unprotected led to labor strife. The need for government intervention became evident. Frequent complaints were made of dangerous working conditions, unsafe machinery, abuse of child labor, discrimination, long hours of work at unfair wages, and frequent on-the-job injuries. Laws at the state and federal levels were enacted to better control the workplace, making it safer for employees. Some of these laws include the Fair Labor Standards Act, Workers' Compensation Act, Occupational Safety and Health Act, Employee Retirement Income Security Act, Social Security Unemployment Compensation Act, the Equal Pay Act, the Americans with Disabilities Act, and the Civil Rights Act.

In 1935, the National Labor Relations Act was passed, giving employees the right to form and join unions. This act provided individual workers bargaining power with large corporations. The National Labor Relations Board (NLRB) is a federal agency that oversees unions and monitors labor practices by both unions and employers. When a union representing employees and an employer negotiate the terms and conditions of employment, this is called collective bargaining. When union members feel that their employer is not complying with demands they have made, the members might go on strike and refuse to work, to pressure their employer to agree to their requests. The people that take the jobs of employees who are on strike are called strike breakers or "scabs." Actions by either unions or employers that violate the National Labor Relations Act are called unfair labor practices. When businesses or the public refuse to do business with a company because they don't like the company's injurious practices, they may refuse to do business with a company until it changes its policies.

Now there are many state and federal laws that protect workers. The Equal Pay Act (EPA) of 1963 was passed to ensure that men and women who did substantially the same work in the same workplace were paid equivalently. In 1964, Title VII of the Civil Rights Act (Title VII) was enacted to prohibit discrimination in employment. No longer could employees be harassed and discriminated against in the workplace based on race, color, sex, religion, and national origin. The Age Discrimination and Employment Act (ADEA) protects workers over age 40 from age discrimination while at work. The Civil Rights Act of 1991 (CRA) provides for monetary damages for intentional discrimination in the workplace. Title I and Title V of the Americans with Disabilites Act of 1990, as amended (ADA), prohibit employment discrimination against qualified individuals with disabilites

345

in the private, state, and local sectors. More recently, Title II of the Genetic Information Nondiscrimination Act of 2008, GINA) prohibits discrimination based on genetic information about an applicant, employee, or former employee. All of these laws are overseen and enforced by the United States Equal Employment Opportunity Commission (EE0).

CASE AND COMMENT

United States Court of Appeals for the Ninth Circuit
Lisa M. Zuress, Plaintiff-Appellant
v.
Michael B. Donley, Acting Secretary, United States Department of the Air Force, Defendant-Appellee
No. 08-17559, D.C. No. 2:08-cv-00606-HRH (Filed June 8, 2010)

Facts: Zuress was employed as a dual status Air Force Reserve Technician at Luke Air Force Base from July 2000 to June 2005. She served in a civilian capacity as a GS-12 Operations Staff Specialist and in a military capacity as an Air Force Reserve Captain. Zuress alleges that the Air Force violated her rights under Title VII after September 2003, when she wrote a letter to senior Defense Department officials describing inappropriate sexual behavior at a base party. Retaliation ensued against her and it escalated when she became a character witness in a coworker's discrimination matter. Zuress realized upon receiving two "average" performance reviews in a row that she would not be promoted and would be ineligible to remain in the reserves. The lack of promotion meant losing her civilian job as well. She submitted military retirement paperwork and went on leave. When she returned she was assigned to a lower grade GS-7 position. Without promotion, she retired three months later from the Air Force Reserve and brought this suit.

Procedural History: This is an appeal from the United States District Court for the District of Arizona, where the court dismissed the plaintiff's amended complaint for lack of subject matter jurisdiction.

Issue: Whether dual-status technicians who perform civilian roles within military departments are protected by federal statutes prohibiting employment discrimination.

Rationale: The National Defense Authorization Act for the Fiscal Year 1998 did not supercede the intra-military immunity doctrine, which prevent lawsuits within the military. The personnel actions that Zuress challenges are integrally related to the military's unique structure and thus her claim is foreclosed. The court disagrees with her argument that National Defense Authorization Act Amendments undermine *Mier v. Owens*. Pursuant to the doctrine of intra-military immunity, "members of the armed forces may not bring an action against the government" and the court cannot entertain a Tile VII claim brought by a dual-class technician.

Ruling: We conclude that the Amendments did not repeal the intra-military immunity Doctrine of *Mier*. Accordingly, we affirm the district court's dismissal of Zuress' Title VII harassment and retaliation claim due to lack of subject matter jurisdiction.

Comment: Note that the court did not address any of the issues raised regarding employment discrimination because the court lacked subject matter jurisdiction. Was there a better legal strategy for Zuress than the one she pursued?

DICTIONARY THESAURUS

Term	
[phonetic pronunciation]	*Note: All dictionary/thesaurus terms appear on flashcards at the back of the book and on the CD-ROM.*

affirmative action
[a.*fer*.me.tiv *ak*.shen]

1. Positive or constructive action rather than inaction or negative or punitive action. 2. When used in conjunction with "plan," "program," or "guidelines," a term applied to the obligation to remedy discrimination based on sex, race, color, creed, or age with respect to, for EXAMPLE, employment, union, membership, or college admission. *See also* Civil Rights Act.

agency shop
[*ay*.jen.see shop]

A collective bargaining agreement states that union membership is optional but that nonmembers must pay the union as much as members pay in dues. Agency shops are prohibited in states with right to work laws.

Americans with Disabilities Act (ADA)
[a.*mare*.i.kenz with dis.e.*bil*.i.tees akt]

A federal statute that prohibits discrimination against disabled persons in employment, public services, and public accommodation.

arbitration
[ar.bi.*tray*.shen]

A method of settling disputes by submitting a disagreement to a person (an arbitrator) or a group of individuals (an arbitration panel) for decision instead of going to court. If the parties are required to comply with the decision of the arbitrator, the process is called binding arbitration; if there is no such obligation, the arbitration is referred to as nonbinding arbitration. Compulsory arbitration is required by law, most notably in labor disputes.

- *n.* adjustment, compromise, mediation, determination ("Compulsory arbitration is the name for arbitration required by law.")

arbitration clause
[ar.bi.*tray*.shen kloz]

A clause in a contract providing for arbitration of controversies that arise out of performance of the contract.

arbitration panel
[ar.bi.*tray*.shen *pan*.el]

A number of arbitrators who hear and decide a case together.

arbitrator
[*ar*.bi.tray.ter]

A person who conducts an arbitration. Generally, the primary consideration in choosing an arbitrator is impartiality and familiarity with the type of matter in dispute.

- *n.* judge, umpire, mediator, intervenor, adjudicator

at will employment
[at will em.*ploy*.ment]

Termination of employment for any cause; may be initiated by employer or employee.

back pay
[bak pay]

Unpaid wages to which an employee is entitled.

back pay order
[bak pay *or*.der]

The order of a court, arbitrator, or administrative agency that employees be given their back pay. Such orders are most common in cases involving the reinstatement of employees who were improperly discharged.

DICTIONARY / THESAURUS *continued...*

boycott
[*boy*.kot]

A joining together in a refusal to do business with a company, unless it changes practices felt to be injurious to those who are joining together, or to some of them, in an attempt to bring about modification of the practice. EXAMPLE: a boycott because of a manufacturer's policy of having most of its labor performed abroad.

certification (of bargaining agent)
[ser.ti.fi.*kay*.shen ov *bar*.gen.ing *ay*.jent]

A formal pronouncement by the National Labor Relations Board, or a similar state agency, that it has determined that a union seeking to represent an employer's employees represents a majority of those employees in an appropriate collective bargaining unit and is therefore their collective bargaining agent. *See also* representation election.

Civil Rights Act
[*sih*.vil rytz akt]

A term that may refer to any or all of the various statutes enacted by Congress relating to civil rights. The Civil Rights Act of 1964 assured access to places of public accommodation, public facilities, and education, without regard to religion, color, race, national origin, or sex; Title VII of that Act prohibited discrimination in employment. The Civil Rights Act of 1991 provided for both compensatory damages and punitive damages for intentional discrimination or unlawful harassment in the workplace on the basis of sex, race, religion, or disability. Additionally, the Age Discrimination in Employment Act and the Americans with Disabilities Act are often classified as civil rights acts. States, as well as the federal government, have legislated extensively in the area of civil rights. *See also* Equal Employment Opportunity Commission.

closed shop
[*klozed* shop]

A place of employment in which all employees are required by a collective bargaining agreement to be members of the union in order to be employed. *Compare* agency shop.

collective bargaining
[ko.*lek*.tiv *bahr*.gen.ing]

The negotiation of terms and conditions of employment between a union, acting on behalf of employees, and an employer or an association of employers. *See also* collective bargaining agreement.

collective bargaining agent
[ko.*lek*.tiv *bahr*.gen.ing *ay*.jent]

A union that engages in collective bargaining on behalf of an employer's employees.

collective bargaining agreement
[ko.*lek*.tiv *bahr*.gen.ing a.*gree*.ment]

An agreement covering wages, hours, and working conditions, entered into between an employer and the union, that is the collective bargaining agent for the employer's employees. *See also* collective bargaining and collective bargaining contract.

collective bargaining contract
[ko.*lek*.tiv *bahr*.gen.ing *kon*.trakt]

An agreement covering wages, hours, and working conditions, entered into between an employer and the union that is the collective bargaining agent for the employer's employees.

collective bargaining unit
[ko.*lek*.tiv *bahr*.gen.ing *yoo*.nit]

An employee group permitted by law to be represented by a collective bargaining agent. EXAMPLES: all of an employer's maintenance employees, all of its drivers, or all employees in the finishing department.

company union
[*kum*.pe.nee *yoo*.nyen]

A labor union whose total membership consists of the employees of a single company and is controlled by the company.

comparable worth
[*kom*.per.ebl werth]

The concept that men and women are entitled to equal pay when their work requires equal skills or duties and is therefore of "comparable worth." Several states have adopted legislation putting this concept into practice in varying degrees. *See also* Equal Pay Act.

concerted activity
[ken.*ser*.ted ak.*tiv*.i.tee]

In labor law, conduct engaged in by an employer's employees, a union, or others for the purpose of supporting collective bargaining demands. Concerted activity that constitutes an unfair labor practice (EXAMPLE: a secondary boycott in which a union boycotts another company to put pressure on the union employees' company) is prohibited by the National Labor Relations Act. *Compare* concerted protected activity.

concerted protected activity
[ken.*ser*.ted pro.*tek*.ted ak.*tiv*.i.tee]

In labor law, conduct engaged in by two or more employees acting together for the purpose of influencing the terms and conditions of their employment, including but not limited to wages and hours. Such activity is protected by the National Labor Relations Act if it falls within the terms of that statute. EXAMPLES: joining a union; striking; picketing.

condition of employment
[kon.*dish*.en ov em.*ploy*.ment]

A matter with respect to which the National Labor Relations Act requires an employer to bargain collectively. EXAMPLES: wages; hours; vacation pay; seniority. *See also* collective bargaining.

deferred compensation
[de.*ferd* kom.pen.*say*.shen]

Compensation paid after the services are rendered (pension and payments made for profit sharing).

discharge
[dis.*charj*]

1. To terminate an employee from employment. 2. To fire an employee. USAGE: "He was discharged from his job."

discrimination
[dis.krim.in.*ay*.shen]

Violations of the Fourteenth Amendment's equal protection clause distinguishing between classes of people in voting, education, employment, and other areas of human activity.

dues
[dooz]

Annual or other regular payments made by a member of a club, union, or association to retain membership.

employ
[em.*ploy*]

To enter into a contract of employment; to hire.

employee
[em.*ploy*.ee]

A person who works for another for pay in a relationship that allows the other person to control the work and direct the manner in which it is done. The earlier legal term for employee was servant.

   Note that statutory definitions of "employee" may differ, depending upon the purpose of the statute. For EXAMPLE, although the distinctions between the definitions of employee in the Social Security Act, the Fair Labor Standards Act, and the National Labor Relations Act may seem insignificant, they may, in any given instance, be critical.

DICTIONARY | THESAURUS *continued...*

employee assistance program
[em.*ploy*.ee e.*sis*.tense *proh*.gram]

An employer-sponsored program, often in conjunction with an insurance company or a health maintenance organization, that provides treatment referrals for employees impaired or disabled by chemical dependency or other problems requiring counseling services. It is often referred to by its abbreviations, EAP.

Employee Retirement Income Security Act
[em.*ploy*.ee re.*tire*.ment *in*.kum see.*kyoo*.re.tee akt]

Better known by its acronym ERISA; a federal statute that protects employee pensions by regulating pension plans maintained by private employers, the way in which such plans are funded, and their vesting requirements. ERISA has important tax implications for both employers and employees. *See also* vested pension.

employer
[em.*ploy*.er]

A person who hires another to work for her for pay in a relationship that allows her to control the work and direct the manner in which it is done. The earlier legal term for employer was master.

employers' liability acts
[em.*ploy*.erz ly.e.*bil*.i.tee aktz]

Now called workers' compensation acts. Employers' liability acts abolished or substantially restricted the defenses previously available to an employer (EXAMPLES: contributory negligence; assumption of risk) when an employee brought suit for an injury incurred on the job pursuant to the Federal Employees' Liability Act (FELA).

employment
[em.*ploy*.ment]

1. The relationship between an employee and an employer. 2. That which occupies a person's time.

- *n.* livelihood, service, business, trade, vocation, occupation, job, profession, work

employment at will
[em.*ploy*.ment at will]

A hiring for an indefinite period of time. In the absence of an agreement to the contrary, all employment is at will and either the employer or the employee may terminate it at any time.

employment discrimination
[em.*ploy*.ment dis.krim.in.*ay*.shen]

Federal statutes prohibit discrimination (unfair treatment or denial of normal privileges) in employment on the basis of sex, age, race, nationality, religion, or being disabled. It is not discrimination if a distinction can be found between the favored class and the unfavored class of employees. *See* discrimination, Civil Rights Act, Americans with Disabilities Act, Equal Pay Act.

Equal Employment Opportunity Commission
[*ee*.kwel em.*ploy*.ment op.er.*tew*.ni.tee kuh.*mish*.en]

A federal agency whose purpose is to prevent and remedy discrimination based on race, color, religion, national origin, age, or sex with respect to most aspects of employment, including hiring, firing, promotions, and wages. The commission, which is known as the EEOC, enforces many federal civil rights acts and antidiscrimination statutes.

Equal Pay Act
[*ee*.kwel pay akt]

A federal statute that requires men and women to be paid equally for the same work. *See also* comparable worth.

Fair Labor Standards Act
[fayr *lay*.ber *stan*.derdz akt]

A federal statute that establishes a maximum work week for certain employees, sets a minimum hourly wage, and imposes restrictions on child labor. The Act covers employers in interstate commerce and other employers, including state and local governments. Additionally, all states have statutes governing hours; most also have minimum wage requirements. *See also* wage and hour acts.

FICA
[fy.kah]

Acronym for Federal Insurance Compensations Act. The federal statute that funds Social Security and Medicare by taxing employers, the wages of employees, and the earnings of the self-employed. Most people are aware of this law because of the FICA deduction that appears on their pay stubs.

green card
[green kard]

A document that evidences an alien's status as a resident alien. It permits the alien to seek and gain employment within the United States.

grievance
[*gree*.venss]

1. A formal complaint filed by an employee or by an employees' union claiming that the employer has violated the collective bargaining agreement. 2. A similar complaint filed against a union by an employer.

hostile environment
[*hoss*.tel en.*vi*.ron.ment]

A situation in which offensive conduct is permitted to infect the workplace, making it difficult or impossible for an employee to work.

job bias
[job *by*.is]

A claim made under employment discrimination after a worker is fired for reasons of race, age, gender, or other disability. *See* Title VII.

labor
[*ley*.ber]

1. In common usage, physical work, although the word refers with equal accuracy to work involving the application of professional or intellectual skills. 2. Work performed for a wage or salary, as opposed to work performed in order to realize a profit. 3. The body or group of persons who work for wages, as a class and as distinguished from management. *See also* labor dispute; unfair labor practice.

- *n.* work, occupation, undertaking, toil, enterprise, task, responsibility, energy, exertion, effort
- *v.* work, agonize, struggle, toil, slave, travail, strain

labor agreement
[*lay*.ber a.*gree*.ment]

See collective bargaining agreement.

labor contract
[*lay*.ber *kon*.trakt]

See collective bargaining agreement.

labor dispute
[*lay*.ber dis.*pyoot*]

A controversy between an employer and its employees or their collective bargaining agent concerning wages, hours, or other working conditions, or concerning union representation.

labor laws
[*lay*.ber lawz]

Federal and state statutes and administrative regulations that govern such matters as hours of work, minimum wages, unemployment insurance, safety, and collective bargaining. EXAMPLES: the National Labor Relations Act; the Fair Labor Standards Act; the Occupational Safety and Health Act.

labor organization
[*lay*.ber or.gan.i.*zay*.shen]

See labor union.

Labor Relations Act
[*lay*.ber re.*lay*.shenz akt]

See National Labor Relations Act.

DICTIONARY	THESAURUS *continued...*

labor relations acts
[*lay*.ber re.*lay*.shenz aktz]

Federal and state statutes that regulate relations between management and labor. EXAMPLE: the National Labor Relations Act.

Labor Relations Board
[*lay*.ber re.*lay*.shenz bord]

See National Labor Relations Act.

Labor Standards Act
[*lay*.ber *stan*.derdz akt]

See Fair Labor Standards Act (FLSA).

labor union
[*lay*.ber *yoo*.nyen]

An association of workers formed for the purpose of engaging in collective bargaining with employers on behalf of workers concerning wages, hours, and other terms and conditions of their employment. *See also* collective bargaining agent.

laborer
[*lay*.ber.er]

A person who performs labor for compensation.

- *n.* worker, employee, help, toiler

lockout
[*lok*.out]

The closing of the workplace by the employer, or to withhold work, to enhance the employer's bargaining position in labor negotiations.

mediation
[mee.dee.*ay*.shen]

The voluntary resolution of a dispute in a nonadversarial manner.

merit
[*mehr*.it]

Worth; quality; value.

merit increase
[*mehr*.it *in*.kreess]

An increase in pay given in recognition of the quality of an employee's work, as opposed to a pay raise granted on the basis of length of service or seniority.

minimum wage
[*min*.i.mum wayj]

See minimum wage laws.

minimum wage laws
[*min*.i.mum wayj lawz]

State and federal statutes establishing a minimum rate of wages to be paid employees. The Fair Labor Standards Act is the federal minimum wage statute. *See also* wage and hour acts.

National Labor Relations Act
[*nash*.en.el *lay*.ber re.*lay*.shenz akt]

Actually, several Acts of Congress, including the Wagner Act and the Taft-Hartley Act, which, together, regulate relations between management and labor by, among other things, prohibiting certain activities (unfair labor practices) that unreasonably hamper employers in the conduct of their business or that interfere with the right of employees to be effectively represented by unions of their choice.

National Labor Relations Board (NLRB)
[*nash*.en.el *lay*.ber re.*lay*.shenz bord]

A federal administrative agency, commonly referred to as the NLRB, created by the National Labor Relations Act for the purpose of enforcing the Act.

pension
[*pen*.shen]

1. A retirement benefit in the form of a periodic payment, usually monthly, made to a retired employee from a fund created by the employer's contributions, or by the joint contributions of the employer and employee, over the period the employee worked for the employer. *See also* pension plan. 2. With respect to a former government employee or a retired member of the military, a regular allowance paid in consideration of the prior service.

- *n.* benefits, annuity, compensation, Social Security, support ("a vested pension")

Pension Benefit Guaranty Corporation
[*pen*.shen *ben*.e.fit gehr.en.*tee* kore.per.*ay*.shen]

A public corporation of the United States government, that, under certain circumstances and within certain limits, guarantees the payment of employer pension plans that terminate without sufficient assets to pay the promised benefits. *See also* Employee Retirement Income Security Act (ERISA).

pension fund
[*pen*.shen fund]

A fund from which a pension is paid.

pension plan
[*pen*.shen plan]

A plan through which an employer provides a pension for its employees' retirement. There are many types of pension plans. Some are funded solely by employer contributions; some are funded jointly by the employer and the employee. Most are regulated by the federal government under the Employee Retirement Insurance Security Act. All pension plans involve significant tax implications. Tax-deferred pension plans are also available to self-employed persons under certain circumstances.

picket
[*pik*.et]

A person who engages in picketing: a demonstrator, striker, or sign holder. ("Mary was a picket in last week's strike.")

- *v.* patrol, march, protest, rally ("We picketed the employer's plant when he committed unfair labor practices.")

picketing
[*pik*.e.ting]

1. In connection with a labor dispute, the presence of employees or others at an employer's place of business for the purpose of influencing other employees or prospective employees to refrain from working, or for the purpose of informing the public, customers, or suppliers of the dispute and inducing them not to do business with the employer. 2. Similar activity by any group of people at any location for the purpose of protesting anything.

polygraph
[*pol*.i.graf]

Commonly called a lie detector, a machine for recording impulses caused by changes in a person's blood pressure, pulse, respiration, and perspiration while under questioning. The results, which are interpreted to indicate the truth or falsity of the answers given, are not admissible as evidence in many states, and in others may be admitted only in limited circumstances for limited purposes. Federal law prohibits employers from administering polygraph tests to employees or applicants for employment except in very restricted circumstances.

- *n.* examination, inspection, lie detector machine

reasonable accommodation
[*ree*.zen.ebl a.kom.o.*day*.shen]

Any change or adjustment to a job or work environment that permits a qualified applicant or employee with a disability to enjoy benefits and privileges of employment equal to those enjoyed by employees without disabilities. *See* Americans with Disabilities Act (ADA).

DICTIONARY	THESAURUS *continued...*

reinstatement
[ree.in.*state*.ment]

The act of restoring a person or thing to a position or condition from which she or it has been removed. EXAMPLES: rehiring an employee who has previously been fired; restoring coverage under an insurance policy that has lapsed for nonpayment.

- *n.* restoration, rehiring, readmittance

representation election
[rep.re.zen.*tay*.shen e.*lek*.shen]

An election conducted by the National Labor Relations Board for the purpose of determining whether a majority of an employer's employees wish to be represented by the union or unions named on the ballot for the purpose of collective bargaining. *See also* certification (of bargaining agent).

secondary boycott
[*sek*.en.dare.ee *boy*.kott]

A boycott applied by a union to third persons to cause them, against their will, not to patronize or otherwise deal with a company with whom the union has a dispute. A secondary boycott is one form of secondary activity.

secondhand smoke
[*sek*.und.hand smok]

Tobacco fumes harming employees confined to a work area is a new cause of action in unsafe work environment cases, and may qualify as a class action.

self-employment
[self-em.*ploy*.ment]

Working for one-self.

self-employment tax
[self-em.*ploy*.ment takz]

The Social Security tax paid by people who are self-employed.

seniority
[see.*nyor*.i.tee]

1. In labor law, the principle that length of employment determines the order of layoffs, recalls to work, promotions, and frequently, rate of pay. 2. The status or state of being senior.

- *n.* tenure, longevity, longer service, station, rank, standing

sexual harassment
[*sek*.shoo.el ha.*rass*.ment]

A form of sex discrimination. Sexual harassment includes unwanted sexual attention from a supervisor. It also includes the toleration by an employer of sexual coercion or "hassling" in the workplace. *See also* Civil Rights Act and Equal Employment Opportunity Commission (EEOC).

strike
[strike]

n. A concerted stoppage of work by a group of employees for the purpose of attempting to compel their employer to comply with a demand or demands they have made.
v. To act together with other employees in refusing to work; to engage in a strike.

- *v.* mutiny, resist, revolt, slow down ("to strike from work")
- *n.* boycott, revolt, walkout, dispute, boycott

strike breaker
[strike *brake*.er]

A person who takes the job of an employee who is on strike.

- *n.* scab

Title VII
[*ty*.tel *sev*.en]

The section of the Civil Rights Act of 1964 dealing with the prohibition of discrimination in employment. *See* job bias.

underemployed
[*un*.der.employd]

Workers employed part-time or in temporary jobs that do not match their educational or skill levels and fail to pay enough to maintain a previous standard of living. For unemployment statistics, the underemployed are excluded, causing the percentage of unemployed to be higher than reported.

unemployment
[un.em.*ploy*.ment]

A term usually applied to the state or status of being involuntarily unemployed.

unemployment compensation
[un.em.*ploy*.ment kom.pen.*say*.shen]

Short for unemployment compensation benefits or unemployment insurance. *See* unemployment compensation acts.

unemployment compensation acts
[un.em.*ploy*.ment kom.pen.*say*.shen aktz]

State statutes that provide for the payment of benefits to persons who are unemployed through no fault of their own. An employee who, for EXAMPLE, has voluntarily left her employment, or has been discharged for willful misconduct, is ineligible to received unemployment compensation benefits. Unemployment compensation is a form of social insurance.

unemployment compensation benefits
[un.em.*ploy*.ment kom.pen.*say*.shen *ben*.e.fits]

See unemployment compensation acts.

unemployment insurance
[un.em.*ploy*.ment in.*shoor*.ense]

See unemployment compensation acts.

unfair labor practice
[un.*fare lay*.ber *prak*.tiss]

An action by either a union or an employer in violation of the National Labor Relations Act or similar state statutes. EXAMPLES: firing an employee because she joins a union; secondary picketing.

unfair labor practice strike
[un.*fare lay*.ber *prak*.tiss strike]

A strike for the purpose of protesting or of inducing an employer to refrain from unfair labor practices.

vested pension
[*vest*.ed *pen*.shen]

A pension that cannot be taken away, regardless of what the employer or the employee does. Note, however, that a pension may vest either fully or partially. *See also* Employee Retirement Income Security Act (ERISA).

wage
[wayj]

Compensation paid to employees, whether by the hour or by some other period of time, or by the job or piece. Wages include all remuneration paid for personal services, including commissions, bonuses, and gratuities, and, under the Fair Labor Standards Act, include board and lodging as well. In one sense, the term "wage" includes salary; in other uses, the term "salary" is reserved for the remuneration paid to executives, professionals, or supervisors, usually on a weekly, biweekly, monthly, or semimonthly basis. *See also* minimum wage laws.

- *n.* allowance, compensation, payment, salary, stipend ("daily wage")

wage and hour acts
[wayj and ower aktz]

Federal and state statutes establishing the minimum wage that must be paid to employees and the number of hours they may work. The Fair Labor Standards Act is the federal wage and hour act. *See also* minimum wage laws.

DICTIONARY | THESAURUS *continued...*

wage and hour laws
[wayj and ower lawz]
See wage and hour acts.

wildcat strike
[*wild*.kat strike]
A strike that is not authorized by the union representing the strikers.

worker
[*wer*.ker]
1. A person who does work. 2. A person who is employed.
- *n.* artisan, breadwinner, employee, laborer, toiler, trader

workers' compensation
[*wer*.kerz kom.pen.*say*.shen]
Short for workers' compensation acts or workers' compensation insurance.

workers' compensation acts
[*wer*.kerz kom.pen.*say*.shen aktz]
State statutes that provide for the payment of compensation to employees injured in their employment or, in case of death, to their dependents. Benefits are paid under such acts whether or not the employer was negligent; payment is made in accordance with predetermined schedules based generally upon the loss or impairment of earning capacity. Workers' compensation laws eliminate defenses by the employer such as assumption of risk, contributory negligence, and fellow servant. Workers' compensation systems are funded through employer contributions to a common fund, through commercially purchased insurance, or both. Occupational diseases are compensable under these acts as well pursuant to Federal Employee's Liability Act (FELA).

workers' compensation insurance
[*wer*.kerz kom.pen.*say*.shen in.*shoor*.ense]
See workers' compensation acts.

Missing Words

Fill in the blanks.

1. Unpaid wages to which an employee is entitled are known as _____.

2. The _____ is a federal statute that requires men and women to be paid equally for the same work.

3. The FICA deduction appears on an employee's pay stub. A(n) _____ is required by federal statute to deduct money from his employee's salary to fund Social Security and Medicare.

4. A(n) _____ is a labor union whose total membership consists of employees of a single company and is controlled by the company.

5. A federal statute that protects employee pensions is known as _____.

6. A concerted stoppage of work by a group of employees for the purpose of compelling their employer to comply with labor demands is a(n) _____.

7. A(n) _____ is the compensation paid to employees, either hourly or by another time period, by the job, or by the piece.

8. Benefits payable according to state statutes to employees injured in their employment is _____.

9. The presence of employees or others at an employer's place of business to influence employees to refrain from working is known as _____.

10. A strike that is not authorized by the union representing the strikers is known as a(n) _____.

11. _____ is the negotiation of terms and conditions of employment between a union and an employer.

12. Benefits paid to employees who are unemployed through no fault of their own are known as _____.

13. When an employer fires an employee for joining a union, this is a(n) _____ in violation of the National Labor Relations Act.

14. A(n) _____ is a place of employment where all employees are required to be members of a union.

15. When a state has _____, the termination of employment may be for any reason and can be initiated by employer or employee.

16. A(n) _____ is a joining together in a refusal to do business with a company unless it changes its practices.

STUDY AID: Use flashcards for this unit before completing the exercises.

Matching

Match the letter of the definition to the term.

_____ 17. affirmative action

    A. method of settling disputes by submitting an agreement to a person or group of individuals instead of to a court

_____ 18. certification

    B. regular payments made to a union

_____ 19. green card

    C. to fire an employee

_____ 20. polygraph

    D. person who takes the job of an employee who is on strike

_____ 21. EEOC

    E. obligation to remedy discrimination based on sex, race, color, creed, or age

_____ **22.** arbitration

F. federal agency that prevents and remedies discrimination

_____ **23.** discharge

G. an act of Congress created to eliminate dangerous conditions in the workplace

_____ **24.** dues

H. document that establishes an alien's status as a resident alien and permits him to work in the United States

_____ **25.** strike breaker

I. commonly called a lie detector

_____ **26.** OSHA

J. NLRB determines that a union seeking to represent employees represents a majority of the employees in an appropriate collective bargaining unit

_____ **27.** wage and hour laws

K. form of sex discrimination

_____ **28.** comparable work

L. equal pay for equal skills or duties

_____ **29.** reinstatement

M. to rehire an employee who was fired

_____ **30.** sexual harassment

N. wage and hour acts

_____ **31.** Title VII

O. prohibits discrimination against disabled persons

_____ **32.** ADA

P. the closing of the workplace by the employer

_____ **33.** lockout

Q. prohibits discrimination in employment and is considered a Civil Rights Act

Multiple Choice

Select the best choice.

_____ **34.** When employment is at will, this means:
   a. only the employer may terminate employment.
   b. only the employee may terminate employment.
   c. neither the employee nor employer may terminate employment.
   d. either the employee or employer may terminate employment at any time.

_____ **35.** Collective bargaining occurs when:
   a. an employee tries to negotiate for numerous benefits in his employment contract.
   b. several employers offer work to one employee.
   c. a union negotiates a contract with an employer on behalf of employees.
   d. an employee directly negotiates an employment contract with an employer.

_____ **36.** In a closed shop situation, all employees:
   a. must belong to a union.
   b. are barred from joining a union.
   c. can only join a union after one year of employment.
   d. none of the above

_____ **37.** When a supervisor repeatedly asks an employee to massage his back, this is an example of:
   a. sex discrimination.
   b. religious discrimination.
   c. age discrimination.
   d. sexual harassment.

_____ **38.** A secondary boycott is an action:
   a. applied by a union against the employer.
   b. applied by the union to the third persons.
   c. resulting in a factory slowdown.
   d. by teachers.

_____ 39. A concerted stoppage of work by a group of employees for the purpose of attempting to compel their employer to comply with their demands is known as:
a. product picketing.
b. hot cargo contract.
c. union solicitation.
d. a strike.

_____ 40. Under the doctrine of comparable worth, men and women are entitled to equal pay:
a. if they are the same age.
b. if they start working on the same day.
c. when their work requires equal skills or duties.
d. all of the above

_____ 41. Under an agency shop agreement, union membership is:
a. optional.
b. required.
c. illegal.
d. none of the above

_____ 42. An employer may hire an employee on the basis of gender if:
a. clients voice a preference.
b. a business is dominated by one gender.
c. an employer is a sole proprietor of a business.
d. sexual characteristics are essential to performance of the job.

_____ 43. Firing an employee for joining a union is an example of:
a. an unfair labor practice.
b. a strike.
c. a boycott.
d. an employer lockout.

_____ 44. Concerted activity is conducted by employees for the purpose of:
a. supporting collective bargaining demands.
b. opposing collective bargaining demands.
c. closing a shop.
d. employee discharge.

True/False

Mark the following T or F.

_____ 45. Conduct engaged in by a company's employees for the purpose of supporting collective bargaining demands is known as a concerted activity.

_____ 46. A method of settling disputes by submitting a disagreement to a person or a group of individuals rather than resorting to the courts is known as arbitration.

_____ 47. Right to work laws prohibit clauses in employment contracts that compel employees to join a union.

_____ 48. When a labor union's total membership consists of employees of a single company and is controlled by the company, this is known as a hiring hall.

_____ 49. A strike to bring about changes in wages, hours, or other conditions of employment is known as a wildcat strike.

_____ 50. When employees are injured on the job, benefits are paid to the employee whether or not the employer was negligent. This is known as workers' compensation insurance.

_____ 51. The National Labor Relations Act prohibits employment discrimination against qualified individuals with disabilities in regard to job application procedures, hiring, compensation, training, promotion, and termination.

_____ **52.** The National Labor Relations Board is a labor organization composed of skilled craft workers.

_____ **53.** An employee assistance program (EAP) is an employer-sponsored program that provides treatment referrals for employees with problems.

_____ **54.** A wildcat strike is defined as a strike to bring about changes in wages, hours, or other conditions of employment.

_____ **55.** Reasonable accommodation is a method of testing food safety.

_____ **56.** A hostile work environment is evidenced by posters of nude women in an office of female and male employees.

Synonyms

Select the correct synonym in parentheses for each numbered item.

57. VESTED
(fixed, variable, undetermined)

58. MERIT
(friendship, feelings, worth)

59. DUES
(collection, payment, account)

60. PICKET
(protest, agree, discharge)

61. SCAB
(strike starter, strike breaker, illegal striker)

62. BOYCOTT
(join, avoid, crossover worker)

63. REINSTATEMENT
(rehire, fire, polling)

64. CERTIFICATION
(lottery, debate, election)

65. SENIORITY
(status, wealth, education)

66. CIVIL RIGHT
(constitutional right, bargaining right, protected activity)

67. GRIEVANCE
(shutdown, relocation, complaint)

68. ARBITRATION
(interrogation, compromise, discharge)

69. AFFIRMATIVE ACTION
(positive action, inaction, punitive action)

70. DISCHARGE
(fire, hire, sell)

71. EMPLOYER
(servant, master, laborer)

72. WAGE
(discharge, compensation, merit)

73. MEDIATION
(resolution, labor dispute, grievance)

74. WORKERS' COMPENSATION ACTS
(federal law, state statutes, local ordinances)

Self-Test

Place the number of the correct term in the appropriate space.

75. conditions of employment

76. labor unions

77. collective bargaining

78. at will

79. company union

80. boycotting

81. closed shop

82. employees

83. employer

84. strike

85. collective bargaining agreement

86. employer's

87. picketing

88. arbitration

89. arbitrator

In the United States, employers and _____ may terminate employment at any time. This is called

_____ employment. When workers join together for the purposes of engaging in _____ with

employers on behalf of workers concerning wages, hours, and other terms and _____, these associations of

workers are known as _____.

There are all different types of unions. A(n) _____ is a labor union whose total membership consists of

employees of a single company. In contrast, a(n) _____ is a place of employment where all employees are

required by a(n) _____ to be members of a union in order to be employed. Sometimes, even though employees

have formed a union, this is no guarantee that employers will comply with all their demands.

A(n) _____ is a stoppage of work by a group of employees to compel an employer to comply with their

demands. When there is a labor dispute, employees might be present at the _____ place of business, to inform

the public and induce them not to do business with the _____; this is called _____. Should the

general public be unhappy with a business or its practices, persons might join together and refuse to do business with a

company unless it changes practices felt to be injurious; this is known as _____.

In the event an employer cannot resolve a dispute with its employees, a(n) _____ might be hired to settle

the dispute by conducting a(n) _____. If the parties are required to follow the decision of the arbitrator, this is

called binding arbitration.

Word Scramble

Unscramble the following words and write the correct word(s) that match(es) the definition for each word or phrase.

90. mummini gawe – state and federal statutes that establish the minimum rate of wages _____

_____

91. graphpoly – a lie detector _____

_____

92. cottboy – to refuse to do business with a company

_____

_____

93. insonpe – a retirement benefit in the form of a periodic payment _____

_____

94. fles-ploymentem – working for oneself _____

_____

95. emmentpunloy pensacomtion – benefits received during unemployment _____

_____

96. ermit – worth, quality, value _____

_____

97. ioryitsen – status or state of being senior _____

_____

98. krites reakber – a person who takes the job of an employee who is on strike _____

_____

99. ikestr – a concerted stoppage of work _____

_____

100. awge and rouh cats – laws that establish the minimum wage _____

_____

101. slexua mentrassha – a form of sex discrimination

_____

_____

102. tionalNa borLa lationsRe dBoar – NLRB _____

_____

103. meriAcans hiwt ilitiesbadis tcA – ADA _____

_____

The Last Word

According to the website of the Workplace Bullying Institute (WBI), statistics show 62 percent of bullies are men and that men target other men 55.5 percent of the time and target women 45.5 percent of the time. Women constitute 38 percent of bullies and target other women 79.8 percent of time and men 20.2 percent of the time.

Bullying is illegal in many states, and bullying in the workplace based on race, religion, or sexual orientation is actionable. Seventeen states have introduced "status-blind" legislation that would enable employees to sue their employers for damages from all manner of harassment claims across gender, race, ethnicity, and disability lines. Many employers who oppose these laws maintain that making a state or federal case over day-to-day workplace issues is akin to killing a fly with a sledge hammer.

However, a joint Zogby/WBI study found almost 50 percent of American workers are victims or witnesses to "repeated malicious mistreatment, verbal abuse, or conduct that is threatening, humiliating, or intimidating, or that interferes with work." Have you ever been bullied by a boss? What is the best way to handle this type of situation?

Access an interactive eBook, chapter-specific interactive learning tools, and more in your Paralegal CourseMate, accessed through www.CengageBrain.com

INDEX

D

N

CIVIL LITIGATION (PRETRIAL)

acknowledgment

[ak.*naw*.lej.ment]

CIVIL LITIGATION (PRETRIAL)

adversary system

[*ad*.ver.sa.ree *sis*.tem]

CIVIL LITIGATION (PRETRIAL)

action

[*ak*.shen]

CIVIL LITIGATION (PRETRIAL)

affidavit

[a.fi.*day*.vit]

CIVIL LITIGATION (PRETRIAL)

action at common law

[*ak*.shen at *kom*.en law]

CIVIL LITIGATION (PRETRIAL)

affidavit of service

[a.fi.*day*.vit ov *ser*.viss]

CIVIL LITIGATION (PRETRIAL)

action at law

[*ak*.shun at law]

CIVIL LITIGATION (PRETRIAL)

affirmation

[a.fer.*may*.shen]

CIVIL LITIGATION (PRETRIAL)

adversary

[*ad*.ver.sa.ree]

CIVIL LITIGATION (PRETRIAL)

affirmative defense

[a.*fer*.ma.tiv de.*fense*]

CIVIL LITIGATION (PRETRIAL)

adversary proceeding

[*ad*.ver.sa.ree pro.*see*.ding]

CIVIL LITIGATION (PRETRIAL)

allegation

[al.e.*gay*.shen]

The system of justice in the United States. Under the adversary system, the court hears the evidence presented by the adverse parties and decides the case.

1. The signing of a document, under oath, where the signer certifies that he is, in fact, the person who is named in the document as the signer. 2. The certificate of the person who administered the oath, for EXAMPLE, a clerk of court, justice of the peace, or notary.
- *n.* confirmation, admission, ratification, declaration, endorsement ("acknowledgment of paternity")

Any voluntary statement reduced to writing and sworn to or affirmed before a person legally authorized to administer an oath or affirmation (EXAMPLE: a notary public). A sworn statement. *See also* verification.
- *n.* affirmation, oath, statement, testimony, avowal, averment, declaration, sworn statement

A judicial or administrative proceeding for the enforcement or protection of a right; a lawsuit. It is important to distinguish a civil action from a criminal action.
- *n.* legal proceeding, lawsuit, dispute, litigation ("an action for divorce")

An affidavit that certifies that process (EXAMPLES: a summons; a writ) has been served upon the parties to the action in a manner prescribed by law.

A lawsuit governed by the common law rather than by statutes.

A formal statement or declaration, made as a substitute for a sworn statement, by a person whose religious or other beliefs will not permit him to swear.
- *n.* statement, oath, declaration, assertion, avowal, confirmation ("out-of-court affirmation")

A lawsuit brought in a court of law as opposed to a court of equity. *Compare* equitable action.

A defense that amounts to more than simply a denial of the allegations in the plaintiff's complaint. It sets up a new matter that, if proven, could result in a judgment against the plaintiff even if all the allegations of the complaint are true. EXAMPLES of affirmative defenses in civil cases include accord and satisfaction, act of God, estoppel, release, and statute of limitations.

1. An opponent; an enemy. 2. The opposite party in a lawsuit.
- *n.* opponent, enemy, competitor, foe, challenger, litigant, opposing party, adverse party

A statement in a pleading of a fact that the party filing the pleading intends to prove.
- *n.* assertion, accusation, avowal, claim, charge

A trial or other proceeding in which all sides have the opportunity to present their contentions; a proceeding involving a contested action.

CIVIL LITIGATION (PRETRIAL)

amend

[a.*mend*]

CIVIL LITIGATION (PRETRIAL)

amendment of pleading

[a.*mend*.ment ov *plee*.ding]

CIVIL LITIGATION (PRETRIAL)

amicus curiae

[a.*mee*.kes *koo*.ree.eye]

CIVIL LITIGATION (PRETRIAL)

amount in controversy

[a.*mount* in *kon*.tre.ver.see]

CIVIL LITIGATION (PRETRIAL)

answer

[*an*.ser]

CIVIL LITIGATION (PRETRIAL)

appear

[a.*peer*]

CIVIL LITIGATION (PRETRIAL)

appearance

[a.*peer*.ense]

CIVIL LITIGATION (PRETRIAL)

appearance docket

[a.*peer*.ense *dok*.et]

CIVIL LITIGATION (PRETRIAL)

bill of particulars

[bill ov per.*tik*.yoo.lerz]

CIVIL LITIGATION (PRETRIAL)

caption

[*kap*.shen]

CIVIL LITIGATION (PRETRIAL)

cause of action

[koz ov *ak*.shen]

CIVIL LITIGATION (PRETRIAL)

change of venue

[chanj ov *ven*.yoo]

1. The action of an attorney in declaring to the court that he represents a litigant in a case before the court (also referred to as "entering an appearance"). 2. The act by which a party comes into court. EXAMPLES: the filing of a complaint by a plaintiff; the filing of an answer by a defendant.

- *n.* actualization, entrance, exhibition, materialization, emergence ("The appearance of his attorney was timely")

To improve; to make better by change or modification; to correct; to adjust. Thus, a motion to amend is a motion by which a party seeks the court's permission to correct an error or omission in a pleading or to modify allegations and supply new ones. *See also* amendment of pleading.

- *v.* correct, remedy, adjust, change, revise, alter, modify

---

A docket kept by the clerk of court in which appearances are entered.

Although every jurisdiction imposes different restrictions, all jurisdictions permit pleadings to be amended for the purpose of correcting errors and omissions and to modify allegations and supply new ones. *See also* amend.

In civil actions, a more detailed statement of the pleading. An adverse party is entitled to be informed of the precise nature of the opposite party's cause of action or defense, in order to be able to prepare for trial and to protect himself against surprise at the trial.

(*Latin*) "Friend of the court." A person who is interested in the outcome of the case, but who is not a party, whom the court permits to file a brief for the purpose of providing the court with a position or a point of view that it might not otherwise have; often referred to simply as an amicus.

A heading. As applied in legal practice, when "caption" is used to mean "heading," it generally refers to the heading of a court paper. EXAMPLE:

Miriam Brown	In the Court of Common
Plaintiff	Pleas of Bucks County,
v.	
Stanley Brown,	
Scott Lang,	Pennsylvania
Defendants	Civil Action No. 1234
	September Term, 2011

- *n.* heading, title, inscription ("the caption of the case")

A term relevant to determining a court's jurisdiction, when jurisdiction is based upon either a minimum dollar amount with which the court is permitted to concern itself, or a maximum amount that represents the upper limit of its jurisdiction.

Circumstances that give a person the right to bring a lawsuit and to receive relief from a court. *See also* complaint.

---

n. A pleading in response to a complaint. An answer may deny the allegations of the complaint, demur to them, admit to them, or introduce affirmative defenses intended to defeat the plaintiff's lawsuit or delay it. One may also assert counterclaims against the plaintiff.

v. 1. To reply. 2. In pleading, to respond to the plaintiff's complaint by denying its allegations or by introducing affirmative defenses containing new matter.

- *n.* defense, reply, denial, rebuttal, refutation, counterclaim ("file an answer to a complaint")
- *v.* reply, respond, defend, controvert ("He answered the plaintiff's complaint by denying the allegations")

Moving the trial of a case from one county or judicial district to another county or judicial district. The most common reasons for a court to permit a change in the venue of a civil trial are "in the interest of justice," or "for the convenience of the parties." A venue change in a criminal trial may be permitted due to the defendant's inability to receive a fair trial because of publicity. The issue is put before the court by means of a motion for change of venue.

To enter an appearance in a case.

- *v.* surface, attend, arrive, come in, materialize ("appear in court")

CIVIL LITIGATION (PRETRIAL)

civil law

[*siv*.el law]

CIVIL LITIGATION (PRETRIAL)

concurrent jurisdiction

[kon.*ker*.ent joo.ris.*dik*.shen]

CIVIL LITIGATION (PRETRIAL)

civil procedure

[*siv*.el pro.*see*.jer]

CIVIL LITIGATION (PRETRIAL)

counterclaim

[*kown*.ter klame]

CIVIL LITIGATION (PRETRIAL)

claimant

[*clay*.ment]

CIVIL LITIGATION (PRETRIAL)

court of equity

[kort ov *ek*.wi.tee]

CIVIL LITIGATION (PRETRIAL)

class action

[klas *ak*.shen]

CIVIL LITIGATION (PRETRIAL)

court of general jurisdiction

[kort ov *jen*.e.rel joo.ris.*dik*.shen]

CIVIL LITIGATION (PRETRIAL)

clear and convincing evidence

[kleer and kon.*vinss*.ing *ev*.i.denss]

CIVIL LITIGATION (PRETRIAL)

court of inferior jurisdiction

[*kort* ov in.*feer*.ee.er joo.ris.*dik*.shen]

CIVIL LITIGATION (PRETRIAL)

complaint

[kom.*playnt*]

CIVIL LITIGATION (PRETRIAL)

court of law

[kort ov law]

Two or more courts having the power to adjudicate the same class of cases or the same matter. *See also* jurisdiction.

---

1. Body of law that determines private rights and liabilities, as distinguished from criminal law. 2. The entire body of law adopted in a country or a state, as distinguished from natural law (sometimes called moral law) and from international law (the law governing relationships between countries). 3. The law of the Roman Empire, or modern law that has been handed down from Roman Law. 4. The name of the body of law by which the State of Louisiana is governed.

A cause of action on which a defendant in a lawsuit might have sued the plaintiff in a separate action. Such a cause of action, stated in a separate division of a defendant's answer, is a counterclaim. *See also* cross-action; cross-claim; cross-complaint.

The rules by which private rights are enforced by the courts and agencies. There are both Federal Rules of Civil Procedure, followed in the federal courts, and rules of civil procedure for each of the states.

A court having jurisdiction of non-money or equitable actions; a court that administers remedies that are equitable in nature, such as an injunction. *Compare* court of law.

One who claims or makes a claim; an applicant for justice; a plaintiff.

- *n.* petitioner, challenger, plaintiff, appellant, litigant, party, pleader

---

Generally, another term for trial court; that is, a court having jurisdiction to try all classes of civil and criminal cases except those that can be heard only by a court of limited jurisdiction.

An action brought by one or several plaintiffs on behalf of a class of persons. A class action may be appropriate when there has been injury to so many people that their voluntarily and unanimously joining in a lawsuit is improbable and impracticable. In such a situation, injured parties who wish to do so may, with the court's permission, sue on behalf of all. A class action is sometimes referred to as a representative action.

A court of original or limited jurisdiction, as opposed to an appellate court, or a court that has jurisdiction to hear many kinds of cases. *See* court of limited jurisdiction.

A degree of proof required in some civil cases, higher than the usual standard of preponderance of the evidence.

---

1. A court having jurisdiction of actions at law, as distinguished from equitable actions. 2. Any court that administers the law of a state or of the United States. *Compare* equitable action.

The initial pleading in a civil action, in which the plaintiff alleges a cause of action and asks that the wrong done to him be remedied by the court. ("Susan was served with a complaint.")

- *n.* petition, charge, pleading. In criminal cases: indictment or accusation

CIVIL LITIGATION (PRETRIAL)

court of limited jurisdiction

[kort ov *lim*.i.ted joo.ris.*dik*.shen]

CIVIL LITIGATION (PRETRIAL)

deposition

[dep.e.*zish*.en]

CIVIL LITIGATION (PRETRIAL)

cross-action

[*kross*-ak.shen]

CIVIL LITIGATION (PRETRIAL)

digest

[*die*.jest]

CIVIL LITIGATION (PRETRIAL)

cross-claim

[*kross*-klame]

CIVIL LITIGATION (PRETRIAL)

discovery

[dis.*kuv*.e.ree]

CIVIL LITIGATION (PRETRIAL)

cross-complaint

[kross-kem.*plaint*]

CIVIL LITIGATION (PRETRIAL)

dismiss

[dis.*miss*]

CIVIL LITIGATION (PRETRIAL)

defendant

[de.*fen*.dent]

CIVIL LITIGATION (PRETRIAL)

diversity jurisdiction

[di.*ver*.se.tee joo.ris.*dik*.shen]

CIVIL LITIGATION (PRETRIAL)

demur

[de.*mer*]

CIVIL LITIGATION (PRETRIAL)

diversity of citizenship

[di.*ver*.se.tee of *sit*.i.zen.ship]

1. The transcript of a witness's testimony given under oath outside of the courtroom, usually in advance of the trial or hearing, upon oral examination or in response to written interrogatories. *See also* discovery. 2. In a more general sense, an affidavit, a statement under oath.

- *n.* testimony, sworn testimony, testimony under oath, affidavit, declaration

---

A court whose jurisdiction is limited to civil cases of a certain type (EXAMPLE: probate court) or that involve a limited amount of money (EXAMPLE: small claims court), or whose jurisdiction in criminal cases is confined to petty offenses and preliminary hearings.

A series of volumes containing summaries of cases organized by legal topics, subject areas, and so on. Digests are essential for legal research. Some digests are limited to certain regions. Digests are updated continually to ensure they are current.

---

1. An action brought by a defendant in a lawsuit against another named defendant based upon a cause of action arising out of the same transaction on which the plaintiff's suit is based. *See also* counterclaim. 2. An independent action brought by a defendant in a lawsuit against the plaintiff.

A means for providing a party, in advance of trial, with access to facts that are within the knowledge of the other side, to enable the party to better try her case. A motion to compel discovery is the procedural means for compelling the adverse party to reveal such facts or to produce documents, books, and other things within his possession or control. *See also* deposition; interrogatories.

- *n.* exposure, uncovering, disclosure, investigation, finding, breakthrough, pretrial device

---

A counterclaim against a coplaintiff or a codefendant.

To order a case, motion, or prosecution to be terminated. A party requests such an order by means of a motion to dismiss.

A complaint a defendant in an action may file: (a) against the *plaintiff*, based upon *any* cause of action she has against him; or (b) against *anyone* (including persons not yet involved in the lawsuit) if she alleges a cause of action based upon the same transactions as those upon which the complaint against her is based.

The jurisdiction of a federal court arising from diversity of citizenship where parties are residents of different states and the jurisdictional amount has been met.

The person against whom an action is brought.

- *n.* accused, respondent, responding litigant, the party charged
- *ant.* plaintiff

A ground for invoking the original jurisdiction of a federal district court, the basis of jurisdiction being the existence of a controversy between citizens of different states.

---

1. To make a demurrer. 2. To object to; take exceptions to; to disagree. When a demurrer is used, it is a method of raising objection to the sufficiency of a pleading and asking that the case be dismissed. In most jurisdictions, demurrers have been replaced by the use of motions or answers, which can perform the same function.

CIVIL LITIGATION (PRETRIAL)

equitable action

[*ek*.wi.tebl *ak*.shen]

CIVIL LITIGATION (PRETRIAL)

interpleader

[in.ter.*pleed*.er]

CIVIL LITIGATION (PRETRIAL)

ex parte

[eks *par*.tay]

CIVIL LITIGATION (PRETRIAL)

interrogatories

[in.te.*raw*.ge.toh.reez]

CIVIL LITIGATION (PRETRIAL)

in personam action

[in peer.*soh*.nam *ak*.shen]

CIVIL LITIGATION (PRETRIAL)

judgment

[*juj*.ment]

CIVIL LITIGATION (PRETRIAL)

in rem action

[in rem *ak*.shen]

CIVIL LITIGATION (PRETRIAL)

jurisdiction

[joo.ris.*dik*.shen]

CIVIL LITIGATION (PRETRIAL)

injunction

[in.*junk*.shen]

CIVIL LITIGATION (PRETRIAL)

jurisdiction in personam

[joo.ris.*dik*.shen in per.*soh*.nam]

CIVIL LITIGATION (PRETRIAL)

interplead

[in.ter.*pleed*]

CIVIL LITIGATION (PRETRIAL)

jurisdiction in rem

[joo.ris.*dik*.shen in rem]

A remedy that requires rival claimants to property held by a disinterested third party (EXAMPLES: a stakeholder; a person who is in debt to the claimants) to litigate their demands without entangling him in their lawsuits.

Although the distinction between a suit in equity and an action at law has been abolished in most states, all actions now being simply civil actions, the concept of an equitable action still exists with respect to the remedy sought, as historically certain types of relief were available only in a court of equity (EXAMPLES: an injunction; specific performance). Equitable actions are designed to remedy injuries that cannot adequately be redressed by an action at law.

Written questions put by one party to another, or, in limited situations, to a witness in advance of trial. Interrogatories are a form of discovery and are governed by the rules of civil procedure. They must be answered in writing. *Compare* deposition.

- *n.* questions, inquiries

Means "of a side" (i.e., by one party). The term refers to an application made to the court by one party without notice to the other party.

---

1. In a civil action, the final determination by a court of the rights of the parties, based upon the pleadings and the evidence; a decision or decree. 2. In a criminal prosecution, a determination of guilt; a conviction.

A legal action whose purpose is to obtain a judgment against a person, as opposed to a judgment against property. Most lawsuits are in personam actions. *See also* jurisdiction in personam. *Compare* in rem action; quasi in rem action.

A term used in several senses: 1. In a general sense, the power and authority of a court to decide lawsuits and bind the parties. EXAMPLES: the right of juvenile courts to hear cases involving juvenile offenders; the power of federal courts to adjudicate federal questions. 2. In a specific sense, the right of a court to determine a particular case; in other words, the power of the court over the subject matter of, or the property involved. 3. The power of a court to hear cases only within a specific territorial area (EXAMPLES: a state; a county; a federal judicial district). *See also* venue. 4. Authority; control; power. 5. District; area; locality. *See also* diversity jurisdiction; subject matter jurisdiction.

- *n.* capacity, authority, authorization, right, charter, judicature, license, sovereignty; territory, region, domain, district, circuit, state, quarter, field, province ("The matter has not been decided in this jurisdiction.")

A legal action brought against property (EXAMPLES: an action to quiet title; a civil forfeiture), as opposed to an action brought against the person.

The jurisdiction a court has over the person of a defendant. It is acquired by service of process upon the defendant or by her voluntary submission to jurisdiction. Voluntary submission may be implied from a defendant's conduct within the jurisdiction, for EXAMPLE, by doing business in a state or by operating a motor vehicle within a state. Jurisdiction in personam is also referred to as personal jurisdiction. *See also and compare* jurisdiction in rem; jurisdiction quasi in rem.

A court order that commands or prohibits some act or course of conduct. It is preventive in nature and designed to protect a plaintiff from irreparable injury to his property or property rights by prohibiting or commanding the doing of certain acts. An injunction is a form of equitable relief.

- *n.* ban, stay, order, enjoinder, interdiction, restraint, mandate, prohibition

---

The jurisdiction a court has over property situated in the state. *See also and compare* jurisdiction in personam; jurisdiction quasi in rem. *See also* in rem action.

To file an interpleader in a lawsuit.

CIVIL LITIGATION (PRETRIAL)

jurisdiction quasi in rem

[joo.ris.*dik*.shen *kway*.sye in rem]

CIVIL LITIGATION (PRETRIAL)

memorandum of law

[mem.o.*ran*.dum ov law]

CIVIL LITIGATION (PRETRIAL)

jurisprudence

[joor.is.*proo*.dense]

CIVIL LITIGATION (PRETRIAL)

motion

[*moh*.shen]

CIVIL LITIGATION (PRETRIAL)

legal research

[*lee*.gl *ree*.serch]

CIVIL LITIGATION (PRETRIAL)

motion for summary judgment

[*mo*.shen for *sum*.e.ree *juj*.ment]

CIVIL LITIGATION (PRETRIAL)

lis pendens

[liss *pen*.denz]

CIVIL LITIGATION (PRETRIAL)

motion to compel discovery

[*mo*.shen to kom.*pel* dis.*kuv*.e.ree]

CIVIL LITIGATION (PRETRIAL)

litigation

[lit.i.*gay*.shen]

CIVIL LITIGATION (PRETRIAL)

motion to dismiss

[*moh*.shen to dis.*miss*]

CIVIL LITIGATION (PRETRIAL)

long arm statutes

[long arm *stat*.shoots]

CIVIL LITIGATION (PRETRIAL)

order

[*or*.der]

A written statement submitted to a court for the purpose of persuading it of the correctness of one's position. Similar to a brief, although usually not as extensive, it cites case law and other legal authority.

The jurisdiction a court has over the defendant's interest in property located within the jurisdiction. *See also and compare* jurisdiction in personam; jurisdiction in rem.

An application made to a court for the purpose of obtaining an order or rule directing something to be done in favor of the applicant. (EXAMPLE: a defendant's motion to dismiss is a formal request to the court that the plaintiff's lawsuit be terminated without further consideration.) The types of motions available to litigants, as well as their form and the matters they appropriately address, are set forth in detail in the Federal Rules of Civil Procedure and the rules of civil procedure of the various states. Motions may be written or oral, depending on the type of relief sought and on the court in which they are made. Some common motions are motion to produce, motion for summary judgment, motion for entry upon land, and motion to dismiss.

  - *n.* request, petition, proposition, plan, demand, offering

---

The science of law; legal philosophy.

  - *n.* philosophy, theory, legal foundation, philosophy of law, system of laws

---

A method of disposing of an action without further proceedings. Under the Federal Rules of Civil Procedure, and the rules of civil procedure of many states, a party against whom a claim, counterclaim, or cross-claim is asserted, or against whom a declaratory judgment is sought, may file a motion for summary judgment seeking judgment in her favor if there is no genuine issue as to any material fact. *See also* motion.

A study of precedents and other authority for the purpose of developing or supporting a legal theory or position. Most legal writing is based upon research and involves application of the law to the facts.

To force a response; to force a response to discovery. A person who fails to answer interrogatories or to respond appropriately to an attempt to take his deposition may be forced to comply by a motion to compel discovery.

A pending suit or pending action. The doctrine of lis pendens states that a pending suit is notice to all, so buying real estate subject to suit binds the purchaser.

Motion requesting a case, motion, or prosecution to be terminated.

A legal action; a lawsuit.

  - *n.* judicial contest, prosecution, action, lawsuit, case, cause ("Massive amounts of litigation have backlogged the courts.")

---

1. A determination made by a court; an order of court.
2. A determination made by an administrative agency.

  - *v.* dictate, require, rule, demand, ordain, prescribe
  - *n.* decree, command, mandate, demand, judgment ("order of the court")

State statutes providing for substituted service of process on a nonresident corporation or individual. Long arm statutes permit a state's courts to take jurisdiction over a nonresident if she has done business in the state (provided the minimum contacts test is met), or has committed a tort or owns property within the state.

CIVIL LITIGATION (PRETRIAL)
order to show cause
[*or*.der to show koz]

CIVIL LITIGATION (PRETRIAL)
pretrial
[pree.*try*.el]

CIVIL LITIGATION (PRETRIAL)
permission to enter upon land
[per.*mish*.en to *en*.ter up.*on* land]

CIVIL LITIGATION (PRETRIAL)
pretrial conference
[pree.*try*.el *kon*.fer.ense]

CIVIL LITIGATION (PRETRIAL)
petition
[pe.*tish*.en]

CIVIL LITIGATION (PRETRIAL)
pretrial motions
[pree.*try*.el *moh*.shenz]

CIVIL LITIGATION (PRETRIAL)
plaintiff
[*plain*.tif]

CIVIL LITIGATION (PRETRIAL)
primary source
[*pry*.mer.ee sors]

CIVIL LITIGATION (PRETRIAL)
pleadings
[*plee*.dingz]

CIVIL LITIGATION (PRETRIAL)
procedural law
[pro.*seed*.jer.el law]

CIVIL LITIGATION (PRETRIAL)
preponderance of the evidence
[pre.*pon*.der.ense ov the *ev*.i.dense]

CIVIL LITIGATION (PRETRIAL)
proceeding
[pro.*seed*.ing]

Prior to trial. "Pretrial" is applied to any aspect of litigation that occurs before the trial begins. USAGE: "pretrial proceedings"; "pretrial motions"; "pretrial conference."

An order of court directing a party to appear before the court and to present facts and legal arguments showing cause why the court should not take a certain action adversely affecting that party's interests. Orders to show cause are often granted ex parte (by one side, without notice to the other party). A party's failure to appear, or having appeared, his failure to show cause, will result in a final judgment unfavorable to him.

A conference held between the judge and counsel for all parties prior to trial, for the purpose of facilitating disposition of the case by, among other actions, simplifying the pleadings, narrowing the issues, obtaining stipulations to avoid unnecessary proof, and limiting the number of witnesses. Often leads to resolution or settlement of case.

During the discovery process, a party might request permission to enter upon the land of another. EXAMPLE: For a "slip and fall" case, the plaintiff's attorney would want to enter on the land of another to see the scene of the accident.

Motions that may be filed prior to the commencement of a trial. EXAMPLES: a motion to suppress; a motion to dismiss.

1. A formal request in writing, addressed to a person or body in a position of authority (EXAMPLES: a city council; an administrative agency), signed by a number of persons or by one person. 2. The name given in some jurisdictions to a complaint or other pleading that alleges a cause of action. 3. An application made to a court ex parte.

- *n.* appeal, request, plea, motion, application
- *v.* plead, seek, solicit, ask, urge, entreat, apply for ("We petitioned the court for mercy.")

An original or firsthand document or reliable works that are generally created at the time the event occurred. These are considered binding authority, or the law itself, as opposed to secondhand information or interpretation or analysis of information. One of the goals of legal research is to find primary sources.

A person who brings a lawsuit.

- *n.* complainant, accuser, suitor, petitioner, opponent, litigant

The means or method by which a court adjudicates cases (EXAMPLES: the Federal Rules of Civil Procedure; the Federal Rules of Criminal Procedure; rules of court), as distinguished from the substantive law by which it determines legal rights.

- *n.* process, system, method, policy, routine, action, operation ("Federal Rules of Civil Procedure")

Formal statements by the parties to an action setting forth their claims or defenses. EXAMPLES of pleadings include: a complaint; a cross-complaint; an answer; a counterclaim. The various kinds of pleadings, and the rules governing them, are set forth in detail in the Federal Rules of Civil Procedure and, with respect to pleading in state courts, by the rules of civil procedure of several states. *See also* amendment of pleading.

1. In one sense, every procedural aspect of a lawsuit, from beginning to end, including all means or process by which a party is able to cause a court to act; a suit; an action. 2. In another sense, any procedural aspect of a lawsuit undertaken to enforce rights or achieve redress. EXAMPLE: a hearing on a motion. 3. A specific course of action.

- *n.* undertaking, course, happening ("The divorce proceeding took longer than I thought."); records, minutes, report, account, transactions ("The proceedings from GALA are kept in a file.")

The degree of proof required in most civil actions. It means that the greater weight and value of the credible evidence, taken as a whole, belongs to one side in a lawsuit rather than to the other side. In other words, the party whose evidence is more convincing has a "preponderance of the evidence" on its side and must, as a matter of law, prevail in the lawsuit because she has met her burden of proof. The expression "preponderance of the evidence" has nothing to do with the number of witnesses a party presents, only with the credibility and value of their testimony.

CIVIL LITIGATION (PRETRIAL)

quasi in rem action

[*kway*.zye in rem *ak*.shen]

CIVIL LITIGATION (PRETRIAL)

sanctions

[*sank*.shenz]

CIVIL LITIGATION (PRETRIAL)

remand

[ree.*mand*]

CIVIL LITIGATION (PRETRIAL)

secondary source

[*sek*.en.dare.ee sorse]

CIVIL LITIGATION (PRETRIAL)

reply

[re.*ply*]

CIVIL LITIGATION (PRETRIAL)

service

[*ser*.viss]

CIVIL LITIGATION (PRETRIAL)

request for admission

[re.*kwest* for ad.*mish*.shen]

CIVIL LITIGATION (PRETRIAL)

service by mail

[*ser*.viss by mail]

CIVIL LITIGATION (PRETRIAL)

request for physical or mental examination

[re.*kwest* for *fiz*.i.kel or *men*.tel eg.zam.i.*nay*.shen]

CIVIL LITIGATION (PRETRIAL)

service by publication

[ser.*viss* by pub.li.*kay*.shen]

CIVIL LITIGATION (PRETRIAL)

request for production

[re.*kwest* for pro.*duk*.shen]

CIVIL LITIGATION (PRETRIAL)

service of process

[ser.*viss* ov *pross*.ess]

An action taken by a tribunal, for EXAMPLE, a court or administrative board, to enforce its judgment, decision, or order. EXAMPLES of sanctions are fines or a penalty, or even the suspension or revocation of a license.

An action that adjudicates only the rights of the parties with respect to property, not the rights of all persons who might have an interest in the property. *See also and compare* in personam action; in rem action.

As opposed to case law, which is binding authority, a secondary source is merely persuasive authority, it is not law itself, but simply commentary upon or a summary of the law. EXAMPLES of secondary sources are legal treatises, law review articles, legal encyclopedias, and dictionaries.

n. The return of a case by an appellate court to the trial court for further hearing or proceedings for a new trial, or for entry of judgment in accordance with the order of the appellate court.
v. To return or send back.

The delivering of process; short for service of process.

- *n.* notice, notification ("service by mail" or "service by posting")

1. In pleading, the plaintiff's response to the defendant's setoff or counterclaim. 2. A response; an answer.

- *n.* rejoinder, replication, retort, refutation, retaliation, response, answer
- *v.* answer, counter, acknowledge, return

In circumstances where permitted by statute, service of process occurs by mailing a copy of a summons, writ, complaint, or other process to the party to be served at his last known address or by mailing it to his attorney.

Written statements concerning a case, directed to an adverse party, that must be admitted or denied. All will be treated by the court as having been established and need not be proven at trial.

In circumstances where permitted by statute, service of process occurs by publishing a copy of a summons, writ, complaint, or other process in a newspaper of general circulation in a particular region.

Demands that can be made during the discovery process. The physical examination or inspection of a party is only requested when the person is claiming bodily harm or hurt (known as personal injury) and has put her physical condition at issue, typically from a car accident or slip and fall. A request for a mental examination is much less common. Again, only where a party has put her mental condition at issue, with a claim of brain damage, distress, fright, or emotional disturbance, can such a request be made. Because of privacy concerns, there are many restrictions on these forms of discovery depending on the jurisdiction.

Delivery of a summons, writ, complaint, or other process to the opposite party, or other person entitled to receive it, in such manner as the law prescribes, whether by leaving a copy at her residence, by mailing a copy to her or her attorney, or by publication.

During the discovery process either party may request that the other side make available for inspection relevant documents or things related to the case that are in its possession. A party is neither required to create or obtain documents it doesn't have in its possession.

CIVIL LITIGATION (PRETRIAL)

statutes of limitations

[*stat*.shootz ov lim.i.*tay*.shenz]

CIVIL LITIGATION (PRETRIAL)

third-party complaint

[third-*par*.tee kum.*plaint*]

CIVIL LITIGATION (PRETRIAL)

subject matter jurisdiction

[*sub*.jekt *mat*.er joo.ris.*dik*.shen]

CIVIL LITIGATION (PRETRIAL)

trial court

[*try*.el kort]

CIVIL LITIGATION (PRETRIAL)

subpoena

[sub.*peen*.ah]

CIVIL LITIGATION (PRETRIAL)

venue

[*ven*.yoo]

CIVIL LITIGATION (PRETRIAL)

subpoena duces tecum

[sub.*peen*.ah *doo*.ses *tee*.kum]

CIVIL LITIGATION (PRETRIAL)

verification

[vehr.i.fi.*kay*.shen]

CIVIL LITIGATION (PRETRIAL)

substantive law

[*sub*.sten.tiv law]

CIVIL LITIGATION (PRETRIAL)

verified

[*vehr*.i.fide]

CIVIL LITIGATION (PRETRIAL)

summons

[*sum*.enz]

CIVIL LITIGATION (PRETRIAL)

verify

[*vehr*.i.fy]

A complaint filed by the defendant in a lawsuit against a third person whom he seeks to bring into the action because of that person's alleged liability to the defendant.

Federal and state statutes prescribing the maximum period of time during which various types of civil actions and criminal prosecutions can be brought after the occurrence of the injury or the offense.

A court that hears and determines a case initially, as opposed to an appellate court; a court of general jurisdiction.

The jurisdiction of a court to hear and determine the type of case before it. EXAMPLE: the jurisdiction of a family court to try cases involving matters of family law.

The county or judicial district in which a case should be tried. In civil cases, venue may be based on where the events giving rise to the cause of action took place or where the parties live or work. Venue is distinguishable from jurisdiction because it is an issue only if jurisdiction already exists and because, unlike jurisdiction, it can be waived or changed by consent of the parties.

- *n.* county, district, zone, area, neighborhood, place of jurisdiction

A command in the form of written process requiring a witness to come to court to testify; short for subpoena ad testificandum [ahd *tes. te.fe.kan*.dem]. The Latin term means "testify under penalty."

A sworn statement certifying the truth of the facts recited in an instrument or document. Thus, for EXAMPLE, a verified complaint is a pleading accompanied by an affidavit stating that the facts set forth in the complaint are true.

- *n.* confirmation, proof, evidence, corroboration

The Latin term duces tecum means "bring with you under penalty." A subpoena duces tecum is a written command requiring a witness to come to court to testify, and at that time to produce for use as evidence the papers, documents, books, or records listed in the subpoena. Depending on the jurisdiction and the documents requested, court approval may be needed for a subpoena. Other subpoenas can be served with an attorney's signature rather than a judge's approval.

Sworn; sworn to; stated under oath.

- *adj.* sworn, sworn to, authenticated

Area of the law that defines rights and responsibilities, law, and facts, as opposed to procedural law, which governs the process by which rights are adjudicated.

---

1. To certify the accuracy or truth of a statement under oath; to make a verification. 2. To establish the accuracy or truth of anything, whether or not by oath.

- *v.* attest, authenticate, confirm, debunk, document, justify, establish, certify; swear, declare, state, avow

In a civil case, the process by which an action is commenced and the defendant is brought within the jurisdiction of the court.

- *n.* citation, mandate, process, notification, command, direction

CIVIL LITIGATION (TRIAL AND APPEAL)

adjudication

[a.joo.di.*kay*.shen]

CIVIL LITIGATION (TRIAL AND APPEAL)

amicus curiae

[a.*mee*.kes *koo*.ree.eye]

CIVIL LITIGATION (TRIAL AND APPEAL)

admissible evidence

[ad.*mis*.ibl *ev*.i.dense]

CIVIL LITIGATION (TRIAL AND APPEAL)

appeal

[a.*peel*]

CIVIL LITIGATION (TRIAL AND APPEAL)

admission

[ad.*mish*.en]

CIVIL LITIGATION (TRIAL AND APPEAL)

appeal bond

[a.*peel* bond]

CIVIL LITIGATION (TRIAL AND APPEAL)

affirm

[a.*ferm*]

CIVIL LITIGATION (TRIAL AND APPEAL)

appellant

[a.*pel*.ent]

CIVIL LITIGATION (TRIAL AND APPEAL)

alternative dispute resolution

[all.*ter*.ne.tiv dis.*pyoot* res.e.*loo*.shen]

CIVIL LITIGATION (TRIAL AND APPEAL)

appellate court

[a.*pel*.et kort]

CIVIL LITIGATION (TRIAL AND APPEAL)

alternative pleading

[all.*ter*.ne.tiv *plee*.ding]

CIVIL LITIGATION (TRIAL AND APPEAL)

appellate jurisdiction

[a.*pel*.et joo.ris.*dik*.shen]

(*Latin*) "Friend of the court." A person who is interested in the outcome of the case, but who is not a party, whom the court permits to file a brief for the purpose of providing the court with a position or a point of view that it might not otherwise have. An amicus curiae is often referred to simply as an amicus.

The final decision of a court, usually made after trial of the case; the court's final judgment.

- *n.* decision, ruling, holding, disposition, pronouncement, verdict, judgment

---

1. The process by which a higher court is requested by a party to a lawsuit to review the decision of a lower court. Such reconsideration is normally confined to a review of the record from the lower court, with no new testimony taken or new issues raised. Review by a higher court may result in affirmance, reversal, modification, or remand of the lower court's decision. 2. The process by which a court or a higher-level administrative body is asked to review the action of an administrative agency. *See also* cross-appeal.

- *n.* petition, review, reexamination ("his appeal to a higher court")

Evidence that a court may admit under the rules of evidence and consider in a case before it.

Security furnished by the party appealing a case to guarantee that the appeal is bona fide and made in good faith.

---

1. A statement of a party to an action that is inconsistent with his claim or position in the lawsuit and which therefore constitutes proof against him. 2. A voluntary statement that something asserted to be true is true. EXAMPLE: the admission of testimony in a trial.

- *n.* confession, acknowledgment, affirmation, declaration, disclosure ("his admission of guilt"); admittance, access, passage ("admission to the bar")

A party who appeals from the lower court to a higher court.

- *n.* appealer, litigant, petitioner, party

In the case of an appellate court, to uphold the decision or judgment of the lower court after an appeal. *Compare* disaffirm.

- *v.* 1. uphold, validate, confirm, ratify ("The decision was affirmed."); declare, assert, maintain, allege ("He affirmed his innocence.") 2. To state formally instead of making a statement under oath; to make an affirmation, a substitute for a sworn statement. This can be used by a person whose religious or other beliefs will not permit him to swear.

A higher court to which the appeal is taken from a lower court.

A term for speedier and less-costly methods for resolving disputes than going to court. EXAMPLES: arbitration; conciliation; mediation; mini-trial; rent-a-judge; summary jury trial. Also known as ADR.

The authority of one court to review the proceedings of another court or of an administrative agency. USAGE: "In our system, the Supreme Court of the United States has ultimate appellate jurisdiction."

A form of pleading in which the pleader alleges facts that may be inconsistent with each other and contradictory. Such pleading is permissible in most jurisdictions as long as the inconsistent statements, standing alone, are sufficient grounds for a lawsuit.

CIVIL LITIGATION (TRIAL AND APPEAL)

appellate review

[a.*pel*.et re.*vyoo*]

CIVIL LITIGATION (TRIAL AND APPEAL)

bench trial

[bench *try*.el]

CIVIL LITIGATION (TRIAL AND APPEAL)

appellee

[a.pel.*ee*]

CIVIL LITIGATION (TRIAL AND APPEAL)

bifurcated trial

[*by*.fer.kay.ted *try*.el]

CIVIL LITIGATION (TRIAL AND APPEAL)

arbitration

[ar.bi.*tray*.shen]

CIVIL LITIGATION (TRIAL AND APPEAL)

brief

[breef]

CIVIL LITIGATION (TRIAL AND APPEAL)

award

[a.*ward*]

CIVIL LITIGATION (TRIAL AND APPEAL)

bringing suit

[*bring*.ing sut]

CIVIL LITIGATION (TRIAL AND APPEAL)

bar

[bar]

CIVIL LITIGATION (TRIAL AND APPEAL)

burden of proof

[*bir*.den ov pruf]

CIVIL LITIGATION (TRIAL AND APPEAL)

below

[be.*loh*]

CIVIL LITIGATION (TRIAL AND APPEAL)

calendar

[*kal*.en.der]

A trial before a judge without a jury; a nonjury trial.

Review of facts by an appellate court of a case appealed to it from a lower court.

A trial that is divided into two parts to provide separate hearings for different aspects of the same matter, for EXAMPLE, guilt and punishment, guilt and sanity, or liability and damages. Bifurcated trials avoid the time and expense of proving damages at trial where liability is not established.

A party against whom a case is appealed from a lower court to a higher court.

- *n.* respondent, defendant

1. A written statement submitted to a court for the purpose of persuading it of the correctness of one's position. A brief argues the facts of the case and the applicable law, supported by citations of authority. 2. A text that an attorney prepares to guide her in the trial of a case. Called a trial brief, it can include lists of questions to be asked of various witnesses, points to be covered, and arguments to be made. 3. An outline of the published opinion in a case, made by an attorney or a paralegal for the purpose of understanding the case.

- *n.* legal argument; summary, abstract, digest, outline, synopsis, review, abridgement, restatement

A method of settling disputes by submitting a disagreement to a person (an arbitrator) or a group of individuals (an arbitration panel) for decision instead of going to court. If the parties are required to comply with the decision of the arbitrator, the process is called binding arbitration; if there is no such obligation, the arbitration is referred to as nonbinding arbitration. Compulsory arbitration, arbitration required by law, most notably occurs in labor disputes. *See also* alternative dispute resolution. *Compare* conciliation; mediation.

Beginning a lawsuit by filing papers that will result in the court's issuing process compelling the defendant to appear in court.

1. The decision, decree, or judgment of an arbitrator or administrative law judge. 2. A jury's determination with respect to damages. 3. A court's order for the payment of damages or costs.

- *v.* To confer, grant, or give

The duty of establishing the truth of a matter; the duty of proving a fact that is in dispute. In most instances the burden of proof, like the burden of going forward, shifts from one side to the other during the course of a trial as the case progresses and evidence is introduced by each side. *See also* prima facie case.

1. The attorneys permitted to practice before a particular court, taken collectively. 2. The court itself, when one speaks of the "case at bar" or the "bar of justice."

- *v.* To prevent. EXAMPLE: The case was barred by the statute of limitations.

A list of cases ready for the court to dispose of, whether by trial or otherwise; a court calendar. A court calendar is also referred to as a docket. *See also* trial calendar.

- *n.* diary, journal, register, schedule, lineup, program, chronology

1. The court below; a lower court. USAGE: "The appeals court may not uphold the judgment of the court below." 2. In a position of lower rank; inferior.

- *adv.* beneath, down, underneath

CIVIL LITIGATION (TRIAL AND APPEAL)

calendar call

[*kal*.en.der kol]

CIVIL LITIGATION (TRIAL AND APPEAL)

court

[kort]

CIVIL LITIGATION (TRIAL AND APPEAL)

certification of record on appeal

[ser.tif.i.*kay*.shen ov *rek*.erd on a.*peel*]

CIVIL LITIGATION (TRIAL AND APPEAL)

court below

[kort be.*loh*]

CIVIL LITIGATION (TRIAL AND APPEAL)

certiorari

[ser.sho.*rare*.ee]

CIVIL LITIGATION (TRIAL AND APPEAL)

court costs

[kort kostz]

CIVIL LITIGATION (TRIAL AND APPEAL)

challenge for cause

[*chal*.enj for koz]

CIVIL LITIGATION (TRIAL AND APPEAL)

court fees

[kort feez]

CIVIL LITIGATION (TRIAL AND APPEAL)

conciliation

[kon.sil.ee.*ay*.shen]

CIVIL LITIGATION (TRIAL AND APPEAL)

court of appeals

[kort ov a.*peelz*]

CIVIL LITIGATION (TRIAL AND APPEAL)

confession of judgment

[ken.*fesh*.en ov *juj*.ment]

CIVIL LITIGATION (TRIAL AND APPEAL)

Court of Appeals of the United States

[kort ov a.*peelz* ov the yoo.*ny*.ted states]

1. A part of government, consisting of a judge or judges, and, usually, administrative support personnel, whose duty it is to administer justice; the judicial branch of government. 2. A place where justice is judicially administered. 3. All judges of the same jurisdiction. For EXAMPLE, all persons who sit as judges of the United States District Court for the Southern District of Texas, taken collectively, constitute "the court" for that judicial district. *Note* that in many instances the words "court" and "judge" are used interchangeably and, in context, have the same meaning.

- *n.* unit of government, forum, chamber, panel, bench, bar, justice, judge, session

---

The reading aloud of the calendar in court, to determine whether the cases listed are ready for trial or to set trial dates.

A term used by an appellate court, or by attorneys appearing before an appellate court, to refer to the trial court.

The trial judge's signed acknowledgment of the questions to be decided on appeal. *See also* appeal.

---

1. Court fees. 2. The expenses involved in litigating an action (EXAMPLES: witness fees; filing fees, the cost of a transcript), including court fees but excluding attorney fees.

(*Latin*) "To be informed." A writ (written order) issued by a higher court to a lower court requiring the certification of the record in a particular case so that the higher court can review the record and correct any actions taken in the case that are not in accordance with the law. The Supreme Court of the United States uses the writ of certiorari to select the state court cases it is willing to review. *See also* certification of record on appeal.

The charges for the services of a public officer, particularly the clerk of court, rendered in connection with litigation. These are fixed by law. EXAMPLES: the fee for a certified copy of a document; filing fees.

An objection, for bias, prejudice, or other stated reason, to a juror being allowed to hear a case. *Compare* peremptory challenge.

Often abbreviated as CA, C.A., or Ct. App. 1. A Court of Appeals. 2. The intermediate appellate court in most states, although it is the highest appellate court in some, including New York. 3. A court in which appeals from a lower court are heard.

The voluntary resolution of a dispute in an amicable manner. One of the primary uses of conciliators, also called mediators, is in settling labor disputes. Professional conciliators are available for that purpose through the Federal Mediation and Conciliation Service. Conciliation differs from arbitration in that a conciliator, unlike an arbitrator, does not render a decision. *See also* alternative dispute resolution; mediation.

The intermediate appellate court in the federal court system, which is divided into 12 geographical circuits (each designated the United States Court of Appeals for that circuit), plus the United States Court of Appeals for the Federal Circuit, which hears appeals in patent, copyright, and customs cases, as well as some appeals from lower courts.

The entry of a judgment upon the admission and at the direction of the debtor, without the formality, time, or effort involved in bringing a lawsuit.

CIVIL LITIGATION (TRIAL AND APPEAL)

court of record

[kort ov *rek*.erd]

CIVIL LITIGATION (TRIAL AND APPEAL)

defendant in error

[de.*fen*.dent in *err*.er]

CIVIL LITIGATION (TRIAL AND APPEAL)

court order

[kort *or*.der]

CIVIL LITIGATION (TRIAL AND APPEAL)

dicta

[*dik*.ta]

CIVIL LITIGATION (TRIAL AND APPEAL)

court reporter

[kort re.*port*.er]

CIVIL LITIGATION (TRIAL AND APPEAL)

direct examination

[de.*rekt* eg.zam.in.*ay*.shen]

CIVIL LITIGATION (TRIAL AND APPEAL)

court reports

[kort re.*ports*]

CIVIL LITIGATION (TRIAL AND APPEAL)

directed verdict

[de.*rek*.ted *ver*.dikt]

CIVIL LITIGATION (TRIAL AND APPEAL)

cross-appeal

[kros-a.*peel*]

CIVIL LITIGATION (TRIAL AND APPEAL)

dismissal

[dis.*miss*.el]

CIVIL LITIGATION (TRIAL AND APPEAL)

cross-examination

[kross-eg.zam.in.*ay*.shen]

CIVIL LITIGATION (TRIAL AND APPEAL)

docket

[*dok*.et]

The party against whom an appeal is taken to a higher court; an appellee.

Generally, another term for trial court.

Plural of dictum, which is short for the Latin term obiter dictum. Dicta are expressions or comments in a court opinion that are not necessary to support the decision made by the court; they are not binding authority and have no value as precedent. If nothing else can be found on point, an advocate may wish to attempt to persuade by citing cases that contain dicta.

1. An adjudication by a court. 2. A ruling by a court with respect to a motion or any other question before it for determination during the course of a proceeding.

The first or initial questioning of a witness by the party who called her to the stand. *Compare* cross-examination.

A person who stenographically (*see also* steno-graphic notes) or by "voice writing" records court proceedings, from which, when necessary, he prepares a transcript that becomes a part of the record in the case.

A verdict that a jury returns as directed by the judge. A judge directs a verdict when the party who has the burden of proof has failed to meet that burden. A motion for directed verdict is the procedural means by which a litigant requests the court to direct a verdict.

Official, published reports of cases decided by courts, filing the opinions rendered in the case, with headnotes prepared by the publisher.

An order for the termination of a civil action without a trial of its issues, or without further trial. Whether a dismissal is a final judgment against the plaintiff depends upon whether it is a dismissal with preju-dice or a dismissal without prejudice.
- *n.* termination, discharge

An appeal filed by the appellee from the same judgment, or some portion of the same judg-ment, as the appellant has appealed from. A cross-appeal is generally made as part of the review proceedings set in motion by the origi-nal appeal.

1. A list of cases for trial or other disposition; a court calendar. 2. A list of cases and a summary of what occurred in these cases, although not a record in the sense of a transcript.
- *v.* To make an entry in a docket

The interrogation of a witness for the oppos-ing party with questions designed to test the accuracy and truthfulness of the testimony the witness gave on direct examination.

CIVIL LITIGATION (TRIAL AND APPEAL)

execution of judgment

[ek.se.*kyoo*.shen ov *juj*.ment]

CIVIL LITIGATION (TRIAL AND APPEAL)

hung jury

[hung *joo*.ree]

CIVIL LITIGATION (TRIAL AND APPEAL)

exhibit

[eg.*zib*.it]

CIVIL LITIGATION (TRIAL AND APPEAL)

impanel

[im.*pan*.el]

CIVIL LITIGATION (TRIAL AND APPEAL)

expert witness

[*eks*.pert *wit*.nes]

CIVIL LITIGATION (TRIAL AND APPEAL)

impartial juror

[im.*par*.shel *joo*.rer]

CIVIL LITIGATION (TRIAL AND APPEAL)

fact finder

[fakt *fine*.der]

CIVIL LITIGATION (TRIAL AND APPEAL)

judgment

[*juj*.ment]

CIVIL LITIGATION (TRIAL AND APPEAL)

high court

[hy kort]

CIVIL LITIGATION (TRIAL AND APPEAL)

judgment notwithstanding the verdict

[*juj*.ment not.with.*stan*.ding the *ver*.dikt]

CIVIL LITIGATION (TRIAL AND APPEAL)

highest court

[*hy*.est kort]

CIVIL LITIGATION (TRIAL AND APPEAL)

judgment NOV

[*juj*.ment en.oh.vee]

A jury that cannot reach a unanimous verdict.

A writ or process for the enforcement of a judgment. A judgment is usually enforced by a sheriff seizing and selling property to satisfy the judgment.

To enroll; to list. The act of the clerk of the court in listing the names of persons who have been selected for jury duty. *See also* jury panel.

- *v.* list, enroll, enter, schedule, docket

1. Any paper or thing offered in evidence and marked for identification. 2. A document attached to and made a part of a pleading, transcript, contract, or other legal paper.

A juror who will render a verdict solely on the basis of the evidence.

A person who is so qualified, either by actual experience or by careful study, as to enable him to form a definite opinion of his own regarding a subject about which persons having no particular training, experience, or special study are incapable of forming accurate opinions.

In a civil action, the final determination by a court of the rights of the parties, based upon the pleadings and the evidence; a decision. *See also* confession of judgment.

A judge, jury, person, board, or body appointed by business, government, or by court, that is empowered to make findings of fact and conclusion with respect to disputed facts. The finding of fact is reasoned or inferred from the evidence.

Also referred to as a judgment NOV, a judgment rendered by the court in favor of a party, notwithstanding the fact that the jury has returned a verdict against that party.

An informal way of referring to the Supreme Court of the United States or the highest court in a state judicial system. *See also* highest court.

Short for judgment non obstante verdicto (judgment notwithstanding the verdict).

The highest court of a state; the Supreme Court of the United States; a court whose decisions are not subject to review by a higher court.

CIVIL LITIGATION (TRIAL AND APPEAL)

judgment on the merits

[*juj*.ment on the *mehr*.its]

CIVIL LITIGATION (TRIAL AND APPEAL)

jury panel

[*joor*.ee *pan*.el]

CIVIL LITIGATION (TRIAL AND APPEAL)

judgment on the pleadings

[*juj*.ment on the *plee*.dingz]

CIVIL LITIGATION (TRIAL AND APPEAL)

jury trial

[*joor*.ee *try*.el]

CIVIL LITIGATION (TRIAL AND APPEAL)

juror

[*joor*.er]

CIVIL LITIGATION (TRIAL AND APPEAL)

leading question

[*lee*.ding *kwes*.chen]

CIVIL LITIGATION (TRIAL AND APPEAL)

jury

[*joor*.ee]

CIVIL LITIGATION (TRIAL AND APPEAL)

mediation

[mee.dee.*ay*.shen]

CIVIL LITIGATION (TRIAL AND APPEAL)

jury challenge

[*joor*.ee *chal*.enj]

CIVIL LITIGATION (TRIAL AND APPEAL)

mistrial

[*mis*.try.el]

CIVIL LITIGATION (TRIAL AND APPEAL)

jury instructions

[*joor*.ee in.*struk*.shenz]

CIVIL LITIGATION (TRIAL AND APPEAL)

notice of appeal

[*noh*.tess ov a.*peel*]

1. The jury list. 2. The jury impaneled for the trial of a particular case. *See also* impanel.

A judgment based on the substantive rights of the parties, as distinguished from a judgment based on procedural points.

A trial in which the jurors are the judges of the facts and the court is the judge of the law. Trial by jury is guaranteed in all criminal cases by the Sixth Amendment, and in many civil cases by the Seventh Amendment. *Compare* bench trial.

A judgment rendered in favor of the defendant when the plaintiff's complaint fails to state a cause of action, or in favor of the plaintiff when the defendant's answer fails to state a legally sufficient defense.

A question put to a witness that suggests the answer the questioner desires. (EXAMPLE: "You did as you were told, didn't you?") Leading questions are generally not allowed on direct examination, but are permitted on cross-examination.

A person on a jury.

- *n.* factfinder, trier of fact, appraiser, arbiter

The voluntary resolution of a dispute in an amicable manner. One of the primary uses of mediators, also called conciliators, is in settling labor disputes. Professional mediators are available for that purpose through the Federal Mediation and Conciliation Service. Mediation differs from arbitration in that a mediator, unlike an arbitrator, does not render a decision. *See also* alternative dispute resolution; conciliation.

A group of women and men selected according to law to determine the truth. Juries are used in various types of legal proceedings, both civil and criminal. *See also* hung jury, petit jury, polling the jury.

- *n.* factfinder, trier of fact, reviewers, panel, venire, array, arbiters

---

A trial that has been terminated by the judge prior to its conclusion because the jury is unable to reach a verdict (*see also* hung jury), because of prejudicial error that cannot be corrected or eliminated by any action the court might take (EXAMPLE: the plaintiff's use of racial slurs), or because of the occurrence of some event that would make it pointless to continue (EXAMPLE: the death of a juror). A mistrial is the equivalent of no trial having been held.

See challenge for cause; peremptory challenge.

The process by which appellate review is initiated; specifically, written notice to the appellee advising her of the appellant's intention to appeal.

Directions given to the jury by the judge just before she sends the jurors out to deliberate and return a verdict, explaining the law that applies in the case and spelling out what must be proven and by whom.

CIVIL LITIGATION (TRIAL AND APPEAL)

oath

[ohth]

CIVIL LITIGATION (TRIAL AND APPEAL)

polling the jury

[*pole*.ing the *joo*.ree]

CIVIL LITIGATION (TRIAL AND APPEAL)

oral argument

[*ohr*.el *ar*.gyoo.ment]

CIVIL LITIGATION (TRIAL AND APPEAL)

preliminary injunction

[pre.*lim*.i.ner.ee in.*junk*.shen]

CIVIL LITIGATION (TRIAL AND APPEAL)

out-of-court settlement

[out-ov-kort *setl*.ment]

CIVIL LITIGATION (TRIAL AND APPEAL)

prima facie case

[*pry*.muh *fay*.shee case]

CIVIL LITIGATION (TRIAL AND APPEAL)

peremptory challenge

[per.*emp*.ter.ee *chal*.enj]

CIVIL LITIGATION (TRIAL AND APPEAL)

rebuttal

[re.*but*.el]

CIVIL LITIGATION (TRIAL AND APPEAL)

perfecting an appeal

[per.*fek*.ting an a.*peel*]

CIVIL LITIGATION (TRIAL AND APPEAL)

record on appeal

[*rek*.erd on a.*peel*]

CIVIL LITIGATION (TRIAL AND APPEAL)

petit jury

[*pet*.ee *joo*.ree]

CIVIL LITIGATION (TRIAL AND APPEAL)

reversal

[re.*ver*.sel]

Individually examining the jurors who participated in a verdict to ascertain whether they unanimously support the verdict.

1. A calling on God to witness what one avers is true. 2. Any form of attestation incorporating an appeal to a sacred or revered being by which a person signifies that he is bound in conscience to perform an act or speak faithfully and truthfully. In most jurisdictions, the question "Do you swear to tell the truth?" has been replaced by "Do you swear or affirm?" In other jurisdictions, the term "oath" has been construed to include affirmation. *See* affirm.

An injunction granted prior to a full hearing on the merits. Its purpose is to preserve the status quo until the final hearing. A preliminary injunction is also referred to as a provisional injunction or temporary injunction, where a permanent injunction is granted after a final hearing on the merits. *See also* temporary restraining order.

A party, through her attorney, usually presents her case to an appellate court on appeal by arguing the case verbally to the court, in addition to submitting a brief. Oral argument may also be made in support of a motion.

A cause of action or defense that is sufficiently established by a party's evidence to justify a verdict in her favor, provided the other party does not rebut that evidence; a case supported by sufficient evidence to justify its submission to the trier of fact and the rendition of a compatible verdict.

1. The ending of a controversy by agreement, before it gets to court. 2. The settlement of a lawsuit after the complaint has been served, and without obtaining or seeking judicial approval.

The stage in a trial or hearing at which a party introduces rebuttal evidence, presenting evidence that denies, refutes, or contradicts. It occurs after the opposite party has rested her case.

A challenge to a juror that a party may exercise without having to give a reason. *Compare* challenge for cause.

The papers a trial court transmits to the appellate court, on the basis of which the appellate court decides the appeal. The record on appeal includes the pleadings, all motions made before the trial court, the official transcript, and the judgment or order appealed from.

Completing all of the steps required by statute for obtaining appellate court review of a judgment.

1. The act of an appellate court in setting aside, annulling, or vacating a judgment or order of a lower court. 2. The act of turning a thing or person around, or being turned around.

The jury in a trial court.

CIVIL LITIGATION (TRIAL AND APPEAL)

reverse

[re.*verse*]

CIVIL LITIGATION (TRIAL AND APPEAL)

summary proceeding

[*sum*.e.ree pro.*seed*.ing]

CIVIL LITIGATION (TRIAL AND APPEAL)

settlement

[*set*.el.ment]

CIVIL LITIGATION (TRIAL AND APPEAL)

summary remedy

[*sum*.e.ree *rem*.e.dee]

CIVIL LITIGATION (TRIAL AND APPEAL)

subpoena

[sub.*peen*.ah]

CIVIL LITIGATION (TRIAL AND APPEAL)

temporary restraining order (TRO)

[*tem*.pe.rer.ee re.*strane*.ing *or*.der]

CIVIL LITIGATION (TRIAL AND APPEAL)

subpoena ad testificandum

[sub.*peen*.ah ad *tes*.te.fe.*kan*.dem]

CIVIL LITIGATION (TRIAL AND APPEAL)

transcript

[*tran*.skript]

CIVIL LITIGATION (TRIAL AND APPEAL)

subpoena duces tecum

[sub.*peen*.ah *doo*.ses *tee*.kum]

CIVIL LITIGATION (TRIAL AND APPEAL)

transcript of the record

[*tran*.skript ov the *rek*.erd]

CIVIL LITIGATION (TRIAL AND APPEAL)

summary jury trial (SJT)

[*sum*.e.ree *joor*.ee *try*.el]

CIVIL LITIGATION (TRIAL AND APPEAL)

trial

[*try*.el]

A proceeding in which a case is disposed of or a trial is conducted in a prompt and simple manner without a jury and without many of the ordinary requirements (such as complaint, summons, indictment, or information). EXAMPLES: a contempt proceeding; trial before a magistrate or a justice of the peace; trial in a small claims court.

Opposite; contrary.

- *v.* To turn around or in the opposite direction. If a judgment is found for the plaintiff, a reverse decision would find for the defendant.

In a civil action, a remedy obtainable in a summary proceeding.

The ending of a lawsuit by agreement. *See also* out-of-court settlement.

- *n.* resolution, termination ("to reach a settlement")

The court is empowered to grant injunctive relief to one party, without notice to the opposite party, if the result would cause "immediate and irreparable harm or loss."

---

n. A command in the form of written process requiring a witness to come to court to testify; short for subpoena ad testificandum.
v. To issue or serve a subpoena.

- *v.* order, command, summon, beckon, demand
- *n.* order, command, mandate, citation, summons, writ, call, directive

---

A hard copy of the court reporter's stenographic notes of a trial (i.e., a record of the proceedings).

(*Latin*) The term ad testificandum means "testify under penalty." A subpoena ad testificandum is a subpoena to testify. Often, the shortened term for this is used: subpoena. *Compare* subpoena duces tecum.

The complete record of a case as furnished to the appellate court when an appeal is taken.

(*Latin*) The term duces tecum means "bring with you under penalty." A subpoena duces tecum is a written command requiring a witness to come to court to testify and, at that time, to produce for use as evidence the papers, documents, books, or records listed in the subpoena.

A hearing or determination by a court of the issues existing between the parties to an action; an examination by a court of competent jurisdiction, according to the law of the land, of the facts or law at issue in either a civil case or a criminal prosecution, for the purpose of adjudicating the matters in controversy. *See also* bench trial; bifurcated trial; trial by jury; mistrial.

- *n.* citation, hearing, litigation, prosecution, suit ("trial by jury")

A court-ordered form of alternative dispute resolution sometimes used by the federal courts in complex cases that would otherwise require a lengthy jury trial. An SJT is a kind of nonbinding capsule trial that allows the parties to obtain the thoughts of jurors with respect to the merits of the case. The facts are presented in simplified form to a reduced jury, questions of admissibility of evidence are decided with the judge in advance, and counsel interviews the jurors after the verdict. Although the verdict is nonbinding, the parties may agree to be bound by it, or they may settle the case based upon the reactions of the jurors.

CIVIL LITIGATION (TRIAL AND APPEAL)

trial by jury

[*try*.el by *joor*.ee]

CIVIL LITIGATION (TRIAL AND APPEAL)

trial jury

[*try*.el *joor*.ee]

CIVIL LITIGATION (TRIAL AND APPEAL)

trial by the court

[*try*.el by the kort]

CIVIL LITIGATION (TRIAL AND APPEAL)

verdict

[*ver*.dikt]

CIVIL LITIGATION (TRIAL AND APPEAL)

trial calendar

[*try*.el *kal*.en.der]

CIVIL LITIGATION (TRIAL AND APPEAL)

**verdict against
the evidence**

[*ver*.dikt a.*genst* the *ev*.i.dense]

CIVIL LITIGATION (TRIAL AND APPEAL)

trial court

[*try*.el kort]

CIVIL LITIGATION (TRIAL AND APPEAL)

verdict contrary to law

[*ver*.dikt *kon*.trare.ee to law]

CIVIL LITIGATION (TRIAL AND APPEAL)

trial de novo

[*try*.el deh *noh*.voh]

CIVIL LITIGATION (TRIAL AND APPEAL)

voir dire examination

[vwa deer eg.zam.i.*nay*.shen]

CIVIL LITIGATION (TRIAL AND APPEAL)

trial judge

[*try*.el juj]

CIVIL LITIGATION (TRIAL AND APPEAL)

witness

[*wit*.nes]

A jury for the trial of a case, as distinguished from a grand jury.

A trial in which the jurors are the judges of the facts and the court is the judge of the law. Trial by jury is guaranteed in all criminal cases by the Sixth Amendment, and in most civil cases by the Seventh Amendment. *Compare* trial by the court. *Also compare* bench trial; *see also* jury trial.

The final decision of a jury concerning questions of fact submitted to it by the court for determination in the trial of a case. In a civil case, the jury may be required to return either a general verdict or a special verdict: making specific findings of fact in response to written questions. *See also* judgment notwithstanding the verdict.

- *n.* adjudication, arbitration, conclusion, decision, decree

---

A trial held before a judge sitting without a jury. A trial by the judge alone is also referred to as a judge trial, a bench trial, or a nonjury trial. *Compare* trial by jury.

A verdict that is contrary to the evidence, or to the weight of the evidence, or that is not supported by sufficient evidence.

A list of cases awaiting trial.

The verdict of a jury that has failed to follow the instructions of the judge with respect to matters of law. *See also* jury instructions.

A court that hears and determines a case initially, as opposed to an appellate court; a court of general jurisdiction.

Examination of a potential juror for the purpose of determining whether she is qualified and acceptable to act as a juror in the case. A prospective juror who a party decides is unqualified or unacceptable may be challenged for cause or may be the subject of a peremptory challenge. "Voir dire" is from old French meaning "to say the truth."

A new trial, a retrial, or a trial on appeal from a justice's court or a magistrate's court to a court of general jurisdiction. A trial de novo is a trial in which the matter is tried again as if it had not been heard before and as if no decision had previously been rendered.

---

1. A person who testifies or gives evidence before a court or at an administrative hearing with respect to something she has observed or of which she has knowledge. *See also* expert witness. 2. A person who is asked to be present at a transaction (for EXAMPLE, the signing of a contract) in order to attest that it took place.

- *v.* 1. To see or observe. 2. To attest; to act as an observer for the purpose of attesting

---

The judge who presides at the trial of a case.

CRIMINAL LAW AND PROCEDURE

accessory

[ak.*sess*.e.ree]

CRIMINAL LAW AND PROCEDURE

arraignment

[a.*rain*.ment]

CRIMINAL LAW AND PROCEDURE

accomplice

[a.*kom*.pliss]

CRIMINAL LAW AND PROCEDURE

arrest

[a.*rest*]

CRIMINAL LAW AND PROCEDURE

actus reus

[*ahk*.tus *ree*.us]

CRIMINAL LAW AND PROCEDURE

arson

[*ar*.sen]

CRIMINAL LAW AND PROCEDURE

affirmative defense

[a.*fer*.ma.tiv de.*fense*]

CRIMINAL LAW AND PROCEDURE

assault

[a.*salt*]

CRIMINAL LAW AND PROCEDURE

aiding and abetting

[*ay*.ding and a.*bet*.ing]

CRIMINAL LAW AND PROCEDURE

assault and battery

[a.*salt* and *bat*.er.ee]

CRIMINAL LAW AND PROCEDURE

alibi

[*al*.i.by]

CRIMINAL LAW AND PROCEDURE

attempt

[a.temt]

The act of bringing an accused before a court to answer a criminal charge made against him and calling upon him to enter a plea of guilty or not guilty. *Compare* preliminary hearing.

- *n.* accusation, incrimination, formal accusal, judicial charge

---

A person who is involved with the commission of a crime but who is not present at the time it is committed. *See also* aiding and abetting.

- *n.* accomplice, abettor, conspirator, collaborator, consort, assistant ("accessory after the fact"); supplement, attachment, addition, extension

---

1. Detention of a person on a criminal charge. 2. Any detention of a person, with or without the intent to take him into custody.

- *v.* apprehend, catch, capture, block, seize ("The thief was arrested."); stop, block, foil, obstruct, hinder
- *n.* apprehension, captivity, capture, confinement, detention, incarceration; stoppage, suspension, halt, cessation ("His arrest was of indefinite duration.")

A person who knowingly and voluntarily helps another person commit a crime; one who acts as an accessory. *See also* aiding and abetting.

The willful and malicious burning of a building. In some jurisdictions, arson includes the deliberate burning of any structure.

- *n.* pyromania, setting a fire, torching

(*Latin*) An "answerable act" (i.e., an act for which one is answerable); a guilty act. In combination with mens rea (a guilty or criminal intent), actus reus is an essential element of any crime. Thus, for EXAMPLE, the act of killing is the actus reus of murder.

An act of force or threat of force intended to inflict harm upon a person or to put the person in fear that such harm is imminent; an attempt to commit a battery. The perpetrator must have, or appear to have, the present ability to carry out the act.

- *v.* abuse, advance, assail, jump, set upon, bash, violate, storm ("The pedestrian assaulted the child.")
- *n.* attack, advance, strike, violation ("The assault was aggressive.")

A defense that amounts to more than simply a denial of the allegations in the plaintiff's complaint. It sets up new matter that, if proven, could result in judgment against the plaintiff even if all the allegations of the complaint are true. EXAMPLES include alibi, double jeopardy, insanity, and self-defense.

An achieved assault; an assault carried out by hitting or by other physical contact. *See also* battery.

Helping or encouraging a person to commit a crime.

An act done with the intent to commit a crime, which would have resulted in the crime being committed except that something happened to prevent it.

The defense that the accused was elsewhere at the time the crime was committed.

- *n.* defense, excuse, explanation, proof, avowal

CRIMINAL LAW AND PROCEDURE

bail

[bayul]

CRIMINAL LAW AND PROCEDURE

burglary

[*ber*.gler.ee]

CRIMINAL LAW AND PROCEDURE

battery

[*bat*.ter.ee]

CRIMINAL LAW AND PROCEDURE

capital crime

[*ka*.pi.tel krime]

CRIMINAL LAW AND PROCEDURE

behavioral health court

[bi.*hav*.yer.le helth kort]

CRIMINAL LAW AND PROCEDURE

capital punishment

[*ka*.pi.tel *pun*.ish.ment]

CRIMINAL LAW AND PROCEDURE

beyond a reasonable doubt

[be.*yond* a *ree*.zen.ebl dout]

CRIMINAL LAW AND PROCEDURE

commutation of sentence

[kom.yoo.*tay*.shun ov *sen*.tense]

CRIMINAL LAW AND PROCEDURE

bigamy

[*big*.e.mee]

CRIMINAL LAW AND PROCEDURE

consecutive sentences

[ken.*sek*.yoo.tiv *sen*.ten.sez]

CRIMINAL LAW AND PROCEDURE

bribery

[*bry*.be.ree]

CRIMINAL LAW AND PROCEDURE

conspiracy

[ken.*spi*.re.see]

At common law, the offense of breaking and entering a dwelling at night with the intent to commit a felony (EXAMPLES: theft; murder). The crime of burglary has been broadened by statute to include entering buildings other than dwellings, with or without a breaking, and regardless of the time of day or night.

- *v.* robbery, larceny, breaking and entering, housebreaking, looting, crime, forcible entry, raiding

---

1. The customary means of securing the release from custody of a person charged with a criminal offense, by assuring his appearance in court and compelling him to remain within the jurisdiction. 2. The security given for a defendant's appearance in court in the form of cash, real property, or a bail bond. 3. The person who is the surety on a bail bond.

- *v.* To secure the release from custody of a person charged with a crime, pending trial, by posting a bail bond
- *n.* bond, guarantee, security, warrant, collateral

A crime punishable by death.

The unconsented-to touching or striking of one person by another, or by an object put in motion by her, with the intention of doing harm or giving offense. Battery is both a crime and a tort. *Compare* assault. *See also* assault and battery.

- *n.* beating, mugging, flogging, hitting, assault, thrashing, injury ("commit a battery")

The death penalty as a punishment for crime.

A newer type of court designed to address the needs of the mentally ill, diverting them to treatment programs in the community, and finding creative and appropriate dispositions in order to avoid recidivism.

The substitution of a less-severe punishment for a harsher punishment.

The degree of proof required to convict a person of a crime. A reasonable doubt is a fair doubt based upon reason and common sense, not an arbitrary or possible doubt. To convict a criminal defendant, a jury must be persuaded of his guilt to a level beyond "apparently" or "probably." Proof beyond a reasonable doubt is the highest level of proof the law requires.

Sentences of imprisonment for crimes in which the time of each is to run one after the other without a break.

The crime of marrying while already married.

An agreement between two or more persons to engage in a criminal act or to accomplish a legal objective by criminal or unlawful means. Conspiracy is a criminal offense (a criminal conspiracy); it is also a wrong that is grounds for a civil action if damage is suffered.

- *n.* connivance, counterplot, frame, plot, scheme, trickery

---

The crime of giving something of value with the intention of influencing the action of a public official, witness, juror, etc.

- *n.* corruption, allurement, cajolery, connivance

CRIMINAL LAW AND PROCEDURE

crime

[kryme]

CRIMINAL LAW AND PROCEDURE

criminal charge

[*krim*.i.nel charj]

CRIMINAL LAW AND PROCEDURE

crime scene investigation

[*kryme* seen in.ves.ti.*gay*.shen]

CRIMINAL LAW AND PROCEDURE

criminal law

[*krim*.i.nel law]

CRIMINAL LAW AND PROCEDURE

criminal

[*krim*.i.nel]

CRIMINAL LAW AND PROCEDURE

criminal offense

[*krim*.i.nel o.*fense*]

CRIMINAL LAW AND PROCEDURE

criminal act

[*krim*.i.nel akt]

CRIMINAL LAW AND PROCEDURE

criminal procedure

[*krim*.i.nel pro.*see*.jer]

CRIMINAL LAW AND PROCEDURE

criminal action

[*krim*.i.nel *ak*.shen]

CRIMINAL LAW AND PROCEDURE

criminal prosecution

[*krim*.i.nel pross.e.*kyoo*.shen]

CRIMINAL LAW AND PROCEDURE

criminal capacity

[*krim*.i.nel ke.*pass*.i.tee]

CRIMINAL LAW AND PROCEDURE

criminal statute

[*krim*.i.nel *stat*.shoot]

An indictment, information, complaint, or other formal charge of the commission of a crime.

An offense against the authority of the state; a public wrong, as distinguished from a private wrong; an act in violation of the penal code; a felony or a misdemeanor. *See also* criminal statute.

- *n.* felony, misdemeanor, criminal act, misconduct, delinquency, corruption, offense, lawlessness

---

Branch of the law that specifies what conduct constitutes crime and establishes appropriate punishments for such conduct.

An inquiry in a criminal matter by law enforcement investigators for the discovery and collection of facts and evidence.

A crime.

adj. 1. Pertaining to crime or punishment. 2. Involving crime; guilty of crime.
n. A person who has been convicted of committing a crime.

- *n.* felon, culprit, violator, offender, delinquent, transgressor
- *adj.* unlawful, felonious, illegal, notorious, blameworthy, noncivil ("criminal intent")

The rules of procedure that govern criminal prosecutions.

Any act punishable as a crime.

The process of arresting, charging, trying, and sentencing a person for the commission of a crime. A criminal sentence generally involves the imposition of a fine, imprisonment, or death. A criminal prosecution is brought by the state, as opposed to a civil action, which is brought by a private party.

A criminal prosecution.

A statute that declares the conduct that it describes to be a crime, and establishes punishment for engaging in it.

A person can be guilty of a crime only if he has the capacity to appreciate the criminal nature of his act. In the eyes of the law, certain persons are conclusively presumed to lack criminal capacity. EXAMPLES: insane persons; persons who have not reached the age of reason, and persons not acting voluntarily.

CRIMINAL LAW AND PROCEDURE

critical stage

[*krit*.i.kel stayj]

CRIMINAL LAW AND PROCEDURE

double jeopardy

[*duh*.bull *jep*.er.dee]

CRIMINAL LAW AND PROCEDURE

cruel and unusual punishment

[*kroo*.el and un.*yoo*.zhoo.el *pun*.ish.ment]

CRIMINAL LAW AND PROCEDURE

embezzlement

[em.*bezl*.ment]

CRIMINAL LAW AND PROCEDURE

culpable

[*kulp*.abl]

CRIMINAL LAW AND PROCEDURE

entrapment

[en.*trap*.ment]

CRIMINAL LAW AND PROCEDURE

death penalty

[deth *pen*.el.tee]

CRIMINAL LAW AND PROCEDURE

exclusionary rule

[eks.*kloo*.zhen.air.ree rule]

CRIMINAL LAW AND PROCEDURE

defense

[de.*fense*]

CRIMINAL LAW AND PROCEDURE

exculpate

[*eks*.kul.pate]

CRIMINAL LAW AND PROCEDURE

degrees of crime

[di.*greez* ov kryme]

CRIMINAL LAW AND PROCEDURE

exculpatory

[eks.*kul*.pe.toh.ree]

A rule originating in the Fifth Amendment that prohibits a second punishment or trial for the same offense.

The point in a criminal proceeding at which a defendant's constitutional right to counsel is violated unless she has counsel or has been advised of her right to counsel.

The fraudulent conversion of property, including but not limited to money, with which a person (EXAMPLES: an employee; a bailee; a trustee) has been entrusted.

- *n.* abstraction, misappropriation, misuse, theft, larceny, pilferage

Forms of punishment for crime prohibited by the Eighth Amendment. The Supreme Court has determined that corporal punishment inflicted by the state is cruel within the meaning of the Constitution, but that capital punishment is not.

Inducing a person to commit a crime she is otherwise not inclined to commit, in order to bring a criminal prosecution against her. A defendant might assert this as an affirmative defense.

Blameworthy; blameable; responsible; at fault.

The rule of constitutional law that evidence secured by the police by means of an unreasonable search and seizure, in violation of the Fourth Amendment, cannot be used as evidence in a criminal prosecution.

Another term for capital punishment.

---

1. Absolve; exonerate; acquit. 2. Condone; excuse; forgive; pardon.

The facts submitted and the legal arguments offered by a defendant in support of his claim that the prosecution's case should be rejected. The term "defense" may apply to a defendant's entire case or to separate grounds, called affirmative defenses, offered by a defendant for rejecting all or part of the case against him.

Tending to free from blame or to acquit of a criminal charge. USAGE: "I think the defendant will be acquitted; virtually all of the evidence was exculpatory."

The grades of crime ranked according to seriousness. EXAMPLES: first degree murder; second degree murder.

CRIMINAL LAW AND PROCEDURE

excusable homicide

[eks.*kyoo*.zebl *hom*.i.side]

CRIMINAL LAW AND PROCEDURE

excuse

[eks.*kyooz*]

CRIMINAL LAW AND PROCEDURE

execute

[*ek*.se.kyoot]

CRIMINAL LAW AND PROCEDURE

extortion

[eks.*tor*.shen]

CRIMINAL LAW AND PROCEDURE

felony

[*fel*.a.nee]

CRIMINAL LAW AND PROCEDURE

felony murder rule

[*fel*.a.nee *mer*.der rule]

CRIMINAL LAW AND PROCEDURE

forensic

[fo.*ren*.sik]

CRIMINAL LAW AND PROCEDURE

forensic pathology

[fo.*ren*.sik path.*aw*.le.jee]

CRIMINAL LAW AND PROCEDURE

forgery

[*for*.jer.ee]

CRIMINAL LAW AND PROCEDURE

fruits of the poisonous tree doctrine

[frut ov the *poy*.zen.es tree dok.*trin]*

CRIMINAL LAW AND PROCEDURE

grand jury

[grand *joo*.ree]

CRIMINAL LAW AND PROCEDURE

homicide

[*hom*.i.side]

Pertaining to or belonging to the courts of justice.

A homicide committed in the course of performing a lawful act, without any intention to hurt (for EXAMPLE, by accident) or committed in self-defense.

Branch of medicine that pertains to the causes of disease and death.

A reason for being relieved of a duty or obligation.

- *v.* pardon, vindicate, exculpate, forbear; absolve, liberate

---

The false making, material alteration, or uttering, with intent to defraud or injure, of any writing that, if genuine, might appear to be legally effective or the basis for legal liability. Forgery is a crime.

- *n.* falsification, fraudulence, misrepresentation, manipulation

To put a person to death in accordance with a sentence of death. Usage: "The prisoner was scheduled to be executed at 9 a.m."

- *v.* eliminate, condemn, assassinate, liquidate, finish, kill, terminate, destroy

---

The constitutional law doctrine that evidence, including derivative evidence, obtained as the result of an illegal search is inadmissible. *See* exclusionary rule.

The criminal offense of obtaining money or other things of value by duress, force, threat of force, fear, or under color of office.

- *n.* coercion, intimidation, fraud, stealing, oppression ("the criminal extortion of funds")

A body whose number varies with the jurisdiction, never less than 6 nor more than 23, whose duty it is to determine whether probable cause exists to return indictments against persons accused of committing crimes. The right to indictment by grand jury is guaranteed by the Fifth Amendment.

A general term for more-serious crimes (EXAMPLES: murder; robbery; larceny), as distinguished from lesser offenses, which are known as misdemeanors. In many jurisdictions, felonies are crimes for which the punishment is death or more than one year of imprisonment. Persons convicted of felonies are generally incarcerated in prisons or penitentiaries, as opposed to local jails.

- *n.* gross offense, serious offense, transgression, wrongdoing, crime

---

The killing of a human being. Homicide may be noncriminal (excusable homicide or justifiable homicide) or criminal (felonious homicide). Excusable or justifiable homicide includes killing by accident or in self-defense. A felonious homicide is either murder or manslaughter. Manslaughter homicide includes negligent homicide and vehicular homicide.

- *n.* murder, manslaughter, slaying, assassination, killing, slaughter, felony, termination of life, extermination

The rule that a death that occurs by accident or chance during the course of the commission of a felony is first degree murder. (EXAMPLE: If, during the course of an armed robbery by robbers A and B, robber A accidentally shoots and kills the storeowner, robber B as well as robber A are both guilty of murder.) The felony murder rule, which is a common law doctrine, has been modified by statute in most states. *See also* murder.

CRIMINAL LAW AND PROCEDURE

identity theft

[eye.*den*.ti.tee theft]

CRIMINAL LAW AND PROCEDURE

incest

[*in*.sest]

CRIMINAL LAW AND PROCEDURE

inculaptory

[in.*kul*.pe.tor.ee]

CRIMINAL LAW AND PROCEDURE

indictment

[in.*dite*.ment]

CRIMINAL LAW AND PROCEDURE

information

[in.fer.*may*.shen]

CRIMINAL LAW AND PROCEDURE

insane

[in.*sane*]

CRIMINAL LAW AND PROCEDURE

insanity

[in.*san*.i.tee]

CRIMINAL LAW AND PROCEDURE

keylogger

[key.*log*.ger]

CRIMINAL LAW AND PROCEDURE

larceny

[*lar*.sen.ee]

CRIMINAL LAW AND PROCEDURE

lesser included offense

[*less*.er in.*kloo*.ded o.*fense*]

CRIMINAL LAW AND PROCEDURE

mala en se

[*mayl*.ah in *saye*]

CRIMINAL LAW AND PROCEDURE

mala prohibita

[*mayl*.ah pro.*hib*.i.tah]

A term for a condition of the mind, which has no medical or scientific meaning and whose legal meaning depends upon the context in which it is used. Insanity as a criminal defense: Different states use different tests or standards for determining whether a criminal defendant was insane (that is, whether she had the capacity to form criminal intent) at the time she committed the crime. The most important of these tests are the M'Naghten rule, irresistible impulse, and, most frequently used, the Model Penal Code's standard—lack of capacity "as a result of mental disease or defect" to appreciate the criminality of one's conduct or to conform one's conduct to the requirements of law. The law also requires that a criminal defendant be sane at the time of trial, and permits imposition of the death penalty only if the person convicted is sane at the time of execution.

The taking of another's personal data without his permission, usually by use of fraud or deception for personal gain. Congress enacted a new law in 1998 making identity theft a federal crime. Often, a person's personal information, such as his Social Security number, birthday, credit card numbers, telephone card numbers, and bank account numbers, are stolen and used to take funds out of his accounts, and the person committing such acts might even assume the victim's identity while carrying out other crimes, creating huge debt in his name and damaging his reputation.

A thief who deposits a virus on computers to record all keystrokes (passwords, credit, bank, and Social Security numbers, etc.) and sends them to a remote location for later retrieval for illegal purposes.

Sexual intercourse between persons so closely related that the law prohibits their marriage to each other.

The crime of taking personal property, without consent, with the intent to convert it to the use of someone other than the owner or to deprive the owner of it permanently. Larceny does not involve the use of force or the threat of force. *Compare* robbery. *Also compare* burglary.

- *n.* theft, embezzlement, burglary, pilferage, misappropriation, stealing

---

That which tends to incriminate. USAGE: "I think the defendant will be convicted because his own testimony was inculpatory." *Compare* exculpatory.

A criminal offense included within the crime for which a defendant has been indicted, and for which he may be convicted under the indictment so long as he is not convicted of the more serious offense; a crime that cannot be committed without at the same time committing one or more other crimes. EXAMPLE: It is impossible to commit first degree murder without also committing second degree murder, voluntary manslaughter, and battery.

---

1. A charge made in writing by a grand jury, based upon evidence presented to it, accusing a person of having committed a criminal act, generally a felony. It is the function of the prosecution to bring a case before the grand jury. If the grand jury indicts the defendant, a trial follows. 2. The formal, written accusation itself brought before the grand jury by the prosecutor. *Compare* information.

(*Latin*) Naturally evil or wicked; immoral; illegal from the very nature of the act on the basis of principles of natural, moral, or public law, independent of the fact that it is punished by the state. EXAMPLES: murder; robbery; incest.

---

1. An accusation of the commission of a crime, sworn to by a district attorney or other prosecutor, on the basis of which a criminal defendant is brought to trial for a misdemeanor and, in some states, for a felony. 2. In some jurisdictions that prosecute felonies only on the basis of indictment by a grand jury, an affidavit alleging probable cause to bind the defendant over to await action by the grand jury.

- *n.* charge, accusation, complaint, allegation ("felony information")

(*Latin*) A wrong that is wrong only because it is prohibited by law. EXAMPLE: driving on the left-hand side of the road. *Compare* mala in se.

Of unsound mind. *See also* insanity.

- *adj.* unsound, deranged, demented, absurd, bizarre, mad

CRIMINAL LAW AND PROCEDURE

malice

[*mal*.iss]

CRIMINAL LAW AND PROCEDURE

Model Penal Code

[*mod*.l *pee*.nel kode]

CRIMINAL LAW AND PROCEDURE

manslaughter

[*man*.slaw.ter]

CRIMINAL LAW AND PROCEDURE

motive

[*moh*.tiv]

CRIMINAL LAW AND PROCEDURE

mens rea

[menz *ray*.ah]

CRIMINAL LAW AND PROCEDURE

murder

[*mer*.der]

CRIMINAL LAW AND PROCEDURE

Miranda rule

[mi.*ran*.da rule]

CRIMINAL LAW AND PROCEDURE

nolo contendere

[*no*.lo kon.*ten*.de.ray]

CRIMINAL LAW AND PROCEDURE

misdemeanor

[mis.de.*meen*.er]

CRIMINAL LAW AND PROCEDURE

parole

[pa.*role*]

CRIMINAL LAW AND PROCEDURE

M'Naghten rule

[me.*naw*.ten rule]

CRIMINAL LAW AND PROCEDURE

plea bargain

[plee *barg*.in]

A proposed criminal code prepared jointly by the Commission on Uniform State Laws and the American Law Institute.

State of mind that causes the intentional doing of a wrongful act without legal excuse or justification; a condition of mind prompting a person to the commission of a dangerous or deadly act in deliberate disregard of the lives or safety of others. The term does not necessarily connote personal ill will. It can and frequently does mean general malice. As an element of murder, all those states of mind that prompt a person to kill another person without legal excuse or justification; an intent to do the person great bodily harm. In the law of defamation, to be actionable, malice must be actual malice or express malice.

The reason that leads the mind to desire a result; that which leads the mind to engage in a criminal act; that which causes the mind to form criminal intent.

The killing of a human being, without premeditation or malice and without legal excuse or justification. Voluntary manslaughter occurs when a homicide is intentional but the result of sudden passion or great provocation. Involuntary manslaughter is an unintentional killing in the course of doing an unlawful act not amounting to a felony or while doing a lawful act in a reckless manner. There are various degrees of manslaughter, which are not consistent from jurisdiction to jurisdiction. *Compare* murder.

The intentional and premeditated killing of a human being (first degree murder); the intentional killing of a human being, without premeditation, but with malice aforethought, express or implied (second degree murder). Under most state statutes, a homicide that occurs during the commission of a felony is first degree murder, as are homicides perpetrated by lying in wait, torture, poison, and other criminal acts from which premeditation or deliberation can be inferred. Similarly, a homicide that results from deliberately doing a dangerous or deadly act with disregard for the safety of others is second degree murder, malice being inferred from the act itself. *Compare* manslaughter. *See also* felony murder rule.

- *n.* liquidation, slaughter, killing, slaying, homicide, execution, unlawful killing

---

An "answerable intent" (i.e., an intent for which one is answerable); an evil intent; a guilty mind; a criminal intent. In combination with actus reus (a guilty or criminal act), mens rea is an essential element of any crime except regulatory crimes or strict liability crimes and some petty offenses and infractions. Mens rea may be inferred or presumed.

(*Latin*) "I do not wish to contest it." A plea in a criminal case, also referred to as no contest, which, although it is essentially the same as a guilty plea, and carries the same consequences with respect to punishment, can be entered only with leave of court, because it is not an admission of responsibility and cannot be used against the defendant in a civil action based upon the same facts.

The Fifth Amendment and the Fourteenth Amendment to the Constitution require that, before a suspect who is in custody may be questioned, he must be informed that he has the right to remain silent and that anything he says may be used against him in court; that he be given the right to have an attorney present during questioning; and that he be advised that if he cannot afford an attorney one will be provided for him. If an interrogation occurs in the absence of these warnings, or in the absence of the suspect's attorney, any confession obtained is inadmissible unless the defendant has intelligently and knowingly waived his "Miranda rights," established by the case *Miranda v. Arizona*.

The release of a person from imprisonment after serving a portion of her sentence, provided she complies with certain conditions. Such conditions vary, depending upon the case, but they generally include stipulations such as not associating with known criminals, not possessing firearms, and not leaving the jurisdiction without the permission of the parole officer. Parole is not an act of clemency; it does not set aside the sentence. The parolee remains in the legal custody of the state and under the control of her parole officer. She may be returned to prison if she breaches the specified conditions. However, due process requires that parole cannot be revoked without a hearing.

- *n.* release, freedom, emancipation, conditional release
- *v.* discharge, release, liberate, let out, disimprison

A crime not amounting to a felony. In many jurisdictions, misdemeanors are offenses for which the punishment is incarceration for less than a year (generally in a jail, rather than in a prison or the penitentiary) or the payment of a fine. EXAMPLE: traffic violation.

- *n.* offense, transgression, wrong, misdeed, violation, trespass, impropriety

---

An agreement between the prosecutor and a criminal defendant under which the accused agrees to plead guilty, usually to a lesser offense, in exchange for receiving a lighter sentence than he would likely have received had he been found guilty after trial on the original charge.

An accused is not criminally responsible if, by defect of reason from disease of the mind, she did not know the nature of the act, or, if so, did not know it was wrong. *See also* insanity.

CRIMINAL LAW AND PROCEDURE

preliminary hearing

[pre.*lim*.i.ner.ee *heer*.ing]

CRIMINAL LAW AND PROCEDURE

prosecutor

[pross.e.*kyoo*.ter]

CRIMINAL LAW AND PROCEDURE

principal

[*prin*.si.pl]

CRIMINAL LAW AND PROCEDURE

racial profiling

[*ra*.shul *pro*.fy.ling]

CRIMINAL LAW AND PROCEDURE

prison

[*priz*.en]

CRIMINAL LAW AND PROCEDURE

rape

[rayp]

CRIMINAL LAW AND PROCEDURE

probable cause

[*prob*.ebl cawz]

CRIMINAL LAW AND PROCEDURE

robbery

[*rob*.e.ree]

CRIMINAL LAW AND PROCEDURE

probation

[pro.*bay*.shen]

CRIMINAL LAW AND PROCEDURE

scienter

[see.*en*.ter]

CRIMINAL LAW AND PROCEDURE

prosecution

[*pross*.e.kyoo.shen]

CRIMINAL LAW AND PROCEDURE

search warrant

[serch *war*.ent]

A public official, elected or appointed, who conducts criminal prosecutions on behalf of her jurisdiction. EXAMPLES: the district attorney of a county; the attorney general of a state; a United States attorney.

A hearing to determine whether there is probable cause to formally accuse a person of a crime; that is, whether there is a reasonable basis for believing that a crime has been committed and for thinking the defendant committed it. If the judge concludes that the evidence is sufficient to hold the defendant for trial, and if the offense is a bailable offense, the court sets bail. If the judge concludes that the evidence is insufficient to bind the defendant over for trial, the defendant is discharged from custody. *See also* probable cause.

Law enforcement's practice of stopping, detaining, or arresting people based on their race or ethnicity rather than their illegal behavior.

A principal of *the first degree* is a person who commits a crime, either in person or through an innocent agent; a principal in *the second degree* is a person who is present at the commission of a crime, giving aid and encouragement to the chief perpetrator.

Sexual intercourse with a woman by force or by putting her in fear or in circumstances in which she is unable to control her conduct or to resist (EXAMPLES: intoxication; unconsciousness). Under the common law definition of the crime, only a female can be raped and only a male can perpetrate the crime. In recent years, however, courts in several states have held that the rape statutes of their jurisdictions are gender-neutral and apply equally to perpetrators of either sex.

- *v.* molest, sexually assault, debauch, defile, ravish ("The woman was raped.")
- *n.* violation, assault, sexual assault, nonconsensual sex, defilement, seduction, abuse

A place of confinement for persons convicted of felonies, as opposed to jail, which is customarily a place of confinement for persons convicted of misdemeanors; a penitentiary.

- *n.* penitentiary, confinement, jail, house of detention, reformatory, guardhouse, pen, cell, facility

---

The felonious taking of money or anything of value from the person of another or from his presence, against his will, by force or by putting him in fear. *Compare* larceny.

- *n.* theft, hold-up, piracy, commandeering, embezzlement, expropriation, abduction

A reasonable amount of suspicion, supported by circumstances sufficiently strong to justify a prudent and cautious person's belief that certain alleged facts are probably true. A judge may not issue a search warrant unless she is shown probable cause to believe there is evidence of crime on the premises. A police officer may not make an arrest without a warrant unless he has reasonable cause, based upon reliable information, to believe a crime has been or is being committed.

Knowledge, particularly guilty knowledge, that will result in one's own liability or guilt.

A sentence that allows a person convicted of a crime to continue to live and work in the community while being supervised by a probation officer instead of being sent to prison. A person may also be sentenced to a term of probation to commence after the expiration of his prison term.

- *n.* conditional release, test period, trial period, parole, furlough, exemption

---

An order in writing issued by a magistrate or other judicial officer, commanding her to search for and seize stolen contraband, or illicit property, or other property evidencing the commission of a crime.

A criminal action brought by the government.

CRIMINAL LAW AND PROCEDURE

self-defense

[self-de.*fense*]

CRIMINAL LAW AND PROCEDURE

violation

[vy.o.*lay*.shen]

CRIMINAL LAW AND PROCEDURE

sentence

[*sen*.tense]

CRIMINAL LAW AND PROCEDURE

year and a day rule

[yere and a day rul]

CRIMINAL LAW AND PROCEDURE

separate counts

[*sep*.ret kounts]

CONSTITUTIONAL LAW

amendment of constitution

[a.*mend*.ment ov kon.sti.*too*.shen]

CRIMINAL LAW AND PROCEDURE

statutes of limitations

[*stat*.shoot of *lim*.i.tay.shenz]

CONSTITUTIONAL LAW

American Civil Liberties Union

[a.*mare*.i.ken *siv*.il *lib*.er.tees *yoon*.yun]

CRIMINAL LAW AND PROCEDURE

stop

[stop]

CONSTITUTIONAL LAW

articles

[*ar*.tiklz]

CRIMINAL LAW AND PROCEDURE

stop and frisk

[stop and frisk]

CONSTITUTIONAL LAW

balancing test

[*bal*.en.sing test]

1. The act of breaking the law; an infringement of the law; a violation of the law. 2. Sometimes used as a synonym for an infraction.

- *n.* abuse, contravention, illegality, misdemeanor, transgression ("a violation of the law")

The use of force to protect oneself from death or imminent bodily harm at the hands of an aggressor. A person may use only that amount of force reasonably necessary to protect himself against the peril with which he is threatened; thus, deadly force may be used in self-defense only against an aggressor who himself uses deadly force.

The rule in prosecution for homicide, in many jurisdictions, that if death does not occur within a year and a day after the occurrence of the wrongful act, it will be presumed that death resulted from some other cause.

The judgment of the court in a criminal case. A criminal sentence constitutes the court's action with respect to the consequences to the defendant of having committed the crime of which she has been convicted. Generally, criminal sentences impose a punishment of imprisonment, probation, fine, or forfeiture, or some combination of these penalties. In some jurisdictions, capital punishment may be imposed in cases involving the commission of a felony of extreme gravity. In some states, depending upon the crime, the jury, rather than the judge, establishes the sentence.

A process of proposing, passing, and ratifying amendments to the United States Constitution or a state or other constitution.

Two or more counts, charging separate offenses, contained in one indictment or information.

A nonprofit organization, commonly called the ACLU, that is concerned with constitutional rights, particularly individual liberties, and engages in litigation and lobbying.

Federal and state statutes prescribing the maximum period of time during which various types of criminal actions and prosecutions can be brought after the occurrence of the injury or offense.

Plural of article. Distinct divisions, parts, clauses, or provisions that, taken as a whole, make up a constitution, charter, statute, contract, or other written statement of principles or mutual understandings.

An arrest; a police officer's action in halting a person's freedom of action, even briefly.

A principle of constitutional law that declares that the constitutional rights of each citizen must, in each instance, be balanced against the danger that their exercise presents to others or to the state. EXAMPLE: freedom of speech does not include the right "to cry fire in a crowded theater" if there is no fire, as others might be hurt.

The detaining of a person briefly by a police officer and "patting him down" with the purpose of ascertaining if he is carrying a concealed weapon.

CONSTITUTIONAL LAW

bicameral

[by.*kam*.er.el]

CONSTITUTIONAL LAW

**Constitution
of the United States**

[kon.sti.*too*.shen of the yoo.*nie*.ted states]

CONSTITUTIONAL LAW

Bill of Rights

[bil ov ritz]

CONSTITUTIONAL LAW

constitutional

[kon.sti.*too*.shen.el]

CONSTITUTIONAL LAW

civilogue

[*siv*.el.log]

CONSTITUTIONAL LAW

constitutional amendment

[kon.sti.*too*.shen.el a.*mend*.ment]

CONSTITUTIONAL LAW

commerce clause

[*kom*.erss kloz]

CONSTITUTIONAL LAW

constitutional convention

[kon.sti.*too*.shen.el ken.*ven*.shen]

CONSTITUTIONAL LAW

constitution

[kon.sti.*too*.shen]

CONSTITUTIONAL LAW

constitutional courts

[kon.sti.*too*.shen.el kortz]

CONSTITUTIONAL LAW

Constitution

[kon.sti.*too*.shen]

CONSTITUTIONAL LAW

constitutional law

[kon.sti.*too*.shen.el law]

The fundamental document of American government, as adopted by the people of the United States through their representatives in the Constitutional Convention of 1787, as ratified by the states, together with the amendments to the Constitution.

Two-chambered, referring to the customary division of a legislature into two houses (a Senate and a House of Representatives).

In accordance with the Constitution of the United States; consistent with the Constitution; not in conflict with the Constitution.

- *adj.* approved, chartered, lawful, democratic, enforceable
- *ant.* unconstitutional

The first 10 amendments to the United States Constitution. The Bill of Rights is the portion of the Constitution that sets forth the rights that are the fundamental principles of the United States and the foundation of American citizenship.

An amendment to a constitution. *See also* amendment of constitution.

In exercising free speech, those in disagreement agree to conduct a civil dialogue while refraining from insulting each other.

A representative body that meets to form and adopt a constitution. (EXAMPLE: The convention that met in Philadelphia in 1787 to draft and adopt the Constitution of the United States.) Article V of the United States Constitution provides for the calling of a convention as a means of amending the Constitution.

The clause in Article I, Section 8, of the Constitution that gives Congress the power to regulate commerce between the states and between the United States and foreign countries. Federal statutes that regulate business and labor (EXAMPLES: the Fair Labor Standards Act; the Occupational Safety and Health Act) are based upon this power. *See also* interstate commerce.

Courts directly established by the Constitution, which are therefore beyond the power of Congress to abolish or alter. EXAMPLE: the Supreme Court of the United States.

The system of fundamental principles by which a nation, state, or corporation is governed. A nation's constitution may be written (EXAMPLE: the Constitution of the United States) or unwritten (EXAMPLE: the British Constitution). A nation's law must conform to its constitution. A law that violates a nation's constitution is unconstitutional and therefore unenforceable.

The body of principles that apply in the interpretation, construction, and application of the Constitution to statutes and to other governmental action. Constitutional law deals with constitutional questions and determines the constitutionality of state and federal laws and of the manner in which government exercises its authority.

The Constitution of the United States.

- *n.* charter, code, formation, written law, supreme law

CONSTITUTIONAL LAW

constitutional limitations

[kon.sti.*too*.shen.el lim.i.*tay*.shenz]

CONSTITUTIONAL LAW

equal protection clause

[*ee*.kwel pro.*tek*.shen kloz]

CONSTITUTIONAL LAW

constitutional questions

[kon.sti.*too*.shen.el *kwes*.chenz]

CONSTITUTIONAL LAW

**equal protection
of the laws**

[*ee*.kwel pro.*tek*.shen ov the lawz]

CONSTITUTIONAL LAW

constitutional right

[kon.sti.*too*.shen.el ryt]

CONSTITUTIONAL LAW

Equal Rights Amendment

[*ee*.kwel rytz a.*mend*.ment]

CONSTITUTIONAL LAW

due process clause

[dew *pross*.ess kloz]

CONSTITUTIONAL LAW

establishment clause

[es.*tab*.lish.ment kloz]

CONSTITUTIONAL LAW

due process of law

[dew *pross*.ess ov law]

CONSTITUTIONAL LAW

executive branch

[eg.*zek*.yoo.tiv branch]

CONSTITUTIONAL LAW

enumerated powers

[e.*nyoo*.me.ray.ted *pow*.erz]

CONSTITUTIONAL LAW

executive privilege

[eg.*zek*.yoo.tiv *priv*.i.lej]

The clause in the Fourteenth Amendment that dictates that no state may "deny to any person within its jurisdiction the equal protection of the laws." *See also* equal protection of the laws.

The provisions of a constitution that limit the legislature's power to enact laws.

Constitutional guarantee that specifies that the rights of all persons must rest upon the same rules under the same circumstances. Put another way, every state must give equal treatment to every person who is similarly situated or to persons who are members of the same class. "Equal protection of the laws" is a requirement for the Fourteenth Amendment. *See also* equal protection clause.

See constitutional law.

A proposed constitutional amendment, passed by Congress in 1972, that failed for lack of ratification by three-fourths of the states. The proposed amendment, generally referred to as the ERA, provided that "equality of rights under the law shall not be abridged by the United States or any state on account of sex."

A right guaranteed by the Constitution of the United States or by a state constitution; a fundamental right. A constitutional right cannot be abrogated or infringed by Congress or by a state legislature.

The provision of the First Amendment that states that "Congress shall make no law respecting an establishment of religion, or prohibiting the free exercise thereof." It means that neither a state nor the federal government can set up a state religion; neither can it pass laws that aid one religion, aid all religions, or prefer one religion over another; neither can it force or influence a person to go to or remain away from a church, synagogue, mosque, or other place of worship, or force him to proclaim a belief or disbelief in any religion.

Actually a reference to two due process clauses, one in the Fifth Amendment and one in the Fourteenth Amendment. The Fifth Amendment requires the federal government to accord "due process of law" to citizens of the United States; the Fourteenth Amendment imposes a similar requirement upon state governments. *See also* due process of law.

1. With the legislative branch and the judicial branch, one of the three divisions into which the Constitution separates the government of the United States. These branches of government are also referred to as departments of government. The executive branch is primarily responsible for enforcing the laws, it includes the President of the United States and all the federal agencies and departments. 2. A similar division exists in state government.

Law administered through courts of justice, equally applicable to all under established rules that do not violate fundamental principles of fairness. Whether a person has received due process of law can only be determined on a case-by-case basis. In all criminal cases, however, it involves, at the very least, the right to be heard by a fair and impartial tribunal, the defendant's right to be represented by counsel, the right to cross-examine witnesses against him, the right to offer testimony on his own behalf, and the right to have advance notice of trial and of the charge sufficient in detail and in point of time to permit adequate preparation for trial. Due process requirements for criminal prosecutions are considerably more rigorous than those for civil cases. "Due process of law" is guaranteed by both the Fifth Amendment and the Fourteenth Amendment. *See also* due process clause.

The privilege of the president of the United States to refuse to make certain confidential communications available to public scrutiny or to review by any branch of government other than the executive branch.

Powers specifically granted by the Constitution to one of the three branches of government. Another term for enumerated powers is express powers. *Compare* implied power.

CONSTITUTIONAL LAW

federalism

[*fed*.er.el.izm]

CONSTITUTIONAL LAW

free exercise clause

[free *ek*.ser.size kloz]

CONSTITUTIONAL LAW

Fifteenth Amendment

[*fif*.teenth a.*mend*.ment]

CONSTITUTIONAL LAW

freedom of expression

[*free*.dum ov eks.*presh*.en]

CONSTITUTIONAL LAW

Fifth Amendment

[fifth a.*mend*.ment]

CONSTITUTIONAL LAW

freedom of religion

[*free*.dum ov re.*lij*.en]

CONSTITUTIONAL LAW

First Amendment

[first a.*mend*.ment]

CONSTITUTIONAL LAW

freedom of speech and of the press

[*free*.dum ov speech and ov the press]

CONSTITUTIONAL LAW

Fourteenth Amendment

[*four*.teenth a.*mend*.ment]

CONSTITUTIONAL LAW

full faith and credit

[fel faith and *kred*.it]

CONSTITUTIONAL LAW

Fourth Amendment

[fourth a.*mend*.ment]

CONSTITUTIONAL LAW

HIPAA

[hi.pa]

The clause in the First Amendment that prevents Congress from prohibiting the "free exercise" of religion. *See also* freedom of religion.

1. Pertaining to a system of government that is federal in nature. 2. The system by which the states of the United States relate to each other and to the federal government.

A term that covers religious freedom, freedom of speech, and freedom of the press, all of which are protected by the First Amendment.

An amendment to the Constitution that provides that "the right of citizens of the United States to vote shall not be denied or abridged by the United States or by any state on account of race, color, or previous condition of servitude."

The First Amendment stipulates that "Congress shall make no law respecting an establishment of religion, or prohibiting the free exercise thereof." This provision guarantees the freedom to believe or not believe and, subject to law, the right to act upon one's religious belief or lack of belief. It also prohibits financial assistance to religion from public funds.

An amendment to the Constitution that guarantees the right to grand jury indictment if one is accused of having committed a serious crime, the right not to be placed in double jeopardy, the right not to be compelled to incriminate oneself, the right to due process of law, and the right not to have one's private property taken by the government without just compensation. The Fifth Amendment applies only to the federal government. Its requirements are made applicable to state and local government through the Fourteenth Amendment.

The First Amendment provides that "Congress shall make no law . . . abridging the freedom of speech or of the press." It embraces the concept that the expression or publication of thought and belief, free from government interference, is essential to the well-being of a free society, and should be limited only to prevent abuse of that right.

An amendment to the Constitution that guarantees freedom of religion, freedom of speech, and freedom of the press, as well as freedom of association (the right "peaceably to assemble") and the right to petition the government for redress of grievances.

A reference to the requirement of Article IV of the Constitution that each state give "full faith and credit" to the "public acts, records and judicial proceedings" of every other state. This means that a state's judicial acts must be given the same effect by the courts of all other states as they receive at home.

An amendment to the Constitution that requires the states (as opposed to the federal government—*compare* Fifth Amendment) to provide due process of law, and to ensure equal protection of the laws, "to any person within (their) jurisdiction." The Fourteenth Amendment also prohibits states from abridging "the privileges and immunities of citizens." *See also* due process clause; equal protection clause; privileges and immunities clause.

This is an acronym for Health Insurance Portability and Accountability Act, which was enacted by Congress in 1996. Title I of the Act protects health insurance coverage of workers and their families when they lose or switch jobs. HIPAA also addresses the security and privacy of health records.

An amendment to the Constitution prohibiting searches without search warrants and requiring that search warrants be issued only upon probable cause.

CONSTITUTIONAL LAW

implied power

[im.*plide pow*.er]

CONSTITUTIONAL LAW

legislature

[*lej*.is.lay.cher]

CONSTITUTIONAL LAW

interstate commerce

[*in*.ter.state *kawm*.ers]

CONSTITUTIONAL LAW

Magna Carta

[*mag*.na *car*.ta]

CONSTITUTIONAL LAW

intrastate commerce

[*in*.tra.state *kawm*.ers]

CONSTITUTIONAL LAW

nanny state laws

[nanny stayt lawz]

CONSTITUTIONAL LAW

judicial branch

[joo.*dish*.el branch]

CONSTITUTIONAL LAW

police power

[po.*leess pow*.er]

CONSTITUTIONAL LAW

legislation

[lej.is.*lay*.shen]

CONSTITUTIONAL LAW

preemption

[pree.*emp*.shen]

CONSTITUTIONAL LAW

legislative branch

[lej.is.*lay*.tiv branch]

CONSTITUTIONAL LAW

prior restraint

[*pry*.er re.*straynt*]

The branch of government that enacts statutory law, usually consisting of two houses, a Senate and a House of Representatives, made up of members representing districts and elected by the voters of those districts. Congress is the national legislature.

- *n.* house, chamber, assembly, parliament, senate, council

The power necessary to carry out a power expressly granted. EXAMPLE: the power of a department of an agency of government to perform such acts as are necessary to achieve the objectives of the statute or constitution under which the agency was established. *Compare* enumerated powers.

(*Latin*) "Great charter," a document that was issued by King John of England in 1215 and is the basis of English and American constitutional protections. Its guarantees relating to life, liberty, and property are embedded in the Constitution of the United States and in every state constitution in the United States.

Commerce between states; that is, from a given point in one state to a given point in another. Most federal statutes dealing with business or labor (EXAMPLES: consumer credit protection acts; the Fair Labor Standards Act), as well as many other federal statutes, are based upon the commerce clause of the Constitution, which gives Congress the power "to regulate commerce . . . among the several states." The term "commerce" is often used as a short reference for "interstate commerce." For EXAMPLE, "affecting commerce" means "affecting interstate commerce" and "engaged in commerce" means "engaged in interstate commerce." *See also* commerce clause. *Compare* intrastate commerce.

---

n. Intrusive state laws legislating or prohibiting those under the age of majority (usually 18) from snowboarding without a helmet, buying soft drinks at school, piercing body parts, getting tattooed, etc.

Commerce that takes place within the boundaries of one state. *Compare* interstate commerce.

---

1. The power of the government to make and enforce laws and regulations necessary to maintain and enhance the public welfare and to prevent individuals from violating the rights of others. 2. The sovereignty of each of the states of the United States that is not surrendered to the federal government under the Constitution. *See also* Tenth Amendment.

---

1. With the legislative branch and the executive branch, one of the three divisions into which the Constitution separates the government of the United States. These branches of government are also referred to as departments of government. The judicial branch, which consists of the court system, is primarily responsible for interpreting the laws. 2. The similar division exists in state government.

The doctrine that once Congress has enacted legislation in a given field, a state may not enact a law inconsistent with the federal statute. Thus, for EXAMPLE, a state may not enact a wage and hour law, applicable to employers who are in commerce, that is inconsistent with the provisions of the Fair Labor Standards Act. A similar doctrine also governs the relationship between the state government and local government.

- *n.* appropriation, substitution, usurpation, replacement, annexation ("preemption doctrine")

Laws (EXAMPLES: statutes, ordinances) enacted by a legislative body (EXAMPLES: Congress; a state legislature; a city council).

- *n.* law, regulation, statute, ordinances, ruling, measure, act

---

The imposition by the government, in advance of publication, of limits that prohibit or restrain speech or publication, as opposed to later punishing persons for what they have actually said or written.

---

1. With the judicial branch and the executive branch, one of the three divisions into which the Constitution separates the government of the United States. These branches of government are also referred to as departments of government. The legislative branch, consisting of the House of Representative and the United States Senate, which together form the United States Congress, is primarily responsible for enacting the laws. 2. A similar division exists in state government.

CONSTITUTIONAL LAW

privileges and immunities clause

[*priv*.i.lejz and im.*yoon*.i.teez kloz]

CONSTITUTIONAL LAW

separate but equal doctrine

[*sep*.ret but *ee*.kwel *dok*.trin]

CONSTITUTIONAL LAW

procedural due process

[pro.*seed*.jer.el doo *pross*.ess]

CONSTITUTIONAL LAW

separation of powers

[sep.e.*ray*.shen ov *pow*.erz]

CONSTITUTIONAL LAW

ratify

[*rat*.i.fy]

CONSTITUTIONAL LAW

stare decisis

[*stahr*.ay de.*sy*.sis]

CONSTITUTIONAL LAW

rational basis

[*rash*.en.el *bay*.sis]

CONSTITUTIONAL LAW

strict scrutiny test

[strikt *skrew*.ten.ee test]

CONSTITUTIONAL LAW

referendum

[ref.e.*ren*.dum]

CONSTITUTIONAL LAW

substantive due process

[*sub*.sten.tiv doo *pross*.ess]

CONSTITUTIONAL LAW

Senate

[*sen*.et]

CONSTITUTIONAL LAW

supremacy clause

[soo.*prem*.e.see kloz]

A doctrine (overruled by *Brown v. Board of Education*), under which the separation of the races in places of public accommodation, including public schools, had been previously held constitutional.

1. Section 2 of Article IV of the Constitution, which provides that "[t]he citizens of each state shall be entitled to all privileges and immunities of citizens in the several states." 2. The clause of the Fourteenth Amendment that provides that "[n]o state shall make or enforce any law which shall abridge the privileges or immunities of citizens of the United States. . . ." These provisions represent a constitutional requirement that a state give out-of-state residents the same fundamental rights as it gives its own citizens.

A fundamental principle of the Constitution that gives exclusive power to the legislative branch to make the law, exclusive power to the executive branch to administer it, and exclusive power to the judicial branch to enforce it. The authors of the Constitution believed that the separation of powers would make abuse of power less likely.

The implication that a person has the right to a proceeding to protect one's rights.

(Latin) Means "standing by the decision." Stare decisis is the doctrine that judicial decisions stand as precedents for cases arising in the future. It is a fundamental policy of our law that, except in unusual circumstances, a court's determination on a point of law will be followed by courts of the same or lower rank in later cases presenting the same legal issue, even though different parties are involved and many years might have elapsed.

To give approval; to confirm.

A term the Supreme Court uses to describe the rigorous level of judicial review to be applied in determining the constitutionality of legislation that restricts a fundamental right or legislation based upon a suspect classification: age, sex, etc.

A reasonable basis, under the law. The courts will not invalidate a statute or overrule an order of an administrative agency that has a "rational basis" in law.

A right grounded in the Fifth and Fourteenth Amendments, the concept that government may not act arbitrarily or capriciously in making, interpreting, or enforcing the law.

Under some state constitutions, the process by which an act of the legislature or a constitutional amendment is referred to the voters at an election for their approval.

- *n.* proposition, proposal, election, questions, mandate, plebiscite

---

The provision in Article VI of the Constitution that "this Constitution and the laws of the United States . . . shall be the supreme law of the land, and the judges in every state shall be bound thereby."

The upper house of Congress. Its 100 members, two from each state, are elected for six-year terms; one-third of the Senate's members are elected every two years.

CONSTITUTIONAL LAW
supreme court
[soo.*preem* kort]

ADMINISTRATIVE LAW
administrative agency
[ad.*min*.is.tray.tiv *ay*.jen.see]

CONSTITUTIONAL LAW
taxing power
[*tak*.sing pow.er]

ADMINISTRATIVE LAW
administrative discretion
[ad.*min*.is.tray.tiv dis.*kresh*.en]

CONSTITUTIONAL LAW
Tenth Amendment
[tenth a.*mend*.ment]

ADMINISTRATIVE LAW
administrative hearing
[ad.*min*.is.tray.tiv *heer*.ing]

ADMINISTRATIVE LAW
abuse of discretion
[a.*byooss* ov dis.*kresh*.en]

ADMINISTRATIVE LAW
administrative law
[ad.*min*.is.tray.tiv law]

ADMINISTRATIVE LAW
adjudicatory
[a.*joo*.di.ka.tore.ee]

ADMINISTRATIVE LAW
administrative law judge
[ad.*min*.is.tray.tiv law juj]

ADMINISTRATIVE LAW
administrative act
[ad.*min*.is.tray.tiv act]

ADMINISTRATIVE LAW
administrative notice
[ad.*min*.is.tray.tiv *no*.tiss]

A board, commission, bureau, office, or department of the executive branch of government that implements the law, which originates with the legislative branch. EXAMPLES: the FBI (Federal Bureau of Investigation); a county public assistance office.

1. The United States Supreme Court. The United States Supreme Court is the highest court in the federal court system. It is established by the Constitution and has both original jurisdiction and appellate jurisdiction. 2. In most states, the highest appellate court of the state. 3. In some states, a trial court.

The power to choose between courses of conduct in the administration of a public office or in carrying out a public duty.

The power of government to levy, assess, and collect taxes.

A hearing before an administrative agency, as distinguished from a hearing before a court.

An amendment to the Constitution that provides that the powers not delegated to the federal government by the Constitution are reserved to the states or to the people.

---

1. The body of law that controls the way in which administrative agencies operate.
2. Regulations and decisions issued by administrative agencies.

A judicial or administrative decision so grounded in whim or caprice, or against logic, that it amounts to a denial of justice.

A person, generally a civil servant, who conducts hearings held by an administrative agency. An administrative law judge is variously referred to as an ALJ, a hearing examiner, or a hearing officer.

Refers to the decision-making or quasi-judicial functions of an administrative agency, as opposed to the judicial functions of a court. Thus, for EXAMPLE, an adjudicatory hearing is a hearing before an administrative agency as opposed to a hearing or trial before a court.

See official notice.

A routine act by a public official, required by law, as opposed to an act based upon a decision involving a degree of choice; a ministerial act. EXAMPLE: the maintaining of court records by the clerk of the court.

ADMINISTRATIVE LAW

Administrative Procedure Act (APA)

[ad.*min*.is.tray.tiv pro.*see*.jer akt]

ADMINISTRATIVE LAW

administrative proceeding

[ad.*min*.is.tray.tiv pro.*see*.ding]

ADMINISTRATIVE LAW

administrative remedy

[ad.*min*.is.tray.tiv *rem*.e.dee]

ADMINISTRATIVE LAW

advisory opinion

[ad.*vize*.e.ree o.*pin*.yen]

ADMINISTRATIVE LAW

affirm

[a.*ferm*]

ADMINISTRATIVE LAW

arbitrary and capricious

[*ar*.bi.trare.ee and ke.*prish*.es]

ADMINISTRATIVE LAW

color

[*kull*.er]

ADMINISTRATIVE LAW

color of right

[*kull*.er ov rite]

ADMINISTRATIVE LAW

COPPA

[*kop*.uh]

ADMINISTRATIVE LAW

de novo review

[de *no*.vo re.*vyoo*]

ADMINISTRATIVE LAW

declaratory judgment

[de.*klar*.e.toh.ree *juj*.ment]

ADMINISTRATIVE LAW

declaratory provision

[de.*klar*.e.toh.ree pro.*vizh*.en]

An apparent legal right; a seeming legal right; the mere semblance of a legal right. Although they may also refer to activity by private persons, terms such as color of authority, color of law, and color of right generally refer to actions taken by a representative of government, which is beyond her authority, but appears legal because of her official status.

A statute enacted by Congress that regulates the way in which federal administrative agencies conduct their affairs and establishes the procedure for judicial review of the actions of federal agencies. The Act is referred to as the APA.

A right based upon color of authority, color of law, or color of office.

A proceeding before an administrative agency, as distinguished from a proceeding before a court.

The Children's Online Privacy Protection Act (COPPA) has been enforced by the Federal Trade Commission (FTC) since 2000 and prohibits website operators from knowingly collecting personally identifiable information (complete name, Social Security number, e-mail address, or telephone number) from children under the age of 13 without parental consent.

A remedy that the law permits an administrative agency to grant.

(*Latin*) Standard of review under which the reviewing body may find the facts and review all issues without deference to the lower body's findings and conclusions.

A judicial interpretation of a legal question requested by the legislative or executive branch of government, or by a private individual or corporation. These opinions have no binding effect.

A judgment that specifies the rights of the parties but orders nothing. Nonetheless, it is a binding judgment and the appropriate remedy for the determination of an actionable dispute when the plaintiff is in doubt as to his legal rights.

In the case of an appellate court, to uphold the decision or judgment of the lower court after the appeal.

Part of a statute or ordinance that states the need that the legislation was enacted to fulfill (i.e., the statute's purpose). Declaratory provisions often begin with the word "whereas."

A reference to the concept in administrative law that permits a court to substitute its judgment for that of an administrative agency if the agency's decision unreasonably ignores the law or the facts of a case.

ADMINISTRATIVE LAW

declaratory relief

[de.*klar*.e.toh.ree re.*leef*]

ADMINISTRATIVE LAW

due process of law

[dew *pross*.ess ov law]

ADMINISTRATIVE LAW

declaratory statute

[de.*klar*.e.toh.ree *stat*.shoot]

ADMINISTRATIVE LAW

Enabling Act

[en.*ay*.bling akt]

ADMINISTRATIVE LAW

delegation of powers

[del.e.*gay*.shen ov *pow*.erz]

ADMINISTRATIVE LAW

Equal Employment Opportunity Commission (EEOC)

[*ee*.kwel em.*ploy*.ment op.er.*tew*.ni.tee kuh.*mish*.en]

ADMINISTRATIVE LAW

department

[de.*part*.ment]

ADMINISTRATIVE LAW

executive

[eg.*zek*.yoo.tiv]

ADMINISTRATIVE LAW

department of government

[de.*part*.ment ov *guv*.ern.ment]

ADMINISTRATIVE LAW

executive agency

[eg.*zek*.yoo.tiv *ay*.jen.see]

ADMINISTRATIVE LAW

due process hearing

[dew *pross*.ess *heer*.ing]

ADMINISTRATIVE LAW

executive branch

[eg.*zek*.yoo.tiv branch]

Law administered through courts, equally applicable to all, that does not violate principles of fairness. Whether a person has received due process of law can only be determined on a case-by-case basis. In all criminal cases, however, it involves, at the very least, the right to be heard by a fair and impartial tribunal, the defendant's right to be represented by counsel, the right to cross-examine witnesses against him, the right to offer testimony on his own behalf, and the right to have advance notice of trial and of the charge sufficient in detail and in point of time to permit adequate preparation for trial. Due process requirements for criminal prosecutions are considerably more rigorous than those for civil cases. "Due process of law" is guaranteed by both the Fifth Amendment and the Fourteenth Amendment.

See declaratory judgment.

A statute that gives the government the power to enforce other legislation, or that carries out a provision of a constitution.

A statute enacted to clarify and resolve the law when the correct interpretation has been in doubt.

A federal agency whose purpose is to prevent and remedy discrimination based on race, color, religion, national origin, age, or sex with respect to most aspects of employment, including hiring, firing, promotion, and wages. The commission, which is known as the EEOC, enforces many federal Civil Rights Acts and anti-discrimination statutes.

---

1. Provisions of the Constitution by which executive powers are delegated to the executive branch of the government, legislative powers to the legislative branch, and judicial powers to the judicial branch. 2. Delegation of constitutional power by one branch of government to another. Such delegation is permissible only if it is consistent with the principle of separation of powers set forth in the Constitution. 3. The transfer of power from the president to an administrative agency.

---

adj. Pertaining to the administration or enforcement of the law.
n. A person who enforces the law, as distinguished from a person who makes the law or a person who interprets the law.

- *n.* chief, supervisor, boss, director, chairperson, president
- *adj.* managerial, presidential, official, administrative

An administrative unit within an organization.

- *n.* branch, section, office, agency, bureau, unit, division

---

See administrative agency.

---

1. One of the three divisions into which the Constitution separates the government of the United States. Used in this sense, the term is synonymous with branch of government. 2. A similar division in state government. 3. An administrative unit within a branch of government. EXAMPLES: the Department of Justice (DOJ); the Department of Commerce (DOC).

---

1. With the legislative branch and the judicial branch, one of the three divisions into which the Constitution separates the government of the United States. These branches of government are also referred to as departments of government. The executive branch is primarily responsible for enforcing the laws. 2. A similar division exists in state government.

An administrative hearing held to comply with the due process clause. EXAMPLE: a parole revocation hearing.

ADMINISTRATIVE LAW

exhaustion of remedy

[eg.*zaws*.chen of *rem*.e.dee]

ADMINISTRATIVE LAW

hearing examiner

[*heer*.ing eg.*zam*.in.er]

ADMINISTRATIVE LAW

fact-finding body

[*fakt*-fine.ding *bod*.ee]

ADMINISTRATIVE LAW

hearing officer

[*heer*.ing *off*.i.ser]

ADMINISTRATIVE LAW

federal agency

[*fed*.er.el *ay*.jen.see]

ADMINISTRATIVE LAW

in camera

[in *kam*.e.ra]

ADMINISTRATIVE LAW

Federal Register

[*fed*.er.el *rej*.is.ter]

ADMINISTRATIVE LAW

inspection laws

[in.*spek*.shen lawz]

ADMINISTRATIVE LAW

Freedom of Information Act (FOIA)

[*free*.dum of in.fer.*may*.shen akt]

ADMINISTRATIVE LAW

judicial review

[joo.*dish*.el re.*vyoo*]

ADMINISTRATIVE LAW

hearing

[*heer*.ing]

ADMINISTRATIVE LAW

license

[*ly*.sense]

The title of the person who functions as a judge with respect to an administrative hearing. In some states, and in the federal system, the title administrative law judge is used instead. *See also* hearing officer.

1. The doctrine that when the law provides an administrative remedy, a party seeking relief must fully exercise that remedy before the courts will intervene. 2. The doctrine, applicable in many types of cases, that the federal courts will not respond to a party seeking relief until she has exhausted her remedies in state court.

Same as hearing examiner, although, in some circumstances, a hearing officer, unlike a hearing examiner, does not have the power to adjudicate, her authority being limited to making recommendations to the appropriate administrative agency. *See also* administrative law judge.

A board or body, usually of an administrative agency, that is empowered to make findings of fact.

(*Latin*) In chambers; in private. A term, referring to a hearing or any other judicial business conducted in the judge's office or in a courtroom that has been cleared of spectators and certain excepted parties.

Any administrative agency, board, bureau, commission, corporation, or institution of the federal government, usually in the executive branch of government.

Federal, state, and local laws designed to promote health and safety by protecting the public from hazards such as the unsanitary processing of food, the improper packaging of articles for sale, or unsafe working conditions. EXAMPLES: food inspection laws administered by the FDA (Food and Drug Administration).

An official publication, printed daily, containing regulations and proposed regulations issued by administrative agencies, as well as other rulemaking and other official business of the executive branch of government. All regulations are ultimately published in the Code of Federal Regulations (CFR).

1. Review by a court of a decision or ruling of an administrative agency. 2. Review by an appellate court of a determination by a lower court.

A federal statute that requires federal agencies to make available to the public, upon request, material contained in their files, as well as information on how the agencies function. The Act contains various significant exemptions from disclosure, including information compiled for law enforcement purposes, and to protect the privacy of individuals. *See* privacy.

1. A special privilege, not a right common to everyone. 2. Permission (EXAMPLES: a marriage license; a fishing license) to do something that, if it were not regulated, would be a right. 3. A privilege conferred on a person by the government to do something she otherwise would not have the right to do. EXAMPLES: the privilege of incorporation; the privilege of operating as a public utility or a common carrier. 4. A requirement imposed as a means of regulating a business. EXAMPLE: a liquor license. 5. Permission to practice a profession, engage in an occupation, or conduct a business. EXAMPLES: a license to practice law; a business license; a real estate license. 6. A certificate evidencing an official grant of permission or authorization. EXAMPLES: a driver's license; a hunting license.

- *n.* privilege, authorization, sanction, permission, entitlement
- *v.* authorize, legitimize, sanction, approve, validate

A proceeding in which evidence is introduced and witnesses are examined so that findings of fact can be made and a determination rendered. Although, in a general sense, all trials can be said to be hearings, not all hearings are trials. The difference is in the degree of formality each requires, with the rules of procedure being more relaxed in hearings. A hearing may be conducted by a court, an administrative agency, an arbitrator, or a committee of the legislature, as well as by many other public bodies.

- *n.* trial, inquiry, litigation, adjudication, review, legal proceedings

ADMINISTRATIVE LAW

licensing

[*ly*.sen.sing]

ADMINISTRATIVE LAW

quasi-judicial

[*kwa*.zi-joo.*dish*.el]

ADMINISTRATIVE LAW

licensor

[*ly*.sen.*sore*]

ADMINISTRATIVE LAW

quasi-legislative

[*kwa*.zi-*lej*.is.lay.tiv]

ADMINISTRATIVE LAW

official notice

[o.*fish*.el *no*.tiss]

ADMINISTRATIVE LAW

rate fixing

[rate *fik*.sing]

ADMINISTRATIVE LAW

official records

[o.*fish*.el *rek*.erdz]

ADMINISTRATIVE LAW

rate making

[rate *may*.king]

ADMINISTRATIVE LAW

privacy

[*pry*.ve.see]

ADMINISTRATIVE LAW

regulation

[reg.yoo.*lay*.shun]

ADMINISTRATIVE LAW

promulgate

[*prom*.ul.gate]

ADMINISTRATIVE LAW

regulatory

[*reg*.yoo.le.tore.ee]

A term applied to the adjudicatory functions of an administrative agency (i.e., taking evidence and making findings of fact and findings of law).

The act or process of granting or issuing a license.

A term applied to the legislative functions of an administrative agency, for EXAMPLE, rulemaking.

The grantor of a license. EXAMPLES: a state (Department of Motor Vehicles); a city (health department); a federal agency (FAA).

See rate making.

The equivalent of judicial notice by an administrative agency; also referred to as administrative notice.

The process engaged in by a public service commission in establishing a rate to be charged to the public for a public service.

Records made by an official of the government in the course of performing her official duties. (EXAMPLE: correspondence; memoranda; data; minutes.) Official records are admissible in the federal courts and in federal administrative proceedings, as well as in most state courts, as an exception to the hearsay rule, to prove the transactions they memorialize.

---

1. The act of regulating. 2. A rule having the force of law, promulgated by an administrative agency; the act of rule making. *See* rule making. 3. A rule of conduct established by a person or body in authority for the governance of those over whom they have authority.

The right of privacy is the right to be left alone. It means that personal information of the kind in the possession of, for EXAMPLE, the government, insurance companies, and credit bureaus may not be made public. The right to privacy, which is implied by the Constitution, is supported, and to some extent enforced, by federal and state privacy acts.

- *n.* confidentiality, noninfringement

Pertaining to that which regulates; pertaining to the act of regulation. *See also* regulation.

---

1. To publish, announce, or proclaim official notice of a public act. 2. To issue a regulation.

ADMINISTRATIVE LAW

regulatory agency

[*reg*.yoo.le.tore.ee *ay*.jen.see]

ADMINISTRATIVE LAW

statutory benefits

[stat.*shoo*.tore.ee *ben*.e.fits]

ADMINISTRATIVE LAW

reporters

[re.*port*.erz]

ADMINISTRATIVE LAW

subpoena

[sub.*pee*.nah]

ADMINISTRATIVE LAW

ripeness doctrine

[*ripe*.ness *dok*.trin]

ADMINISTRATIVE LAW

substantial evidence

[sub.*stan*.shel *ev*.i.dense]

ADMINISTRATIVE LAW

rulemaking

[*rool*.may.king]

ADMINISTRATIVE LAW

substantial evidence rule

[sub.*stan*.shel *ev*.i.dense rool]

ADMINISTRATIVE LAW

separation of powers

[sep.ar.*ay*.shun ov *pow*.erz]

ADMINISTRATIVE LAW

substantive due process

[*sub*.stan.tiv doo *pross*.ess]

ADMINISTRATIVE LAW

statute

[stat.*shoot*]

ADMINISTRATIVE LAW

summary judgment

[*sum*.e.ree *juj*.ment]

Benefits that are provided because the law requires it. EXAMPLES: workers' compensation coverage, unemployment insurance, veterans' benefits, and Social Security.

An administrative agency empowered to promulgate and enforce regulations. *See also* regulation.

n. A command in the form of written process requiring a witness to come to court to testify; short for subpoena ad testificandum.
v. To issue or serve a subpoena.

1. Court reports, as well as official, published reports of cases decided by administrative agencies. 2. Court reporters.

Evidence that a reasonable person would accept as adequate to support the conclusion or conclusions drawn from it; evidence beyond a scintilla. *See also* substantial evidence rule.

The doctrine that an administrative agency or a trial court will not hear or determine a case, and an appellate court will not entertain an appeal, unless an actual case or controversy exists.

The rule that a court will uphold a decision or ruling of an administrative agency if it is supported by substantial evidence. *See also* substantial evidence.

The promulgation by an administrative agency of a rule having the force of law (i.e., a regulation).

A right grounded in the Fifth and Fourteenth Amendments. The government may not act arbitrarily or capriciously in making, interpreting, or enforcing the law. A person is entitled to both substantive due process and procedural due process.

A fundamental principle of the Constitution that gives exclusive power to the legislative branch to make the law, to the executive branch to administer it, and to the judicial branch to enforce it. The authors of the Constitution believed that the separation of powers would make abuse of power less likely.

A method of disposing of an action without further proceedings. A party against whom a claim is made may move for summary judgment in her favor, if there is no genuine issue of any material fact.

A law enacted by a legislature; an act.

ADMINISTRATIVE LAW

sunshine law

[*sun*.shine law]

TORTS AND PERSONAL INJURY

assault

[a.*salt*]

TORTS AND PERSONAL INJURY

absolute liability

[ab.so.*loot* ly.e.*bil*.i.tee]

TORTS AND PERSONAL INJURY

assault and battery

[a.*salt* and *bat*.er.ee]

TORTS AND PERSONAL INJURY

act

[akt]

TORTS AND PERSONAL INJURY

assumption of risk

[a.*sump*.shen ov risk]

TORTS AND PERSONAL INJURY

actionable

[*ak*.shen.abl]

TORTS AND PERSONAL INJURY

attractive nuisance

[a.*trak*.tiv *noo*.sense]

TORTS AND PERSONAL INJURY

actual damages

[*ak*.chew.al *dam*.e.jez]

TORTS AND PERSONAL INJURY

attractive nuisance doctrine

[a.*trak*.tiv *noo*.sense *dok*.trin]

TORTS AND PERSONAL INJURY

ad damnum clause

[ad *dahm*.num clawz]

TORTS AND PERSONAL INJURY

battery

[*bat*.ter.ee]

An act of force or threat of force intended to inflict harm upon a person or to put the person in fear that such harm is imminent; an attempt to commit a battery. The perpetrator must have, or appear to have, the present ability to carry out the act. Accordingly, a child's threat of injury to an adult is rarely considered an assault.

State and federal statutes requiring that meetings and records of administrative agencies be open to the public.

An achieved assault; an assault carried out by hitting or by other physical contact. *See also* battery.

Liability for an injury whether or not there is fault or negligence. EXAMPLE: When fire works or dangerous explosives are used and someone is injured, liability is automatically imposed against the user of the dangerous explosives. *See also* strict liability.

The legal principle that a person who knows and deliberately exposes herself to a danger assumes responsibility for the risk, rather than the person who actually created the danger. Assumption of risk is often referred to as voluntary assumption of risk, and applies to risky sports such as boxing and race car driving.

n. That which is done voluntarily; putting one's will into action.
v. To put a conscious choice into effect; to do.

- *n.* performance
- *v.* perform, do, behave, enact, execute, transact

An unusual mechanism, apparatus, or condition that is dangerous to young children but is so interesting and alluring as to attract them to the premises on which it is kept. EXAMPLES: an abandoned mine shaft; an abandoned house; a junked car. *See also* nuisance.

Conduct is actionable if it furnishes a ground for legal action. EXAMPLES of actionable conduct include defamation, negligence, and trespass.

The principle in the law of negligence that a person who maintains an attractive nuisance on his property must exercise reasonable care to protect young children against its dangers, or be held responsible for any injury that occurs, even though the injured child trespassed upon his property or was otherwise at fault.

Monetary compensation for a loss or injury that a plaintiff has suffered rather than a sum of money awarded by way of punishing a defendant or to deter others. *Compare* punitive damages. *See also* damage.

The unconsented-to touching or striking of one person by another, or by an object put in motion by him, with the intention of doing harm or giving offense. Battery is both a crime and a tort. *Compare* assault. *See also* assault and battery.

The clause in a complaint that sets forth the plaintiff's demand for damages and the amount of the claim. This is generally substantially more than the plaintiff expects to actually recover.

TORTS AND PERSONAL INJURY

breach of duty

[breech ov *dew*.tee]

TORTS AND PERSONAL INJURY

compensatory damages

[kem.*pen*.se.to.ree *dam*.ejez]

TORTS AND PERSONAL INJURY

breach of warranty

[breech ov *war*.en.tee]

TORTS AND PERSONAL INJURY

consent

[ken.*sent*]

TORTS AND PERSONAL INJURY

business invitee

[*biz*.ness in.vy.*tee*]

TORTS AND PERSONAL INJURY

contribution

[kon.tri.*byoo*.shen]

TORTS AND PERSONAL INJURY

care

[kayr]

TORTS AND PERSONAL INJURY

contributory negligence

[kon.tri.*byoo*.tor.ee *neg*.li.jense]

TORTS AND PERSONAL INJURY

causation

[kaw.*zay*.shen]

TORTS AND PERSONAL INJURY

conversion

[ken.*ver*.zhen]

TORTS AND PERSONAL INJURY

comparative negligence

[kem.*par*.i.tiv *neg*.li.jense]

TORTS AND PERSONAL INJURY

culpable negligence

[kulp.abl *neg*.li.jense]

Damages recoverable in a lawsuit for actual loss or injury suffered by the plaintiff as a result of the defendant's conduct. Also called actual damages, they may include expenses, loss of time, reduced earning capacity, bodily injury, and mental anguish.

The failure to do that which a person is bound by law to do, or the doing of it in an unlawful manner. *See also* duty.

Agreement; approval; acquiescence, being of one mind. Consent necessarily involves two or more persons because, without at least two persons, there cannot be a unity of opinion or the possibility of thinking alike.

- *v.* agree, accept, allow, approve, concede, yield, comply, sanction, ratify
- *n.* agreement, approval, acquiescence, concession, allowance, permission

---

The violation of an express warranty or implied warranty. EXAMPLE: If a product in its promotional material promises to remove rust and it doesn't, there is a breach of warranty.

---

1. A payment of his share of a debt or judgment by a person who is jointly liable. 2. The right of a person who has satisfied a shared indebtedness to have those with whom she shared it contribute in defraying its cost.

- *n.* indemnification, restitution, reparation, repayment, satisfaction

---

A person who comes upon premises at the invitation of the occupant, and who has business to contract. If a business invitee is injured as a result of some hazard on the premises, she is more likely to be able to hold the owner or occupant responsible at law than would a social guest or trespasser.

A failure by the plaintiff to exercise reasonable care that, in part at least, is the cause of an injury. Contributory negligence defeats a plaintiff's cause of action for negligence in states that have not adopted the doctrine of comparative negligence. *Compare* comparative negligence.

---

1. Custody; safekeeping. 2. Attention; awareness; caution. Care is a word that must always be interpreted in the context in which it appears. It is extremely important as a standard for determining negligence. The context determines the level of care that the law requires under the circumstances. A person should use care not to harm others or their property.

- *n.* custody, safekeeping, interest, regard, attention, awareness, caution
- *v.* beware, be cautious, guard, watch, support, supervise

Control over another person's personal property that is wrongfully exercised; control applied in a manner that violates that person's title to or rights in the property. Conversion is both a tort and a crime. EXAMPLE: If a man takes a jacket that belongs to someone else, he has converted it when he takes it, hems it, and wears it.

- *n.* theft, larceny, misappropriation, deprivation, embezzlement

---

The act of causing; the producing of a result. Causation is one of the elements needed to hold a defendant liable in a torts case. *See also* proximate cause.

- *n.* production, origination, root

Both in the law of negligence and as used in criminal negligence and manslaughter statutes, a conscious and wanton disregard of the probability that death or injury will result from the willful creation of an unreasonable risk. EXAMPLE: when a person carries a loaded gun on a crowded bus, where she is likely to be bumped, and the gun goes off, injuring bus-riders.

The doctrine adopted by most states that requires a comparison of the negligence of the defendant with the negligence of the plaintiff: the greater the negligence of the defendant, the lesser the level of care required of the plaintiff to permit her to recover. The plaintiff's negligence does not defeat her cause of action, but it reduces the damages she is entitled to recover. *Compare* contributory negligence.

TORTS AND PERSONAL INJURY

damage

[*dam*.ej]

TORTS AND PERSONAL INJURY

exculpatory clause

[eks.*kul*.pe.toh.ree clawz]

TORTS AND PERSONAL INJURY

dangerous instrumentality

[*dane*.jer.*ess* in.stroo.men.*tal*.i.tee]

TORTS AND PERSONAL INJURY

excusable

[eks.*kyoo*.zebl]

TORTS AND PERSONAL INJURY

defamation

[def.e.*may*.shen]

TORTS AND PERSONAL INJURY

excusable neglect

[eks.*kyoo*.zebl neg.*lekt*]

TORTS AND PERSONAL INJURY

degree of care

[de.*gree* ov kayr]

TORTS AND PERSONAL INJURY

excusable negligence

[eks.*kyoo*.zebl *neg*.li.jenss]

TORTS AND PERSONAL INJURY

duty

[*dew*.tee]

TORTS AND PERSONAL INJURY

false imprisonment

[fals im.*priz*.en.ment]

TORTS AND PERSONAL INJURY

emotional distress

[ee.*moh*.shen.l dis.*tress*]

TORTS AND PERSONAL INJURY

foreseeable

[for.*see*.ebl]

A clause in a contract or other legal document excusing a party from liability for his wrongful act. EXAMPLE: a provision in a lease relieving a landlord of liability for trespass.

The loss, hurt, or harm to person or property that results from injury that, in turn, is the negligent or deliberate invasion of a legal right. Although the words damage, damages, and injury are often treated as synonyms, there are important differences in their meanings. Injury is the illegal invasion of a legal right (i.e., a wrong); damage is the loss, hurt, or harm that results from the injury; and damages are the compensation awarded for that which has been suffered. Additional damages may be awarded if the damage resulted from an injury that was inflicted recklessly or with malice. *See also* punitive and special damages.

- *n.* loss, hurt, harm, destruction, impairment
- *ant.* benefit

That which may be forgiven or overlooked.

- *adj.* pardonable, forgivable, permissible ("excusable negligence")

A thing so dangerous (EXAMPLES: explosives; hazardous waste; a gun) that if it causes injury, the law may impose liability even though there was no negligence. A dangerous instrumentality is a basis for absolute or strict liability.

Dilatory neglect that may be forgiven or overlooked by a court, upon a showing of good reason therefore. For EXAMPLE: A court may authorize the opening of a default judgment after expiration of the time normally allowed. The court may authorize belated action in some circumstances if the failure to act was due to excusable neglect.

Libel or slander; the written or oral publication, falsely and intentionally, of anything that is injurious to the good name or reputation of another person. For EXAMPLE: If a person tells a friend that his accountant is a liar and a thief, and knows this is not a true statement, this is an example of slander.

- *n.* libel, slander, defamatory statement, deprecation, belittlement
- *ant.* praise

See excusable neglect.

A relative standard by which conduct is tested to determine whether it constitutes negligence. EXAMPLES: due care; extraordinary care; ordinary care; reasonable care.

The unlawful restraint by one person of the physical liberty of another. Like false arrest, to which it is closely related, it is both a tort and a crime.

1. A legal obligation, whether imposed by the common law, statute, court order, or contract. (USAGE: "When a right is invaded, a duty is violated.") A tort is committed only when there has been a breach of duty resulting in injury. 2. Any obligation or responsibility.

- *n.* responsibility, requirement, assignment, mandatory act, pledge, obligation

---

That which may be anticipated or known in advance; that which a person should have known. In the law of negligence, a person is responsible for the consequences of his acts only if they are foreseeable. *See also* proximate cause.

- *adj.* imminent, prospective, forthcoming

Mental anguish. Nonphysical harm that may be compensated for by damages in some types of lawsuits. Mental anguish can be as limited as the immediate mental feelings during an injury, or as broad as prolonged grief, shame, humiliation, and despair. The misdeed must be so outrageous that a reasonable person would suffer severe emotional distress. Emotional distress can be either the result of intentional, reckless, or negligent acts.

TORTS AND PERSONAL INJURY

Good Samaritan doctrine

[good se.*mehr*.i.ten *dok*.trin]

TORTS AND PERSONAL INJURY

injury

[*in*.jer.ee]

TORTS AND PERSONAL INJURY

gross negligence

[grose *neg*.li.jenss]

TORTS AND PERSONAL INJURY

intent

[in.*tent*]

TORTS AND PERSONAL INJURY

hedonic damages

[hee.*don*.ik *dam*.e.jez]

TORTS AND PERSONAL INJURY

intentional injury

[in.*tent*.shen.al *in*.je.ree]

TORTS AND PERSONAL INJURY

immunity

[im.*yoo*.ni.tee]

TORTS AND PERSONAL INJURY

intentional tort

[in.*tent*.shen.al tort

TORTS AND PERSONAL INJURY

imputed negligence

[im.*pewt*.ed *neg*.li.jenss

TORTS AND PERSONAL INJURY

intervening cause

[in.ter.*veen*.ing kaws]

TORTS AND PERSONAL INJURY

injunction

[in.*junk*.shen]

TORTS AND PERSONAL INJURY

invasion of privacy

[in.*vay*.zhen ov *pry*.ve.see]

The invasion of a legal right; an actionable wrong done to a person, her property, or her reputation. (*Compare* "damage," which is the loss, hurt, or harm resulting from "injury.") An injury is not limited to physical harm done to the body; an injury to the body (that is, a personal injury) may mean death as well as mere physical harm.

- *n.* wrong, damage, loss, detriment, harm, offense
- *ant.* benefit

When a person stops to help an injured person in serious danger, through the negligent acts of another, the rescuer cannot be charged with contributory negligence. In this instance, the rescuer risks her life to save another person. However, the attempt must be reasonable and not reckless. Generally, this protection is provided by state statute. Some jurisdictions refer to this as the rescue doctrine.

Purpose; the plan, course, or means a person conceives to achieve a certain result. Intent is an essential element of intentional torts but not for negligence. Intent is not, however, limited to conscious wrongdoing, and may be inferred or presumed. *See also* malice.

- *n.* determination, scheme, plan, resolve, goal, will and premeditation

Willfully and intentionally acting, or failing to act, with a deliberate indifference to how others may be affected. *See also* negligence.

An injury inflicted by positive, willful, and aggressive conduct, or by design, as opposed to an injury caused by negligence or resulting from an accident. *See also* injury.

Damages awarded by some courts for the loss of enjoyment of life's pleasures. For EXAMPLE: A mother who is injured and can no longer hug her children might seek hedonic damages.

A harm or wrong inflicted by positive, willful, and aggressive conduct, or by design, as opposed to damage caused by negligence or resulting from an accident.

An exemption granted by law, contrary to the general rule. It is a privilege. Immunity may be granted to an individual or a class of persons. *See* Federal Torts Claim Act.

A cause that intrudes between the negligence of the defendant and the injury suffered by the plaintiff, breaking the connection between the original wrongful act or omission and the injury, and itself becoming the proximate cause of the injury.

The negligence of one person that, by reason of her relationship to another person, is chargeable to the other person. EXAMPLE: A parent might be responsible for the acts of his child.

A violation of the right of privacy. *See also* privacy; which is the right to be left alone. EXAMPLE: If an individual's personal income tax forms or medical records are published in the newspaper without her consent, this is an example of a violation of the right to privacy.

A court order that commands or prohibits some act or course of conduct. It is preventive in nature and designed to protect a plaintiff from irreparable injury to his property or property rights by prohibiting or commanding the doing of certain acts. EXAMPLE: a court order prohibiting unlawful picketing. An injunction is a form of equitable relief.

TORTS AND PERSONAL INJURY

joint and several liability

[joynt and *sev*.rel ly.e.*bil*.i.tee]

TORTS AND PERSONAL INJURY

malice

[*mal*.iss]

TORTS AND PERSONAL INJURY

joint tortfeasors

[joynt *tort*.fee.zerz]

TORTS AND PERSONAL INJURY

malicious prosecution

[mel.*ish*.us pross.e.*kyoo*.shen]

TORTS AND PERSONAL INJURY

last clear chance doctrine

[last cleer chayns *dok*.trin]

TORTS AND PERSONAL INJURY

malpractice

[mal.*prak*.tiss]

TORTS AND PERSONAL INJURY

liability

[ly.e.*bil*.i.tee]

TORTS AND PERSONAL INJURY

misrepresentation

[mis.rep.re.zen.*tay*.shen]

TORTS AND PERSONAL INJURY

libel

[*lie*.bul]

TORTS AND PERSONAL INJURY

necessity

[ne.*sess*.i.tee]

TORTS AND PERSONAL INJURY

loss of consortium

[loss ov ken.*sore*.shem]

TORTS AND PERSONAL INJURY

negligence

[*neg*.li.jense]

1. State of mind that causes the intentional doing of a wrongful, danger-ous, or deadly act without legal excuse or justification in deliberate disregard of the lives or safety of others. The term does not necessarily connote personal ill will. It can mean general malice. *Compare* intent. 2. In the law of defamation, to be actionable malice must be actual malice or express malice, as distinct from implied or constructive malice. 3. In the law of damages, additional damages may be awarded if the damage to the plaintiff resulted from an injury inflicted recklessly or with malice. *See also* punitive damages.

The liability of two or more persons who jointly commit a tort (joint tortfeasors). They are re-sponsible individually as well as together.

Civil suit commenced maliciously and without probable cause. After the termination of such a suit in the defendant's favor, the defendant has the right to bring an action against the original plaintiff for the tort of "malicious prosecution."

Two or more persons whose acts, together, contribute to producing a single injury to a third person or to property. Joint tortfeasors are jointly and severally liable. *See also* joint and several liability.

The failure of a professional to act with rea-sonable care; misconduct by a professional in the course of engaging in her profession. For EXAMPLE: Attorneys, physicians, accoun-tants, psychiatrists, and even priests have been charged with malpractice of their duties.

A rule of negligence law by which a negligent defendant is held liable to a plaintiff who has negligently placed himself in peril, if the defendant had a later opportunity than the plaintiff to avoid the occurrence that resulted in injury. In some jurisdictions, the doctrine is referred to as the discovered peril doctrine and in others as the humanitarian doctrine.

The statement of an untruth; a misstatement of fact designed to lead one to believe that something is other than it is; a false statement of fact designed to deceive. EXAMPLE: A jeweler stating to a customer that an inexpensive silver ring is made of platinum would be a misrepresentation.

Although broadly speaking "liability" means legal re-sponsibility, it is a general term whose precise meaning depends upon the context in which it appears. A person's responsibility after she has committed a tort that causes injury. *See also* absolute liability; joint and several liability; product liability; strict liability; vicarious liability.

- *n.* responsibility, debt, obligation, indebtedness

---

1. That which is necessary; that which must be done. 2. That which is compelled by natural forces and cannot be resisted.

A false and malicious publication, expressed either in printing, writing, or by signs and pictures, tending to harm a person's reputation and expose him to public hatred, contempt, or ridicule. *Note* that "libel" is not "liable." *Compare* slander. *See also* malice; defamation.

- *n.* defamation, slander

The failure to do something that a reasonable person would do in the same circumstances, or the doing of something a reasonable person would not do. Negligence is a wrong generally characterized by carelessness, inattentiveness, and neglectfulness rather than by a positive intent to cause injury. *See also* comparative negligence; contributory negligence; gross negligence.

- *n.* thoughtlessness, default, breach of duty, oversight, irresponsibility, carelessness, recklessness, inattentiveness ("the doctor's negligence caused the tumor to go undetected")

The loss of a spouse's assistance, companion-ship, and a spouse's ability to have sexual rela-tions. If such loss results from a tort, it gives rise to a cause of action.

negligence in law

[*neg*.li.jense in law]

omission

[o.*mish*.en]

negligence per se

[*neg*.li.jense per say]

ordinary negligence

[*or*.di.ner.ee *neg*.li.jense]

negligent

[*neg*.li.jent]

pain and suffering

[payn and *suf*.e.ring]

negligent homicide

[*neg*.li.jent *hom*.i.side]

principal

[*prin*.si.pl]

nominal damages

[*nom*.i.nel *dam*.e.jez]

privacy

[*pry*.ve.see]

nuisance

[*noo*.sense]

product liability

[*pro*.dukt ly.e.*bil*.i.tee]

1. Not doing something required by the law.
2. A failure to act; a failure to do something that ought to be done.

- *n.* breach, neglect, disregard, exclusion, oversight

1. A breach of the duty to use care; the failure to observe a duty established by law that proximately causes injury to the plaintiff. *See also* proximate cause. 2. Negligence per se.

The failure to exercise the degree of care that a reasonably prudent person would have exercised in similar circumstances; the failure to exercise ordinary or due care. *Compare* gross negligence. *See* negligence.

Negligence that is beyond debate because the law, usually a statute or ordinance, has established a duty or standard of care that the defendant has violated, as a result of which he has caused injury to the plaintiff. EXAMPLE: failure to stop at a stop sign, as required by law, which is the proximate cause of injury to another driver or a pedestrian. *See also* absolute liability; negligence in law; strict liability.

Mental anguish or physical pain. Damages may be recoverable if the pain and suffering is caused by a tort.

1. Being responsible for an act of negligence.
2. Careless; inattentive; lax. 3. Reckless.

- *adj.* careless, inattentive, reckless, irresponsible

In an agency relationship, the person for whom the agent acts and from whom the agent receives her authority to act.

The crime of causing the death of a person by negligent or reckless conduct.
EXAMPLE: While driving drunk, the driver strikes and kills a pedestrian.

A reference to the right of privacy. The right of privacy is the right to be left alone. The right of privacy means, among other things, that a person's writings that are not intended for public consumption (EXAMPLES: a diary; personal letters) cannot be made public, that a person's photographs may not be publicly distributed, and that a person's private conversations may not be listened in on or recorded. It also means that personal information of the kind in the possession of, for EXAMPLE, the government, insurance companies, and credit bureaus may not be made public. The right to privacy, which is grounded in the Constitution, is supported, and to some extent enforced, by federal and state privacy acts.

Damages awarded to a plaintiff for a small or symbolic amount ($1.00) where no actual damages have been incurred, but the law recognizes the need to vindicate the plaintiff.

The liability of a manufacturer or seller of an article for an injury caused to a person or to property by a defect in the article sold. A product liability suit is a tort action in which strict liability is imposed. The manufacturer or seller of a defective product may be liable to third parties (EXAMPLE: bystanders) as well as to purchasers. A contractual relationship is not a requirement in a product liability case.

Anything a person does that annoys or disturbs another person in her use, possession, or enjoyment of her property, or that renders the ordinary use or possession of the property uncomfortable (EXAMPLES: noise; smoke; a display of public indecency; an encroachment). What constitutes a nuisance in a particular case depends upon numerous factors, including the type of neighborhood in which the property is located, the nature of the act or acts complained of, their proximity to the persons alleging injury or damage, their frequency or continuity, and the nature and extent of the resulting injury, damage, or annoyance.

- *n.* annoyance, inconvenience, bother, intrusion, aggravation, hindrance, problem
- *ant.* benefit

TORTS AND PERSONAL INJURY

proximate cause

[*prok*.si.mit cawz]

TORTS AND PERSONAL INJURY

slander

[*slan*.der]

TORTS AND PERSONAL INJURY

prudent person

[*proo*.dent *per*.sun]

TORTS AND PERSONAL INJURY

special damages

[*spesh*.el *dam*.e.jez]

TORTS AND PERSONAL INJURY

punitive damages

[*pyoo*.ni.tiv *dam*.e.jez]

TORTS AND PERSONAL INJURY

statutes of limitations

[*stat*.shoots ov lim.i.*tay*.shenz]

TORTS AND PERSONAL INJURY

reasonable care

[*ree*.zen.ebl kayr]

TORTS AND PERSONAL INJURY

strict liability

[strikt ly.e.*bil*.i.tee]

TORTS AND PERSONAL INJURY

reasonable person test

[*ree*.zen.ebl *per*.sun test]

TORTS AND PERSONAL INJURY

sudden emergency doctrine

[*sud*.en e.*mer*.jen.see *dok*.trin]

TORTS AND PERSONAL INJURY

res ipsa loquitur

[race *ip*.sa *lo*.kwe.ter]

TORTS AND PERSONAL INJURY

supervening cause

[soo.per.*veen*.ing cawz]

A false and malicious oral statement tending to hurt a person's reputation or to damage her means of livelihood. *Compare* libel. *See also* malice; defamation.

- *n.* defamation, slur, vilification, denigration, ("slander of character")

As an element of liability in a tort case, that cause which, unbroken by any intervening cause, produced the injury, and without which the result would not have occurred; the primary cause; the efficient cause. *Note* that the proximate cause of an injury is not necessarily the final cause or the act or omission nearest in time to the injury.

Damages that may be added to the general damages in a case, and arise from particular (special) circumstances of the case. For EXAMPLE: a dry cleaning bill or a round-trip airline ticket.

A reasonable person, or ordinary prudent person. *See also* reasonable person test.

Federal and state statutes prescribing the maximum period of time during which the various types of civil actions and criminal prosecutions can be brought after the occurrence of the injury or offense.

Damages that are awarded over and above compensatory damages or actual damages because of the wanton, reckless, or malicious nature of the wrong done by the defendant. Such damages bear no relation to the plaintiff's actual loss and are often called exemplary damages, because their purpose is to make an example of the defendant to discourage others from engaging in the same kind of conduct in the future.

Liability for an injury whether or not there is fault or negligence; absolute liability. The law imposes strict liability in product liability cases. EXAMPLE: a defective gas pedal that sticks and the car accelerates by itself, causing injury.

Due care or ordinary care. The degree of care exercised by a reasonable person. *See also* reasonable person test.

The principle that a person who is placed in a position of sudden emergency, not created by his own negligence, will not be held responsible if he fails to act with the degree of care that the law would have required of him had he had sufficient time for thought and reflection.

A standard for determining negligence, which asks: "What would a reasonable person have done in the same circumstances?" In short, it measures the failure to do that which a person of ordinary intelligence and judgment would have done in the same circumstances, or the doing of that which a person of ordinary intelligence and judgment would not have done.

In the law of negligence, a new or additional event that occurs subsequent to the original negligence and becomes the proximate cause of injury.

(*Latin*) Means "the thing speaks for itself." When an instrumentality (i.e., a thing) causes injury, an inference or rebuttable presumption arises that the injury was caused by the defendant's negligence, if the thing or instrumentality was under the exclusive control or management of the defendant and the occurrence was such as in the ordinary course of events would not have happened if the defendant had used reasonable care. EXAMPLE: The utility company may properly be held liable under the doctrine of res ipsa loquitur for a gas explosion that destroys a building in which its equipment is functioning imperfectly.

TORTS AND PERSONAL INJURY

supervening negligence

[soo.per.*veen*.ing *neg*.li.jense]

TORTS AND PERSONAL INJURY

unavoidable casualty

[un.a.*voyd*.abl *kazh*.you.al.tee]

TORTS AND PERSONAL INJURY

tort

[tort]

TORTS AND PERSONAL INJURY

unavoidable cause

[un.a.*voyd*.abl cawz]

TORTS AND PERSONAL INJURY

tortfeasor

[*tort*.fee.zer]

TORTS AND PERSONAL INJURY

unintentional tort

[un.in.*ten*.shen.el tort]

TORTS AND PERSONAL INJURY

tortious

[*tore*.shus]

TORTS AND PERSONAL INJURY

vicarious liability

[vy.*kehr*.ee.us ly.e.*bil*.i.tee]

TORTS AND PERSONAL INJURY

trespass

[*tress*.pas]

TORTS AND PERSONAL INJURY

willful and malicious injury

[*will*.ful and mal.*ish*.ess *in*.jer.ee]

TORTS AND PERSONAL INJURY

unavoidable accident

[un.a.*voyd*.abl *ak*.si.dent]

TORTS AND PERSONAL INJURY

willful and wanton act

[*will*.ful and *want*.en akt]

An occurrence or accident that is beyond human foresight or control.

The negligence of a defendant who is held liable under the last clear chance doctrine; the negligence of a defendant whose conduct is the supervening cause of an injury.

In the law of negligence, a cause that could not have been avoided by the exercise of due diligence and foresight; an accidental cause.

A wrong involving a breach of duty and resulting in an injury to the person or property of another. A tort is distinguished from a breach of contract in that a tort is a violation of a duty established by law, where a breach of contract results from a failure to meet an obligation created by the agreement of the parties. Although the same act may be both a crime and a tort, the crime is an offense against the public that is prosecuted by the state in a criminal action; the tort is a private wrong that must be pursued by the injured party in a civil action. *See also* intentional injury; joint tortfeasors.

- *n.* wrong, civil wrong, violation, breach of duty

A tort that is not done with an intent or knowingly, An unintentional tort is a harm or injury caused by negligence or resulting from an accident. EXAMPLE: A person not paying attention while driving might veer into another car, injuring the occupants. While there was no intent, harm was caused by the driver's negligence.

A person who commits a tort. *See also* joint tortfeasors.

Liability imposed upon a person because of the act or omission of another. EXAMPLES: the liability of an employer for the conduct of her employees; the liability of a principal for the conduct of her agent, the liability of the owner of a car for the conduct of the driver.

1. Involving a tort; wrongful. 2. Pertaining to a tort.

An injury to a person or property inflicted intentionally and deliberately, without cause and with no regard for the legal rights of the injured party.

1. An unauthorized entry or intrusion on the real property of another. 2. In the widest sense of the term, any offense against the laws of society or natural law; any wrong; any violation of law. 3. Any misdeed, act of wrongdoing, or sin.

- *n.* breach, contravention, entry, encroachment, obtrusion, poaching

1. An act or conduct that the perpetrator knows or should know is likely to result in injury, but about which he is indifferent. EXAMPLES: reckless driving, or shooting a gun in a crowded movie theater. 2. A deliberate and intentional wrong.

An inevitable accident; an inescapable peril; an occurrence that could not reasonably have been foreseen or prevented.

TORTS AND PERSONAL INJURY **willful neglect** [*will*.ful neg.*lekt*]	CONTRACTS **accord and satisfaction** [a.*kord* and sat.is.*fak*.shen]
TORTS AND PERSONAL INJURY **willful negligence** [*will*.ful *neg*.li.jense]	CONTRACTS **adhesion contract** [ad.*hee*.zhen *kon*.trakt]
TORTS AND PERSONAL INJURY **wrongful death** [*rong*.ful deth]	CONTRACTS **age of majority** [aj ov ma.*jaw*.ri.tee]
TORTS AND PERSONAL INJURY **wrongful death action** [*rong*.ful deth *ak*.shen]	CONTRACTS **agreement** [a.*gree*.ment]
TORTS AND PERSONAL INJURY **wrongful death statutes** [*rong*.ful deth *stat*.shoots]	CONTRACTS **anticipatory breach** [an.*tiss*.i.pe.tore.ee breech]
CONTRACTS **acceptance** [ak.*sep*.tens]	CONTRACTS **avoid** [a.*voyd*]

An agreement between two persons, one of whom is suing the other, in which the claimant accepts a compromise (usually a lesser amount) in full satisfaction of his claim.

The deliberate or intentional failure of a person to perform a duty to others as required by law. EXAMPLES of such duties include: the duty of a parent to care for a child in some circumstances; the duty of a spouse to provide care to his or her partner; the obligation of a public official to perform a duty required by virtue of her office.

A contract prepared by the dominant party (usually a form contract) and presented on a take-it-or-leave-it basis to the weaker party, who has no real opportunity to bargain about its terms. *See also* contract.

Reckless disregard of a person's safety, evidenced by the failure to exercise ordinary care to prevent injury after discovering an imminent peril. *See also* negligence.

The age at which a person may legally engage in conduct in which she could not previously engage because she was a minor. EXAMPLES: entering into a binding contract; enlisting in the military service; voting; making a valid will.

A death that results from a wrongful act, such as negligence by a doctor in surgery.

1. A contract. 2. A concurrence of intention; mutual assent. *See also* meeting of the minds. 3. A coming together of parties with respect to a matter of opinion.

- *n.* contract, bargain, compact, arrangement, pact, concurrence, compliance, alliance

An action arising under a wrongful death statute. The personal representative of the decedent brings an action on behalf of the decedent's beneficiaries that alleges that the death of the decedent was attributable by the negligent act of another. *See* wrongful death statutes.

The announced intention of a party to a contract that she does not intend to perform her obligations under the contract; an announced intention to commit a breach of contract. *Compare* repudiation.

State statutes that allow the personal representative of the decedent to bring an action on behalf of the decedent's statutory beneficiaries (EXAMPLES: spouse; children) if the decedent's death was the result of the defendant's wrongful act. This action is for the wrong to the beneficiaries.

To cancel, annul, evade, or escape.

1. The assent by the person to whom an offer is made, to the offer as made by the person making it. This is necessary for a binding contract. 2. Unspoken consent to a transaction by a failure to reject it. *See also* offer and acceptance. *Compare* rejection.

CONTRACTS
bargain
[*bar*.gen]

CONTRACTS
competent
[*kom*.pe.tent]

CONTRACTS
bilateral
[by.*lat*.er.el]

CONTRACTS
consideration
[ken.sid.e.*ray*.shen]

CONTRACTS
bilateral contract
[by.*lat*.er.el *kon*.trakt]

CONTRACTS
contract
[*kon*.trakt]

CONTRACTS
boilerplate language
[*boy*.ler.plate *lang*.wej]

CONTRACTS
counteroffer
[*koun*.ter.off.er]

CONTRACTS
breach of contract
[breech ov *kon*.trakt]

CONTRACTS
cure
[kyur]

CONTRACTS
capacity
[ke.*pass*.i.tee]

CONTRACTS
damages
[*dam*.e.jez]

1. Having legal capacity. 2. Capable; qualified. 3. Sufficient; acceptable.

- *adj.* eligible, qualified, capable, fit, polished, efficient, responsible, able
- *ant.* uncapable

---

n. An agreement between two or more persons; a contract.
v. To negotiate; to talk about the terms of a contract.

- *n.* treaty, pact, settlement, deal, agreement, transaction, contract, covenant, stipulation

---

1. The reason a person enters into a contract; that which is given in exchange for performance or the promise to perform; the price bargained and paid; the inducement. Consideration is an essential element of a valid and enforceable contract. A promise to refrain from doing something one is entitled to do also constitutes consideration. 2. Motivation, incentive, inducement.

- *n.* value, incentive, recompense, inducement, reward, benefit ("Consideration is an essential element of a valid and enforceable contract.")

---

1. Involving two interests. 2. Having two sides.

---

n. An agreement entered into, for adequate consideration, to do, or refrain from doing, a particular thing. The Uniform Commercial Code defines a contract as the total legal obligation resulting from the parties' agreement. In addition to adequate consideration, the transaction must involve an undertaking that is legal to perform, and there must be mutuality of agreement and obligation between at least two competent parties. *See also* bilateral contract. *Compare* unilateral contract.
v. To enter into a contract.

- *n.* agreement, understanding, bargain, compact, mutual promise, covenant, accord, arrangement, promise, assurance
- *v.* agree, promise, engage, undertake, covenant, bargain, obligate, pledge

---

A contract in which each party promises performance to the other, the promise by the one furnishing the consideration for the promise from the other. EXAMPLE: a contract for home heating oil (the dealer promises to deliver oil, the homeowner promises to pay). *Compare* unilateral contract.

A position taken in response to an offer, proposing a different deal. This negates the original offer. It is considered a rejection of the offer and the proposal of a new counteroffer. Under the UCC, a counteroffer is considered a proposal of additional terms and the original offer is not considered withdrawn.

Language common to all legal documents of the same type. Attorneys maintain files of such standardized forms for use where appropriate. *Compare* adhesion contract.

---

1. Under the Uniform Commercial Code, a seller has the right to correct ("cure") his failure to deliver goods that conform to the contract if he does so within the period of the contract. 2. To remedy.

- *n.* recovery, improvement, remedy, restoration, correction

---

Failure, without legal excuse, to perform any promise that forms a whole or a part of a contract, including the doing of something inconsistent with its terms. Clear and absolute refusal to perform a contract.

The sum of money that may be recovered in the courts as financial reparation for an injury or wrong suffered as a result of breach of contract or a tortious act.

- *n.* restoration, compensation, restitution, repayment, recovery, reparation, expenses

---

Competency in law. USAGE: "Generally, a minor does not have the capacity to enter into contracts." A person's ability to understand the nature and effect of an act he has engaged in.

CONTRACTS

disaffirm

[dis.e.*ferm*]

CONTRACTS

enforceable

[en.*forss*.ebl]

CONTRACTS

entire output contract

[in.*tire out*.put *kon*.trakt]

CONTRACTS

equity

[*ek*.wi.tee]

CONTRACTS

executed contract

[ek.se.*kyoot*.ed *kon*.trakt]

CONTRACTS

executory contract

[ek.se.kyoo.*tor*.ee *kon*.trakt]

CONTRACTS

express contract

[eks.*press kon*.trakt]

CONTRACTS

formal contract

[*for*.mel *kon*.trakt]

CONTRACTS

implied contract

[im.*plide kon*.trakt]

CONTRACTS

impossibility

[im.poss.i.*bil*.i.tee]

CONTRACTS

impracticability

[im.prak.ti.ke.*bil*.i.tee]

CONTRACTS

incompetency

[in.*kawm*.pe.ten.see]

A contract whose terms are stated by the parties. *Compare* implied contract.

To disclaim; to repudiate; to renounce; to disavow; to deny.

- *v.* disavow, recant, negate, veto, rescind, renege, renounce, deny, repudiate
- *ant.* affirm

---

1. A signed, written contract, as opposed to an oral contract. 2. A contract that must be in a certain form to be valid. EXAMPLE: a negotiable instrument. *Compare* informal contract.

That which can be put into effect or carried out, referring to legal rights. EXAMPLES: a contract; a judgment. If an enforceable contract is breached, a party might seek relief through the court system.

- *adj.* binding, lawful, effective
- *ant.* unenforceable

Implied contracts are of two types: contracts implied in fact, which the law infers from the circumstances, conduct, acts, or the relationship of the parties rather than from their spoken words; and contracts implied in law, which are quasi-contracts or constructive contracts imposed by the law, usually to prevent unjust enrichment.

A contract in which the seller binds herself to the buyer to sell to the buyer the entire amount of a product she manufactures, and the buyer binds himself to buy all of the product. *See also* requirement contract.

That which cannot be done. *Compare* impracticability. When a contract becomes impossible to perform, a party is relieved of the duty of performance. EXAMPLE: A party cannot sell a house that has just burned to the ground.

- *n.* futility, insurmountability, infeasibility, unattainability, failure, unfeasibility, difficulty, failure

A system for ensuring justice in circumstances where the remedies customarily available under the conventional law are inadequate; a system of jurisprudence less formal and more flexible than the common law, available in particular types of cases to better ensure a fair result. EXAMPLE: Instead of awarding money damages, a court might order the opposing party to stop doing a certain act, such as operating a noisy business near a residential area.

A legal term unique to the Uniform Commercial Code, from the provision of the UCC that excuses a seller from the obligation to deliver goods when delivery has become unrealistic because of unforeseen circumstances. *Compare* impossibility of performance; legal impossibility. *See also* Uniform Commercial Code.

A contract whose terms have been fully performed. *Compare* executory contract.

---

1. The condition, state, or status of an incompetent person. 2. Lack of capability to perform a required duty. *Compare* competent.

A contract yet to be performed, each party having bound herself to do or not to do a particular thing. *Compare* executed contract.

CONTRACTS

infancy

[*in*.fen.see]

CONTRACTS

mailed

[maled]

CONTRACTS

informal contract

[in.*for*.mel *kon*.trakt]

CONTRACTS

majority

[ma.*jaw*.ri.tee]

CONTRACTS

intention

[in.*ten*.shen]

CONTRACTS

meeting of the minds

[*meet*.ing ov the mindz]

CONTRACTS

invitation

[in.vi.*tay*.shen]

CONTRACTS

misrepresentation

[mis.rep.re.zen.*tay*.shen]

CONTRACTS

lapse

[laps]

CONTRACTS

mistake

[mis.*take*]

CONTRACTS

liquidated damages

[*lik*.wi.dated *dam*.e.jez]

CONTRACTS

mutual assent

[*myo*.choo.el a.*sent*]

Describes an item when it is appropriately enveloped or packaged, addressed, and stamped, and deposited in a proper place for the receipt of mail. In contract law, acceptance of an offer takes place when the acceptance is mailed, unless the parties have made another arrangement or a statute provides otherwise. This is sometimes referred to as the "mailbox rule."

---

1. The status of a person who has not reached the age of majority and who therefore is under a civil disability; nonage; minority, generally under the age of 18. 2. A civil disability resulting from the fact that one has not yet attained one's majority. 3. The period of life during which one is a very young child.

- *n.* childhood; inception, start, conception

Legal age; full age; the age at which a person acquires the capacity to contract; the age at which a person is no longer a minor. The age of majority varies from state to state and differs depending upon the purpose.

- *n.* legal age, full age, age of responsibility

A contract not in the customary form, often an oral contract. *Compare* formal contract.

The mutual assent of the parties to a contract with respect to all of the principal terms of the contract. A meeting of the minds is essential to the creation of a legally enforceable contract.

Purpose; plan; object; aim; goal. The intention of the parties is the most important factor in interpreting a contract.

- *n.* course, purpose, route, propensity, plan, object, aim, goal ("the intention of the parties")

The statement of an untruth; a misstatement of fact designed to lead one to believe that something is other than it is; a false statement of fact designed to deceive.

- *n.* fraud, deception, deceit, distortion, fabrication, exaggeration

---

An express or implied request by a person for another person to make an offer. EXAMPLE: An advertisement in a newspaper is really an invitation for the public to make an offer to purchase an item.

---

1. An erroneous mental conception that influences a person to act or to decline to act; an unintentional act, omission, or error arising from ignorance, surprise, imposition, or misplaced confidence. "Mistake" is a legal concept especially significant in contract law because, depending upon the circumstance, it may warrant reformation or rescission of a contract. 2. An error; a misunderstanding; an inaccuracy.

- *n.* misconception, inaccuracy, confusion ("a mistake of identity")

---

n. A termination or extinguishment, particularly of a right or privilege; a forfeiture caused by a person's failure to perform some necessary act or by the nonoccurrence of some contingency. *v.* To cease: to expire: to terminate. EXAMPLE: An offer can lapse after a reasonable time.

A meeting of the minds; consent; agreement.

A sum agreed upon by the parties at the time of entering into a contract as being payable by way of compensation for loss suffered in the event of a breach of contract; a sum similarly determined by a court in a lawsuit resulting from breach of contract.

CONTRACTS
mutual mistake
[*myoo*.choo.el mis.*take*]

CONTRACTS
oral contract
[*ohr*.el *kon*.trakt]

CONTRACTS
offer
[*off*.er]

CONTRACTS
performance
[per.*form*.ense]

CONTRACTS
offer and acceptance
[*off*.er and ak.*sep*.tense]

CONTRACTS
promise
[*prom*.iss]

CONTRACTS
offeree
[off.er.*ree*]

CONTRACTS
promisee
[prom.i.*see*]

CONTRACTS
offeror
[off.er.*ror*]

CONTRACTS
promisor
[prom.i.*sore*]

CONTRACTS
option
[*op*.shen]

CONTRACTS
quantum meruit
[*kwan*.tum *mehr*.oo.it]

A contract that is not in writing. Unless the subject of an oral contract is covered by the statute of frauds, it is just as valid as a written contract; often, however, its enforceability is limited because its terms cannot be proven. *See also* contract, informal contract.

- *n.* parol contract

Both sides of a transaction or contract have different perceptions of fact or law. This may warrant the changing or canceling of a contract.

1. The doing of that which is required by a contract at the time, place, and in the manner stipulated in the contract; that is, according to the terms of the contract. 2. Fulfilling a duty in a manner that leaves nothing more to be done.

- *n.* fulfillment, effort, production

n. 1. A proposal made with the purpose of obtaining an acceptance, thereby creating a contract. *See also* offer, acceptance, mailed. 2. A tender of performance. 3. A statement of intention or willingness to do something. 4. A proposal; a proposition; a bid. *See also* counteroffer.
v. To propose for acceptance or rejection.

- *v.* present, propose, provide, award, suggest
- *n.* proposal, suggestion, endeavor, proposition, submission, bid

1. An undertaking that binds the promisor to cause a future event to happen; an offer that, if supported by consideration, and if accepted, is a contract. 2. An assurance that a thing will or will not be done. It gives the person to whom it is made the right to demand the performance or nonperformance of the thing if she acted in reliance and to her detriment. 3. Under the Uniform Commercial Code, "a written undertaking to pay money signed by the person undertaking to pay."

- *v.* affirm, swear, vow, pledge, covenant, vouch ("I promise I will do this for you.")
- *n.* oath, declaration, affirmation, vow, pledge, assurance, endorsement, covenant

Essential elements in the creation of a legally enforceable contract, reflecting mutual assent or a meeting of the minds. In the case of a bilateral contract, acceptance is the offeree's communication that she intends to be bound by the offer; in the case of a unilateral contract, the offeree accepts by performing in accordance with the terms of the offer.

A person to whom a promise is made.

A person to whom an offer is made. *Compare* offeror.

A person who makes a promise.

A person who makes an offer.

(*Latin*) Literally, it means "as much as is deserved." This doctrine makes a person liable to pay for goods or services she accepts, while knowing the other party expects to be paid, even if no contract exists.

An offer, combined with an agreement supported by consideration not to revoke the offer for a specified period of time; a future contract in which one of the parties has the right to insist on compliance with the contract, or to cancel it, at his election. In other words, "option" is short for option contract.

- *n.* advantage, offer, choice, preference, prerogative ("option to purchase")

CONTRACTS
quasi-contract
[*kway*.zye *kon*.trakt]

CONTRACTS
rescission
[ree.*sizh*.en]

CONTRACTS
ratify
[*rat*.i.fy]

CONTRACTS
restitution
[res.ti.*tew*.shen]

CONTRACTS
reformation
[ref.er.*may*.shun]

CONTRACTS
revocation of offer
[rev.e.*kay*.shen ov *off*.er]

CONTRACTS
rejection
[re.*jek*.shun]

CONTRACTS
statute of frauds
[*stat*.shoot ov frawdz]

CONTRACTS
repudiation
[re.pyoo.dee.*ay*.shun]

CONTRACTS
third-party beneficiary contract
[third-*par*.tee ben.e.*fish*.er.ee *kon*.trakt]

CONTRACTS
requirement contract
[re.*kwire*.ment *kon*.trakt]

CONTRACTS
unconscionable
[un.*kon*.shen.ebl]

The abrogation, annulment, or cancellation of a contract by the act of a party. Rescission may occur by mutual consent of the parties, pursuant to a condition contained in the contract, or for fraud, failure of consideration, material breach, or default. It is also a remedy available to the parties by a judgment or decree of the court. More than mere termination, rescission restores the parties to the status quo existing before the contract was entered into.
- *n.* unmaking, termination, withdrawal, voidance, extricating

An obligation imposed by law to achieve equity, usually to prevent unjust enrichment. A quasi-contract is a legal fiction that a contract exists where there has been no express contract. EXAMPLE: a contract implied on the theory of quantum meruit.

In both contract and tort, a remedy that restores the status quo. Restitution returns a person who has been wrongfully deprived of something to the position he occupied before the wrong occurred; it requires a defendant who has been unjustly enriched at the expense of the plaintiff to make the plaintiff whole, either, as may be appropriate, by returning property unjustly held, by reimbursing the plaintiff, or by paying compensation. *See also* unjust enrichment.
- *n.* compensation, repayment, amends, dues, recompense, reparation

To give approval, to confirm.
- *v.* sanction, confirm, countersign, agree, affirm, authorize
- *ant.* repudiate

The withdrawal of an offer by an offeror before it has been accepted. An offer can be withdrawn anytime before acceptance.

To modify or correct the contract to reflect the intent of the parties. An equitable remedy available to a party to a contract provided she can prove that the contract does not reflect the true agreement.

A statute, existing in one form or another in every state, that requires certain classes of contract to be in writing and signed by the parties. Its purpose is to prevent fraud or reduce the opportunities for fraud. A contract to guarantee the debt of another is an EXAMPLE of an agreement that the statute of frauds requires to be in writing.

1. Any act or word of an offeree, communicated to an offeror, conveying her refusal of an offer.
2. The act of rejecting.
- *n.* abandonment, disallowance, denial, refusal, waiver

A contract made for the benefit of a third person, other than the parties making the contract. EXAMPLE: Parents buy life insurance for the benefit of their children.

A denial of the validity of something; a denial of authority.
- *n.* denial, rejection, renunciation, repeal, retraction, nullification, disaffirmation

Morally offensive, reprehensible, or repugnant. An unconscionable contract is a contract in which a dominant party has taken unfair advantage of a weaker party, who has little or no bargaining power, and has imposed terms and conditions that are unreasonable and one-sided. A court may refuse to enforce an unconscionable contract. *See* adhesion contract.
- *adj.* excessive, preposterous, exorbitant, unscrupulous inexcusable, unequal, grossly unfair

A contract under which one party agrees to furnish the entire supply of specified goods or services required by the other party for a specified period of time, and the other party agrees to purchase his entire requirement from the first party exclusively. *See also* entire output contract.

CONTRACTS
undue influence
[*un*.dew *in*.flew.ense]

CONTRACTS
valid
[*val*.id]

CONTRACTS
unenforceable
[un.en.*forss*.ebl]

CONTRACTS
void contract
[voyd *kon*.trakt]

CONTRACTS
Uniform Commercial Code (UCC)
[*yoon*.i.form ke.*mersh*.el kode]

CONTRACTS
voidable
[*voyd*.ebl]

CONTRACTS
unilateral contract
[yoon.i.*lat*.er.el *kon*.trakt]

CONTRACTS
voidable contract
[*voyd*.ebl *kon*.trakt]

CONTRACTS
unilateral mistake
[yoon.i.*lat*.er.el mis.*take*]

AGENCY
agency
[*ay*.jen.see]

CONTRACTS
unjust enrichment
[un.*just* en.*rich*.ment]

AGENCY
agency by estoppel
[*ay*.jen.see by es.*top*.el]

Effective; sufficient in law; legal; lawful; not void; in effect. USAGE: "Valid contract"; "valid marriage"; "valid defense."

- *adj.* legal, lawful ("valid contract")

Inappropriate pressure exerted on a person for the purpose of causing him to substitute his will with the will or wishes of another.

A contract that creates no legal rights; the equivalent of no contract at all. *Compare* voidable contract.

That which cannot be put into effect or carried out. USAGE: "unenforceable contract." Compare enforceable.

Something that is defective but valid unless disaffirmed by the person entitled to disaffirm.

- *adj.* avoidable, reversible, revocable, nullifiable ("a voidable contract")

One of the Uniform Laws, which have been adopted in much the same form in every state. It governs most aspects of commercial transactions, including sales, leases, negotiable instruments, deposits and collections, letters of credit, bulk sales, warehouse receipts, bills of lading and other documents of title, investment securities, and secured transactions.

A contract that may be avoided or disaffirmed by one of the parties because it is defective; for EXAMPLE, a contract induced by fraud.

A contract in which there is a promise on one side only, the consideration being an act or something other than another promise. In other words, a unilateral contract is an offer that is accepted not by another promise but by performance. EXAMPLE: The Acme Company promises Winton Electronics that if it buys products from Acme, Winton will be the sole Chicago distributor of Acme products. *Compare* bilateral contract.

A relationship in which one person acts for or on behalf of another person at the other person's request. *See also* implied agency.

A misconception by one, but not both, parties to a contract with respect to the terms of the contract.

An agency created by appearances that lead people to believe that the agency exists. It occurs when the principal, through negligence, permits her agent to exercise powers she never gave him, even though she has no knowledge of his conduct. *See also* estoppel, apparent authority; implied agency; implied authority.

The equitable doctrine that a person who unjustly receives property, money, or other benefits that belong to another may not retain them and is obligated to return them. The remedy of restitution is based upon the principle that equity will not permit unjust enrichment.

AGENCY

agency by ratification

[*ay*.jen.see by rat.i.fi.*cay*.shen]

AGENCY

apparent authority

[a.*par*.ent aw.*thaw*.ri.tee]

AGENCY

**agency coupled
with an interest**

[*ay*.jen.see *cup*.ld with an *in*.trest]

AGENCY

commission agent

[ke.*mish*.en *ay*.jent]

AGENCY

agency in fact

[*ay*.jen.see in fakt]

AGENCY

consignee

[ken.sine.*ee*]

AGENCY

agency relationship

[*ay*.jen.see re.*lay*.shun.ship]

AGENCY

consignment

[ken.*sine*.ment]

AGENCY

agent

[*ay*.jent]

AGENCY

consignment contract

[ken.*sine*.ment *kon*.trakt]

AGENCY

apparent agent

[a.*par*.ent *ay*.jent]

AGENCY

consignor

[ken.sine.*or*]

Authority that an agent is permitted to exercise, although not actually granted by the principal. *See also* agency by estoppel.

A relationship in which one misrepresents one's self as an agent to a principal, when in fact one is not, while the principal accepts the unauthorized act.

An agent who buys or sells on commission; a fee or payment calculated on a percentage basis. *See* factor.

See power coupled with an interest.

The person to whom a carrier is to deliver a shipment of goods; the person named in a bill of lading to whom the bill promises delivery; the person to whom goods are given on consignment, either for sale or safekeeping. *Compare* consignor. *See also* factor.

- *n.* receiver, salesperson, representative, seller
- *ant.* consignor

An agency created by the agreement of the principal and the agent, as distinguished from an agency created by operation of law. EXAMPLE: an agency by estoppel.

The entrusting of goods either to a carrier for delivery to a consignee or to a consignee who is to sell the goods for the consignor.

- *n.* entrusting, distribution, committal, transmittal

The relationship that exists in law between a principal and an agent.

A consignment of goods to another (the consignee) with the understanding either that she will sell them for the consignor and forward the proceeds, or, if she does not, that she will return them to the consignor. A consignment is also known as a bailment for sale.

One of the parties to an agency relationship, specifically, the one who acts for and represents the other party, who is known as the principal. The word implies service as well as authority to do something in the name of or on behalf of the principal (EXAMPLE: a person who represents a business person in contract negotiations). Although one can be both an employee and an agent, the usual distinction between the two is that the manner in which an employee does his work is controlled and directed by his employer; in contrast, an agent is free to use independent skill and judgment, his principal's concern being the results he produces, not how he does his work. *See also* del credere agent; general agent; managing agent; special agent; universal agent.

- *n.* assistant, delegate, emissary, assignee, deputy, functionary, proxy, representative

A person who sends goods to another on consignment; the person named in a bill of lading as the person from whom goods have been received for shipment. *Compare* consignee.

- *n.* shipper, sender
- *ant.* consignee

One who is, in law, an agent because she has obvious authority. EXAMPLE: a nurse in uniform working at a doctor's office, who greets patients in the waiting room.

AGENCY

del credere agent

[*del kreh.de.reh ay.jent*]

AGENCY

fiduciary

[fi.*doo*.she.air.ee]

AGENCY

deviation doctrine

[dee.vee.*ay*.shen *dok*.trin]

AGENCY

fiduciary duty

[fid.*doo*.she air.ee *dew*.tee]

AGENCY

employee

[em.*ploy*.ee]

AGENCY

frolic and detour

[*froll*.ik and *de*.tur]

AGENCY

employer

[em.*ploy*.er]

AGENCY

general agent

[*jen*.e.rel *ay*.jent]

AGENCY

estoppel

[es.*top*.el]

AGENCY

implied agency

[im.*plide ay*.jen.see]

AGENCY

factor

[*fak*.ter]

AGENCY

implied authority

[im.*plide* aw.*thaw*.ri.tee]

A person who is entrusted with handling the money or property of another person. EXAMPLES: attorney and client; guardian and ward; trustee and beneficiary.

(*Italian*) An agent who guarantees his principal against the default of those with whom he contracts.

Duty to act loyally and honestly with respect to interests of another; the duty the law imposes upon a fiduciary.

The rule that if an agent has digressed only slightly from the instructions of the principal, the principal is not excused from liability for the agent's negligence.

The negligent conduct of an employee or agent who has departed from doing the employer's or principal's business to do something unrelated to work, for which the employer/principal is not liable.

A person who works for another for pay in a relationship that allows the other person to control the work and direct the manner in which it is done. The earlier legal term for employee was servant. *Compare* independent contractor. *Also compare* agent. *Note* that statutory definitions of "employee" may differ, depending upon the purpose of the statute. For EXAMPLE, although the distinctions between the definitions of employee in the Social Security Act, the Fair Labor Standards Act, and the National Labor Relations Act may seem insignificant, they may, in any given instance, be critical.

- *n.* servant, worker, agent, laborer, helper, personnel, jobholder

---

An agent authorized to perform all acts connected with the business of his principal. *Compare* special agent. *See also* agent; managing agent.

A person who hires another to work for her for pay in a relationship that allows her to control the work and direct the manner in which it is done. The earlier legal term for employer was master.

- *n.* master, contractor, director, boss, chief
- *ant.* employee

An actual agency, the existence of which is proven by deductions or inferences from the facts and circumstances of the situation, including the words and conduct of the parties. *Compare* estoppel; apparent authority.

A prohibition imposed by law against uttering what may actually be the truth. A person may be estopped by his own *acts or representations* (that is, not be permitted to deny the truth or significance of what he said or did) if another person who was entitled to rely upon those statements or acts did so to her detriment. This type of estoppel is also known as equitable estoppel or estoppel in pais.

- *n.* impediment, prohibition, restraint, ban, bar

The authority of an agent to do whatever acts are necessary to carry out her express authority. EXAMPLE: An attorney retained to commence a legal action has the implied authority to file such pleadings as she feels are appropriate.

A person employed to receive goods from a principal and to sell them for compensation, usually in the form of a commission referred to as factorage. A factor is a bailee (person to whom property is entrusted) who is sometimes called a consignee or commission merchant (e.g., sale of right to collect accounts in exchange for a commission).

- *n.* ingredient, determinant, consideration, instrumentality, point; bailee, consignee, commission, merchant

AGENCY

imputed

[im.*pew*.ted]

AGENCY

power coupled with an interest

[*pow*.er *cup*.ld with an *in*.trest]

AGENCY

imputed knowledge

[im.*pew*.ted *nawl*.edj]

AGENCY

power of attorney

[*pow*.er ov a.*tern*.ee]

AGENCY

imputed negligence

[im.*pew*.ted *neg*.li.jenss]

AGENCY

principal

[*prin*.sipl]

AGENCY

independent contractor

[in.de.*pen*.dent *kon*.trak.ter]

AGENCY

respondeat superior

[res.*pon*.dee.at soo.*peer*.ee.or]

AGENCY

managing agent

[*man*.e.jing *ay*.jent]

AGENCY

servant

[*ser*.vent]

AGENCY

master

[*mas*.ter]

AGENCY

special agent

[*spesh*.el *ay*.jent]

1. A power of appointment that includes an interest in the thing itself. 2. A power that gives an agent an interest in the subject of the agency. EXAMPLE: the power and interest of a partner in a business who is given the right to manage the business as security for loans he has made to the partnership.

1. That which is attributed to a person, not because he personally performed the act (or personally had knowledge or notice), but because of his relationship to another person for whose acts, omissions, knowledge, or notice he is legally responsible. USAGE: "The neglect by his paralegal in this matter will be imputed to attorney Jones." *See also* agency. 2. Blamed; implicated; ascribed; charged.

- *adj.* attributed, blamed, implicated, ascribed, charged ("The paralegal's neglect is the attorney's imputed neglect.")

A written instrument by which a person appoints another as his agent or attorney in fact and confers upon her the authority to perform certain acts. A power of attorney may be "full" (a general power of attorney) or "limited" (a special power of attorney). The power to sell property without specifying which property, or to whom, is an EXAMPLE of a general power of attorney; the power to sell a particular piece of property to a particular person is an EXAMPLE of a special power of attorney.

1. An agent's knowledge that is binding upon his principal because of their agency relationship. 2. Knowledge of facts charged to a person because anyone of ordinary common sense would know them. 3. That which a person has a duty to know and the means of knowing.

In an agency relationship, the person for whom the agent acts and from whom the agent receives her authority to act. *See also* undisclosed principal.

The negligence of one person that, by reason of her relationship to another person, is chargeable to the other person. EXAMPLE: An employer is liable for the negligence of his employee that occurs within the scope of employment.

(*Latin*) Means "Let the master respond." The doctrine under which liability is imposed upon an employer for the acts of its employees committed in the course and scope of their employment. Similarly, respondeat superior makes a principal liable for a tort committed by her agent, and a master responsible for the negligence of his servant.

As distinguished from an employee, a person who contracts to do work for another person in her own way, controlling the means and method by which the work is done but not the end product. An independent contractor is the agent of the person with whom she contracts. *Compare* employee.

An outdated term for employee. *See also* master. *See also and compare* agent; employee; independent contractor.

A person to whom a corporation has given general powers involving the exercise of judgment and discretion in conducting the corporation's business. *See* agent. *See also* general agent.

An agent authorized to perform a particular or specific act connected with the business of her principal. *Compare* general agent.

1. An outdated term for employer. *See also* employer; master; servant. 2. A person who has control or authority over others.

- *n.* officer, official, employer, boss, director, leader, commandant, head ("office master")

AGENCY

third party

[thurd *par*.tee]

AGENCY

vicarious liability

[vy.*kehr*.ee.us ly.e.*bil*.i.tee]

AGENCY

third-party beneficiary

[thurd-*par*.tee ben.e.*fish*.er.ee]

INTELLECTUAL PROPERTY

abandonment of trademark

[a.*ban*.den.ment ov *trade*.mark]

AGENCY

third person

[thurd *per*.sen]

INTELLECTUAL PROPERTY

abstract

[*ab*.strakt]

AGENCY

undisclosed agency

[un.dis.*klozed ay*.jen.see]

INTELLECTUAL PROPERTY

access

[*ak*.sess]

AGENCY

undisclosed principal

[un.dis.*klozed prin*.sipl]

INTELLECTUAL PROPERTY

amendment to allege use

[a.*mend*.ment to a.*lej* yoose]

AGENCY

universal agent

[yoon.i.*ver*.sel *ay*.jent]

INTELLECTUAL PROPERTY

arbitrary mark

[*ar*.bi.trare.ee mark]

Liability imposed upon a person because of the act or omission of another. EXAMPLES: the liability of an employer for the conduct of its employees; the liability of a principal for the conduct of her agent. *See also* respondeat superior.

A person who is not a party to an agreement, instrument, or transaction, but who may have an interest in the transaction. *See also* third person.

Loss of trademark rights resulting from non-use of the mark; demonstrated by sufficient evidence that the owner intends to discontinue use of the mark. May also occur when a mark has lost its distinctiveness or through the owner's misuse of trademark rights.

The intended beneficiary of a contract made between two other persons. A third-party beneficiary may sue to enforce such a contract (e.g., the child of a couple who signed a separation agreement guaranteeing college tuition for the child).

Summary of the invention that enables the reader to determine the character of the patentable subject matter.

As the term is used in the law, either a person who has an interest in a transaction or a person who has an interest in an action (i.e., a party or a third party).

The reasonable opportunity of the defendant to view or hear the copyrighted work.

A situation in which a person who is in fact an agent for another deals with a third person as if he were the principal, the fact that he is an agent being unknown or hidden. *See also* undisclosed principal.

Amendment to an intent-to-use application indicating use of a mark in commerce; the amendment can only be filed before approval of the mark for publication (or, if there is a rejection, within six months of the response period).

The unrevealed principal in a situation involving an undisclosed agency.

Word or image that has a common meaning that does not describe or suggest the goods or services with which it is associated.

An agent who is authorized to do everything her principal is entitled to delegate.

INTELLECTUAL PROPERTY
architectural work
[ar.ka.*tek*.cha.ral werk]

INTELLECTUAL PROPERTY
collective mark
[ku.*lek*.tiv mark]

INTELLECTUAL PROPERTY
audiovisual works
[aw.dee.o.*vizh*.u.al werkz]

INTELLECTUAL PROPERTY
copyright
[*kop*.ee.rite]

INTELLECTUAL PROPERTY
author
[*aw*.ther]

INTELLECTUAL PROPERTY
copyright infringement
[*kop*.ee.rite in.*frinj*.ment]

INTELLECTUAL PROPERTY
authorization of agent
[aw.ther.i.*zay*.shen ov *ay*.jent]

INTELLECTUAL PROPERTY
copyright notice
[*kop*.ee.rite *no*.tiss]

INTELLECTUAL PROPERTY
automated database
[*awt*.toh.may.ted *day*.tah.base]

INTELLECTUAL PROPERTY
derivative work
[*de*.riv.e.tiv werk]

INTELLECTUAL PROPERTY
basic registration
[*ba*.sik rej.is.*tray*.shen]

INTELLECTUAL PROPERTY
design patent
[de.*zine pat*.ent]

A trademark or service mark used to identify a trade association, fraternal society, or union. *See* trademark and service mark.

The design of a building as embodied in any tangible medium of expression, including a building, architectural plans, or drawings; it includes the overall form as well as the arrangement and composition of spaces and elements in the design, but does not include individual standard features.

n. The right of an author, granted by federal statute, to exclusively control the reproduction, distribution, and sale of her literary, artistic, or intellectual productions for the period of the copyright's existence. Copyright protection extends to written work, music, films, sound recordings, photographs, paintings, sculpture, and some computer programs and chips. The symbol © is used to show copyright protection. *See also* intellectual property; literary property.
v. To acquire a copyright.

- *n.* authority, grant, license, permit, privilege authorization

Works that consist of a series of related images that are intrinsically intended to be shown by the use of machines or devices, such as projectors, viewers, or electronic equipment, together with accompanying sounds, if any, regardless of the nature of the material objects, such as films or tapes, in which the works are embodied.

Using any portion of a copyrighted material without the consent of the copyright owner. *Compare* fair use doctrine.

1. A person who produces a written work. 2. A person who originates something; a maker. In copyright law, a person can be an author without producing any original material, provided she does something beyond copying, such as compiling or editing.

- *n.* producer, maker, originator, biographer, inventor, creator, planner

A notice specifically required in a special form by law in each copy of a published work. EXAMPLE: © or the word copyright.

Inventor's or patent owner's authorization of representation by a patent agent.

A work based upon one or more preexisting works, such as a translation, musical arrangement, dramatization, fictionalization, motion picture version, sound recording, art reproduction, abridgment, condensation, or any other form in which a work may be recast, transformed, or adapted. A work consisting of editorial revisions, annotations, elaborations, or other modifications that, as a whole, represent an original work of authorship is also a derivative work.

A body of facts, data, or other information assembled into an organized format suitable for use in a computer and comprising one or more files.

A patent of a design that gives an original and pleasing appearance to an article.

The primary copyright record made for each version of a particular work.

INTELLECTUAL PROPERTY
device
[de.*vice*]

INTELLECTUAL PROPERTY
distinctive
[dis.*tink*.tiv]

INTELLECTUAL PROPERTY
dilution
[dil.*loo*.shen]

INTELLECTUAL PROPERTY
divisional application
[da.*vizh*.an.el ap.li.*kay*.shen]

INTELLECTUAL PROPERTY
disclaimer
[dis.*klame*.er]

INTELLECTUAL PROPERTY
doctrine of equivalents
[*dok*.trin ov ee.*kwiv*.e.lentz]

INTELLECTUAL PROPERTY
disparagement
[dis.*pa*.rej.ment]

INTELLECTUAL PROPERTY
dramatic works
[dra.*mat*.ik werkz]

INTELLECTUAL PROPERTY
disparagement of goods
[dis.*pa*.rej.ment ov goodz]

INTELLECTUAL PROPERTY
drawing (trademark)
[*draw*.ing *trade*.mark]

INTELLECTUAL PROPERTY
display publicly
[dis.*play pub*.lik.lee]

INTELLECTUAL PROPERTY
evaluation agreement
[i.val.yoo.*ay*.shen a.*gree*.ment]

Characteristic, distinguishing, particular, un-common, idiosyncratic, salient, not indentical, clearly different.

1. In patent law, an invention. 2. An emblem such as a business logo or a union label. 3. An apparatus; machine, appliance, or contrivance.

- *n.* instrument, mechanism, contraption, invention, construction, apparatus ("an eating device")

Application made for an independent invention that has grown out of an earlier application; a method of dividing an original application that contains two or more inventions. Trademark applications may also be divided.

The adverse effect of use of a similar mark on the reputation of a distinctive mark, even though the use may not confuse consumers as to the source of the goods or services; occurs when the defendant's use weakens or reduces the distinctive quality of the mark. A claim of dilution is available only under state laws, sometimes known as antidilution statutes.

Right of patent owner to prevent sale, use, or manufacture of a discovery or invention if it em-ploys substantially the same means to achieve substantially the same results in substantially the same way as that claimed.

Statement that a trademark owner asserts no exclusive right in a specific portion of a mark, apart from its use within the mark.

Narrative presentations (and any accompanying music) that generally use dialogue and stage directions as the basis for a theatrical exhibition.

Discredit; detraction; dishonor; denunciation; disrespect.

A substantially exact representation of the mark as used (or, in the case of intent-to-use appli-cations, as intended to be used). A drawing is required for all federal trademark applications and for many state trademark applications.

Criticism that discredits the quality of merchan-dise or other property offered for sale.

Contract by which one party promises to submit an idea and the other party promises to evaluate the idea. After the evaluation, the evaluator will either enter into an agreement to exploit the idea or promise not to use or disclose the idea.

To show a copy of a copyrighted work, either directly or by means of a film, slide, television image, or any other device or process where the public is gathered or the work is transmit-ted or otherwise communicated to the public.

INTELLECTUAL PROPERTY
exclusive jurisdiction
[eks.*kloo*.siv joo.ris.*dik*.shen]

INTELLECTUAL PROPERTY
infringement
[in.*frinj*.ment]

INTELLECTUAL PROPERTY
exclusive license
[eks.*kloo*.siv *ly*.sense]

INTELLECTUAL PROPERTY
infringement of copyright
[in.*frinj*.ment ov *kop*.ee.rite]

INTELLECTUAL PROPERTY
exhaustion doctrine
[eg.*zaws*.chen *dok*.trin]

INTELLECTUAL PROPERTY
infringement of patent
[in.*frinj*.ment ov *pat*.ent]

INTELLECTUAL PROPERTY
fair use doctrine
[fayr yoos *dok*.trin]

INTELLECTUAL PROPERTY
infringement of trademark
[in.*frinj*.ment ov *trade*.mark]

INTELLECTUAL PROPERTY
generic
[jen.*err*.ik]

INTELLECTUAL PROPERTY
intangible
[in.*tan*.jibl]

INTELLECTUAL PROPERTY
idea
[eye.*dee*.uh]

INTELLECTUAL PROPERTY
intangible asset
[in.*tan*.jibl *ass*.et]

A violation of a right or privilege. EXAMPLE: violation of a copyright.

- *n.* violation, misfeasance, invasion, encroachment, interference, breach ("infringement of patent")

A court's sole authority to hear a certain type of case.

Using any portion of copyrighted material without the consent of the copyright owner. *Compare* fair use doctrine. *See also* copyright.

Agreement by patent holder to restrict the grant of proprietary rights to one person.

The manufacture, use, or sale of a patent or process patent without the authorization of the owner of the patent.

When a patented product (or product resulting from a patented process) is sold or licensed, the patent owner loses some or all patent rights as to the resale of that particular article.

A use or imitation of a trademark in such manner that a purchaser of goods is likely to be deceived into believing that they are the goods of the owner of the trademark.

The principle that entitles a person to use copyrighted material in a reasonable manner, including a work's theme or idea, without the consent of the copyright owner. EXAMPLE: teachers photocopying one page of a magazine for students to read.

---

adj. Without physical substance; nonmaterial. *Compare* tangible property.
n. A thing that may or may not have value, but has no physical substance; an intangible asset or intangible property. EXAMPLES: a copyright; goodwill. *Compare* tangible property.

- *adj.* nonphysical, abstract, imperceptible, impalpable

---

1. Pertaining to a kind, class, or group. 2. General; inclusive. A generic marker or term would lack the distinctiveness for trademark protection. USAGE: A generic drug.

Intangible property that has value. *Compare* tangible property.

Concept, thought, belief, proposal in the mind of the inventor to be applied to an invention.

INTELLECTUAL PROPERTY

intangible property

[in.*tan*.jibl *prop*.er.tee]

INTELLECTUAL PROPERTY

licensee

[ly.sen.*see*]

INTELLECTUAL PROPERTY

intellectual property

[in.te.*lek*.choo.el *prop*.er.tee]

INTELLECTUAL PROPERTY

literary property

[*lit*.e.re.ree *prop*.er.tee]

INTELLECTUAL PROPERTY

internet piracy

[*in*.ter.net *py*.re.see]

INTELLECTUAL PROPERTY

literary work

[*lit*.e.re.ree werk]

INTELLECTUAL PROPERTY

invention

[in.*ven*.shen]

INTELLECTUAL PROPERTY

logo

[*loh*.go]

INTELLECTUAL PROPERTY

inventor

[in.*ven*.ter]

INTELLECTUAL PROPERTY

misappropriation of trade secret

[*mis*.a.pro.pree.*ay*.shen ov trayd *see*.kret]

INTELLECTUAL PROPERTY

license

[*ly*.sense]

INTELLECTUAL PROPERTY

moral rights

[*mor*.el rytz]

A person to whom the owner of a patent, copyright, or trademark grants a right to use.

---

1. A right unrelated to a physical thing. EXAMPLES: a right to sue (i.e., a cause of action); a right to inherit property. 2. Property that has no intrinsic value, but evidences something of value. EXAMPLE: a stock certificate (which evidences a share in the ownership of the corporation that issued it). *Compare* tangible property.

The interest of an author, or anyone to whom he has transferred his interest, in his own work; the exclusive right of an author to use and profit from his own written or printed intellectual production. *See also* intellectual property; literary work; infringement of copyright.

Property (EXAMPLES: copyrights; patents; trade secrets) that is the physical or tangible result of original thought. Modern technology has brought about widespread infringement of intellectual property rights. EXAMPLE: the unauthorized reproduction and sale of videotapes, audiotapes, and computer software. *See also* infringement of copyright, infringement of patent, literary property, piracy.

In copyright law, "works, other than audiovisual works, expressed in words, numbers, or other verbal or numerical symbols or induced, regardless of the nature of the material objects, such as books, periodicals, manuscripts, phone records, film, tapes, disks, or cards, in which they are embodied."

Theft conducted on the Internet by illegally copying, downloading, or distributing unauthorized software.

Graphic symbols that function as a mark. *See also* trademark.

---

1. The act of creating something patentable. *See also* patent, device. 2. The thing that has been invented. 3. The act of creating something new.

- *n.* finding, discovery, creation

Improper acquisition of a trade secret by a person who has reason to know that the trade secret was obtained by improper means, or the disclosure or use of a trade secret without consent by a person who either had a duty to maintain secrecy or who used improper means to acquire the secret.

A person who creates an invention.

- *n.* author, maker, creator, devisor

Rights that protect the professional honor and reputation of an artist by guaranteeing the right to claim or disclaim authorship of a work and the right to prevent, in certain cases, distortion, mutilation, or other modification of the work.

---

1. A special privilege, not a right common to everyone. 2. Authorization by the owner of a patent to make, use, or sell the patented article; permission by the owner of a trademark or copyright to use the trademark or to make use of the copyrighted material.

INTELLECTUAL PROPERTY

motion picture

[*moh*.shen *pik*.chur]

INTELLECTUAL PROPERTY

patent rights

[*pat*.ent rytz]

INTELLECTUAL PROPERTY

patent

[*pat*.ent]

INTELLECTUAL PROPERTY

patentability

[*pat*.ent.a.bil.a.tee]

INTELLECTUAL PROPERTY

Patent and Trademark Office

[*pat*.ent and *trade*.mark *off*.iss]

INTELLECTUAL PROPERTY

patentable

[*pat*.ent.ebl]

INTELLECTUAL PROPERTY

patent infringement

[*pat*.ent in.*frinj*.ment]

INTELLECTUAL PROPERTY

patentee

[pat.en.*tee*]

INTELLECTUAL PROPERTY

patent medicine

[pat.*ent med*.i.sin]

INTELLECTUAL PROPERTY

pioneer patent

[*py*.e.neer *pat*.ent]

INTELLECTUAL PROPERTY

patent pending

[*pat*.ent *pen*.ding]

INTELLECTUAL PROPERTY

piracy

[*py*.re.see]

The rights a patentee receives with respect to her invention as a result of having been granted a patent for it.

Audiovisual works consisting of a series of related images that, when shown in succession, impart an impression of motion with sound, if any.

The quality of being patentable.

n. 1. The exclusive right of manufacture, sale, or use granted by the federal government to a person who invents or discovers a device or process that is new and useful. *See also* device, invention. 2. The grant of a right, privilege, or authority by the government. The abbreviation "Pat." is often used.
v. To obtain a patent upon an invention.

- *n.* permit, license, certificate, trademark, right, legal right

Entitled to receive a patent. To be patentable, an idea must include every essential characteristic of the complete and practical invention.

Authorized by the Constitution and established by Congress, this office of the federal government registers all trademarks and grants all patents issued in the United States. Its duties also include examining patents, hearing and deciding appeals from inventors and trademark applicants, and publishing the *Official Gazette.*

A person who receives a patent.

See infringement of patent.

A patent in a new field; a totally new device; a basis patent.

An over-the-counter medication; a medication concocted by a manufacturer, often according to a secret formula. Note that a patent medicine is generally not patented; however, it is often protected by trademark.

A term for infringement of copyright or for using literary property without permission, plagiarism.

- *n.* plagiarism, infringement, appropriation ("Printing an article without the author's permission is piracy.")

The status of a patent application while it is being determined if the invention is new and useful. The symbol used for this is "Pat. Pend."

INTELLECTUAL PROPERTY

public use

[*pub*.lik yoos]

INTELLECTUAL PROPERTY

trademark

[*trayd*.mark]

INTELLECTUAL PROPERTY

registration

[rej.is.*tray*.shen]

INTELLECTUAL PROPERTY

trademark infringement

[*trayd*.mark in.*frinj*.ment]

INTELLECTUAL PROPERTY

service mark

[*ser*.viss mark]

INTELLECTUAL PROPERTY

trademark license

[*trayd*.mark *ly*.sense]

INTELLECTUAL PROPERTY

tangible property

[*tan*.jibl *prop*.er.tee]

INTELLECTUAL PROPERTY

trade name

[trayd naym]

INTELLECTUAL PROPERTY

trade dress

[trayd dres]

INTELLECTUAL PROPERTY

trade secret

[trayd *see*.kret]

INTELLECTUAL PROPERTY

trade libel

[trayd *ly*.bel]

INTELLECTUAL PROPERTY

transfer of copyright ownership

[tranz.*fer* ov *kop*.ee.rite *oh*.ner.ship]

A mark, design, title, logo, or motto used in the sale or advertising of products to identify them and distinguish them from the products of others. A trademark is the property of its owner and, when registered under the Trademark Act, is reserved for the exclusive use of its owner. The symbol ® is used to indicate a registered trademark. *Compare* service mark, trade name. *See also* collective mark.

- *n.* logo, brand, identification, mark, design, initials, logotype, stamp

---

In patent law, any use of an invention other than a secret or experimental use. If such a use continues for one year or more, prior to the date of patent application, this will prevent the issuance of a patent.

Use of a substantially similar mark by a junior user that creates a likelihood of consumer confusion. *See also* infringement of trademark.

The act of registering.

- *n.* recording, reservation, enrollment, filing, listing

Agreement granting limited trademark rights to another.

A mark design, title, or motto used in the sale or advertising of services to identify the services and distinguish them from the services of others. A service mark is the property of its owner and, when registered under the Trademark Act, is reserved for the exclusive use of its owner. *Compare* trademark.

The name under which a company does business. The goodwill of a company includes its trade name. *Compare* trademark.

Property, real or personal, that has physical substance; property that can be physically possessed. EXAMPLES: real estate; automobiles; jewelry.

Confidential information concerning an industrial process or the way in which a business is conducted. Trade secrets are of special value to a business and are the property of the business. EXAMPLE: a secret ingredient in a fried chicken recipe.

The size, shape, texture, color, graphics, and other distinct features of a product that constitute its total appearance used to promote the sale of the product.

An assignment, mortgage, exclusive license, transfer by will or intestate succession, or any other change in the ownership of any or all of the exclusive rights in a copyright, whether or not it is limited in time or place of effect, but not including a nonexclusive license.

A libel that defames the goods or products a person produces in her business or occupation, as opposed to a libel against the person herself.

INTELLECTUAL PROPERTY

transmit

[tranz.*mit*]

INTELLECTUAL PROPERTY

utility patents

[yoo.*til*.i.tee *pat*.entz]

INTELLECTUAL PROPERTY

tying

[*tye*.ing]

INTELLECTUAL PROPERTY

visually perceptible copy

[*vizh*.yoo.e.lee per.*sep*.ta.ble *kop*.ee]

INTELLECTUAL PROPERTY

unfair competition

[un.*fare* kom.pe.*tish*.en]

INTELLECTUAL PROPERTY

work of authorship

[werk ov *aw*.ther.ship]

INTELLECTUAL PROPERTY

useful article

[*yoos*.ful *ar*.tikl]

INTELLECTUAL PROPERTY

work of visual art

[werk ov *vizh*.yoo.ul art]

INTELLECTUAL PROPERTY

usefulness

[*yoos*.ful.ness]

INTELLECTUAL PROPERTY

work made for hire

[werk mayd for hyer]

INTELLECTUAL PROPERTY

use in commerce

[yoos in *kom*.erss]

INTELLECTUAL PROPERTY

writ of seizure

[rit ov *seez*.zher]

The most common type of patent, granted on the basis that the invention is of benefit to society.

To communicate a copyrighted work by any device or process where images or sounds are received beyond the place from which they are sent.

A copy that can be visually observed when it is embodied in a material object, either directly or with the aid of a machine or device.

Business practice in which the purchase of a patented item is tied to a second, nonpatented item. An unjustified tying arrangement is patent misuse (also called tie-in). EXAMPLE: when someone uses the electronic product of one company, he must use a special device from another company for the first product to function.

Creation of intellectual or artistic effort fixed or embodied in a perceptible form and meeting the statutory standards of copyright protection.

A collection of common law principles that protect against unfair business practices. The use or imitation of another firm's name, mark, logo design, or title for the purpose of creating confusion in the public mind and causing the public to believe that a competitor's business or product is one's own. Such practices are illegal.

Under the Copyright Act of 1976, either (1) a painting, drawing, print, or sculpture, existing in a single copy, in a limited edition of 200 copies or fewer that are signed and consecutively numbered by the author, or, in the case of a sculpture, in multiple cast, carved, or fabricated sculptures of 200 or fewer that are consecutively numbered by the author and bear the signature or other identifying mark of the author; or (2) a still photographic image produced for exhibition purposes only, existing in a single copy that is signed by the author.

An article having an intrinsic utilitarian function that is not merely to portray the appearance of the article or to convey information. An article that is normally a part of a useful article is considered a useful article.

1. A work prepared by an employee within the scope of his or her employment. 2. A work specially ordered or commissioned for use as a contribution to a collective work, as a part of a motion picture or other audiovisual work, as a translation, as a supplementary work, as a compilation, as an instructional text, as a test, as answer material for a test, or as an atlas, if the parties expressly agree in a written instrument signed by them that the work shall be considered a work made for hire.

An invention must be new and have a use or purpose and must work (i.e., be capable of performing its intended purpose).

Order of the court directing the federal marshal to seize and hold infringing merchandise; granted only upon payment of a bond.

Use of a trademark by placing it on goods or containers, tags or labels, displays associated with the goods (or, if otherwise impracticable, on documents associated with the goods), and selling or transporting the goods in commerce regulated by the United States.

INTELLECTUAL PROPERTY
writing

[*write*.ing]

TAX LAW
adjusted basis

[a.*just*.ed *bay*.siss]

TAX LAW
accelerated depreciation

[ak.*sel*.e.ray.ted de.pree.shee.*ay*.shen]

TAX LAW
adjusted gross income

[a.*just*.ed *grose in*.kum]

TAX LAW
accrued income

[a.*krewd in*.kum]

TAX LAW
amended return

[a.*mend*.ed re.*tern*]

TAX LAW
accrued interest

[a.*krewd in*.trest]

TAX LAW
amortization

[am.er.ti.*zay*.shen]

TAX LAW
ad valorem tax

[ad va.*lore*.em takz]

TAX LAW
amortize

[*am*.er.tize]

TAX LAW
adjusted

[a.*just*.ed]

TAX LAW
appreciation

[a.pree.she.*ay*.shen]

For the purpose of calculating the amount of income tax due, the original cost of property offset for such things as casualty losses and depreciation.

1. Anything that is written. The Uniform Commercial Code defines "written" or "writing" to include "printing, typewriting, or any other intentional reduction (or words) to tangible form." 2. The expression of ideas by visible letters, numbers, or other symbols.

An income tax term for gross income less the deductions (generally, business expenses) permitted by law. *Compare* taxable income.

Rapid depreciation of the value of a capital asset in order to produce larger tax deductions during the early years of the life of the asset. *Compare* straight-line depreciation. *See also* depreciation.

Within the limitations prescribed by law, amended tax returns may be filed to correct inaccuracies and omissions in the original return. *See also* return.

Income that a person has earned but has not yet claimed. *See also* income; earned income.

The act of amortizing. *See also* amortize.

Interest that has been earned but has not yet been paid.

1. To gradually pay off a debt by regular payments in a fixed amount over a fixed period of time. 2. To depreciate an intangible asset (EXAMPLES: stock; bills).

A tax established in proportion to the value of the property to be taxed. EXAMPLE: a tax of $3 on an antique worth $100 and $9 on an antique worth $300, the tax being 3 percent of the value, as distinguished from a $5 tax regardless of the value of the antique.

An increase in the value of something. *Compare* to depreciation.

1. Corrected; balanced. 2. Brought into line.

TAX LAW

assessment

[a.*sess*.ment]

TAX LAW

capital

[*ka*.pi.tel]

TAX LAW

assessor

[a.*sess*.er]

TAX LAW

capital assets

[*ka*.pi.tel *ass*.ets]

TAX LAW

audit

[*aw*.dit]

TAX LAW

capital gain

[*ka*.pi.tel gayn]

TAX LAW

auditor

[*aw*.dit.er]

TAX LAW

capital gains tax

[*ka*.pi.tel gaynz takz]

TAX LAW

back taxes

[back *tak*.sez]

TAX LAW

death taxes

[deth *tak*.sez]

TAX LAW

basis

[*bay*.siss]

TAX LAW

declaration of estimated tax

[dek.le.*ray*.shen ov *ess*.ti.may.ted takz]

adj. Relating to wealth.
n. 1. Broadly, the total assets of a business.
2. Money or property used for the production
of wealth. 3. An owner's equity in a business.

- n. cash, stock, wealth, holdings, financial
  assets, funds, resources

---

1. Imposing of tax on the basis of a listing
and valuation of the property to be taxed.
2. Requiring a payment above and beyond that
which is normal. EXAMPLE: the imposition of a
15 percent penalty on property taxes paid after
a certain date.

All assets except those excluded from that category by the Internal Revenue Code.

A public official who makes an assessment of
property, usually for purposes of taxation.

- n. charger, estimator, collector

Financial gain resulting from the sale or exchange of capital assets. *See also* gain.

---

1. A formal or official examination and verification of accounts,
vouchers, and other financial records as, for EXAMPLE, a
tax audit or an independent audit of a company's books and
records. 2. Any verification of figures by an accountant.

- n. analysis, review, scrutiny, verification ("The audit is
  complete.")
- v. analyze, balance, investigate, examine, monitor, probe
  ("The accountant audited the books.")

Income tax upon financial gain resulting from
the sale or exchange of capital assets. *See also*
gain.

---

1. A person who conducts an audit. 2. A civil
servant whose duty it is to examine the accounts of state officials to determine whether
they have spent public funds in accordance with
the law.

- n. accountant, bookkeeper, cashier,
  inspector

Another term for inheritance taxes or estate
taxes.

---

1. Taxes that are owed from a prior date.
2. Taxes on which the ordinary processes
for collection have been exhausted.

A formal estimate of income anticipated during the
forthcoming tax year, required under federal and
state tax codes from corporations, trusts, and estates, and individuals who receive income that is not
subject to withholding (generally, income other than
wages). Such declarations must be accompanied by
payment of the estimated tax.

In tax law, the cost of property as of a
certain date, upon which depreciation can be
computed and gain or loss can be calculated
when the property is sold or exchanged.

- n. cost ("the tax basis of the property")

TAX LAW
deductible
[de.*duk*.tibl]

TAX LAW
direct tax
[dye.*rekt* takz]

TAX LAW
deduction
[de.*duk*.shen]

TAX LAW
earn
[urn]

TAX LAW
deferred
[de.*ferd*]

TAX LAW
earned
[urnd]

TAX LAW
deferred income
[de.*ferd in*.kum]

TAX LAW
earned income
[urnd *in*.kum]

TAX LAW
dependent
[dee.*pen*.dent]

TAX LAW
earned income credit
[urnd *in*.kum *kred*.it]

TAX LAW
depreciation
[dee.pree.shee.*ay*.shen]

TAX LAW
equalization of taxes
[ee.kwe.li.*zay*.shen ov *tak*.sez]

A tax (also called a property tax or an ad valorem tax) levied directly on real or personal property based upon value, or directly upon income (i.e., an income tax). Such a tax should be distinguished from an indirect tax, which is levied upon the importation, consumption, manufacture, or sale of articles and upon the privilege of doing business or engaging in a profession.

Expenses that a taxpayer is permitted to subtract, in whole or in part, in computing her taxable income. EXAMPLES: interest on the mortgage on one's home; casualty losses; charitable contributions. *See also* deduction.

- *adj.* removable, allowable, discountable

Receive as a result of labor or services.

- *v.* gain, draw, win, acquire ("earn wages")

---

1. The amount allowed a taxpayer in reduction of gross income for the purpose of determining adjusted gross income. 2. That which may be taken away or subtracted, particularly money.

- *n.* subtraction, withdrawal, removal, exemption, allowance ("the home office deduction")

---

1. Received as a result of labor or service.
2. Gained; acquired.

Put off to a future time; postponed.

Income received for work or for the performance of some service. Unearned income includes dividends, interest, etc.

A tax law term for payments received before they are earned. (EXAMPLE: payment of $1,000 in 2010 to a tutor who is to provide 20 lessons in 2011)

A tax credit on earned income for low income workers with dependent children, as defined by the Internal Revenue Code.

In tax law, a person whose relationship to the taxpayer is such that the taxpayer is entitled to claim her as an exemption when filing his income tax return. EXAMPLE: a child of the taxpayer who is less than 19 years of age.

- *n.* minor, charge, ward

Carried out by boards of equalization; the process of adjusting the total assessments on all real estate in a tax district to equalize them with the total assessments in other tax districts in the state, the goal being equality and uniformity in taxation.

---

1. The lessening in worth of any property caused by wear, use, time, or obsolescence. *Compare* appreciation. 2. In computing income tax, a deduction allowed for the gradual loss of usefulness of a capital asset used in business or in the production of income.

- *n.* devaluation, reduction, deflation
- *ant.* appreciation

TAX LAW

estate tax

[es.*tate* takz]

TAX LAW

gain

[gayn]

TAX LAW

exemption

[eg.*zemp*.shen]

TAX LAW

gift tax

[gift takz]

TAX LAW

extension of time

[eks.*ten*.shen ov time]

TAX LAW

gross

[grose]

TAX LAW

Federal Insurance Contributions Act

[*fed*.er.el in.*shoor*.ense kon.tri.*byoo*.shenz akt]

TAX LAW

gross estate

[grose es.*tate*]

TAX LAW

FICA

[fy.ka]

TAX LAW

gross income

[grose *in*.kum]

TAX LAW

fiscal year

[*fis*.kel yeer]

TAX LAW

head of household

[hed ov *house*.hold]

1. Earnings; profits; proceeds; return; yield; interest; increase; addition. 2. Excess of revenue over expense. *Compare* loss.

- *n.* acquisition, profit, appreciation, enhancement

A tax imposed by the federal government and most states upon the transmission of property by a deceased person. The tax is imposed upon the net estate of the decedent without reference to the recipient's relationship to the decedent or to the amount a recipient receives. An estate tax is a transfer tax. *See also* inheritance, or death, taxes.

A tax on the transfer by gift, by a living person, of money or other property. The federal government and most states impose gift taxes. By comparison, there are distinctly different tax consequences if the transfer of the gift occurs upon the death of the donor (*see also* estate tax). Additionally, special tax considerations apply to gifts made by living persons in contemplation of death. A gift tax is a transfer tax.

---

1. An allowance granted by way of a deduction when computing one's taxable income. EXAMPLES: a tax exemption for a dependent; a personal exemption. 2. The person for whom an exemption may be claimed in an income tax return.

Without deduction; as a whole; entire; total. EXAMPLES: gross earnings; gross income; gross pay. *Compare* net income.

---

1. Modification of an obligation by giving additional time for performance. 2. An enlargement of time.

---

1. The value of all property left by a decedent, before payment of taxes and expenses. 2. The value of all taxable property in a decedent's estate.

The federal statute that funds Social Security and Medicare by taxing employers, the wages of employees, and the earnings of the self-employed. Most people are aware of this law because of the FICA deduction that appears on their pay stub.

---

1. Total income. 2. The whole or entire profit from a business. 3. Under the Internal Revenue Code, "all income from whatever source derived," before allowance for deductions or exemptions. *Compare* net income. *See also* adjusted gross income.

See Federal Insurance Contributions Act.

A single person, other than a surviving spouse, who provides a home for certain persons, generally dependents. Also, married persons who live apart are each a head of household. A head of household is entitled to pay federal income tax at a lower rate than other single persons.

An accounting period of 12 consecutive months. Both businesses and individuals may choose any such 12-month period as their tax year. A fiscal year is often referred to by its abbreviation, FY.

TAX LAW

income

[*in*.kum]

TAX LAW

IRS

TAX LAW

income tax

[*in*.kum takz]

TAX LAW

Internal Revenue Service

[in.*tern*.el *rev*.e.new *ser*.viss]

TAX LAW

income tax return

[*in*.kum takz re.*tern*]

TAX LAW

joint return

[joynt re.*tern*]

TAX LAW

individual retirement account

[in.de.*vid*.joo.el re.*tire*.ment a.*kount*]

TAX LAW

loss

[loss]

TAX LAW

inheritance tax

[in.*hehr*.i.tense taks]

TAX LAW

marital deduction

[*mehr*.i.tel de.*duk*.shen]

TAX LAW

Internal Revenue Code

[in.*tern*.el *rev*.e.new kode]

TAX LAW

net income

[net *in*.kum]

Abbreviation for Internal Revenue Service.

The gain derived from capital or from labor, including profit gained through a sale or conversion of capital assets. *See also* adjusted gross income; earned income; gross income; net income; taxable income.

  - *n.* wages, salary, earning, profit, livelihood

Popularly known as the IRS, the organization that administers and enforces the Internal Revenue Code. The Internal Revenue Service is an agency within the Department of the Treasury.

A tax based on income, personal or corporate. The Internal Revenue Code, which is the federal tax law, taxes income from "whatever source derived." Many states and municipalities tax income as well.

A single income tax return filed by a husband and wife reporting their combined incomes. Although married persons are entitled to file separately, their total tax liability is usually greater if they do.

See tax return.

The term is also applied extensively in tax law, where it is used in contradistinction to gain, and refers to transactions involving an excess of expense over revenue.

Under the Internal Revenue Code, individuals who are not included in an employer-maintained retirement plan may deposit money (up to an annual maximum amount set by the Code) in an account for the purchase of retirement annuities. No tax is paid on income deposited to an IRA, and the proceeds are taxable only when they are withdrawn.

In computing the taxable estate, a deduction allowed under both the federal estate tax and gift tax with respect to property passing from one spouse to the other.

A tax on the privilege of taking the property of a decedent by descent or under a will, but not as a tax on the decedent's right to dispose of his property or a tax on the property itself. *Compare* estate tax. *See* death taxes.

Gross income less ordinary and necessary expenses; taxable income. *Compare* gross income.

A compilation of all federal statutes that impose taxes (EXAMPLES: income tax, estate tax; gift tax; excise tax) or provide for the administration of such laws.

TAX LAW

penalty

[*pen*.el.tee]

TAX LAW

tax bracket

[takz *brak*.et]

TAX LAW

return

[re.*tern*]

TAX LAW

tax credit

[takz *kred*.it]

TAX LAW

Roth IRA

[Rawth *eye*.rah]

TAX LAW

tax evasion

[takz e.*vay*.zhen]

TAX LAW

straight-line depreciation

[strayt-line de.*pree*.shee.*ay*.shen]

TAX LAW

tax exemption

[takz eg.*zemp*.shen]

TAX LAW

tax

[takz]

TAX LAW

tax return

[takz re.*tern*]

TAX LAW

tax audit

[takz a*w*.dit]

TAX LAW

taxable

[*tak*.sebl]

A taxpayer's tax rate category. "Tax bracket" is synonymous with tax rate, and is based upon the amount of the taxpayer's taxable income.

An additional charge because of a delinquency in making payment. The IRS imposes such a penalty on taxpayers who file late tax returns. *Note* that a penalty is not interest, and is usually assessed in addition to interest.

- *n.* sanction, sentence, forfeiture, castigation, retribution, punishment

---

A credit that reduces the amount of income tax owed by a taxpayer, as opposed to a deduction, which merely reduces a taxpayer's taxable income. *See also* exemption.

A formal accounting of a person's income; for EXAMPLE, a tax return.

Willfully avoiding payment of taxes legally due; for EXAMPLE, fraudulently concealing or understating one's income. Tax evasion is also referred to as tax fraud and is a felony.

A type of retirement account permitted under the tax laws that allows a tax reduction on some of the money deposited for retirement. Individuals pay income tax and then make their contributions with post-tax dollars. The principal grows tax-free. There are no further taxes when the money is withdrawn for retirement.

---

1. Freedom from the obligation to pay taxes.
2. A personal exemption under the Internal Revenue Code. *See also* exemption.

A method of depreciating an asset at an even pace by subtracting its estimated salvage value from its cost and dividing the remainder by the number of years of its estimated useful life. *Compare* accelerated depreciation. *See also* depreciation.

---

1. A formal accounting that every person who has income is required to make to the government every tax year; the form on which a taxpayer reports his taxable income annually and on the basis of which he pays his income tax.
2. Independent of income, any formal accounting required by law to be made to any taxing authority with respect to property, gifts, estates, sales, or the like. *See also* return, amended return, declaration of estimated tax, joint return.

An involuntary charge imposed by the government (whether national, state, or local, or any of their political subdivisions) upon individuals, corporations, or trusts, or their income or property, to provide revenue for the support of the government. Taxes may be imposed on, among other things, sales, gifts, and estates, and may be called, among other things, imposts, duties, excises, levies, and assessments. EXAMPLES of different types of taxes include: ad valorem tax, capital gains tax, estate tax, excise tax, export tax, franchise tax, gift tax, income tax, inheritance taxes, intangibles tax, luxury tax, occupation tax, payroll tax, privilege tax, property tax, sales tax, school taxes, and transfer tax.

- *n.* levy, assessment, tribute, impost, exaction, imposition, capitulation, tithe ("a graduated tax")
- *v.* assess, levy, exact, collect, require

Subject to tax; liable to taxation.

- *adj.* liable to taxation, assessable, chargeable, exactable ("a taxable gift")

An examination by the IRS of a taxpayer's books and records to determine the accuracy of his income tax return.

TAX LAW

taxable income

[*tak*.sebl *in*.kum]

TAX LAW

withholding tax

[with.*hole*.ding takz]

TAX LAW

taxation

[tak.*say*.shen]

WILLS, TRUSTS, AND ESTATES

administrator

[ad.*min*.is.tray.ter]

TAX LAW

taxing

[*tak*.sing]

WILLS, TRUSTS, AND ESTATES

administrator cum testamento annexo

[ad.*min*.is.tray.ter kum tes.ta.*men*.to an.*eks*.o]

TAX LAW

taxpayer

[*taks*.pay.er]

WILLS, TRUSTS, AND ESTATES

administrator de bonis non

[ad.*min*.is.tray.ter day *boh*.nis non]

TAX LAW

W-2 wage and tax statement

[W-2 wayj and takz *stayt*.ment]

WILLS, TRUSTS, AND ESTATES

advance directive

[ad.*vanse* de.*rekt*.iv]

TAX LAW

W-4 form

[W-4 form]

WILLS, TRUSTS, AND ESTATES

attest

[a.*test*]

Federal and state income tax and FICA contributions deducted by an employer from the pay of employees and remitted by the employer to the IRS.

With respect to liability for federal income tax; in the case of an individual, adjusted gross income, less itemized deductions, or the standard deduction plus personal exemptions; in the case of a corporation, gross income less deductions.

A person who is appointed by the court to manage the estate of a person either who died without a will or whose will failed to name an executor or named an executor who declined or was ineligible to serve. The administrator of an estate is also referred to as a personal representative.

- *n.* representative, executor, trustee ("the estate's administrator")

The act or process of levying, assessing, and collecting taxes; the act of taxing.

The court-appointed administrator of the estate of a decedent whose will failed to name an executor or whose named executor cannot or refuses to serve. Cum testamento annexo, a Latin phrase meaning "with will attached," is often abbreviated CTA. *Compare* administrator DBN.

The act or process of levying, assessing, and collecting a tax; taxation.

The court-appointed administrator of the estate of a decedent whose executor has died or resigned. De bonis non, a Latin phrase meaning "goods not administered," is often abbreviated DBN. *Compare* administrator CTA.

A person who is under a legal obligation to pay a tax; a person who has paid a tax.

A term for the various instruments a person can use to ensure that her wishes with respect to health care are carried out if she is no longer able to speak for herself. EXAMPLES: a health-care proxy; a living will. *See* durable power of attorney.

A form issued to a taxpayer annually showing earnings summary as well as withholding taxes.

To swear to; to bear witness to; to affirm to be true or genuine. *See also* attestation.

- *v.* adjure, announce, assert, aver, certify, swear, support, sustain

A document in which taxpayers state the number of exemptions claimed for employer's payroll purposes per IRS regulations.

WILLS, TRUSTS, AND ESTATES

attestation

[a.tes.*tay*.shen]

WILLS, TRUSTS, AND ESTATES

bypass trust

[*bi*.paz trust]

WILLS, TRUSTS, AND ESTATES

attestation clause

[a.tes.*tay*.shen clawz]

WILLS, TRUSTS, AND ESTATES

codicil

[*kod*.i.sil]

WILLS, TRUSTS, AND ESTATES

attesting witness

[a.*test*.ing *wit*.nes]

WILLS, TRUSTS, AND ESTATES

competency

[*kom*.pe.ten.see]

WILLS, TRUSTS, AND ESTATES

beneficiary

[ben.e.*fish*.ee.air.ee]

WILLS, TRUSTS, AND ESTATES

curtesy

[*ker*.te.see]

WILLS, TRUSTS, AND ESTATES

bequeath

[be.*kweeth*]

WILLS, TRUSTS, AND ESTATES

decedent

[de.*see*.dent]

WILLS, TRUSTS, AND ESTATES

bequest

[be.*kwest*]

WILLS, TRUSTS, AND ESTATES

decedent's estate

[de.*see*.dents es.*tate*]

Also called a credit shelter trust or credit trust. This is used for estate planning purposes so that a deceased spouse's estate passes or goes to a trust instead of to the surviving spouse. This is generally used by married couples to pass money on to their children and bypass as much government estate taxes as is possible.

The act of witnessing the signing of a document, including signing one's name as a witness to that fact.

- *n.* endorsement, affirmation, certification, testimony, evidence ("an attestation clause")

An addition or supplement to a will, which adds to or modifies the will without replacing or revoking it. A codicil does not have to be physically attached to the will.

- *n.* addition, supplement, appendix, accessory, addendum, attachment, extension ("codicil to a will")

A clause, usually at the end of a document such as a deed or a will, that provides evidence of attestation. EXAMPLES: "signed, sealed, and delivered in the presence of"; "witness my hand and seal."

---

1. Legal capacity. The ability to execute binding contracts, wills, etc. 2. A testator is considered competent if she understands the general nature and extent of her property, potential beneficiaries of the estate, and the purpose of a will. 3. The right to sue and be sued.

A person who witnesses the signing of a document. *See also* attestation.

The rights a man had under common law with respect to his wife's property. These rights have now been modified in every state, and the rights are extended to a wife in her husband's property.

---

1. A person who receives a benefit. 2. A person who has inherited or is entitled to inherit under a will. 3. A person for whom property is held in trust. 4. A person who is entitled to the proceeds of a life insurance policy when the insured dies. 5. A person designated by statute as entitled to the proceeds of a legal action such as a wrongful death action.

- *n.* heir, recipient, successor, legatee, assignee

A legal term for a person who has died. *See also* decedent's estate.

- *n.* deceased, testator, intestate, dead individual, departed

---

To leave personal property or money by will; such a gift is called a bequest or a legacy. A gift of real property by will is properly called a devise, although the courts generally construe "bequeath" as synonymous with "devise" when it is used in connection with a testamentary gift of real estate.

- *v.* grant, give, assign, remit, leave, provide

The total property, real and personal, that a decedent owns at the time of her death.

Technically, a gift of personal property by will, (i.e., a legacy), although the term is often loosely used in connection with a testamentary gift of real estate as well. *Compare* devise. *See also* bequeath.

- *n.* gift, devise, endowment, heritage, legacy

WILLS, TRUSTS, AND ESTATES

devise

[de.*vize*]

WILLS, TRUSTS, AND ESTATES

**durable power
of attorney**

[*dew*.rebl *pow*.er of a.*tern*.ee]

WILLS, TRUSTS, AND ESTATES

devisee

[de.vie.*zee*]

WILLS, TRUSTS, AND ESTATES

elective share

[e.*lek*.tiv share]

WILLS, TRUSTS, AND ESTATES

devisor

[de.*vie*.zor]

WILLS, TRUSTS, AND ESTATES

estate

[es.*tate*]

WILLS, TRUSTS, AND ESTATES

discretionary trust

[dis.*kresh*.en.air.ee trust]

WILLS, TRUSTS, AND ESTATES

estate of inheritance

[es.*tate* ov in.*herr*.i.tense]

WILLS, TRUSTS, AND ESTATES

distribution

[dis.tre.*byoo*.shen]

WILLS, TRUSTS, AND ESTATES

estate per autre vie

[es.*tate* per *oh*.tre vee]

WILLS, TRUSTS, AND ESTATES

dower

[*dow*.er]

WILLS, TRUSTS, AND ESTATES

estate planning

[es.*tate* *plan*.ing]

A power of attorney that remains effective even though the grantor becomes mentally incapacitated. Some durable powers of attorney become effective only where a person is no longer able to make decisions for herself. EXAMPLES: A health-care proxy; a living will. *See* advance directive.

n. A gift of real property by will, although it is often loosely used to mean a testamentary gift of either real property or personal property. *Compare* bequest; legacy. *v.* 1. To dispose of real property by will. By comparison, "bequeath" is a word used in wills to transfer personal property. However, the term "devise and bequeath" applies to both real property and personal property. *Compare* bequest; legacy.

- *v.* confer, bequeath, convey, endow ("She devised her business operation to her daughter.")
- *n.* inheritance, legacy, transfer, conveyance ("the devise of the family jewels")

In some states, the share a surviving spouse may elect to take in the estate of the deceased spouse. In such jurisdictions, it replaces dower. *See* dower.

The beneficiary of a devise.

---

1. The property left by a decedent; (i.e., a decedent's estate). 2. The right, title, and interest a person has in real or personal property, either tangible or intangible. Estates in real property (estates in land or landed estates) include both freehold estates (EXAMPLES: a fee simple; a fee tail; a life estate) and estates less than freehold (EXAMPLES: estates for years; estates at will). 3. The property itself.

- *n.* assets, wealth, property, fortune, personality, effects

A testator who makes a devise.

Also known as a fee, a freehold interest in land that is inheritable; (i.e., an interest that the tenant is not only entitled to enjoy for his own lifetime, but which, after his death, if he leaves no will, his heirs will inherit under the intestate laws).

A trust in which broad discretion is vested in the trustee and is to be exercised by her in carrying out the purposes of the trust.

An estate that is to last for the life of a person other than the tenant. EXAMPLE: "I give Blackacre to my son-in-law, Samuel Jones, for as long as my daughter, Mary Brown Jones, shall live."

1. The act of the administrator of an estate in allocating the decedent's property among his heirs, or by an executor of the estate where the decedent left a will. 2. Allocation.

Pre-death arrangement of a person's property and estate best calculated to maximize the estate for the beneficiaries during and after the person's life.

The legal right or interest that a wife acquires by marriage in the property of her husband. Dower no longer exists, or has been modified in most states, but every state retains aspects of the concept for the protection of both spouses. *See* elective share.

WILLS, TRUSTS, AND ESTATES

estate tax

[es.*tate* takz]

WILLS, TRUSTS, AND ESTATES

fiduciary duty

[fi.*do*.she.air.ee *dew*.tee]

WILLS, TRUSTS, AND ESTATES

estate upon condition

[es.*tate* up.*on* ken.*dish*.en]

WILLS, TRUSTS, AND ESTATES

forced heirs

[forst airs]

WILLS, TRUSTS, AND ESTATES

execute

[*ek*.se.kyoot]

WILLS, TRUSTS, AND ESTATES

guardian ad litem

[*gar*.dee.en ad *ly*.tem]

WILLS, TRUSTS, AND ESTATES

executed

[*ek*.se.*kyoot*.ed]

WILLS, TRUSTS, AND ESTATES

heir hunters

[air *hunt*.erz]

WILLS, TRUSTS, AND ESTATES

executor

[eg.*zek*.yoo.tor]

WILLS, TRUSTS, AND ESTATES

holographic will

[hol.o.*graf*.ik will]

WILLS, TRUSTS, AND ESTATES

fiduciary

[fi.*do*.she.air.ee]

WILLS, TRUSTS, AND ESTATES

inter vivos trust

[*in*.ter *vy*.vos trust]

The duty to act loyally and honestly with respect to the interests of another; the duty the law imposes upon a fiduciary.

A tax imposed by the federal government and most states upon the transmission of property by a deceased person. The tax is imposed upon the net estate of the decedent without reference to the recipient's relationship to the decedent or to the amount a recipient receives. An estate tax is a transfer tax.

Those persons whom the testator or donor cannot deprive of the portion of his estate reserved for them by the law, except in cases where he has reason to disinherit them (i.e., person's spouse).

An estate whose existence, enlargement, or termination is conditioned upon the happening of a particular event. Such conditions are either expressed in the deed, will, or other instrument that creates the estate, or they are implied by law.

A person appointed by the court to represent and protect the interests of a minor or an incompetent person during litigation.

To sign a document. USAGE: "I will not rest until I execute my will."

- *v.* accomplish, perform, achieve, administer, complete ("She was quick to execute her obligations under the contract.")

Persons, often lawyers, who troll probate court filings from public administrators. When documents show missing heirs to a rich estate, hunters locate heirs and offer inheritance information—for a fee.

1. Completed, performed, or carried out.
2. Signed

- *adj.* cut, signed

A will that is entirely written and signed by the testator in his own handwriting. In many states, the requirement that the signing of a will be witnessed is not imposed in the case of a holographic will, because a successful counterfeit of another person's handwriting is very difficult; the requirement that the will be entirely in handwriting is therefore thought to be sufficient protection against forgery.

A person designated by a testator to carry out the directions and requests in the testator's will and to dispose of his property according to the provisions of his will. *Compare* administrator.

- *n.* administrator, fiduciary, custodian, personal representative

Living trust.

adj. That which is based upon trust or confidence; the relationship between a fiduciary and his principal.
n. A person who is entrusted with handling money or property for another person. EXAMPLES: attorney and client; guardian and ward; trustee and beneficiary.

WILLS, TRUSTS, AND ESTATES

intestacy

[in.*tess*.te.see]

WILLS, TRUSTS, AND ESTATES

lapsed devise

[lapsd de.*vize*]

WILLS, TRUSTS, AND ESTATES

intestate

[in.*tess*.tate]

WILLS, TRUSTS, AND ESTATES

legacy

[*leg*.e.see]

WILLS, TRUSTS, AND ESTATES

intestate estate

[in.*tess*.tate es.*tate*]

WILLS, TRUSTS, AND ESTATES

legatee

[leg.e.*tee*]

WILLS, TRUSTS, AND ESTATES

intestate laws

[in.*tess*.tate lawz]

WILLS, TRUSTS, AND ESTATES

legator

[leg.a.tor]

WILLS, TRUSTS, AND ESTATES

intestate succession

[in.*tess*.tate suk.*sesh*.en]

WILLS, TRUSTS, AND ESTATES

letters of administration

[*let*.erz ov ad.*min*.is.tray.shen]

WILLS, TRUSTS, AND ESTATES

issue

[*ish*.oo]

WILLS, TRUSTS, AND ESTATES

living trust

[*liv*.ing trust]

A devise that was good when the will was made but has failed since then because of the death of the legatee before the death of the testator.

The status of the estate or property of a person who dies without leaving a valid will. *See also* intestate. *Compare* testacy.

Accurately, a gift of personal property by will, although the term is often used loosely to mean any testamentary gift; a bequest. *Compare* devise.

- *n.* grant, bequest, endowment, present; tradition, history, meaning ("the legacy of River Phoenix")

---

adj. Pertaining to a person, or to the property of a person, who dies without leaving a valid will. EXAMPLE: "John died without a will and left an intestate estate." *See also* intestacy. *Compare* testate.
n. 1. A person who dies without leaving a valid will. USAGE: "John is an intestate." 2. The status of a person who dies without leaving a valid will. USAGE: "John died intestate." *See also* intestacy. *Compare* testate.

A person who receives personal property as a beneficiary under a will, although the word is often used loosely to mean a person who receives a testamentary gift of either personal property or real property. *Compare* devisee, legator.

- *n.* recipient, devisee, beneficiary, donee, legal heir

The estate of a person who dies without leaving a valid will.

A person who makes a gift of property in a will to the legatee.

State statutes that set forth the rules by which property passes when a person dies intestate. *See also* intestate succession.

The formal document issued by the probate court appointing an administrator for an estate.

Inheritance from a person who dies intestate. *Compare* testate succession.

---

1. An inter vivos trust. A trust created during the lifetime of its creator and becomes effective in his lifetime, as opposed to a testamentary trust which takes effect at death. 2. An active trust.

All persons who are descendants of one ancestor, including all future descendants. However, when used in a will, "issue" will be taken to mean children or grandchildren, or all living descendants of one ancestor, including all future descendants, if that is the testator's intention.

WILLS, TRUSTS, AND ESTATES

nuncupative will

[*nung*.kyoo.pay.tiv will]

WILLS, TRUSTS, AND ESTATES

probate

[*proh*.bate]

WILLS, TRUSTS, AND ESTATES

per capita

[per *kap*.i.ta]

WILLS, TRUSTS, AND ESTATES

publication clause

[pub.li.*kay*.shen klawz]

WILLS, TRUSTS, AND ESTATES

per stirpes

[per *ster*.peez]

WILLS, TRUSTS, AND ESTATES

right to die

[ryt to dy]

WILLS, TRUSTS, AND ESTATES

pour-over trust

[por-*oh*.ver trust]

WILLS, TRUSTS, AND ESTATES

surety

[*shoor*.e.tee]

WILLS, TRUSTS, AND ESTATES

predecease

[pree.di.*ses*]

WILLS, TRUSTS, AND ESTATES

surrogate

[*ser*.e.get]

WILLS, TRUSTS, AND ESTATES

pretermitted heir

[pree.ter.*mit*.ed air]

WILLS, TRUSTS, AND ESTATES

testacy

[*tes*.te.see]

n. 1. The judicial act whereby a will is adjudicated to be valid. 2. A term that describes the functions of the probate court, including the probate of wills and the supervision of the accounts and actions of administrators and executors of decedents' estates.
v. 1. To prove a will to be valid in probate court. 2. To submit to the jurisdiction of the probate court for any purpose.

- *v.* validate, authenticate, certify, establish, substantiate ("The court must probate this will")
- *n.* validation, adjudication, verification, confirmation

A will declared orally by a testator during his last illness, before witnesses, and later reduced to writing by a person who was present during the declaration.

- *n.* oral will; deathbed will

Portion of a will that states that the instrument reflects the wishes of the testator.

(*Latin*) Means "by the head"; by the individual. 1. For each person. 2. A method of dividing an estate in which all persons who are equally related to the decedent share equally in the estate. EXAMPLE: Bill has two living children, Mary and Sam, and two grandchildren by Adam, a deceased child. If Bill's $900,000 estate is divided per capita among his heirs, Mary and Sam each receive $450,000 and Adam's children receive nothing. *Compare per stirpes.*

This refers to the right of a person to determine what limits, if any, she wishes to impose with respect to efforts to prolong her life if she becomes gravely ill. *See living will.*

(*Latin*) Means "by the root"; according to class; by representation. This is a method of dividing or distributing an estate in which the heirs of a deceased heir share the portion of the estate that the deceased heir would have received had he lived. EXAMPLE: Bill has two living children, Mary and Sam, and two grandchildren by Adam, a deceased child. If Bill's $900,000 estate is divided per stirpes among his heirs, Mary and Sam each receive $300,000, and Adam's children each receive $150,000, sharing the $300,000 portion that Adam would have received had he lived.

A person who promises to pay the debt or to satisfy the obligation of another person.

Provision in a will that directs that the property be distributed into a trust.

In some states, the title of a judge who presides in probate court.

To die before another person.

The status of the estate or property of a person who dies without leaving a valid will. *Compare* intestacy. *See also* testate.

A child of a testator who is omitted from the testator's will. Generally the right of such a child to share in the decedent's estate depends on whether the omission was intentional or unintentional. If there is an unintentional omission, a statute might provide that such child shall share in the estate as though the testator died without a will.

WILLS, TRUSTS, AND ESTATES

testament

[*tes*.te.ment]

WILLS, TRUSTS, AND ESTATES

testamentary trust

[tes.te.*men*.ter.ee trust]

WILLS, TRUSTS, AND ESTATES

testamentary

[tes.te.*men*.ter.ee]

WILLS, TRUSTS, AND ESTATES

testate

[*tes*.tate]

WILLS, TRUSTS, AND ESTATES

testamentary capacity

[tes.te.*men*.ter.ee ke.*pass*.i.tee]

WILLS, TRUSTS, AND ESTATES

testate estate

[*tes*.tate es.*tate*]

WILLS, TRUSTS, AND ESTATES

testamentary gift

[tes.te.*men*.ter.ee gift]

WILLS, TRUSTS, AND ESTATES

testate succession

[*tes*.tate suk.*sesh*.en]

WILLS, TRUSTS, AND ESTATES

testamentary instrument

[tes.te.*men*.ter.ee *in*.stroo.ment]

WILLS, TRUSTS, AND ESTATES

testator

[*tes*.tay.ter]

WILLS, TRUSTS, AND ESTATES

testamentary intent

[tes.te.*men*.ter.ee in.*tent*]

WILLS, TRUSTS, AND ESTATES

trust

[trust]

A trust created by will.

1. A will. The terms "testament," "will," "last will," and "last will and testament" are synonymous.
2. A declaration of faith, belief, or principle.

- *n.* attestation, colloquy, covenant, demonstration, statement, exemplification, testimonial, will, last will

adj. Pertaining to a person, or to the property of a person, who dies leaving a valid will. *See* testacy.
n. 1. A person who dies leaving a valid will.
2. The status of a person who dies leaving a valid will. *Compare* intestate.

Pertaining to a will; pertaining to a testament.

The estate of a person who dies leaving a valid will.

The mental capacity of a testator, at the time of making her will, to be able to understand the nature of her act and, generally if not precisely, the nature and location of her property and the identity of those persons who are the natural objects of her bounty.

Taking property under a will rather than by inheritance. *Compare* intestate succession.

1. A gift that is the subject of a testamentary disposition. 2. A generic term for a legacy, bequest, or devise.

A person who dies leaving a valid will.

An instrument whose language clearly indicates that its author intended to make a disposition of his property, or some of his property, to be effective upon his death. A will is an EXAMPLE of a testamentary instrument.

A fiduciary relationship involving a trustee who holds trust property for the benefit or use of a beneficiary. Property of any description or type may properly be the subject of a trust. The trustee holds legal title to the trust property (also called the res or corpus of the trust); the beneficiary holds equitable title. A trust is generally established through a trust instrument, such as a deed of trust or a will, by a person (known as the settlor) who wishes the beneficiary to receive the benefit of the property but not outright ownership. A trust may, however, also be created by operation of law: implied trust.

For a court to admit a will to probate, it must determine that the testator intended the instrument to be her last will.

WILLS, TRUSTS, AND ESTATES

trust estate

[trust es.*tate*]

WILLS, TRUSTS, AND ESTATES

trust officer

[trust *off*.i.ser]

WILLS, TRUSTS, AND ESTATES

trust fund

[trust fund]

WILLS, TRUSTS, AND ESTATES

trust property

[trust *prop*.er.tee]

WILLS, TRUSTS, AND ESTATES

trust funds

[trust fundz]

WILLS, TRUSTS, AND ESTATES

trustee

[trust.*ee*]

WILLS, TRUSTS, AND ESTATES

trust indenture

[trust in.*dent*.sher]

WILLS, TRUSTS, AND ESTATES

trustee ad litem

[trust.ee ad *ly*.tem]

WILLS, TRUSTS, AND ESTATES

trust instrument

[trust i*n*.stroo.ment]

WILLS, TRUSTS, AND ESTATES

Uniform Probate Code

[*yoon*.i.form *pro*.bate kod]

WILLS, TRUSTS, AND ESTATES

trust inter vivos

[trust i*n*.ter *vy*.vose]

WILLS, TRUSTS, AND ESTATES

vested

[*vest*.ed]

An officer of a financial institution who manages trust funds.

Phrase sometimes used to mean the property held by the trustee for the benefit of the beneficiary, and sometimes used to mean the interest that the beneficiary has in the property.

Property that is the subject of a trust. It is also referred to as the trust res, the res of the trust, or the corpus of the trust.

1. A fund held in trust by a trust company or other trustee. *See also* trust funds. 2. A fund that, although not held in trust in the technical sense, is held under a relationship "of trust" that gives one the legal right to impose certain obligations upon the holder of the funds.

The person who holds the legal title to trust property for the benefit of the beneficiary of the trust, with such powers and subject to such duties as are imposed by the terms of the trust and the law.

- *n.* guardian, fiduciary, custodian

Money held in a trust account. *See also* trust fund.

A trustee appointed by the court, as opposed to a trustee appointed in a trust instrument.

An instrument stating the terms and conditions of a trust.

An act promulgated in 1969 to streamline and make the probate process more uniform throughout the country. The law was intended to be adopted by all the states; however, less than half have adopted it or some portion of it.

A document in which a trust is created. EXAMPLES: a deed of trust; a will.

1. That which cannot be taken away; indefeasible. 2. Absolute; definite; established; fixed. USAGE: "He had a vested devise."

A trust that is effective during the lifetime of the creator of the trust.

- *n.* living trust

WILLS, TRUSTS, AND ESTATES

will

[will]

REAL PROPERTY
AND LANDLORD/TENANT

color of title

[*kull*.er ov *ty*.tel]

WILLS, TRUSTS, AND ESTATES

will contest

[will *kon*.test]

REAL PROPERTY
AND LANDLORD/TENANT

condition subsequent

[ken.*dish*.en *sub*.se.kwent]

REAL PROPERTY
AND LANDLORD/TENANT

abstract of title

[*ab*.strakt ov *ty*.tel]

REAL PROPERTY
AND LANDLORD/TENANT

condominium

[kon.de.*min*.ee.um]

REAL PROPERTY
AND LANDLORD/TENANT

adverse possession

[*ad*.verse po.*zesh*.en]

REAL PROPERTY
AND LANDLORD/TENANT

contract for sale of land

[*con*.trakt for sale ov land]

REAL PROPERTY
AND LANDLORD/TENANT

broker

[*broh*.ker]

REAL PROPERTY
AND LANDLORD/TENANT

convey

[kon.*vay*]

REAL PROPERTY
AND LANDLORD/TENANT

chain of title

[chayn ov *ty*.tel]

REAL PROPERTY
AND LANDLORD/TENANT

conveyance

[kon.*vay*.ense]

That which gives the appearance of title, but is not title in fact; that which, on its face, appears to pass title but fails to do so. EXAMPLE: a deed to land executed by a person who does not own the land.

An instrument by which a person (the testator) makes a disposition of her property, to take effect after her death.

- *n.* bequest, bestowal, declaration, disposition, estate, legacy ("last will and testament")
- *v.* bequest, confer, devise, legate, probate ("to will an estate to someone")

In a contract, a condition that divests contractual liability that has already attached (or causes the loss of property rights granted by deed or will) upon the failure of the other party to the contract, deed, or will, to comply with its terms. EXAMPLE: An insurer's obligation to cover losses to a person's home can be void, if she leaves her doors unlocked and she is robbed, provided her insurance contract specified that unoccupied homes must be kept locked.

n. An attempt to defeat the probate of a will, commonly referred to as an attempt to "set aside the will."

A multi-unit dwelling, each of whose residents owns her individual apartment absolutely while holding a tenancy in common in the areas of the building and grounds used by all the residents. *Compare* cooperative apartment house.

- *n.* home, multi-unit dwelling, separate ownership

A short account of the state of the title to real estate, reflecting all past ownership and any interests or rights, such as a mortgage or other liens, which any person might currently have with respect to the property. An abstract of title is necessary to verify title before purchasing real property. *See also* chain of title; search.

A contract in which one party agrees to sell and the other to purchase real estate. *Note* that a contract for the sale of land is not a deed, but merely an agreement to transfer title.

The act of occupying real property in an open, continuous, and notorious manner, under a claim of right, hostile to the interests of the true owner for a period of years. In this manner, the occupier might claim ownership of the property. *See also* tacking.

1. To transfer title to property from one person to another by deed, bill of sale, or other conveyance. 2. To transfer, to transmit.

A person whose business is to bring buyer and seller together; an agent who, for a commission, negotiates on behalf of his principal in connection with entering into contracts or buying and selling any kind of property. A broker does not generally take possession of the property with respect to which he deals. There are both buyer and seller brokers.

- *n.* agent, middleman, proxy, representative, emissary, mediator, intermediary

1. The transferring of title to real property from one person to another. 2. Any document that creates a lien on real property or a debt or duty arising out of real estate. EXAMPLES: a lease; a mortgage; an assignment. 3. Any transfer of title to either real property or personal property.

The succession of transactions through which title to a given piece of land was passed from person to person from its origins to the present day. *See also* abstract of title; search.

REAL PROPERTY
AND LANDLORD/TENANT

conveyancing

[kon.*vay*.ense.ing]

REAL PROPERTY
AND LANDLORD/TENANT

covenant running with the land

[*kov*.e.nent *run*.ing with the land]

REAL PROPERTY
AND LANDLORD/TENANT

cooperative apartment house

[koh.*op*.er.a.tive a.*part*.ment hows]

REAL PROPERTY
AND LANDLORD/TENANT

deed

[deed]

REAL PROPERTY
AND LANDLORD/TENANT

co-ownership

[koh-*ohn*.er.ship]

REAL PROPERTY
AND LANDLORD/TENANT

deed of covenant

[deed ov *kov*.e.nent]

REAL PROPERTY
AND LANDLORD/TENANT

covenant

[*kov*.e.nent]

REAL PROPERTY
AND LANDLORD/TENANT

deed of gift

[deed ov gift]

REAL PROPERTY
AND LANDLORD/TENANT

covenant appurtenant

[*kov*.e.nent a.*per*.te.nent]

REAL PROPERTY
AND LANDLORD/TENANT

deed of quitclaim

[deed ov *kwit*.klame]

REAL PROPERTY
AND LANDLORD/TENANT

covenant for quiet enjoyment

[*kov*.e.nent for *kwy*.et en.*joy*.ment]

REAL PROPERTY
AND LANDLORD/TENANT

deed of release

[deed ov re.*leess*]

A covenant that passes with the land when the land is conveyed. Such a covenant imposes upon the next purchaser, and all subsequent purchasers, both the liability for performance and the right to demand performance.

The act of transferring title to or creating a lien on real estate by deed, mortgage, or other instrument.

n. 1. Document by which real property, or an interest in real property, is conveyed from one person to another. 2. An act or action; something done or completed. *v.* To transfer or convey by deed.

- *v.* transfer, convey, grant
- *n.* instrument, release, assignment, conveyance, contract ("warranty deed")

A multi-unit dwelling in which each tenant has an interest in the corporation or other entity that owns the building as well as a lease entitling her to occupy a particular apartment within the building. *Compare* condominium.

See deed of warranty.

Ownership of property by more than one person. *See also* joint tenancy; tenancy in common.

A deed conveying property without consideration.

n. In a deed, a promise to do or not to do a particular thing, or an assurance that a particular fact or circumstance exists or does not exist. *See also,* for EXAMPLE, covenant for quiet enjoyment; covenant appurtenant. *v.* To contract; to pledge; to make a binding promise.

- *n.* agreement, promise, pledge, vow, bond, compact, commitment ("covenant not to sue")

See quitclaim deed.

See covenant running with the land.

See quitclaim deed.

A covenant that title is good and that therefore the grantee will be undisturbed in her possession and use of the property.

REAL PROPERTY
AND LANDLORD/TENANT

deed of trust

[deed ov trust]

REAL PROPERTY
AND LANDLORD/TENANT

easement

[*eez*.ment]

REAL PROPERTY
AND LANDLORD/TENANT

deed of warranty

[deed ov *war*.en.tee]

REAL PROPERTY
AND LANDLORD/TENANT

easement in gross

[*eez*.ment in grose]

REAL PROPERTY
AND LANDLORD/TENANT

demise

[de.*mize*]

REAL PROPERTY
AND LANDLORD/TENANT

easement of access

[*eez*.ment ov *ak*.sess]

REAL PROPERTY
AND LANDLORD/TENANT

domicile

[*dom*.i.sile]

REAL PROPERTY
AND LANDLORD/TENANT

easement of light and air

[*eez*.ment ov lite and air]

REAL PROPERTY
AND LANDLORD/TENANT

dominant tenement

[*dom*.i.nent *ten*.e.ment]

REAL PROPERTY
AND LANDLORD/TENANT

eminent domain

[*em*.i.nent doh.*main*]

REAL PROPERTY
AND LANDLORD/TENANT

dower

[*dow*.er]

REAL PROPERTY
AND LANDLORD/TENANT

estate

[es.*tate*]

1. A right to use the land of another for a specific purpose. EXAMPLE: a right of way given by a landowner to a utility company to erect and maintain power lines. 2. A right to use water, light, or air. *See also* easement of light and air.

- *n.* privilege, liberty, servitude, advantage, right of way

---

A deed that creates a trust in real estate and is given as security for a debt. A deed of trust is in the nature of a mortgage, but differs from a mortgage in that it is executed in favor of a disinterested third person as trustee, where a mortgage is executed directly to the creditor to be secured.

An easement in gross does not exist so that the owner of adjoining property may better enjoy his property; rather, it is a personal interest in the use of another's land, unrelated to his own (EXAMPLE: a right to take water from the property of another). An easement in gross may be a right in either real property or personal property, depending upon its intended duration. *See also and compare* dominant tenement; servient tenement.

---

1. A deed that contains title covenants. 2. A deed that contains covenants concerning the property conveyed and is a separate document from the deed that actually conveys the property.

The right of an owner of real property bordering a public road to come from and go to the highway without being obstructed.

---

n. 1. A deed. 2. The transfer of property by will. *v.* To convey; to pass on by will or inheritance.

- *v.* bequeath, transmit, confer, endow
- *n.* conveyance, transfer

An easement for the enjoyment of light and air unobstructed by structures on the adjoining premises. This is particularly important to land owners in large cities where there are many multi-story buildings that are next to each other.

The relationship the law creates, between a person and a particular locality or country. Domicile is a person's permanent home or permanent abode. While a person may have only one domicile, she may have many residences.

The power of the government to take private property for a public use or public purpose without the owner's consent, if it pays just compensation. The process by which this is done is called condemnation.

- *n.* condemnation, expropriation, compulsory acquisition

Real property that benefits from an easement that burdens another piece of property, known as the servient tenement. *Compare* servient tenement.

---

1. The property left by a decedent (i.e., a decedent's estate). 2. The right, title, and interest a person has in real or personal property, either tangible or intangible. Estates in real property (estates in land or landed estates) include both freehold estates (EXAMPLES: a fee simple; a fee tail; a life estate) and estates less than freehold (EXAMPLES: estates for years; estates at will). 3. The property itself.

- *n.* assets, wealth, property, fortune, personality, effects

---

The legal right or interest that a wife acquires by marriage in the property of her husband. Dower, which was very important under the common law, ensured that a widow was able to live upon and make use of a portion of her husband's land, usually one-third, as long as she lived. Dower, as such, no longer exists or has been substantially modified in most states, but every state retains aspects of the concept for the protection of both spouses (EXAMPLES: elective share; election by spouse; election under the will). *Note* that "dower" is not "dowry."

REAL PROPERTY
AND LANDLORD/TENANT

eviction

[ee.*vik*.shen]

REAL PROPERTY
AND LANDLORD/TENANT

fee estate

[fee es.*tate*]

REAL PROPERTY
AND LANDLORD/TENANT

Fair Housing Act

[fayr *how*.zing akt]

REAL PROPERTY
AND LANDLORD/TENANT

fee simple

[fee *sim*.pl]

REAL PROPERTY
AND LANDLORD/TENANT

fair market value

[*fayr mar*.ket *val*.yoo]

REAL PROPERTY
AND LANDLORD/TENANT

fee simple absolute

[fee *sim*.pl *ab*.so.loot]

REAL PROPERTY
AND LANDLORD/TENANT

Fannie Mae

[*fan*.ee may]

REAL PROPERTY
AND LANDLORD/TENANT

fee simple estate

[fee *sim*.pl es.*tate*]

REAL PROPERTY
AND LANDLORD/TENANT

**Federal Housing
Administration**

[*fed*.er.el *how*.zing ad.min.is.*tray*.shen]

REAL PROPERTY
AND LANDLORD/TENANT

fee tail

[fee tayl]

REAL PROPERTY
AND LANDLORD/TENANT

fee

[fee]

REAL PROPERTY
AND LANDLORD/TENANT

fee tail female

[fee tayl *fee*.male]

A fee in land; an estate in fee.

The act of putting a tenant out of possession of premises that she has leased.

- *n.* expulsion, ouster, ejection, dislodgement, removal, dispossession

Also known as a fee simple absolute; the most complete estate in land known to the law. It signifies total ownership and control. It may be sold or inherited free of any condition, limitation, or restriction by particular heirs. *Compare* fee tail.

Another name for the Civil Rights Act of 1968, which prohibits practices that deny housing to anyone because of race, color, religion, or national origin.

See fee simple.

Actual value; value in money. The amount a buyer will pay and a seller will accept when neither is under pressure to buy or sell and both have a reasonable degree of knowledge of the relevant facts. Fair market value is virtually synonymous with actual cash value, fair cash value, and fair value. When there is no market, it is sometimes necessary for a court to construct a fair market value, relying upon expert testimony with respect to a hypothetical buyer and seller in the same circumstances.

See fee simple.

From the initials FNMA, Federal National Mortgage Association, it is the agency that supplies a market for mortgages insured by the Federal Housing Administration.

An estate in land that is given to a person and her lineal descendants only, the heirs in general being deprived of any interest in the estate. In the absence of lineal descendants, the estate reverts to the donor. A fee tail estate given only to the donor's female lineal descendants is called a fee tail female; a fee tail estate limited to the donor's male lineal descendants is called a fee tail male. *See also* reversion. *Compare* fee simple.

Commonly referred to as the FHA; an agency of the United States that supports the availability of housing and of a sound mortgage market by insuring bank mortgages granted to borrowers who meet its standards.

See fee tail.

An estate in real property that may be inherited. When "fee" is used without words of limitation (for EXAMPLE, base fee, conditional fee, determinable fee, or qualified fee), it always means fee simple.

- *n.* estate, property, inheritance, holding ("absolute fee")

REAL PROPERTY
AND LANDLORD/TENANT

fee tail male

[fee tayl male]

REAL PROPERTY
AND LANDLORD/TENANT

fixture

[*fiks*.cher]

REAL PROPERTY
AND LANDLORD/TENANT

flipping

[*flip*.ping]

REAL PROPERTY
AND LANDLORD/TENANT

flopping

[*flop*.ping]

REAL PROPERTY
AND LANDLORD/TENANT

foreclosure

[for.*kloh*.zher]

REAL PROPERTY
AND LANDLORD/TENANT

foreclosure decree

[for.*kloh*.zher de.*kree*]

REAL PROPERTY
AND LANDLORD/TENANT

foreclosure defense

[for.*kloh*.zher de.*fenz*]

REAL PROPERTY
AND LANDLORD/TENANT

foreclosure sale

[for.*kloh*.zher sayl]

REAL PROPERTY
AND LANDLORD/TENANT

future interest

[fyu.cher *in*.trest]

REAL PROPERTY
AND LANDLORD/TENANT

grant

[grant]

REAL PROPERTY
AND LANDLORD/TENANT

grantee

[gran.*tee*]

REAL PROPERTY
AND LANDLORD/TENANT

grantee-grantor indexes

[gran.*tee*-gran.*tor in*.dek.sez]

To avoid foreclosure on technical grounds, attorneys representing foreclosed clients take probing depositions from lenders' employees to find lapses in judgment, flaws in the process, or wrongdoing.

See fee tail.

A sale of mortgaged premises in accordance with a foreclosure decree.

An article, previously personal property, that, by being physically affixed to real estate, has become part of the real property; something so connected to a structure for use in connection with it that it cannot be removed without doing injury to the structure. EXAMPLES: a chandelier; an outdoor television antenna; a furnace.

- *n.* attachment, permanent addition, immovable object

An estate or interest in land or personal property, including money, whether vested or contingent, that is to come into existence at a future time. EXAMPLES: a remainder; a reversion; payments or income to be received in the future.

In an illegal "flip" the value of the property is inflated (through high comparable sales and exaggerated appraisals, etc.) to induce the mortgage lender to fund more than the property's true value. Usually a deal is worked with the seller to recoup the difference between the real (lower) selling price and the amount of the buyer's mortgage money. Another way is for the buyer to obtain a "cash out" loan that can be worth up to 125 percent of the property's worth. This scenario only works in a hot, or seller's, market, where home prices are rapidly rising. *See* flopping.

---

n. 1. A word used in conveying real property; a term of conveyance. 2. The conveyance or transfer itself. 3. That which is conveyed, conferred, or given. EXAMPLE: land. *v.* 1. To convey; to bequeath; to devise. USAGE (in a deed): "grant, bargain and sell."

- *v.* relinquish; award, donate, assign, allot
- *n.* allocation, gift, contribution, privilege, endowment, donation

The near opposite of flipping, it occurs in a softening or down real estate market. The "flop" works by deflating the value of a property to a price where the lender accepts less than is owed in a short sale. Then the buyer (perhaps in cahoots with a broker who may already have another buyer) quickly sells the property to the new party at a higher market price. *See* flipping.

The person to whom a grant is made; the party in a deed to whom the conveyance is made. *Compare* grantor.

1. A legal action by which a mortgagee terminates a mortgagor's interest in mortgaged premises. *See also* mortgage. 2. The enforcement of a lien, deed of trust, or mortgage on real estate, or a security interest in personal property, by any method provided by law.

- *n.* blockage, obstruction, confiscation, prohibition, removal, dispossession, removal, eviction

---

See grantor-grantee indexes.

A decree that orders the sale of mortgaged real estate, the proceeds to be applied in satisfaction of the debt.

REAL PROPERTY
AND LANDLORD/TENANT

grantor

[gran.*tor*]

REAL PROPERTY
AND LANDLORD/TENANT

grantor-grantee indexes

[gran.*tor*-gran.*tee in*.dek.sez]

REAL PROPERTY
AND LANDLORD/TENANT

home

[home]

REAL PROPERTY
AND LANDLORD/TENANT

homestead

[*home*.sted]

REAL PROPERTY
AND LANDLORD/TENANT

joint tenancy

[joynt *ten*.en.see]

REAL PROPERTY
AND LANDLORD/TENANT

land

[land]

REAL PROPERTY
AND LANDLORD/TENANT

land contract

[land *kon*.trakt]

REAL PROPERTY
AND LANDLORD/TENANT

land sale contract

[land sale k*on*.trakt]

REAL PROPERTY
AND LANDLORD/TENANT

land use regulation

[land yoos reg.yoo.*lay*.shen]

REAL PROPERTY
AND LANDLORD/TENANT

landlord

[*land*.lord]

REAL PROPERTY
AND LANDLORD/TENANT

landlord's lien

[*land*.lordz leen]

REAL PROPERTY
AND LANDLORD/TENANT

landowner

[*land*.oh.ner]

A contract for sale of land; installment land contract.

The person who makes a grant; the party in a deed who makes the conveyance. *Compare* grantee.

A contract for sale of land; installment land contract.

Volumes maintained in most county courthouses that list every deed, mortgage, secured transaction, and lien of every type ever recorded in the county. All transactions are alphabetically indexed, both by grantor (the grantor-grantee index) and by grantee (the grantee-grantor index).

Government regulation of the way in which land is used. Zoning statutes and ordinances are EXAMPLES of land use regulation. *See also* zoning.

A word whose legal significance may be either "house," "residence," or "domicile," depending upon the context in which it appears.

- *n.* residence, domicile, house, abode, domain; native land, birthplace, motherland, fatherland

An owner of real property who leases all or a portion of the premises to a tenant. A landlord is also called a lessor; a tenant is called a lessee.

- *n.* lessor, landowner, possessor, proprietor
- *ant.* lessee

The right to own real property free and clear of the claims of creditors, provided the owner occupies the property as her home.

A lien for rent that is in arrears, that a landlord has on a tenant's personal property located on the leased premises.

An estate in land (EXAMPLES: a fee simple estate; a life estate; an estate for years) or in personal property (EXAMPLE: a savings account) held by two or more persons jointly, with equal rights to share in its enjoyment. The most important feature of a joint tenancy is the right of survivorship, which means that upon the death of a joint tenant the entire estate goes to the survivor (or, in the case of more than two joint tenants, to the survivors, and so on to the last survivor). *See also* tenancy by the entirety. *Compare* tenancy in common.

A person who owns real property.

- *n.* landlord, owner, proprietor, possessor, title holder

The soil and everything attached to it, whether naturally (EXAMPLES: trees; water; rocks) or by man (EXAMPLES: buildings; fixtures; fences), extending from the surface downward to the center of the earth and upward endlessly to the skies. "Land" is property used interchangeably with "real estate," "real property," and "realty." "Property" is often used by itself to mean "land." *See also* covenant running with the land. 2. An interest in land or an estate in land. EXAMPLES: a fee simple; a life estate.

- *n.* real estate, property, earth, terrain, soil, ground, nation, realty, territory, acreage

REAL PROPERTY
AND LANDLORD/TENANT

lands, tenements, and hereditaments

[landz, *ten*.e.mentz, and he.red.i.ta.mentz]

REAL PROPERTY
AND LANDLORD/TENANT

listing agreement

[*list*.ing a.*gree*.ment]

REAL PROPERTY
AND LANDLORD/TENANT

lease

[lees]

REAL PROPERTY
AND LANDLORD/TENANT

lot

[lot]

REAL PROPERTY
AND LANDLORD/TENANT

lease with option to purchase

[lees with *op*.shen to *per*.chess]

REAL PROPERTY
AND LANDLORD/TENANT

lot book

[lot book]

REAL PROPERTY
AND LANDLORD/TENANT

legal description

[*lee*.gl des.*krip*.shen]

REAL PROPERTY
AND LANDLORD/TENANT

mechanic's lien

[me.*kan*.iks *lee*.en]

REAL PROPERTY
AND LANDLORD/TENANT

levy

[*lev*.ee]

REAL PROPERTY
AND LANDLORD/TENANT

metes and bounds

[meets and bowndz]

REAL PROPERTY
AND LANDLORD/TENANT

life estate

[life es.*tate*]

REAL PROPERTY
AND LANDLORD/TENANT

mortgage

[*more*.gej]

A contract between an owner of real property and a real estate agent under which the agent is retained to secure a purchaser for the property at a specified price, for a commission.

A term found in deeds and other documents relating to land, which expresses the most inclusive interest a person can own in real property (i.e., an inheritable interest in the land and everything on it or under it) (EXAMPLES: structures, minerals), and all rights arising out of it (EXAMPLES: the right to collect rent; the right to harvest timber).

A tract or parcel into which land has been divided.

1. A contract for the possession of real estate in consideration of payment of rent, ordinarily for a term of years or months, but sometimes at will. The person making the conveyance is the landlord or lessor; the person receiving the right of possession is the tenant or lessee. 2. Under the Uniform Commercial Code, a contract transferring the right to possession and use of personal property ("goods") for a term in return for consideration.

See plat book.

A lease that provides the lessee with the option, at the end of the term (or, under some leases, at any time during the term), to purchase the property for a specified sum.

A lien created by law for the purpose of securing payment for work performed or materials furnished in constructing or repairing a building or other structure.

In deeds and mortgages, a description of the real estate that is the subject of the conveyance, by boundaries, distances, and size, or by reference to maps, surveys, or plats. *See also* metes and bounds.

A property description, commonly in a deed or mortgage, that is based upon the property's boundaries and the natural objects and other markers on the land. *See also* legal description.

The seizure of property by the sheriff under writ to ensure payment of a judgment debt or to pay it. Such a levy is called levy of execution.

A written pledge of real property to secure a debt, usually to a bank.

An estate that exists as long as the person who owns or holds it is alive. Its duration may also be the lifetime of another person (EXAMPLE: "to Sarah so long as Sam shall live").

REAL PROPERTY
AND LANDLORD/TENANT

mortgage insurance

[*more*.gej in.*shoor*.ense]

REAL PROPERTY
AND LANDLORD/TENANT

plat book

[plat book]

REAL PROPERTY
AND LANDLORD/TENANT

mortgage loan

[*more*.gej lown]

REAL PROPERTY
AND LANDLORD/TENANT

plot

[plot]

REAL PROPERTY
AND LANDLORD/TENANT

mortgage note

[*more*.gej note]

REAL PROPERTY
AND LANDLORD/TENANT

possibility of reverter

[pos.i.*bil*.i.tee ov re.*ver*.ter]

REAL PROPERTY
AND LANDLORD/TENANT

partition deed

[par.*tish*.en deed]

REAL PROPERTY
AND LANDLORD/TENANT

property

[*prop*.er.tee]

REAL PROPERTY
AND LANDLORD/TENANT

perpetuity

[per.pe.*tyoo*.i.tee]

REAL PROPERTY
AND LANDLORD/TENANT

quitclaim deed

[*kwit*.klame deed]

REAL PROPERTY
AND LANDLORD/TENANT

plat

[plat]

REAL PROPERTY
AND LANDLORD/TENANT

real property

[real *prop*.er.tee]

An official book of plat maps. *See also* plat.

1. Insurance purchased by a mortgagor that pays the mortgage if the mortgagor is unable to because of death or disability. 2. Insurance purchased by a mortgagee insuring him against loss resulting from the mortgagor's inability to make payment. Mortgage insurance is a form of credit insurance.

Same as plat.

- *n.* plat, field, land, area

A loan secured by a mortgage.

A type of future interest that remains in a grantor when, by grant or devise, he has created an estate in fee simple determinable or fee simple conditional, the fee automatically reverting to him or his successors upon occurrence of the event by which the estate is limited. EXAMPLE: Sam conveys Blackacre to the school district with the condition that it should revert back to Sam or his assigns when the school district ceases to use the land for school purposes. In these circumstances, Sam owns a possibility of reverter. *See also* reversion.

A note that evidences a loan for which real estate has been mortgaged.

1. The right of a person to possess, use, enjoy, and dispose of a thing without restriction (i.e., not the material object itself, but a person's rights with respect to the object). 2. Ownership or title, either legal or equitable. 3. In the more common sense, real property and personal property; tangible property and intangible property; corporeal property and incorporeal property. 4. Anything that can be owned.

- *n.* possessions, investments, holdings, capital ("his property at death"); realty, territory, acreage ("a beautiful piece of property")

A deed that achieves a partition or splitting of real estate.

A deed that conveys whatever interest the grantor has in a piece of real property, as distinguished from the more usual deed, which conveys a fee and contains various convenants including title covenants.

A limitation of a contingent future interest in violation of the rule against perpetuities.

- *n.* eternity, continuation, indefiniteness, forever

Land, including things located on it or attached to it directly (EXAMPLE: buildings) or indirectly (EXAMPLE: fixtures). *See also* property.

- *n.* real estate

A map of a tract of land, showing the boundaries of the streets, blocks, and numbered lots. A plat is also referred to as a "plat map" or a "plot."

- *n.* map, plan, chart, sketch, diagram ("we needed to see the plat of the city")

REAL PROPERTY
AND LANDLORD/TENANT

recording

[ree.*kore*.ding]

REAL PROPERTY
AND LANDLORD/TENANT

recording acts

[ree.*kore*.ding aktz]

REAL PROPERTY
AND LANDLORD/TENANT

remainder

[ree.*mane*.der]

REAL PROPERTY
AND LANDLORD/TENANT

remainderman

[ree.*mane*.der.man]

REAL PROPERTY
AND LANDLORD/TENANT

residence

[*rez*.i.dence]

REAL PROPERTY
AND LANDLORD/TENANT

restrictive covenant

[ree.*strik*.tiv *kov*.e.nent]

REAL PROPERTY
AND LANDLORD/TENANT

reversion

[re.*ver*.zhen]

REAL PROPERTY
AND LANDLORD/TENANT

reversionary interest

[re.*ver*.zhen.a.ree *in*.trest]

REAL PROPERTY
AND LANDLORD/TENANT

revert

[re.*vert*]

REAL PROPERTY
AND LANDLORD/TENANT

riparian land

[ry.*pare*.ee.en land]

REAL PROPERTY
AND LANDLORD/TENANT

robo signers

[*row*.bow *syne*.erz]

REAL PROPERTY
AND LANDLORD/TENANT

search

[serch]

1. A future interest in land to take effect in favor of the grantor of the land or his heirs after the termination of a prior estate he has granted; in other words, the returning of the property to the grantor or his heirs when the grant is over. (EXAMPLE: "I leave Blackacre to Joe Jones for life, and after his death to my heirs." The grantor's heirs have a reversionary interest in Blackacre, which will vest when Joe Jones dies; Joe Jones's interest is a life estate.) A reversion arises by operation of law. *Compare* remainder. 2. The interest or estate of an owner of land during the period of time for which he has granted his possessory rights to someone else. Thus, in the above EXAMPLE, the grantor and his heirs may also be said to have a reversionary interest in Blackacre during Joe Jones's life. A landlord's interest in premises that she has leased to a tenant is another EXAMPLE of a reversionary interest.

- *n.* remainder, future interest, residue, estate, interest; return, throwback

---

A copy or a record of a transaction for the sale of land. *See also* recording acts.

A future interest (i.e., the right to the future enjoyment of a reversion).

State statutes that provide for the recording of instruments, particularly those affecting title to real estate (EXAMPLES: a deed; a mortgage; a tax lien) and security interests in personal property (EXAMPLES: a conditional sale contract; a security agreement). There are several types of recording acts. In notice act states, an instrument that is not recorded is invalid with respect to a person who subsequently purchases the property who has no actual knowledge of the unrecorded transaction. In race act states, actual notice is immaterial because, in the event of conflicting claims of ownership, absolute priority is given to the first person who "wins the race to the courthouse" to record her instrument. Race-notice acts, which are in effect in some jurisdictions, combine various features of notice acts and race acts.

- *n.* recording laws, recording statutes

---

1. With respect to an interest in land, to come back to a former owner or her heirs at a future time. USAGE: "After Bill dies, the life estate in Blackacre that Sam granted to Bill will revert to Sam, and if Sam is also dead, it will revert to Sam's heirs." *See also* reversion. 2. Turn backward.

---

1. An estate in land to take effect immediately after the expiration of a prior estate (known as the particular estate), created at the same time and by the same instrument. EXAMPLE (in a will): "I will leave my land to Joe Jones for life, and after his death to Sarah Green and her heirs." The interest or estate of Sarah Green and her heirs is a remainder; Joe Jones's interest is a life estate. *Compare* reversion. 2. That which is left over; the residue.

- *n.* balance, residue, surplus, excess, remains; estate, interest, property

---

Land along the bank of a river or stream. Only land within the watershed of the river or stream is considered to be riparian.

A person entitled to receive a remainder.

---

n. Document processors for mortgage lenders who rapidly sign papers in robotic fashion, without being familiar with the details of the loan or even reading the mortgage documents.

One's home; the place where a person lives with no present intention of moving. Although in a given context "residence" may have the same meaning as "domicile," the terms are not synonymous, because, while a person may have many residences, she can only have one domicile.

A title search or examination of all mortgages, liens, debts, etc., that affect ownership of land in order to verify title.

---

1. A covenant in a deed prohibiting or restricting the use of the property (EXAMPLE: the type, location, or size of buildings that can be constructed on it). A covenant prohibiting the sale of real property to persons of a particular race is unenforceable because it is an unconstitutional restraint on alienation. 2. A covenant not to sue.

REAL PROPERTY
AND LANDLORD/TENANT

servient tenement

[*serv*.ee.ent *ten*.e.ment]

REAL PROPERTY
AND LANDLORD/TENANT

tenancy for life

[*ten*.en.see for life]

REAL PROPERTY
AND LANDLORD/TENANT

short sale

[short sayl]

REAL PROPERTY
AND LANDLORD/TENANT

tenancy for years

[*ten*.en.see for yeerz]

REAL PROPERTY
AND LANDLORD/TENANT

survey

[*ser*.vey]

REAL PROPERTY
AND LANDLORD/TENANT

tenancy from month to month

[*ten*.en.see from month to month]

REAL PROPERTY
AND LANDLORD/TENANT

tacking

[*tack*.ing]

REAL PROPERTY
AND LANDLORD/TENANT

tenancy from year to year

[*ten*.en.see from yeer to yeer]

REAL PROPERTY
AND LANDLORD/TENANT

tenancy

[*ten*.en.see]

REAL PROPERTY
AND LANDLORD/TENANT

tenancy in common

[*ten*.en.see *in kahm*.en]

REAL PROPERTY
AND LANDLORD/TENANT

tenancy by the entirety

[*ten*.en.see by the en.*ty*.re.tee]

REAL PROPERTY
AND LANDLORD/TENANT

tenant

[*ten*.ent]

A life estate.

Real property that is subject to an easement that benefits another piece of property, known as the dominant tenement.

A tenancy under a lease or other contract for the period of a year or for a stated number of years.

In real estate transactions, a sale in which the lender accepts less than what is owed on the mortgage, usually to avoid the time, trouble, and costs of foreclosing.

1. A tenancy in which no definite term is agreed upon and the rate is so much per month (i.e., a tenancy under a month-to-month lease). 2. A tenancy at will. 3. The tenancy of a hold-over tenant (i.e., a tenancy at sufferance). *Compare* tenancy from year to year.

n. 1. The method by which the boundaries of land are determined. 2. A map, plat, or other document reflecting a surveyor's determination of the boundary or boundaries of land.
v. 1. To determine the boundaries of land.

- *v.* appraise, outline, assay, canvass, measure ("to survey the land")
- *n.* analysis, study, audit

A tenancy in which no definite term is agreed upon and the rate is so much per year. A tenancy from year to year may also be a tenancy at sufferance or a tenancy at will. *Compare* tenancy from month to month.

With respect to acquiring title to land by adverse possession, a doctrine allowing an adverse possessor to add her period of possession to that of a previous possessor to establish continuous possession. *See also* adverse possession.

A tenancy in which two or more persons own an undivided interest in an estate in land, for EXAMPLE, in a fee simple estate or a life estate, or in personal property, for EXAMPLE, in a savings account. As opposed to joint tenants, tenants in common have no right of survivorship; when a tenant in common dies, her interest passes to her heirs rather than to her cotenant or cotenants. *Compare* tenancy by the entirety.

1. The right to hold and occupy realty or personalty by virtue of owning an interest in it. 2. Possession of a realty under a lease; the relationship existing between a landlord or lessor and a tenant or lessee. 3. A term for the interest a tenant has under the lease.

- *n.* holding, leasing, occupancy, residence, rental

1. A person who holds or possesses realty or personalty by virtue of owning an interest in it. 2. A person who occupies realty under a lease with a landlord; a lessee. *See also* tenancy.

- *n.* lessee, occupier, renter, boarder, leaseholder, inhabitant, roomer

A form of joint tenancy in an estate in land or in personal property that exists between husband and wife by virtue of the fact that they are husband and wife. As with a conventional joint tenancy, a tenancy by the entirety is a tenancy with right of survivorship. "Tenancy," in this context, means ownership of the jointly held estate or interest, whether, for EXAMPLE, it is a fee simple estate, a life estate, a savings account, or the like. *Compare* tenancy in common.

REAL PROPERTY
AND LANDLORD/TENANT

tenantable

[*ten*.nen.tebl]

REAL PROPERTY
AND LANDLORD/TENANT

warranty deed

[war.en.*tee* deed]

REAL PROPERTY
AND LANDLORD/TENANT

tenants in common

[*ten*.entz in *kahm*.en]

REAL PROPERTY
AND LANDLORD/TENANT

warranty of habitability

[war.en.*tee* ov hab.it.e.*bil*.i.tee]

REAL PROPERTY
AND LANDLORD/TENANT

timeshare

[*tym*.shair]

REAL PROPERTY
AND LANDLORD/TENANT

waste

[wayst]

REAL PROPERTY
AND LANDLORD/TENANT

trespass

[*tress*.pas]

REAL PROPERTY
AND LANDLORD/TENANT

zone

[zone]

REAL PROPERTY
AND LANDLORD/TENANT

variable rate mortgage

[*vair*.ee.ebl rate *more*.gej]

REAL PROPERTY
AND LANDLORD/TENANT

zoning

[*zone*.ing]

REAL PROPERTY
AND LANDLORD/TENANT

variance

[*var*.ee.ense]

REAL PROPERTY
AND LANDLORD/TENANT

zoning board

[*zone*.ing bord]

A deed that contains title covenants.

Premises that are habitable or ready to live in because plumbing, electricity, heat, and water are all in working condition.

A warranty implied by law that leased premises are fit to occupy.

Two or more owners of property under a tenancy in common.

---

1. The destruction, misuse, alteration, or neglect of premises by the person in possession, to the detriment of another's interest in the property. EXAMPLE: a tenant's polluting of a pond on leased land. 2. That which is left over, useless or even dangerous. EXAMPLES: hazardous waste; solid waste; toxic waste.

- *n.* decay, desolation, disuse, improvidence, misapplication, squandering; badlands, barrens, brush

Interval ownership of a single condominium unit by multiple owners in weekly shares. In practice, each owner buys use of the unit for the week(s) he wants. Pro rata annual fees are assessed to each owner for maintenance/taxes. Ownership is transferable.

---

n. 1. An area or district created by a zoning board in accordance with zoning regulations. 2. A distinct area that is unlike the surrounding areas.
v. To engage in zoning.

- *n.* area, belt, circuit, district, realm, territory, tract sector

An unauthorized entry or intrusion by one (trespasser) onto the real property of another.

The creation and application of structural, size, and use restrictions imposed upon the owners of real estate within districts or zones in accordance with zoning regulations or ordinances. Although authorized by state statutes, zoning is generally legislated and regulated by local government. Zoning is a form of land use regulation and is generally of two types: regulations having to do with structural and architectural design; and regulations specifying the use(s) to which designated districts may be put; for EXAMPLE, commercial, industrial, residential, or agricultural.

Another term for an adjustable rate mortgage, one in which the percentage rate changes annually, or in some stipulated period.

An administrative agency of a municipality that administers zoning regulations or ordinances.

In zoning law, an exception from the strict application of a zoning ordinance, granted to relieve a property owner of unnecessary hardship. A variance allows the land owner to use the land in a matter that the law would not otherwise permit.

FAMILY LAW
adoption
[a.*dop*.shen]

FAMILY LAW
antenuptial
[*an*.te.*nup*.shel]

FAMILY LAW
adult
[a.*dult*]

FAMILY LAW
antenuptial agreement
[*an*.te.*nup*.shel a.*gree*.ment]

FAMILY LAW
adultery
[a.*dul*.ter.ee]

FAMILY LAW
arrears
[a.*reerz*]

FAMILY LAW
affiliation proceeding
[a.*fil*.ee.ay.shun pro.*see*.ding]

FAMILY LAW
bigamy
[*big*.e.mee]

FAMILY LAW
alimony
[*al*.i.moh.nee]

FAMILY LAW
ceremonial marriage
[sehr.e.*mone*.ee.el *mehr*.ej]

FAMILY LAW
annulment of marriage
[a.*nul*.ment ov *mar*.ej]

FAMILY LAW
child
[child]

Before marriage.

- *adj.* prenuptial, premarital

The act of creating the relationship of parent and child between persons who do not naturally share that relationship.

- *n.* acceptance, embracement, approval, assumption ("their adoption of a hostile stance"); fostering, fosterage, raising ("adoption of the homeless child")

See prenuptial agreement.

A grown person; one who is no longer a child. "Adult" is not a technical legal word.

Payments past due. EXAMPLE: A person may be in arrears in alimony payments or in arrears on a mortgage.

- *n.* unpaid debts, obligations, delinquency, overdue payments ("arrears in alimony")

Sexual intercourse by a married person with a person who is not his or her spouse.

- *n.* infidelity, affair, unfaithfulness, cuckoldry

The crime of marrying while already married to another.

A judicial proceeding to establish the paternity of an illegitimate child and to compel the father to contribute to its support. *See also* paternity suit.

A marriage performed by an appropriate religious or civil official, after the parties have met all legal requirements (EXAMPLE: securing a marriage license). *See also* solemnization of marriage. *Compare* common law marriage.

Ongoing support payments by a divorced spouse, usually payments made for maintenance of the former spouse. Alimony is not child support. *See also* palimony.

- *n.* support, maintenance, sustenance, allowance

---

1. A very young person. *Compare* minor.
2. Offspring; progeny; descendent. *Compare* heir. "Child" is not a technical legal term with a definite meaning. Its meaning is always subject to construction in the context in which it is used.

- *n.* kid, adolescent, minor, youth, juvenile

The act of a court in voiding a marriage for causes existing at the time the marriage was entered into (EXAMPLE: the existing marriage of one of the parties). Annulment differs from divorce in that it is not a dissolution of the marriage but a declaration that no marriage ever existed.

FAMILY LAW
child abuse
[child a.*byooss*]

FAMILY LAW
common law marriage
[*kom*.en law *mar*.ej]

FAMILY LAW
child abuse reporting acts
[child a.*byooss* re.*port*.ing aktz]

FAMILY LAW
community property
[ke.*myu*.ni.tee *prop*.er.tee]

FAMILY LAW
child stealing
[child *steel*.ing]

FAMILY LAW
condonation
[kon.do.*nay*.shen]

FAMILY LAW
child support
[child se.*port*]

FAMILY LAW
connivance
[ke.*nie*.vense]

FAMILY LAW
civil union
[*sih*.vil *yoon*.yen]

FAMILY LAW
consortium
[kon.*sore*.shum]

FAMILY LAW
cohabitation
[ko.ha.bi.*tay*.shen]

FAMILY LAW
cruelty
[*kroo*.el.tee]

A marriage entered into without ceremony, the parties agreeing between themselves to be husband and wife, followed by a period of cohabitation where the parties hold themselves out as actually married. Common law marriages are valid in some states but invalid in most. *Compare* ceremonial marriage.

The physical, sexual, verbal, or emotional abuse of a young person. Child abuse includes the neglect of a child. It is a crime in every state. *See also* child abuse reporting acts.

A system of law under which the earnings of either spouse are the property of both the husband and the wife, and property acquired by either spouse during the marriage (other than by gift, under a will, or through inheritance) is the property of both. States that have adopted this system are called community property states. *Compare* equitable distribution.

State statutes that make specified persons (EXAMPLES: physicians, teachers) responsible for reporting suspected child abuse.

The forgiveness by one spouse of the other's conduct that constitutes grounds for divorce. Condonation is a defense to a divorce action based upon the conduct that has been condoned.

- *n.* forgiveness, pardon, overlooking, clemency, discharge, acquittal

---

The taking or removal of a child from a parent or from a person awarded custody. This is also the crime committed when a child is abducted from the custody of one parent by the other, although it is commonly called parental kidnapping.

As a defense in an action for divorce, fraudulent consent by one spouse to the other spouse's engaging in conduct that constitutes grounds for divorce. *Compare* no-fault divorce.

- *n.* conspiracy, collusion, consent, overlooking, condoning

---

1. Money paid, pending divorce and after divorce, by one parent to the other for the support of their children. *See also* support.
2. The obligation of parents to provide their children with the necessities of life.

The rights and duties of both husband and wife, resulting from marriage. They include companionship, love, affection, assistance, comfort, cooperation, and sexual relations. *See also* loss of consortium.

An alternative to full marriage for gay couples, also known as "civil partnership." The state confers the rights of inheritance, joint ownership of property, health benefits, and other civil rights to same-sex couples.

The infliction of physical or mental pain or distress. As a ground for divorce, "cruelty" means physical violence or threats of physical violence, or mental distress willfully caused.

- *n.* brutality, harshness, spitefulness, viciousness, torture, violence
- *ant.* sympathy, kindness

---

1. Living together as man and wife, although not married to each other. 2. Living together. 3. Having sexual intercourse.

- *n.* living together, common law marriage, alliance, union, residing together
- *ant.* separation

FAMILY LAW

curtesy

[*ker*.te.see]

FAMILY LAW

divorce

[di.*vorss*]

FAMILY LAW

custody

[*kuss*.te.dee]

FAMILY LAW

divorce a vinculo matrimonii

[di.*vorss* ah *vin*.kyoo.loh mat.ri.*moh*.ni.eye]

FAMILY LAW

decree

[de.*kree*]

FAMILY LAW

divorce from bed and board

[di.*vorss* from bed and bord]

FAMILY LAW

desertion

[de.*zer*.shen]

FAMILY LAW

domestic relations

[de.*mes*.tick re.*lay*.shenz]

FAMILY LAW

dissolution of marriage

[dis.e.*loo*.shen ov *ma*.rej]

FAMILY LAW

elder law

[*el*.der law]

FAMILY LAW

divided custody

[di.*vy*.ded *kuss*.te.dee]

FAMILY LAW

equitable adoption

[*ek*.wi.tebl e.*dop*.shen]

A dissolution of the marital relationship between husband and wife. *Compare* alimony. *See also* no-fault divorce.

- *n.* separation, division, break, break-up, parting, disunion
- *v.* rescind, dismiss, annul, cease, dissolve

The rights a husband had under the common law with respect to his wife's property. Today these rights have been modified in every state in various ways, but all states that retain curtesy in some form extend the same rights to both spouses. *Note* that "curtesy" is not "courtesy."

A decree that dissolves the marriage because of matrimonial misconduct. Also called absolute divorce. *Compare* no-fault divorce.

As applied to persons, physical contact. (EXAMPLES: Parents customarily "have physical custody" of their children; although, in the event of divorce, one parent may have sole custody, or both parents have joint custody or divided custody.) Custody carries with it the obligation on the part of the custodian to maintain and care for the person in his charge for the duration of their relationship.

- *n.* care, control, protection, possession, management, restraint

---

A decree that terminates the right of cohabitation, and adjudicates matters such as custody and support, but does not dissolve the marriage itself. *Compare* divorce a vinculo matrimonii; no-fault divorce.

---

n. The final order of a court. For all practical purposes, the distinction between decrees and judgments no longer exists, and all relief in all civil actions, whether legal or equitable, is obtained by means of judgment.
v. To order, to dictate, to ordain, to enact, to command.

- *n.* mandate, commandment, directive, ordinance, statute, decision, ruling

---

The field of law relating to domestic matters, such as marriage, divorce, support, custody, and adoption; family law.

---

1. As a ground for divorce, a voluntary separation of one of the parties to a marriage from the other without the consent of or without having been wronged by the second party, with the intention to live apart and without any intention to return to the cohabitation. 2. The criminal abandonment of a child in neglect of the parental duty of support.

A field of law with statutes and regulations designed to protect the elderly. Elder law encompasses a variety of legal issues such as wills, trusts and estates, long-term care, guardianships, elder abuse, health care, Social Security, Medicaid, and Medicare.

---

1. The termination of a marriage, whether by annulment, divorce a vinculo matrimonii, or no-fault divorce. 2. A term for divorce in some no-fault states.

The principle that a child may enforce in equity a promise to adopt him, at least to the extent that he will be given rights of inheritance with respect to the property of the person who made the promise.

An arrangement under which the child of divorced parents lives a portion of the time with one parent and a portion of the time with the other. Legal custody, however, remains at all times with one of the parents. *Compare* joint custody. *See also* custody.

FAMILY LAW
equitable distribution
[*ek*.wi.tebl dis.tri.*byoo*.shen]

FAMILY LAW
foster parent
[*foss*.ter *pair*.ent]

FAMILY LAW
family
[*fam*.i.lee]

FAMILY LAW
gay marriage
[gay *mehr*.ej]

FAMILY LAW
family court
[*fam*.i.lee kort]

FAMILY LAW
guardian ad litem
[*gar*.dee.en ad *ly*.tem]

FAMILY LAW
family law
[*fam*.i.lee law]

FAMILY LAW
HLA testing
[HLA *test*.ing]

FAMILY LAW
foreign divorce
[*forr*.en di.*vorss*]

FAMILY LAW
imputed income
[im.*pew*.ted *in*.kum]

FAMILY LAW
foster child
[*foss*.ter child]

FAMILY LAW
incompatibility
[in.kum.pat.e.*bil*.e.tee]

A person who rears a foster child.

Some jurisdictions permit their courts, in a divorce case, to distribute all property obtained during the marriage on an "equitable" basis. In deciding what is equitable, the court takes into consideration factors such as the length of the marriage and the contributions of each party, including homemaking. *Compare* community property.

The relationship of two men or two women legally united as spouses, first legalized by Massachusetts and other foreign jurisdictions. *See also* civil union.

1. A word of great flexibility, the meaning of which varies according to the context in which it appears. In its most common usage, it means the persons who live under one roof and under one head or management. A family is not necessarily limited to a father and mother (or a father or mother) and children. 2. In another of its common uses, "family" refers to persons who are of the same bloodline or are descended from a common ancestor.

- *n.* classification, progeny, descendants, household, family unit, issue

A person appointed by the court to represent and protect the interests of a minor or an incompetent person during litigation.

A court whose jurisdiction varies from state to state. It may hear domestic relations cases; it may hear juvenile court matters; it may also try child abuse cases and oversee paternity suits.

Abbreviation of human leukocyte antigen testing. An HLA blood test is a paternity test.

Area of the law concerned with domestic relations.

1. The benefit a person obtains through performance of her own services or through the use of her own property. Generally, this is not subject to taxes. EXAMPLE: if you are a carpenter and make repairs to your home, these services would not be subject to tax. 2. Benefits that accrue when no money is received. EXAMPLE: when an employer offers free health insurance to employees and their families, this would be imputed income.

A divorce granted in a state or country other than the couple's state of residence.

Conflict in personality and temperament. As a requirement for no-fault divorce, a conflict so deep it cannot be altered or adjusted, rendering it impossible for the parties to continue to live together in a normal marital relationship.

A child brought up by a person who is not her biological parent. *Compare* adoption.

FAMILY LAW
infant
[in.*fent*]

FAMILY LAW
juvenile offender
[*joo*.ve.nile o.*fen*.der]

FAMILY LAW
irreconcilable differences
[ir.rek.en.*sy*.lebl *dif*.ren.sez]

FAMILY LAW
legitimacy
[le.*jit*.i.mes.ee]

FAMILY LAW
irremedial breakdown of marriage
[ir.re.*mee*.dee.el *brake*.down of *mehr*.ej]

FAMILY LAW
loss of consortium
[los ov kun.*sore*.shem]

FAMILY LAW
joint custody
[joynt *kuss*.te.dee]

FAMILY LAW
maintenance
[*main*.ten.ense]

FAMILY LAW
juvenile
[*joo*.ve.nile]

FAMILY LAW
majority
[ma.*jaw*.ri.tee]

FAMILY LAW
juvenile court
[*joo*.ve.nile kort]

FAMILY LAW
marital agreement
[*mehr*.i.tel a.*gree*.ment]

A minor who breaks the law. A juvenile offender is sometimes referred to as a delinquent child or a youthful offender.

A person who has not reached the age of majority and who therefore is under a civil disability; non-age, minority. The period of life when one is a young child.

The state of having been born to parents who are married to each other.

A requirement for divorce or dissolution of marriage in some states with no-fault divorce laws. The term itself means that because of dissension and personality conflicts, the marriage relationship has been destroyed and there is no reasonable expectation of reconciliation. *See also* irremedial breakdown of marriage.

The loss of a spouse's assistance or companionship, or the loss of a spouse's ability or willingness to have sexual relations. If such loss results from a tort, it gives rise to a cause of action in favor of the partner of the spouse injured by the tort. *See also* consortium.

A requirement for no-fault divorce in some states. *See also* irreconcilable differences.

- *n.* irretrievable breakdown of marriage

The support of a person. *See also* support.

- *n.* upkeep, conservation, preservation, care, protection, help, aid, finances, alimony, subsistence, livelihood ("maintenance for her health")

An arrangement whereby both parties to a divorce retain legal custody of their child and jointly participate in reaching major decisions concerning the child's welfare.

Legal age; full age, the age at which a person acquires the capacity to contract; the age at which a person is no longer a minor. The age of majority varies from state to state and differs depending on the purpose. EXAMPLES: eligibility for a driver's license; eligibility to vote; the right to buy alcoholic beverages. *Compare* minor.

adj. Young, youthful, immature.

- *n.* infant, youth, youngster, minor, teenager, ward, teen
- *adj.* childish, inexperienced, sophomore, irresponsible, infantile, adolescent
- *ant.* adult

An agreement between two people who are married to each other (a postnuptial agreement), or two people who are about to marry (a prenuptial agreement), with respect to the disposition of the marital property or property owned by either spouse before the marriage, with respect to the rights of either in the property of the other, or with respect to support.

A court having special jurisdiction over juvenile offenders, as well as abused and neglected children.

FAMILY LAW

marriage

[*mehr*.ej]

FAMILY LAW

non-marital children

[non-*mehr*.i.tel *chil*.drin]

FAMILY LAW

marriage certificate

[*mehr*.ej ser.*tif*.i.ket]

FAMILY LAW

palimony

[*pal*.i.moh.nee]

FAMILY LAW

marriage license

[mehr.ej *ly*.sense]

FAMILY LAW

partition

[par.*tish*.en]

FAMILY LAW

merger in judgment

[*mer*.jer in *juj*.ment]

FAMILY LAW

paternity

[pa.*ter*.ni.tee]

FAMILY LAW

minor

[*my*.ner]

FAMILY LAW

paternity suit

[pa.*ter*.ni.tee sute]

FAMILY LAW

no-fault divorce

[no-fawlt di.*vorss*]

FAMILY LAW

prenuptial agreement

[pree.*nup*.shel a.*gree*.ment]

Children not related to or connected with the marriage.

1. The relationship of a man and a woman legally united as husband and wife. Marriage is a contract binding the parties until one dies or until a divorce or annulment occurs. 2. The act of becoming married; the marriage ceremony. *See also* common law marriage, gay marriage, and civil union.

- *n.* matrimony, wedlock, nuptial state, nuptials, sacrament, espousal ("to be joined in marriage")
- *ant.* divorce

Alimony paid upon the break-up of a live-in relationship between two people who were not married to each other. In some states, such payment may be ordered by a court if the parties entered into an express contract or if the court finds the existence of an implied contract. In others, court-ordered palimony is based upon quantum meruit. In still others, palimony is considered to be contrary to public policy and is not recognized by the law.

A certificate that evidences a marriage, prepared by the person officiating at the ceremony and usually required by state law. *Compare* marriage license.

A division made between two or more persons of land or other property belonging to them as co-owners, usually pursuant to a divorce action.

Authorization to marry issued by the state in which the ceremony is to occur. It is a condition precedent to a ceremonial marriage. *Compare* marriage certificate.

The status of being a father.

- *n.* fatherhood, derivation, ancestry, lineage, descent

The extinguishment of a cause of action by entry of a judgment. EXAMPLE: the obligation to pay money under a separation agreement is superseded by a judgment for alimony.

A proceeding to establish the paternity of a child born out of wedlock, usually for the purpose of compelling the father to support the child. *See also* affiliation proceeding.

A person who has not yet attained her majority; a person who has not reached legal age; a person who has not acquired capacity to contract. *See* infant. *Compare* majority.

An agreement between a man and a woman who are about to be married, governing the financial and property arrangements between them in the event of divorce, death, or even during the marriage. Prenuptial agreements are also called antenuptial agreements, antenuptial settlements, or premarital agreements. *See also* marital agreement.

A term for the requirements for divorce in jurisdictions in which the party seeking the divorce need not demonstrate that the other party is at fault. The requirements differ from state to state. EXAMPLES include irreconcilable differences, irremedial breakdown of marriage, and irretrievable breakdown of marriage.

FAMILY LAW
reconciliation
[rek.en.sil.ee.*ay*.shen]

FAMILY LAW
solemnize
[*saw*.lem.nize]

FAMILY LAW
recrimination
[re.krim.i.*nay*.shen]

FAMILY LAW
spouse
[spouse]

FAMILY LAW
same-sex marriage
[same-sex *mehr*.ej]

FAMILY LAW
step-parent
[step-*pare*.ent]

FAMILY LAW
separation
[sep.e.*ray*.shen]

FAMILY LAW
support
[sup.*ort*]

FAMILY LAW
separation agreement
[sep.e.*ray*.shen a.*gree*.ment]

FAMILY LAW
surrogate
[*ser*.e.get]

FAMILY LAW
solemnization of marriage
[saw.lem.neh.*zay*.shen ov *mehr*.ej]

FAMILY LAW
surrogate motherhood
[*ser*.e.get *muth*.er.hood]

The performance of a formal ceremony; to act with formality. *See also* solemnization of marriage.

The act of resolving differences. In domestic relations law, a resumption of cohabitation by spouses who have been living apart.

- *n.* restoration, conciliation, rapprochement, concordance, rapport

A husband or wife, a marriage partner.

- *n.* wife, husband, mate, companion, partner

A defense in an action for divorce based upon the misconduct by the plaintiff that would itself be grounds for divorce if the defendant had brought an action against the plaintiff.

- *n.* countercharge, retort, rejoinder, counterattack, reprisal, blame, retribution

A wife, in her relationship to her spouse's child by a former marriage; a husband, in his relationship to his spouse's child by a former marriage.

See gay marriage and civil union.

To provide funds or other means of maintenance of a person.

The status of a husband and wife who live separately. The state of being apart or coming apart.

- *n.* detachment, disrelation, disassociation, partition, parting, rupture, disunion, alienation

A person who acts for another.

- *n.* alternate, substitute, agent, vicarious, actor, delegate, proxy, stand-in ("surrogate mother")

An agreement between husband and wife who are about to divorce or to enter into a legal separation, settling property rights and other matters (EXAMPLES: custody, child support, visitation, alimony) between them. Separation agreements are subject to court approval. *See also* marital agreement.

The status of a woman who "hosts" the fertilized egg of another woman in her womb or who is artificially inseminated with the sperm of a man who is married to someone else and to whom (with his wife) she has agreed to assign her parental rights if the child is delivered.

The performance of the marriage ceremony.

FAMILY LAW

tenancy by the entirety

[*ten*.en.see by the en.*ty*.re.tee]

LEGAL ETHICS

American Association for Paralegal Education (AAfPE)

[a.*mare*.i.ken a.so.see.*ay*.shen for pa.re.*lee*.gal ed.yoo.*kay*.shen]

FAMILY LAW

tender years

[*ten*.der yerz]

LEGAL ETHICS

American Bar Association

[a.*mare*.i.ken bar a.so.see.*ay*.shen]

FAMILY LAW

visitation

[viz.i.*tay*.shen]

LEGAL ETHICS

attorney

[a.*tern*.ee]

FAMILY LAW

void marriage

[voyd *mehr*.ej]

LEGAL ETHICS

attorney at law

[a.*tern*.ee at law]

FAMILY LAW

wedlock

[*wed*.lok]

LEGAL ETHICS

attorney fees

[a.*tern*.ee feez]

LEGAL ETHICS

abuse of process

[a.*byoos* ov *pross*.ess]

LEGAL ETHICS

attorney in fact

[a.*tern*.ee in fakt]

A national organization of paralegal teachers and educational institutions that provides technical assistance and supports research in the paralegal field, promotes standards for paralegal instruction, and cooperates with the American Bar Association and others in developing an approval process for paralegal education.

A form of joint tenancy in an estate in land or in personal property that exists between husband and wife by virtue of the fact that they are husband and wife. As with a conventional joint tenancy, a tenancy by the entirety is a tenancy with right of survivorship. "Tenancy," in this context, means ownership of the jointly held estate or interest, whether, for EXAMPLE, it is a fee simple estate, a life estate, a savings account, or the like.

The country's largest voluntary professional association of attorneys commonly referred to as the ABA. Its purposes include enhancing professionalism and advancing the administration of justice.

A term used to describe minors, particularly when they are very young. USAGE: "a child of tender years."

An attorney at law or an attorney in fact. Unless otherwise indicated, generally means attorney at law.

- *n.* lawyer, counselor, advocate, legal advisor, barrister, counsel, legal eagle

Short for visitation rights (i.e., the right of a divorced parent who does not have custody of his child to visit the child at such times and places as the court may order).

A person who is licensed to practice law; a lawyer.

A marriage absolutely prohibited by law. EXAMPLE: marriage with a person who is not of age.

Compensation to which an attorney is entitled for her services. This is usually a matter of contract between the attorney and the client. *See also* retainer. However, where authorized by statute, a court may enter an order in a lawsuit directing the payment of a party's attorney fees by the opposite party. In some types of cases, attorney fees are set by a statute that also requires that the fees be paid by the defendant if the plaintiff or claimant prevails in the action. EXAMPLE: Under many Workers' Compensation acts, the claimant's attorney is entitled to a specified percentage of the claimant's award. *See also* contingent fee.

The state of being married; marriage.

- *n.* marriage, matrimony, connubiality, union

An agent or representative authorized by his principal, by virtue of a power of attorney, to act for her in certain matters.

The use of legal process in a manner not contemplated by the law to achieve a purpose not intended by the law. EXAMPLE: causing an ex-husband to be arrested for nonsupport of his child in order to secure his agreement with respect to custody. *Compare* malicious use of process.

LEGAL ETHICS

attorney of record

[a.*tern*.ee of *rek*.erd]

LEGAL ETHICS

certified legal assistant (CLA)

[*ser*.ti.fide *lee*.gul uh.*sis*.tent]

LEGAL ETHICS

attorney-client privilege

[a.*tern*.ee-*klie*.ent *priv*.i.lej]

LEGAL ETHICS

Chinese Wall

[chy.*nez* wol]

LEGAL ETHICS

attorney's lien

[a.*tern*.eez leen]

LEGAL ETHICS

client

[*klie*.ent]

LEGAL ETHICS

attorney's work product

[a.*tern*.eez werk *prod*.ukt]

LEGAL ETHICS

Code of Judicial Conduct

[kohd ov joo.*dish*.el *kon*.dukt]

LEGAL ETHICS

canon

[*kan*.on]

LEGAL ETHICS

commingling of funds

[ko.*ming*.ling ov fundz]

LEGAL ETHICS

censure

[*sen*.shoor]

LEGAL ETHICS

competent

[*kom*.pe.tent]

A legal assistant who has been certified by the National Association of Legal Assistants after passing NALA's examination.

The attorney who has made an appearance on behalf of a party to a lawsuit and is in charge of that party's interests in the action.

The code of ethics prohibits the practice of law where there is a conflict of interest. In order to retain such a case, the attorney or employee with the conflict of interest must conduct herself as if there were a "Chinese Wall" around the case file and the staff working on the case. The person with the conflict of interest cannot handle the case or talk about the case with the persons assigned to the file. In a small town, the chances of a conflict of interest can occur with great frequency. Also with large law firms, an employee might switch her employment, and it is quite possible that the new employer has a case representing a defendant where she worked on the plaintiff's side of the same case.

Nothing a client tells his attorney in connection with his case can be disclosed by the attorney, or anyone employed by him or his firm, without the client's permission. *See also* privileged; privileged communication.

---

1. A person who employs an attorney. 2. A person who discusses with an attorney the possibility of hiring the attorney.

- *n.* customer, consumer, patron
- *ant.* seller

A lien that an attorney has upon money or property of her client (including papers and documents) for compensation due her from the client for professional services rendered. It is a possessory lien.

A set of principles and ethical standards promulgated by the American Bar Association, and subsequently adopted by a majority of states, which establish ethical standards, both personal and professional, for judges. *See also* ethics.

See work product; work product rule.

The act of an agent, broker, attorney, or trustee in mingling his own funds with those of his client, customer, or beneficiary. Such conduct is unethical and often illegal as well.

A law or rule. Canons of ethical conduct state the standards of behavior expected of attorneys. *See* Rules of Professional Conduct.

- *n.* law, rule, statute, act, code, order, standard, criterion, measure, ethic, norm

---

1. Having legal capacity. 2. Capable; qualified. 3. Sufficient; acceptable.

Severe criticism; condemnation.

- *n.* disapproval, rebuke, reproach, reprimand, criticism, condemnation, denunciation, disapproval, castigation
- *v.* condemn, criticize, scold, reprimand, admonish, reprove, chastise, denigrate

LEGAL ETHICS

confidential communication

[kon.fi.*den*.shel kum.yoo.ni.*kay*.shen]

LEGAL ETHICS

disciplinary rules

[*dis*.i.plin.eh.ree rulz]

LEGAL ETHICS

confidential relationship

[kon.fi.*den*.shel re.*lay*.shen.ship]

LEGAL ETHICS

disqualified judge

[dis.*kwal*.i.fide juj]

LEGAL ETHICS

confidentiality

[kon.fi.den.shee.*al*.i.tee]

LEGAL ETHICS

double billing

[*dub*.el *bil*.ing]

LEGAL ETHICS

conflict of interest

[*kon*.flikt of *in*.trest]

LEGAL ETHICS

duty of candor

[*dew*.tee ov *kan*.der]

LEGAL ETHICS

contingent fee

[kon.*tin*.jint fee]

LEGAL ETHICS

escrow

[*es*.kroh]

LEGAL ETHICS

disbarment

[dis.*bahr*.ment]

LEGAL ETHICS

escrow account

[*es*.kroh e.*kount*]

Rules and procedures for sanctioning attorneys guilty of professional misconduct. All jurisdictions have adopted such rules. Sanctions may include disbarment, suspension, probation, or reprimand. *See also* Rules of Professional Conduct.

See privileged communication.

A judge who is disqualified to act in a particular case because of personal interest in the subject matter of the suit or because of his preconceived mental attitude. *See also* recusation.

A fiduciary relationship, and any informal relationship between parties in which one of them is duty-bound to act with the utmost good faith for the benefit of the other. Although the terms "confidential relationship" and "fiduciary relationship" are often used interchangeably, there is a distinction between them. "Fiduciary relationship" is a term correctly applicable to legal relationships (EXAMPLES: guardian and ward; trustee and beneficiary; attorney and client), whereas "confidential relationship" includes these as well as every other relationship in which one's ability to place confidence is important, such as, for EXAMPLE, business transactions in which one party relies upon the superior knowledge of the other.

To bill twice for the same product or service.

See privileged; privileged communication.

The obligation to be honest. EXAMPLE: Attorneys are charged with the duty of candor.

---

1. The existence of a variance between the interests of the parties in a fiduciary relationship. EXAMPLE: the conduct of an attorney who acts both for her client and for another person whose interests conflict with those of her client. 2. The condition of a public official or public employee whose personal or financial interests are at variance or appear to be at variance with his public responsibility. EXAMPLE: ownership, by the Secretary of Defense, of stock in a company that contracts with the Department of Defense for the manufacture of military equipment.

A written instrument (EXAMPLES: stock, bonds, a deed), money, or other property deposited by the grantor with a third party (the escrow holder) until the performance of a condition or the happening of a certain event, upon the occurrence of which the property is to be delivered to the grantee.

- *adj.* separate, designated, specified ("keep the money in an escrow account")

A fee for legal services, calculated on the basis of an agreed-upon percentage of the amount of money recovered for the client by his attorney. *See also* attorney fees; fee.

A bank account in the name of the depositor and a second person, the deposited funds being returnable to the depositor or paid to a third person upon the happening of a specified event (EXAMPLE: money for the payment of property taxes that a mortgagor pays into the escrow account of the mortgage company or bank).

The revocation of an attorney's right to practice law. *See also* Rules of Professional Conduct.

- *n.* banishment, discharge, dismissal, ejection, eviction, removal

LEGAL ETHICS

escrow contract

[*es*.kroh *kon*.trakt]

LEGAL ETHICS

frivolous suit

[*friv*.e.les soot]

LEGAL ETHICS

escrow holder

[*es*.kroh *hole*.der]

LEGAL ETHICS

grievance

[*gree*.venss]

LEGAL ETHICS

ethics

[*eth*.iks]

LEGAL ETHICS

IOLTA

[eye.*ol*.ta]

LEGAL ETHICS

fee

[fee]

LEGAL ETHICS

Juris Doctor

[*joor*.is *dok*.ter]

LEGAL ETHICS

fiduciary duty

[fi.*doo*.shee.air.ee *dew*.tee]

LEGAL ETHICS

legal assistant

[*lee*.gl e.*sis*.tent]

LEGAL ETHICS

frivolous pleading

[*friv*.e.les *plee*.ding]

LEGAL ETHICS

loyalty

[*loy*.el.tee]

A lawsuit brought with no intention of determining an actual controversy. EXAMPLE: an action initiated for purposes of harassment.

A contract that describes the rights of the parties to an escrow.

---

1. Any complaint about a wrong or an injustice. 2. Formal complaint filed by a client who is unhappy with an attorney's work.

- *n.* complaint, protest, allegation, accusation, objection

The third party to an escrow.

Acronym for Interest on Lawyers' Trust Accounts. In states with IOLTA programs, lawyers who hold funds belonging to clients deposit such money into a common fund, the interest on which is used for charitable, law-related purposes such as legal services to the poor. Some states' IOLTA programs are voluntary, some are mandatory.

---

1. A code of moral principles and standards of behavior for people in professions such as law or medicine (EXAMPLES: the Code of Judicial Conduct (for judges); the Rules of Professional Conduct (for attorneys). 2. A body of moral principles generally.

- *n.* principles, values, morals, mores, criteria, canon, rules

---

The primary degree given by most law schools. It is commonly expressed in its abbreviated form, JD or J.D. Although a person might have a JD degree, it doesn't necessarily mean that the person has taken and passed the bar examination or received a license to practice law.

---

1. A charge made for the services of a professional person, such as a lawyer or physician. *See also* attorney fees; contingent fee. 2. A statutory charge for the services of a public officer. EXAMPLE: court fees.

A legal assistant is the same as a paralegal. *See* paralegal.

- *n.* paralegal, lawyer's assistant

The duty to act loyally and honestly with respect to the interests of another; the duty the law imposes upon a fiduciary.

Adherence to law or to the government; faithfulness to a person or to a principle.

- *n.* allegiance, fealty, devotion, bond, faith, support ("He has shown great loyalty to his country.")

A pleading that is good in form but false in fact and not pleaded in good faith.

LEGAL ETHICS

malicious prosecution

[ma.*lish*.ess pross.e.*kyoo*.shen]

LEGAL ETHICS

paralegal

[*pehr*.e.leeg.el]

LEGAL ETHICS

malicious use of process

[ma.*lish*.ess use ov *pross*.ess]

LEGAL ETHICS

privileged

[*priv*.i.lejd]

LEGAL ETHICS

meritorious defense

[mehr.i.*toh*.ree.us de.*fense*]

LEGAL ETHICS

privileged communication

[*priv*.i.lejd kem.yoon.i.*kay*.shen]

LEGAL ETHICS

National Association of Legal Assistants (NALA)

[*nash*.en.el a.so.see.*ay*.shen of *leeg*.el a.*sis*.tents]

LEGAL ETHICS

privileged relationship

[*priv*.i.lejd re.*lay*.shen.ship]

LEGAL ETHICS

National Association of Legal Secretaries (NALS)

[*nash*.en.el a.so.see.*ay*.shen of *leeg*.el *sek*.re.tare.eez]

LEGAL ETHICS

probation

[pro.*bay*.shen]

LEGAL ETHICS

National Federation of Paralegal Associations (NFPA)

[*nash*.en.el fed.e.*ray*.shen of pehr.e.*leeg*.el a.so.see.*ay*.shenz]

LEGAL ETHICS

pro bono publico

[pro *bone*.oh *poob*.li.koh]

The terms *paralegal* and *legal assistant* are used interchangeably. In 1997 the ABA adopted the following definition, "A legal assistant or paralegal is a person, qualified by education, training or work experience who is employed or retained by a lawyer, law office, corporation, governmental agency or other entity and who performs specifically delegated substantive legal work for which a lawyer is responsible." A paralegal is a person who, although not an attorney, performs many of the functions of an attorney under an attorney's supervision and control.

- *n.* legal assistant, paraprofessional, aide, lay advocate, legal technician, lawyer's assistant

---

A criminal prosecution or civil suit commenced maliciously and without probable cause. After the termination of such a prosecution or suit in the defendant's favor, the defendant has the right to bring an action against the original plaintiff for the tort of "malicious prosecution."

Entitled to a privilege; possessing a privilege.

- *adj.* protected, excused, immune, exempt, elite ("a privileged class"); confidential, secret, exceptional, top-secret ("privileged records")

The use of process for a purpose for which it was intended, but out of personal malice or some other unjustifiable motive (EXAMPLE: to extort money) and without probable cause. It is, in effect, a form of malicious prosecution.

A communication between persons in a confidential relationship or other privileged relationship (EXAMPLES: husband and wife; physician and patient; attorney and client). The contents of such communications may not be testified to in court unless the person possessing the privilege waives it.

A defense that goes to the merits of the case; a defense warranting a hearing, although it may not be a perfect defense or a defense assured of succeeding.

A relationship of a type such that communications between the parties to the relationship are protected by law against disclosure (i.e., are "privileged") unless the party whom the law protects waives the right to protection. *See also* privileged communication.

A national organization of legal assistants and paralegals whose purpose is to enhance professionalism and the interests of those in the profession, as well as to advance the administration of justice generally. Among its other undertakings, NALA has established a "Code of Professional Responsibility" for paralegals and legal assistants and provides professional certifications, continuing education, and assistance in job placement. A person who receives certification through NALA is entitled to so indicate by the use of "CLA" (Certified Legal Assistant) after his name.

A sentence that allows a person convicted of a crime to continue to live and work in the community while being supervised by a probation officer, instead of being sent to prison.

A national organization of legal secretaries whose purpose is continuing legal education and professionalism. Membership in NALS provides publications, seminars and workshops, and other educational tools. NALS also grants professional legal secretary certification to qualified applicants.

(*Latin*) Means "for the public good." An attorney who represents an indigent client free of charge is said to be representing her client pro bono. Many bar associations require their members to perform a specified amount of pro bono work for the public.

An association of paralegal and legal assistant organizations nationwide whose purpose is to enhance professionalism and the interests of those in the profession, as well as to advance the administration of justice. Among its other undertakings, NFPA has established the "Affirmation of Responsibility," a code of professional conduct for paralegals and legal assistants, and provides continuing education and assistance in job placement.

LEGAL ETHICS

pro hac vice

[pro hak *vy*.see]

LEGAL ETHICS

recusation

[rek.yoo.*zay*.shun]

LEGAL ETHICS

pro se

[pro say]

LEGAL ETHICS

reprimand

[*rep*.ri.mand]

LEGAL ETHICS

professional corporation

[pro.*fesh*.en.el kore.per.*ay*.shen]

LEGAL ETHICS

retainer

[re.*tane*.er]

LEGAL ETHICS

professional ethics

[pro.*fesh*.en.el *eth*.iks]

LEGAL ETHICS

retaining lien

[re.*tane*.ing leen]

LEGAL ETHICS

professional legal secretary

[pro.*fesh*.en.el *leeg*.el *sek*.re.teh.ree]

LEGAL ETHICS

Rules of Professional Conduct

[rulz ov pro.*fesh*.en.el *kon*.dukt]

LEGAL ETHICS

professional misconduct

[pro.*fesh*.en.el mis.*kon*.dukt]

LEGAL ETHICS

sanction

[*sank*.shen]

The act of challenging a judge or a juror for prejudice or bias. *See also* disqualified judge.

(*Latin*) Meaning "for this occasion," an attorney who is not a member of the bar of a particular state may be admitted for one particular case.

A severe and solemn rebuke or censure for disobedience or wrongdoing.

- *n.* admonishment, castigation, censure, reprehension, chiding, lecture, warning, reproval
- *v.* chastise, rebuke, reprove, admonish, castigate, deprecate

(*Latin*) Means "for one's self." Refers to appearing on one's own behalf in either a civil action or a criminal prosecution, rather than being represented by an attorney.

---

1. The act of hiring an attorney. 2. A preliminary fee paid to an attorney at the time she is retained, in order to secure her services. 3. In certain circumstances, the right of a person (EXAMPLE: an executor) who is rightfully in possession of funds belonging to a person who owes him money (EXAMPLE: money belonging to the decedent's estate that he is administering) to retain an amount sufficient to satisfy the obligation.

- *n.* fee, contract, engagement fee, compensation, remuneration

A corporation formed for the purpose of practicing a profession (EXAMPLES: law; medicine; psychotherapy; dentistry) and to secure certain tax advantages. The members of a professional corporation remain personally liable for professional misconduct. Professional corporations often identify themselves by the abbreviation PC. Thus, for EXAMPLE, a professional corporation composed of attorneys Jessica Smith and Sam Smith might be named "Smith and Smith, Esqs., PC."

An attorney's possessory lien, which attaches to a clients' money, paper, or property that the attorney held during the course of his retainer. An attorney has a right to keep such property until a client pays the attorney's fee.

See ethics. *See also* Code of Judicial Conduct; Rules of Professional Conduct.

Rules promulgated by the American Bar Association that detail an attorney's ethical obligations to her client, the courts, and opposing counsel. With variations, these rules have been adopted by most states and incorporated into their statutory codes of ethics. *See also* ethics.

A person who has met the requirements for certification by the National Association of Legal Secretaries.

---

n. Action taken by a state bar association or a state's highest court when an attorney has been found to have committed an ethical violation. EXAMPLES of sanctions against attorneys include the imposition of a private or public reprimand, revocation or suspension of license to practice law.
v. To punish; to penalize.

- *v.* punish, ban, boycott ("The bar sanctioned the erring attorney.")
- *n.* ban, boycott, decree, injunction, penalty, sentence, punishment ("unimposed sanctions")

1. Malpractice. 2. In the case of an attorney, violating the disciplinary rules of a jurisdiction in which he practices. *See also* Rules of Professional Conduct.

LEGAL ETHICS

solicitation

[so.liss.i.*tay*.shen]

LEGAL ETHICS

work product rule

[werk *prod*.ukt rool]

LEGAL ETHICS

special counsel

[*spesh*.el *koun*.sel]

INSURANCE LAW

adjuster

[a.*just*.er]

LEGAL ETHICS

suspend

[sus.*pend*]

INSURANCE LAW

annuity

[a.*nyoo*.i.tee]

LEGAL ETHICS

suspended

[sus.*pen*.ded]

INSURANCE LAW

annuity policy

[a.*nyoo*.i.tee *pol*.i.see]

LEGAL ETHICS

unauthorized practice of law

[un.*aw*.ther.ized *prak*.tiss ov law]

INSURANCE LAW

bad faith

[bad fayth]

LEGAL ETHICS

work product

[werk *prod*.ukt]

INSURANCE LAW

beneficiary

[ben.e.*fish*.ee.air.ee]

The rule that an attorney's work product is not subject to discovery. This includes the materials produced by persons working for the attorney.

---

1. The act of an attorney in seeking clients. An attorney is permitted to solicit clients but must adhere to the code of ethics. It could be an ethical violation in which an attorney sends dozens of pizzas to an ambulance company's staff at lunch time each week, putting pressure on them to refer all patients to the attorney. 2. Inviting a business transaction.

- *n.* petition, requisition

A person who makes a determination of the value of a claim against an insurance company for the purpose of arriving at an amount for which the claim will be settled. An adjuster may be an agent for the insurance company or an independent adjuster.

- *n.* reconciler, arbitrator, intermediary, intervenor, mediator

---

An attorney, employed by the attorney general of the United States or a state, to assist in a particular case as a prosecutor.

---

1. A yearly payment of a fixed sum of money for life or for a stated number of years.
2. A right to receive fixed periodic payments (yearly or otherwise), either for life or for a stated period of time.

Most annuities are in the form of insurance policies. When payments are made until the death of the beneficiary, the annuity is a life annuity. When payments will be terminated if the beneficiary acts in a specified way (EXAMPLE: accepting full-time employment), the annuity is a term annuity. A contingent annuity is payable upon the occurrence of some stated event beyond the control of the beneficiary (EXAMPLE: the death of the beneficiary's father). A joint and survivorship annuity is paid to two beneficiaries and, after one of them dies, to the survivor (EXAMPLE: continued payment to a widow of an annuity that, prior to her husband's death, was paid to her and her husband jointly). A retirement annuity is generally payable upon retirement from employment.

- *n.* payment, income, pension, subsidy, stipend, allotment

---

1. To temporarily remove an attorney's right to practice law. USAGE: "The bar association suspended the attorney's law license for six months." 2. To temporarily withdraw a privilege. *See also* suspended.

- *v.* withdraw, revoke ("suspend his license")

An insurance policy that provides for or pays an annuity.

Temporarily inactive or temporarily not effective.

A devious or deceitful intent, motivated by self-interest, ill will, or a concealed purpose. The opposite of good faith. Bad faith is stronger than negligence, but may or may not involve fraud. EXAMPLE: An insurance company engages in bad faith when it refuses, with no basis for its action, to pay a claim.

Engaging in the practice of law without the license required by law. EXAMPLES: giving a legal opinion to a client, setting legal fees, or signing legal documents.

A person who receives a benefit.

Material prepared by counsel in preparing for the trial of a case. EXAMPLES: notes; memoranda, and legal pleadings.

INSURANCE LAW
benefit
[*ben*.e.fit]

INSURANCE LAW
collision insurance
[ke.*lizh*.en in.*shoor*.ense]

INSURANCE LAW
binder
[*bine*.der]

INSURANCE LAW
comprehensive coverage
[kom.pre.*hen*.siv *kuv*.e.rej]

INSURANCE LAW
business interruption insurance
[*biz*.ness in.ter.*up*.shen in.*shoor*.ense]

INSURANCE LAW
comprehensive insurance
[kom.pre.*hen*.siv in.*shoor*.ense]

INSURANCE LAW
cancellation
[kan.sel.*ay*.shen]

INSURANCE LAW
contribution between insurers
[kon.tra.*byoo*.shen be.*tween* in.*shoor*.erz]

INSURANCE LAW
cancellation clause
[kan.sel.*ay*.shen kloz]

INSURANCE LAW
deductible
[de.*duk*.tibl]

INSURANCE LAW
coinsurance
[*ko*.in.*shoor*.ense]

INSURANCE LAW
disability clause
[dis.e.*bil*.i.tee kloz]

Automobile insurance that protects the owner or operator of a motor vehicle from loss due to damage done to his property by another.

A payment made under an insurance policy, pension, annuity, or the like.

- *n.* aid, asset, advantage, profit, gain, utility

A package of coverage provided by a policy of comprehensive insurance that protects against a myriad of perils (collision, theft, etc.).

1. An interim memorandum, used when an insurance policy cannot be issued immediately, evidencing either that insurance coverage is effective at a specified time and continues until the policy is issued, or that the risk is declined and giving notice of that fact. 2. An earnest money deposit that preserves a buyer's right to purchase real estate.

- *n.* deposit, pledge, stake, collateral, escrow, security ("a binder on the deal")

Insurance that provides coverage for various risks (EXAMPLES: fire; theft; flood; wind; hail), each of which could also be covered under separate policies.

Insurance protecting against loss from the interruption of business, as distinguished from coverage upon merchandise or other property used in the business. *See also* insurance.

The obligation of an insurance company that has issued a policy covering the same loss as that insured by another insurance company to contribute proportionally to the other insurer who has paid the entire loss.

The act of a party to a contract ending the contract after the other party has been guilty of breach of contract. Cancellation should be contrasted with termination, which provides the party ending the contract with fewer remedies.

- *n.* abandonment, reversal, recall, nullification, revocation, termination, withdrawal, rescission ("cancellation of the insurance policy")

In insurance, portion of a loss that the insured must pay from his own pocket before the insurance company will begin to make payment. USAGE: "Because my policy has a $500 deductible, my insurance company will pay only $2,000 of the $2,500 damage to my car."

A provision in a contract that allows the parties to cancel the contract without obligation. Also known as an escape clause.

- *n.* escape clause

A clause in an insurance policy providing for a waiver of premiums in the event of the insured's disability.

A division of the risk between the insurer and the insured. EXAMPLE: a health insurance policy under which the insurance company is obligated to pay 80 percent of every claim and the insured pays 20 percent.

INSURANCE LAW

disability insurance

[dis.e.*bil*.i.tee in.*shoor*.ense]

INSURANCE LAW

group insurance

[groop in.*shoor*.ense]

INSURANCE LAW

double indemnity

[*du*.bel in.*dem*.ni.tee]

INSURANCE LAW

health insurance

[helth in.*shoor*.ense]

INSURANCE LAW

double insurance

[*du*.bel in.*shoor*.ense]

INSURANCE LAW

homeowners policy

[*home*.ohn.erz *pol*.i.see]

INSURANCE LAW

exclusion

[eks.*kloo*.zhen]

INSURANCE LAW

indemnification

[in.dem.ni.fi.*kay*.shen]

INSURANCE LAW

fire insurance

[*fy*.er in.*shoor*.ense]

INSURANCE LAW

indemnify

[in.*dem*.ni.fy]

INSURANCE LAW

fraud

[frawd]

INSURANCE LAW

indemnity insurance

[in.*dem*.ni.tee in.*shoor*.ense]

1. A contract providing life, accident, or health insurance for a group of employees. The terms of the contract are contained in a master policy; the individual employee's participation is demonstrated by a certificate of insurance that she holds. 2. A contract providing life, accident, or health insurance for any defined group of people. The contract is a master policy and is entered into between the group policyholder (for EXAMPLE, the American Automobile Association) and the insurance company for the benefit of the policyholder's members.

Insurance that provides income in the event of disability.

Insurance that indemnifies the insured for medical expenses incurred as a result of sickness or accident.

A benefit payable under an insurance policy at twice face value if loss occurs under certain conditions. EXAMPLE: under a life insurance policy, the death of the insured by accidental, as opposed to natural, causes.

An insurance policy that insures homeowners against most common risks, including fire, burglary, and civil liability.

Coverage of the same risk and the same interest by different insurance companies. *See also* contribution between insurers.

---

1. The act of indemnifying or being indemnified. 2. Payment made by way of compensation for a loss. *See also* indemnity insurance.

- *n.* restitution, amends, compensation, insurance, payment, reparation

---

1. A provision in an insurance policy that removes a specified risk, person, or circumstance from coverage. *See also* exception. 2. The act of keeping out or apart.

- *n.* rejection, omission, dismissal, elimination, disallowance, nonacceptance, repudiation

---

1. To compensate or reimburse a person for loss or damage. 2. To promise to compensate or reimburse in the event of future loss or damage. *See also* indemnity insurance.

- *v.* compensate, reimburse, secure, make amends, guarantee, restore, repay, redeem

---

Insurance that indemnifies the insured against loss to property (EXAMPLES: a house, the contents of a house; a commercial building) due to fire.

Insurance providing indemnification for actual loss or damage, as distinguished from liability insurance, which provides for payment of a specified sum upon the occurrence of a specific event regardless of what the actual loss or damage may be.

Deceit, deception, or trickery that is intended to induce, and does induce, another person to part with anything of value or surrender some legal right.

INSURANCE LAW

indemnity policy

[in.*dem*.ni.tee *paw*.li.see]

INSURANCE LAW

insurance agent

[in.*shoor*.ense *ay*.jent]

INSURANCE LAW

insurability

[in.shoor.e.*bil*.i.tee]

INSURANCE LAW

insurance binder

[in.*shoor*.ense *bine*.der]

INSURANCE LAW

insurable

[in.*shoor*.ebl]

INSURANCE LAW

insurance broker

[in.*shoor*.ense *broh*.ker]

INSURANCE LAW

insurable interest

[in.*shoor*.ebl *in*.trest]

INSURANCE LAW

insurance carrier

[in.*shoor*.ense *kehr*.ee.er]

INSURANCE LAW

insurance

[in.*shoor*.ense]

INSURANCE LAW

insurance company

[in.*shoor*.ense *kum*.pe.nee]

INSURANCE LAW

insurance adjuster

[in.*shoor*.ense a.*just*.er]

INSURANCE LAW

insurance contract

[in.*shoor*.ense *kon*.trakt]

A person authorized by an insurance company to represent it when dealing with third persons in matters relating to insurance. *Compare* insurance broker.

See indemnity insurance.

See binder.

Having the qualities needed to be insurable: no preexisting health conditions, nonsmoker, under certain ages, etc.

A person who acts as an intermediary between the insured and the insurer, who is not employed by any insurance company. The broker solicits insurance business from the public, and having obtained an order, either places the insurance with a company selected by the insured, or, if the insured does not select a carrier, then with a company of the broker's choice. Depending upon the circumstances, an insurance broker may represent either the insured, or the insurer, or both. *Compare* insurance agent.

Capable of being insured. EXAMPLE: as a condition of purchasing life insurance, being in sound health at the time the policy is issued.

A company engaged in the business of issuing insurance policies; an insurance company.

An interest from whose existence the owner derives a benefit and whose nonexistence will cause her to suffer a loss. The presence of an insurable interest is essential to the validity and enforceability of an insurance policy because it removes it from the category of a gambling contract. An insurable interest in life insurance, for EXAMPLE, is: (a) one's interest in his own life; (b) one's natural interest in the continued life of a blood relative; (c) any reasonable expectation of financial benefit from the continued life of another (one's debtor, business partner, etc.).

A company engaged in the business of issuing insurance policies.

A contract (the policy) by which one party (the insurer), in return for a specified consideration (the premium), agrees to compensate or indemnify another (the insured) on account of loss, damage, or liability arising from an unknown or contingent event (the risk). There are almost as many kinds of coverage as there are risks. EXAMPLES of some of the most common types of insurance are accident insurance, automobile insurance, credit life insurance, disability insurance, fire insurance, flood insurance, health insurance, homeowners' insurance, liability insurance, life insurance, major medical insurance, malpractice insurance, mortgage insurance, and title insurance.

The law does not permit a person to insure against the consequences of acts or transactions that violate public policy, for EXAMPLE, gambling losses. Most importantly, the law requires a person to have an insurable interest in whatever she wishes to insure.

- n. indemnification, assurance, coverage, policy, warranty, covenant, security, guarantee, indemnity against contingencies, safeguard

The formal name for an insurance policy.

See adjuster.

INSURANCE LAW

insurance policy

[in.*shoor*.ense *pol*.i.see]

INSURANCE LAW

malpractice insurance

[mal.*prak*.tiss in.*shoor*.ense]

INSURANCE LAW

insurance premium

[in.*shoor*.ense *pree*.mee.um]

INSURANCE LAW

marine insurance

[ma.*reen* in.*shoor*.ense]

INSURANCE LAW

insure

[in.*shoor*]

INSURANCE LAW

material misrepresentation

[mah.*teer*.e.al mis.rep.re.zen.*tay*.shen]

INSURANCE LAW

insured

[in.*shoord*]

INSURANCE LAW

no-fault insurance

[no-fawlt in.*shoor*.ense]

INSURANCE LAW

insurer

[in.*shoor*.er]

INSURANCE LAW

personal liability

[*per*.sen.el ly.a.*bil*.i.tee]

INSURANCE LAW

life insurance

[life in.*shoor*.ense]

INSURANCE LAW

preexisting condition clause

[pree.eg.*zis*.ting ken.*dish*.en kloz]

A type of liability insurance that protects professional persons (EXAMPLES: attorneys; physicians; psychotherapists) from liability for negligence and other forms of malpractice. It is also called professional liability insurance.

A contract to compensate or indemnify a person for loss arising from a contingent occurrence.

An insurance policy covering the risk of loss to a ship or its cargo from the perils of the sea.

Money paid to an insurer for an insurance policy.

A fraudulent or deliberately inaccurate statement that is intended to cause, or causes, a person to act in reliance. Also called a fraudulent misrepresentation.

1. To enter into a contract of insurance as an insurer; to issue an insurance policy.
2. To guarantee.

- *v.* obtain insurance, secure against loss, underwrite, guard, safeguard, shield, back

A type of automobile insurance required by law in many states, under which the insured is entitled to indemnification regardless of who was responsible for the injury or damage. Proof of negligence is not a condition of liability under such a policy. *See also* insurance.

A person protected by an insurance policy; a person whose property is protected by an insurance policy. One need not be the named insured (i.e., named in the policy) to be covered. A standard automobile insurance policy, for EXAMPLE, usually covers any person operating the insured vehicle with the permission of the named insured.

Liability to satisfy a judgment, debt, or other obligation from one's personal assets.

Generally, an insurance company; that is, the party who assumes the risk under an insurance policy and agrees to compensate or indemnify the insured.

- *n.* indemnitor, indemnifier, guarantor, assurer, surety, underwriter

A provision in a health insurance policy that excludes from coverage, for a specified period of time, medical conditions that existed when the insured purchased the policy.

A contract (the policy) in which the insurer, in exchange for the payment of a premium, agrees to pay a specified sum to a named beneficiary upon the death of the insured. *See also* straight life insurance; term life insurance; whole life insurance.

INSURANCE LAW

premium

[*pree*.mee.yum]

INSURANCE LAW

risk

[rizk]

INSURANCE LAW

proof of loss

[proof ov loss]

INSURANCE LAW

self-insurance

[self-in.*shoor*.ense]

INSURANCE LAW

reinsurance

[ree.in.*shoor*.ense]

INSURANCE LAW

straight life insurance

[strate life in.*shoor*.ense]

INSURANCE LAW

reinsurer

[ree.in.*shoor*.er]

INSURANCE LAW

subrogation

[sub.ro.*gay*.shen]

INSURANCE LAW

replacement value

[ree.*plaiss*.ment *val*.yoo]

INSURANCE LAW

term life insurance

[term life in.*shoor*.ense]

INSURANCE LAW

rider

[*ry*.der]

INSURANCE LAW

title insurance

[*ty*.tel in.*shoor*.ense]

1. The chance of loss or injury; the hazard or peril of loss that is protected by an insurance policy. EXAMPLES: fire, flood; sickness.
2. A gamble; a peril.

Money paid to an insurance company for coverage by an insurance policy.

Protecting one's property or business by establishing a fund out of which to pay for losses instead of purchasing insurance. Self-insurance is a means through which employers may provide workers' compensation and health coverage to their employees as an alternative to securing workers' compensation insurance and health insurance.

A written statement of the dollar amount of a loss sustained, submitted by an insured. Proof of loss is a standard requirement of casualty insurance policies.

Life insurance in which the cash surrender value of the policy increases as the insured makes premium payments throughout her lifetime. Straight life insurance is also referred to as whole life insurance or ordinary life insurance. *Compare* term life insurance.

A contract between two insurance companies under which the second company (the reinsurer) insures the first company (the insurer) against loss due to policyholders' claims.

The substitution of one person for another with respect to a claim or right against a third person; the principle that when a person has been required to pay a debt that should have been paid by another person, she becomes entitled to all of the remedies that the creditor originally possessed with respect to the debtor. (EXAMPLE: After the insurance company that insures Lloyd's car indemnifies him for the damage done to his car by Mary's negligence, the insurance company has the same cause of action against Mary as Lloyd originally had.) Subrogation is sometimes referred to as substitution.

- *n.* displacement, substitution, transfer, transference, exchange, switch, supplanting

An insurance company's insurance company. *See also* reinsurance.

Life insurance that provides protection only for a stated number of years and has no cash surrender value. *Compare* life insurance; straight life insurance; whole life insurance.

In the context of an insurance loss, the cost of replacing insured property at its current value, as opposed to its original cost; that is, at what it costs now, not what it cost when it was purchased.

An insurance policy in which the insurer agrees to indemnify the purchaser of realty, or the mortgagee, against loss due to defective title.

A sheet or sheets of paper, written or printed, attached to a document, that refer to the document in a manner that leaves no doubt of the parties' intention to incorporate it into the document. Riders are most frequently used with insurance policies to make additions or changes to the original policy.

- *n.* attachment, extension, insertion, supplement, addendum

INSURANCE LAW **umbrella policy** [um.*brel*.a *pah*.li.see]	COMMERCIAL LAW **accommodation loan** [a.kom.o.*day*.shen loan]
INSURANCE LAW **waiver** [*way*.ver]	COMMERCIAL LAW **accommodation paper** [a.kom.o.*day*.shen *pay*.per]
INSURANCE LAW **whole life insurance** [hole life in.*shoor*.ense]	COMMERCIAL LAW **alteration** [al.ter.*ay*.shen]
INSURANCE LAW **workers' compensation insurance** [*wer*.kerz kom.pen.*say*.shen in.*shoor*.ense]	COMMERCIAL LAW **asset** [*ass*.et]
COMMERCIAL LAW **acceptance** [ak.*sep*.tense]	COMMERCIAL LAW **assignment** [a.*sine*.ment]
COMMERCIAL LAW **acceptor** [ak.*sep*.tor]	COMMERCIAL LAW **assignment for the benefit of creditors** [a.*sine*.ment for the *ben*.e.fit of *kred*.it.terz]

A loan made as a favor, without benefit or without adequate benefit to the person making the loan.

An insurance policy that provides coverage over and above the liability limitations of the insured's basic liability insurance policies.

A bill or note signed as a favor to another person, known as the accommodated party, to enable that person to receive a loan. The person who grants the favor is the accommodation party or accommodation maker. If the accommodated party and the accommodation party sign jointly, they are known as co-makers. If the accommodated party defaults on the note, the accommodation party is fully liable.

The intentional relinquishment or renunciation of a right, claim, or privilege a person knows he has.

- *n.* abandonment, abdication, forgoing, refusal, relinquishment, renunciation

An erasure, writing, or typing that modifies the content of an instrument or document. EXAMPLE: changing the date on a check (as opposed to securing or writing a new check). Because an instrument can be altered by a person entitled to do so, an alteration is not necessarily a forgery.

- *n.* change, modification, conversion, switch, correction

Straight life insurance or ordinary life insurance, as opposed to term life insurance or group insurance.

Anything of value owned by a person or an organization. Assets include not only all real property and personal property, but intangible property such as bills, notes, stock, and accounts receivable.

State statutes provide for the payment by the employer of compensation to employees injured in their employment or, in case of death, to their dependents, without the need to prove any negligence on the part of the employer.

A transfer of property, or a right in property, from one person to another.

1. With respect to negotiable instruments, the agreement of the bank or other drawer to honor a draft, check, or other negotiable instrument. Acceptance, which must be indicated on the instrument, in writing, is an acknowledgment by the drawee that the drawer has sufficient funds on deposit to cover the draft. *See also* certified check. 2. In the law of sales, the acceptance of the goods that are the subject of the sale has an important bearing upon the passage of title from the buyer to the seller per the contract.

- *n.* acquisition, reception, adoption, compliance, consent, acknowledgment
- *ant.* rejection, opposition

An assignment and transfer by a debtor of all her property to a trustee to collect any amounts owned, to sell the property, and to distribute the proceeds among her creditors.

A drawee who has accepted a draft. *See also* acceptance.

COMMERCIAL LAW
attachment
[a.*tach*.ment]

COMMERCIAL LAW
cashier's check
[kash.*eerz chek*]

COMMERCIAL LAW
attachment lien
[a.*tach*.ment *leen*]

COMMERCIAL LAW
certificate of deposit
[ser.*tif*.i.ket ov de.*poz*.it]

COMMERCIAL LAW
bearer
[*bare*.er]

COMMERCIAL LAW
certified check
[*ser*.ti.fide chek]

COMMERCIAL LAW
bearer instrument
[*bare*.er *in*.stroo.ment]

COMMERCIAL LAW
chattel paper
[*chat*.el *pay*.per]

COMMERCIAL LAW
bearer paper
[*bare*.er *pay*.per]

COMMERCIAL LAW
check
[chek]

COMMERCIAL LAW
cash
[kash]

COMMERCIAL LAW
collateral
[ko.*lat*.er.el]

A bill of exchange, drawn by a bank upon bank funds, and accepted by virtue of the act of issuance. The bank's insurance of the check is a guaranty that it will be honored. A cashier's check is the equivalent of cash. *Compare* certified check.

The process by which a person's property is figuratively brought into court to ensure satisfaction of a judgment that may be rendered against him. In the event judgment is rendered, the property may be sold to satisfy the judgment.

- *n.* seizure, confiscation, garnishment, dispossession

A voucher issued by a bank acknowledging the receipt of money on deposit that the bank promises to repay to the depositor. There are two kinds of certificates of deposit: demand certificates and time certificates. Demand certificates are ordinary savings accounts; the deposit can be withdrawn at any time, without penalty. Time certificates, which pay a higher rate of interest, are designed not to be cashed for a specified number of months or years. A certificate of deposit is often referred to simply as a CD. A treasury certificate is a form of certificate of deposit issued by the United States Treasury.

A lien that arises when property is attached; it is perfected when judgment is entered.

A check upon which the bank has stamped the words "certified" or "accepted," certifying that the check is drawn upon sufficient funds and will be honored when it is presented for payment. A certified check is the equivalent of cash. *See also* acceptance. *Compare* cashier's check.

The holder of a negotiable instrument payable to "bearer" or to "cash" (i.e., a negotiable instrument not payable to a named person). The Uniform Commercial Code defines a bearer as the person in possession of an instrument, document of title, or certificated security payable to bearer or indorsed in blank.

- *n.* carrier, recipient, courier, possessor, holder, payee

As defined by the Uniform Commercial Code, a document that reflects both a debt and a security interest in specific goods. *See also* secured transaction.

A negotiable instrument payable to bearer or to cash, or that is in any form that does not specify a payee.

A written order ("pay to the order of") directed to a bank to pay money to the person named. *See also* cashier's check; certified check; traveler's check; draft; negotiable instrument.

- *n.* draft, note, negotiable instrument, bank note, inspection, examination

---

Commercial paper payable to bearer or to cash, or in any other form that does not designate a specific payee.

Stocks, bonds, or other property that serve as security for a loan or other obligation; property pledged to pay a debt.

- *n.* deposit, security, endorsement, pledge, promise

Coin, money; money in hand, either in coin, currency, or other legal tender. A cashier's check or a certified check is the equivalent of cash, because payment is essentially guaranteed.

- *n.* coin, money, funds, currency, notes, legal tender
- *v.* make change, pay, draw, liquidate, redeem ("to cash a check")

COMMERCIAL LAW

commercial paper

[ke.*mer*.shel *pay*.per]

COMMERCIAL LAW

credit bureau

[*kred*.it *byoo*.roh]

COMMERCIAL LAW

consignment

[ken.*sine*.ment]

COMMERCIAL LAW

credit card

[*kred*.it kard]

COMMERCIAL LAW

consumer

[kon.*soo*.mer]

COMMERCIAL LAW

The Credit Card Accountability, Responsibility and Disclosure Act of 2009

[the k*re*.dit kard *a*.kount.a.*bil*.i.tee
and dis.*klo*.shur akt ov 2009]

COMMERCIAL LAW

consumer credit protection acts

[kon.*soo*.mer *kred*.it pro.*tek*.shen aktz]

COMMERCIAL LAW

creditor

[*kred*.it.or]

COMMERCIAL LAW

consumer goods

[kon.*soo*.mer gudz]

COMMERCIAL LAW

debt

[det]

COMMERCIAL LAW

credit

[*kred*.it]

COMMERCIAL LAW

defense

[de.*fense*]

A company that collects information concerning the financial standing, credit, and general reputation of others, which it furnishes to subscribers for a fee.

Negotiable instruments, including checks, drafts, certificates of deposit, and promissory notes. Commercial paper is regulated by Article 3 of the Uniform Commercial Code.

A card issued for the purpose of enabling the owner to obtain goods, services, or money on credit.

The entrusting of goods either to a carrier for delivery to a consignee or to a consignee who is to sell the goods for the consignor.

- *n.* entrusting, distribution, committal, transmittal

n. The Act's key changes to credit card law included:

Banning retroactive rate increases on existing balances, requiring 45 days notice of rate increases, mandating that statements be mailed 21 days before the due date, and over-limit fees can be charged only after a cardholder authorizes such transactions.

A person who buys and uses products or services and who is affected by their cost, availability, and quality, as well as by laws regulating their manufacture, sale, and financing.

- *n.* buyer, client, patron, purchaser, vendee, customer

A person to whom a debt is owed by a debtor.

Also known as truth in lending acts; federal and state statutes that require, among other things, that contracts for the sale of consumer goods involving credit be written in plain language, that the finance charges be stated as a uniform annual percentage rate, and that goods purchased on credit or with credit cards be returnable within specified periods of time. *See also* credit.

An unconditional and legally enforceable obligation for the payment of money (EXAMPLES: a mortgage; an installment sale contract) and obligations imposed by law without contract (EXAMPLES: a judgment, unliquidated damages). A debt not presently due is nonetheless a debt.

- *n.* obligation, liability, debit, dues, commitment, encumbrance

As defined by the Uniform Commercial Code, articles used primarily for personal, family, or household purposes.

With respect to commercial paper, a legal basis for denying one's liability on an instrument.

Trust placed in a person's willingness and ability to pay when the obligation to pay is extended over a period of time without security.

- *n.* rating, trust, standing, authority, loan, mortgage ("He has good credit.")

COMMERCIAL LAW
deficiency
[de.*fish*.en.see]

COMMERCIAL LAW
draw
[draw]

COMMERCIAL LAW
demand loan
[de.*mand* lone]

COMMERCIAL LAW
drawee
[draw.*ee*]

COMMERCIAL LAW
demand note
[de.*mand* note]

COMMERCIAL LAW
drawer
[draw.*er*]

COMMERCIAL LAW
demand paper
[de.*mand pay*.per]

COMMERCIAL LAW
execution
[ek.se.*kyoo*.shen]

COMMERCIAL LAW
dishonor
[dis.*on*.er]

COMMERCIAL LAW
filing
[*file*.ing]

COMMERCIAL LAW
draft
[draft]

COMMERCIAL LAW
filing laws
[*file*.ing lawz]

1. To create, make, or sign a negotiable instrument. 2. To take or accept an advance. 3. To withdraw money from a bank account.

- *v.* extract, deplete, exhaust, withdraw ("Do you wish to draw on your savings account?")
- *ant.* deposit
- *n.* extraction, withdrawal, depletion, advance ("I made a draw on my checking account.")

---

1. The amount still due the creditor after foreclosure of a mortgage or other security.
2. Shortage, undersupply, lack.

- *n.* insufficiency, lack, shortage, inadequacy, absence, scantiness, want
- *ant.* adequacy

The person upon whom a draft is drawn; the person to whom a draft is presented for acceptance and payment. The drawee of a check is always a bank. *Compare* drawer.

A loan that is callable (total payment is demanded) at any time.

The maker of a draft. *Compare* drawee.

A promissory note payable when payment is demanded.

---

1. A writ of process for the enforcement of a judgment. 2. The act of an officer in serving a writ or process. 3. The signing of a document or instrument.

- *n.* fulfillment, achievement, performance, conclusion ("the execution of a contract")

Commercial paper payable when payment is demanded.

The act of depositing a document with a public officer to preserve it as one of the records of his office.

To refuse to accept or pay a negotiable instrument when it is duly presented for acceptance or payment, or when presentment is excused and the instrument is not accepted or paid.

- *ant.* accept

Statutes that require the filing of an instrument as a condition of its complete effectiveness.

An order in writing by one person on another (commonly a bank) to pay a specified sum of money to a third person on demand or at a stated future time. EXAMPLE: a check.

- *n.* money order, check, banknote, negotiable paper ("a bank draft")

COMMERCIAL LAW

financing statement

[*fine*.an.sing *state*.ment]

COMMERCIAL LAW

holder in good faith

[*hole*.der in good faith]

COMMERCIAL LAW

forge

[forj]

COMMERCIAL LAW

honor

[*on*.er]

COMMERCIAL LAW

garnishment

[*gar*.nish.ment]

COMMERCIAL LAW

indorse

[in.*dorse*]

COMMERCIAL LAW

holder

[*hole*.der]

COMMERCIAL LAW

indorsee

[in.dor.*see*]

COMMERCIAL LAW

holder for value

[*hole*.der for *val*.yoo]

COMMERCIAL LAW

indorsee in due course

[in.dor.*see* in dew korss]

COMMERCIAL LAW

holder in due course

[*hole*.der in dew kors]

COMMERCIAL LAW

indorsement

[in.*dorse*.ment]

A person who takes or holds property, including a negotiable instrument, without knowledge of any defect in title.

A notice of the existence of a security interest in goods, which a creditor is entitled to file with the appropriate public officer, usually the secretary of state. The designated public office varies from state to state. Note that "financing statement" is not "financial statement."

To pay or accept a negotiable instrument when it is duly presented. *Compare* dishonor. *See also* acceptance.

- *v.* credit, redeem, make good ("The store honors personal checks.")

To commit a forgery; to make falsely with intent to defraud or injure any writing that, if genuine, might appear to be legally effective or the basis for legal liability. Forgery is a crime.

- *v.* counterfeit, duplicate, imitate, reproduce, construct. *See* utter.

To sign one's name on the back of a document, especially a check. *See also* indorsement.

A proceeding by a creditor to obtain satisfaction of a debt from money or property of the debtor that is in the possession of a third person or is owed by such a person to the debtor. EXAMPLE: Because Ron owes back taxes, the IRS (the creditor, also called the garnishor or plaintiff) initiates a garnishment against Ron (the debtor, also called the defendant) by serving a notice of garnishment of Ron's wages upon his employer, the ABC Company (the garnishee). Note that a garnishment is distinguished from an attachment by the fact that the money or property reached by the garnishment remains in the hands of the third party until there is a judgment in the action involving the basic debt.

- *n.* attachment, levy, appropriation, collection

The person to whom a negotiable instrument is indorsed by name. *Compare* bearer. *See also* indorse.

A person who has the legal right to enforce a negotiable instrument or who is entitled to receive, hold, and dispose of a document of title and the goods to which it pertains. With respect to an instrument payable to or in the name of "bearer," the person in possession is the holder; with respect to an instrument payable to or in the name of an identified person, that person is the "holder" if she is in possession of the instrument.

- *n.* owner, possessor, bearer, keeper, recipient

A person who in good faith, in the ordinary course of business, for value, acquires a negotiable instrument duly indorsed to her, indorsed generally, or payable to bearer.

A person who has given consideration for a negotiable instrument that he holds.

The writing of one's name on the back of a negotiable instrument, by which a person transfers title to the paper to another person.

A holder of a negotiable instrument who gave value for it and took it in good faith and without notice of any claim or defense against it.

COMMERCIAL LAW	COMMERCIAL LAW
indorser	**maker**
[in.*dor*.ser]	[*may*.ker]
COMMERCIAL LAW	COMMERCIAL LAW
installment payments	**merchant**
[in.*stall*.ment *pay*.ments]	[*mer*.chent]
COMMERCIAL LAW	COMMERCIAL LAW
judgment	**mortgage**
[*juj*.ment]	[*more*.gej]
COMMERCIAL LAW	COMMERCIAL LAW
lien	**negotiable**
[*leen*]	[ne.*go*.shebl]
COMMERCIAL LAW	COMMERCIAL LAW
lien creditor	**negotiable instrument**
[leen *kred*.i.tor]	[ne.*go*.shebl *in*.stroo.ment]
COMMERCIAL LAW	COMMERCIAL LAW
liquidated debt	**negotiate**
[*lik*.wi.day.ted det]	[ne.*go*.shee.ate]

A person who obligates himself by executing a check, promissory note, draft, or other negotiable instrument. *See also* drawer.

The person who indorses a negotiable instrument. *Compare* indorsee.

---

1. A person who regularly trades in a particular type of goods. 2. Under the Uniform Commercial Code, "a person who deals in goods of the kind or otherwise by his occupation holds himself out as having knowledge or skill peculiar to the goods involved in the transaction." The law holds a merchant to a higher standard than it imposes upon a casual seller.

Payments at fixed intervals until the entire principal and interest on an obligation are satisfied. Installment payments are made under installment contracts, installment notes, or installment sale contracts, as well as other types of agreements. Commercial installment sales and installment loans are regulated by consumer credit protection acts.

---

n. 1. A pledge of real property to secure a debt. Which one of at least three possible legal principles defines the rights of the parties to a given mortgage depends upon the state in which the mortgaged property is located. In states that have adopted the lien theory, the mortgagee (creditor) has a lien on the property; the mortgagor (debtor) retains legal title and is entitled to possession unless his interest is terminated by a foreclosure decree. In title theory states, a mortgage transfers title and a theoretical right of possession to the mortgagee; title reverts to the mortgagor upon full payment of the mortgage debt. A third group of states employs hybrid versions of the lien and title theories, with characteristics of both. 2. A written agreement pledging real property as security.
v. 1. To place real property under a mortgage. 2. To obligate; to pledge.

In a civil action, the final determination entered by a court after it renders its decision on the rights of the parties, based upon the pleadings and the evidence.

- *n.* decree, holding, ruling, conclusion, opinion, award, sentence, finding, adjudication, verdict, arbitration ("the judgment of the court"), decision

---

Transferable by indorsement or delivery.
EXAMPLE: a negotiable instrument.

- *adj.* transferable; assignable; alienable; open; undetermined; malleable
- *ant.* nonnegotiable, fixed

A claim or charge on, or right against, personal property, or an encumbrance on real property, for the payment of a debt. A lien may be created by statute (EXAMPLES: a tax lien, an attachment lien) or by agreement between the parties (EXAMPLES: a mortgage on real estate; a security agreement covering personal property). In some instances, a lien permits the creditor to retain the debtor's property in his possession until the debt is satisfied. Such a lien is called a possessory lien.

- *n.* debt, obligation, mortgage, interest ("The mortgage is a lien on the house.")

Under the Uniform Commercial Code, a signed writing that orders or provides payment of money if: it is unconditional, it is in a fixed amount, it is payable on demand to bearer or to order or at a definite time, and it "does not state any undertaking or instruction by the person promising or ordering payment to do any act in addition to the payment of money." (EXAMPLES: a check; a money order; a certificate of deposit; a bond; a note, a bill of lading; a warehouse receipt.) Negotiable instruments are also referred to as commercial paper or negotiable paper.

- *n.* draft, check, bond, note, money order, instrument

A creditor whose debt is secured by a lien. EXAMPLES: an execution creditor; a judgment creditor.

To transfer a negotiable instrument to a third person by indorsement or delivery.

A debt that has been paid or for which it is certain as to how much is due. *See also* debt.

COMMERCIAL LAW
negotiation
[ne.go.shee.*ay*.shen]

COMMERCIAL LAW
perfecting a security interest
[per.*fek*.ting a se.*kyoo*.ri.tee *in*.trest]

COMMERCIAL LAW
nonnegotiable
[non.ne.*go*.shebl]

COMMERCIAL LAW
possession
[poh.*zesh*.en]

COMMERCIAL LAW
nonnegotiable instrument
[non.ne.*go*.shebl *in*.stroo.ment]

COMMERCIAL LAW
presentment
[pre.*zent*.ment]

COMMERCIAL LAW
note
[note]

COMMERCIAL LAW
primary liability
[*pry*.mer.ee ly.e.*bil*.i.tee]

COMMERCIAL LAW
order paper
[*or*.der *pay*.per]

COMMERCIAL LAW
promissory note
[*prom*.i.sore.ee note]

COMMERCIAL LAW
payor
[pay.*or*]

COMMERCIAL LAW
purchase money security interest
[per.ches *mun*.ee se.*kyoo*.ri.tee *in*.trest]

Under the Uniform Commercial Code, a method of protecting a security interest in goods against the claims of other creditors by filing a financing statement with the appropriate public officer (usually the secretary of state). However, a security interest in consumer goods is perfected without such filing.

The act of transferring a negotiable instrument to a third person by indorsement or delivery.

- *n.* agreement, compromise, mediation, discussion

Occupancy and dominion over property; a holding of land legally, by one's self (actual possession) or through another person such as a tenant (constructive possession). The holding may be by virtue of having title or an estate or interest of any kind. One need not have a resident on the land to be in actual possession of it.

- *n.* dominion, proprietorship, ownership, holding, guardianship, keeping ("I have possession of my family's land.")

---

1. A document or instrument not transferable by indorsement or delivery. EXAMPLES: a lease, a deed; a mortgage. 2. Not subject to negotiation.

- *adj.* nontransferable, non-assignable

A demand to accept (presentment for acceptance) or to pay (presentment for payment) a negotiable instrument, made to the drawee by a person, usually the payee or holder, entitled to enforce the instrument.

An instrument that is not negotiable.

The liability of a person who, by the terms of the instrument he has executed, or because of some other legal obligation he has incurred, or by virtue of his legal relationship to an injured party, is absolutely required to make payment, satisfy the obligation, or assume full responsibility for the injury; the liability of a maker or principal, as distinguished from that of a guarantor or indorser. *Compare* secondary liability.

A written promise by one person to pay another person a specified sum of money on a specified date; a term used interchangeably with promissory note. A note may or may not be negotiable, depending upon its form. *See also* negotiable instrument.

A written promise to pay a specific sum of money by a specified date or on demand. A promissory note is negotiable if, in addition, it is payable to the order of a named person or to bearer. *See also* negotiable instrument.

A negotiable instrument (i.e., an instrument that recites an unconditional promise to pay a fixed amount of money, and that is payable to order and meets all the other requirements of negotiability).

A security interest created when a security agreement is executed by a purchaser of personal property.

---

1. A person who makes a payment or is obligated to make a payment. 2. The person who makes a check, bill, or note.

COMMERCIAL LAW

repossession

[ree.po.*zesh*.en]

COMMERCIAL LAW

security interest

[se.*kyoor*.i.tee *in*.trest]

COMMERCIAL LAW

secondary liability

[*sek*.en.dare.ee ly.e.*bil*.i.tee]

COMMERCIAL LAW

sight draft

[site draft]

COMMERCIAL LAW

secured

[se.*kyoord*]

COMMERCIAL LAW

special indorsement

[*spesh*.el in.*dors*.ment]

COMMERCIAL LAW

secured creditor

[se.*kyoord kred*.it.er]

COMMERCIAL LAW

time draft

[time draft]

COMMERCIAL LAW

secured transaction

[se.*kyoord* tranz.*ak*.shen]

COMMERCIAL LAW

traveler's check

[*trav*.lerz chek]

COMMERCIAL LAW

security

[se.*kyoor*.i.tee]

COMMERCIAL LAW

Uniform Commercial Code (UCC)

[*yoon*.i.form ke.*mersh*.el kode]

1. Under the Uniform Commercial Code, "an interest in personal property or fixtures which secures payment or performance of an obligation." *See also* purchase money security interest. 2. With respect to real property, a mortgage or other lien.

---

1. A remedy of the seller upon default by the buyer under a conditional sale contract or other security agreement. 2. A taking of possession by the owner of real estate after the occupant relinquishes possession or forfeits the right to possession.

- *n.* recapture, restoration, retrieval, seizure, reacquisition, recovery

---

A bill of exchange or draft payable upon presentment to the drawee. It is the equivalent of a check that is payable on demand.

Liability that does not come about until the primary obligor fails to meet her obligation; the liability of a guarantor or indorser as distinguished from that of a maker or principal. *Compare* primary liability.

An indorsement that specifies the person to whom or to whose order the instrument is to be payable (e.g., "pay to the order of Lisa Whitney").

Made certain of payment; given security. *Compare* unsecured.

- *adj.* guaranteed, protected, insured, sheltered ("a secured debt")

A draft payable at a fixed or determinable future time.

A creditor who has a perfected security lien for a debt in the form of an encumbrance on property of the debtor. EXAMPLES: a mortgagee; a lienee.

An instrument, usually one of a set, purchased from a bank or other financial institution and similar in many respects to a cashier's check. Traveler's checks must be signed by the purchaser at the time of purchase and countersigned when cashed.

A transaction that creates or provides for a security interest in personal property. EXAMPLE: a secured loan.

One of the Uniform Laws, which have been adopted in much the same form in every state. The UCC governs most aspects of commercial transactions, including sales, leases, negotiable instruments, deposits and collections, letters of credit, bulk sales, warehouse receipts, bills of lading and other documents of title, investment securities, and secured transactions.

---

1. Singular of securities. 2. Collateral; a pledge given to a creditor by a debtor for the payment of a debt or for the performance of an obligation. EXAMPLES: a mortgage; a lien; a deposit.

- *n.* warranty, bail, surety, escrow, collateral, debenture, assurance ("security for the mortgage")

COMMERCIAL LAW

unsecured

[un.se.*kyoord*]

BANKRUPTCY

bankruptcy

[*bank*.rupt.see]

COMMERCIAL LAW

utter

[*ut*.er]

BANKRUPTCY

Bankruptcy Abuse Prevention and Consumer Protection Act

[*bank*.rupt.see a.*byooss* pre.*vent*.shen and kon.*soo*.mer *pro*.tek.shen act]

BANKRUPTCY

arrangement with creditors

[a.*raynj*.ment with *kred*.i.terz]

BANKRUPTCY

Bankruptcy Code

[*bank*.rupt.see code]

BANKRUPTCY

assets

[*ass*.ets]

BANKRUPTCY

bankruptcy courts

[*bank*.rupt.see kortz]

BANKRUPTCY

automatic stay

[awto.*mat*.ik sta]

BANKRUPTCY

bankruptcy estate

[*bank*.rupt.see es.*tate*]

BANKRUPTCY

bankrupt

[*bank*.rupt]

BANKRUPTCY

bankruptcy judge

[*bank*.rupt.see juj]

1. The circumstances of a person who is unable to pay his debts as they come due.
2. The system under which a debtor may come into court (voluntary bankruptcy) or be brought into court by his creditors (involuntary bankruptcy), either seeking to have his assets administered and sold for the benefit of his creditors and to be discharged from his debts (a straight bankruptcy), or to have his debts reorganized (a business reorganization or a wage earner's plan).

- *n.* insolvency, failure, disaster, defaulting
- *ant.* solvency

A term describing debts or obligations for which no security has been given or no perfected security lien exists.

Enacted in 2005, it is a significant overhaul in bankruptcy that is less favorable than previous bankruptcy legislation for debtors.

To put counterfeit money or forged checks into circulation. *See* forge.

Federal bankruptcy legislation. There have been six major statutes, enacted respectively in 1800, 1841, 1867, 1898, 1978, and 2005. The last of these is the Bankruptcy Abuse Prevention and Consumer Protection Act.

---

1. A proceeding, also called a composition, by which a debtor who is not insolvent may have her failing finances rehabilitated by a bankruptcy court under an agreement with her creditors. *See also* composition with creditors. 2. The plan worked out by the bankruptcy court; also referred to as an arrangement for the benefit of creditors. *See also* bankruptcy.

Federal courts that hear and determine only bankruptcy cases.

Property of any value.

All of the property of the debtor at the time the petition in bankruptcy is filed.

When a bankruptcy petition is filed with the court clerk, a hold arises that bars creditors from all debt collection efforts against debtors. *See* stay.

A judge of a bankruptcy court.

---

1. A person who is unable to pay her debts as they come due; an insolvent person. 2. A person who is entitled to the protection of the Bankruptcy Code.

- *adj.* insolvent, indigent, wiped out, penniless, destitute, broke, out of business

BANKRUPTCY

bankruptcy petition

[*bank*.rupt.see pe.*tish*.en]

BANKRUPTCY

Chapter 13

[*chap*.ter ther.*teen*]

BANKRUPTCY

bankruptcy proceedings

[*bank*.rupt.see pro.*see*.dings]

BANKRUPTCY

Chapter 12

[*chap*.ter twelv]

BANKRUPTCY

bankruptcy trustee

[*bank*.rupt.see trus.*tee*]

BANKRUPTCY

composition with creditors

[kom.po.*zish*.en with *kred*.i.terz]

BANKRUPTCY

bond

[bond]

BANKRUPTCY

creditor

[*kred*.it.er]

BANKRUPTCY

Chapter 11

[*chap*.ter ee.*lev*.en]

BANKRUPTCY

creditor beneficiary

[*kred*.it.er ben.e.*fish*.ee.ar.ee]

BANKRUPTCY

Chapter 7

[*chap*.ter *sev*.en]

BANKRUPTCY

creditors' meeting

[*kred*.it.erz *meet*.ing]

Under a Chapter 13 proceeding of the Bankruptcy Code, an individual debtor who is a wage earner and who files a repayment plan acceptable to his creditors will be given additional time in which to meet his obligations, generally three to five years.

See petition in bankruptcy.

Chapter 12 of the Bankruptcy Code addresses the debts of "family farmers" or "family fishermen," with regular annual income. Under this chapter, debtors propose a plan to repay all or part of their debts to creditors over a period of three to five years. Chapter 12 is more streamlined, less complicated, and less expensive than Chapter 11 (also a reorganization plan) and better meets the needs of the family farmer or fishermen. *See* bankruptcy.

Any proceedings under the Bankruptcy Code; any proceedings relating to bankruptcy.

---

1. An agreement between a debtor and her creditors under which, in exchange for prompt payment, the creditors agree to accept amounts less than those actually owed in satisfaction of their claims. *See also* arrangement with creditors. 2. Proceedings under Chapter 13 of the Bankruptcy Code for debt readjustment.

See trustee in bankruptcy.

A person to whom a debt (secured by collateral or unsecured) is owed by a debtor. *See also* general creditor, secured creditor, and unsecured creditor.

- *n.* lender, assignee

The written instrument that evidences a debt. Trustees and receivers appointed by the court are required to file for a bond in order to take control of the property of the debtor, or to reorganize the debtor's business.

A creditor who is the beneficiary of a contract made between the debtor and a third person.

Under Chapter 11 of the Bankruptcy Code, the debtor is permitted to continue business operations until a reorganization plan is approved by his creditors. The debtor is not discharged from bankruptcy until the debts are paid off, which could take several years. *See* bankruptcy.

The first meeting of creditors of a debtor, required for the purpose of allowing the claims of creditors, questioning the debtor under oath, and electing a trustee in bankruptcy.

A straight bankruptcy is called a Chapter 7 proceeding because it is conducted under Chapter 7 of the Bankruptcy Code. A debtor has his assets collected and sold for the benefit of his creditors, and then is discharged from his debts (a straight bankruptcy). *See* bankruptcy.

BANKRUPTCY

debtee

[*det*.ee]

BANKRUPTCY

forfeit

[*for*.fit]

BANKRUPTCY

debtor

[*det*.er]

BANKRUPTCY

fraudulent conveyance

[*fraw*.je.lent ken.*vay*.ense]

BANKRUPTCY

debtor in possession

[*det*.er in po.*zesh*.en]

BANKRUPTCY

garnishment

[*gar*.nish.ment]

BANKRUPTCY

discharge in bankruptcy

[dis.*charj* in *bank*.rupt.see]

BANKRUPTCY

general creditor

[*jen*.e.rel *kred*.it.er]

BANKRUPTCY

dismissal

[dis.*miss*.el]

BANKRUPTCY

homestead exemption

[*home*.sted eg.*zemp*.shen]

BANKRUPTCY

exemptions

[eg.*zemp*.shenz]

BANKRUPTCY

involuntary bankruptcy

[in.*vol*.en.te.ree *bank*.rupt.see]

To lose, particularly as result of default or neglect, or commission of a crime. One may forfeit money, property, or rights.

A person who lends to a debtor.

- *n.* creditor, lender

1. The act of a debtor in making payment to one of her creditors by paying him with the intention of defrauding other creditors. 2. Under the Bankruptcy Code, a transfer of property to a creditor that gives him an advantage over other creditors. Although such a transfer may be disallowed by the trustee in bankruptcy, it is not necessarily a criminal act. *See also* preference.

1. A person who owes money to another person. 2. A person who owes anything to another person. *See also* debtee.

- *n.* borrower, buyer

Attachment of debtor's wages by a creditor.

A debtor who continues to operate his business while undergoing a business reorganization under the jurisdiction of the bankruptcy court. *See also* bankruptcy.

One who is not entitled to priority because the creditor's claim is not secured by a mortgage or other lien.

The release of a debtor from an obligation to pay, pursuant to a bankruptcy proceeding.

- *v.* To perform an obligation or duty; to satisfy a debt. USAGE: "All his debts were discharged by bankruptcy."

Under homestead exemption statutes, the immunity of real property from execution for debt, provided the property is occupied by the debtor as the head of the family. This can vary by state law, with some states allowing for 100 percent immunity, even for mansions.

The release of the debtor's case in totality from protection and jurisdiction of the bankruptcy court.

A bankruptcy initiated by one's creditors. *See also* bankruptcy; bankruptcy proceedings. *Compare* voluntary bankruptcy.

Earnings and property allowed to be retained by a debtor free from claims of creditors in bankruptcy. EXAMPLES: a wedding band, a family bible.

BANKRUPTCY

judgment creditor

[*juj*.ment *kred*.i.ter]

BANKRUPTCY

lien

[leen]

BANKRUPTCY

liquidation

[lik.wi.*day*.shen]

BANKRUPTCY

moratorium

[more.e.*toh*.ree.um]

BANKRUPTCY

nondischargeable debt

[non.dis.*charj*.ebl det]

BANKRUPTCY

petition in bankruptcy

[pe.*tish*.en in *bank*.rupt.see]

BANKRUPTCY

petitioner

[pe.*tish*.en.er]

BANKRUPTCY

petitioning creditor

[pe.*tish*.en.ing *kred*.it.er]

BANKRUPTCY

preference

[*pref*.e.rense]

BANKRUPTCY

preferential assignment

[pref.e.*ren*.shel a.*sine*.ment]

BANKRUPTCY

preferential debts

[pref.e.*ren*.shel detz]

BANKRUPTCY

preferential transfer

[pref.e.*ren*.shel *tranz*.fer]

A person seeking relief by a petition.

- *n.* pleader, litigant, applicant, asker, supplicant ("The petitioner asked for relief.")
- *ant.* respondent

A creditor who has secured a judgment against his debtor that has not been satisfied.

A creditor who initiates proceedings against his debtor in a bankruptcy court. *See also* bankruptcy proceedings; petition in bankruptcy.

A claim on personal or real property for the payment of a debt or mortgage.

---

1. The act of a debtor in paying one or more of his creditors without paying the others. "Preference" is often confused with priority. However, a priority exists by operation of law; a preference is a transaction that, depending upon the circumstances, the law may consider voidable. *See also* priority. 2. Under the Bankruptcy Code, a transfer of property by an insolvent debtor to one or more creditors to the exclusion of others, enabling such creditors to obtain a greater percentage of their debt than other creditors of the same class. Such a transaction may constitute a voidable preference and be disallowed by the trustee in bankruptcy. *See also* fraudulent conveyance. 3. The right of one person over other persons. *See also* voidable preference.

- *n.* partiality, election, advantage; priority

---

1. The extinguishment of a debt by payment or straight bankruptcy. 2. The ascertainment of the amount of a debt or demand by agreement or by legal proceedings. *See also* bankruptcy; receivership.

- *n.* elimination, abolition, rescission

An assignment for the benefit of creditors by which the assignor gives a preference to certain of her creditors; any assignment that prefers one creditor over another.

A period during which a person, usually a debtor, has a legal right to postpone meeting an obligation. An individual creditor may declare a moratorium with respect to her debtor, or a moratorium may be imposed by legislation and apply to debtors as a class.

- *n.* grace period

Debts that, under the Bankruptcy Code, are payable before all other debts. EXAMPLE: wages owed employees.

Any voidable or fraudulent preferences, taxes, child support, or other debts that cannot be legally discharged in bankruptcy. *See also* voidable preference.

See preference and preferential assignment.

A document filed in a bankruptcy court initiating bankruptcy proceedings. *See also* bankruptcy, petitioning creditor, bankruptcy petition.

BANKRUPTCY

priority

[pry.*aw*.ri.tee]

BANKRUPTCY

secured creditor

[se.*kyoord kred*.it.er]

BANKRUPTCY

proof of claim

[proof ov klam]

BANKRUPTCY

stay

[stay]

BANKRUPTCY

receiver

[re.*seev*.er]

BANKRUPTCY

straight bankruptcy

[strait *bank*.rupt.see]

BANKRUPTCY

receivership

[re.*seev*.er.ship]

BANKRUPTCY

trustee in bankruptcy

[trust.*ee* in *bank*.rupt.see]

BANKRUPTCY

reorganization

[ree.or.ge.ni.*zay*.shun]

BANKRUPTCY

unsecured creditor

[un.se.*kyoord kred*.it.er]

BANKRUPTCY

schedule in bankruptcy

[*sked*.jool in *bank*.rupt.see]

BANKRUPTCY

voidable preference

[*void*.ebl *pref*.rense]

One who has security for a debt owed in the form of an encumbrance on the property of the person in bankruptcy.

1. In bankruptcy law, the right of a secured creditor to receive satisfaction before an unsecured creditor. 2. The status of that which is earlier or previous in point of time, degree, or rank; precedence. *See also* preference.

- *n.* lead, order, superiority, primacy, preference, precedence, right, seniority, rank

---

The Bankruptcy Code provides for automatic stops to further pro-ceedings, usually temporarily; to restrain; to hold back; to suspend foreclosures or executions on certain types of debts upon filing of bankruptcy petition. *See also* moratorium and automatic stay.

- *v.* hinder, postpone, intermit, obstruct, suspend ("stay the creditor's foreclosure")
- *n.* deferment, halt, remission, reprieve, standstill, suspension

In bankruptcy, a statement in writing, signed by a creditor, setting forth the amount owed and the basis of the claim.

See Chapter 7.

A person appointed by the court to take custody of property in a receivership. In the case of the assets or other property of an insolvent debtor, whether an individual or corporation, the duty of a receiver is to preserve the assets for sale and distribution to the creditors. In the case of assets or other property that is the subject of litigation, the duty of a receiver is to preserve the property or fund in litigation, receive its rent or profits, and apply or dispose of them as the court directs. Such a receiver is called a pendente lite receiver. If the property in dispute is a business, the receiver may have the additional responsibility of operating the business as a going concern. *See* bond.

- *n.* trustee, supervisor, administrator, depository, overseer, manager, collector

---

A person appointed by a bankruptcy court to collect any amounts owed the debtor, sell the debtor's property, and distribute the proceeds among the creditors.

A proceeding by which the property of an insolvent debtor, or property that is the subject of litigation, may be preserved and appropriately disposed of by a person known as a receiver, who is appointed and supervised by the court. A corporation as well as an individual may be "in receivership." *See also* receiver.

One who has received no security for the debt owed by the person in bankruptcy.

See Chapter 11.

Under the Bankruptcy Code, a preference is voidable if it takes place within a specified number of days before the filing of the petition in bankruptcy and if it allows the creditor to obtain more than she would have received from the bankruptcy court.

A schedule filed by a debtor listing, among other things, all of his property, its value, his creditors, and the nature of their claims.

LABOR AND EMPLOYMENT
arbitration
[ar.bi.*tray*.shen]

LABOR AND EMPLOYMENT
back pay order
[bak pay *or*.der]

LABOR AND EMPLOYMENT
arbitration clause
[ar.bi.*tray*.shen kloz]

LABOR AND EMPLOYMENT
boycott
[*boy*.kot]

LABOR AND EMPLOYMENT
arbitration panel
[ar.bi.*tray*.shen *pan*.el]

LABOR AND EMPLOYMENT
certification
(of bargaining agent)
[ser.ti.fi.*kay*.shen ov *bar*.gen.ing *ay*.jent]

LABOR AND EMPLOYMENT
arbitrator
[*ar*.bi.tray.ter]

LABOR AND EMPLOYMENT
Civil Rights Act
[*sih*.vil rytz akt]

LABOR AND EMPLOYMENT
at will employment
[at will em.*ploy*.ment]

LABOR AND EMPLOYMENT
closed shop
[klozed shop]

LABOR AND EMPLOYMENT
back pay
[bak pay]

LABOR AND EMPLOYMENT
collective bargaining
[ko.*lek*.tiv *bahr*.gen.ing]

The order of a court, arbitrator, or administrative agency that employees be given their back pay. Such orders are most common in cases involving the reinstatement of employees who were improperly discharged.

A method of settling disputes by submitting a disagreement to a person (an arbitrator) or a group of individuals (an arbitration panel) for decision instead of going to court. If the parties are required to comply with the decision of the arbitrator, the process is called binding arbitration; if there is no such obligation, the arbitration is referred to as nonbinding arbitration. Compulsory arbitration is required by law, most notably in labor disputes.

- *n.* adjustment, compromise, mediation, determination ("Compulsory arbitration is the name for arbitration required by law.")

A joining together in a refusal to do business with a company, unless it changes practices felt to be injurious to those who are joining together, or to some of them, in an attempt to bring about modification of the practice. EXAMPLE: a boycott because of a manufacturer's policy of having most of its labor performed abroad.

A clause in a contract providing for arbitration of controversies that arise out of performance of the contract.

A formal pronouncement by the National Labor Relations Board, or a similar state agency, that it has determined that a union seeking to represent an employer's employees represents a majority of those employees in an appropriate collective bargaining unit and is therefore their collective bargaining agent. *See also* representation election.

A number of arbitrators who hear and decide a case together.

A term that may refer to any or all of the various statutes enacted by Congress relating to civil rights. The Civil Rights Act of 1964 assured access to places of public accommodation, public facilities, and education, without regard to religion, color, race, national origin, or sex; Title VII of that Act prohibited discrimination in employment. The Civil Rights Act of 1991 provided for both compensatory damages and punitive damages for intentional discrimination or unlawful harassment in the workplace on the basis of sex, race, religion, or disability. Additionally, the Age Discrimination in Employment Act and the Americans with Disabilities Act are often classified as civil rights acts. States, as well as the federal government, have legislated extensively in the area of civil rights. *See also* Equal Employment Opportunity Commission.

A person who conducts an arbitration. Generally, the primary consideration in choosing an arbitrator is impartiality and familiarity with the type of matter in dispute.

- *n.* judge, umpire, mediator, intervenor, adjudicator

A place of employment in which all employees are required by a collective bargaining agreement to be members of the union in order to be employed. *Compare* agency shop.

Termination of employment for any cause; may be initiated by employer or employee.

The negotiation of terms and conditions of employment between a union, acting on behalf of employees, and an employer or an association of employers. *See also* collective bargaining agreement.

Unpaid wages to which an employee is entitled.

LABOR AND EMPLOYMENT

collective bargaining agent

[ko.*lek*.tiv *bahr*.gen.ing *ay*.jent]

LABOR AND EMPLOYMENT

concerted activity

[ken.*ser*.ted ak.*tiv*.i.tee]

LABOR AND EMPLOYMENT

collective bargaining agreement

[ko.*lek*.tiv *bahr*.gen.ing a.*gree*.ment]

LABOR AND EMPLOYMENT

concerted protected activity

[ken.*ser*.ted pro.*tek*.ted ak.*tiv*.i.tee]

LABOR AND EMPLOYMENT

collective bargaining contract

[ko.*lek*.tiv *bahr*.gen.ing *kon*.trakt]

LABOR AND EMPLOYMENT

condition of employment

[kon.*dish*.en ov em.*ploy*.ment]

LABOR AND EMPLOYMENT

collective bargaining unit

[ko.*lek*.tiv *bahr*.gen.ing *yoo*.nit]

LABOR AND EMPLOYMENT

deferred compensation

[de.*ferd* kom.pen.*say*.shen]

LABOR AND EMPLOYMENT

company union

[*kum*.pe.nee *yoo*.nyen]

LABOR AND EMPLOYMENT

discharge

[dis.*charj*]

LABOR AND EMPLOYMENT

comparable worth

[*kom*.per.ebl werth]

LABOR AND EMPLOYMENT

discrimination

[dis.krim.in.*ay*.shen]

In labor law, conduct engaged in by an employer's employees, a union, or others for the purpose of supporting collective bargaining demands. Concerted activity that constitutes an unfair labor practice (EXAMPLE: a secondary boycott in which a union boycotts another company to put pressure on the union employees' company) is prohibited by the National Labor Relations Act. *Compare* concerted protected activity.

A union that engages in collective bargaining on behalf of an employer's employees.

In labor law, conduct engaged in by two or more employees acting together for the purpose of influencing the terms and conditions of their employment, including but not limited to wages and hours. Such activity is protected by the National Labor Relations Act if it falls within the terms of that statute. EXAMPLES: joining a union; striking; picketing.

An agreement covering wages, hours, and working conditions, entered into between an employer and the union, that is the collective bargaining agent for the employer's employees. *See also* collective bargaining; collective bargaining contract.

A matter with respect to which the National Labor Relations Act requires an employer to bargain collectively. EXAMPLES: wages; hours; vacation pay; seniority. *See also* collective bargaining.

An agreement covering wages, hours, and working conditions, entered into between an employer and the union that is the collective bargaining agent for the employer's employees.

Compensation paid after the services are rendered (pension and payments made for profit sharing).

An employee group permitted by law to be represented by a collective bargaining agent. EXAMPLES: all of an employer's maintenance employees, all of its drivers, or all employees in the finishing department.

---

1. To terminate an employee from employment. 2. To fire an employee. USAGE: "He was discharged from his job."

A labor union whose total membership consists of the employees of a single company and is controlled by the company.

Violations of the Fourteenth Amendment's equal protection clause distinguishing between classes of people in voting, education, employment, and other areas of human activity.

The concept that men and women are entitled to equal pay when their work requires equal skills or duties and is therefore of "comparable worth." Several states have adopted legislation putting this concept into practice in varying degrees. *See also* Equal Pay Act.

LABOR AND EMPLOYMENT

dues

[dooz]

LABOR AND EMPLOYMENT

employers' liability acts

[em.*ploy*.erz ly.e.*bil*.i.tee aktz]

LABOR AND EMPLOYMENT

employ

[em.*ploy*]

LABOR AND EMPLOYMENT

employment

[em.*ploy*.ment]

LABOR AND EMPLOYMENT

employee

[em.*ploy*.ee]

LABOR AND EMPLOYMENT

employment at will

[em.*ploy*.ment at will]

LABOR AND EMPLOYMENT

employee assistance program

[em.*ploy*.ee e.*sis*.tense *proh*.gram]

LABOR AND EMPLOYMENT

employment discrimination

[em.*ploy*.ment dis.krim.in.*ay*.shen]

LABOR AND EMPLOYMENT

Employee Retirement Income Security Act

[em.*ploy*.ee re.*tire*.ment *in*.kum see.*kyoo*.re.tee akt]

LABOR AND EMPLOYMENT

Equal Employment Opportunity Commission

[*ee*.kwel em.*ploy*.ment op.er.*tew*.ni.tee kuh.*mish*.en]

LABOR AND EMPLOYMENT

employer

[em.*ploy*.er]

LABOR AND EMPLOYMENT

Equal Pay Act

[*ee*.kwel pay akt]

Now called workers' compensation acts. Employers' liability acts abolished or substantially restricted the defenses previously available to an employer (EXAMPLES: contributory negligence; assumption of risk) when an employee brought suit for an injury incurred on the job pursuant to the Federal Employees' Liability Act (FELA).

Annual or other regular payments made by a member of a club, union, or association to retain membership.

1. The relationship between an employee and an employer. 2. That which occupies a person's time.

- *n.* livelihood, service, business, trade, vocation, occupation, job, profession, work

To enter into a contract of employment; to hire.

A hiring for an indefinite period of time. In the absence of an agreement to the contrary, all employment is at will and either the employer or the employee may terminate it at any time.

A person who works for another for pay in a relationship that allows the other person to control the work and direct the manner in which it is done. The earlier legal term for employee was servant.

Note that statutory definitions of "employee" may differ, depending upon the purpose of the statute. For EXAMPLE, although the distinctions between the definitions of employee in the Social Security Act, the Fair Labor Standards Act, and the National Labor Relations Act may seem insignificant, they may, in any given instance, be critical.

Federal statutes prohibit discrimination (unfair treatment or denial of normal privileges) in employment on the basis of sex, age, race, nationality, religion, or being disabled. It is not discrimination if a distinction can be found between the favored class and the unfavored class of employees. *See* discrimination, Civil Rights Act, Americans with Disabilities Act, Equal Pay Act.

An employer-sponsored program, often in conjunction with an insurance company or a health maintenance organization, that provides treatment referrals for employees impaired or disabled by chemical dependency or other problems requiring counseling services. It is often referred to by its abbreviations, EAP.

A federal agency whose purpose is to prevent and remedy discrimination based on race, color, religion, national origin, age, or sex with respect to most aspects of employment, including hiring, firing, promotions, and wages. The commission, which is known as the EEOC, enforces many federal civil rights acts and antidiscrimination statutes.

Better known by its acronym ERISA; a federal statute that protects employee pensions by regulating pension plans maintained by private employers, the way in which such plans are funded, and their vesting requirements. ERISA has important tax implications for both employers and employees. *See also* vested pension.

A federal statute that requires men and women to be paid equally for the same work. *See also* comparable worth.

A person who hires another to work for her for pay in a relationship that allows her to control the work and direct the manner in which it is done. The earlier legal term for employer was master.

LABOR AND EMPLOYMENT
Fair Labor Standards Act
[fayr *lay*.ber *stan*.derdz akt]

LABOR AND EMPLOYMENT
labor
[*ley*.ber]

LABOR AND EMPLOYMENT
FICA
[fy.kah]

LABOR AND EMPLOYMENT
labor agreement
[*lay*.ber a.*gree*.ment]

LABOR AND EMPLOYMENT
green card
[green kard]

LABOR AND EMPLOYMENT
labor contract
[*lay*.ber *kon*.trakt]

LABOR AND EMPLOYMENT
grievance
[*gree*.venss]

LABOR AND EMPLOYMENT
labor dispute
[*lay*.ber dis.*pyoot*]

LABOR AND EMPLOYMENT
hostile environment
[*hoss*.tel en.*vi*.ron.ment]

LABOR AND EMPLOYMENT
labor laws
[*lay*.ber lawz]

LABOR AND EMPLOYMENT
job bias
[job *by*.is]

LABOR AND EMPLOYMENT
labor organization
[*lay*.ber or.gan.i.*zay*.shen]

1. In common usage, physical work, although the word refers with equal accuracy to work involving the application of professional or intellectual skills. 2. Work performed for a wage or salary, as opposed to work performed in order to realize a profit. 3. The body or group of persons who work for wages, as a class and as distinguished from management. *See also* labor dispute; unfair labor practice.

- *n.* work, occupation, undertaking, toil, enterprise, task, responsibility, energy, exertion, effort
- *v.* work, agonize, struggle, toil, slave, travail, strain

A federal statute that establishes a maximum work week for certain employees, sets a minimum hourly wage, and imposes restrictions on child labor. The Act covers employers in interstate commerce and other employers, including state and local governments. Additionally, all states have statutes governing hours; most also have minimum wage requirements. *See also* wage and hour acts.

See collective bargaining agreement.

Acronym for Federal Insurance Compensations Act. The federal statute that funds Social Security and Medicare by taxing employers, the wages of employees, and the earnings of the self-employed. Most people are aware of this law because of the FICA deduction that appears on their pay stubs.

See collective bargaining agreement.

A document that evidences an alien's status as a resident alien. It permits the alien to seek and gain employment within the United States.

A controversy between an employer and its employees or their collective bargaining agent concerning wages, hours, or other working conditions, or concerning union representation.

---

1. A formal complaint filed by an employee or by an employees' union claiming that the employer has violated the collective bargaining agreement. 2. A similar complaint filed against a union by an employer.

Federal and state statutes and administrative regulations that govern such matters as hours of work, minimum wages, unemployment insurance, safety, and collective bargaining. EXAMPLES: the National Labor Relations Act; the Fair Labor Standards Act; the Occupational Safety and Health Act.

A situation in which offensive conduct is permitted to infect the workplace, making it difficult or impossible for an employee to work.

See labor union.

A claim made under employment discrimination after a worker is fired for reasons of race, age, gender, or other disability. *See* Title VII.

LABOR AND EMPLOYMENT

Labor Relations Act

[*lay*.ber re.*lay*.shenz akt]

LABOR AND EMPLOYMENT

labor relations acts

[*lay*.ber re.*lay*.shenz aktz]

LABOR AND EMPLOYMENT

Labor Relations Board

[*lay*.ber re.*lay*.shenz bord]

LABOR AND EMPLOYMENT

Labor Standards Act

[*lay*.ber *stan*.derdz akt]

LABOR AND EMPLOYMENT

labor union

[*lay*.ber *yoo*.nyen]

LABOR AND EMPLOYMENT

laborer

[*lay*.ber.er]

LABOR AND EMPLOYMENT

lockout

[*lok*.out]

LABOR AND EMPLOYMENT

mediation

[mee.dee.*ay*.shen]

LABOR AND EMPLOYMENT

merit

[*mehr*.it]

LABOR AND EMPLOYMENT

merit increase

[*mehr*.it *in*.kreess]

LABOR AND EMPLOYMENT

minimum wage

[*min*.i.mum wayj]

LABOR AND EMPLOYMENT

minimum wage laws

[*min*.i.mum wayj lawz]

The closing of the workplace by the employer, or to withhold work, to enhance the employer's bargaining position in labor negotiations.

See National Labor Relations Act.

The voluntary resolution of a dispute in a non-adversarial manner.

Federal and state statutes that regulate relations between management and labor. EXAMPLE: the National Labor Relations Act.

Worth; quality; value.

See National Labor Relations Act.

An increase in pay given in recognition of the quality of an employee's work, as opposed to a pay raise granted on the basis of length of service or seniority.

See Fair Labor Standards Act (FLSA).

See minimum wage laws.

An association of workers formed for the purpose of engaging in collective bargaining with employers on behalf of workers concerning wages, hours, and other terms and conditions of their employment. *See also* collective bargaining agent.

State and federal statutes establishing a minimum rate of wages to be paid employees. The Fair Labor Standards Act is the federal minimum wage statute. *See also* wage and hour acts.

A person who performs labor for compensation.
- *n.* worker, employee, help, toiler

LABOR AND EMPLOYMENT

National Labor Relations Act

[*nash*.en.el *lay*.ber re.*lay*.shenz akt]

LABOR AND EMPLOYMENT

picket

[*pik*.et]

LABOR AND EMPLOYMENT

National Labor Relations Board (NLRB)

[*nash*.en.el *lay*.ber re.*lay*.shenz bord]

LABOR AND EMPLOYMENT

picketing

[*pik*.e.ting]

LABOR AND EMPLOYMENT

pension

[*pen*.shen]

LABOR AND EMPLOYMENT

polygraph

[*pol*.i.graf]

LABOR AND EMPLOYMENT

Pension Benefit Guaranty Corporation

[*pen*.shen *ben*.e.fit gehr.en.*tee* kore.per.*ay*.shen]

LABOR AND EMPLOYMENT

reasonable accommodation

[*ree*.zen.ebl a.kom.o.*day*.shen]

LABOR AND EMPLOYMENT

pension fund

[*pen*.shen fund]

LABOR AND EMPLOYMENT

reinstatement

[ree.in.*state*.ment]

LABOR AND EMPLOYMENT

pension plan

[*pen*.shen plan]

LABOR AND EMPLOYMENT

representation election

[rep.re.zen.*tay*.shen e.*lek*.shen]

A person who engages in picketing: a demonstrator, striker, or sign holder. ("Mary was a picket in last week's strike.")

- v. patrol, march, protest, rally ("We picketed the employer's plant when he committed unfair labor practices.")

Actually, several Acts of Congress, including the Wagner Act and the Taft-Hartley Act, which, together, regulate relations between management and labor by, among other things, prohibiting certain activities (unfair labor practices) that unreasonably hamper employers in the conduct of their business or that interfere with the right of employees to be effectively represented by unions of their choice.

---

1. In connection with a labor dispute, the presence of employees or others at an employer's place of business for the purpose of influencing other employees or prospective employees to refrain from working, or for the purpose of informing the public, customers, or suppliers of the dispute and inducing them not to do business with the employer. 2. Similar activity by any group of people at any location for the purpose of protesting anything.

A federal administrative agency, commonly referred to as the NLRB, created by the National Labor Relations Act for the purpose of enforcing the Act.

Commonly called a lie detector, a machine for recording impulses caused by changes in a person's blood pressure, pulse, respiration, and perspiration while under questioning. The results, which are interpreted to indicate the truth or falsity of the answers given, are not admissible as evidence in many states, and in others may be admitted only in limited circumstances for limited purposes. Federal law prohibits employers from administering polygraph tests to employees or applicants for employment except in very restricted circumstances.

- n. examination, inspection, lie detector machine

---

1. A retirement benefit in the form of a periodic payment, usually monthly, made to a retired employee from a fund created by the employer's contributions, or by the joint contributions of the employer and employee, over the period the employee worked for the employer. See also pension plan. 2. With respect to a former government employee or a retired member of the military, a regular allowance paid in consideration of the prior service.

- n. benefits, annuity, compensation, Social Security, support ("a vested pension")

Any change or adjustment to a job or work environment that permits a qualified applicant or employee with a disability to enjoy benefits and privileges of employment equal to those enjoyed by employees without disabilities. See Americans with Disabilities Act (ADA).

A public corporation of the United States government, that, under certain circumstances and within certain limits, guarantees the payment of employer pension plans that terminate without sufficient assets to pay the promised benefits. See also Employee Retirement Income Security Act (ERISA).

The act of restoring a person or thing to a position or condition from which she or it has been removed. EXAMPLES: rehiring an employee who has previously been fired; restoring coverage under an insurance policy that has lapsed for nonpayment.

- n. restoration, rehiring, readmittance

A fund from which a pension is paid.

An election conducted by the National Labor Relations Board for the purpose of determining whether a majority of an employer's employees wish to be represented by the union or unions named on the ballot for the purpose of collective bargaining. See also certification (of bargaining agent).

A plan through which an employer provides a pension for its employees' retirement. There are many types of pension plans. Some are funded solely by employer contributions; some are funded jointly by the employer and the employee. Most are regulated by the federal government under the Employee Retirement Insurance Security Act. All pension plans involve significant tax implications. Tax-deferred pension plans are also available to self-employed persons under certain circumstances.

LABOR AND EMPLOYMENT

secondary boycott

[*sek*.en.dare.ee *boy*.kott]

LABOR AND EMPLOYMENT

strike

[strike]

LABOR AND EMPLOYMENT

secondhand smoke

[*sek*.und.hand smok]

LABOR AND EMPLOYMENT

strike breaker

[strike *brake*.er]

LABOR AND EMPLOYMENT

self-employment

[self-em.*ploy*.ment]

LABOR AND EMPLOYMENT

Title VII

[*ty*.tel *sev*.en]

LABOR AND EMPLOYMENT

self-employment tax

[self-em.*ploy*.ment takz]

LABOR AND EMPLOYMENT

underemployed

[*un*.der.employd]

LABOR AND EMPLOYMENT

seniority

[see.*nyor*.i.tee]

LABOR AND EMPLOYMENT

unemployment

[un.em.*ploy*.ment]

LABOR AND EMPLOYMENT

sexual harassment

[*sek*.shoo.el ha.*rass*.ment]

LABOR AND EMPLOYMENT

unemployment compensation

[un.em.*ploy*.ment kom.pen.*say*.shen]

n. A concerted stoppage of work by a group of employees for the purpose of attempting to compel their employer to comply with a demand or demands they have made.
v. To act together with other employees in refusing to work; to engage in a strike.

- *v.* mutiny, resist, revolt, slow down ("to strike from work")
- *n.* boycott, revolt, walkout, dispute, boycott

A boycott applied by a union to third persons to cause them, against their will, not to patronize or otherwise deal with a company with whom the union has a dispute. A secondary boycott is one form of secondary activity.

A person who takes the job of an employee who is on strike.

- *n.* scab

Tobacco fumes harming employees confined to a work area is a new cause of action in unsafe work environment cases, and may qualify as a class action.

The section of the Civil Rights Act of 1964 dealing with the prohibition of discrimination in employment. *See* job bias.

Working for oneself.

Workers employed part-time or in temporary jobs that do not match their educational or skill levels and fail to pay enough to maintain a previous standard of living. For unemployment statistics, the underemployed are excluded, causing the percentage of unemployed to be higher than reported.

The Social Security tax paid by people who are self-employed.

A term usually applied to the state or status of being involuntarily unemployed.

---

1. In labor law, the principle that length of employment determines the order of layoffs, recalls to work, promotions, and frequently, rate of pay. 2. The status or state of being senior.

- *n.* tenure, longevity, longer service, station, rank, standing

---

Short for unemployment compensation benefits or unemployment insurance. *See* unemployment compensation acts.

A form of sex discrimination. Sexual harassment includes unwanted sexual attention from a supervisor. It also includes the toleration by an employer of sexual coercion or "hassling" in the workplace. *See also* Civil Rights Act and Equal Employment Opportunity Commission (EEOC).

LABOR AND EMPLOYMENT

unemployment compensation acts

[un.em.*ploy*.ment kom.pen.*say*.shen aktz]

LABOR AND EMPLOYMENT

unemployment compensation benefits

[un.em.*ploy*.ment kom.pen.*say*.shen *ben*.e.fits]

LABOR AND EMPLOYMENT

unemployment insurance

[un.em.*ploy*.ment in.*shoor*.ense]

LABOR AND EMPLOYMENT

unfair labor practice

[un.*fare lay*.ber *prak*.tiss]

LABOR AND EMPLOYMENT

unfair labor practice strike

[un.*fare lay*.ber *prak*.tiss strike]

LABOR AND EMPLOYMENT

vested pension

[*vest*.ed *pen*.shen]

LABOR AND EMPLOYMENT

wage

[wayj]

LABOR AND EMPLOYMENT

wage and hour acts

[wayj and ower aktz]

LABOR AND EMPLOYMENT

wage and hour laws

[wayj and ower lawz]

LABOR AND EMPLOYMENT

wildcat strike

[*wild*.kat strike]

LABOR AND EMPLOYMENT

worker

[*wer*.ker]

LABOR AND EMPLOYMENT

workers' compensation

[*wer*.kerz kom.pen.*say*.shen]

Compensation paid to employees, whether by the hour or by some other period of time, or by the job or piece. Wages include all remuneration paid for personal services, including commissions, bonuses, and gratuities, and, under the Fair Labor Standards Act, include board and lodging as well. In one sense, the term "wage" includes salary; in other uses, the term "salary" is reserved for the remuneration paid to executives, professionals, or supervisors, usually on a weekly, bi-weekly, monthly, or semimonthly basis. *See also* minimum wage laws.

- *n.* allowance, compensation, payment, salary, stipend ("daily wage")

State statutes that provide for the payment of benefits to persons who are unemployed through no fault of their own. An employee who, for EXAMPLE, has voluntarily left her employment, or has been discharged for willful misconduct, is ineligible to received unemployment compensation benefits. Unemployment compensation is a form of social insurance.

Federal and state statutes establishing the minimum wage that must be paid to employees and the number of hours they may work. The Fair Labor Standards Act is the federal wage and hour act. *See also* minimum wage laws.

See unemployment compensation acts.

See wage and hour acts.

See unemployment compensation acts.

A strike that is not authorized by the union representing the strikers.

An action by either a union or an employer in violation of the National Labor Relations Act or similar state statutes. EXAMPLES: firing an employee because she joins a union; secondary picketing.

---

1. A person who does work. 2. A person who is employed.

- *n.* artisan, breadwinner, employee, laborer, toiler, trader

---

A strike for the purpose of protesting or of inducing an employer to refrain from unfair labor practices.

Short for workers' compensation acts or workers' compensation insurance.

A pension that cannot be taken away, regardless of what the employer or the employee does. Note, however, that a pension may vest either fully or partially. *See also* Employee Retirement Income Security Act (ERISA).

LABOR AND EMPLOYMENT

workers' compensation acts

[*wer*.kerz kom.pen.*say*.shen aktz]

LABOR AND EMPLOYMENT

workers' compensation insurance

[*wer*.kerz kom.pen.*say*.shen in.*shoor*.ense]

State statutes that provide for the payment of compensation to employees injured in their employment or, in case of death, to their dependents. Benefits are paid under such acts whether or not the employer was negligent; payment is made in accordance with predetermined schedules based generally upon the loss or impairment of earning capacity. Workers' compensation laws eliminate defenses by the employer such as assumption of risk, contributory negligence, and fellow servant. Workers' compensation systems are funded through employer contributions to a common fund, through commercially purchased insurance, or both. Occupational diseases are compensable under these acts as well pursuant to Federal Employee's Liability Act (FELA).

See workers' compensation acts.

collective bargaining

collective bargaining agreement

collective bargaining contract

collective bargaining unit

company union

comparable worth

concerted activity

concerted protected activity

condition of employment

deferred compensation

discharge

discrimination

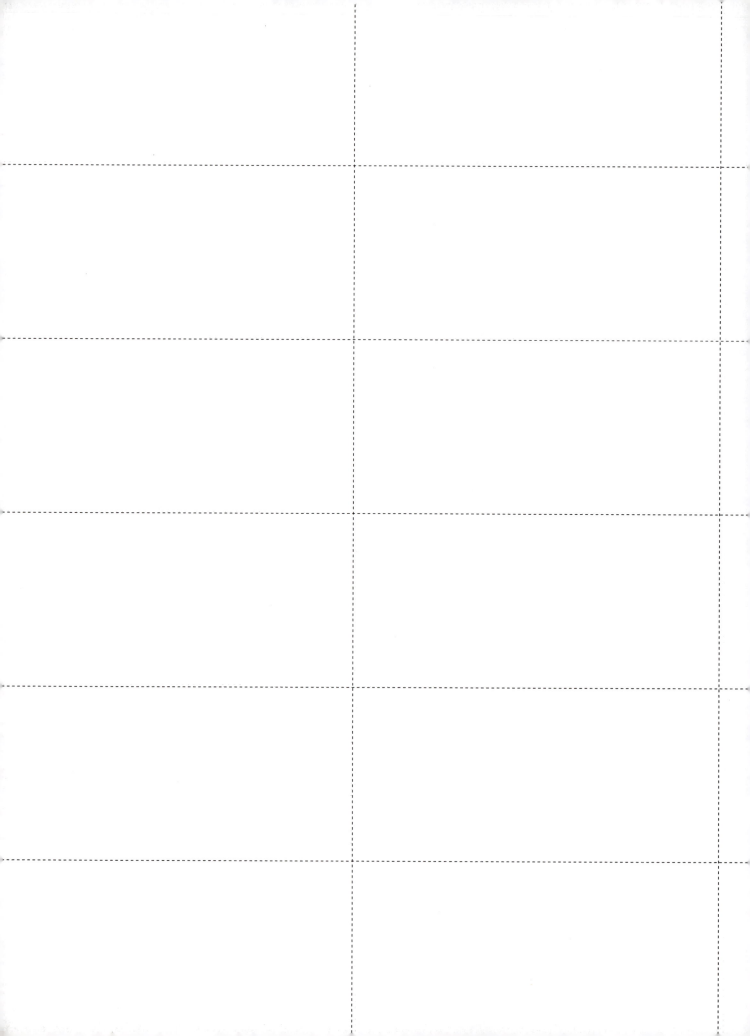